BCL-3ided

INDIA'S ECONOMIC PROBLEMS
An Analytical Approach

INDIA'S ECONOMIC PROBLEMS
An Analytical Approach

SECOND EDITION

Edited by
J.S. Uppal
Professor of Economics
State University of New York at Albany

St. Martin's Press
New York

Printed in India

Library of Congress Catalog Card Number 78-62033

ISBN 0-312-41409-9

First published in the United States of America in 1979

Foreword

Indian economics has long since come of age. In addition to the excellence of research at several long-established centres such as the Indian Statistical Institute and the Gokhale Institute, we also now have the establishment of new constellations of research in Trivandrum (under Dr. K. N. Raj), in Bangalore (under Dr. V. K. R. V. Rao), in Ahmedabad (under the initial leadership of Dr. D.T. Lakdawala) and in other areas of the country. Much of this research has been truly indigenous and this is a source of pride for us.

At the same time, a number of young Indian economists have now left a strong imprint on the international scene: in the theory of international trade, in welfare economics, in planning theory, in econometrics, and so on. Many of our economists now edit international journals (not on the basis of their regional origin but on the tougher basis of individual professional achievement), lead research projects, have been elected to Fellowships in distinguished professional societies, and are at the very top of the professional elite. And this has happened, not merely in the United Kingdom where our achievements must be discounted because we have traditional ties and also because the excellence of economics research has declined with the ebb of the Empire, but also in the United States which has been the centre of basic and fundamental research in the subject since the War.

How far have the vast achievements of the Indian economists been reflected in the quality of teaching in our country? This has been a much slower process.

Some of the economists of excellence have been drawn away into official work—something that is unavoidable and even socially desirable in a poor country—whereas many have been overwhelmed by the pressures of educational expansion into struggling to maintain, rather than improve, standards. Nonetheless, at some of the universities there have been steady improvements and this is reflected again in the ease with which the students of these universities tend to get into fellowship programmes for Ph.Ds. at the world's top Economics Departments such as MIT and Harvard, and in fact are sought actively by the next-best Departments such as Stanford, Berkeley, and Rochester.

This steady trend in the improved teaching of the best Indian universities needs to be strengthened by *both* diffusion to other universities—even equality of opportunity to students from different parts of the country requires that this be considered a top priority—*and* the contribution of the better-trained economists to the writing of better and more suitable textbooks and teaching materials.

Hence, I am glad to see that this group of US based Indian economists has seen fit to make its own contribution in this regard by adding this collection of essays on the Indian economy to the growing literature on the Indian economy which is now becoming available to students at the Indian universities. It is to be hoped that the university bodies in charge of recommending reading materials to their students in B.A. and M.A. courses will take cognizance of such materials and utilize them with profit.

Professor of Economics
Massachusetts Institute of Technology

JAGDISH N. BHAGWATI

Preface to the Second Edition

The early appearance of this edition has been encouraged by a highly favourable reception of the first. It is gratifying to note that this book is being widely used all over India by students, especially at the MA level, candidates for the various competitive examinations, and also by professional economists in research organizations.

In 1976, I had an opportunity to visit several universities in India to lecture on Indian economic problems as a Fulbright Visiting Professor, at the Gokhale Institute of Politics and Economics, Poona. I received valuable suggestions from students and professors to make this book more responsive to recent curriculum changes for MA examinations. Several laudable reviews on this book, containing suggestions for making the book more useful, have also been taken into account. Most important, the events in the Indian economy have changed quite fast, especially during the last two years, 1975–77: the imposition and removal of the Emergency during these years have necessitated serious consideration of several economic plans and policies.

All the chapters in this revised edition have been rewritten incorporating the above considerations. Some new chapters—Elements of Gandhian Economics, Black Money—have been added in view of their importance in the current economic thinking in the country. The statistics have been updated; the theoretical content of the relevant economic issues has been sharpened in all the chapters. An effort has been made to reduce variations in different chapters on coverage of material, methods of analysis, and writing styles.

It is sincerely hoped that this modest attempt on the part of some "Indian economists abroad" will continue to be useful to the "students of India" to whom this book is dedicated. All royalties from the sale of this book will continue to be contributed to the Prime Minister's Relief Fund for India.

State University of New York at Albany   J.S. Uppal

Preface to the Second Edition

Preface to the First Edition

In recent visits to India, I had the privilege of exchanging views with my former colleagues about the teaching of economics in the colleges and universities there and abroad. Many of them complained that most of the books on Indian economics now being used are too descriptive—they fail to analyse critically the economic problems facing Indian society. The result is that students, especially at the undergraduate level, do not learn to examine such problems within a theoretical and logical framework. They are unable to grasp as fully as they might the cause-and-effect relationships between different policy variables. Their knowledge of the Indian economy is often restricted to a set of statements, many of which may be based merely on "conventional wisdom".

These books have another limitation. They are usually cast in a narrow framework. Little effort is made to compare India's problems to those of other developing countries, or, for that matter, to those of more advanced countries in their earlier stages of development. Students thus end up with a rather parochial view of the Indian economy in a day and age when societies have so much to learn from one another and from the rich store of human experience—sometimes known as the "knowledge explosion".

In view of those deficiencies in the currently used books on the Indian economy, we—as economists who were raised in India, educated there as well as in western countries, and who are now teaching abroad—have tried to produce this anthology that would present the economic problems of India in a more analytic manner. The book is intended primarily for undergraduate students, though students working on the master's degree and studying for competitive examinations will also find it beneficial.

Each economist has contributed a paper on an Indian economic problem closely related to his major interest and field of specialization. The papers are comprehensive in that they discuss the problems in their various aspects—including the nature and the causes of the problems, their importance in the process of India's economic development, the Indian government's attempts to solve the problems, and possible solutions based on experiences of other developing countries. It is hoped that a fruitful international perspective has been attained by this reference to the experience of other countries together with the inclusion of western views on Indian economic problems.

The contributors were asked to place emphasis on linking the apparatus of theoretical economic analysis with the facts of Indian economic conditions. The papers are meant to be neither exercises in theoretical analysis nor journalistic presentations of economic facts. They seek to strike a reasonable balance between abstract theory and living reality, difficult though that objective may be.

Events in the Indian economy are moving fast. Since the manuscript went to the press in 1972, several developments have taken place in the economy which the reader should be aware of. These developments, along with the relevant chapter numbers may be noted here: (i) There has been the unprecedented inflationary trend, whose explanation may be sought in factors like the drought in 1972–73, deficit financing and the energy crisis (Chapter 19); (ii) Licensing has been liberalised, by the industrial policy statement of February 2, 1973, which identifies core industries of national importance in which foreign concerns and large houses (with assets of not less than Rs. 20 crores) will be eligible to participate (Chapter 8); (iii) The summary of the Approach to the Fifth Plan, has been given in the document 'Towards an Approach to the Fifth Plan' (Chapter 10); (iv) The Report of the Banking Commission, 1972 has also been made available (Chapter 17); (v) The recommendations of the Sixth Finance Commission and recent allocations by the Finance Commission to various states throw light on the Centre-State relations and the regional priorities the government has set down (Chapter 21).

As with every compilation of articles by different authors, some differences in treatment remain in spite of the editor's efforts. There are variations in coverage of material, methods of analysis, and writing styles. This is the price that must be paid for the inclusion of analysis by 25 experts in one volume. The editor is grateful to the contributors for their efforts and hopes that readers will find that the merits of this composite volume outweigh the disadvantages of its multiple authorship.

The book is dedicated to the students of India by "Indian economists based abroad". All royalties from the sale of this book will be contributed to the Prime Minister's Relief Fund for India.

State University of New York at Albany   J.S. UPPAL

The Contributors

J.S. Uppal: (b. 1927) has an M.A. in Economics from the Punjab University. After teaching at the Government College, Ludhiana, and Mahindra College, Patiala (Punjab, India) for some years, he proceeded to the University of Minnesota where he took the M.A. (1961) and Ph.D. (1965) degrees. He has taught at the University of Hawaii, Michigan State University and is now Professor of Economics at the State University of New York at Albany. Professor Uppal's other books are: *Economic Development in South Asia* (St. Martin's Press, New York, 1977) *Can Cities Survive? The Fiscal Plight of American Cities* (St. Martin's Press, New York, 1974); *Disguised Unemployment in an Underdeveloped Economy* (Asia Publishing House, New York, 1973); *Africa—Problems in Econo-* *mic Development* (The Free Press, The Macmillan Co., 1972); and *India and China: Studies in Comparative Development* (The Free Press, The Macmillan Co., 1971). Professor Uppal has also published papers in professional journals, including the *Oxford Economics Papers*, *Indian Economic Journal*, *Canadian Journal of Economics*, *Journal of Developing Areas*, *Economia Internationale*, and *Asian Survey*. He has been a recipient of the John Cowel Fellowship, Ford Foundation Fellowship and research grants from the State University of New York Research Foundation. In 1976, he was a Fulbright Visiting Professor at the Gokhale Institute of Politics and Economics, Poona (India).

Jaleel Ahmad: M.S. (Pittsburgh); Ph.D. (Massachusetts Institute of Technology); Associate Professor of Economics, Concordia University, Montreal, Canada; and Consultant to the United Nations Conference on Trade and Development, Geneva, Switzerland.

Ramsinh K. Asher: B. Com. (Bombay University); M.B.A. & M.A. (Syracuse University); Assistant Professor of Economics, Bowie State College, Bowie, Maryland, U.S.A.

V.N. Balasubramanyam: M.A. (Mysore University); A.M.; Ph.D. (Illinois University); Senior Lecturer in Economics, University of Lancaster, U.K.

Balwir Singh Cheema: M.A. (Punjab University); Ph.D. (American University, Washington); Associate Professor of Economics, Wittenberg University, Springfield, Ohio, U.S.A.

Vikas Chitre: M.A. (University of Bombay); Ph.D. (University of Rochester); formerly taught at the University of Toronto (Canada), the University of Adelaide (Australia); and Professor and Head of the Department of Economics, University of Jodhpur (Rajasthan); presently Professor of Economics, Gokhale Institue of Politics and Economics, Poona (India)

Ram L. Chugh: M.A. (Punjab University); Ph.D. (Wayne State University); Associate Professor of Economics, State University of New York College at Potsdam, New York.

James Cutt: Studied Economics at the University of Edinburgh; Ph.D. (University of Toronto); former Assistant Professor of Economics, York University, Toronto, Canada; presently on the faculty of Economics, the Australian National University, Canberra, Australia.

Romesh Diwan: B.A. (Punjab University); M.A. (Delhi School of Economics); Ph.D. (University of Birmingham); formerly Lecturer, Punjab University; Lecturer, University of Glasgow; Economist, United Nations; presently Professor of Economics, Rensselaer Polytechnic Institute, Troy, New York.

G.C. Dorai: B.A. (Punjab University); M.A. (Delhi University); Ph.D. (Wayne State University); former Lecturer Sri Venkateswara College, Delhi; Wheaton College, Norton, Mass., U.S.A.; presently Associate Professor of Economics, The William Paterson College of New Jersey Wayne, New Jersey, U.S.A.

A. Thomas Eapen: B.Sc. (Madras University); M.B.A.; Ph.D. (University of Michigan); Associate Professor of Economics, State University of New York, Binghamton, New York, U.S.A.

Prem P. Gandhi: M.A. (Delhi University); M.B.A. (New York University); Ph.D. (New School for Social Research); Professor of Economics, State University College at Plattsburgh, New York, U.S.A.

Surendra N. Kulshreshtha: M.S. (Agra University); Ph.D. (University of Manitoba); formerly taught Agricultural Economics, R.B.S. College; affiliate of the Agra University; presently Professor of Agricultural Economics, University of Saskatchewan, Saskatoon, Canada; and Transportation Expert with the Sulawesi Regional Development Study, a joint project of the Canadian International Development Agency and Republic of Indonesia.

Sudhin K. Mukhopadhyay: B. A.; M. A. (University of Calcutta); Ph.D. (Economics : University of Minnesota); Fulbright scholar; formerly with the Indian Statistical Institute, Emory University, and University of Minnesota; presently Reader in Economics and Director of several research projects on the economics of agricultural and human resource development, University of Kalyani, West Bengal, India.

Inder Pal Nijhawan: M.A. (Delhi School of Economics); Ph.D. (University of North Carolina); Associate Professor of Economics, Fayetteville State University; and Associate Member of Graduate Faculty, North Carolina State University, U.S.A.

Ulaganathan Sankar: B.A. (Madras University); M.A. (Annamalai University); Ph.D. (University of Wisconsin); formerly Lecturer in Economics, Annamalai University; Research Associate, Gandhian Institute of Studies, Varanasi; Professor of Economics, University of Wisconsin, Milwaukee, U.S.A.; presently Professor of Economics, Madras University, Madras, India.

Mahmood A. Zaidi: B.A.; M.A. (University of California, Los Angeles); Ph.D. (University of California, Berkeley); formerly instructor in Economics at both the Los Angeles and Berkeley campuses of University of California; presently Professor, Industrial Relations Center, and Director of Graduate Study, University of Minnesota, Minneapolis, Minnesota, U.S.A.

Contents

Part One

THE NATIONAL ECONOMY

The Indian Economy and the Five-Year Plans

J. S. UPPAL

India suffers from underdevelopment, as shown by various economic and social indicators. The per capita income in India—an important measure of relative economic development—is among the lowest in the world. In terms of US dollars, it was only $110 in 1972, with an average annual growth-rate of only 1.1 per cent during the period 1960–1972. The low per capita income and slower growth rates are a reflection of the general state of economic underdevelopment of the economy. Some of the major causes of India's economic underdevelopment are:

Excessive Dependence on Agriculture

About three-quarters of India's population work in agriculture, contributing about 50 per cent to her total income: this indicates a comparatively lower productivity of agricultural than of non-agricultural labour. For example, according to the National Income Committee, the average productivity per worker in India in agriculture for the year 1950–51 was Rs. 500, while it was Rs. 1,700 in large-scale industries, and Rs. 1,500 in commerce, transportation and communications.[1] Histori-

cally, as countries have developed, the proportion of the population working in agriculture has diminished. For example, in the US, this ratio fell from about 75 per cent in 1810 to 10 per cent in 1970. With industrial development and general growth of the economy, the agricultural sector becomes more productive and fewer people are needed to produce a given quantity of output.

Deficiency of Capital

Deficiency of capital is another basic characteristic of underdevelopment. It is reflected in two ways. First, the amount of capital available per head is very low: the figures on per capita production of two crucial capital goods, steel and electricity, are 31 lb and 188 KW for India, against the corresponding figures of 1,584 lb and 11,960 KW for the US. In the agricultural sector of the Indian economy, the capital investment per head has been reduced to the point where with an increasing labour force, the marginal productivity has become extremely low: approaching zero. Secondly, the low rate of capital formation, particularly during 1950–70, was grossly inadequate for the achievement of any significant growth rate. We have discussed these issues in detail in Chapter 13.

Low Labour Productivity
Low labour productivity is both a symptom and cause of underdevelopment. It is at the root of much of the poverty in underdeveloped countries like India. The extremely low productivity of agricultural labour in India can be observed from Table 1.1.

Table 1.1. **Average Annual Productivity of Agricultural Labour, 1970**

(in US dollars)

Country	Average Annual Productivity
India	124
Pakistan	176
West Germany	3,495
United Kingdom	2,057
Japan	2,265
USA	2,408

SOURCE: 1. World Bank, *Trends in Developing Countries,* Washington D.C., 1973.
2. United Nations, *Statistical Year Book 1974,* New York, 1975.

Labour productivity in the non-agricultural sector is similarly low.

The reasons for low productivity are many and varied, and they include both social and economic factors. One important cause is the growing scarcity of such cooperative inputs as land and capital, which, together with rapid population growth, places an increasing burden on land. We have examined this situation in detail in Chapter 5. It is pertinent to point out some important aspects affecting agricultural output. Because of increasing population pressure, the amount of cultivated land per capita has declined from 1.11 acres in 1921 to 0.62 acres in 1971. The decline in area of cultivable land can be counteracted by increase in capital investment (improved technology, use of fertilizers, expanded irrigation facilities, etc.), as has been done in other land-scarce countries such as Japan. But unfor-

tunately, because of the low rate of capital formation, Indian farmers have not been able to resort to this remedy. The result is that overall productivity in agriculture has not risen sufficiently to meet the increasing demands of a rapidly increasing population. The overall increase in agricultural productivity per acre in India during the period 1950–70 was around 2 per cent per year against a corresponding annual population growth of 2.5 per cent. In recent years, the use of improved inputs (new varieties of seeds, more and better fertilizers, expanded irrigation facilities, etc.), has resulted in impressive increases in agricultural outputs in certain areas. This is referred to in the literature as the Green Revolution—providing evidence that it is mostly lack of capital investment that accounts for low labour productivity, especially in agriculture.

Unemployment and Underemployment
Another important aspect of underdevelopment in India is the prevalence of serious unemployment, as well as underemployment. Though estimates differ for different regions in the country, the figure of 15 per cent of the labour force being unemployed or seriously underemployed can be used as a rough approximation. The problem is more acute in the rural areas, where about one-quarter of the work force is "surplus". We discuss the nature, extent and causes of this phenomenon in Chapter 12, but it is important to note that unemployment is both a cause and effect of underdevelopment. Population increase without a corresponding increase in other inputs, inevitably results in part of the work force being without work. This non-utilization of the crucial factor of production—labour—results in loss of goods and services that the unemployed could have produced. A country is thus made poorer by the extent of its unemployment. However, the poorer the country, the less its ability to save the capital needed to create employment opportunities. Thus, efficient utilization of manpower is an essential prerequisite for economic development. We note here the existence of a vicious circle: unemployment—poverty—low investments—unemployment.

Lack of Infrastructure

Inadequate economic and social overheads, such as power, transportation and communications (also called forward linkages, or infrastructure) tend to aggravate the already serious problems related to agricultural and industrial growth. Though India has made impressive gains in creating a social and economic infrastructure since Independence, these are highly inadequate against the increasing demand from economic planning and development.

Inequalities in Income and Wealth Distribution

Maldistribution of national income results in extreme economic disparities among different groups, with a small group tending to own a large proportion of the country's wealth and resources. A committee appointed by the Indian Planning Commission presented a grim picture of the distribution of the national income in 1960, with the poorest 10 per cent of the population earning only 1.3 per cent and 0.7 per cent of aggregate income in the urban and rural sectors respectively, and economic power concentrated in the hands of a few big companies in the private sector.[2] Analysing the changes in income distribution, the Committee observed:

> Even after 10 years of planning and despite fairly heavy schemes of taxation on the upper incomes, there is a considerable measure of concentration in urban incomes. This would also hold for rural incomes as in their cases, even the burden of taxation is not heavy on the higher ranges of incomes.[3]

Statistics on income distribution in India collected in an All-India Rural Household Survey, show that between 1962 and 1967–68, the gap, in fact, widened: the share in the national income going to the upper 20 per cent of households increased from 48 per cent to 53 per cent, that of the lowest 20 per cent decreased from 5.9 per cent to 4.9 per cent.[4] The United Nations' estimates of Lorenz-ratios,[5] indicating distribution of income in India over time and by broad sectors of the economy, are given in Table 1.2. The declining Lorenz-ratios show increas-

Table 1.2. Estimates on Lorenz-Ratios in India: 1960-68

	Rural	Urban	Total
1960–61	0.34	0.47	0.38
1961–62	0.30	0.35	0.32
1967–68	0.28	0.31	0.30

SOURCE: 1. H.B. Chenerey *et al., Redistribution with Growth* (London: Oxford University Press, 1974), pp. 6–16, 253–90.

2. United Nations, *Economic and Social Survey of Asia and the Pacific, 1974*, Bangkok, 1975, p. 58.

ing inequalities in income distribution among both urban and rural populations.

This disparity in income distribution, which historically, contributed to capital formation and economic development in some presently advanced countries, for example, Japan, the US and UK, has not helped low-income countries like India, since the wealth of the economic elite is in absolute terms quite small in relation to the needs of these countries. Also, such wealth tends to be diverted to conspicuous consumption, or be dissipated in unproductive forms of expenditure (e.g., real estate, gold, dowries and social ceremonies), rather than invested to augment the productive capacity of the country's economy. The persistence of inequalities over a long period of time tends to foster apathy and cynicism among the majority of people. Those in the lowest income brackets would tend to dismiss the "planning process" as a "rich man's racket".

Low Levels of Consumption

The low levels of earnings and inequities in income distribution in India are reflected in tragically low levels of consumption of even such necessities of life as food, housing, and essential clothing. In India, the monthly per capita consumer expenditure in 1963–64 was Rs. 22.37 in rural areas, and Rs. 32.96 in urban areas, of which 70.1 per cent and 54.4 per cent, respectively, was spent on food.[6] On the basis of various criteria, such as cost of "minimum essential food" and "expenditure to buy food for minimum caloric requirements",

Indian economists have variously estimated the proportion of the Indian population living below the poverty line during the period 1968–70 to be between 41 and 53 per cent.[7] Comparing figures over time, most estimates indicate that the proportion of the population living below the poverty line has increased or remained substantially the same during the period 1960–70.[8] Surveys of food consumption in India made in 1960 show that 63.2 per cent of the rural population and 32.49 per cent of the urban population suffered from nutritional deficiency.[9] The comparable figures for 1967–68 indicate that the deficiency had by then worsened considerably compared to 1960–61, especially in the rural areas.[10]

Education
One area in which India has recorded impressive gains is in the expansion of educational facilities, especially at the secondary and college levels. According to the United Nation's estimates, the annual growth rates in education in India for First Level (age 6–13, primary middle schools), Second level (age 14–18, high school) and Third level (college level) were 5.4 per cent, 7.1 per cent and, 11.0 per cent respectively during the period 1960–70.[11] There has also been a rapid increase in the number of technically trained personnel. Presently India ranks third in the world (after the US and USSR) in the absolute number of technically trained workers.

What is the impact of this pattern of increased educational facilities on the process of economic development in India? In the literature on the role of education in economic development, it is generally held that there is a positive and high correlation between education and economic development.[12] This generalization is evidently based on the assumption that education, besides contributing to the enrichment of students, modernizing their outlook and so on, develops their capacity and will for positive economic activity. Unfortunately, India's educational system has not proved conducive to instilling these positive attitudes. According to a 1972 Task Force on Education appointed by the Government of India:

We have unfortunately, at present, a top heavy,

lopsided, educational structure which does not seem to be commensurate with the socio-economic needs of the society. This is not, however, a recent phenomenon, it has its roots in the pre-Independence period, only it has become more acute of late.[13]

Thus, India has more educated persons than the economy can presently absorb. Being unemployed, they are unable to contribute their talents to economic development and in fact constitute a burden on the national economy.

The incidence of unemployment among educated persons in India reveals two disquieting tendencies: first, the rate of unemployment, paradoxically, increases with the level of education and second, during the period 1960–70, the rate of increase in unemployment was greater for college graduates than for the holders of high school diplomas.[14] Even engineers and other persons with advanced technical education are facing unemployment in India. Thus, at the present level of development, the expansion of educational facilities, especially beyond secondary level, is not contributing to any significant extent to economic expansion. What is needed is a reconstruction of the educational system to meet India's development needs and also to strike a better balance between the number of graduates emerging from institutions of higher education and the demand for such skills and services. Despite repeated government proclamations during the last 25 years, there has been no noticeable effort in India to change her educational system to make it conducive to planned economic growth.

This discussion of various features of the Indian economy shows that the country possesses all the major symptoms of economic underdevelopment : low per capita income; population growth preceding economic development, which acts as a retarding factor in the development process; and low agricultural productivity arising essentially from lack of capital investment in land and in the essential economic overheads or infrastructure. With scarcity of capital relative to the abundant supply of labour, India may be said to be suffering from severe structural imbalance in regard to her factor-endowment situation.

Underdevelopment: A Historical Perspective

Historically, at least during the present century, India has remaind poor, with per capita income at static low levels. Data on the changes in output in pre-independence India are given in Table 1.3.

There were negative rates of growth in per capita output during the three decades 1916–1945, largely explained by the low productivity in agriculture. Over the five decades under review, agricultural output increased by only 12 per cent, whereas total population increased by 34 per cent. This imbalance is partly a reflection of the fact that the area under cultivation per head decreased from 1.11 acre in 1921 to 0.94 acre in 1941. The considerable increase in industry and mining did not affect total productivity significantly because of its minor share (less than 5 per cent) in the value of total output.

After Independence, India adopted ambitious plans for economic and social development. India's five-year plans, beginning in 1950–51, incorporated strategies to promote rapid and balanced economic development; to strengthen the economy at its base; and to initiate institutional changes that would facilitate rapid advances in future. More than 25 years have elapsed since the first of these five-year plans was formulated. The country has had heavy investments both in domestic and foreign resources. In 1977, India is in the midst of its Fifth Five-Year Plan. Though we will discuss the Indian plans in a later section, it may be pointed out that the performance of the Indian economy has been rather mixed. Whereas the overall achievements of the five-year plans have been less than impressive, some progress is observed from the changes in some important economic indicators. We will discuss this point in greater detail in a later section. For quick and convenient reference some figures on the growth of the economy are given in Table 1.4.

The growth rates are grossly inadequate to meet increased demands arising from a considerable growth in population and some rise in incomes. But they do represent some progress in India, which viewed historically, had been virtually stagnant over the last century. K.N. Raj observed in 1965 :

The rate of economic growth that has been achieved in India since 1950–51 is 2 to 3 times as high as the rate recorded in British administration. As a result, the percentage increase in national income in the last thirteen years has been higher than the percentage increase realized in India over the entire preceding half a century.[15]

Comparing the performance of the Indian

Table 1.3. Long-Term Changes in Net Output in India: 1896–1945

	1896–1904	1905–15	1916–25	1926–35	1936–45
Per capita output[a]	158	159	164	155	144
Per capita output[b]	100	101	104	98	91
Agricultural crops[b]	100	106	108	110	112
Industry and mining[b]	100	154	200	267	420
Population[b]	100	107	108	119	134
Decennial rate of percentage growth in per capita income	1	3	—6	—7	—5

[a]In rupees, 1952–53 prices
[b]Index —1896–1905-100

SOURCE: 1. S. Kuznets (ed.), *Economic Growth: Brazil, India and Japan*, (Durham: Duke University Press, 1955), pp. 120–124.

2. Surendra J. Patel, *Essays on Economic Transition* (New York: Asia Publishing House, 1965), p. 44.

Table 1.4. Annual Growth Rates :   Some Economic Indicators in India

(constant prices 1960–61)

Years	Growth National Product	Per Capita Income	Agricultural Production	Industrial Production	Population Growth
1951–56	3.5	1.6	4.2	8.2	1.9
1956–61	4.7	2.5	4.5	6.6	2.8
1961–66	2.6	0.3	−1.1	5.7	2.5

SOURCE: 1. *Economic Survey*, 1972–73, 1975–76.

2. Commerce Research Bureau, *Basic Statistics Relating to the Indian Economy*, Bombay, 1972.

3. Jagdish N. Bhagwati and Padma Desai, *India: Planning for Industrialization*, (New York: Oxford University Press, 1970), pp. 61–83.

4. Jagdish N. Bhagwati and T.N. Srinivasan, *Foreign Trade Regimes and Economic Development: India* (New York: National Bureau of Economic Research, 1975), pp. 1–32.

economy under the first three five-year plans, with that of pre-Independence India, Max Millikan observed :

The growth rate of nearly 4 per cent in this period represents a noticeable acceleration over the annual growth rate of British India for the first half of the twentieth century, which has been estimated at no more than 1 per cent, and compares very favourably with the growth rates of the presently advanced countries during their earlier development history.[16]

By mentioning some achievements of planning in India, we are not playing down the desperate economic plight of its millions, whose per capita income is one of the lowest in the world. There is, however, no denying the fact that planning in India, in the words of A.H. Hanson, "effected a break with economic stagnation. Dynamism has been created in the hitherto static economies and today, instead of the stagnation of the previous decades, clearly and unmistakably the economy has been pushed into motion…"[17]

The forces that have pushed the Indian economy into motion, moreover, have directly or indirectly created counterforces, all of which tend to act as a brake on India's future progress. Intuitively, this might be a plausible explanation of the slow progress of the Indian economy during the last two decades of economic

planning. We will come back to this point in the next section while explaining Leibenstein's hypothesis.

The Persistence of Underdevelopment

Why do underdeveloped countries continue to subsist at low income levels and why do efforts for development not put these economies on a "self-sustaining" path of economic growth? Economists have pondered over these questions, which are quite pertinent to the Indian economy both during the pre- and post-Independence periods. Some of the hypotheses suggested on these crucial questions are:

The Vicious Circle Hypothesis

The well-known vicious circle theory, associated with the names of Hans Singer (1949) and Ragnar Nurkse (1953), tries to explain the continuing and self-perpetuating low incomes in an underdeveloped economy, by a mutually reinforcing circle. It postulates a circular relationship between lack of capital, income and savings thus: Low incomes——→Low capacity to save——→Lack of capital——→Low productivity and low incomes.

This view has been criticised as being too simplistic: placing too much emphasis on income as a determinant of savings to the neglect of other socioeconomic factors. In our view, this hypothesis, though simplistic, does emphasise the crucial importance of savings and capital formation in the economic development process. Applying this hypothesis to the Indian economy, one can see that during the period 1950–70 with savings rates between 6 and 9 per cent (an investment rate of between 7 and 11 per cent) of the national income and the capital output ratio of 30; the national income would increase only by 3–3.5 per cent, with per capita income increasing at more than 1–1.5 per cent. From this negligible increase in per capita income, it is unrealistic to expect higher private savings, the lack of which is an important cause of lower incomes. We have discussed this issue fully in Chapter 13.

The vicious circle hypothesis also raises another crucial question of public policy in economic development. Economic development would require the breaking of this circle, and especially of the links between income and savings, irrespective of the economic and political structure of the society. Historical experience of the present developed economies shows that different methods were adopted to break this circle. The Communist countries, e.g., USSR, squeezed capital from the landowners, and also through reduction in the consumption of the working classes. Capitalistic countries, e.g.. USA and UK, encouraged the owners of the means of production to amass huge profits by paying lower wages (less than the productivity) to the working classes. Some countries, e.g., Japan, taxed agriculture to finance industrial development. The experiences of developed countries clearly suggest different techniques that can be adopted by the developing countries to break the "vicious circle" of underdevelopment.

Low Income-Level Equilibrium
Another explanation for the persistence of underdevelopment is furnished by the Leibenstein hypothesis :
1. It is useful to characterize a backward economy as an equilibrium system whose equilibrium state (or states) possesses a degree of "quasi-stability" with respect to per capita income.
2. If the equilibrium of a backward

economy is disturbed, the forces or influences that tend to raise per capita income set in motion, directly or indirectly, forces that have the effect of depressing per capita income.
3. In the disequilibrium state (in the backward economy), for at least the lower incomes above the equilibrium levels, the effects of the income-depressing forces are greater than the effects of the income-raising forces.[18]

The static nature of the Indian economy, before Independence, clearly corresponds to Leibenstein's quasi-stability condition. Changes in some economic variables— introduction of railways and roads, huge investments in modern technology in textile industry and plantations—did occur, creating sporadic increases in the income levels. But, as Leibenstein notes, these stimulants did not lead to sustained growth in per capita incomes but to a "pattern of change that leads to an eventual return to the low, underdeveloped equilibrium income".[19]

As noted earlier, massive investments under five-year plans on economic and social improvement programmes have created strong forces which raised per capita income, expanded the infrastructure and achieved some economic development. But these productive forces evoked counterforces that have tended to retard further economic development and growth. Karl von Vorys describes the effect of these counterforces as a "problem of accelerated reaction".[20] Moreover, during the later stages of economic development in India (1960–70), these counterforces have tended to accelerate more rapidly than the forces of development, and "those counterforces unless controlled, may very well not only slow down economic development but bring it to a standstill".[21]

What are some of these major counterforces which are inhibiting the growth of the Indian economy? It is an essential task of economic planning and policy to identify these counterforces and adopt appropriate policies to counteract them. In our opinion, these counterforces include (i) Population explosion, (ii) Low capital formation, and (iii) Revolution of rising expectations giving rise to increased demand for goods and services. We have discussed these factors in separate chapters, but it is pertinent to mention that these counterforces have been created or at least accentuated by the planning process in India. The population explosion is caused by a drastic decline in the death rate, brought about to a great extent by various improved health and sanitation measures adopted under five-year plans. Consequently, India's population has now reached a stage where any further increase in numbers diminishes rather than increases the per capita income. Increased expectations, or Revolution of Rising Expectations, arising from the clearly-stated well-publicised objectives of various five-year plans, have stepped up the demand for goods and services to the point that the economy has not been able to generate capital required for sustained economic expansion. As discussed in Chapters 3 and 13, the future success of planning in India will be largely determined by the extent to which the problems of "population explosion" and low "capital formation" are successfully dealt with.

Economic Planning: Indian Five-Year Plans
A study of Indian economic history brings out clearly certain factors that have greatly influenced the general attitudes in India towards formulating economic plans and policies for development. It is generally believed by students of Indian history that, in the eighteenth century, India was industrially more advanced and materially more prosperous than Europe. The ruthless policies adopted by the East India Company resulted in the destruction of Indian industries and consequent "ruralization", unemployment and impoverishment of the Indian people. British policies in India from the middle of the nineteenth century prevented industrialization, despite the country's rich resources of industrial raw materials. The blame for "underdevelopment" and poverty was thus laid squarely on the British Government. Independence from alien rule was seen as the solution to the poverty problem, and this was the main slogan and rallying point of Indian nationalism.

Also, there were strong sentiments against the laissez faire policies of capitalism, which were believed to have brought about the ruin of the Indian economy and to have arrested economic growth. A study of the political and economic thinking of the Indian leadership before independence, as stated in various Economic Plans— Plan by the National Planning Committee (1938); the Bombay Plan (1944), the Gandhian Plan and the People's Plan, shows a strong commitment to (i) democratic socialism, (ii) active state participation in various aspects of the economy to achieve "social" as opposed to private gain, and (iii) comprehensive economic planning covering all facets of national life. In presenting this brief historical account, we wish to stress the point that much of India's economic policy and plan objectives are rooted in her history.

Within about three years of achieving independence, the Indian Planning Commission was set up to draw up plans for economic development. The Planning Commission was instructed to

1. make an assessment of the material, capital and human resources of the country, including technical personnel, and formulate a plan for the most effective and balanced utilization of the country's resources;

2. determine priorities, define the stages in which the plan should be carried out, and propose the allocation of resources for the due completion of each stage; and

3. indicate the factors which are tending to retard economic development, and determine the conditions which, in view of the current social and political situation, should be established for the successful execution of the Plan.

Since 1950, India has completed the First Five-Year Plan, 1950–51 to 1955–56; Second Five-Year Plan, 1955–56 to 1960–61; Third Five-Year Plan, 1960–61 to 1965–66; Annual Plans, 1966–67 to 1968–69; and Fourth Five-Year Plan, 1969–70 to 1974–75. The country is now in the middle of the Fifth Five-Year Plan (1974–75 to 1979–80).

The texts of these plan documents provide detailed explorations on the problems and prospects of the Indian economy. Each plan is built on the experience of the earlier one, and contains a discussion on patterns of investment, including the planning strategies proposed to accomplish production targets in the different sectors of the economy. The Planning Commission reports on the progress of each plan, recommending alterations necessitated by the rapid social, economic, and political changes in the country. The Indian plans display a high level of understanding of the nature and problems of the Indian economy. In fact, the Indian plans are recognized as one of the finest contributions to the literature on development economics and are widely read and used by planners and economists throughout, the world. (It is ironic that the nation that can prepare such fine plans cannot solve her economic problems by implementing them).

The First Five-Year Plan (1950–51 to 1955–56) aimed

1. to correct the disequilibrium in the economy caused by the Second World War and the 1947 partition of the country; and

2. to initiate a process of development for raising national income to improve the standards of living.

Priority was given to development of agriculture and the social and economic infrastructure, including irrigation and power projects. The basic criterion for determining economic and planning policies was declared to be a "socialistic pattern of society" (discussed in the next section). The Plan aimed at increasing the rate of investment from 5 per cent to about 7 per cent of the national income. The First Plan succeeded in achieving most of its targets: national income increased by 17.5 per cent (against the target of 12.5 per cent), agricultural and industrial production increased by 21.0 per cent and 41.0 per cent respectively. Rates of investment improved from about 5 per cent in 1950–51 to 7.3 per cent in 1955–56. At the end of the First Plan, the Indian economy had price stability with near self-sufficiency in food and other essential raw materials. It was, however, held in certain quarters that the success of the First Plan was due to favourable monsoons, and the existing "idle capacity" in the industrial sector rather than the plan policies.

Emboldened by the success of the First Plan, the Planning Commission formu-

lated an ambitious Second Five-Year Plan (1955–56 to 1960–61) with these objectives:

1. an increase of 25 per cent in the national income;

2. rapid industrialization with particular emphasis on the development of basic and heavy industries;

3. provision of employment opportunities; and

4. reduction in inequalities in income and wealth distribution.

The rate of investment was to increase from 7 per cent of the national income to about 11 per cent by 1960–61. The development strategy seemed to be "big push" with "unbalanced" approach. Industrialization and mineral development were considered "growing points" or "leading sectors" and were, accordingly, accorded highest priority in the allocation of plan resources. The achievements of the Second Plan were lower than the targets. The increase in national income was 23.5 per cent, against the target of 25 per cent. With a population increase of 11.0 per cent (against the expected figure of 6.0 per cent) the increase in per capita income was only 12.5 per cent. Agricultural production, especially of foodgrains, jute, cotton and oil seeds, received a serious setback. Heavy and basic industries, e.g., steel and cement, which have a long gestation period were behind schedule. The upshot of the fall in output, against the increasing demands from increased spending, created scarcities and increased inflationary pressures (for details see Chapter 16). There were also serious balance-of-payment difficulties on account of the high foreign-exchange component in planned industrial projects. The planners blamed the fall in agricultural production on the failure of monsoons in 1957–58 and 1959–60, but the fact remains that growth in agricultural production did not keep pace with the increasd demand on this sector from the process of industialization. The unemployment situation did not ease at all and in fact the Second Plan period ended with a bigger backlog of unemployed manpower.

Realizing that unsatisfactory growth of agriculture was an important limiting factor in the process of economic planning, the Third Five-Year Plan (1960–61 to 1965–66) emphasised that agriculture must be given priority. The process of industrialization through heavy industries was, however, to continue. The major objectives of the Third Plan were to

1. secure an increase in national income of over 6 per cent per year and at the same time to ensure a self-sustaining growth for the economy,

2. achieve self-sufficiency in foodgrains and increase agricultural production to meet the demands for industrialization,

3. expand basic industries: steel, chemicals, fuel and power,

4. utilize fully the manpower resources of the country and ensure substantial expansion in employment opportunities, and

5. achieve greater equality of opportunity.

The Third Plan postulated an increase of 30 per cent in agricultural production: 70 per cent in industry, and 30 per cent in national income. Unfortunately, the progress of the Third Plan also fell far short of target. The increase in national income was less than half of the targeted amount; food production increased by only 2 per cent per year, against the targeted rate of 6 per cent; industrial production too fell short of target: an annual average rate of 5.7 per cent against the targeted 7.5 per cent. The Third Plan period started with an unemployment figure of 7.0 million, while it ended with a much higher backlog of 9.6 million, indicating that the problem of unemployment was in fact accentuated during the Third Plan. The inflationary pressure created during the Second Plan continued to increase during the Third Plan.

What did go wrong during the Third Plan period? First, there was trouble on the Indo-Chinese borders in 1962, and hostilities with Pakistan in 1965. These events forced diversion of some of the planned resources to the defence budget. Secondly, the serious monsoon failure in 1964–65 and bad weather conditions during 1965–66 caused a decline in agricultural production. It was also felt that the major cause of failures in

various sectors was the lack of proper implementation of plan provisions.

The serious international problems and natural calamities faced during the Third Plan period—the Chinese invasion, the Indo-Pakistan conflict, two years of severe drought—increasing inflationary pressures, etc.,—delayed the finalization of the Fourth Plan. Instead, between 1966–1969, three Annual Plans were formulated, mainly to cope with the prevailing pressing problems and increasing food production; introducing anti-inflationary measures ; providing employment opportunities. The Annual Plans had mixed results. The year 1966–67 saw another drought, food production did not register any appreciable increase against increasing demands, necessitating food imports amounting to 8.7 million tons in 1967. The poor performance of agriculture adversely affected industrial output, especially in industries utilizing agricultural raw materials. The increase in industrial production was only 0.3 per cent during 1966–67. The savings rate declined to 8.2 per cent from the earlier-year figure of 10.2 per cent. This poor performance put pressures on price levels, further increasing the inflationary trend. In the years 1967–68 and 1968–69, a new agricultural strategy of increasing the application of new and improved inputs, mainly fertilizers, in selected areas of the country, was adopted to increase agricultural output surely and quickly. Good monsoons during this period along with the new agricultural strategy, had beneficial results in increasing the agricultural output, including an increase in the supply of raw materials and the resultant improved industrial output. The price index registered some decrease, easing inflationary pressures in the economy.

With the background of some economic recovery with eased pressures on prices, the Fourth Five-Year Plan was introduced covering the period 1969–1974. The basic strategy of the Fourth Plan was "growth with stability" and it had the following specific objectives:

1. to achieve an annual growth in national income of 5.5 per cent (and per capita income of about 3 per cent). Food production to increase by 31 per cent

during the Plan period;

2. to achieve price stability through building buffer stocks of foodgrains and other essential commodities;

3. to achieve self reliance by gradually ending dependence on foreign aid;

4. to achieve social justice and equality in income and wealth distribution; and

5. growth of employment opportunities to absorb the increasing labour force.

The rate of private savings was to be stepped up from 11.2 per cent of the national income in 1968–69 to 14.5 per cent by 1974–75. During the first two years, 1969–70, and 1970–71, the achievements of the Fourth Plan were on the target. National income increased at the annual rate of 5.5 per cent. But, unfortunately from 1971–72, the economy was subjected to heavy strain. It started with the heavy refugee influx from Bangladesh followed by the conflict with Pakistan, and the hike in the prices of critical raw materials—gasoline and fuels. The tempo of the green revolution slowed down. The Indian economy was also affected by the international economic situation characterized by high inflation arising from shortages of critical raw materials and fuel price increases. During the years 1971–72 and 1972–73, agricultural production declined by 0.4 per cent and 8.0 per cent respectively. The decrease in food production was much greater than these ratios. Growth rate of industrial production fell to 3.0 per cent in 1970–71 and 4.4 per cent during 1972–73. The shortages created in the economy against the growing demand for consumer goods added to the spiral of inflation. Wholesale prices increased by 10 per cent during 1972–73 and 22.6 per cent in 1973–74. The consumer price index (1960–100), which was 174 in 1968–69 shot up to 275 per cent by March 1975. The increase in real national income was nominal and even negative during this period. Galloping inflation was accompanied by the usual social and economic evils including hoarding, and black marketing. Serious labour unrest was indicated by strikes and labour troubles. The common man was losing faith in the goals of economic planning and dismissed the plan as

nothing more than a futile academic excercise. Academic circles[22] characterized the deteriorating economic situation as a "crisis" and there were persistent demands for bold action to curb "inflation", "indiscipline", and "fall in production".

It was in the midst of this crisis in the Indian economy that the Planning Commission released *Towards an Approach to the Fifth Plan* (May 1972) and later *Draft Fifth Plan* (1974–1979). With the broad objective of "the removal of poverty and the attainment of economic self-reliance", the Fifth Five-Year Plan stresses the following goals;

1. Implementation of a National Programme of Minimum Needs : providing basic necessities; elementary education for all children up to the age of 14; public health facilities; provision of drinking water; home sites for landless labour; roads and electricity and slum clearance and environmental improvement;

2. Self-reliance : according to the Planning Commission, "it is, thus, visualized that by 1985–86, we would be in a position to meet the maximum amount of foreign exchange requirements, including debt service charges, from our own resources, thus obviating the need for any significant inflow of concessional aid".[23] This objective assumes a self-sustaining growth rate of 6.2 per cent per year, growth of exports at 7.6 per cent; and a progressive substitution of imports during the plan period;

3. Removal of Poverty: through a direct attack on the problems of unemployment, and underemployment. According to the Planning Commission, "the twin causes of poverty are underdevelopment and inequality.... The problem cannot be overcome within the foreseeable future by efforts in one direction only... Growth and reduction in inequality are both indispensable to a successful attack on mass poverty.... The strategy for elimination of poverty thus rested on two major factors, a rising rate of growth of domestic product combined with declining rate of growth of population"[24];

4. Expansion of Employment : "The Fifth Plan envisages substantial additional

opportunities for wage employment in the non-agricultural sector.... Expanded, fuller and more productive self-employment is anticipated in agriculture, cottage industry, road transport, trade and service sector".[25] For increasing employment opportunities, the Plan suggests "generating additional employment by undertaking area-based land improvement programmes or by giving incentives to small units in sectors where these have the potentiality to be competitive with large-scale units".[26] As regards providing jobs to technical personnel, the Plan asserts "the solution for the fuller employment of scientists, engineers and technicians must eventually be found in an upsurge of industrial growth and vigorous expansion of productive research and development activities.[27]

The Fifth Plan provides for an annual 5.7 per cent rate of growth in the national income with a growth rate of 4 per cent per year in agriculture and 8 per cent for the manufacturing sector. With an anticipated increase in population at the rate of 1.8 per cent, the per capita increase in income would be at the rate of 3.9 per cent during the Fifth Plan period.

The release of the *Fifth Five-Year Plan* did not ease the growing pessimism and frustration in the country since there was *not* much new and basically different in it. The nation was drifting towards chaos under the heavy stresses and strains of mounting economic problems. In June 1975, the Indian Government declared a national emergency, and the Prime Minister issued a 20-point programme embodying programmes to tackle these problems. We will come to this point in a later section.

Table 1.5 gives a breakdown on outlays in the five-year plans, which would indicate the relative priorities accorded to different sectors.

Development Strategy in Five-Year Plans

Development planning involves a deliberate choice between various policy alternatives and instruments with which to attack the problems of a developing economy. Every policy alternative has varying social and economic implications

which have to be weighed carefully with the objectives of planning. A study of the Indian plans shows their preference for certain strategies, which in some cases are stated succinctly.

Mathematical Models
Overall, the methodology adopted in the plans was based on simple neoclassical models of economic growth. The First Plan, though a collection of on-going projects, contained projections for the next 25 years based on the simple Harrod-Domar model[28]

$$\Delta I \times \frac{1}{\alpha} = I \delta$$

where I represents the rate of investment in a given period, α the marginal propensity to save and δ the output-capital ratio, or the potential social average productivity of investment. From this equation, we can derive the value of ΔI at which the additional output from investment will be equal to additional aggregate demand generated during the period. Thus for given values of α and δ we can compute rates of investment, income, and consumption which would be consistent with steady growth of the economy. For the First Plan, I_0 (rate of investment in the base year 1950–51) was taken to be about 5 per cent of the national income; δ was estimated at 0.33, and it was estimated that α could be raised to 0.20 during the First Plan and 0.50 in the subsequent plans. On this assumption, it was shown that the rate of investment could be raised from 5 per cent of the national income in 1950–51, to about 7 per cent by the end of the First Plan, 11 per cent by the end of the Second, and 20 per cent by 1967–68. Assuming population increase at an annual average rate of 1.25 per cent, the consumption levels would continue to increase with the proposed marginal savings rates mentioned above. On the basis of all the implicit assumptions, the per capita income could be doubled by 1977, compared to its level in 1950–51.

The Second Plan was based on the Mahalanobis two sector (consumer goods and producer goods) model which emphasises the physical aspects of planning and investment. It was demonstrated[29] that if

Table 1.5. Total Public Sector Outlays During the Five-Year Plans (including State's shares)

(rupees in crores)

Head	First Plan	Second Plan	Third Plan	Fourth Plan	Fifth Plan
1. Agriculture and allied sectors	290 (14.8)	549 (11.7)	1089 (12.7)	2353.5 (15)	4730 (12.7)
2. Irrigation and flood control	434 (22.2)	430 (9.2)	665 (7.8)	1272.0 (8.1)	2681 (7.2)
3. Power	149 (7.6)	452 (9.7)	1252 (14.6)	2911.8 (18.5)	6190 (16.7)
4. Village and small industries	42 (2.1)	187 (4.0)	241 (2.8)	244.7 (1.6)	— —
5. Industry and minerals	55 (2.8)	938 (20.1)	1726 (20.1)	2873.6 (18.3)	8939 (24.0)
6. Transport and communications	518 (26.4)	1261 (27.0)	2112 (24.6)	3062 (19.5)	7115 (19.1)
7. Social Services—health, education, and family planning	472 (24.1)	855 (18.3)	1492 (17.4)	3006.2 (19.0)	6709 (18.0)
Total	1960 (100)	4672 (100)	8577 (100)	15724 (100)	37250 (100)

NOTE: Figures in brackets are proportion of expenditures on different heads to the total plan outlays.

SOURCE: 1. Government of India, Planning Commission, *Draft Fifth Five-Year Plan, 1974–79.* Vol. I (New Delhi, 1973), p. 83.

2. ———, Publications Division, *India: A Reference Manual*, New Delhi, 1976, p. 175.

α_0 = the initial investment rate

λ_c and λ_k = the fractions of net investment used in consumer goods sector c and capital goods sector k respectively.

β_c and β_k = the ratios of increment of income to investment in sectors c and k respectively; and

Y_0, C_0, K_0, Y_t, C_t & K_t = the national income, consumption, and investment in the base year and in period t respectively

$$K_t = (1 + \lambda_k \beta_k)^t K_0$$

and

$$Y_t = Y_0 \left[1 + \alpha_0 \frac{\lambda_k \beta_k + \lambda_c \beta_c}{\lambda_k \beta_k} \{(1 + \lambda_k \beta_k)^t - 1\} \right]$$

It was assumed that β_c would be normally greater than β_k. Thus, the larger the percentage investment in consumer goods industries, the larger would be the income generated. However, after "a critical range of time—the larger the investment in investment goods industries, the larger will be the income generated". The logic of this view is that a higher rate of investment (i.e., a greater proportion of productive factors used for accumulation) would result in a smaller volume of output being available for consumption in the short run but that, over the long run, it would produce a higher growth-rate of consumption; the difference would be that there is a choice to be made between investment in capital goods and investment in consumer goods industries. In this model, applied to the Second Five-Year Plan, β was taken as 0.50, β_k as 0.20 and λ_k was fixed at 0.33. With the values of λ_k taken as 0.33, β and β_k as 0.50 and 0.20 respectively, it is obvious that the marginal propensity to save would need to be only around 0.13.

The Third Five-Year Plan brought more sophistication to the planning excercise. An attempt was made to achieve greater inter-industry consistency in some detail. However, basically the Third Plan was a continuation of Second Plan policies and choices, i.e., with emphasis on heavy industries. In the Fourth Plan, there was a shift away from emphasis on heavy industry, and stress laid on agriculture. But this was again changed in the Fifth Plan.

Development Strategy
Emphasis on Heavy and Capital Goods Industries It is commonly believed in the underdeveloped countries that "industrialization", specially of "basic and heavy industries" is a prerequisite of economic development. Steel plants and other large-scale industries are now international status symbols. The historical experience of some of the western advanced countries suggests that development of agricultural, then consumer goods industries, and last, of heavy basic industries are the typical stages of economic growth. Some advanced countries, specially the Soviet Union, skipped the earlier stages and started their plans directly with development of heavy industries. The Soviet Union still continues to have problems with her agriculture; but, it is commonly believed in the underdeveloped countries that Russia has become a powerful nation by putting emphasis on industrialization, specially of heavy industries, in her plan policies.

As regards India, the absence of heavy industries has always been considered the major obstacle to her development. This view stems from the argument that Indian industrial development has been lopsided. During the pre-independence period, while India had fairly well-developed consumer goods industries (e.g., cotton textiles), the basic and capital goods industries were conspicuously absent. This lack of basic industries persisted despite the fact that she had ample supplies of industrial raw materials. Nehru used to characterize steel and fertilizer plants as "temples of the modern India". While the First Plan emphasised infrastructures —power projects, transport and communi-

cations, from the Second Plan onwards development of large-scale industries and mineral development were accorded priority in the allocation of plan outlays, as in Table 1.5. As explained above, the Mahalanobis model—the basis of the Second Plan—emphasised investment in the heavy and basic industries to accelerate the level of national income. According to the development strategy implicit in the Mahalanobis model, and five-year plans, small-scale and cottage industries would be developed to meet the demands for consumer goods, and to provide employment specially in the rural sector. The Indian Planning Commission seems to have rejected the suggestion that, rather than heavy investments in costly "machines to make machines" to increase the productive capacity of the economy, better and faster results would be achieved by investments in her "export-oriented industries". The rationale for rejecting this view was that the possibilities of enlarging India's exports were limited on account of their highly elastic demand in the world market and also facilities for the manufacturing of simple consumer goods, like cotton textiles, would become so generally available among nations that it would be unsafe to rely on their exports in the long run.

"Growth Orientation" The main emphasis in the five-year plans was to achieve the highest of attainable growth rates. Nehru once remarked: "Production comes first and I am prepared to say that everything we should do should be judged from the point of view of the production".[30] It was assumed that all other objectives, e.g., greater employment opportunities and eradication of poverty, would somehow follow from increase in national income. In other words, increase in grotwh rate of national income was a primary goal and the other objectives were derivative and secondary. This assumption, running explicitly in all the plans was implicitly stated in the Fifth Plan:

> In elaborating our strategy of development in earlier plan documents, we seem to have assumed that fast rate of growth of national income will by itself create more and

fuller employment and produce higher living standards of the poor.[31]

The Planning Commission ignored the fact that the strategy of "production orientation" without change in the pattern of ownership of the means of production might result in further maldistribution of income and wealth. As noted in an earlier section, this is what seems to have happened in the Indian economy during the last two decades.

Socialist Pattern of Society:
Growth of the Public Sector
The long-term goal of Indian Planning has been to transform the economy into a Socialistic Pattern of Society, and most of the plan policies and development strategies reflect this goal. Though the formal resolution on this issue was passed at the Avadi session of the Indian National Congress in 1955, the Indian leadership was definitely committed to this goal much before Independence. The view that the laissez faire (or "market economic system") system adopted by the British Government during their two centuries of occupation of India was the major obstacle to economic development, was widely held.

The major Indian leaders, specially Mahatma Gandhi, Tagore and Nehru, were greatly influenced by socialist ideas and they articulated them freely in their writings and speeches, with a great impact on the nation's thinking. In 1938, the National Planning Committee set up by the All-India National Congress suggested planning for the economic development of India following the path of a socialistic society within a democratic framework.[32] Nehru, the chief architect of economic planning rejected the sociopolitical system prevailing in India before Independence:

Our economy and social structure have outlived their days and it has become a matter of urgent necessity for us to refashion them so that they may promote the happiness of all our people in things material and spiritual... *we must aim at a classless society,* based on cooperative effort, *with opportunities for all.*[33]

Nehru rejected Capitalism for India, stating that "a system which is based purely on the acquisitive instinct of society is immoral". Nehru made it quite clear in 1954 that

The picture I have in mind is definitely and absolutely a socialistic picture of society. I am not using the word in a dogmatic sense at all. I mean largely that the means of production should be socially owned and controlled for the benefit of society as a whole. There is plenty of room for private enterprise there, provided the main aim is kept clear.[34]

The economic policy formulated in pursuance of the above statements is reflected in the Constitution of India. Articles 38, 39 and 41 are particularly relevant:

The state shall strive to promote the welfare of the people by securing and protecting, as effectively as it may, a social order in which justice...social, economic and political, shall inform all institutions of national life (Article 38).

The state shall, in particular, direct its policy towards securing...
a. that the citizens, men and women, equally, have the right to an adequate means of livelihood;
b. that the ownership and control of the material resources of the community are so distributed as best to subserve the common good; and
c. that the operation of the economic system does not result in the concentration of wealth and means of production to the common detriment (Article 39).

The state shall, within the limits of its economic capacity and development, make effective provision for securing the right to work, to education, and to public assistance in cases of unemployment, old age, sickness and disablement, and in other cases of undeserved want (Article 41).

In December 1954, the Indian Lok Sabha clearly stated India's economic policy in a resolution containing the following clauses:

1. The objective of economic policy should be a Socialistic Pattern of Society, and
2. Towards this end the tempo of economic activity in general and industrial development in particular should be stepped up to the maximum possible extent.

The Second Five-Year Plan explained the concept Socialistic Pattern of Society further, to mean that the basic criterion for determining the lines of advance must not be private profit, but social gain. More specifically

1. major decisions were to be made by "agencies informed by social purpose".
2. benefits were to accrue more and more to the "relatively less privileged classes of society".
3. there was to be a "progressive reduction of the concentration of incomes, wealth, and economic power".
4. greater opportunities for "vertical mobility of labour" were to be given to the small man.
5. the public sector of the economy was to undergo rapid expansion.

The Third Five-Year Plan emphasised the reduction of inequalities in income and wealth distribution and a more even distribution of economic power. The Fourth Five-Year Plan not only places emphasis on the above objectives, but also suggests further nationalization of enterprises. The Prime Minister—the Chairman of the Planning Commission —asserts

the overriding inspiration must be a burning sense of social justice. While increased production is of the utmost importance, it is equally important to remove, or reduce, and prevent the concentration of wealth and economic power.... A reorientation of our socio-economic institutions in this spirit is, accordingly, a first necessity.[35]

The above statements clearly state the major objectives of the socialist society as

1. rapid economic growth through planning,
2. more equitable distribution of income and wealth, and
3. fuller employment.

The means of achieving these objectives

might help all of these objectives, while others might aid one objective at the expense of the others.

The instruments of public policy for achieving the goals of socialistic society in broad terms were

1. economic planning for rapid economic development
2. growth of public sector
3. nationalization
4. land reforms
5. redistributive policies to redistribute income and wealth.

For an understanding of the nature of India's socialistic society, the following remarks made by Padma Desai and Jagdish Bhagwati are highly pertinent:

Nearly all traditional socialist doctrines lead in the direction of public ownership of the means of production, and (failing total control of the means of production) they equally point in the direction of public ownership of the "key" sectors of production. The specific shape given to these doctrines in the Indian context however, was in the Fabian-type gradualism which characterized the transition to public ownership, in *toto* and of the key sectors.[36]

This Fabian-type gradualism in India's economic policy meant some specific policies:

1. Nationalization of the existing capital stock was ruled out and Government sought to increase the share of the public sector in total investment so that Government's share in the total capital stock becomes dominant. The share of the public sector in total investment increased from 54.0 per cent in the Second Five-Year Plan to 58.6 per cent and 63.7 per cent in the Third and Fourth Plans respectively. The dominant industries in the key sector included steel and other heavy industries, e.g., fertilizers, machine tools, and ship-building. The successive Industrial Policy Resolutions focused on reservation of these areas for public sector investment rather than on the take-over of existing private sector industries (for example the case of the Tata Iron and Steel Company).
2. The private sector was allowd to contribute in the industrialization of

medium type and consumer goods industries, while the economy was being transformed into one dominated by the public sector incorporating the heavy and basic industries.

3. The devices of substantial targeting and comprehensive industrial licensing, were used to control and direct the level and composition of industrial production and investment in the economy.

4. Licensing and other controls were used to prevent the concentration of industrial wealth and power in a small number of families and groups.

The growth of the public sector and its relationship with the private is discussed in detail in Chapter 9.

In the domain of agriculture, the major components of the strategy were (a) security of tenure, (b) abolition of absentee landownership, and (c) cooperative farming and marketing. These are discussed in detail in Chapter 6.

More equal distribution of income and wealth and eradication of poverty were to be achieved by

1. land reform measures
2. growth of public sector
3. increase in per capita income, and
4. provision of employment opportunities.

It is important to point out that no radical policy, e.g., nationalization of land for state farming or redistribution among the landless labourers, was contemplated. In other words, the five-year plans did not suggest any structural changes in the ownership patterns either in the agricultural or industrial sectors. The outcome of the Indian Socialistic Society is discussed in a later section.

Self Reliance The Fifth Five-Year Plan has set the achievement of "economic self-reliance" as one of the strategic goals of planning in India. The idea is however not new. Besides some odd references to it in the earlier plans, self-reliance was mentioned several times, specially during national crises such as Independence, periods of food scarcity, and international conflicts. The roots of self-reliance can also be traced to the *swadeshi* movement launched during the twenties, and to the Gandhian idea of village-level self-suffi-

ciency. A review of the five-year plans would show that "self-reliance" involves:

1. a long-term equilibrium in the balance of payments. Rather than depend on foreign loans and grants in these days of uncertain international relations, the country should be able to finance its imports by generating sufficient export surpluses.

2. self-sufficiency in food and other essential raw materials.

3. self-sufficiency in defence and other strategic defence-related industries.

4. self-sufficiency in highly technically qualified personnel and knowhow.

5. self-sufficiency in the capital goods essential for economic development of the country.

To achieve the goal of self-reliance, the Fifth Plan seeks "a dynamic self-reliance where the rate of economic growth is accelerated, while, at the same time, developing the capacity to sustain it essentially from our own resources. It is thus envisaged that by 1985–86, economic growth would be basically self-sustaining at a rate of 6.2 per cent per annum, which would be the highest ever attained by the economy on a sustained basis."[37] The five-year plans have recommended specific policies including domestic capital formation to "end dependence on foreign capital": export promotion and import substitution; expansion and diversification of technical services.

Comprehensiveness The Indian plans are comprehensive in the sense that they cover many aspects of the society, from the gross national product to the arts and music, from the welfare of the lower castes to improvement of transport and communication systems. According to the Second Five-Year Plan, the Indian plans are intended to

accelerate the institutional changes needed to make the economy more dynamic and more progressive in terms no less of social than economic ends. Development is a continuous process; it touches all aspects of community life and has to be viewed comprehensively. Economic planning, thus extends itself into extra-economic spheres, educational and cultural.[38]

Some writers have criticised this approach for spreading scarce resources too thinly, instead of concentrating on areas of high growth-potential.[39] The Indian plans, however, provide for the development not only of the production of goods and services, but also social services and civilizing activities. It is obvious that the planning technique which considers all "social objectives higher than mere material gains" would produce a lower growth rate.

Democratic Planning and Federal Political Structure The Indian plans are formulated and implemented within a democratic and federal structure. The Planning Commission is an advisory committee, charged with the responsibility of preparing plans in consultation with diverse political and economic interests. The Commission first prepares a draft plan which is subjected to critical review all over the country by various interest groups. Taking into account all the dissenting views, the Commission then revises the plan and presents it to Parliament for approval. After this approval, the plan is broken up into different segments and forwarded to various Central ministries and State governments for implementation of the plan provisions falling under their jurisdiction, according to the division of power under the Constitution. There are various coordinating agencies, e.g., the National Development Council, to coordinate between the different levels. From this very brief review of the administrative structure of planning in India, the following points should be stressed:
  1. Planning in India is an open process.
  2. The Planning Commission is an advisory committee. It prepares the plan but has no authority to implement it.
  3. Implementation of the plan is left to various levels of government in the Indian federal set-up : Centre, States, and local governments, according to the demarcation of functions provided for in the Indian Constitution.
  4. The success of the plan depends on public cooperation and mass participation.

In the Indian democratic set-up, Government has no authority to restrain private consumption, force private capital formation or force people to work, as we find in totalitarian regimes. Gunnar Myrdal[40] characterizes India as a "soft state" where the obligation on the part of the masses to make sacrifices for economic development cannot be easily enforced.

Bhatt describes how democratic planning within a federal structure imposes considerable constraints:

> The functioning of a democratic process in a poor country with a large size and intense religious, linguistic and cultural diversity creates sometimes such irrational and conflicting demands on the economic system as the system cannot meet without adversely impinging on the growth process.[41]

It is important to keep in mind the social and political environment within which Indian plans are formulated and implemented, especially while comparing the Indian performance with that of totalitarian regimes like China. In a totalitarian society the government has rigid control on key economic variables such as choice between consumption and savings; leisure and work; and also rigid control on the national resources. In such a society, there is minimal dissension against the decisions of the central planning authority and any conflicting demands can be resolved easily. In such a society, the implementation of plan policies, thus, becomes much easier than in democratic societies like India.

Development Performance: 25 Years of Planning in India

1975 was a corner-stone in the history of planning in India. It saw the completion of a quarter-century of planning—the First to the Fourth Plans, including the Annual Plans. Though the Indian economy had made significant progress in certain aspects, some serious problems—galloping inflation, rising unemployment especially among educated persons, adverse balance of payments, labour unrest—have cropped up. Various studies concluded that many of the egalitarian policies emphasised in all the plans, e.g., land reforms, reducing income inequalities and removal of poverty, had been largely a failure. A feeling was developing among a large section of the people that the five-year plans had not made any difference to their deteriorating social and economic lot. Several studies published during 1970–75, on the state of the Indian economy and impact of the five-year plans, presented the rather grim picture of the Indian economy and planning being in a state of crisis.[42] It was widely suggested that nothing short of bold steps could save the economy. In view of mounting economic difficulties and in recognition of the fact that growing pessimism and disillusionment among the masses was injurious to democratic planning, the Indian government issued on 1 July 1975, the 20-point Programme to invigorate the planning process. Thus 1975 marks an important stage in Indian planning.

Development Gains
India's development performance during 1950–1977, can be reviewed in terms of some major economic indicators in Table 1.6.

Growth in the Gross National Product
The growth rate of the gross national product and also the per capita income can be interpreted in two ways. A comparison of the growth rate during the period 1950–75, with that in the pre-Independence period, to repeat Max Millikan's remarks, "represents a notable acceleration over the annual growth rate of British India for the first half of the twentieth century, which has been estimated at no more than one per cent, and compares very favourably with the growth rates of the presently advanced countries during their earlier development".[43] In this sense, the growth of the Indian economy represents a significant break in the virtual stagnation during the first half of the present century as shown in Table 1.3. The growth of the economy during the last two decades is, however, not impressive judged from (i) the target or planned growth-rates, which are higher than the realized rates, except during the First Plan, and (ii) comparison with other underdeveloped countries. As Jagdish Bhagwati remarks :

> It is now clear that the Indian economic performance, while a definite improvement over that in the pre-Independence period, is less than satisfying whether one takes the "capitalistic" index of growth rates of income or the "socialist" indices of eradication of poverty and reduction of income inequality. International comparisons show that our growth rate during the last two decades since planning began has been bettered by a number of other countries of different sizes, political persuasions and economic ideologies : Taiwan, South Korea, Brazil and Israel are only a few of the examples that may be mentioned.[44]

The increase in already grossly inadequate per capita income at a very small average annual rate of about 1.3 per cent does not speak well for the effectiveness of economic planning.

Growth of Infrastructure and Basic Industries
There has been considerable progress in the provision of infrastructure and the basic industries. Road kilometerage increased from 4 lakhs in 1951 to 11.5 lakhs in 1974. Railway-route length increased from 53,596 kms in 1951 to 60,234 kms in 1974. Shipping tonnage increased to 39 lakh grt in 1976, from 3.7 in 1951. The electric power generated jumped from 530 crore Kwh in 1951 to 5,898 crore Kwh in 1975. The cultivated area under irrigation increased from 2.09 crore hectares in 1950–51 to 4.0 crore hectares in 1974. The growth of certain basic industries was, spectacular. The production of steel increased from 1.47 million tons in 1950–51 to 7.4 million tons in 1976. The increase in aluminium output during this period rose from 4,000 tons in 1950–51 to 126,600 in 1974–75. A similar high rate of growth has been achieved in mechanical engineering industries (machine tools, railway wagons, power-driven pumps, diesel engines), electrical engineering industries (power transformers, electric motors, electric cables and wires), chemical and

Table 1.6. Some Indicators of Economic Growth in India

	(1950–1967)				(Average Annual Growth Rates)			
Indicators	1950–51 1955–56	1955–56 1960–61	1960–61 1965–66	1966–67 1970–71	1973 1974	1974 1975	1975 1976	1976 1977
1. Gross National Product (at 1960–61 Prices)								
a. Target	2.5	5.0	5.0	5.5	—	—	—	—
b. Actual	3.5	4.7	2.6	3.7	5.4	0.3	8.5	1.5
2. Per Capita Income: (1960–61 prices)								
a. Target	1.3	3.8	2.8	—	—	—	—	—
b. Actual	1.6	2.5	0.3	1.6	3.2	−1.7	6.6	0.4
3. Population Growth:								
a. Predicted	1.2	1.2	2.2	—	—	—	—	—
b. Actual	1.9	2.2	2.3	2.1	2.2	2.0	1.9	1.9
4. Agricultural Production	4.2	4.3	−1.1	−0.1[a]	10.7	−3.5	15.6	−5.0
5. Foodgrain Production	4.9	4.4	2.0	1.1[a]	−7.9	−4.6	21.0	−8.0
6. Industrial Production	8.2	6.6	5.7	4.1[a]	2.0	2.8	6.1	10.6

[a]Figures for 1964–65/1969–70.

SOURCE: 1. Commerce Research Bureau, *Basic Statistics Relating to Indian Economy*, Bombay, 1972.

        2. Government of India, *Economic Survey*, New Delhi, 1973–74, 74–75, 75–76, 76–77.

        3. Government of India, Planning Commission, *Five-Year Plans, I–IV*.

        4. Jagdish Bhagwati and T.N. Srinivasan, *Foreign Trade Economic Development—India* (New York: Columbia University Press, 1975).

allied industries (fertilizers, cement and petroleum products). While the general index of industrial production (1960 = 100) increased from 54.8 in 1950 to 201.8 in 1975, the index for basic and key industries registered much higher increases as shown in Table 1.7.

We have discussed the growth of some of these industries in Chapter 7. While India has a long way to go in developing the infrastructure and basic industries required to meet the growing demands of the economy, there has been spectacular progress in this sector if we compare the situation in 1974–75 with that in 1950. The present level of development, in infrastructure and the basic industries, is adequate to make the Indian economy one of self-sustaining growth.

Table 1.7. Index of Industrial Production 1951–74
(1960=100)

Group	1951	1974
General index	54.8	201.8
Rubber products	56	269.0
Chemicals	42.4	301.8
Petroleum	11.0	350.0
Machinery	22.2	432.0
Electricity	35.7	405.8

SOURCE: 1. Government of India, Ministry of Information, *India 1976*.

        2. Government of India, Planning Commission, *Fourth Five-Year Plan 1969–74*.

*Education, Social Services and
Development of Human Capital*
As mentioned earlier another area in
which India has made impressive gains
is in the expansion of educational facilities
and provision of social services like
public health and sanitation measures.
During 1951–71, the literacy rate went
up from 16.6 per cent to 30.0 per cent.
Ninety per cent of the children in the
age group 6–11 were in school in 1976,
compared to 33.0 per cent in 1950. There
were 9 crore students (at primary and
secondary levels) in schools in 1976
compared to 2.2 crores in 1950. The
number of pupils studying arts, science
and commerce at the university level
increased from 3.6 lakh in 1950 to 32
lakh in 1975. The number of universities
registered an increase from 27 in 1950
to 96 in 1976. Several educational, scientific and social science research councils
have been started and contributions by
Indian scholars to international journals
of repute have received world-wide
acclaim. This impressive growth in
educational and research facilities would
normally be a great asset in economic
development. Unfortunately, as noted
earlier there are several disquieting features
in the field of education. The Indian
educational system continues to be
lopsided and largely inconsistent with the
needs of economic development. (We
discuss this matter fully in Chapter 12.)
We have also noted earlier that educational
facilities, specially at the advanced level,
seem to have expanded beyond the
present absorption capacity of the Indian
economy. During the last decade, there
has been a phenomenal rise in export
consultancy services, involving a large
number of technically trained personnel
in industrial, technological and management fields going to other underdeveloped
countries in the Middle East, South-East
Asia and Africa. The foreign exchange
earnings from such services rose to $5.50
million in 1975–76, compared to the
average export earning of $1.37 to $1.52
million during the period 1970–71 to
1974–75—an increase of nearly 400 per
cent.[46]

There has also been a vast improvement
in the provision of health facilities during
the last two decades. The number of
doctors and hospital beds has increased
by more than two-and-a-half times and
that of nurses by more than five times.
In the rural areas, there were about
7,000 primary health centres in April
1976, while none existed before 1950.
Epidemics of malaria, TB, smallpox,
cholera, and plague, which took a heavy
toll of life, are no longer big killers. The
death rate has come down from 27.4
per thousand per year in 1950, to 11.3
in 1976, and the life expectancy at birth
has increased from 32 years to 53 years
during the same period. This impressive
improvement in health facilities, highly
desirable for human welfare, has,
however, accentuated the already serious
problem of a population explosion. Here
is an example that supports the
Leibenstein hypothesis, discussed earlier,
that the planning process itself creates
factors that retard further economic
development.

Savings and Investment
As discussed earlier, in a democratic
society with a large number of people
living under subsistence levels, it is not
realistic to expect much domestic savings
and investment. As Barbara Ward remarks, "in democratic India, where people
are being asked for the first time in history
to vote themselves through the tough
period of primitive accumulation, savings
are lower".[47] She goes on to say:
"Savings for them entail tapping off a
margin from current consumption when
consumption is already so low that it is
barely enough to sustain life. Even
though the hope is that five to ten years
from now, conditions will be better, can the
people be persuaded—least of all by free
vote—to submit themselves to an even
worse plight now?"[48]

We discuss the problems of savings and
investment in detail in Chapter 13. It
might be pointed out that while inadequate
savings have continued to be an impedi-
ment to economic growth, India's record
in increasing the rate of capital formation,
specially the domestic part of it, is fairly
impressive and better than that of any of
the few democratic underdeveloped countries. In 1950, India's gross investment

was 7.0 per cent of the national income (6.6 per cent domestic and 0.4 per cent foreign capital). The corresponding ratio increased to 13.7 per cent (12.2 per cent domestic and 1.5 per cent foreign capital), in 1973–74. In Septembr 1976, the Reserve Bank of India reported the rate of investment to be 16.0 per cent. Granted, this rate of investment will have to be increased further to achieve the annual average rate of growth of 5.5 per cent envisaged in the Fifth Five-Year Plan. The increase in the rates of saving and investment achieved during the last 25 years, as explained above, is, however, an impressive achievement in a democratic society.

Shortcomings of Planning in India
While we have outlined the major development gains from a quarter-century of planning, we should not overlook some of the serious shortcomings and failures encountered during this period. Some of these failures had created a feeling of pessimism and disillusionment among a large section of people. We have already discussed the inadequate and slow rate of economic growth both compared with other developing countries, and in view of the target rates in the five-year plans. What are the other major failures of India's five-year plans? To discuss this matter, we should remind ourselves of the basic premise of the plans, i.e., development along socialistic lines to secure rapid economic growth and expansion of employment, reduction of disparities in income and wealth, prevention of concentration of economic power and creation of the values and attitudes of a free and equal system.

Whither India's Socialistic Society
We have discussed the nature of the Indian Socialist Society and its major instruments of public policy, i.e. (i) growth of the public sector and nationalization; (ii) land reforms; and (iii) redistributive policies to reduce inequalities in income and wealth. As we have mentioned earlier, the incidence of poverty and disparity in income distribution have in fact increased since the start of economic planning. Land reform measures (see

Chapter 6) have largely failed to achieve their objectives : providing security of tenure to cultivators, decreasing the rent charged, and confining ownership rights to the actual tillers.

As discussed in Chapter 9, there has been a large expansion of the public sector (Increase in total investment: Rs. 25 crore in 1951 to Rs. 7,261 crore in March 1975 in public enterprises whose number increased from 5 to 129 during this period). Some questions have been raised on the performance of government undertakings. Shortcomings such as delays in completion of these projects; over-capitalization due to inadequate planning; delays and avoidable expenditures during construction; surplus machine capacity; and large overhead expenditure, have been found in public undertakings.[49] Until 1972–73, the dividend on share capital was quite low—which is cited as a symptom of the low profitability of public enterprises compared to the private sector. Since 1972–73 and more specially during 1975–76, there has been some improvement in this respect. An important reason for emphasis on the public sector as an instrument of socialistic society was the expectation that while the returns from private business go to comparatively rich private owners, the benefits of the public undertakings would accrue to the "common man". It was also thought that profits from public undertakings would be an important source of capital formation. Neither of these hopes was realized. Commenting on the distribution of the benefits of public undertakings, Minhas remarks:

Whether it was the operation of public enterprises or the construction of infrastructure facilities in the field of irrigation, flood control, power, transport, etc., or the operation of a licensing system for control of investments and imports, or the distribution of food and fertilizers, etc., the basic fact of the distribution of public largesse to the not-so-poor was ever present.[50]

Due to the low profitability of public enterprises, the public sector fell below the target in contributing to capital formation. The ratio of Government savings, which include profits from public enterprises, to the national income has been quite low : 1.2 per cent in 1955–56 to 2.8 per cent in 1973–74. According to Desai and Bhagwati "the public sector has not generated the expected surpluses of investment and growth".[51]

The land reform measures, whether relating to security of tenure or reduction of rent charged, or grant of ownership rights to the actual tillers, have largely failed. We have discussed the agrarian structure and land reforms in Chapter 6. Other measures to achieve more equal distribution of income and wealth have been ineffective. We will discuss this matter further.

On the basis of the ineffectiveness of various instruments of public policy designed to achieve a socialist society, it is contended in the words of Koshal:

...the objectives of India's socialistic society which has been influenced on ideological ground has remained more or less a decorative piece in the government's pronouncements, and a hardy perennial in all the plans. Even after 25 years of independence and 23 years of planning, we have not made any significant progress towards the objective of a socialistic society.[52]

Some critics call India's socialist society nothing more than a mixed economy in which the public sector has taken over those functions for which private enterprise does not have sufficient resources.[53] In this sense, India's socialist society is grounded more or less in pragmatism. Minhas has, however, strong views about Indian socialism :

Let us, however, try to see what Indian Socialism has turned out to mean in practice. The socialistic intentions of independent India were pitted against the outmoded attitudes of a strongly feudal and caste status-conscious society, which has been unwilling to accept the rigorous code of private as well as public behaviour implied in the concept of socialism.[54]

A great deal of constructive effort is needed to enforce the redistributive measures already enacted, introduce changes in the pattern of ownership of means of production and also to remove the outmoded attitudes of a "strongly feudal and status-conscious society" which stand in the way of socialistic principles.

Inflationary Pressures Inflation is a typical outcome of economic planning, involving huge investments in an under-developed country, characterized by serious shortages of essential inputs, and balance of payment problems, increasing demands from huge investment spending, population increase, and growing expectations and economic rigidities. In the Indian economy, there were heavy increases in inflationary pressures specially after 1965–66. The index number of wholesale prices (1961–62=100) which stood at 132 in 1965–66, increased to 188 during 1971–72. The following year, it went up to 207 (an increase of 19 points in one year). In 1973–74, the index number shot up to 254 and in September 1974 it increased further to 329. These are very high increases, amongst the highest in the world, over a short span of time. These high inflationary pressures contributed to social and political tensions and the process of inflation fed on itself from black marketing and hoarding of basic necessities, creating further hardships for the masses in general and low-income population in particular. (We discuss the nature, causes and implications of inflation in the Indian economy in Chapter 16.)

Failure of Redistributive Measures : and Poverty We have noted earlier the existence of serious inequalities in income and wealth distribution in the Indian economy, and reduction of these inequalities as one of the crucial tasks of planning. We also noted that according to a United Nations study, the estimates of Lorenz-ratios (indicating distribution of income) show that during the period 1960–68, the inequalities in income distribution had in fact increased. In 1964, the Committee on Distribution of Income appointed by the Indian Planning Commission had reported, as already stated earlier, that there was a considerable measure of concentration in urban as well as rural incomes even after 10 years of planning and despite several redistributive fiscal measures.

Alleviation of poverty has consistently been one of the major objectives of the five-year plans, yet several studies on the incidence of poverty have indicated that the proportion of population under the poverty line has increased, or at the best remained constant. Ojha computed the magnitude of poverty during 1960–61 and 1967–68 on the basis of consumption expenditure to buy a certain amount of essential caloric intake.[55] For 1960–61, he estimated 184.2 million persons in rural areas (51.82 per cent of the rural population) and 6 million urban dwellers (7.6 per cent of the urban population) lived below the poverty line. On an all-India basis, Ojha estimated 190 million persons (44 per cent of the total population) to be below the poverty level. Over time, "compared to 1960–61 the nutritional deficiency in rural areas widened considerably in the rural population in 1967–68".[56] Compared to the 52.0 per cent of the rural population in 1960–61, 70 per cent of the population was found to be below poverty level . More or less similar conclusions were arrived at by Dandekar and Rath,[57] about 40 per cent of the rural population, i.e., about 160 million persons in 1967–68 subsist at a level of living which is nutritionally highly deficient in terms of caloric intake.[57] In the urban sector, about 50 per cent of the population was estimated to be below the poverty level. Thus, according to Dandekar and Rath, in all about 200 million persons in 1967–68 were below the poverty level. Bardhan also holds a similar view, that the percentage of rural population below the poverty line had gone up from 38 per cent in 1960–61 to 54 per cent in 1968–69. The Fifth Five-Year Plan is cognizant of the continuing abject poverty : according to the Planning Commission "economic development during the two decades since the inception of planning has resulted in a sizeable increase in average per capita income—yet large numbers have remained poor".[58] How do we explain this paradox of "sizeable increase in per capita income" and "persistence of poverty"? According to the Fifth Five-Year Plan "one reason for the failue of planning to make a major dent on poverty has been the inadequate rate of economic growth".[59] In our view, the fault lies first in the inappropriateness of the strategy applied and secondly in the ineffectiveness of the measures designed to alleviate poverty. Efforts to reduce inequalities in income and wealth distribution by emphasis on increase in growth rate in a society characterized by unequal distribution and private ownership of the means of production, are not likely to succeed without an alteration of the pattern of ownership. The closest we came to changing the ownership pattern was by legislating "ceiling on ownership of land". As discussed in Chapter 6, the laws in this respect were defied more than observed. The remarks in the Fourth Plan that "the process of development might lead, in the absence of purposive intervention by the state, to greater concentration of wealth and income",[60] seems to support our contention above, but the "purposive intervention" referred to by the Planning Commission have been rather soft measures (e.g., licensing, anti-monopolies legislation, progressive taxation, ceiling on land ownership, security of tenure to cultivators) which would not change the pattern of ownership of the means of production, essential for reducing maldistribution of income. Another policy measure designed to reduce poverty was the provision of employment opportunities, especially in the rural areas. Failure to achieve this objective also contributed to the persistence of poverty among large numbers of the Indian population.

Failure in Manpower Utilization and Unemployment In a labour-abundant economy like India, another major determinant of economic growth and welfare of the general population would be the proper utilization of manpower. The Indian economy, from the very begining of planning, has been beset with serious unemployment problem. (We have devoted Chapter 12 to an examination of the nature, causes and magnitude of unemployment in India.) Each five-year plan devoted considerable attention to explaining the gravity of the unemployment situation, and provided for a solution of the problem as one of the major objectives of planning in India. A review of the employment pattern since 1950 shows the disquieting fact there was more unemployment at the end of each of the four five-year and three annual plans, than at their beginning (Table 1.8). It will be noted from item 7 that the rate of unemployment was successively higher at the end than at the beginning of each plan. The Planning Commission stopped releasing estimates on unemployment in 1969, but, commenting on the employment situation after the Fourth Five-Year Plan, the Planning Commission remarks "... it would appear that employment generation has not kept pace with the growth of the labour force. The situation of unemployment among educated and technically qualified persons also continues to cause concern".[61] It may also be pointed out the estimates of unemployment rates (item 7 in Table 1.8) grossly underestimate the extent of idle manpower, since in an underdeveloped economy like India, underemployment rather than unemployment is a more appropriate indicator of manpower utilization. (We discuss this in detail in Chapter 12.)

How do we explain the failures of planning in India in the crucial aspects: lower growth-rate; persistence of inequalities in income and wealth distribution and non-

utilization of manpower, which were, as a matter of fact, the major objectives of all the five-year plans? There are obviously several reasons for these failures, but we shall mention only a few.

1. *Crisis of Implementation* The most important cause of poor performance was lack of implementation of most plan policies, whether they were aimed at creating employment opportunities, or were distributive measures including land reforms. In our discussion of India's economic problems, we will point out the wide gaps between targets and achievements; between the high-sounding goals, and actual attainments; the promises to the masses, and actual distribution of the benefits from plans. Various views have been expressed on the causes of this lack of implementation. To Bhagwati and Desai, it is "merely a *symptom of the attitudes and habits...it* reflects a certain lack of empiricism in the Indian make-up : which typically leads to intentions being confused with action".[62]

(a) *Bureaucracy: Alliances with Vested Interests* Several commissions and committees[63] appointed by Government blamed the bureaucracy, including the civil service, which seriously lacked in knowledge of technical tools and skills for economic management, but was charged with implementation of the plan

Table 1.8. Unemployment and the Five Year Plans

(in millions)

	Plan I	Plan II	Plan III	Annual Plans
	1951–56	1956–61	1961–66	1966–69
1. Labour force at the beginning	185.2	197.0	215.0	229.0
2. Net addition to the labour force	9.0	11.8	17.0	14.0
3. Backlog of unemployment at the beginning of the plan	3.3	5.3	7.1	14.0
4. Total (2+3)	12.3	17.1	24.1	23.6
5. Additional jobs created	7.0	10.0	14.5	1.4
6. Backlog of unemployed at the end of plan: (4–5)	5.3	7.1	9.6	22.2
7. Unemployment as percentage of labour force	2.9	3.6	4.5	9.6

SOURCE: *Reserve Bank of India Bulletins, 1969, 1970, 1975.*

policies, including management of government, commercial and industrial undertakings. The bureaucracy is also accused of serving the interests of the ruling classes and being indifferent to the needs of the underprivileged. In the alliances formed in the Indian political set-up for control of political and economic power, and for receiving the benefits of economic development, bureaucrats seem to have aligned themselves with the diverse vested interests of landowners and industrialists, rather than been faithful executors of plan policies. In the face of such alliances, as Gunnar Myrdal remarks, "measures designed to aid the lowest strata in the population have ordinarily been poorly enforced, if at all".[64] See Chapter 6 for an explanation of the collusion between bureaucrats and landowners which has been a principal cause of failure in implementation of land reform measures.

(b) *Administrative Constraints* According to Hanson,[65] the slack in implementation of plan policies is due to the administrative structure of the Planning Commission and working of the federal system in the Indian political system. The Planning Commission being an advisory committee, recommends the Plan to the Central Government, which, in turns transmits it to the States for implementation at State and local government levels. This dichotomy, in plan formulation, and its execution by numerous administrative units at state and local levels, stands in the way of implementation.

(c) *Rigid Social Structure* Kinship, and hereditary relationships based on the caste system and social factors, still continue to dominate Indian society especially in the rural sector. Traditionally, the ownership of means of production, including land, vests in the higher castes and dominant social groups, and the labour, including agricultural labourers, comes from the lower social classes. In such an atmosphere, it is difficult for the economically and socially weaker classes to achieve the rights granted them under various plan provisions. According to Minhas, the socialistic intentions of independent India, "were pitted against

the outmoded attitudes of a strongly feudal and class-conscious society, which has been unwilling to accept the rigorous code of private as well as public behaviour implied in the concept of socialism".[66] The Planning Commission is aware of this sociological factor and explains the problems of implementation of land reforms measures thus :

> When there is a pressure on land and the social and economic position of tenants in the village is weak, it becomes difficult for them to seek the protection of law. Moreover, resort to legal process is costly and generally beyond the means of tenants. Thus, in many ways, despite the legislation, the scales are weighed in favour of the continuance of existing terms and conditions.[67]

2. Inappropriate Plan Strategies We had explained earlier the development strategies implicit in Indian plans. These strategies are :
1. industrialization: emphasis on heavy and capital goods industries,
2. growth orientation,
3. socialistic society and growth of the public sector, and
4. self reliance.
As already explained, the premises of these development strategies were that industrialization, especially of heavy industries involving huge investments, would stimulate growth, thus creating employment opportunities sufficient to absorb the labour force. The socialistic policies—land reforms legislation, progressive income tax, growth of the public sector, regulation and control of the private sector—would somehow direct the benefits from economic growth towards the economically weaker sections of the society. We have already explained how "experience has now shown that these promises of our policies have been either misguided or inadequate or unrealistic in our political framework. In short, a serious restructuring of our policies is called for".[68] How could heavy investment in capital-intensive large-scale and heavy industries ease unemployment in a labour-abundant economy? How could the benefits of economic growth accrue to economically weaker sections in an

economy with concentration of ownership of means of production in upper classes? These are some of the crucial questions that need to be seriously considered in reconstructing future economic policies.

The shortcomings of planning dominated the economic scene during 1972–73 and 1973–74. The results of these shortcomings were aggravated by crop failures, war with Pakistan over Bangladesh, and a heavy influx of refugees. The conditions, characterized as "crisis in Indian economy" and "crisis in economic planning", necessitated bold steps not only to reduce the growing strain on the economy, but also to continue on the path of economic planning in which a large section of the population was losing faith.

Twenty-Point Programme

The Indian government announced a 20-point programme in July 1975 to supplement the continuing Fifth Five-Year Plan. The objective of this programme was to reemphasise existing economic policies and reaffirm the national commitment to implement them successfully under emergency provisions simultaneously announced. These twenty points were:

1. Continuance of steps to bring down prices of essential commodities. Streamlined production, procurement and distribution of essential commodities. Strict economy in government expenditure.

2. Implementation of agricultural land ceilings and speedier distribution of surplus land and compilation of land records.

3. Stepping up of provision of house sites for landless and weaker sections.

4. Bonded labour, wherever it exists, will be declared illegal.

5. Plan for liquidation of rural indebtedness. Legislation for moratorium on recovery of debt from landless labourers, small farmers and artisans.

6. Review of laws on minimum agricultural wages.

7. Five million more hectares to be brought under irrigation. National programme for use of underground water.

8. An accelerated power programme. Super thermal stations under central control.

9. New development plan for development of handloom sector.

10. Improvement in quality and supply of people's cloth.

11. Socialization of urban and urbanizable land. Ceiling on ownership and possession of vacant land and on plinth area of new dwelling units.

12. Special squads for valuation of conspicuous construction and prevention of tax evasion. Summary trials and deterrent punishment of economic offenders.

13. Special legislation for confiscation of smuggler's properties.

14. Liberalisation of investment procedure. Action against misuse of import licences.

15. New schemes for workers' association in industry.

16. National permit scheme for road transport.

17. Income tax relief to middle classes; exemption limit placed at Rs. 8,000.

18. Essential commodities at controlled prices to students in hostels.

19. Books and stationery at controlled prices.

20. New apprenticeship scheme to enlarge employment and training, especially of weaker sections.

The Prime Minister, Indira Gandhi, had prefaced the new programme with the request : "Please do not expect magic remedies and dramatic results. There is only one magic which can remove poverty and that is hard work sustained by clear vision, iron will and strict discipline". What has the 20-point programme achieved? Mrs Gandhi's Government claimed that the results were highly commendable. The Reserve Bank of India in its *Annual Report, 1975–76*, echoed the Government view that the Indian economy had never had it so good as in the year ending June 1976, and that it was moving to higher levels of saving, investment, and growth in an environment of price stability.[69] The

Government claimed that the growth-rates in both the national and the per capita income were the highest ever achieved in the post-Independence period. Industrial production grew at 6.0 per cent; food production touched the 119-million ton mark, which, it was claimed, had made India not only self-sufficient but had also enabled the building of reserves for any future crop failure caused by natural calamities. The electric power generated increased by 21.6 per cent and the goal of electrification of all Indian villages was very close to realization. Output in the steel industry increased by 18.0 per cent during the year 1975–76 over the earlier year. The rate of savings and investments stood at 14.5 per cent and 16.0 per cent respectively of the national income, bringing India closer to the goal of self-reliance. Inflationary pressure had eased with the wholesale price index, decreasing by 7.8 per cent over the previous year, with a corresponding decline in consumer prices. India was among the few countries in the world where the rate of change in price level was negative. These achievements, according to the 1976 Report of the World Bank.[70] were due to the following factors:

(1) Bumper harvest in 1975–76 (2) successful anti-inflationary resources (3) increase in the electric power generated which reduced the earlier deficiency in supply of electricity (4) increase in the production of petroleum products and coal by 10 per cent over the previous year (5) due to increased discipline in the industrial sector, a huge reduction in man-hours formerly lost through strikes and labour trouble (6) greater efficiency in the administrative services and close to full utilization of capacity in public sector undertakings (7) increase in export earnings by 7 per cent over the previous year and overall improvement in the balance of payments position.

On the basis of these findings, the World Bank remarked that conditions were once again ripe for an up-turn in the growth of the Indian economy.

Some doubts have, however, been expressed on this overoptimistic view of the Indian economy during the emergency period, June 1975–March 1977. K.N. Raj

has advised caution in interpreting these gains : "… a significant increase in output in one or two years does not necessarily mean the establishmeant of a new trend. In fact, such increases have taken place earlier, such as in 1968 and 1969 when the growth of industrial production averaged 6.5 per cent and again in 1972 when it was over 7 per cent."[71] These short-run achievements "…are usually a reflection of particular favourable circumstances in certain years, such as arising out of bumper harvests in the years immediately preceding."[72] In spite of the 8.5 per cent increase in the gross national product during the one particular year 1975–76, the annual average rate of growth of the economy for the three-year period 1974–75 to 1976–77, comes to only 3.5 per cent.[73] Similarly, in spite of the 15.6 per cent increase in food production during the year 1975–76, the rate of growth of foodgrain output recorded over the period 1964–65 to 1975–76 would still be no more than 2.6 per cent per year.[74] Thus the favourable performance of the economy during 1975–76 should not offer ground for much complacency.

There have also been some critical comments on the implications of the economic performance during the Emergency. K.N. Raj maintains that a significant part of the growth of industrial output during the period was in the public sector area such as steel.[75] The weighted average rate of growth for the public sector during April–December 1975 was about 15 per cent. Adjusting this figure for the overall increase in industrial production, gives us only a 1.0 per cent growth rate for the private sector.[76] This slight growth rate in the private sector, would indicate a rather recessionary situation with increase in unemployment. With the expansion in the public sector industries mentioned above, and recession conditions in the consumer goods industries in the private sector, some enterprises such as steel accumulated large unsaleable stocks. Some of this unsold and unused iron and steel had to be dumped in the international market, which amounts to India subsidising other countries.[77]

It is maintained that the development

strategy followed during the emergency period concentrated on "industrial production" and "export promotion". For this purpose, labour strikes were banned, prices controlled, wages frozen, and different types of incentives were provided to investors, domestic or foreign, for introduction of capital-intensive technology. To boost export earnings, even essential consumer goods were exported. The common man—specially those in the lower-income group—suffered in various ways. In addition to the increasing unemployment due to recession conditions in the industrial sector, especially among the unskilled and uneducated, the real wages of workers decreased as a result of increasing prices and frozen wages. The per capita net availability of essential consumer goods such as food. sugar, vanaspati and textiles also declined. Net per capita availability of cloth declined from 14.43 metres in 1974 to 13.31 metres per day in 1975.[78] Except for the drought years of 1958 and 1966–67, the net per capita availability of foodgrains (430 grams per day in 1976) was lower than it has been since 1956, when it was 431 grams per day.[79]

Commenting on the decline in the general price level during the years 1974–75 and 1975–76, K.N. Raj attributes it not only to the bumper harvest during 1975–76 but also to the slowing down of the rate of net capital formation (expressed as a percentage of the net domestic output), and reliance on larger import surpluses.[80] According to K.N. Raj, "Insofar as reduction in the rate of investment merely postpones and accentuates the problem of absorbing the growing number of unemployed and underemployed people, one can legitimately say that the reduction in prices has been achieved in part at the expense of the additional employment that could have been created."[81]

The Economy During 1976–77

The year 1976–77, during which the Emergency prevailed for several months, saw the lifting of Emergency measures, followed by elections to the Lok Sabha and State legislatures. The *Economic Survey 1976–77* depicts a rather un-favourable state in the economy. While the overall performance has been regarded as "uneven",[82] the *Economic Survey* admits that "the hope that the economy had shaken off the stagnation of the first four years of this decade and resumed the path of high growth, did not materialize."[83] The figures in the last column in Table 1.6 show that the growth rate declined sharply from 8.5 per cent in 1975–76 to 1.5 per cent in 1976–77. Taking the rate of increase in population at 1.9 per cent, would give a minus figure of -0.4 per cent in increase in per capita incomes. This decline in the growth rate can be explained by the decrease in agricultural production to the extent of –5.0 per cent during this period. There was a 10.6 per cent increase in industrial production, but as the *Economic Survey* cautions, it cannot be assumed to indicate a more cheerful trend.[84] The industrial structure remains beset with serious problems such as serious power shortages, uneconomic size, low capacity-utilization, lack of adequate maintenance, poor financial resources, and also poor management. Moreover most of the increased industrial output occurred in the public sector heavy industries, and shortages in the essential consumer goods continue to put pressure on the price level.

The price level, which had decreased between September 1974 and March 1976 due to various factors—the bumper harvest of 1975–76, use of emergency provisions under MISA, and the climate of fear among traders, etc.—started rising again after March 1976. Between March 1976 and February 1977, prices rose by 15.5 per cent. The wholesale price index (1970–71 $= 100$), which had declined by 11.6 per cent between 28 September 1974 and 20 March 1976, had risen by 11.9 per cent by 26 March 1977.[85] The All-India Industrial Workers Consumer Price Index (1960 $= 100$) rose from 286 in March 1976 to 312 in March 1977.[86] It may be noted that after March 1976, with the Emergency still intact, there has been an almost uninterrupted rise in prices, which seems to have wiped out the entire decline in prices occurring between September 1974 and March 1976.

There were several causes for the sharp

increase in prices after March 1976, including forecasts of declining agricultural and food production during 1976–77, the resultant shortages of raw materials for agro-industries, shortages of essential consumer goods, growing industrial unrest (not reported in the controlled Press) because of the decline in the real wages of workers.

On the basis of these observations on the performance of the economy during the Emergency period, it seems that though the economy did experience some short-run gains from June 1974 to March 1976, most of these gains were wiped out in the following months, especially during the year 1976–77.

The Indian Economy and the Janata Party Government

The end of the Emergency in March 1977 saw the bitter defeat of the Congress Party and the assumption of power by a coalition of various opposition parties under the banner of the Janata Party. The 1977–78 outlook and the tasks before the new Government are outlined in the 1976–77 *Economic Survey* released by the Government.[87] It calls for "a careful watch on the price situation", and suggests some measures such as strict fiscal and monetary discipline, avoidance of unproductive expenditure; greater mobilization of resources through improvement of the yield of existing taxes, and imaginative fiscal policy. The public distribution system will be strengthened to achieve price stability in essential commodities e.g., cereals, edible oil, kerosene oil and other domestic fuels, and to ensure their availability to weaker sections of the population. The new Government is aware that "the volume of unemployment is large and it is growing". Policies aiming at removing unemployment and eliminating destitution and poverty will receive greater emphasis. The solution of the two related problems of unemployment and poverty will be sought through a higher rate of growth through increased investment expenditure "orientated towards employment generation in sectors like agriculture, irrigation and small scale and rural industries."

It is too early as yet to judge the performance of the Janata Party government. It is still busy with teething troubles, including restoration of the constitution mutilated during the Emergency. At this stage, one can merely evaluate the economic contents of its election manifesto.[88]

A. Institutional Changes
    1. End of destitution in ten years
    2. Deletion of private property as a fundamental right
    3. Decentralization of the economy
    4. People's active participation in the planning process

B. Increase in Production
    1. Production and distribution of basic goods for mass consumption
    2. Achievement of full employment by the end of the Seventh Five-Year Plan
    3. Production by small-scale and cottage industries and reservation of spheres for these enterprises

C. Development of Agriculture
    1. Higher priority to rural sector
    2. Agrarian reforms
    3. Improvements in terms of trade between agricultural/rural goods and industrial goods

D. De-urbanisation
    1. Development of new village movement
    2. Reduction in urban-rural disparities
    3. Dispersal of development process

E. Removal of Inequalities
    1. Stress on value of austerity
    2. Reduction in income/wealth disparities
    3. Recognition of wage-earners' rights

These economic goals are based on Gandhian ideas and they constitute an alternative strategy of development planning: the Gandhian Strategy or Decentralization Strategy, in contrast to the Development Strategy of Industrial Development and Export Promotion adopted in the past. According to Romesh Diwan, "The fundamental difference between these two strategies... lies in the fact that Industrial Strategy builds on the welfare of the 'elite' while Gandhian Strategy builds on the welfare of the large and poor majority; hoping to eliminate elitism in the process."

The implementation of these policies is an important and difficult task. Their implementation by the Janata Party government will depend upon (a) a firm commitment to these goals by the various parties forming the coalition, and (b) the decisiveness and firmness with which the policies are pursued. There are some fears on the degree of unanimity of views, and commitment, among political groups with diverse views on fundamental issues like distributive measures, including land reforms, and the role of the public sector in the economy. It is also not certain to what extent the Janata Party government will be able to command compliance from the bureaucracy, which has had close ties with business and landed interests, for implementation of the policies and programmes implicit in the new strategy.

Only time will show to what extent the new strategy has been successfully implemented by the new government. The budget proposals for the fiscal year 1977–78 contain some provisions which seem consistent with the new strategy. True, several of the budget proposals were formulated even before the Janata Party had fully assumed office: provisions such as greater allocation of budgetary resources to agriculture, preferential tax treatment for industries in rural areas, tax concessions for the small-scale sector, and extension of investment allowances for small units, indicate a movement towards the new policies. *The Economic Survey, 1976–77*, issued by the Janata Party government reaffirms its strong commitment to new programmes and policies.

If the new strategy is to have a chance, drastic steps will have to be taken to remove the serious socioeconomic hurdles that continue to stand in the way of India's economic development and welfare of her teeming millions.

REFERENCES

1. Quoted in Ruddar Datt and K.P.M. Sundharam, *Indian Economy* (New Delhi : S. Chand, 1976), p. 36.
2. Government of India, Planning Commission, *Report of the Committee on the Distribution of Income and Levels of Living*, Part I (New Delhi, 1964), p. 28.
3. Ibid., p. 28.
4. National Council of Applied Economic Research, *All India Household Income, Savings and Consumer Expenditure* (New Delhi, 1972) pp. 26–29.
5. Quoted in H.B. Chenerey *et al.*, *Redistribution with Growth* (London : Oxford University Press, 1974), pp. 6–16.
6. Government of India, *National Sample Survey*, 18th Round 1963–64, New Delhi, 1970.
7. A.J. Fonesca (ed.): *Challenge of Poverty in India* (Delhi: Vikas, 1972,) pp. 34–75.
8. Ibid., pp. 34–75.
9. Ibid., p. 40.
10. Ibid., p. 41.
11. United Nations, *Economic Survey of Asia and Far East*, Bangkok, 1973, p. 40.
12. See T.W. Schultz, *The Economic Value of Education* (New York: Columbia University Press, 1963) for an excellent treatment of this topic.
13. Government of India, *Report of the Working Group on Education*, New Delhi, 1972, pp. 11–12.
14. United Nations, *Economic Survey*, chs. 1–6; also Government of India, *Report of the Committee on Unemployment* New Delhi, 1973.
15. K.N. Raj, *Indian Economic Growth : Performance and Prospects* (Delhi: Allied Publishers, 1965), p. 2.
16. Max F. Millikan, "Economic Development: Performance and Prospects", *Foreign Affairs*, vol. 46, no. 3, April 1968, p. 532.
17. A.H. Hanson, *The Process of Planning* (London: Oxford University Press, 1966), p. 526.
18. Harvey Leibenstein, *Economic Backwardness and Economic Growth* (New York: Wiley, 1963), p. 16.
19. Ibid., p. 34.
20. Karl von Vorys, "Some Aspects of the Economic Development of India", *World Politics*, **13**, 1960–61 p. 585.
21. Ibid., p. 585.
22. For example see B.S. Minhas, *Planning and the Poor* (New Delhi: S. Chand, 1974); Ashoka Mehta, *India To-Day* (New Delhi: S. Chand, 1974); and B.M. Bhatia, *India's Deepening Economic Crisis* (New Delhi: S. Chand, 1974).
23. Government of India, Planning Commission, *Draft Fifth Five-Year Plan*, vol. I, New Delhi, p. 4.
24. Government of India, Planning Commission, *Towards an Approach to the Fifth Plan*, New Delhi, 1972, p. 1.
25. Ibid., pp. 3–4.
26. Ibid., p. 4.

27. Ibid., p. 6.
28. For an excellent treatment of this, see K.N. Raj, "Growth Models and Indian Planning" in C.D. Wadhwa (ed.), *Some Problems of India's Economic Policy* (New Delhi: Tata-McGraw Hill, 1973), pp. 15 and 16.
29. Ibid., pp. 16–20; and Ryutaro Komiya, "A Note on Professor Mahalanobis' Model of Indian Economic Planning", pp. 32–41.
30. Quoted in Lawrence Veit, *India's Second Revolution* (New York: McGraw Hill, 1976), p. 200.
31. *Approach to the Fifth Plan*, p. 3.
32. Quoted in R. Koshal, "Socialist Society—An Analysis of India's Economic Policy," in J.S. Uppal (ed.), *India's Economic Problems* (New Delhi: Tata-McGraw Hill, 1975), p. 133.
33. Ibid., pp. 144–145.
34. Quoted in Baldev R. Nayar, *The Modernization Imperative and Indian Planning* (New Delhi: Vikas, 1972), p. 5.
35. *Fourth Five-Year Plan*.
36. Padma Desai and Jagdish Bhagwati, Socialism and Indian Economic Policy, Paper presented at the 1974 meeting of the American Economic Association, p. 4 (mimeographed).
37. *Draft Fifth Five-Year Plan*, Vol. I, p. 4.
38. *Second Five-Year Plan*, p. 3.
39. For example, see M.R. Pai, *Planning in India : A Commentary* (Bombay: Popular Prakashan, 1966), pp. 1–56.
40. Gunnar Myrdal, *Asian Drama : An Inquiry into the Poverty of Nations* (New York: Pantheon, 1968), p. 66.
41. V.V. Bhatt, *Two Decades of Development —The Indian Experiment* (Bombay: Vora, 1973), p. 30.
42. Minhas, *Planning and the Poor*; Mehta, *India Today;* and B.M. Bhatia, *India's Economic Crisis*.
43. Millikan, "Economic Development", p. 532.
44. Jagdish Bhagwati, "India in the International Economy", Institute of Public Enterprise, Hyderabad, 1973, p. 1.
45. Government of India *Report of Committee on Distribution of Income*, p. 28.
46. Information Service of India *India News*, Washington D.C., Oct. 29, 1976.
47. Barbara Ward, *The Rich Nations and the Poor Nations* (New York: Norton, 1962), p. 5.
48. Ibid., p. 125.
49. See Government of India, *Report of the Study Plan on Public Sector Undertakings* (New Delhi), 1967; and Jagdish Bhagwati and Padma Desai, *India : Planning for Industrialization* (London: Oxford University Press, 1970).
50. Minhas, *Planning and the Poor*, p. 10.
51. Desai and Bhagwati, *Socialism and Indian Economy*.
52. Koshal, *Socialist Society*, pp. 144–45.
53. Hanson, *Planning Process*, Ch. 12.
54. Minhas, *Planning and the Poor*, p. 10.
55. P.D. Ojha, "A Configuration of Indian Poverty", in Fonesca, *Challenge of Poverty*, p. 40.
56. Ibid., p. 41.
57. V.M. Dandekar and N. Rath, "Poverty in India—Dimensions and Trends", *Economic and Political Weekly*, 2 January 1971.
58. *Draft Fifth Plan*, p. 66.
59. Ibid., p. 6.
60. *Fourth Five-Year Plan*, pp. 14–15.
61. *Draft Fifth Plan*, p. 267.
62. Bhagwati and Desai, *India: Planning for Industrialization*, pp. 5–6.
63. Government of India, *Report of the Study Team on Public Sector Undertakings*, New Delhi, June 1967.
64. Myrdal, *Asian Drama*, p. 762.
65. See Hanson, *Planning Process*, Chs. 9–10.
66. Minhas, *Planning and the Poor*, p. 10.
67. *Third Five-Year Plan*, p. 229.
68. Bhagwati, "India in the International Economy", p. 4.
69. Quoted in *Economic and Political Weekly*, Vol. XI, No. 38, 18 September 1976, p. 1517.
70. Quoted in Indian Information Service, *India News*, Washington DC, 28 May 1976.
71. K.N. Raj, "The Economic Situation", *Economic and Political Weekly*, Vol. XI, No. 27, 3 July 1976, p. 995.
72. Ibid.
73. Government of India, *Economic Survey, 1976–77*, New Delhi, 1977, p. 1.
74. Raj, "The Economic Situation", p. 994.
75. Ibid., p. 995.
76. Ashok Bhargava and Gopalan Balachandran, "Economic Issues", Paper presented at the Second Conference of the Association of Indian Economic Studies at Mt. Clair, New Jersey, USA, August 1977, p. 3 (mimeographed).
77. Ibid., p. 6.
78. Ibid., p. 4.
79. Ibid., p. 4.
80. Raj, "The Economic Situation," p. 996.
81. Ibid., p. 996.
82. *Economic Survey, 1976–77*, p. 3.
83. Ibid., p. 3.
84. Ibid., p. 46.
85. Ibid., p. 1.
86. Ibid.
87. Ibid., pp. 45–49.
88. For an excellent discussion on this point see Romesh Diwan, "Economic Policies of the Janata Government", A Working Paper prepared for the Workshop at the Second Conference of the Association of Indian Economic Studies, Mt. Clair, New Jersey, USA, August 1977 (mimeographed).
89. Ibid., pp. 6–7.

BIBLIOGRAPHY

Vera Anstay: *The Economic Development of India*. London. Longmans, Green, 1929.

V.V. Bhatt: *Two Decades of Development*. Bombay. Vora, 1973.

Pramit Chaudhuri: *Aspects of Indian Economic Development*. London. Allen & Unwin, 1973.

J.S. Uppal and K. Chen: *India and China : Studies in Comparative Development*. New York Free Press, 1973.

H.B. Chenery *et al.*: *Redistribution with Growth*. London. Oxford University Press, 1974.

A.H. Hanson: *The Process of Planning*. London. Oxford University Press, 1966.

E.A.G. Robinson and M. Kidron (eds.): *Economic Development in South Asia*. London. St. Martin's Press, 1970.

John Mellor: *The New Economics of Growth*. Ithaca, New York. Cornell University Press, 1976.

D. Bright Singh: *Economics of Development*. Bombay. Asia Publishing House, 1963.

J. Bhagwati and P. Desai: *India: Planning for Industrialization*. New York. Oxford University Press, 1970.

———— and T.N. Srinivasan: *India*. New York. Columbia University Press, 1975.

J.S. Uppal: *Economic Development in South Asia*. New York. St. Martin's Press, 1977.

Lawrence A. Veit: *India's Second Revolution*. New York. McGraw-Hill, 1976.

C.D. Wadhva (ed.): *Some Problems of India's Economic Policy*. New Delhi. Tata McGraw Hill, 1973.

Tarlok Singh: *India's Development Experience*, New Delhi. MacMillan, 1974.

2

Structural Changes in the Indian Economy

MAHMOOD A. ZAIDI
AND
SUDHIN K. MUKHOPADHYAY

The Net Domestic Product of India increased from Rs. 92,600 million in 1950–51 to Rs. 1,92,190 million in 1970–71 (at 1959–60 and 1960–61 prices respectively).[1] During the same period of time the composition of the national product also changed. The share of agriculture, animal husbandry, and ancillary activities declined from 50 per cent to about 40 per cent, while the share of industries and services went up correspondingly. These are some indications that the economy of India has been developing.

Discussions of economic development generally deal with such changes in the aggregates of national product or its industrial composition. Such aggregative studies are important to understand the broad movements of the economy. But it has to be remembered that there is much

more to economic development than what surfaces via these highly aggregated magnitudes. What, after all, is an economy? It is a web of numerous activities carried out by the different constituent units—firms, industries, sectors, regions, etc., that generate the macroeconomic magnitudes like national income or consumption. As economic development takes place, i.e., as there is a sustained change in the economic aggregates, there usually occurs a change in the network of activities lying behind the simple aggregates. In the words of W.W. Leontief, "it is necessary to penetrate below the surface of global statistics and such round terms as 'development'. Each economic system—developed or developing—has a complicated internal structure. Its performance is determined by the mutual relations of its differentiated component parts, just as the motion of the hands of a clock is governed by the gears inside".[2] At different levels of economic development the volume and nature of

The authors of this paper would like to thank Edward Coen, Professor of Economics at the University of Minnesota, and the editor, for helpful comments and encouragement.

the activities of the internal structure are generally different. So, in order to ascertain the nature of the development and to predict the requirements of various inputs for development and to facilitate the formulation of national plans for economic development, it is important to examine the internal mechanism of the economy within its broad macroframework.

The purpose of this chapter is to present a simplified picture of the "internal structure" that lies behind the changing global aggregates of the Indian economy. After some introductory comments in this section, a methodology of studying economic structure is discussed in simple terms in section II, and section III deals with some actual measures of the changing economic structure of India.

Economists have long been aware of the need to examine the mechanism of interrelated changes in the economy as a whole and theories were developed as early as the eighteenth century by the French economist Francois Quesnay in the famous Tableau Economique, and in the nineteenth century by Leon Walras in his general equilibrium theory. But in spite of their elegance and depth, these ideas remained far removed from the possibility of actual application to particular economies. The task of constructing a network of interrelated economic changes through equations and measuring them empirically had been considered extremely difficult. In reality, this network consists of flow of goods and services between the microelements of an economy and the flows involve too many variables and complicated interrelations. So, rather than attempting to study the economy in its total framework, economic analysis had long been content with a partial equilibrium approach, making the restrictive assumption that there is no significant change outside the given portion of the economy under investigation.

But since the nineteen thirties, due mostly to the research contributions of W.W. Leontief, the theoretical conceptualization of general equilibrium has been rendered empirically verifiable.

The method, known as "input-output" analysis, makes possible an analysis of the detailed statistical picture of the entire economy. The disaggregated structure of the economy and changes in it are now amenable to quantitative measurement.

Input-Output Analysis—a Simple Exposition

It has been suggested that in order to understand the mechanism of economic development at the macro level and to formulate plans for aiding and influencing development, it is necessary to know the internal structure of the economy. Input-output analysis is a modern technique designed to study this internal structure and its changes.

The input-output analysis is developed by treating the economy like a fabric which is woven together by the flows of trade or transactions of goods and services that ultimately link the different branches or industries of the economy. The economy is first divided into a number of sectors or branches. Then a simple double-entry method of book-keeping is adopted to record the flows between different sectors or branches. The transactions are set up in the form of a two-way table of horizontal rows and vertical columns. The horizontal rows of figures show the way the output of each sector is distributed among all the different sectors of the economy. These sectors will include both production and consumption, so that part of the output of a sector will go as intermediate goods or inputs into production sectors, and part will go to final consumption, be it private or governmental consumption. On the other hand, the vertical columns show how each sector receives its inputs in the form of goods and services from the various sectors of the economy. The two-way input-output table shows each figure belonging both to a row and a column; it stands as the output of one sector being used as input for another sector. Of course, the output of a sector is used also as its own input in most cases. For example, paddy seeds are the output of the agriculture sector used as an input in the same sector. So the total gross output of a sector may be looked upon in an input-output framework as the sum of the flow of goods to the productive sectors and to final consumption, and the sum of the total gross outputs of all the sectors is the gross national product of the economy.

The input-output relations can be understood clearly with the help of a simple tabular presentation. In Table 2.1 the economy is divided into two production sectors, 1 and 2[3]. Let X represent output and C represent final consumption. The subscripts refer to the sectors.

Table 2.1

To From	Production sector		Final consump- tion	Total gross output
	1	2		
Sector				
1	x_{11}	x_{12}	C_1	X_1
2	x_{21}	x_{22}	C_2	X_2

x_{11} represents the output of sector 1 that is used as input in sector 1 itself. Similarly x_{12}, for instance, stands for the output of sector 1 used as input in sector 2. The column of Total Gross Output gives the sum of the output of each sector that is used as input as well as final consumption. This relationship can be written in the form of two balance equations corresponding to the two sectors, namely :

$$x_{11} + x_{12} + C_1 = X_1 \qquad (1)$$
$$x_{21} + x_{22} + C_2 = X_2 \qquad (2)$$

The grand total of the sectoral outputs will give us the gross total output of the economy. Thus input-output analysis gives us a glimpse into the flows of goods and services that take place behind the global aggregates of gross output.

Input-output analysis enables us to go beyond a simple exposition of the volumes of intersectoral transaction as indicated in Table 2.1. The central concept of input-output analysis is that there is a fundamental relationship between the volume of output of a sector and the inputs used by it. For example, if sector 2 represents cotton textiles industry,

then there is a relationship between how much textiles are produced (i.e., output of the sector 2, X_2) and the amount of cotton that is used by it as input. And if sector 1 includes cotton farming, the entry x_{12} in Table 2.1 will represent the flow from sector 1 to sector 2, so X_2 and x_{12} are interdependent. Input-output analysis shows how in this way every entry in the table is dependent on the other.

These relationships indicate the structure of the technology of the economy and are measured by calculating the ratio or coefficient of each input to the total output in the production of which the input is used. For an industry or sector we get these input coefficients by dividing the column-wise entries for this industry by its gross output figure. For example, from Table 2.1, x_{12}/X_2 is the input coefficient of product 1 in industry 2. This coefficient is usually denoted as a_{12}. Similarly, we can compute $a_{22} = x_{22}/X_2$; $a_{11} = x_{11}/X_1$; $a_{21} = x_{21}/X_1$. The input coefficients corresponding to Table 2.1 are shown in Table 2.2.

Table 2.2

$$\begin{bmatrix} a_{11} & a_{12} \\ a_{21} & a_{22} \end{bmatrix}$$

Each element in Table 2.1 shows how much of the input of an input-supplying sector is needed to produce one unit of output of the receiving sector. That is, to produce one unit of output, sector 1 needs, for example, a_{11} units of its own output, and a_{21} units of input from sector 2. Table 2.2 provides a picture of the economy's technological structure at the time to which the table refers.

The input-coefficients of a sector are the measures of its *direct* requirements of inputs per unit of output produced. But to produce the inputs, the supplying sectors would in their turn also require inputs. For example, to produce textiles, an input of cotton is required, but the production of cotton in turn, would need the use of possibly some farm machinery or fertilizer which again would need inputs of iron and steel, chemicals, and so on. Thus, to produce a given amount of input in an industry, there is not only a direct input requirement, but *indirect* or secondary requirements for outputs from industries which supply the first industry, and so on through successive outputs and inputs until the effect of the final demand for the first industry's output has been traced to its last reverberation in the remotest part of the economy. Input-output analysis provides us with this useful information relating to the supplies of different goods and services which are needed to produce a given set of final goods.[4]

The Internal Structure of the Indian Economy

The technical structure of an economy reflected in its input-coefficients is determined by engineering considerations, custom or institutional arrangements, and by relative prices of inputs. The data on input-output analysis, on the basis of which the input coefficients are calculated, are the flows of goods and services within the economy that lie behind the summary measures like gross national product. Since the level of the gross national product varies with levels of development, it is usually observed that the pattern of transactions between different sectors are similar for economies which are at a relatively high level of development. The input-output tables of countries at low levels of development, with a relatively small gross national product, usually display a pattern that is different from the pattern displayed by the developed countries. At very low levels of development, the mode of production is largely self-contained, i.e., there is very little or no interaction between the sectors of the economy. As economic development proceeds, there emerges increasing interaction between sectors and there is more trade, i.e., more flow of goods and services. This is because the economy moves to higher levels of technology where, due to both engineering and institutional reasons, there is increased specialization within sectors and more interdependence between sectors. For example, consider two sectors such as the agriculture and chemical industries. At a low development level of agriculture, there is hardly

any flow of chemicals, e.g., fertilizer and pesticides, into agriculture, but the flow is substantial in a modernized agriculture. Also, before the development of modern steel plants in India, there was no scope for the flow of iron ore (mining sector) to the steel industry (manufacturing sector).

Several input-output tables have been prepared for India that make it possible to examine how the structure of the Indian economy has changed. Table 2.3 provides us with a view of the structure of the Indian economy in 1952–53, 1959, 1964–65 and 1970–71. This table has been prepared on the basis of larger input-output tables. For simplicity, the larger tables have been aggregated here to only two sectors, the interrelationships between which are displayed in the flows. Sector 1 is called the *primary complex* because it consists mostly of primary activities and such industries as are primarily engaged in the processing of primary products. Sector 2 consisting of all other industries is called the *secondary complex*. Such a classification of the economy might throw light on the two crucial sectors and their interrelationships along with the development of the Indian economy. Table 2.3 shows the intermediate outputs, i.e., outputs used as inputs. These, added to the output for final consumption (not shown here) would give gross output.

Table 2.3 shows how the flow of goods between the primary and secondary complexes have increased during the period. This indicates that in 1952–53, which was the beginning of planning for economic development in India, not only was the gross national product of India relatively low, but the volume of input-output transactions inside the economy was also at a rather low level compared to the volume of transactions in later years.

But it is not only in the volume of intermediate goods that the Indian economy has changed, the structure of its technology has also changed considerably as indicated by the coefficients in Tables 2.4 and 2.5. As was noted earlier, such structures reflect engineering and institutional factors. These factors are relatively stable, rendering the input-

Table 2.3. Input-Output Transactions, India

(Rupees in millions)

To \\ From	1952–53		1959		1964–65		1970–71	
	Primary complex	Secondary complex	Primary complex	Secondary complex	Primary complex	Secondary complex	Primary complex	Secondary complex
Primary complex	2,892	456	35,193	1,004	36,765	3,331	49,635	5,661
Secondary complex	397	826	2,604	5,245	3,705	18,670	11,249	35,648

SOURCE: The data for 1952–53 are taken from the 19 sector input-output table prepared by the Indian Institute of Public Opinion; the 1959 data are from the 29 sector table in P.N. Mathur and R. Bharadwaj (eds.), *Economic Analysis in Input-Output Framework*, (Poona: Input-Output Research Association, 1965); and the 1964–65 and 1970–71 tables are based on the 77 sector Input-Output Tables, in Government of India, Planning Commission, *Draft Fourth Five-Year Plan: Material and Financial Balances, 1964–65, 1970–71 and 1975–76* (New Delhi, September 1966). The 1952–53 figures are at 1952–53 prices, 1959 data are at 1959 prices and the 1964–65 and 1970–71 data are at 1960–61 prices. It should be mentioned that relative price differences do have some effect on the structures but it has been assumed to be negligible in the present study.

Table 2.4. Input Coefficients, India

	1952–53		1959		1964–65		1970–71	
	Primary complex	Secondary complex	Primary complex	Secondary complex	Primary complex	Secondary complex	Primary complex	Secondary complex
Primary complex	0.222	0.103	0.303	0.061	0.268	0.062	0.268	0.106
Secondary complex	0.029	0.124	0.023	0.281	0.027	0.347	0.061	0.670

Table 2.5. Total Input Coefficients, India

	1952–53		1959		1964–65		1970–71	
	Primary complex	Secondary complex	Primary complex	Secondary complex	Primary complex	Secondary complex	Primary complex	Secondary complex
Primary complex	1.293	0.169	1.447	0.122	1.371	0.130	1.404	0.451
Secondary complex	0.047	1.279	0.055	1.40	0.057	1.536	0.259	3.112

NOTE: Total Input Coefficients are measured by taking $(I-A)^{-1}$, where I is the identity matrix and A is the input coefficient matrix in Table 2.4.

coefficient structures quite stable over time[5] in most countries. However, it may be argued that in a country like India, which is at a low level of development, changes in the input-coefficients are likely to be greater than in an advanced country like the USA, which is already on a high technological level. This is mainly because a more mature and stable economy is generally less prone to change than an economy in the very early stages of development. Also at the initial stages of development of an economy, the bases on which the rates of change are calculated, for example the level of income, are low so that the rates of change appear to be rather large, compared with more developed economies where the same absolute amount of change will mean a smaller rate of change because of a larger denominator.

Table 2.4 shows the input coefficients for both sectors in India for selected years. The first point of difference with the volume of transactions in Table 2.3 is that, proportionately speaking, the coefficients in Table 2.4 have changed much less than the volumes in Table 2.3, indicating that the coefficients are more stable than the volumes. Secondly, all the transactions in Table 2.3 showed increase over time, but all the coefficients in Table 2.4 did not change in the same direction. For example, the input required from the secondary complex per unit of primary complex output decreased slightly while input from the secondary complex per unit of secondary complex output increased. Again, between 1952–53 and 1964–65, input required from the primary complex per unit of primary complex output increased while the same input per unit of secondary complex output decreased. In 1970–71, however, a noticeable change seems to have taken place in the increased use of inputs from the secondary complex in the primary complex. This shows that the structure of the Indian economy changed in such a way that different sectors moved in different directions in regard to their input use. Moreover, both in the transactions and in the coefficients the entries on the main diagonals of each table, i.e., the upper left-hand and the lower right-hand entries, are larger relative to the other two entries. This signifies a considerable dependence of each sector on inputs from within the sector itself rather than from outside. In general this is a characteristic of a developing economy like India.

The input-coefficients reflect only the direct input required per unit of output. But the secondary effects of the production of one unit of any sector's output for final consumption are not reflected in Table 2.4. For this purpose, Table 2.5 has been computed to show the total (direct plus indirect) inputs required to produce one extra unit of each sector's output for the market. Table 2.5 shows that the total input requirements in India did not change in the same way as the direct input requirements in Table 2.4. To produce one rupee's worth of primary goods, it was necessary to have a total input from the primary sector worth Rs. 1.293 in 1952–53 which rose to Rs. 1.371 in 1964–65 and Rs. 1.404 in 1970–71. Similarly, to produce secondary output worth one rupee the total input requirement from the primary sector was worth Re. 0.169, 0.122, 0.130 and 0.451 in 1952–53, 1959, 1964–65 and 1970–71 respectively. The structure of production of the Indian economy changed so that the total input requirements per unit of final goods from the primary sector increased with respect to both sectors. This indicates an increase in the use of industrial inputs in Indian agriculture during the period. On the other hand, the total input requirements for the secondary complex increased with respect to inputs from itself but decreased with respect to inputs from the primary sector.

Changes in the structure of an economy have important implications for the generation not only of output from different sectors of the economy, but also in the creation of employment. An economic activity has implications for employment, first, through the direct employment of labour to work in the given sector, and second, indirectly through creating demand for intermediate output from other sectors. As we have seen in Tables 2.4 and 2.5, structural changes in any one sector may result either in an increase or a decrease in the input coefficient associated with each supplying sector. Thus the net effect on employment potential caused by a structural change depends both on the degree and direction of change in each input coefficient, and the corresponding employment potential of each sector. On the basis of the employment potentials of the primary and secondary complexes of India and the nature of changes in the input coefficients it seems that the employment potential of the Indian economy has increased substantially.[6]

Conclusion

Studies of economic development commonly deal with changes in the aggregative magnitudes of the end results of economic activity, like national income or consumption. But behind these expressions there lies an interconnected network of numerous transactions of outputs between the different branches of the economy. In order to understand the mechanism of economic development and to formulate plans for economic growth, it is necessary to study this internal structure. Input-output analysis provides a useful tool for such study. Based on two-way tables of the flows of outputs between sectors that use those outputs as their inputs for producing the final goods for consumption, input-output analysis has made possible a general equilibrium analysis of the detailed structure of the economy. The extent to which the different branches of the economy are connected by the flows of intermediate goods is rather small in the earlier stages of development which are characterized by very little intersectoral trade. As the economy moves along the path of development there is more specialization within sectors and increased interdependence between sectors and so the intersectoral flows of outputs become larger. This is illustrated by the Indian economy which has displayed an increase in the volumes of transactions between sectors during 1952–53 and 1970–71. The internal structure of the Indian economy has changed in such a way that to produce the same amount of output it required in total a much higher amount of input from the industrial sector in 1970–71 than in 1952–53. This shows the increased use of industrial inputs in the Indian economy; in other words, this is an indication of the industrialization of India.

REFERENCES

1. Reserve Bank of India, *Report on Currency and Finance, 1974–75*, vol. II (Bombay, 1976).
2. W.W. Leontief, "The Structure of Development", *Input-Output Economics* (New York: Oxford University Press, 1966), pp. 41–42. Readers are referred to this article for a simple and authoritative treatment of input-output analysis.
3. Theoretically, it is possible to disaggregate the economy into any number of sectors. The level of disaggregation depends on the purpose of analysis and the availability of data.
4. The coefficient matrix of the total (direct plus indirect) input requirements are known as Leontief Inverse, and computed by inverting the $(I-A)$ matrix, where I is the identity matrix and A is the matrix of coefficients (e.g., Table 2.2).
5. Leontief, "Structure of Development".
6. See authors' "Economic Development, Structural Change and Employment Potential", *Journal of Development Studies* vol. 11, no. 2, January 1975. Reprinted in Frances Stewart (ed.), *Employment, Income Distribution and Development* (London: Frank Cass, 1975).

Part Two

THE HUMAN FACTOR

3

Population Growth in India

RAM L. CHUGH

India's Population Growth: Facts and Figures

India ranks second in the world in terms of population, and seventh in terms of land area. She supports nearly 15 per cent of the world's population on 2.4 per cent of the world's land area and shares only 1.5 per cent of the world's income. India's population in 1971 was 548 million and it is currently estimated to be 603 million. The present population exceeds the combined populations of the United States and the Soviet Union. In contrast to India, these two countries together cover about 21.3 per cent of the world's land area, share nearly 40 per cent of the world's income, and support only 12 per cent of the world's population. To provide another interesting comparison, the population of India nearly equals the population of all the states of Africa and Latin America put together. These comparisons are made to stress the high density of population in India. For a predominantly agricultural economy, the population pressure is very high. At the present rate of growth, estimated to be 2.2 per cent a year, India's population is increasing at the rate of 13 million a year—as if the entire population of a country like Australia is added to it every year. What does the addition of nearly 13 million people mean to India's economy? It means making available every year, among other things, "tons of food, 2.5 million houses, 4 million jobs, 126,500 schools, 372,500 teachers and 188 million metres of cloth".[1] Thus, such a massive annual increase in population imposes a heavy burden on an already overburdened economy and almost completely wipes out the progress which the country makes.

Let us examine the pattern of India's population growth from an historical perspective. According to the estimates of Kingsley Davis, the population of the Indian subcontinent was 125 million in 300 B.C., and it remained much the same for about 2000 years.[2] The major reason for the zero growth was the existence of high birth- and death-rates which, in the long run, balanced each other. "With the establishment of British rule and the restoration of a measure of internal peace in the sense of averted wars, and the setting-up of a skeleton health and medical service",[3] the pattern of population growth was gradually modified. Population increased at a very slow rate until 1921, after which it increased fairly rapidly. The population of India for the period 1891 to 1971 is given in Table 3.1.

Table 3.1. Growth of India's Population 1891-1971

Census year	Population in millions (adjusted to the present area)	Increase or decrease in millions
1891	236.7	——
1901	236.3	−0.4
1911	252.1	15.8
1921	251.4	−0.7
1931	279.0	27.6
1941	316.7	37.7
1951	361.1	44.4
1961	439.2	78.1
1971	548.0	109.0

SOURCE: S. Chandrasekhar, *India's Population: Facts, Problem and Policy* (Delhi: Meenakshi, 1967), p. 4.

The figure for 1971 is from the 1971 Census.

The above figures show that the population growth of India prior to 1921 was not only slow but also sporadic. After 1921, the population increased at a steady pace and then at an accelerating rate. The year 1921 is regarded as the year of the "great divide" in the demographic history of India. Thus, for example, the population increased by 15 million during the three decades of 1891 to 1921, but during the next three decades of 1921-51, it increased by 110 million, which is seven times the increase in the previous period. During the next two decades of 1951-61 and 1961-71, the population increased by 78 million and 109 million respectively. These increases are phenomenal: it took India hundreds of years to attain a population of 250 million in 1921, but only 45 years to double it. And, at the current rate of growth, the population will double every 32 years. Such an accelerating growth-rate was not foreseen by Indian planners. The first two five-year plans were formulated on the assumption that

the population would grow at an annual rate of 1.25 per cent which, as we know now, was a serious underestimation. The actual rate of growth was closer to 2 per cent, as shown by the 1961 census. The findings of the 1961 census were a shocking revelation and were responsible for bringing a new sense of urgency to the family planning programme. If the current trends of population growth are projected into the future, the resulting figure is even more terrifying. It is anticipated that at the present rate of growth, India's population will reach the billion mark before the end of this century, and there is nothing which it can do to stop this. According to demographers, even if India were to take drastic measures to reduce its birth rate to the replacement level by 1985, its population will still reach the billion mark by A.D. 2000.[4] This is the inevitable consequence of an age structure which is heavily skewed toward the younger age-group. Nearly 42 per cent of the present population is below 15 years of age and this group has many fertile years ahead.

The skyrocketing of India's population is an entirely new phenomenon which has seriously aggravated the problems of economic development. Demographers call it a period of population explosion to dramatize the severity of the situation. Figure 3.1 portrays the "vertical" nature of this demographic explosion.

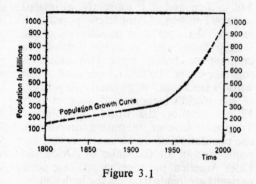

Figure 3.1

Causes of India's Exploding Population Growth

The difference between a nation's birth and death rates determines its population growth. Consequently, differential movements in these two rates can provide an explanation of the pattern of population growth. For instance, the main reason for the slow and erratic growth of population prior to 1921 was the prevalence of high birth and death rates, leaving little room for population expansion. After 1921, the death rate declined sharply. But the decline in the death rate was not accompanied by a similar reduction in the birth rate. The death rate declined from 47 per thousand in 1911–20 to 15 per thousand in 1972, while the birth rate fell from 48 per thousand to only 37 per thousand during the same period.[5] It is the imbalance between these two rates, brought about mainly by the sudden and rapid decline in the death rate, which is responsible for the explosive growth of India's population. The trends in India's birth and death rates are given in Table 3.2.

Table 3.2. India's Birth and Death Rates: 1901–1970

	Estimated birth rate	Estimated death rate	Increase in population
1901–10	49.2	42.6	6.6
1911–20	48.1	47.2	0.9
1921–30	46.4	36.3	10.1
1931–40	45.2	31.2	14.0
1941–50	39.9	27.4	12.5
1951–60	41.7	22.8	18.9
1961–70	39.0	17.0	22.0

SOURCE: S.P. Jain, "Some Aspects of Mortality", in Ashish Bose *et al.* (ed.), *Population in India's Development, 1947–2000* (Delhi: Vikas, 1974), p. 320.

The figures indicate that the decline in the death rate was slow until 1950, and that thereafter it was quite rapid. The birth rate, on the other hand, has remained high and relatively stable. The figures indicate the widening gap between these two rates (See Figure 3.2). The main challenge is to reduce this gap not by increasing the death rate but by reducing the birth rate.

Causes of Decline in Death Rate

The dramatic decline in the death rate has been brought about by developments in modern science and technology.

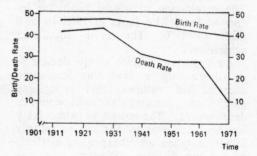

Figure 3.2

Famines, epidemics, diseases and other disasters which used to take a heavy toll of human life have been greatly controlled. With the application of science and technology to agriculture, the supply of food has kept pace with the demand. Moreover, distribution of food has been considerably facilitated by improvements both in the means of transportation and in the methods of food storage. As a result, famines have been virtually eliminated. That does not mean there are no periodic food shortages due either to the failure of monsoons or to some other natural calamity, but such situations can now be met by quick imports. The international community has so far responded splendidly to any threat of famine in any part of the world, and international cooperation has been responsible for staving off many deaths. Similarly, deaths from epidemics like cholera, plague, and smallpox, have been greatly reduced because of the widespread use of immunization, antibiotics, and other products of modern medicine. The eradication of malaria by DDT has had a spectacular effect in reducing the death rate. Better water supplies and improved sanitary conditions brought about mainly by public health programmes have helped reduce the incidence of death.

The successful attack on the factors

causing high mortality is reflected in an increased life expectancy at birth and also in a sharp reduction in the Infant Mortality Rate. The latter has dropped from 232 per thousand in 1901 to 131 in 1972. Although this rate is still high compared to rates in the West, the decline is dramatic and represents considerable progress. The expectation of life at birth has increased from 23.6 years in 1901 to 51.0 years in 1972. This is a significant achievement.

An important feature of the decline in the death rate is that this has been accomplished without there being any parallel corresponding significant economic development. The reduction in mortality has been achieved by the use of mostly imported quick and inexpensive methods of fighting diseases. Western countries had to struggle hard to attain a similar decline in their death rates—it took them 70 to 80 years to achieve a decline in mortality which took India hardly 20 years.

Causes of the High Birth Rate
The birth rate in India continues to be very high.[6] Efforts to reduce it have not yet been successful. There are various reasons for the continuing high birth-rate.

1. "Marriage [in India] is not merely a necessary social institution but a quasi-religious duty"[7]: nearly 99 per cent of the eligible males and females marry at least once in their lifetime.

2. There is a low marriage age for both males and females. The average age of marriage, according to the 1971 census, was 17.1 years for females and for males 22.4 years. Early marriage is greatly facilitated by the institution of the joint family system. The married partners need not be economically self-supporting and the husband does not need to have any independent household. Thus, there are no economic obstacles to marriage. The low age at marriage for females contributes to the high birth-rate in two ways. First, it prolongs the period of child bearing, and second, the fertility in the younger age-group is very high. It is estimated that in 1961 nearly 70 per cent of females in the age group of 15–19 years was already married. The corresponding figure for

a developed country like Sweden is only 3.7 per cent.[8]

3. The widely prevalent desire to have sons also leads to a high birth rate. This desire is based primarily on economic grounds, but it also has a religious basis. Sons are expected to provide economic support to their parents when they are sick, unemployed or old. For a country like India with no comprehensive social security programme, this desire is understandable. Because of the high mortality in the past, it was necessary for a couple to have a large number of children in order to ensure the survival of one or two. This attitude still continues even though there has been a sharp decline in mortality.

4. The decline in maternal mortality and increase in life expectancy have also led to higher birth rates. This is a necessary consequence of improvements in health facilities.

5. There is also no widespread use of family planning methods among either the urban or the rural population, especially among the latter who constitute 80 per cent of the total. Most people regard children as a gift of God, and uncontrolled procreation is regarded as one of the laws of normal life.

These factors when taken into conjunction with the entire social and economic structure of the country, tend to maintain the birth rate at a high level. In reality, the birth rate of a country is a highly complex phenomenon and is determined by socioeconomic, cultural, religious, and biological factors. All these factors are interrelated in a very complicated manner. Because of their interdependence, it is extremely difficult to indicate precisely the manner in which each of these influences the birth rate. Thus, an adequate explanation for the existence of a high birth rate for a poor country like India which is still caught in its age-old traditions, religious taboos, and rigid social institutions, is rather difficult.

The next section attempts to provide an economic explanation for the existence of the high birth rate in India, but it is strongly emphasised that economic factors must be studied in conjunction with non-economic factors.

An Economic Theory of Family Formation[9]

An economic explanation for differing levels of birth rates in different countries is based on the theory of cost-benefit analysis. It is argued that, in a poor country, costs of raising children are low and benefits large, and there is an economic incentive for having large families. Conversely, costs of raising children for an average family in a rich country are very high and the benefits small, and this necessitates a small-size family. Let us now analyse this theory in detail.

The underlying economic rationale for different sizes of families is the familiar principle of utility maximization. This approach treats a couple as a consumer unit and a child as a special kind of consumer-producer good. A child is like a consumer good because he satisfies certain needs of his parents, and he is like a producer good because investment made in him yields a stream of economic returns. These attributes make a child an economic asset, and thus worth having. There are, however, costs of acquiring and maintaining a child which make him not a free good but one with a price tag. A child, therefore, is a source of both benefits and costs. Like any consumer, a couple also operates within a given budget constraint and has to allocate its limited resources among several competing assets (one of which happens to be a child) in such a way as to maximize their utility. Consequently, a rational couple is hypothesised as weighing the satisfaction and other returns anticipated from a child against the costs of raising him, before deciding to have one. A couple is expected to have a child if expected benefits exceed costs. They would stop having children when the additional benefits from the last child equal the additional costs. The last child becomes the marginal unit and satisfies the equilibrium condition of equating marginal benefits with marginal costs. Because couples differ in their budget constraints and in their preference functions, we find differing sizes of families.

Costs and Benefits of Having Children

A child imposes two kinds of costs on his parents. These are financial, and opportunity costs. The first covers the complete cost of acquiring and maintaining a child until he is grown up. Expenses for prenatal care, delivery, postnatal care, food, clothing, shelter, medical care, and education, which are caused by a child, are included in financial costs. Some of these may be borne by the State, thus reducing the cost for the parents. The second covers the earnings foregone by the working mother during the period of her confinement, and expenses of extra-parental care. It is argued that the costs of raising children are directly related to the economic status of the parents.

Parents expect to enjoy two types of benefit from their offspring. These are economic, and noneconomic. The former includes the economic contribution which a child is expected to make to his family's income when he grows up. The latter includes the joy experienced by the parents of having a child at home, playing with him, and seeing him grow to adulthood. The desire to have a male child who will continue the family line and perform religious rites at the time of the parents' death is also part of the noneconomic benefits. While economic benefits are assumed to be inversely related to the economic status of the parents, the noneconomic benefits are dependent upon several factors, such as social, cultural, religious, and psychological factors.

Differing Birth Rates in Countries

Using the cost-benefit approach to family formation, one can now rationalize the existence of high birth-rates in developing countries and of low birth-rates in developed countries.

Developing Countries

In a typical developing country like India, nearly 80 per cent of the people live in villages and work on land: their living standards are very low. In such a system, where the people are poor and illiterate, costs of raising children are low and constitute a very small drain of the family budget. In most cases, prenatal care is rare, and delivery takes place within the house, usually with the help of a village midwife whose fee is nominal. Food, clothing and shelter do not impose an additional financial burden because most of it comes through reallocation within the existing budget. Medical and educational expenses are negligible. Most often, a child does not reach secondary school level. Similarly, opportunity costs are almost zero because women generally do not work outside the home, and there are thus no extraparental care expenses. Moreover, the institution of the joint family system makes it easier to raise a child because the burden of looking after him does not fall exclusively on the parents. Consequently, the costs of acquiring and maintaining children are low in a "poor' society.

On the other hand, the benefits are relatively large. A child starts helping his family on the farm at an early age. He learns the skills of farming by observing others, and does not require any outside training. At the time of harvest, a farmer normally needs a lot of labour, and the availability of nonwage family labour makes a big family an asset. And, as already stated, because of lack of social security programmes in such countries, children are the best form of social insurance.

Since the costs of raising children are low and the benefits large, there is an economic incentive for having a large number of children. In other words, it is with a large number of children that a couple satisfies the equilibrium condition of equating marginal costs and marginal benefits.

Developed Countries
In a typical developed country, nearly 80 per cent of people live in urban areas and derive their income from nonfarm occupations. In such a society the average living standard, literacy, and mobility are high. As a consequence, costs of raising children are also very high. An average family spends a considerable sum of money for prenatal care, hospital delivery, postpartum care for both mother and infant. The annual cost of upkeep which includes food, clothing, shelter, medical care and education, is very high and constitutes a sizable

part of the family's budget. Opportunity costs both in terms of earnings foregone by the working mother, and expenses for extraparental care are not insignificant. There is a strong desire on the part of the parents to maintain their living standards even when the family grows large. In fact, it is observed that parents often desire that their children enjoy even higher standards, which means more investment in them. In short, costs of raising children in developed countries are high, and impose a heavy financial burden on an average family.

Moreover, parents do not ordinarily expect economic support from their children. Most often, when a child becomes an earner he leaves his parents' home. The existence of extensive welfare programmes makes the economic argument for a large family redundant. A child is thus mainly a source of noneconomic benefits but the psychological satisfaction which parents derive from their children would tend to decline sharply with the addition of each child.

Thus, in developed countries children are more a burden than an asset, and this necessitates a small-size family.

Graphic Presentation
This analysis can be presented diagrammatically to illustrate the behaviour of two typical couples—one belonging to a developing country and the other to a

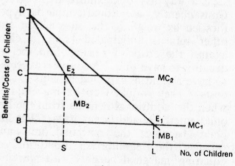

Fig. 3.3

developed country—in arriving at the equilibrium size of their family. In Figure 3.3, the vertical axis represents the benefits and costs of having children, and the horizontal axis indicates the number of children. MC_1 and MC_2 refer to the marginal costs of raising children for an average couple in developing and developed countries respectively. The costs of raising the first child equals OB in a developing country and OC in a developed country. It is assumed that the cost of raising further children stays constant at these levels. This is indicated by the horizontal marginal cost curves. MB_1 and MB_2 refer to the marginal benefits which an average couple expects in a developing and developed economy respectively. OD indicates the benefits expected from the first child and, for the sake of simplicity, these are assumed identical for each couple in both countries. But the marginal benefits from additional children drop slowly for the couple in the developing country, and at a much faster rate for the couple in the developed economy. These differing rates of marginal benefits are indicated by differing slopes of marginal benefit curves.

The couple in the developing country reaches an equilibrium size of family at point E_1 where MB_1 intersects MC_1. The other couple in the advanced economy attains an equilibrium at point E_2 where MB_2 intersects MC_2. These points are represented by letters S and L on the horizontal axis, indicating that a couple with a low economic status would have a larger number of children than a couple with a higher economic status.

Limitations of This Approach
Even though the cost-benefit approach to family formation has explained the existence of differential family sizes, the presentation of this approach has been at a rather elementary level.[10] The inherent limitations of this approach necessitate caution in accepting the validity of the analysis in its entirety. First, it assumes that an average couple is rational and well-informed. Secondly, it assumes that family planning techniques are known and contraceptives are available and accessible so that a couple has children not by chance but by choice. This knowledge may not exist among most couples in a poor country. Thirdly, this is a micro approach which analyses

each family in isolation. The social costs and benefits of differing family sizes are not discussed. Fourthly, the approach does not discriminate between the sex of the child. This may have no relevance in a developed country but it has great significance for an average couple in a developing country. Lastly, this is mainly an economic approach and treats the child as a consumer-producer good which to some sounds dehumanized.

Despite these limitations, it is generally felt that this approach does provide a reasonably sound explanation for differing sizes of family. The analysis also contains some policy implications for controlling population growth. For example, a government may succeed in reducing the desirability of a large-size family by adopting measures such as compulsory education, declaring child labour illegal, and devising a suitable social-security programme.

Having discussed the causes for the rapidly-growing population of India, we now examine its impact on economic development.

Population Growth and Economic Development

The major task facing developing countries like India is to bring about economic development, and raise the living standards of the people. A rising living standard means improvement in the economic well-being of the people. For most people in India, it means access to more and better food, clothing, shelter, education, and medical facilities. For lack of a better indicator, economic development is still measured by rising real per capita incomes, which is the growth of real national income adjusted for growth in population. And, if standards of living are to improve, it is essential that the rate of economic development be higher than the rate of population growth. As we shall see, a rapidly growing population makes the task of economic development more difficult. In fact, most developing countries are discovering that their efforts to advance into the modern industrial age are being thwarted by a rapid growth in population, and that they need to work hard even to stay at the same place. The reason is that the expanded outlay on food, shelter, clothing, and other social services for meeting the needs of a growing population, limits the availability of funds for capital formation.

Demographers draw a distinction between two kinds of investment—demographic, and economic. The former refers to the investment required to maintain the per capita income of the growing population at a constant level, and the latter to the investment required for raising the per capita income. While the first is determined by the rate of population growth, the second is determined by the population growth and the rate of increase in per capita income desired. There can be no economic development without economic investment. In developing countries, demographic investment itself constitutes a major part of the total annual investment. According to World Bank estimates, "in the mid 1960's, almost two-thirds of the total annual investment in a sample of 22 developing countries was required to maintain per capita income at a constant level leaving only about a third to raise living standards. The corresponding figures for a representative sample of 19 developed countries were one-quarter and three-quarters".[11] This helps explain why India has not made any significant gain in per capita income. Most of the investments are used primarily to provide an increasing population with a constant living standard. Reviewing the economic and social progress the country has made, the Fourth Five-Year Plan said: "Per capita real income in 1965–66 was about the same as it was in 1960–61, the results of the meagre growth rate of national income having been completely neutralized by the 2.5 per cent rate of population growth".[12] Clearly, the major objective of economic development—raising living standards—is being jeopardised by the population explosion.

Population Growth and Capital Requirements
Investment is a necessary condition for economic growth. A country with a fast-growing population needs to devote a larger proportion of its national income to capital formation than a country with a slow-growing population, to obtain the same increase in the per capita income. How much a country should actually invest depends upon the rate of economic growth desired and its capital-output ratio. The rate of growth in per capita income can be obtained by subtracting the rate of population growth from the rate of economic growth. The capital-output ratio indicates the amount of capital required to produce one unit of output. This ratio is about 3:1 for most developing countries such as India. This means that a country needs 3 units of capital to get 1 unit of output. The investment required to achieve a certain rate of economic growth can be estimated by multiplying the rate by the capital-output ratio. For instance, if a developing country with its population growing at 3 per cent per year desired its per capita income to increase at 2 per cent per year, it will have to grow at 5 per cent per year, and it will need to invest 15 per cent of its national income annually. On the other hand, if the population of this country was increasing at 1 per cent per year, it will need to invest 9 per cent per year to get the same increase in per capita income.

Using this analysis, Table 3.3 gives the rates of investment which India must make to obtain different rates of growth in per capita income.

To keep the per capita income from falling, India must invest 6.6 per cent of its national income annually. The entire amount becomes demographic investment. An investment of 9.6 per cent will be required to obtain an annual increase of 1 per cent in per capita income. If India wants per capita income to rise at 3 per cent per year so as to double it every 23 years, it must invest 15.6 per cent per year. And, if the aim is to double the per capita income in one decade, India must achieve a growth rate of 7 per cent per year in per capita income, and for that it must be prepared to invest as much as 27.9 per cent per year.

Currently, India's per capita income is growing around 1 per cent per year. At this rate, it will double in 70 or 80 years, which is a long way to go. The gross domestic savings are estimated to

Table 3.3. Investment Required for Different Rates of Growth

(percentage)

Population growth (%)	Growth in per capita income	Growth of national income	Capital-output ratio	Investment required
2.2	0	2.2	3:1	6.6
2.2	1.0	3.2	3:1	9.6
2.2	3.0	5.2	3:1	15.6
2.2	7.0	9.2	3:1	27.6

rise from 12.2 per cent in 1973–74 to 15.7 per cent in 1978–79.[13] If these savings can actually be mobilized, India should be able to achieve an annual growth-rate of 3 per cent in per capita income by the end of the Fifth Plan. This projection and the ones in Table 3.3 are based on the assumption that population continues to grow at the current rate. A decline in this rate will accelerate the process of economic development.

Consequences of the Population Explosion
The foregoing analysis indicates that a country with a fast-growing population needs to invest a large amount to raise the per capita income. Unfortunately, a rapidly growing population has certain features which hamper the process of economic development, by reducing the availability of investible funds. These features are: (1) higher dependency-ratio; (2) increasing demand for food; (3) unemployment problem; and (4) diversion of investment to social services. The implications of these for economic development will now be examined.

Higher Dependency-Ratio
The population of a country can be divided into two groups: economically active, and economically inactive. The former refers to the population in the age group of 15–59 years which is a working population, and the latter to the population in the age group of below 15 and over 59 years. This is the non-working group which depends for its consumption needs on the economically active group. In most developing countries, the economically productive group constitutes nearly 55 per cent of the population, and the corresponding figure for developed countries is around

65 per cent. This implies a higher dependency-ratio in developing countries, i.e., a working adult supports a relatively larger number of people than his counterpart in a developed country. A higher dependency-ratio is a necessary consequence of population explosion. A high birth-rate results in an age structure heavily skewed toward younger people. And also reduction in infant mortality inceases the number of dependent children. A higher dependency-ratio has an adverse effect on the availability of savings. A worker has to meet his own consumption needs and those of his dependents before he can think of saving.

According to the 1971 census, productive and nonproductive consumers constituted 52 and 48 per cent of India's population. It is anticipated that with a further decline in the death rate and with no change in the birth rate, the dependency ratio will rise. The problem in India is even worse because not every one in the working age-group is gainfully employed. Consequently, the actual percentage of dependents is much higher.

Population Growth and Demand for Food
The most widely shared fear about population growth is that it will outrun the food supply and bring pe ple close to starvation. The Malthusian spectre of overpopulation, based on the assumption that the food supply will not be able to keep up with the demand, has long been invalidated in most of the developed countries where agriculture has made a tremendous advance. But the picture of mass starvation and hunger still hangs like Damocles' sword over most developing countries. In most of these, the supply of food has not kept pace with demand,

With population growing at an explosive rate, these countries will witness an accelerating demand for food in the coming decades. Food and other farm products constitute major consumption items for an average family. It is estimated that the average income elasticity of demand for food is around 0.8, which is very high.

In India, until recently, the demand for food exceeded the supply, and the deficit was met by imports. During the Third Plan period alone, India imported 25 million tons of foodgrains. While imports of foodgrains constituted only 5 to 6 per cent of the total demand, it did mean a great loss of valuable foreign exchange, which could have been utilized for imports of capital goods. It is felt that India has now reached the stage of self-sufficiency in food both because of the relative success of the Green Revolution and because of the increased emphasis on agriculture in the Fourth and Fifth Plans. The success of the Green Revolution has brought a new sense of confidence and hope to Indian agriculture. But will the trend of increased agricultural production continue? India has brought most of its land under cultivation. The Fourth Plan expected to increase the area under cultivation by only an additional 2 per cent. Thus, increase in output has to come through intensive cultivation and higher yields per acre. The Fourth Plan estimated that the output of food and other farm products must increase at the rate of 5 per cent a year so as to be self-sufficient. To meet these goals, India will require a successive series of green revolutions, which means huge investments in the agricultural sector. Dr. Lester R. Brown, a leading expert in agriculture says:[14]

...the new seeds [do not] offer a solution to the food problem, but they do buy some precious time, perhaps an additional 10–15 years in which to stabilize world population growth. If within 15 years we are not well on our way to stabilize world population growth, Dr. Borlaug's monumental contribution will have been in vain. Let it not be so.

It may be possible to increase food production to meet increasing demand by the application of advances in science and technology. But, as mentioned earlier, this will call for huge investments which will have to be diverted from other areas. It is the diversion of investment to agriculture from other crucial sectors which causes the planners great concern. If population growth could be controlled and the demand for food did not increase so rapidly, India's investible resources could be used in nonagricultural areas, such as industry, communication, and transportation.

Population Growth and the Employment Problem
Another serious consequence of a rapidly growing population is the resultant manpower explosion—the swelling stream of fresh entrants to an already glutted labour market, making the unemployment situation still worse. Despite great efforts to create more jobs in the five-year plans, the unemployment problem in India is much more serious today than at any time before. Every plan period ends with a greater backlog of unemployed people. For example, the backlog of unemployment at the end of the Second Plan was 9 million. The additional labour force expected during the Third Plan was estimated at 17 million. The Third Plan anticipated the creation of additional employment for 14 million, thus ending with a backlog of 12 million. This figure includes open unemployment. But in India nearly one-fourth of the labour force is underemployed. It is anticipated that during the seventies and eighties, the manpower problem will become extremely serious. This will be the result of the extraordinary expansion of population which occurred in the fifties and sixties. The babies born then will enter the labour market in the seventies and eighties. And, "no programme of family planning, public or private, surgical or spiritual, chemical or mechanical, will have the slightest effect whatsoever on the labour force explosion of the 70's".[15] It is expected that nearly 90 million people will enter the labour force during the seventies alone.

To provide jobs for such a rapidly

growing labour force is an extremely difficult task and requires huge investment and careful planning. But for a developing country like India, it is difficult to mobilize resources on such a large scale. In short, a rapidly expanding population makes it even more difficult to raise employment and per capita income simultaneously.

Diversion of Investment to Social Services
In addition to the diversion of investments discussed above, a rapidly growing population also leads to increased expenditure on social services, such as health, education, and housing. A rising population means a growing proportion of young people, which creates a heavy demand for these services. Undoubtedly, expenditure on these services adds to the productive capacity of the nation by improving the quality of the labour force, but such investments are ordinarily capital-intensive and have long gestation periods. These investments constitute a sizable part of the total annual investments and the proportion is expected to go up as population keeps growing. During the Third Plan, Rs. 9.36 billion were spent on education, health, and housing and urban development. The Fifth Plan has made provision for Rs. 17.26 billion for education, Rs. 7.96 billion for health, and Rs. 5.43 billion for housing and urban development.[16] This outlay does not include non-plan expenditure by Government and expenditure by the private sector. Expenditures on such a large scale impose a great burden on the limited resources of the country. If population growth could be reduced, some of these resources could then be diverted to other projects. Coale and Hoover have shown that if India could reduce its population growth by half between 1956–81, the country could save as much as Rs. 60–65 billion during the thirty-year period of 1956–86 from housing and education alone.[17]

This discussion has shown that while a rapidly growing population requires large investment to raise living standards, it also reduces the availability of investible funds, thereby making the task of economic development extremely difficult. The serious threat which rapid population growth poses for India's development plans was strongly stressed in the Fourth Plan:[18]

Population growth on this scale can be a crippling handicap since our population in relation to resources is already large, incomes are low and economic development is a desperate need. The speed at which a country develops depends largely upon its ability to direct a larger part of its growing resources to investment rather than current consumption. A growing population with a high proportion of dependent children will find it increasingly difficult to do so. If population keeps growing rapidly, the major part of investment and national energy and efforts may be used up for merely maintaining the existing low living standards. Population growth thus presents a very serious challenge.

Population growth must slow down. The resources of India are not limitless, they cannot sustain a rapidly growing population for all time. But what factors will bring about a slowdown? To answer this question, let us look at the pattern of population growth experienced by the advanced countries.

The Theory of Demographic Transition

The theory of demographic transition postulates a three-stage relationship between economic development and population growth. According to this theory, as a country advances economically, its population passes through the stages of low growth, high growth, and then finally low and stable growth. These stages of population growth are shown in Figure 3.4, where the horizontal axis indicates different levels of economic development, and the vertical axis, population.

During the first stage, a country is at a low level of economic development. Agriculture is the major occupation, and it is conducted in the most primitive manner. The average living standard is extremely low. Most people are illiterate, and are ruled by age-old customs and religious beliefs. Such a society is characterized by a high and relatively stable birth rate and a high but fluctuating

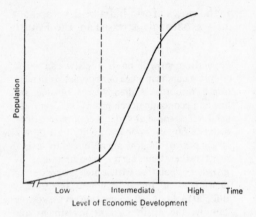

Fig. 3.4

death rate, leaving little room for population expansion. The rate of population growth in this stage is below one per cent a year.

As an economy advances, the living standards of the people improve. They eat better and live better. Developments in science and technology, and medicine, make available the means to control the forces of death. As a result, the death rate begins to decline. The birth rate still continues to be at a high level because of resistance to changing long-established customs and traditions. The imbalance between the high birth rate and the declining death rate leads to high population growth. The rate of population growth ranges between 1 and 3 per cent a year. Demographers call this a period of population explosion. This is a stage of disequilibrium because the population of a country cannot keep growing at a high rate indefinitely.

As economic development continues, the structure of the economy undergoes a change. Industry comes to dominate, and this creates a massive shift of population from rural to urban areas. Most people are literate and highly mobile. The status of women also changes, and women join the labour force in increasing numbers. These factors tend to make children more of a burden than an asset. Thus small families are preferred, and this leads to a decline in the birth rate. At this stage, we ultimately have a low birth rate, a low death rate, and a low but stable population growth, of around 1 per cent a year.

All developed countries have passed through these stages and are now in the final stage. Some demographers have observed that when a country becomes highly affluent, there is a tendency for the birth rate to go up, as has happened in the United States during the postwar period. This is regarded as a very temporary phenomenon. It is estimated that most European countries entered the second stage in the latter part of the eighteenth century and remained at that stage for nearly 100 years.

Most developing countries today are at the second stage, and are experiencing population explosions. To answer the question whether the population explosion can continue indefinitely we must first ask whether these countries will also experience the same type of demographic transition.

Relevance of Demographic Transition Theory to Developing Countries
Will a developing country like India follow a similar population cycle? Many population experts do not think so. They cite several factors which they feel hinder the application of the transitional theory to the presently overpopulated developing countries. They base their arguments on the contrasts they observe between the economic conditions and demographic situation in the developing countries today, with those prevailing in the developed countries at the corresponding stage of their development. They emphasise the following differences.[19]

1. The decline in the death rate in the developed countries was slow and gradual, and was the result of overall economic development. On the other hand, the decline in the death rate in the developing countries has been sudden and rapid and it has not been accompanied by any economic development.

2. Developed contries never experienced birth rates above 40 during their development period. Moreover, after a time lag, these countries registered a decline in their birth rates. On the other hand, birth rates in developing countries today range between 40 and 60. And, no

significant decline in their birth rates has yet been observed even though death rates have declined considerably.

3. Thus, the magnitude of the population explosion being experienced by developing countries today is much greater. Such high rates of population growth were never experienced by developed countries.

4. Developing countries today are relatively more densely populated than were developed countries during the corresponding period.

5. Developing countries today are at a much lower level of economic development than the developed countries were at the corresponding stage.

6. The opportunities for large-scale international migration which existed during the eighteenth and nineteenth centuries do not exist any longer.

7. Unlike most developed countries, developing countries today have no colonies to exploit.

Because of these differences, there is little hope that developing countries will automatically follow the traditional demographic cycle and attain demographic equilibrium. According to Myrdal, "the population cycle which would restore near balance between births and deaths, is not in sight in any of the South Asian countries".[20] Developing countries today are caught in a kind of low-income level equilibrium trap, and a rapidly growing population hinders the process of economic development, and thus holds back the completion of the demographic transition. Demographers therefore stress the need for an active population control policy, and argue that an economic development programme unaccompanied by such a policy cannot show much progress. In fact, during the recent past, several studies have been conducted which have shown that a developing country will grow faster (economically) with reduced population growth.

One such study which is of relevance to India, has been conducted by Coale:[21] here, the question is asked, what will the effect on income per consumer be if a country decides to reduce its fertility rate by 50 per cent over a 25-year period. India is used as a case study. The findings

indicate that income per consumer would grow faster with reduced fertility. It is shown that after 30 years, income per consumer in a population with reduced fertility would be 40 per cent higher than income per consumer in a population with unchanged fertility. The difference in income would increase to 100 per cent after 60 years, and to 600 per cent after 150 years. The study demonstrates very clearly that a country stands to gain, and will grow at a faster rate, if it is able to reduce its population growth.

Population Policy in India

The Indian Planning Commission itself recognized in the beginning that a rapidly growing population can be a menace to economic development and advocated the need for family planning. The Government of India took a courageous stand on this question and displayed great foresight by adopting family planning as an integral part of its overall national development programme. In fact, India is credited to be the first country in the world to adopt family planning as a state policy.

The first indication of the official attitude toward the population problem was contained in the First Plan which, inter alia, stated that "there is no doubt that given a situation in which shortage of capit equipment rather than of labour is the main limiting factor in development, a rapidly growing population is apt to become more a source of embarrassment than of help to a programme for raising standards of living".[22] And it advocated the need for "reduction of the birth rate to the extent necessary to stabilize the population at a level consistent with the requirements of national economy".[23]

Accordingly, a sum of Rs. 6.5 million was made available for family planning. Since the reaction of the people to this new public policy was not known, a cautious approach to the family planning programme was suggested.

The need for population control was stressed even more strongly in the Second Plan, which stated:[24]

The logic of facts is unmistakable and there

is no doubt that under conditions prevailing in countries like India, a high rate of population growth is bound to affect adversely the rate of economic advance and living standards per capita. Given the overall shortage of land and capital equipment relatively to population as in India, the conclusion is inescapable that an effective curb on population growth is an important condition for rapid improvement in incomes and in levels of living.

During the Second Plan period, the family planning programme was organized on a nation-wide basis. A Central Family Planning Board was instituted and a Director of Family Planning was appointed in the Ministry of Health at the Centre. Similar boards were also formed at the state level and family planning officers were appointed to head these. It was expected that such an organizational set-up would help generate a country-wide awareness of the population issue and the need to check population growth through family planning. The principal method for expanding the programme was still to be the birth control clinics which were to be increased during the Plan. A sum of Rs. 50 million was allocated for family planning.

Even though both plans indicated an official desire to control population growth, actual implementation of the programme was half-hearted and lacked a sense of urgency. Both plans failed to spend the full amount allocated. The First Plan spent hardly 25 per cent of its budgeted amount, and the Second only 45 per cent. The Second Plan did no doubt create a general awareness of the need for family planning, but the programme lacked enthusiastic support, leadership, and a sense of direction. Several reasons have been advanced for the indifference with which the programme was implemented. First, India was the first country in the world to launch a publicly-supported family planning programme, and was thus breaking new ground. Government was not sure of the kind of response such a programme would receive from political parties, religious groups, and the public at large. It therefore adopted a very cautious and exploratory approach. Secondly, the programme relied heavily on the traditional clinical-referral approach, and treated family planning as a medical rather than a social and economic problem. Thirdly, and perhaps the most important, the planners seriously underestimated the rate of population growth. The Second Plan estimated the rates of population growth to be 12.5 per cent for the decade 1951–60, 13.3 per cent for 1961–70, and 14.0 per cent for 1971–80.[25] The family planning programme was based on such projections.

But this indifference did not last long. The results of the 1961 census were a shocking revelation to planners and brought a new seriousness and determination to the family planning programme. This was reflected in the subsequent plans. For instance, the Third Plan emphasised that "the objective of stabilizing the growth of population over a reasonable period must be at the very centre of planned development".[26] And it strongly recommended that "the greatest stress has to be placed in the Third and subsequent five-year plans on the programme for family planning".[27] This indicated a clear recognition of the gravity of the country's population problem and the resolve to check it. A sum of Rs. 500 million was provided for family planning—more than nine times the combined allocation of funds under the previous two plans. The programme was to be suitably reorganized so as to reach people in both urban and rural areas. The Plan emphasised the need for educating the people through various media, and for motivating them to accept the norm of a small family size. The programme was to be expanded through the clinical-cum-extension approach, though, towards the middle of the Plan period, the emphasis shifted towards the extension approach.

The Fourth Plan described family planning as a programme of "the highest priority". It reiterated that "in order to make economic development yield tangible benefits for the ordinary people, it is necessary that the birth rate be brought down as early as possible".[28] It proposed that the programme should aim at reducing the birth rate from 39 per thousand to 25 per thousand within the next 10–12 years. This was the first time that a five-year plan had contained a specific recommendation for setting a particular target for reducing the birth rate. It was suggested that, to achieve this goal, the programme should expand its activities, and encourage eligible couples to adopt family planning as a way of life through "(i) group acceptance of the small sized family; (ii) personal knowledge about family planning methods; and (iii) ready availability of supplies and services".[29] A sum of Rs. 3.30 billion was provided for implementing the programme.

The time-and-target oriented approach to family planning introduced in the Fourth Plan is being continued in the Fifth Plan. The *Draft Fifth Plan* calls for reducing the birth rate to 30 per thousand by 1978–79 and to 25 per thousand by 1983–84. To achieve these goals, the targets set for the Fifth Plan period include 18 million sterilizations, 5.9 million IUD insertions, and 8.8 million users of conventional contraceptives by 1978–79.[30] The Plan also calls for an increasing integration of family planning services with other health-related services, such as maternity, child care, and nutrition, through the help of specially trained "multipurpose" workers. The Plan provides for an outlay of Rs. 5.16 billion for implementation of the family planning programme.

The problem of population growth is also being attacked through changes in socioeconomic factors. Some of these changes are: raising the age at marriage for both males and females, improving the economic and social status of women, making education compulsory, declaring child labour illegal, and providing old-age security programmes. It is expected that these changes, in addition to family planning, will help reduce the birth rate. The recent passage of the liberal abortion bill by the Parliament was also a step to this end. There is no doubt that India is now strongly determined to control its runaway population growth.

The Family Planning Programme in India
The family planning programme as it exists today has the following essential features:

1. The guiding philosophy of the programme is to educate people about the need for family planning, and to motivate them to accept it on a voluntary basis. "In its implementation, the programme shuns any force, coercion or compulsion and depends on long-term education and motivation of the people on a sustained basis".[31] The knowledge, attitude and practice surveys on family planning have shown that the majority of Indian couples, nearly 70 per cent urban and 50 to 70 per cent rural, favour family planning on a voluntary basis.

2. The programme has adopted the "cafeteria approach" which means making available a variety of medically tested and proven contraceptives, such as sterilization, IUD, pills, condoms, foam tablets, jellies, and other conventional contraceptives. The objective is to allow the couple to choose the method which suits them best. Even though there are several contraceptives "on the shelf", the programme has relied heavily on sterilization and on IUD. Efforts are made to make family planning services available to clients as close to their place of residence as possible. A large network of rural and urban birth clinics has been established. At present, there are 1,975 urban Family Welfare Planning centres, 5,132 main rural centres and 33,370 rural subcentres where family planning advice and supplies are available.[32]

3. In 1965 when the government accepted the interuterine contraceptive device (IUD) as one of the contraceptives, the family planning programme got a real breakthrough and the movement gained momentum. Since then, the programme has become time- and target-oriented. Currently, the goal is to reduce the birth rate to 30 per thousand by 1978–79. To accomplish this, annual targets for sterilizations, IUD insertions, and other contraceptives are specified for each state. These targets are fixed on the basis of the state's population and its past performance.

4. The actual implementation of the programme is in the hands of the state governments. But it is a centrally-sponsored programme and is entirely financed by the Central Government.

In 1966, a separate Department of Family Planning was created at the Centre to coordinate the family planning programmes at the centre and in the states. At present, there are 21 State Family Planning Bureaus and 334 District Bureaus. For family planning services to reach the people, every state has developed an organizational set-up from the state headquarters to the peripheral level.

5. The family planning programme is highly flexible and dynamic. It allows for periodic evaluation of its working both by internal and external agencies. The Programme Evaluation Organization of the Planning Commission and other officially appointed committees have frequently investigated the working of the programme. The United Nations, at the request of the Government of India, sent two missions—one in 1965 and the other in 1969—to evaluate the performance of the programme and to suggest measures to improve its working. Such periodic evaluations have helped the programme to improve its efficacy. Similarly, the programme also encourages research in the medical and biological aspects of family planning. Field studies to investigate the attitude of the people toward family planning are often conducted.

Performance of the Family Planning Programme

Despite such emphasis on family planning, India's population explosion continues at an almost unabated rate. The programme has not succeeded in bringing about any significant decline in the birth rate and its overall performance has been below expectation. For example, the Fourth Plan had aimed at reducing the birth rate from 39 per 1000 to 32 per 1000 by 1973–74; and for achieving this goal, 28 million couples were expected to be protected by 1973–74. However, at the end of 1973–74, only 15 million couples had been protected and the birth rate had declined by only 2 points[33]. Judging from the achievements of the family planning programme since its inception, one can safely say that the programme has not yet made any spectacular progress the way similar programmes have done in South Korea and Taiwan. It is, however, argued that even though the programme was officially launched in 1952 it suffered from a great deal of uncertainty and lack of initiative for a long time, and it was only in 1965 that the programme got a real start. It is therefore too early to judge its performance. Its success or failure will not be known until the 1980 census. Nonetheless, the following comments can be made on its performance up till now.

1. The initial response to the IUD insertion programme was amazingly high. In 1965 when the programme was introduced, nearly 0.8 million insertions were made and the number shot up to 1 million in the following year. Such excellent progress within the first two years led to great optimism about the programme, and much higher targets were fixed for the next several years. It was anticipated that at the rate the programme had gained acceptance, India would be able to reduce the birth rate within a short period of time. The optimism, however, proved to be short-lived, and the programme soon suffered a setback. The rate of IUD insertions began to decline at an increasing rate. In the year 1967–68, only 0.67 million insertions were made and the number declined to 0.48 million in the following year. The main reason for this backlash was the lack of follow-up medical facilities to deal with the complications experienced by the users. In some cases the loop would be expelled involuntarily, while some experienced pain and bleeding. The lack of post-insertion medical facilities created a great deal of anxiety and misgiving in the users which spread in turn to potential users. Thus, the IUD insertion programme which was supposed to have performed a miracle for India, proved a failure because it was not carefully planned. The *Draft Fifth Plan* has recommended policies for actively promoting the IUD programme and has stressed the need for providing proper post-insertion care for users.

2. Fortunately the decline in the IUD insertion programme was somewhat offset by the increasing popularity of sterilization. During the five-year period of the Fourth Plan (1969–74), nearly 9 million sterilizations were performed, of which 6.2 million were carried out during the last

three years. This is the highest number of sterilizations any country has ever attained both in absolute number and as a percentage. Initially, the Central Government was reluctant to include sterilization among other contraceptive methods, mainly because of its irreversibility. But some states like Tamil Nadu, Kerala, Maharashtra, and Gujarat went ahead with the sterilization programme, and were able to register considerable success. Subsequently, the Central Government also accepted it as a part of the nationwide family planning programme. The programme offers monetary incentives to individuals to compensate them for loss of wages and other out-of-pocket expenses incurred in coming to the clinic. The amount of incentive differs from state to state. So far the programme has been executed on a voluntary basis. But some states are thinking of making it compulsory for couples with more than 2 or 3 children. Dr. Chandrasekhar, an eminent demographer and a former Central Minister for Health and Family Planning is one of the staunchest supporters of compulsory sterilization. He considers sterilization to be the most suitable method for Indian conditions. Impressed with the success which sterilization programmes have had in certain states, he argues "Had India embarked on this policy fifteen years ago with fervour the country by now could have cut its birth rate by half".[34]

3. One of the reasons for the slow progress of family planning is the lack of effective organization and manpower. "Clearly, the limitations of the family planning programme arise not from finances but essentially from considerations of organization and personnel which affect the scale and intensity at which the programme can be implemented."[35] The Fourth Plan contained specific provisions for expansion of training facilities to meet the manpower needs of the programme. One of the factors contributing to the dearth of personnel (especially medical staff) is that the expansion of family planning depends heavily on the traditional clinical approach. It has been indicated before that despite the cafeteria approach, the programme relies greatly on sterilization

and on IUD. Both these methods require individual medical attention, and in the case of the latter there is also need for follow-up medical service. If the programme can popularize other family planning methods requiring little or no medical services, the manpower problem will be less serious.

4. The results of surveys indicate that most couples (urban and rural) accept the norm of a small size family and would be willing to practise birth control if such knowledge was made available to them. It has, however, been observed that the willingness to learn about birth control only expresses interest, and no strong motivation to translate this into practice even if such facilities are made available. This kind of behaviour has been observed by the Indian-Harvard-Ludhiana Population Study: "While 80 per cent of the couples reported willingness to learn a contraceptive method, only 45 per cent used some method at some time during the study period and after about 2 1/2 years of sustained efforts, only 17 per cent of the couples were found practising".[36] The results of field experiences in other areas are even more disappointing. For example, the results of the pilot experiment in the city of Madras indicated that while 92 per cent of the women were desirous of limiting their families, only 4 per cent did anything about it.[37] Obviously, there is something which prevents these people from translating their desires into action. The major reason seems to be their resistance to altering long-established norms. Family planning is something new, and its acceptance implies breaking away from the age-old tradition of uncontrolled procreation. Thus, while there is no visible opposition to the programme, there is no enthusiastic support for it either among the people. The programme cannot make any significant progress unless it succeeds in destroying various forces which inhibit people from practising family planning. This appears to be the most difficult task. These obstacles can be overcome only through a well-organized massive educational programme designed to motivate them to actually practise family planning. This is a basic condition for the success of the programme.

Recent Developments and Future Prospects

The national population policy calls for a reduction of the country's birth rate from the present level of 35–36 per thousand to 30 per thousand by 1978–79, and to 25 per thousand by 1983–84. To achieve these goals, it is estimated that the proportion of couples protected against conception will have to increase from the current 16–17 per cent to 33 per cent by 1978–79 and to 45 per cent by 1983–84.[38] In terms of numbers of new acceptors, the first target would require 18 million sterilizations, 5.9 million IUD insertions, and 8.8 million users of conventional contraceptives during the 1974–79 period. This is the magnitude of the task facing the family planning programme.

Will the family planning programme succeed in meeting these goals? The record of its past performance would make one doubtful. However, during the last two years (1975–77) several new and far-reaching developments affecting the family programme have taken place. Some of these major developments are summarised below:

1. In February 1976, the Central Government announced a scheme of incentives and penalties to persuade couples to limit their families to two or three children. The scheme was designed to encourage sterilization after a couple has had three children, and applied to government employees in the union territory of Delhi. Couples who limit their families to two or three children become "eligible" to receive various government amenities, such as free medical care, housing, housing loans, education, and get preference for other government services. Couples with more than three children become "ineligible" to receive these services— i.e., couples with large families are penalized. New employees have to sign a pledge to limit their families to two or three childen, or to lose their jobs. This scheme is expected to be extended to central employees in the rest of the country.

2. Several state governments (Haryana, Punjab, UP, Tamil Nadu) have also announced similar schemes for their employees. It had appeared that the system of incentives and penalties for encouraging couples to limit the size of their families would become an integral part of the population policy of India.

3. In April 1976, the Union Minister of Health and Family Planning issued a national population policy statement containing several new measures at a joint meeting of the Central Councils of Health and Family Planning in New Delhi. The Minister indicated that necessary steps (by law and otherwise) would be undertaken by the Central Government to implement these measures. The policy statement contained these measures:[39] (i) The minimum age of marriage will be raised to 18 for females and to 21 for males. (ii) The number of seats in the Lok Sabha and other elected bodies will be frozen at the 1971 population level. (iii) Wherever population size is a factor in determining the share of states in the central resources, the 1971 population will be used as the basis. (iv) Eight per cent of the Central Government's assistance to State plans will be based on their performance in the area of family planning. (v) Registration of marriage will be made compulsory. (vi) Efforts will be directed to raising the level of education among females and to improving the nutritional status of children. (vii) The scope of "population education" in both formal and nonformal sectors will be expanded. (viii) A new cell, named Population Education and Training Cell, will be created under the Department of Family Planning. (ix) Monetary compensation to states for sterilization will be increased. (x) A new strategy for disseminating information about family planning throughout the country will be evolved.

After the announcement of this population policy, seveal steps were taken to implement it. For example, a bill for increasing the minimum age of marriage was introduced in the Parliament. Monetary compensation to states for sterilization had also been increased.

4. Believing that public opinion was receptive to the adoption of more stringent measures for family planning, some states thought of making sterilization compulsory. Maharashtra passed such a bill, making sterilization compulsory for

couples having three (living) children. Three other states—Haryana, Punjab, and UP—have also drafted similar bills. There was, however, bitter opposition to compulsory sterilization from the general public. Opposition to compulsory sterilization was, in fact, an important issue in the 1977 elections. The Government of. India has recently given assurances that there would be no compulsory sterilization in the country and that the goal of family planning would be achieved through voluntary programmes. The family planning programmes at the state level as well, are in the process of being reviewed in the light of the Central Government policy.

The year 1976 may be regarded a landmark in the family planning movement of India. One hopes that the momentum gained over the past few months will be maintained, or even accelerated, so as to meet the Fifth and Sixth Five-Year Plan targets. The population problem of India is extremely serious and its solution requires a great and sustained effort. It is, therefore, hoped that the strong political support which the programme had enjoyed in 1976–77 will continue for some time. Further, it is hoped that the family planning programme itself will take full advantage of the present favourable climate towards family planning in India and will direct its energies towards fully implementing the new population policy.

REFERENCES

1. S.P. Sinha, "India's Uphill Battle", *Far Eastern Economic Review*, vol. LXXVI, no. 18 (29 April 1972), p. 57.
2. Kingsley Davis, *The Population of India and Pakistan*, (Princeton: Princeton University Press, 1951), Ch. 4.
3. S. Chandrasekhar, *India's Population: Facts, Problems and Policy* (Delhi: Meenakshi Press, 1967), p. 3.
4. See Population Reference Bureau, "India: Ready or Not, Here They Come", *Population Bulletin*, vol. XXVI, no. 5 (November 1970).
5. 1972 figures are from Department of Commerce, *World Population: 1973* (Washington, D.C.: U.S. Government Printing Office, 1974), p. 10.
6. India's birth rate is not any higher than the birth rates of other developing countries. But considering the already excessive population of India, the present birth rate constitutes a serious threat.
7. Chandrasekhar, *India's Population*, p. 15.
8. Gunnar Myrdal, *Asian Drama*, vol. 2 (New York: The Twentieth Century Fund, 1968), p. 1432. The Sweden figure is for the year 1950.
9. The discussion in this section is based on the work of Warren C. Robinson and David E. Horlacher, "Population Growth and Economic Welfare", *Reports on Population/Family Planning*, no. 6 (New York: The Population Council) February 1971.
10. For example, spacing of children, economies and diseconomies resulting from a large number of children, have not been taken into consideration.
11. World Bank, *Population Planning*, Sector Working Paper (Washington, D.C., March 1972), p. 5.
12. Government of India, Planning Commission, *Fourth Five-Year Plan, 1969–1974*, New Delhi, 1970, p. 5.
13. Government of India, Planning Commission, *Draft Fifth Five-Year Plan*, vol. 1 (New Delhi: Publication Division, 1973), p. 42.
14. Lester R. Brown, "Nobel Peace Prize: Developer of High Yield Wheat Receives Award", *Science*, vol. 170, No. 3957 (October 1970) p. 519.
15. Population Reference Bureau, "India: Ready or Not", p. 10.
16. *Draft Fifth Plan*, vol. 1, p. 85.
17. A.J. Coale and E.M. Hoover, *Population Growth and Economic Development in Low Income Countries* (Princeton: Princeton University Press, 1958), p. 254.
18. *Fourth Plan*, p. 31.
19. Cf. Ashish Bose, "The Population Puzzle in India", *Economic Development and Cultural Change*, vol. 7, no. 3 (April 1959), pp. 245–46. The article contains a useful summary of these differences.
20. Myrdal, *Asian Drama*, vol. 2, p. 1402.
21. A.J. Coale, "Population and Economic Development", in Phillip H. Hauser (ed.), *The Population Dilemma* (Englewood Cliffs: Prentice-Hall, 1963).
22. Government of India, Planning Commission, *The First Five-Year Plan* (New Delhi: Government of India Press, 1960), p. 18
23. Ibid., p. 522.
24. Government of India, Planning Commission, *The Second Five-Year Plan* (New Delhi: Publication Division, 1956), p. 7.
25. *The Second Plan*, p. 8.
26. Government of India, Planning Commission, *Third Five Year Plan* (New Delhi: Government of India Press), p. 675.
27 Ibid., p. 675.
28. *The Fourth Plan*, p. 391.

29. Ibid., p. 391.
30. *The Draft Fifth Plan*, vol. 2, p. 240–41.
31. Govind Narain, *India: The Family Planning Programme Since 1965*. Studies in Family Planning, No. 35 (New York: The Population Council, November 1968), p. 1. Mr. Narain provides an excellent review of the working and performance of the family planning programme in India.
32. Pravin Visaria and Anrudh K. Jain, *India, Country Profiles* (New York: The Population Council, May 1976), p. 28.
33. See D. Banerji, "Family Planning in India- Some Inhibiting Factors", in Ashish Bose et al. *Population In India's Development, 1947–2000* (Delhi: Vikas, 1974), pp. 405–14, for a critical review of the performance of the family planning programme in India.
34. S. Chandrasekhar, *India's Population*, p. 47.
35. Government of India, *The Third Plan*, p. 676.

36. As quoted in M.V. Raman, "Attitudes toward Family Size and Fertility Control in India —An Assessment", *Proceedings of the World Population Conference*, vol. 2 1965 (New York: United Nations, 1967), p. 166.
37. R.A. Gopalaswami, "Family Planning: Outlook for Government Action", in Clyde V. Kiser (ed.), *Research in Family Planning* (Princeton University Press, 1962), p. 73.
38. K.C. Seal, "The Family Planning Programme in India", in Ashish Bose et al., *Population in India's Development*, p. 381. Also, see *Draft Fifth Plan*, p. 241–41.
39. For a detailed review of the development in India's population policy see Visaria and Jain, *India*, pp. 24–45.
40. *The New York Times*, 16 September 1976, p. 9.
41. Ibid., p. 9.

BIBLIOGRAPHY

Agarwala, S.N.: *India's Population Problems*. Bombay. Tata-McGraw Hill, 1972.

Bose, Ashish et al. (eds.): *Population in India's Development, 1947–2000*. New Delhi. Vikas, 1974.

Chandrasekhar, S.: *India's Population: Facts, Problems and Policy*. New Delhi. Meenakshi, 1967.

Coale, Ansley J. and Hoover, Edgar M.: *Population Growth and Economic Development in Low-Income Countries*. Princeton. Princeton Univesity Press, 1958.

Dow, Thomas E.: "The Population of India". *Current History* vol. 54, no. 320 (April 1968), pp. 219–24, 241–42.

Davis, Kingsley: "The Amazing Decline of Mortality in Underdeveloped Areas". *American Economic Review* vol. 46 (May 1956). pp. 305–318.

Hauser, Phillip M. (ed.): *The Population Dilemma*. Englewood Cliffs, N.J. Prentice-Hall, 1963.

Higgins, Benjamin: *Economic Development*. New York. W.W. Norton, 1968.

Jones, Gavin W.: *The Economic Effect of Declining Fertility in Less Developed Countries*. New York. The Population Council, 1969.

Madalgi, S.S.: *Population and Food Supply in India*. New Delhi. Lalvani Publishing House, 1970.

Myrdal, Gunnar: *Asian Drama*, vols. 2 and 3. New York. The Twentieth Century Fund, 1968.

Narain, Govind: *India: The Family Planning Programme Since 1965*. Studies in Family Planning No. 35. New York. The Population Council, November 1968.

Ohlin, Govan: *Population Control and Economic Development*. Paris. OECD Development Centre, 1967.

Robinson, Warren C. and Horlacher, David E.: *Population Growth and Economic Welfare*. Reports on Population/Family Planning, No. 6. New York. The Population Council, February 1971.

Population Reference Bureau: "India: Ready or Not, Here They Come". *Population Bulletin* vol. XXVI, no. 5. November 1970.

United Nations: *An Evaluation of the Family Planning Programme of the Government of India*. New York. United Nations, 24 November 1969.

Uppal, J.S.: *Economic Development in South Asia*. New York. St. Martins, 1977.

Visaria, Pravin and Jain, Anrudh, K., *India. Country Profiles*. New York. The Population Council, May 1976.

Watson, Walter, B. and Lapham, Robert J.: *Family Planning Programs: World Review 1974*, Studies in Family Planning. New York. The Population Council, August 1975.

Zaiden, George: "Population Growth and Economic Development", *Finance and Development* vol. 6, no. 1. March 1969. pp. 2–8.

4

Socio-Political Institutions, Cultural Values, and Attitudes: Their Impact on Indian Economic Development

INDER P. NIJHAWAN

Noneconomic Aspects of Economic Development

The precise role of noneconomic factors in economic problems in general, and economic development in particular, is subject to considerable controversy. The controversy stems from and centres around the following issues:

Recognition
Economists have for two centuries debated on whether or not the boundaries of economics should be delimited to encompass other disciplines. Opinions are sharply divided. The major arguments against the study of "noneconomic" phenomena within the purview of economic science are as follows:

1. Specialization presupposes a narrow scope of study. Therefore, there is need to restrict the scope of economics exclusively to the study of economic phenomena.[1]

2. "Noneconomic" factors are difficult to measure and therefore lack objectivity.[2]

3. Sociopolitical factors change but slowly. Therefore, in the short-term analysis they can justifiably be treated as parameters. From this premise, the moral is derived that less developed countries should not strive to change the social and cultural milieu as they cannot afford to wait (owing to pressure of population and rising aspirations) for economic development in the long run, which would result from changes in these noneconomic factors. It is, therefore, recommended that the less developed countries should instead focus attention on the economic factors which are crucial to the immediate increase in per capita income.[3]

4. Some economists deem changes in the social and political milieu to be the

consequence rather than the cause of economic growth.[4] It is, therefore, logical that change in economic variables must precede change in the sociopolitical framework.

This atomistic conception of the social process provoked strong reactions. It was forcefully asserted that "economic man" is a myth.[5] It was argued that the "unity of social life" and the inseparable connection between its elements precludes any division of concrete reality into political, social, cultural, ethical, and economic parts. Apart from the whole being something greater than the sum of its parts, any attempt to comprehend reality by atomism would be misleading and even dangerous.[6] The relevance of economics, after all, is to social and cultural reality. The tendency to abstract from the social whole will make prediction perilous.

J.R. Hicks believes that since policy is a reconciliation of political, social, cultural, sociological, and economic considerations, any attempt to recommend policy without due consideration of "noneconomic" factors will be singularly misleading.[7] In the same vein Boulding asserts "... there is no such thing as economics—there is only Social Science applied to economic problems".[8]

Thus, from analytical, operational, and policy standpoints, "noneconomic" factors cannot realistically be precluded from economic analysis.

Identification

"Noneconomic factors" is a loose term used to cover a wide variety of factors. However, not all factors branded "noneconomic" and stressed by different economists could be critical to economic development; if it were so, no country in the world could be adequately developed. This leads to the problem of identification: which of the several "noneconomic" factors are relevant to economic growth? On this issue a consensus of opinion is singularly lacking.

Chronologically, the origin of the term "noneconomic factors" is to be traced to the reaction against free competition and its concomitant unequal distribution of income. The United Nations' Research Institute for Social Development includes in social factors any phenomenon or variable immediately influencing welfare.

Parson[9] and Levy[10] stress that the relation of the individual to society is a critical one in the transformation process. Economic development presupposes the existence of rationality in cognition, universalism in membership, and specificity in relationship. The former implies that the individual's interpretation of the universe must be based on reason rather than on superstition. Universalism in membership presumes absence of nepotism and selection of roles in society by merit; and specificity in relationship requires that production relations be governed by contract, rather than by friendly and family ties. Kuznets[11] is merely endorsing the views of Parson and Levy when he singles out secularism, egalitarianism, and nationalism as preconditions of the Industrial Revolution.

Lerner[12] pinpoints the critical importance of the behavioural deviance in economic change. Hagen[13] stresses the relationship between personality, society, and economic growth. Like Hagen, McClelland[14] also attempts to study variables which produce innovative and creative personalities. The number of people with achievement is one of the most important determinants of economic development.

Ralph Linton[15] however, believes that most of the factors which affect adoption and integration of new ideas by society can be explained more effectively in terms of cultural rather than psychological factors. Like Linton, Sole[16] also singles out certain specific types of cognition and culture as the most significant "noneconomic" factors in economic transformation. Religion is considerably stressed by Max Weber[17] and R. Tawney.[18] Erich Fromm,[19] Hoselitz,[20] and Rostow[21] pinpoint the importance of institutional factors in economic development and believe that a proper institutional framework is a precondition for "take off". Mead[22] stresses the relevance of the size of the social unit to economic development. According to Denison[23] education is the single most important social factor, which accounted for as much as 23 per cent of growth in the USA between

1909–1929. Hoselitz[24] and Wolf[25] stress the importance of values and institutions in economic transformation. Adelman and Morris[26] adopt a broader definition of "noneconomic factors" and define sociopolitical factors in terms of extent of dualism, extent of urbanization, character of basic social organization, importance of indigenous middle class, extent of social mobility, extent of literacy, extent of mass communication, degree of modernization of outlook, degree of national integration and sense of national unity, extent of centralization of political power, strength of democratic institutions, degree of freedom of political opposition and press, degree of competitiveness of political party system, strength of labour movement, political strength of traditional elite, degree of administrative efficiency, extent of leadership commitment to economic development, and extent of political stability.

Surely not all these factors are important for Indian economic development. Therefore, the problem of identification arises.

Causal Relationship
Another issue which has plagued economists for a long time is whether sociocultural factors determine or are determined by economic development. According to Marx,[27] the mode of production is the fundamental determinant of the sociopolitical structure, which in turn determines and ideas institutional framework. Hagen,[28] on the other hand, believes that cultural personality is the basic explanatory variable in economic development. Hagen regards economic variables as mere parameters or conditioning circumstances within which specific types of cultural change spark off the process of economic development.

Katona[29] hypothesises that economic processes are the result of people's behaviour and are influenced by different patterns of behaviour. Tinbergen[30] and Rostow[31] take the middle ground and treat the relationship between economic and "noneconomic" factors as one of interaction.

Suffice it to say that the role assigned to social processes in the economic development of India, and the consequent policy recommendations, vary according to whether these social processes are considered the cause or consequence of economic change.

Methodology
Even if issues of recognition, identification, and causal relationship are resolved satisfactorily, there remains the fundamental problem of methodology. Often, attempts to extend growth analysis to include "noneconomic" factors are frustrated by the absence of empirical knowledge about the manner in which they operate. There are two distinct approaches: (1) economists can widen the scope of their positive research to encompass "noneconomic" variables, and (2) economic theory can be supplemented with the theories developed in other social sciences which deal with "noneconomic" phenomena. In the latter approach, the study of interaction between "economic" and "noneconomic" variables is through a clearly defined division of the field of research, rather than by an integrated attack on the concrete problems. The emphasis, therefore, is on synthesis of knowledge rather than on integration and assimilation. The former approach is adopted by Hicks,[32] Tinbergen,[33] Viner,[34] Marschak,[35] and Boulding.[36] The latter approach is recommended and practised by Rostow.[37]

Methodological Considerations and the Framework for Analysis

These four fundamental issues and the controversy which centres around those issues (summarised above) broadly provide the framework for analysing the role of sociopolitical factors in the economic transformation of India. The first issue pertains to relative weight, the second to selection of relevant factors, the third to direction of relationship between economic growth and social processes, and the fourth to methods of analysing the relationship. The relative weight of sociopolitical factors in Indian economic development can be determined by Denison's type study[38] where growth in each input is compared with growth in output, and by weighing the inputs against each other, their relative contribution to total output can be ascertained. While

Denison's type study will provide an analytical framework, data problems will preclude any such study in the Indian context. Besides, as in the Denison model, unexplained variation (growth in GNP not explained by growth of labour, natural resources, capital and technology) will be attributed to the whole gamut of factors; among which would also be noneconomic factors. This will pose the further problem of disentangling the noneconomic variables from economic variables, and assessing the relative weight of each.

In the absence of empirical data and the lack of an appropriate analytical framework to disentangle the contribution of "noneconomic" vis-a-vis "economic" factors, it will not be possible to determine empirically the relative weight of sociopolitical factors in the economic development of India.

Difficulties in measuring "noneconomic" factors and their relative contributions to growth of total output make it hard to identify the sociopolitical factors which are critical for the success of planned economic development in India. Among the "noneconomic" factors, those frequently discussed in the literature of Indian growth are: religion, attitude towards life, political stability, traditions and customs, values, the caste system, and sociopolitical institutions. Other factors such as class structure, literacy, degree of social tension, national integration and national unity, degree of freedom of political opposition and press, strength of labour movement, degree of administrative efficiency, behavioural deviance, the number of people with n achievement, and size of social unit, have received little, if any, attention in the Indian literature. It may well be that these factors are not pertinent to and/or are less important in the Indian context. However, any such conclusion should be based on analysis rather than on presumption and, if possible, vindicated by empirical data. Of late, some attempts have been made to quantify some of the variables enumerated above. Literacy, educational attainment, political stability, and n achievement have been measured with some degree of success.[39] However,

economists still debate the relevance of proxy variables used for measurement. Measurement of more encompassing concepts such as "social development" and "national integration" is particularly shaky.

In what follows, we shall discuss some of the factors iterated above without implying that these alone are of the greatest import in the Indian context.

As regards the direction of relationship between sociopolitical and economic variables, it is now generally conceded, and it is assumed in this paper, that economic and "noneconomic" variables act upon each other rather than be tied in a cause-effect fashion.[40]

Analytically, there are two distinct approaches to a study of the interaction of economic and noneconomic variables.[41] According to some psychologists and economists, the individual's internal state (comprising motives, needs and personality) is the most important determinant of human behaviour and actions. Others stress the environment (reflected in and by values, norms, etc.) as the sole explanation of human behaviour.

Kunkel[42] calls the former, psychodynamic models, and the latter behavioural models. The two approaches have different implications from the standpoint of economic development. Psychodynamic models, by their very nature, are somewhat of a fait accompli. To the extent that man's internal state, consisting of innate and acquired characteristics, is largely determined in early childhood, changes in the behaviour of adults would either be difficult or could, at best, occur over a long period of time.[43] Additionally, innate nature being unconscious, its exact determinants can hardly be identified.

Behavioural models, at least analytically, afford considerable scope for change in behaviour, at any stage, without substantial lapse in time. The main determinants of behaviour are the rewarding and punishing consequences of certain activities which are determined by the economic and social environment. Since the mechanism of reward and punishment is amenable to change, social behaviour can be tailored to the needs and requirements of economic transformation.

Discussion on the role of sociopolitical factors in economic development in general and in India in particular, is often marred by an unconscious blending of psychodynamic and behavioural models. Since in what follows we shall use the behavioural model in the Indian context, (see Chart 4.1) it is essential to summarise its main features briefly.[44]

1. It is evident from Chart 4.1 that the distinction between "economic" and "noneconomic" variables is academic. Behaviour (which determines the activities and, hence, rate of growth), is influenced by both "noneconomic" and "economic" factors.

variables are changed simultaneously with economic factors, considerable increase in output can be achieved without substantial changes in the latter. For example, in the case cited above, if taboos on saving are removed, slight changes in the interest rate may be enough to generate sufficient resources for economic development (assuming saving is interest-sensitive).

4. It is equally clear from Chart 4.1 that it is erroneous to believe that social and psychological fetters on economic development can be removed or weakened by changing the values, attitudes, and personality of individuals in less developed countries.[45] Values and attitudes state the

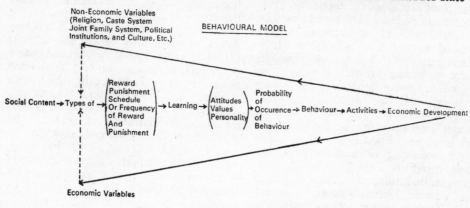

Chart 4.1

2. It is wrong to argue[45] that changes in economic variables can, by themselves, spark off the process of economic growth. For example, in a society where frugality is equated with miserliness owing to social customs, or culture, or religion, people learn to have an unfavourable attitude towards thrift. This reduces the probability of saving, and, therefore, when income increases, people tend to spend rather than save. Low marginal and average propensity to save result in, ceteris paribus, low rate of investment, and other things remaining the same, low rate of growth. In a situation such as this, only a substantial or no amount of rise in interest rates (economic variable) may overcome the stigma on saving, and hence, facilitate an increase in per capita output.

3. It is evident that if sociopolitical

probability of occurrence of behaviour. They are the symptoms of inferences from behaviour, and not the causes of changes in behaviour.

5. Behavioural changes conducive to substantial increase in per capita income, in most cases, result from changes in types and frequency of stimuli and/or presence or absence of punishment.

Sociopolitical Institutions, Values, and Attitudes

In this section, we shall attempt to analyse how "noneconomic" factors impinge on the process of transformation in the Indian economy. The behavioural model illustrated by Chart 4.1 will provide the analytical framework.

Among the "noneconomic" factors, Hinduism has been subject to the maximum controversy and debate.[47] The exact mechanism by which the Hindu religion impinges on economic change is rarely, if ever, spelled out in detail. However, broadly the relationship postulated is as follows :

Religious Teachings and Interpretation ———→ Values and Attitudes ———→ Actions ———→ Economic Development.

The model does not explain how and why religious teachings are internalized in the form of values and then translated into actions. The link between religious teachings and behaviour, therefore, remains clouded. The basic links are clearly laid out in the behavioural model. The effect of religious teachings on economic development can be elucidated by an example. The philosophy of renunciation in Asia is traced to the holy scriptures. It is often argued that this philosophy militates against economic growth. If people are taught that human desires are the source of misery and unhappiness, and that lasting mental peace can only be attained through renunciation, it follows that there is religious merit in reducing desires or not indulging in material pleasures. People, therefore, learn to value deprivation more than affluence. Limited aspirations warrant limited efforts to attain them. Thus, a worker may not work the whole day if it takes half-a-day's work to earn two meals. Government might spend crores of rupees on irrigation projects to boost production on farms and yet fail to induce farmers to use the new facilities if the existing ones are enough to provide subsistence to the farmer and his family. The net result, among other things, would be small marketable surplus, inadequate division of labour, and constrained supply of efforts. Thus, the philosophy of renunciation will run counter to the assumption of nonsatiation which is the very premise of economic development.

Having discussed the mechanism by which religion impinges on economic change, we shall now attempt to answer the fundamental question: whether Indian religion is conducive or inimical to industrialization. This calls for identification of the basic tenets of Hinduism. Hinduism is not a religion based on any single accepted creed or dogma. Because Hinduism lacks a single or unified pattern of thought, it can at best be defined in terms of certain concepts : (1) It is polytheistic in the sense that it recognizes and sanctions many gods and godesses; (2) It is monistic because it subscribes to one supreme spirit—Brahma; (3) Monism and polytheism are apparently contradictory terms but they can be reconciled by the concept of incarnation—all divine beings are incarnations of the supreme spirit; (4) God is omnipresent; (5) The material world and material things are illusions—*maya*;(6) There is transmigration of soul from one body to another; (7) The endless chain of rebirths embodied in transmigration is not accidental; whether the soul will enter the womb of a human being or an animal is determined in accordance with the laws of *karma*—actions; (8) Emancipation from the pain and misery of the cycle of rebirth can only be attained by achieving *moksa*, i.e., by union with Brahma; (9) When *moksa* is attained, the liberated soul achieves supreme bliss or *nirvana*; (10) Salvation of soul can be attained by three different ways: (a) by *dharma*—right conduct; (b) by *yoga*, which releases an individual from empirical conciousness and unites him or her with the supreme spirit; (c) by devotion or *bhakti*.

Needless to say the aforementioned concepts do not exhaust the list. Besides, Hinduism is a way of life; it is a body of customs and amalgamation of many religious ideas. Accordingly, it cannot be adequately defined by and contained in the narrow confines of any one religion or set of concepts. Its complexity is heightened by the fact that it seems to be practised at two levels: one based on popular beliefs, and the other on esoteric principles. It is, therefore, not surprising that the basic tenets of Hinduism are subject to considerable controversy and some writers characterize it as dualism of thought.[48] There are certain elements in Hindu philosophy which are "other worldly". The varied versions of this view are: asceticism: the world is essentially an illusion, human desires are the source of misery and unhappiness; and law of *karma*: relating present rewards to past actions and present actions to future life.

However, there are other elements which sanction the materialistic values of an industrialized society. The *Shukranitisara*, for example, lauds wealth as the means to all pursuits and favours its accumulation by "... legitimate ways, as by learning, service, valour, agriculture, commerce, the practice of crafts and even by mendicancy".[49] The *Bhagavad Gita*, and the theory of *Varnashrama Dharma*, like Protestant ethic, exhort every one to do his duty to the best of his ability, whatever his station in life. No wonder the *Mahabharata* denounces poverty as a sin and asserts "he that has no wealth has neither this world nor the next".[50] Similarly, the *Panchatantra* attributes most evils and vices to lack of money.[51] In some quarters it is even argued that Hindu philosophy contains and sanctions all the "character traits" of Protestant ethic such as :

...A belief in an orderly universe subject to deterministic laws, the ability to anticipate a course of events and behave accordingly, with the possibility of control based on knowledge; a strong sense of responsibility for one's actions and their consequences; and a capacity to organize one's life under a systematic methodical discipline which will maximize the goals one has set oneself.[52]

The authority of the *Bhagavad Gita* and other Hindu scriptures is invoked to substantiate the sanction of the typical "character traits" of Protestant ethic in Hindu philosophy.

It is, therefore, evident that Hinduism is a blend of disparate and conflicting elements—some elements which are conducive and others that are inimical to economic growth. The controversy originates in and revolves around the relative weight of "this worldly" and "other worldly" elements in Hindu philosophy. Dr. T.M.P. Mahadevan, in his address to the Thirtieth Indian Philosophical Congress, disparages the role of material goods and material pursuits in Indian philosophy.[54] Instead, he invokes the authority of the *Vedas* to prove that nonmaterialism is a dominant theme of the Hindu religion. "If he [man] should be saved, he must be made

to turn back from his meaningless race of material power. Not by adding things to oneself can one be happy. True happiness lies within".[55]

Singer, on the other hand, argues that Hinduism contains not only all the "character traits" of Protestant ethic (religion which is highly conducive to economic growth), but Hindus in their day-to-day activities are as materialistic as Western men.[56] Srinivas[57] endorses Singer's viewpoint when he claims that the abject poverty of the Indian farmer and the constant threat of starvation forces him to be nothing but practical: he cannot afford to be "other-worldly".

[The peasant] is naturally deeply interested in agriculture and everything related to it—land, rain, water, manure, cattle, labour, pests, etc.,—one often comes across pretty strict bookkeeping, even between the members of elementary family. Money from the sale of surplus crops belongs to man, while the money obtained by the sale of milk, butter butter-milk, eggs and fowl belongs to the wife. The better-off peasant teaches his son the value of money and thrift early in life.[58]

It is no wonder that Max Weber thinks "the acquisitiveness of Indians of all strata left little to be desired and nowhere to be found so little antichrematism and such evaluation of wealth".[59]

Singer forcefully argues that "this worldly" and "other worldly" elements are not necessarily incompatible.[60] It is possible for an Indian to believe in meditation and *karma* and yet possess all the "character traits" (frugality, rationality, hard work, and spirit of adventure, etc.) essential for economic development. Singer quotes several instances (based on personal observations and interviews) where belief in *karma* did not prevent a Hindu householder from discharging his worldly duties, or in the case of merchants, from the pursuit and accumulation of wealth. The most befitting example is provided by the *banyas*—traditionally a business community in India—who, while they worship the Goddess of Wealth, are very miserly in the personal use of the wealth they amass.[61]

To resolve the issue of relative weight

and ascertain the extent of belief of the younger generation in "other worldly" elements in Hinduism, we took a random sample of 61 students in a girls' school and 46 students in a boys' school at Kalkaji Colony in New Delhi. The sample is statistically neither large nor representative enough to yield meaningful results. However, we state them for what they are worth.

Surprisingly enough, not even one respondent (of a sample of 107) listed "other worldly" tenets such as asceticism, *karma*, and renunciation, among the fundamental tenets of Hinduism. A majority of the respondents deem the following to be the salient tenets of Hinduism: truth always triumphs; union is strength; honesty is the best policy; loving one and all; non-violence; respect for elders and teachers; God is omnipresent and resides in every being.

The survey results cannot permit generalization owing to the statistical inadequacy of the survey. However, this evidence coupled with the evidence presented earlier does suggest that "other worldly" elements are not the dominant theme of Hinduism.

Thus, we may sum up:

(1) Hinduism contains "this worldly" as well as "other worldly" elements;

(2) "other worldly" elements, even though preached often, are not practised very much;

(3) these two categories are not mutually exclusive; and

(4) the Hindu religion sanctions most of the character traits of Protestant ethic— often considered prerequisites of economic development.[62]

However, religion may impinge on Indian economic development by a different route. It may (1) drain the surplus, and (2) affect the investment preference in a manner which is inimical to economic growth. ·

The ceremonies pertaining to deity and demon in Hinduism are so elaborate and warrant such an enormous investment of food, money, and effort, as to absorb a significant proportion of the savings of an average household. No breakdown of expenditure on religious ceremonies is available. However, the total expenditure on ceremonies in rural India is

estimated at 7.2 per cent of per capita income.

It is often hypothesised that the bulk of household savings in India is diverted to unproductive assets like currency and gold. It has been estimated that the stock of gold in India constitutes about 10 per cent of total tangible wealth in India.[64] There are several diverse factors which explain the investor's predilection for gold. However, part of the explanation lies in the sanction received in the Hindu religion. Its importance springs from three factors: (1) It is treated as the metal of God. Idols and temples are often either gold-plated or are in fact made of gold. Lord Srivenkateswara's temple in Southern India and the Golden Temple at Amritsar are classic examples. (2) Gold is often used in the worship of and to propitiate the Goddess of Wealth. The amount of gold donated as charity to some of the temples in India (e.g., Lord Srivenkateswara's temple of Tirupati) defies imagination. (3) Gold ornaments are part of the attire on religious occasions.

The effect of gold hoarding on the growth potential of India can scarcely be understated. Contrary to the generally-held view that investment in gold involves only a transfer of purchasing power or assets from the purchaser to the seller, it does also affect the availability of real resources, consumption (saving), investment, employment, the price level, allocation and growth of entrepreneurial skill, and organization of resources.[65]

Another factor related to, but not necessarily contained in religion, is the "world view" of the masses.[66] The basic component of the world view is the perception and interpretation of the relationship between activities (actions) and consequences (results). An individual may find, perceive, or interpret this relationship to be (1) capricious, or (2) systematic and orderly. In the former, the consequences are often distributed randomly and there is no direct, logical, and explicable connection with the activity. Thus, a foreign element like luck (*naseeb*), providence, spirits, God, etc., must be invoked to explain the consequences— good or bad.

In the systematic-universe view, correlation between contingency and activities is strong and predictable. There is, therefore, little or no scope for intervention from nonhuman elements. What is knowable, predictable, and strongly correlated to human activities is evidently also controllable. There is, no doubt, a constant struggle between man and nature, but man is not deemed powerless or inferior to nature.

It is instructive to examine briefly the factors which affect the world view of the masses. The three most important sources of world view are : (1) personal experiences; (2) observation of other's experiences; (3) knowledge of events, experiences described in stories, proverbs, religious teachings, etc. Since the formulation of the world view involves interpretation of the relationship between actions and results, the maintenance and form of the world view may differ among different members of the same community—even though experiences, observations, and source of knowledge of events are the same.

Having examined the forms of world views and their sources, it will be useful to analyse the role of the world view in the industrialization of less-developed countries in general, and of India in particular. The basic links involved are explained in the behavioural model mentioned earlier. The world view will affect the interpretation of the relationship between contingency and actions. If the universe is deemed capricious, the individual will learn to expect little or no correlation between actions and results. This will result in a fatalistic attitude. Owing to uncertainty about the future arising out of the capricious-universe view, and the overridding importance of nonhuman elements like luck, providence, and spirits, men learn to be subservient to the physical environment.

An attitude of helplessness and resignation pervades the masses. These attitudes impinge on all activities including saving, investment, long-range perspective, supply of efforts, and family planning. If a higher standard of living and amassing of wealth is treated as the result of providence rather than something springing from hard work and saving, there is little rationale for saving, hard work, innovations, and

enterprise. The Indian farmer, owing to the *zamindari* system, demonstrated this attitude of resignation. No matter how hard he worked or how much he improved his cultivation techniques, the lion's share of the produce was appropriated by the landlord. The farmer was thus forced to believe that he was fated to be poor. Behavioural response regarding family size is no different. If more children are born, it is believed that God must have ordained it. It is also believed that if God thus increases the size of the family, He will also provide the means to feed them.

Similarly, the attitude of "here and now" pervades all spheres of life. Households avoid assets which yield returns only over a long period of time or are relatively illiquid or involve considerable risk. No wonder that in India there is a marked preference for assets like gold, land, and inventories, rather than bonds and stocks. As stated earlier, preference for these assets, far from increasing the productive capacity of the economy, adversely affects the saving, investment, entrepreneurial skill, and organization of resources.

Planning and capital formation presuppose a long-range perspective. In a society where the future is not only uncertain, but also distrusted owing to the capricious-universe view, the desire and incentive to save, invest, and plan are conspicuously lacking. Entrepreneurship and innovations also warrant a long-range perspective because the rewards of these activities do not accrue over a short period.

However, the adverse effects of the capricious-universe view should not be overstressed. A fatalistic attitude or faith in nonhuman elements may not be inimical to industrialization if the former is invoked to rationalize one's failure despite efforts. God helps those who help themselves, is a common aphorism in India. Thus, the fatalistic attitude may not necessarily imply inaction or sloth, or lack of desire and incentives to save, invest, and innovate. Singer rightly argues that the fatalistic attitude "does not create man's condition —it 'explains' and 'justifies' it. Whatever a man can or cannot do may be explained with referrence to the law of *karma* but this explanation does not determine what he will or will not do".[67] In fact, a fatalistic attitude may be a blessing in disguise. Often, individuals undertake extremely risky ventures in the name of God. Since failure is not entirely accounted for by the individual's efforts, the individual may never cease trying. Each failure may strengthen the need to propitiate the Almighty, but leave the will to work intact. It is no wonder that India's achievement score (index of initiative, enterprise, and entrepreneurial skill) ranks high[68] and the household saving-rate compares favourably with that in many advanced countries of the world,[69] low per capita income notwithstanding.

Related to the capricious-universe view is the oft-repeated allegation: the Indian farmer is irrational and, therefore, his behavioural response runs counter to most theories in economics which are founded on the rationality premise. An ardent supporter of the irrationality premise is Kusum Nair.[70] She argues forcefully that the aspirations of the Indian farmer have a low ceiling. Therefore, the "nonsatiety" assumption is not valid in the Indian context. Nair quotes several instances (from her extensive all-India village survey) of the "perverse" behavioural response of the Indian masses. She cites the examples of a worker who having earned enough to sustain himself for the day, stops work after lunch, and a farmer who refuses to utilize the irrigation facilities made available by a million-rupee irrigation project, because his annual requirements of food are met by the existing facilities. The backward-sloping supply curve of labour and foodgrains is a trite proposition in the Indian context.

The opponents of the "irrationality" premise, however, argue that the Indian farmer is as rational as his counterpart in advanced countries. The "practical" and "down-to-earth" approach of the Indian peasant has been stressed elsewhere in this chapter. The point can be further illustrated with reference to the use of the Indian wooden plough—usually considered outdated as a method of farming,—which is often cited as the proof of the Indian farmer's "irrational" behaviour. Recent research has, however, shown that it is not necessarily outmoded. It is argued that for certain types of crop where the moisture content of the soil is critical, deep ploughing is inappropriate. Since the wooden plough does not dig deep, it is particularly suitable for these crops. The wisdom and knowledge of the Indian peasant regarding changes in weather and the consequent need for crop rotation is indicated by innumerable research studies.

It must however be conceded that a few examples in support of the rationality or irrationality premise are not enough to vindicate either of these hypotheses.

There is, however, an indirect way of testing the hypotheses empirically. If it were possible to gauge the efficiency with which existing resources are allocated and utilized within the given institutional framework in rural India or/and show whether or not the institutional framework responds to profit considerations—the rationality premise can be refuted or proved.[71] Hopper's study shows that the Indian farmer uses his resources rationally, as each resource is employed to the point where its earning is equal to its estimated marginal product.[72] Similarly, Raj Krishna illustrates how farmers in Punjab switched to new varieties of cotton when they were convinced that long-staple cotton would sell in larger quantities and at a higher price than the old varieties.[73]

Desai, however, reaches a conclusion diametrically opposed to that of Hopper's. Invoking the linear programming technique, Desai shows that actual returns to farming are significantly less than the optimum-reflecting inefficiency. However, Desai's argument does not refute the "rationality premise". The peasant may attempt to maximize his profits and yet fail to allocate resources in an optimum manner owing to ignorance or inadequate knowledge. Since the analytical models used by Hopper and Desai are subject to considerable limitations and the scope of the study is narrow (Hopper's study, for example, is based on selected crops and Desai bases his study on data from 40 farms in two districts) their conclusions must be accepted with a pinch of salt.

Regarding the institutional framework, Hanumantha Rao argues that the choice of institutional arrangements in rural India is, in most cases, based on predominantly economic considerations.[75] The peasant resorts to crop-sharing only if returns are certain; when returns are uncertain he chooses the fixed contractual payment system. Similarly, Raj argues that notwithstanding the sanctity of the cow in Hindu belief, Hindus sometimes slaughter them if "ecological and price considerations make it economically advantageous to do so".[76]

Thus, available evidence, even though limited and shaky, does not support the hypothesis that the Indian peasant is "irrational". If anything, the success of the "green revolution", refutes the irrationality premise.

Another "noneconomic" factor which has attracted the attention of Indian and foreign economists alike, is the caste system in India. The caste system is interlaced with Hinduism. The Upanishads clearly state whether the soul will enter the womb of a Brahmin, Kshatriya, Vaishya, or the womb of an outcaste will be determined by the law of *karma*. Hinduism exhorts each individual member of the caste to fulfill the function of his or her caste. Dereliction of the duty assigned to an individual in a caste is a sin. Here caste is apparently based on occupation. However, according to some philosophers,[77] caste distinctions were originally based on colour: the Aryan conquerors divided the society into two castes to separate their own race from the "black-skinned" people whom they were fighting and subjugating. It is, therefore, maintained that it was only in the later period that occupation became a criterion for distinguishing between different castes.

There are four major castes in India: (1) Brahmins (priests and educators); (2) Kshatriyas (warriors); (3) Vaishyas (farmers, traders, and artisans); (4) Shudras (labourers, servants and slaves). At present, there are hundreds of subdivisions of these major castes, and occupation is no longer the criterion for differentiating different castes. Caste today simply refers to a particular group of families with common customs, traditions, and rituals, and whose members can share meals with each other and marry each other without being "polluted".

It is often hypothesised that the caste system in India is inimical to economic growth. The assumptions underlying this hypothesis are:
1. The close and rigid ties between caste and occupations prevent the occupational mobility vital to economic transformation. As a rule, Brahmins were associated with the priestly occupation and government service, Vaishyas with business and trade, the Kshatriyas specialized in military and government careers, and the Shudras in scavenging, sweeping, tanning, and shoemaking.
2. Occupational structure is governed by caste and traditions rather than by merit and skill.
3. The caste system tends to limit the loyalty of individuals to a group and hence prevents or obstructs the development of the sense of nationhood, which is considered an important prerequisite of economic development.[78]
4. In certain quarters it is argued that the institution of the caste system blunts the sense of adventure: "Crossing the sea meant becoming outcaste."[79] This will militate against the growth and formation of entrepreneurial skill and scientific and technical progress.

Yet most of these assumptions are incorrect: the link between caste and occupation is not as rigid as is generally assumed. More than one caste often has the same occupation. Agriculture, which absorbs nearly 60–65 per cent of the Indian population, is not the prerogative of any one caste. Similarly, in the Indian army, people belonging to different castes rub shoulders with one another. Recent studies by anthropologists and sociologists particularly stress that whenever better and more favourable opportunities arose, people seized them regardless of their nature, and of caste.[80] It is no wonder that Brahmins enter the army, Vaishyas hold high-ranking jobs in the Government of India, Shudras practise trade and business, and Kshatriyas are teachers. Occupational and vertical mobility is particularly marked among the Shudras— sometimes called the untouchables. Recently, in the proximity of Delhi, "some of the outcaste groups have deliberately given up their traditional occupations and taken to construction labour as a way of affirming their changed status".[81]

It is equally wrong to argue that the caste system restricts geographical mobility. Historically there has been little or no connection between caste and area. Travelling abroad was restricted to a few, due to the prohibitive financial cost rather than caste restrictions.

The effect of the caste system on entrepreneurial skill formation is equally uncertain. Acquisition of wealth was sanctioned for all castes even though the mode of acquisition differed. As a matter of fact, the caste system was responsible for the growth of a special class—Vaishya or *banya*—whose main objective was to perform, practise, and specialize in entrepreneurial activities. As Gore pointed out:

> The [Vaishyas] worshipped and propitiated the Goddess of Wealth. Their pursuit of wealth was single-minded. In search of it they took considerable financial and personal risks. The long trade-routes which passed through mountains and overseas could not have been maintained by people who were afraid to take risks of this kind. The Vaishya will leave his country and migrate hundreds of miles in search of a suitable place for his work.[82]

No wonder in terms of *n* achievement motive (one of the most important determinants of entrepreneurial skill) India ranks high; the achievement score is estimated to be 2.11.[83]

However, it cannot be denied that sometimes roles in Indian society are chosen on the basis of caste rather than merit and capacity. This results in nepotism, waste of ability and, hence, loss of potential output. Loss of output will be substantial if selection in the upper rungs of the political and economic hierarchy is caste-rooted. Fortunately, selection for key governmental and economic services in India is made on the basis of competitive examinations—thus excluding caste.

Nationalism is often regarded as one of the prerequisites of "take off". The caste system, insofar as it limits the loyalty of the individual to a caste or group, militates against nationalism.

The role of the family structure in Indian economic development has been subject to considerable discussion. It is often hypothesised that the extended or joint family system inhibits or obstructs the process of transformation. Under the joint family system, kinship is extended to include not merely immediate family members but also distant relatives: cousins, nephews, uncles, etc. There are common rights and obligations. It is this feature of shared obligations and rights which is deemed inimical to savings, investment, mobility, risk taking, and labour supply. Since the fruits of labour are shared, individuals stint in supplying the labour. Similarly, it is argued, there is little incentive to invest in and undertake uncertain ventures because whereas the risks are borne by the investor, the fruits are shared by all the family members. This also dampens the spirit of entrepreneurship and innovation. Similarly the basic motivation for saving is lacking because family members share the cost of insurance for dependents and security against old age. Filial obligations and ties also limit geographical and occupational mobility. The institution of the joint family system is also extended to management and operation of business enterprise. Often, recruitment in these family enterprises is based on familial considerations rather than on competence.

It is evident that most of the disadvantages of the joint family system spring from the tacit assumption that there is a fundamental discontinuity or cleavage between the initiator and the beneficiary. While the existence of this discontinuity cannot be denied, its extent seems to be blown out of proportion. It can be argued that in most cases, family members not merely share the fruits but also the risk, labour, and management responsibility of the family projects. There are several instances where the joint family system was instrumental in undertaking risky ventures rather than being a deterrent to it. The joint family system, through its "network of family obligations, particularly among business communities, does provide a way of spreading risks and of collecting capital at a lower cost than would be required on the open market".[84] In certain cases, the money is apportioned according to effort, capital input, and responsibility, even though returns are deposited in the common pool. Similarly, the effect of the joint family system on supply of effort should be examined empirically. Logically, one may argue that family ties, family honour, and welfare, coupled with monetary stimuli, are better motivating factors than mere monetary rewards and impersonal arrangements. Japan presents a classic illustration of this, where great increase in production is achieved "within a paternalistic, particularistic, diffuse, and nonrationalized form of social organization, common in large, technologically advanced companies".[85]

The distinct, but characteristic, features of most Japanese industries are: (1) lifetime commitment to labour; (2) familistic management; and (3) seniority system. Most of these features are common to enterprises run by a joint family.

The joint family system also improves the quality of the labour force by handing down its skills from one generation to another.

Similarly, the effect of the joint family system on saving is uncertain. Even though the reasons for the origin and existence of this institution are complex, the contribution of economic factors can hardly be denied. Economies arising out of joint consumption and better utilization of certain indivisible items of consumption —such as house, car, furniture, electricity, and other appliances, reduce consumption expenditure and hence provide a larger saving margin out of a given income. It is true that the extended family obligations can be a drain on the family savings, but if these obligations are not fulfilled by the family, the state may have to bear this burden. Thus, the overall saving rate may not be adversely affected.

The effects of the joint family system on Indian economic development are mixed. The arguments are far from conclusive, owing to lack of empirical data. Even if it is granted that it restricts occupational and geographical mobility and also dampens the incentives to save, invest, and work, its relative weight will depend on the prevalence of the institution in India. It can be safely surmised that the joint family system is disintegrating in urban areas and even in rural India it is no longer as attractive as it used to be in the past.

The role of political institutions in Indian economic development has received relatively little attention, and yet it is one of the most important determinants of economic transformation. Its importance stems from its control over the contingencies (taxes, subsidies, differential remuneration) which, according to the behavioural model postulated, are the critical determinants of the behavioural activities, and, hence, industrialization. Through its control on the contingencies and their schedule of reinforcement, political institutions can establish and reinforce types of behaviour which are conducive to industrialization, and discourage those which affect it adversely.

Political institutions assume paramount importance in the Indian context because India is a unique case where the process of planned economic development is conceived within the democratic framework. Detailed planning encompassing the entire economy presupposes coercive powers to an extent that can be ruled out under democracy. Since, in democracy, authority is vested with the masses rather than with the chosen few, constant fear of losing votes results in policies and a framework which militate against a fast rate of growth. The point can be elucidated by certain examples. Nowhere has Indian planning failed so miserably as in agriculture (the "green revolution" is a recent phenomenon). The sluggishness in Indian agriculture cannot be attributed solely to the inadequacy of special inputs like irrigation facilities, fertilizers, seeds, and farm equipment. The fact that such facilities as are available have not been fully utilized clearly reveals that the trouble lies somewhere else as well. Part of the explanation must be sought in the democratic institutions which put a powerful lever —the vote—in the hands of the "common man", which makes the implementation of a plan an uphill task. Speaking frankly, Mr. Dhebar once said, "Whenever they tackled the problem of landlordism, the question, 'What will happen to Congress if *zamindari* is abolished?' raised its ugly head". The fear of losing votes thwarted any attempt to introduce sweeping changes in the institutional and organizational framework in the agriculture sector. The introduction of modern inputs within the framework of outdated and outmoded production relations which militate against any improvement in production is bound to prove abortive. Lajdgensky's report in this connection is revealing.

The disappointing performance on the savings front is no less patent. There is no other road to economic development than that of withholding an increasing share of national income from consumption, and using it for investment. In any case, the consumption of the masses should be reduced or, if not actually reduced, it should not be allowed to rise as fast as income.

History has known only two ways of achieving this. It may be done by allowing the capitalist to increase the share of profits in national income, and then ploughing back the profits in expanding industries, and/or letting the state amass the savings through taxation and other coercive measures. The first method was the modus operandi of capitalist development and the second, that of socialist. But, in India, both methods are subject to severe limitations. The application of the first method will run counter to our avowed objective of reduction in inequality of income and wealth. The method of taxation and other coercive measures are also subject to severe limitations for the same reason. Agriculture produces within itself half of the national income, but the burden of taxation does not in any case exceed 7 per cent of the aggregate income. Scarcity of resources on the one hand and the high marginal propensity to live off the peasantry on the other, merely emphasise the need for mopping up large resources from agriculture. But the masses, since they are poor and have the ballot paper, cannot be taxed. The rich peasants, since they control the precious votes or the political machinery of the state itself, must be exempted. Uttar Pradesh faced a veritable political crisis as a result of its government's attempt to increase land tax by a moderate amount.

The fate of the compulsory deposit scheme as originally conceived is another case in point. The original scheme had to be shelved, not because resources were not desperately needed, but because of vehement opposition from Chief Ministers.

The much-controverted gold control rules are another instance of how the implementation of a plan, like its formulation, is largely a political process. The goldsmiths offered tooth-and-nail resistance to Government's attempt to prevent gold smuggling, which was a serious drain on the lamentably small, but precious, foreign exchange resources. The goldsmiths were singularly active in Rajkot where the Swatantra party candidate gained a thundering victory over his rival—the Congress candidate. The latter singled out the unpopularity of gold control rules as the most important reason for his defeat. It is no wonder that the gold control scheme was soon shelved.

Thus, the problem of resource mobilization becomes difficult in most underdeveloped countries, both because of their much greater poverty and also because of new ideology which had no real counterpart in [the] early history of developed countries, but is now being spread by their generous support—that the purpose of economic development is to raise the level of living of masses of people. It becomes more difficult insofar as democratic governments are being adopted, giving the vote to the masses".[86]

The day-to-day strikes by one section or the other of the community, whether justified or otherwise, do corroborate the contention, that, "the task of organizing a democracy for rapid and coordinated advance along several lines is one of special difficulty".[87]

Emergency rule and the recent amendments to the Indian Constitution have naturally sparked off speculation regarding its impact on Indian Economic Development. Whether or not these changes in the political framework will, ceteris paribus, stimulate the growth in per capita income will depend on how and to what extent they will alter, reinforce and affect the rewarding and punishing consequences of the presence and/or absence of a certain behaviour (activities). A closer scrutiny of the recent legislative acts reveals that the majority of these are directed towards affecting the reward/punishment mechanism. For example, the family planning policy for civil servants, land reforms, urban ceilings, new restrictions on labour union activities, the proposed 59 clause 44th Amendment, etc., are intended to remove or reduce impediments and hurdles in implementation of socioeconomic reforms. While several achievements on the economic scene (such as a miraculous decrease in rate of inflation, sizeable improvement in food production and distribution, decline in absenteeism and strikes in factories, etc.) are visible, it would be inaccurate to attribute these gains entirely to the Emergency. Besides, the short-term effects should be distinguished from the long-term ones.

Present Policies and the Call of the Future

It is evident that the whole gamut of non-economic factors impinges on economic development in a wide variety of ways. The precise mechanism by which influence is exerted is rarely, if ever, delineated. However, following Kunkel, a behavioural model is postulated to explain the interaction between economic and non-economic factors. It is assumed that the process of transformation is dependent on certain activities which are determined by behaviour. It is further postulated that most behavioural patterns are induced, learned, and determined by the nature and type of contingency. It follows, therefore, that by appropriate changes in contingencies, certain types of behaviour can be altered and other types can be established and/or reinforced. For example, the capricious-universe view can be altered by building a framework in which rewards and efforts are strongly correlated. In the Indian context this would necessitate a change in the production relations on land, better irrigation facilities to save peasants from the vagaries of nature, a more objective and competitive type of examination for selection and evaluation. The massive expenditure on

irrigation projects in the Indian plans and land reform programme with its stress on "land to the tiller", if implemented, should gradually change the capricious-universe view. The Community Development Programme with its stress on self-help and village level planning should also alter the fatalistic attitude of rural people.

As stated earlier, Indian religion is characterized by "this worldly" and "other worldly" elements. Our survey of two schools in Delhi (though hardly an adequate or representative sample) shows virtually little knowledge of these "other worldly" elements among the younger generation. A deliberate policy to underscore materialistic elements vis-a-vis nonmaterialistic elements can reduce some of the inimical effects of religion on industrialization.

The grip of the caste system and the joint family system in India is apparently weakening. The Gandhian Movement against untouchability and the avowed policy of Government to uplift this minority by granting scholarships and reserving a certain quota of posts for Harijans are steps in the right direction. The role of competitive examinations in this context cannot be understressed.

In general, two factors are of critical significance from the standpoint of policy: (1) communication, and (2) education.[88]

1. Communication: Since most behaviour patterns are learned, the role of the mass media in economic development is self-evident. In rural India, where much of the information is derived from observations within the village, from personal experience, knowledge imparted by adults, by stories, proverbs, and past incidents, there is considerable uncertainty and lack of knowledge about the outer world. Yet it is in rural India that the hold of religion, the caste system, and the joint family system is the greatest. Evidently, the craving for money will be limited if the image of "good living" is only provided by the rich person in the village. Communication with the outer world and the broadening of horizons beyond the narrow confines of a village, are desideratura if some of the existing behavioural patterns are to be changed and

new ones are to be established to further economic development.

2. Education. Assuming behaviour patterns are learned, education can serve as a powerful tool for reinforcing, shaping, and establishing the types of behaviour pattern which are conducive to industrialization. Education not only enables individuals to know and grasp the range of alternatives available and activities required, but also to interpret, verify, and countercheck the information gathered from hearsay, stories, myths, from parents, and friends within the village. By means of education, the individual can gain access to historical knowledge. Extension of horizons through knowledge of the rest of the world permits subjects to look beyond the purview of personal experiences and observations. It also enables the individual to relate himself to the environment and successfully manipulate it. Kunkel rightly points out that the capricious-universe view can be partly changed by education, even if personal experiences point towards it. In Kunkel's words:

... education may provide a youth with information concerning the principles of national and regional governments, ideals of justice, the operation of economic systems, law, etc. The study of national and regional history as a series of interrelated events, with more or less logical sequence of human activities and governmental, economic, and political forms, would help the individual gain the conception of a systematic universe and lengthened time perspective.[89]

Education is no panacea. But it can, to some extent, reduce the inimical influence of noneconomic factors on economic development.

Recent research experiments in South India reveal how psychotherapeutic techniques can be used successfully to inculcate and/or stimulate entrepreneurial activities.[90] An achievement training-course was organized through the Small Industries Extension Training Institute at Hyderabad. Comparisons between the pre- and post-course candidates showed marked improvement in achievement motivation and consequent

entrepreneurial activities. Though the results are tentative, it does suggest that behaviour and personality changes are not only theoretically conceivable, but also practicable.

Conclusions

1. The role of noneconomic factors in economic development is subject to considerable controversy. The fundamental issues involved pertain to (a) relative weight of noneconomic factors vis-a-vis economic factors; (b) identification of noneconomic factors most pertinent to economic change; (c) direction of relationship between economic and sociopolitical phenomenon; and (d) the methods of analysing the relationship. There is no consensus of opinion on any of these issues owing to lack of relevant and/or sufficient data.

2. There are two distinct approaches to the study of interaction between economic and noneconomic factors: though the (a) psychodynamic model; and (b) behavioural model. The latter approach is deemed more appropriate for the study in question.

3. Philosophers generally agree that there is dualism of thought in Hinduism: there are certain tenets which are "this worldly" and others which are "other worldly". The controversy stems from their relative weight in Hinduism in practice. Our survey (even though statistically inadequate) reveals that the younger generation does not deem "other worldly" tenets important, let alone practise them. It was argued that, even if some people believe in these tenets, it does not necessarily prevent them from performing activities which further economic development. It was shown that Hinduism exhibits all the "character traits" of the Protestant ethic which, according to Max Weber, are most conducive to industrialization. However, it was established that certain religious activities in India may (a) absorb a relatively high proportion of lamentably small surplus, and (b) result in a pattern of asset preference which is inimical to economic growth.

4. The "capricious-universe" view of

the Indian masses can obstruct the process of economic expansion through its effect on saving, investment, and supply of labour and family planning. However, the crux of the matter is whether a fatalistic attitude creates man's condition or "explains" and 'justifies" it. If the latter provides the *raison d'etre* for a fatalistic attitude, its inimical effects should not be overstressed.

5. It is often argued that "economic man" is a myth in the Indian context. The available evidence (even though limited and shaky) does not support the view that the Indian peasant is irrational.

6. It is hypothesised that the caste system in India obstructs the process of economic expansion by (a) limiting occupational and geographical mobility; (b) breeding nepotism; (c) obstructing the development of a sense of nationhood; and (d) discouraging formation of entrepreneurial skill by blunting the sense of adventure. Available evidence does not support allegations (a) and (d), which are more critical from the standpoint of economic development.

7. The major disadvantages of the joint family system (such as its adverse effects on saving, investment, mobility, labour supply, and risk-taking) stem from the tacit assumption that there is a fundamental discontinuity between the initiator and the beneficiary. Since the family members are not bound to each other by any contractual arrangement, a wide variation in the criteria and method of apportioning the income is conceivable. It is our contention that in most families not only the fruits but also the obligations are shared by everyone. The joint family system has certain advantages (such as sharing possible risks, familistic management, lifetime commitment to enterprise, and economical utilization of fixed inputs) which should be underscored.

8. Democracy and planning are often regarded as a contradiction in terms. Even though the Indian experience refutes this contention, it cannot be denied that the democratic framework and the consequent stress on winning votes do impair the rate of growth.

9. Among other policy instruments, communication and education are of paramount importance in abating or removing the inimical effects of socio-political factors on Indian economic development.

REFERENCES

1. Vincent J. Trascio, *Pareto's Methodological Approach to Economics* (Chapel Hill: University of North Carolina, 1966), p. 56.
2. Sarjent, Florence, *Industrial Organization* (London: Macmillan, 1958).
3. United Nations, *Economic Survey of Asia and Far East* (Bangkok, 1962).
4. Karl Marx, *Capital, A Critique of Political Economy* (New York: The Modern Library, 1956).
5. Schumpeter, *History of Economic Analysis* (New York: Oxford University Press, 1954).
6. Schumpeter, *Economic Analysis*, Chapter III.
7. John R. Hicks, *Essays in World Economics* (Oxford: Clarendon Press, 1956).
8. K. Boulding, *A Reconstruction of Economics* (New York: John Wiley, 1950), p. vii.
9. T. Parson, *Toward a General Theory of* (Cambridge, Massachusetts: Cambridge University Press, 1951).
10. M.J. Levy, *The Structure of Society* (Princeton: Princeton University Press, 1952).
11. S. Kuznets, *Modern Economic Growth* (London: The University Press, 1965), ch. 1.
12. D. Lerner, *The Passing of Traditional Society* (Glencoe: Free Press, 1958).
13. E. Hagen, *On the Theory of Social Change: How Economic Growth Begins* (Illinois: Dorsey Press, 1962).
14. David McClelland, *The Achieving Society* (Princeton: D. Van Nostrand, 1961).
15. Ralph Linton, "Cultural and Personality Factors Affecting Economic Growth", in David E. Norvack and Robert Lekachmon (eds), *Development and Society* (New York: St. Martin's Press, 1964).
16. Robert A. Sole, *Economic Organization and Social Systems* (New York: Free Press, 1955).
17. Max Weber, *Protestant Ethic and Spirit of Capitalism* (New York: Scribner, 1956).
18. R.H. Tawney, *Religion and Rise of Capitalism* (New York: Harcourt and Brace, 1952).
19. Erich Fromm, *Psychoanalysis and Religion* (New York: Yale University, 1950).
20. Bert F. Hozelitz, "Non-Economic Factors in Economic Development", in B. Okun and R.W. Richardson (eds), *Studies in Economic Development* (New York: Holt, Rinehart and Winston, 1961).
21. W.W. Rostow, *Stages of Economic Growth*

(London: Cambridge University); *The Process of Economic Growth* (New York: Norton, 1962).

22. M. Mead, *Cultural Patterns and Technical Change* (Paris: UNESCO, 1953).
23. E. Denison, *The Sources of Economic Growth in the U.S. and the Alternative before the U.S.*, Committee for Economic Development, Supplementary Paper Number B, (New York, 1962).
24. Bert F. Hoselitz, "A Sociological Approach to Economic Development" in Hoselitz (ed.) *Sociological Aspects of Economic Growth* (New York, Glencoe: Free Press, 1960), pp. 23–84.
25. Charles Wolf, Jr., "Institutions and Economic Development" in Okun and Richardson, *Studies in Economic Development*.
26. Irma Adelman and Cynthia Taft Morris, "An Econometric Model of socioeconomic and political change in underdeveloped countries", *American Economic Review*, vol. 58, December 1968.
27. Marx, *Capital*.
28. E. Hagen, *Theory of Social Change*.
29. George Katona, *Psychological Analysis of Economic Behaviour* (New York: McGraw-Hill, 1951).
30. J. Tinbergen, "Social Factors in Economic Development", *Zeitschrift des Staatswists*, 1968.
31. Rostow, *Process of Economic Growth*.
32. Hicks, *Essays in World Economics*.
33. Tinbergen, "Social Factors in Economic Development".
34. Jacob Viner, *International Trade and Economic Development* (Oxford: Clarendon Press), p. 2.
35. Jacob Marschak, "Measurement for Policy and Prediction", in J. Hood and T.C. Koopmans (eds), *Studies of Economic Method* (New York: John Wiley, 1950), p. 10.
36. Kenneth Boulding, *A Reconstruction of Economics* (New York: John Wiley, 1959), p. vii.
37. Rostow, *Process of Economic Growth*.
38. Denison, *Sources of Economic Growth*.
39. See UNESCO, *Social Aspects of Economic Development in Latin America*, vol. I (Paris, 1963), pp. 88–89; D. Lerner, *The Passing of Traditional Society*; S.M. Lipset, *Political Man: the Social Bases of Politics* (New York: Doubleday, 1960); David McClelland, *The Achieving Society*; and Adelman and Morris, "Econometric Model of Development".
40. See G. Myrdal, *Asian Drama: an Inquiry into the Poverty of Nations* (New York: Twentieth Century Fund, 1968); Viner, *International Trade and Economic Development*; Marshack, "Measurement for Policy and Prediction"; and Boulding, *Reconstruction of Economics*.
41. For an excellent discussion this subject, see John H. Kunkel, *Society and Economic Growth* (New York: Oxford University Press, 1970), pp. 16–25.
42. Kunkel, *Society and Economic Growth*.
43. Hagen and McClelland's Models provide classic illustrations in point.
44. For details, see Kunkel, *Society and Economic Growth*.
45. See J. Bhagwati, *The Economics of Underdeveloped Countries* (New York: McGraw-Hill, 1970), p. 100.
46. McClelland and Hagen are champions of this belief.
47. See M. Singer, "Religion and Social Changes in India: The Max Weber Thesis, Phase Three", *Economic Development and cultural Change*, 1966; John Goheen, "A Comment on Professor Singer's Cultural Values in India's Economic Development", *Economic Development and Cultural Change*, October 1958; M.N. Srinivas, "A Note on Mr. Goheen's Note", *Economic Development and Cultural Change*, October 1958.
48. Ibid.
49. Srinivas, "Mr. Goheen's Note".
50. *Mahabharata* XII, Ch. 8, quoted by Gokhale, p. 52.
51. Tr. A.W. Ryder, p. 211; quoted by Ajit Dasgupta, "India's Cultural Values and Economic Development: A Comment", *Economic Development and Cultural Change*, October 1958, p. 101.
52. Singer, *Religion and Social Change*, p. 501.
53. Ibid.
54. "The Rediscovery of Man", Proceedings of Thirtieth Indian Philosophical Congress, December 1955, quoted by Goheen.
55. "The Rediscovery of Man", quoted by Goheen, p. 3.
56. Milton Singer, "Cultural Values in Indian Economic Development", *Annals of American Academy and Social Sciences*, pp. 81–91.
57. Srinivas, "Goheens Note", p. 4.
58. Ibid.
59. Max Weber, *Religion in India* (Glencoe: Free Press, 1958), p. 4.
60. Singer, *Religion and Social Change*, p. 501.
61. Ibid.
62. Max Weber overstressed the role of Protestant ethic in the rise of capitalism. Even if we identify all religions conducive to economic development with Protestant ethic, there is enough evidence in history to prove that the same traits elsewhere did not spark off the process of economic change. As a matter of fact, there are several instances where altogether different "character traits" in religion facilitated industrialization. Japanese religion is a classic illustration in point.
63. Richard D. Lambert and Bert F. Hoselitz, *The Role of Saving and Wealth in Southern Asia and the West* (UNESCO, 1963), p. 307.
64. Hugh Patrick, "Financial Development and Economic Development", *Economic Development and Cultural Change*, January 1966.
65. For details refer to my dissertation, *Asset Preference and Economic Development—with special reference to India* (University of North Carolina at Chapel Hill: January 1971).
66. For a lucid and detailed discussion on this subject, see Kunkel.
67. Singer, *Religion and Social Change*.
68. See McClelland, *The Achieving Society*.

69. See "Asset Preference and Economic Development".
70. Kusum Nair, *Blossoms in the Dust* (New York: Frederick A. Praeger, 1962).
71. For a detailed and lucid discussion, see Jagdish Bhagwati and Sukhamoy Chakravarty, "Contributions to Indian Economic Analysis: A Survey", *American Economic Review*, vol. LIX, no. 4, part 2 (September 1969). The following section is based on this survey article.
72. W.D. Hopper, "Allocation Efficiency in a Traditional Indian Agriculture", *Journal of Farm Economics*, August 1965.
73. Raj Krishna, "Farm Response in the Punjab (India–Pakistan): A Case Study of Cotton", Unpublished Ph.D. dissertation, University of Chicago, 1961.
74. D.K. Desai, *Increasing Income and Production in Indian Farming* (Bombay: Indian Society of Agriculture Economics, 1963).
75. C.H. Hanumantha Rao, "Entrepreneurship, Management and Farm Tenure Systems", February 1967, mimeographed.
76. K. N. Raj, "Investment in Livestock in Agrarian Economies: A Theoretical and Empirical Analysis", December 1967, mimeographed.
77. Edward M. Burns and Philip L. Ralph, *World Civilization* (New York: W.M. Norton, 1964).
78. Kuznets, op. cit.
79. Srinivas, op. cit., p. 5.
80. See M. N. Srinivas, *Religion and Society Among the Coorgs of South India* (London: Oxford University Press); N.A. Toothi, *Vaishnavas of Gujrat* (London: Longmans, 1935).
81. M.S. Gore, "India", in Lambert and Hoselitz, p. 181.
82. Ibid., p. 187.
83. David G. McClelland, *Motivational Trends in Society* (New York: General Learning Press, 1971).
84. Lambert and Hoselitz, p. 400.
85. Robert N. Marsh and Hiroshi Mannari, "A New Look at Lifetime Commitment in Japanese Industry", *Economic Development and Cultural Change*, vol. 20, no. 4, July 1972.
86. Gunnar Myrdal, *Economic Theory in Underdeveloped Regions* (Bombay: Vora and Co., 1958), pp. 94–95.
87. Government of India Planning Commission, *First Five Year Plan* (New Delhi), p. 8.
88. For details, see Kunkel, *Society and Economic Growth*.
89. Ibid, p. 245.
90. David McClelland and David G. Winter, *Motivating Economic Achievement* (New York: Free Press, 1969).

BIBLIOGRAPHY

Adelman, Irma and Cynthia Taft Morris : "An Econometric Model of Development". *American Economic Review.* December 1968.

Boulding, Kenneth: A Reconstruction of Economics. New York. John Wiley, 1950.

Goheen, John: A Comment on Professor Singer's "Cultural Values in India's Economic Development". *Economic Development and Cultural Change.* July 1958.

Hagen, Everette: *On the Theory of Social Change: How Economic Growth Begins.* Illinois. Dorsey Press, 1962.

Hoselitz, Bert F: "Non-Economic Factors in Economic Development". In Bernard Okun, and Richard W Richardson (eds), *Studies in Economic Development.* New York. Holt, Rinehart and Winston, 1961.

Karve, D.G.: "Comments," *Economic Development and Cultural Change.* July 1968

Karve, Irawati: "What is Caste?", and "Caste and Occupation". *Economic Weekly,* 22 March 1958.

Kindleberger, C.E.: *Economic Development.* New York. McGraw Hill, 1966.

Kunkel, John H.: *Society and Economic Growth.* New York. Oxford University Press, 1970.

Lambert, Richard and Bert F. Hoselitz (eds): *The Role of Savings and Wealth in Southern Asia and the West.* UNESCO, 1963.

Lambert, Richard: "The Social and Psychological Determinants of Savings and Investments in Developing Societies". in Hoselitz, Bert F, and Wilbert E. Moore (eds). *Industrialization and Society.* The Hague. UNESCO, 1963.

McClelland, Davig G.: *The Achieving Society.* Princeton. D. Van Nostrand, 1961.

Mishra, V.B.: *Hinduism and Economic Growth.* New York. Oxford University Press, 1962.

Myrdal, Gunnar: *Asian Drama: An Inquiry into the Poverty of Nations.* New York. Twentieth Century Fund, 1968.

Raulet, Harry and J.S. Uppal: "The Social Dynamics of Economic Development in Rural Punjab". *Asian Survey,* April 1970.

Singer, Milton: "Cultural Values in India's Economic Development". *Annals of American Academy and Social Science,* 1956.

———: "India's Cultural Values and Economic Development: A Discussion: A Postscript". *Economic Development and Cultural Change,* July 1958.

———:"Religion and Social Change in India, The Max Weber Thesis, Phase Three". *Economic Development and Cultural Change,* July 1966.

Srinivas, M.N.: "A Note on Mr. Goheen's Note". *Economic Development and Cultural Change,* July 1958.

Tawney, R.H.: *Religion and Rise of Capitalism.* New York. Harcourt and Brace, 1952.

Uppal, J.S.: *Economic Development in South Asia.* New York. St. Martin's Press, 1977.

Weber, Max: *Religion of India.* Glencoe. The Free Press, 1958.

————: *Protestant Ethic and Spirit of Capitalism.* New York. Scribner, 1956.

Part Three

THE ECONOMIC SECTOR

5

Agriculture in India: Problems and Prospects

ROMESH DIWAN

That system alone will prevail which the villagers after mutual discussions and understandings approve of. No system or arrangement would be thrust upon them from outside. If each of them prefers separate individual cultivation of land, he can do so; and if two, four or even more persons want to come together or even if the whole village wants to have collective farming they are welcome to follow their inclination. All will, however, work with complete unanimity. If the opinion seems to be divided, both the experiments will be undertaken. But the ownership of the land will vest in the village as a whole and consequently there would be real village self-government in each village.

—ACHARYA VINOBA BHAVE
on BHOODAN AND GRAMDAN

The word "agriculture" comes from the Latin words: *agri*, fields, *culture*, cultivation. Accordingly, Webster Collegiate Dictionary defines it as "the art or science of cultivating the ground; the production of crops and livestock on a farm; farming". In economic literature, this term has been given a much broader meaning. It encompasses everything pertaining to the activity of farming. The basic purpose of farming used to be the production of "wage goods". "Wage goods"[1] are goods such as wheat, rice and maize that are consumed by people at large to satisfy their basic needs of existence. These are the necessities of life. Without these goods people will literally die. Over time, farming activity has been extended to the production of raw materials[2] used in the manufacture of industrial goods. Examples of raw materials are cotton, jute and rubber. They are different from wage-goods insofar as raw materials cannot be consumed directly by the people. They have to be processed before they can be consumed. It should be mentioned, however, that some of these raw materials, duly processed (sometimes in homes), do enter into the consumption of people at large. Some of these, therefore, may be classified as wage-goods since they relate to the social necessities. Thus, sugar and cotton would relate to wage goods. Jute, on the other hand, is strictly a raw material. Even though the distinction between wage goods and raw materials depends upon the nature and structure of consumption of the society, it is still a useful and analytically meaningful distinction. In this chapter, we will divide the total agricultural production into these two categories.

Sometimes a distinction is made between agriculture and plantations. A plantation economy also produces both wage goods[3] like tea, and raw materials such as cocoa, rubber, cotton, and sugarcane. However, the distinction is an important one and follows from the way plantation economy was introduced. While agricultural activity was fundamental to the very existence of the society, plantation activity was superimposed on an existing socioeconomic structure by an alien investor. While the purpose of the output of agricultural production was consumption by members of the country in which production took place, the purpose of the output of plantation economy was purely export to the country of the investor.[4] As a result, the institutional set-up was, and still is, very different in the plantation economy. As countries which were ruled by foreign governments become independent, they make, and are still, making attempts to integrate the plantation economy with the agricultural economy. This process of integration has its own problems. In this chapter, our analysis will focus only on the agricultural economy.

Total Agricultural Output

Since wage goods satisfy the basic needs of the members of a society, the society, to exist, has to obtain these goods. There are two[5] ways it can do this : (i) produce these goods itself, and (ii) produce other goods, say non wage goods, and exchange these non wage goods for wage goods by trading with another country which produces wage goods and is willing (or can be pressured) to exchange. Generally, countries with large land areas, such as Brazil, Canada, China, France, India, Nigeria, USA, and USSR, produce wage goods themselves. It is only countries with small land areas and high density of population, like Belgium, Britain, the Netherlands, that obtain wage goods both by producing themselves and through trade.

In the context of India, production of wage goods is essential. It is particularly so if we examine the nature of the Indian economy. A large part of the total production in the Indian economy is carried on in the agriculture sector Table 5.1 corroborates this observation.

Table 5.1 Share of Agriculture in National Income

Year	Percentage of agriculture in national income
1960–61	52.5
1965–66	44.2
1969–70	45.2
1974–75	41.2

SOURCE: Government of India, *Economic Survey*, 1975–76 (New Delhi: Manager of Publications, 1976).

NOTES: 1. The year refers to the agricultural year July to June.
2. The estimates of percentage are based on the data for 1960–61 prices (revised series).

Thus, half of the total production in the economy is accounted for by the agriculture sector: agriculture is the most important activity in the country.

The question that arises is, is the production from agriculture enough, or sufficient, to satisfy the basic needs of the members of the Indian society? Before attempting to answer this it is necessary to understand what we mean by "the production from agriculture". Also, the percentage share of agriculture in Table 5.1 is estimated by dividing the "total agricultural output" by the national income. To appreciate and interpret the numbers in Table 5.1, therefore, it is necessary to define the term, "total agricultural output" which is basically the same thing as "production from agriculture". "Total agricultural output" is a fictional concept, but an useful one for analytical purposes. "Total agricultural output" is made up of various types of agricultural production, such as wage goods and raw materials. This much is obvious. Yet, there is no easy way to define the total agricultural output as a simple sum of the various types of production. The problem is that different productions are measured in different units: for example, wheat is measured in *maunds* and tons and cotton in bales. How then does one add, say, wheat to cotton? Thus, how does a particular total agricultural output, say, composed of 10 tons of wheat and 10 bales of cotton, compare with another total agriculture output, say, composed of 15 tons of wheat and 5 bales of cotton? To put this question in a more precise form, let us assume[6] that agricultural production is made up only of two commodities, one representing wage goods and the other raw materials, and let A, A_1 and A_2 denote the amount of total agricultural output, wage goods, and raw material respectively. Then, the question is: is $A = A_1 + A_2$?[7]

Since A is a purely fictional quantity, in the sense that one cannot find a quantity called A in the real world, and A_1 and A_2 are real-life quantities the sum does not make sense. The reason is that the quantities A_1 and A_2 are measured in different units, and accordingly, cannot be added together.

In order to express A as the sum of A_1 and A_2, it is necessary to represent all them quantities in the same units. There are various ways of doing so. One of them is to write A, A_1 and A_2 in value terms. Thus if we write p, p_1, p_2 for the price per unit of A, A_1, and A_2 respectively, we may write the equation[8]

$$pA = p_1A_1 + p_2A_2 \qquad (1)$$

Equation (1) means that the total money spent on total agricultural output is equal to the total money spend on wage goods and on raw materials. This makes sense since it is a sum in money terms. In other words, we are adding up quantities in the same units. It may be pointed out, however, that p like A is a fictional concept. (pA), on the other hand, is a real life number, even though both p and A are fictional.

If we divide equation (1), we get[9]

$$A = (p_1/p) A_1 + (p_2/p) A_2; = c_1A_1 + c_2A_2; c_1 = p_i/p \ (i = 1, 2) \quad (2)$$

We can thus define the concept "total agricultural output" as a weighted sum of the production of wage goods and raw materials. It will be noticed that even though a simple sum does not make sense, a weighted sum does seem legitimate. The simple sum is possible only in the particular case when $c_1 = c_2 = 1$. This, it will be appreciated is a very stringent condition indeed.[10]

We have suggested that A_1 and A_2 are real life quantities while A is a fictional quantity. The implication of this statement is that we can find data on actual quantities of A_1 and A_2 (see Table 5.2). Before we analyse these data, it needs to be mentioned that we cannot write a similar row for the "total agriculture output". Total agricultural output can be expressed only in the form of an index number. Thus, we present the data in Table 5.2 along with the data on "total agricultural output" in Table 5.3. These tables suggest that over 13 years or so, since 1960, the total agricultural output has increased by 40 per cent; or at the rate of approximately 3 per cent per year. However, this increase has not been evenly spread over individual commodities. It is wheat whose produc-

Table 5.2. Production of Agricultural Commodities
(in million tons)

Commodity/Year	1955–56	1960–61	1965–66	1968–69	1973–74
Rice	28.6	11.0	30.6	39.8	44.1
Wheat	8.8	34.6	10.4	18.6	21.8
Cereal	57.6	69.6	62.4	83.6	94.7
Pulses	11.7	12.7	9.9	10.4	10.0
Cotton	4.2	5.5	4.8	5.4	5.74
Tea	0.31	0.32	0.37	0.40	

SOURCE: *Economic Survey*, 1975–76, p. 63.

Table 5.3. Index Numbers of Agricultural Production
(triennium ending 1961–62=100)

Commodity/Year	1960–61	1965–66	1968–69	1973–74
Rice	101.8	90.0	116.5	129.9
Wheat	98.8	93.4	157.1	195.7
Total Cereal	101.6	90.9	120.0	138.2
Pulses	105.5	82.4	84.3	82.5
Cotton	119.1	104.0	119.4	143.3
Tea	96.2	112.8	120.5	141.4
Total Agricultural Output	142	132	159	

SOURCE: *Economic Survey*, 1975–76, p. 62.

NOTES: 1. The actual figures have been rounded off to whole numbers.

2. The original table gives far more detail. Necessary notes regarding these data are also given there.

tion has increased the fastest; at the rate of 8 per cent per year. Other fast-growing crops are maize, cotton, and sugarcane, all of these at approximately 5 per cent per year. Coffee and rubber have grown still faster, at the rate of 11 and 17 per cent per year respectively. On the other hand, pulses have remained virtually at the same level as in 1950. Production of jute has actually decreased.

From equation (2) we can see that increase in A can come about in many ways. Thus it is quite possible to have an increase in the total agricultural output along with a decrease in one of the commodities. In other words, we can have a situation where the people at large are actually becoming poorer (the wage-goods are decreasing) even when the total agricultural output is increasing. It is, therefore, important to look into the production of individual commodities, and one must be very careful in interpreting the quantity "total agricultural output".[11]

There are other ways of determining the weights.[12] We suggest one. Equation (2) can be derived by formulating weights from the amount of manual labour used in producing one unit of the agricultural commodity—"labour per unit of production". Thus if we write n, n_1 and n_2 for labour used per unit of A, A_1 and A_2, we get back equation (2) except that now $c_i = n_i/n$ ($i = 1, 2$).[13]

Sufficiency of Agricultural Production

In Tables 5.1, 5.2, and 5.3 we notice the following: (i) Agricultural production forms a large part of total production in the economy. (ii) The production of foodgrains (cereals and pulses) has gone up from 55 thousand tons in 1950–57 to 95 thousand tons in 1968–69. (iii) Total agricultural production has grown at the rate of 3 per cent per year. By themselves, these facts are quite interesting. However, the fundamental question is: do they suggest that India is producing "enough" wage goods to satisfy the needs of the members of its society? Obviously, we cannot answer this question from the facts above. We need more information, of two types: (i) What is meant by "enough"? (ii) What is the size and nature of the members of the Indian society?

Before we can answer this question, there is a prior one why should production be "enough" to satisfy the needs of the members of the society? This question is of value, world views, etc., and not of facts. We can answer: by definition, the consumption of wage goods is essential for the very existence of the members of the society, or it dies. Thus, the production of these goods has to be at least as much as the needed consumption for existence otherwise some members will die and the society will shrink in size. On the other hand, if the production is greater than the needed consumption, then the members will be healthier, so that they can produce more. Also in theories of economic development, it is generally believed that excess of this production is necessary for the development of industry. In other words, this surplus production provides the base on which an industrial sector can be built. Without this surplus, there is no way of having an industrial sector.

Now we come back to our question: is production "enough" to satisfy the needs of the members of the society? (By "enough" we mean the very minimum of food that is needed for mere existence). Experts on nutrition have estimated that in Indian climatic conditions an intake of around 2,000–2,400 calories is adequate for living. These calorie requirements differ with the type of work, age, etc. In that case, is the production sufficient to provide at least 2,000–2,400 calories for all the members? There are two ways of looking at this question. One, we can estimate the total amount of calories produced, expressing all types of food production in terms of calories. Estimates of this nature have been made. Professor K.N. Raj[14] produced evidence to this effect.

> His [K.N. Raj] evidence is based on the fact that on nutritional grounds the average foodgrains requirements of an adult under Indian conditions is 13 ounces per day. Taking into consideration the age composition and provision for seed and wastage, the average requirement would be 15½ ounces per day. From the data he concludes that in no year in the last decade and a half has the per capita availability of foodgrains fallen below this level and, except in two years (1951–52 and 1952–53), it would have been possible to ensure this from domestic production.[15]

The other approach is to analyse the conditions of actual consumption. Very meagre data are available on the actual consumption of wage goods by the people at large.[16] Estimates of consumption can be, and are, made from the expen-

Table 5.4. Distribution of Consumer Expenditure by Major Items

Monthly per capita expenditure (Rs)	Per centage of population	Annual per capita expenditure (Rs)	Percentage distribution of total expenditure				
			Food grains and sub-stitutes	Other items of food	Fuel and light	Clothing	Others
Rural							
0–8	6.38	79.3	64.42	18.25	8.74	1.23	7.36
8–11	11.95	116.6	63.57	17.43	8.56	2.51	7.93
11–13	9.88	147.2	60.25	19.09	7.36	5.70	7.60
13–15	9.82	170.8	58.12	20.44	7.48	4.63	9.33
15–18	13.79	200.0	54.50	23.66	6.93	5.23	9.67
18–21	11.44	237.3	50.31	24.10	6.67	6.97	11.95
Urban							
0–8	2.15	77.6	63.79	17.87	8.93	0.63	8.78
8–11	2.49	118.3	52.67	26.65	8.23	1.13	11.32
11–13	7.19	145.0	48.32	27.35	8.64	2.27	13.42
13–15	6.86	169.7	45.73	29.11	8.03	2.87	14.26
15–18	10.71	201.2	41.72	31.37	7.38	3.57	15.96
18–21	11.40	235.7	37.17	33.40	7.49	3.41	18.53
21–24	9.68	271.7	36.45	33.81	7.12	3.94	18.68
24–28	11.04	315.4	32.72	34.56	6.91	5.29	20.52

SOURCE: Constructed from V.M. Dandekar and Nilkantha Rath, "Poverty in India", *Economic and Political Weekly*, 20 March 1971, Tables 1.2 and 1.3, p. 26–27.

ditures on consumption. Recently, Dandekar and Rath[17] have made a somewhat detailed analysis of the actual consumption of a large section of the population. They provide the evidence in Table 5.4.

Dandekar and Rath argue and few disagree, that "in 1960–61, an annual per capita consumer expenditure of Rs 170 was essential to give a diet adequate at least in respect of calories"[18] in the rural areas. In urban areas the equivalent expenditure is Rs 271. Using the minimal needed annual expenditure, one can derive the conclusions regarding consumption from Table 5.4. Dandekar and Rath conclude, that in 1960–61, about one-third of the rural population and nearly half of the urban population lived on diets inadequate even in respect of calories.[19] The implication is that a sizable proportion, more than two-fifths, of the Indian society does not get even an adequate diet. On the other hand, the production in the country is sufficient to provide an adequate diet.

There are two reasons for this contradiction. One, the contradiction arises from the problem of maldistribution. This author has argued that the explanation lies in separate analyses of the urban and rural situation.[20] Two, the actual production of foodgrains is just not sufficient, particularly when one takes into consideration the inequalities generated by regional disparities. In other words, there may be a problem of distribution, but the total output is not sufficient if we wish to remove the poverty of the masses. The policy, therefore, has to be in terms of increasing the production and not merely distributing what is already being produced.

In this chapter we will not discuss the problem relating to distribution of output, but shall concentrate on issues concerning production. The important question here is: why does Indian agriculture not produce sufficiently large quantities of wage goods and raw materials? It must be mentioned here that the sufficiency of raw materials is determined by the size of the industrial sector. We have not discussed the question whether sufficient quantities of raw materials are

produced. The total agricultural output index gives a weightage of 66.9 per cent to total foodgrains production and only 33.1 per cent to total nonfoodgrains production. We leave the reader with the assertion that the production of raw materials also is not sufficient for India's needs.[21]

Productivity in Agriculture

Thus, we come back to our question: why does Indian agriculture not produce sufficiently large quantities? To answer it we must first understand the factors that determine production. Production of a commodity generally, and agricultural commodity particularly, is influenced by two major facts concerning: (a) the technological relationships between inputs and outputs, and (b) the institutional set-up in the producing country. *These factors, technology, and institutional framework, are not independent of each other:* they are heavily interdependent, though we shall study them separately to shed light on their characteristics. The technological relationship analyses various methods of producing the particular commodity. It refers to the question: how can, and does, actual production take place? The emphasis here is on the alternative forms of combining the different inputs. The institutional set-up, on the other hand, deals with the relationship between decision makers and actual producers. It is concerned with some of the basic decisions regarding production: (i) What will be produced? (ii) Why will it be produced? and (iii) Who will produce it? (iv) How will the production be distributed between the producers and decision makers?

Technological Relationships

Production is a process in which a certain number of inputs are so combined as to result in the production of a particular commodity. For example, if wheat is the particular commodity desired to be produced it will require the inputs of (i) land, (ii) seeds and manure, (iii) water, (iv) sunshine, (v) time, (vi) energy, and (vii) tools. There are large variations in the types of these inputs. Land can be more or less fertile. Water can be obtained through rain or irrigation; in its turn, may be from water tanks, tube-wells, canals, etc. Seeds can be of different varieties, with varying resistance to insects. The timing of sunshine is very important.[22] Different methods of production require more or less time. Energy comes in various forms: (a) human, (b) animal, (c) electrical, and (d) mechanical. In economic literature, human energy is separated from other forms of energy. Human energy is of two types: (i) mental, and (ii) physical. Mental energy involves the capacity for decision-making while physical energy involves the performance of physical tasks. Physical energy can be substituted by other forms of energy.[23] The important thing here is that in a human being one form of energy cannot be separated from another. The tools needed are fully dependent upon the form the energy takes. Thus electric energy can be obtained only through an electric generator. Mechanical energy, on the other hand, requires a different motor. The ploughs suited to pulling by bullocks are of a different nature from the ploughs fitted to a tractor. The purpose of tools is, basically, to facilitate the use of energy. It will be noticed that all the various inputs are heavily interdependent. The relation between them is of both complimentarity and substitution.

A particular combination of these inputs generates a particular technique of production. Since every particular input has a number of forms, the combination of these forms gives a very large number of techniques indeed.[24] We will pick out and concentrate on only two of these techniques, which are well defined and very distinct.[25] These are discussed both in popular and academic literature. They are termed *desi* and farangi, or old and new, traditional and modern, pre-modern and modern, low and high yielding, high and low quantity, Asian and Western, etc.[26] It will be noticed that all of these are emotive words, implying that one is better than the other. To avoid value judgements (not that these are not important), and help facilitate understanding and analysis, we shall call them Techniques I and II

Technique I

Technique I is a method of production which has been used in India; and also in Asia, for several centuries. Over such a long time, it has been improved to the point of being perfected. It has conformed to the resources of India. The seeds used are highly resistant to any sort of disease, so that even in bleak years there is a minimal production. Water is obtained from whatever sources are available. (It is because of this that Indian agriculture is called a gamble). The energy used is a low one and in the form of bullocks. The tools are those that can be pulled by bullocks. The production per acre of land by this method is low. On the other hand, the costs of production per acre of land are also low, so that even a poor farmer can adopt this method of production. The risk factor is slight. It is a method which is ecologically sound. It is labour intensive and not capital intensive.

Technique II

Technique II is a method of production that has been introduced in India in the very recent past. In this method, the seeds used have very little resistance to disease, so that insecticides are extremely important. The manuring involves intensive doses of fertilizers. Fertilizers are effective only if there are large quantities of water available. Since a large quantity of water is essential, the water-supply cannot depend upon rain alone. Water has to be obtained either from canals or from tubewells; ordinary persian wells are not sufficient since these do not deliver large quantities of water. Thus, if canal water is not available, there is need for a large capital investment in tubewells, fertilizers and insecticides. Large doses of energy are needed for this method, so that simple bullock power is not sufficient any longer. Such doses of energy can only be channelled through machinery like tractors, etc., which involves further capital investment. Since machinery and tubewells have their own economies of scale, the land holding for using this method should be comparatively large. The production per acre of land is high[26] and so is the cost per acre of land. The risk factor is also high. A poor farmer cannot adopt this method. The method is capital intensive and ecologically unsound. Since this method has been used extensively in Western countries, it conforms to their resource mix.

Production Function

In economic theory, the methods of production are analysed by the means of a production function; an abstracted, simplistic and somewhat unrealistic device. The production function is generally represented by a mathematical equation:

$$A_1 = f(L, K, Ld)$$

Where A_1, L, K and Ld stand for the final output, quantity of labour employed, quantity of capital used, and acreage of land used in production. It will be noticed that seed, manure, water, tools, bullocks, etc., have all been aggregated into the capital, K. The function completely ignores inputs like time and sunshine. However, these are fairly constant for a particular method of production. Function f is a general form and can express a particular relationship; e.g., linear homo-geneous function.[27] f also determines a particular technique of production. Thus, f_1 implies one method of production and f_2 another.

The implication of the production function is that if we increase the units of the inputs L, K and Ld, then the output A_1 will increase. If a 1 per cent increase in all the inputs leads to more than, equal to, and less than 1 per cent increase in output, we have increasing, constant, and diminishing returns to scale respectively. It is generally believed that the law of diminishing returns to scale operates in agriculture. It will be noticed that a 1 per cent increase in all the inputs does not change the proportions between inputs. These are written as K/L, L/K, K/Ld, Ld/k, L/Ld, Ld/L. Sometimes the increase may take place only in one input; say L. In that case, the total output will change, but so will the proportions. In the textbooks, production function is expressed in this form. To elucidate some of the concepts and concerns, we make use of these two concepts. Thus, taking L as the variable input, holding both Ld and K constant, we may draw the graphs as in Graph 5.1.[28] The two curves I and II represent the total output of A_1. The curve I is drawn by

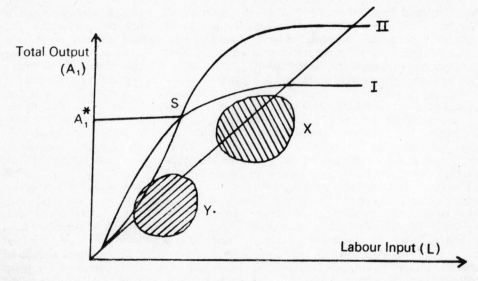

Graph 5.1

holding K and Ld constant at a particular value, say K^* and Ld^*. Similarly, II assumes that K and Ld are constant, however, at a different value, say K^{**} and Ld^{**}. In this particular example, for every level of output beyond A_1^*, the output on curve II is higher than on curve I. Since the labour employed in both cases is the same, it implies that output per unit of labour on curve II is higher than output per unit of labour on curve I. Output per unit of labour (A_1/L) is also known as labour productivity, sometimes simply productivity.

Labour productivity in Indian agriculture is considered quite low. Table 5.5 compares productivity in India with that of other countries.

Table 5.5. Average Labour Productivity Per Year in Agriculture

Country	Average Productivity in US Dollars
India	105
Norway	973
United Kingdom	2,057
Canada	2,126
Japan	2,265
USA	2,408
New Zealand	3,481
West Germany	3,495

SOURCE: Ruddar Dutt and K.P.M. Sundharam, *Indian Economy* (New Delhi: Niraj Prakashan, 1971), p. 321.

NOTES: 1. There are a million problems in comparing productivity for the whole agriculture. More meaningful comparisons should be made between particular commodities.

2. It is not clear what years these estimates relate to.

Even though there are large pitfalls in making comparisons, the large difference in the estimates for India and Western countries does suggest that the labour productivity in Indian agriculture is not high.

Before one analyses the evidence on productivity, it is important to ask first, what is the relevant concept of productivity? Just as we have labour productivity,

we can also define land productivity and capital productivity. In the context of Indian agriculture, it is land and not labour which is, perhaps, the scarce input. A case can, therefore, be made for land productivity (A_1/Ld); i.e., output per unit of land. Table 5.6 gives data on land productivity and trends therein.

Thus the land productivity has been growing in the production of foodgrains at the rate of 1.65 in the past 20 years.

Table 5.6. Rates of Growth of Agricultural Production and Land Productivity (1949-50 to 1968-69)

(Growth rate per cent per year)

Commodity	Production	Area	Land Productivity
Rice	3.02	1.22	1.78
Wheat	4.20	2.26	1.90
All foodgrains	2.79	1.19	1.65
Cotton	3.93	1.91	1.98
Sugarcane	3.97	2.74	1.20
All commodities	2.92	1.37	1.53

SOURCE: *Fourth Five-Year Plan*, p. 117.

NOTE: If we write P_d for productivity, and define it as A_1/Ld;

then $\dfrac{\dot{A_1}}{A_1} = \dfrac{\dot{Ld}}{Ld} + \dfrac{\dot{P_d}}{P_d}$ Dots represent rates of change and the three values represent the columns respectively.

Causes of Low Labour Productivity

Coming back to the evidence of labour productivity, the question arises: why is labour productivity so low in India? There are many causes for this, some of which lie in the institutional set-up. The institutional set-up affects very strongly the motives for, and capacity of labour to work on, production. We shall study these in the next section. The other reasons are purely technological. From Graph 5.1 it is obvious that labour productivity under technique II is larger than under technique I.

Some economists maintain that India is in the area X on the graph. Professor

Radha Sinha[29] calls it the "pre-modern high level equilibrium trap". By this he means that in India we have reached the limit posed by the existing technology: technique I. No amount of juggling with the factors would help. Actually, he has made an interesting use of the graph to elucidate his argument. He maintains that actual production is always less than the potential output defined by the curve. The difference lies in the various imperfections and institutional limitations. The total output cannot be increased beyond the curve. The only way to increase it is to shift the whole curve. This is possible if there is a change in the method of production: technique II. His point is that in the case of India we have already reached the point of virtual maximum. This is also the contention of some other economists, like T.W. Schultz.[30]

The implication of Professor Radha Sinha's argument is that further increases in production can only come from the use and hence availability of the "new" type of inputs like "new" seeds, fertilizers, insecticides, tubewells, etc., the inputs needed for the "green revolution". These inputs have to be either (i) produced domestically, or (ii) obtained by imports from abroad. In case (i), the increases in agricultural production depend upon the growth of the industrial sector. In case (ii), they depend upon the increase in trade with Western countries. In any case, endogenous increases in agricultural production are not possible. From now on, the agricultural sector is tied up with the industrial sector or the Western economy. Another interesting implication is that contrary to the earlier situation where industry depends upon agriculture (for demand of the industrial output and the supply of industrial inputs), now it is agriculture that depends upon industry for the agricultural inputs.

Institutional Framework

So far, we have concentrated on the methods of production and the technical relations between the output and its inputs. The production process, however, is also influenced in a large measure by the institutional set-up. Some social scientists, including economists, argue that the method of production itself depends upon the nature of institutions.[31] In any case, some of the most important and very basic questions regarding production are defined, if not completely determined, by the nature and type of the institutions. Some of the basic questions are: Why produce? What to produce? and, Who should produce?

We have used the term "institutions" without in any way defining it. Either one can define the particular institutions prevalent in India or outline the general nature of the institutional framework. We follow the latter method, and distinguish between three major institutional types of framework, namely, (i) feudalism, (ii) capitalism, and (iii) socialism. These are, unfortunately, amorphous terms, and there is, therefore, a large area where there can be, and generally is, a lot of disagreement. Our purpose here is not to engage in defining these systems but the rather limited one of, hopefully, bringing out the different principles involved in these forms. It is asserted that a particular form can be created from various combinations of these three systems. Actually, various combinations of the principles of these three systems do generate a large number of rather complex institutional types of framework.[32]

Feudalistic Modes of Production

The fundamental basis of feudalistic agriculture is the relationship between the landlord (or *zamindar*[33]) and the actual tiller of the land. The land belongs to the landlord. The tiller of the land is attached to the land; hence to the landlord. Various names have been given to the tiller. In Britain he was called "the serf"; in the USA, he was the "nigger". The nigger or the serf was basically a slave. To my knowledge, there is no such extreme case in India, though some tenancy laws did tend to serfdom and slavery.[34] The legal structure in the feudalistic system is that the landlord had legal rights over his slaves or serfs.

The *zamindari* system in India, in any form, represents a feudalistic institution. The *zamindari* system, some remnants of which are visible in today's India, emerged during the British occupation of India. One of the forms of British exploitation of the Indian masses involved the collection of land revenue. Some of the Indian intermediaries, who performed the dirty work of the British masters and collected the land revenue to pass it on to the British superiors, eventually became the *zamindars*.

In the feudal system, the relations between the tiller and the landlord are well defined. Not only is the tenant attached to the land, but the land is also attached to the tenant. It is the *zamindar* who owns the land and decides what to produce. Since he also owns the tenants and the tenants are needed to produce whatever he desires, he has to provide for their subsistence. Thus he is forced to produce enough wage goods to maintain the tenants at their "level-of-existence". To that extent, the tenant's livelihood is secure. However, the landlord has to live himself, too. And this at the luxury level. Thus the tenants have to produce those goods which can maintain the landlord and his class at the "level-of-luxury". Consequently the limits of production in feudalism are defined by the limits of consumption of the *zamindars*. It needs to be emphasised that the *zamindar* class itself did not participate in production. The *zamindars*, like feudal lords elsewhere in the world, spent their lives in luxury. The production was made up of two types: (i) necessary production, from the social point of view, to keep producers (tenants) alive and in production, (ii) surplus production, savings, from the social point of view, to keep the landlords in luxury. In the case of the Indian *zamindari* system, this surplus had to be divided between the *zamindar*, the petty exploiter, and the occupying British government, the super-exploiter.

Since production is carried on by the tenant, there is a limit to exploitation. Beyond a certain point, the exploitation becomes counterproductive to the *zamindar*—not to the British exploiter.[36] (Also the *zamindar* spends his time in luxurious living and has thus little time to supervise exploitation)!

At the production end, there is no incentive for either the tenant or the *zamindar* to increase the quantity of production. Investment in land by the landlord involves reduction in time and expenditures for consumption.[37] Also there is no way to make tenants work harder. On the other hand, the tenant has no resources to invest in greater production. Further, the gains of any additional improvements will be appropriated by the landlord, and so there is no incentive for him to produce more. Hence, the institution of *zamindari* is not capable of producing high yields per acre. Major studies show that labour as well as land productivity is low in such a system. The institution of *zamindari* encourages the method of production which is land intensive, i.e., it uses more land per unit of output; in other words land productivity is very low indeed.[38] Production is carried on purely by custom or tradition. Some economists argue that the method of production described under technique I is also suitable to the *zamindari* system; the emphasis in this method of production being on using the least amount of inputs.

Economists argue that the reasons why the productivity in India is low, can be sought in this institution. If we go back to Graph 5.1 (p. 96), these economists argue that the situation in India is in the region *Y*. Thus, if the institutional framework can be changed so as to make more production worth the while of the tenants or tillers or farmers, then even with technique I, productivity can be increased. It is on this basis that they argue for land reforms. However, *zamindari* has been, legally at least, abolished in all states by the laws pertaining to "land ceilings".

Capitalistic System of Production
Development of the capitalistic system of production involves the generalization of commodity production. "Everything that is the object of economic life, everything that is produced is henceforth a commodity, all foodstuffs, all consumer goods, all raw materials, all means of production, including labour power itself."[39] In other words, everything is now produced to be sold in the market for exchange. Production is not decided on because it

satisfies a basic human need, but because it can be exchanged for money. This process extends also to the producer and the worker. "The producer separated from his means of production is no longer master of the products of his labour and can live only by selling, that is, by making a commodity of, his own labour power, in exchange for a wage which enables him to acquire these means of life. The transition from petty commodity production to capitalistic production properly so-called is thus marked by two parallel phenomena. On the one hand, the transformation of labour power into a commodity, on the other, the transformation of means of production into capital."[40]

In terms of agricultural production, it means that owning land is no longer a matter of prestige and the prerogative of the aristocracy. There is no one to lord over the land. Instead land is now a means of production, hence, capital. The owner now is not a landlord but a capitalist[41]: the motivation of the capitalist is to make as large a profit as he can. To do so, he must choose those crops which are most profitable. The most profitable crops are those where the difference in price and cost per unit is the largest. There are two ways to make profits:[42] (i) to produce crops that are in high demand, whose price is high, assuming the cost of production is the same, and (ii) to produce as large a quantity as possible. Since the very purpose of production in the capitalistic system is to make a profit, the system is conducive to production in larger quantities. However, it is quite possible that a part, even a large part, of this production may not be socially useful.[43]

In this system, the actual tiller of the land becomes a wage-earner. The capitalist treats the actual tiller of land like any piece of capital. The wage-earner is now a commodity. The capitalist will employ the tiller so long as it is profitable for him. If the production is not profitable, the tiller of the land loses his job and becomes unemployed. Thus under this system, though actual production is liable to be greater than under feudalism, the actual tiller of the land has no security, and generally speaking the wage rate is not high. The actual tiller then remains poor and loses the little security he had under feudalism.

Since the capitalist has no personal relation with the actual tiller of the land, he can easily substitute other forms of energy for the human energy. The change in the form of energy may be more productive of output, but it certainly is very destructive of the human being whose energy is being substituted.

In the history of Indian agriculture, the *ryotwari* system[44] or peasant proprietorship, provided the capitalistic institutions of production. By and large, land holdings were not so large as to need the employment of wage labour. The family itself worked hard. One of the reasons why labour productivity in Punjab is higher than in other states is because of the early introduction of this institution in Punjab. Of course, there are other reasons as well: availability of more water, larger size of holdings, etc., The land reform movement is basically a movement to develop capitalistic institutions—and wind up feudalistic ones. This happens because ceilings are being placed on the ownership of land. Thus a particular family cannot hold land which is beyond a certain size. Since the *zamindari* system involves the ownership of a large area of land, ceilings on land will replace feudalism by capitalism.

Green Revolution

The example, par excellence, of the capitalistic modes of production in Indian agriculture are the farms that have been involved in what has been euphorically called the Green Revolution. What has happened is that some of the capitalistic farmers, with comparatively larger holdings, centred in Punjab and Haryana, buttressed by large doses of "aid" by Government in the form of research, raw materials (fertilizers, insecticides, "better" type seeds, etc.), and subsidies support (insurance of buying the output at a particular price and allowing prices for tools and implements, etc.), as well as "aid" by some of the aid-giving agencies of the USA in India, have successfully substituted technique II for technique I.

The nature of the capitalistic mode of production is judged by the evidence from Ashok Rudra.[45] According to this evidence, only large farmers can make the type of investment needed for technique II (Table 5.7).

Table 5.7. Capital Expenditure on Some Items on the Big Farms in Punjab (1967–68)
(in rupees)

Size and Group in Acres	Tractors	Tubewells and Equipment	Repairs	Building[a] Land Repairs etc.
20–25	1,900	2,000	500	1,100
30–40	4,400	2,200	900	1,850
50–75	7,600	4,700	1,900	3,500
100–150	21,000	—	7,000	6,750

[a]Expenditure on buildings, etc., is an average of two years (1966–68).

SOURCE: Rudra, "Big Farmers of Punjab".

With such large capital expenditure, the capitalist has to decide whether to invest in industry or agriculture. Investment in agriculture becomes rational only if it is profitable. There is now some evidence that the investment in technique II is more profitable than investment in technique I. This evidence is contained in Table 5.8, giving information on productivity, expenditures and incomes on the production of different varieties of wheat in a particular area. The different varieties of wheat involve different techniques of production. Thus, *desi* wheat involves technique I and the Mexican variety *kalyan* is produced by technique II.

The switch to technique II from technique I has resulted in both larger profits and output. Since the capitalist farmer is interested in larger profits, and Government in increase in the quantity of foodgrain production, both these interests have coincided in technique II. Government is, thus, encouraging the spread of technique II. The result has been a continuous growth in the use of technique II. All the indices confirm this growth process. Table 5.9 gives the data on the targeted and actual area under the technique II type of production. Technique II is sometimes referred to as High Yielding Varieties (HYV) of seeds.

Also, the consumption of fertilizers has increased rapidly as suggested by Table 5.10.

Table 5.8. Yield, Income, Expenditure and Profit per Acre in Different Varieties of Wheat in Amritsar (Punjab)

Varieties	Yield (in maunds)	Income (Rs.)	Expenditure (Rs.)	Profit (Rs.)
Desi	16.84	521	124	397
Kalyan	38.45	1,223	390	833

NOTES: 1. Profit is defined as income-expenditure.

2. Income is defined as output multiplied by price.

SOURCE: H. Laxminarayan, "The Small Farmer Should be the Strategy Base", *Yojana*, 8 December 1968, p. 5.

Table 5.9. Area Under High Yielding Varieties of Seeds (Thousand hectares)

Foodgrains	1966–67 Target	1966–67 Actual	1968–69 Target	1968–69 Actual	1969–70 Target
Rice	1,315	887	3,440	2,630	3,240
Wheat	644	540	2,023	4,050	4,050
Total foodgrains	2,860	1,837	8,499	8,500	10,920

SOURCE: Datt and Sundharam, *Indian Economy*, p. 486.

Table 5.10. Consumption of Fertilizers
(in 100 tons)

Year	Consumption
1950–51	69
1955–56	130
1960–61	289
1965–66	785
1968–69	1760
1973–74	3839

SOURCE: Datt and Sundharam, *Indian Economy*, p. 332.

The growth of consumption of fertilizers is obviously large. In the past 20 years it has virtually increased 20 times.

The effect of the introduction of technique II has been to increase both the output and land productivity. Table 5.11 gives some idea of the magnitudes.

Table 5.11. Production and Average Yield of Principal Crops
(Production in million tons)

	1960–61	1964–65	1969–70
Rice	34.6	39.0	40.4
	(1,013)	(1,073)	(1,073)
Wheat	11.0	12.3	20.1
	(851)	(913)	(1,209)
Maize	4.1	4.7	5.7
	(926)	(1,009)	(968)
Bajra	3.2	4.4	5.3
	(286)	(380)	(426)
Jawar	9.8	9.7	9.7
	(533)	(503)	(522)

NOTE: Figures in brackets refer to yield in kilograms per hectare (the land productivity).

SOURCE: Datt and Sundharam, *Indian Economy*, p. 435.

Since technique II has demonstrated its capacity to increase the total output and since Government accords high priority to the increase in the production of foodgrains, the technique is here to stay. In 1968–69, some 17 million acres were under technique II. In view of the technicalities of production required by technique II, it can be used only in irrigated areas. The total irrigated area in 1968–69 was 67 million acres. Technique II, thus, can be extended to 50 million acres more. Assuming technique II produces an additional (to technique I) 0.6 tons per acre of foodgrains, the extension of technique II will produce an additional 30 million tons of foodgrains. Considering that in 1968–69 the total output was around 95 million tons, the additional 30 million tons should virtually "solve the problem of food and agriculture in India". Hence, the "new strategy" or the "new technology", as our technique II is generally called, seems very attractive indeed.

Prospects

The need for increased foodgrain production continues with population growth. Government policy has recognized this fact. Since the Bengal famine in 1943, Government policy, through the medium of the Grow More Food Campaign and Five-Year Plans, has been fully involved in the promotion of increased production. The following policy steps have been taken:

1. More area has been brought under cultivation.

2. Irrigation has been extended to a larger area.

3. Foodgrains have been imported in large quantities.

4. More financial resources have been provided to encourage investment in agricultural production.

5. Attempts have been made to change the institutional framework by the so-called land-reforms legislation.

6. Research has been conducted in varieties of seeds and technical relations of inputs that lead to higher production.

7. Supplies of inputs like fertilizers, insecticides, etc., have been imported to encourage the adoption and spread of technique II.

8. Price-support policies have been promulgated to ensure profitability in production.

The current emphasis of policy is to spread technique II further. So far this technique covers only 25 per cent of the irrigated area. Even if it is extended to the whole irrigated area, it will still not cover all the area in the country. However, even this extension forms a very large task. The problems arise from two sources: (i) availability of the supply of the necessary inputs, (ii) contradictions of technique II itself. Again, these are interrelated. Let us take them individually.

Availability of Supplies of Inputs
Ranjit Sau[46] has estimated the cost of production in technique II (Table 5.12).

Table 5.12. **Cost Per Acre of Wheat Under Technique II**

Item	Expenses (Rs)	% of Total Cost
Current		
Human labour	54.54	10.7
Bullock labour	66.08	10.9
Seeds	14.22	2.7
Insecticides	10.00	1.9
Irrigation	30.00	5.8
Fertilizer and Manure	195.00	38.5
Total Current	359.84	70.5
Capital	150.00	29.5
(interest on capital depreciation and other charges on marketing)		
Total Costs	509.84	100

SOURCE: Sau, "Resource Allocation in Indian Agriculture".

The largest costs in production are those of fertilizers, capital equipment and irrigation. Adequate supplies of both fertilizers and capital equipment are not produced in the country. By and large, these have to be imported. The extension of technique II, thus, implies a large demand for these inputs. Since the domestic industrial production is small, the question arises, can these be imported in sufficiently large quantities? The only way it is possible is by changing the composition of imports.

Again, no studies have been made regarding the availability of water for extended periods of production through this technique. At the moment, water may not be a scarce resource. However, there is the experience of Western countries which suggests that water itself may become a scarce resource.

Contradictions of Technique II
Any capitalistic system has its inner contradictions. These may be listed under two separate headings: (a) economic contradictions, (b) ecological contradictions.

Economic Contradictions
Unemployment Technique II requires large doses of energy which cannot be supplied by human and bullock labour. Accordingly, successful adoption requires capital investment in tools and implements such as tractors. As Table 5.12 suggests, the capital costs are 150 per cent of the total costs of human and bullock labour. Generally, tools and implements displace human labour. Martin Billings and Arjan Singh have done a study[47] to this effect. They conclude that by 1983–84, the displacement of labour will be of the order of 17.4 per cent of the total agricultural labour force; one person in every six. In other terms, 146 million man-days will be replaced. Fifty-five per cent of it will be done by tractors and pumpsets and 37 per cent by thrashers and reapers.

In itself, displacement of labour is not undesirable. If the displaced labour is fully employed elsewhere in industry, there is no problem. Actually, the theories of economic development hold the hope of development in just such a process of employing displaced labour. However, in the context of India, it may be extremely undesirable. In spite of the planning efforts and preoccupation of the planning body with employment policy, the economic system in India in the past 20 years has not been able to employ those people who freshly join the labour force. If you add the displacement of another 17 per cent, the unemployment problem will be so large as literally to generate a political revolution.

Imports The effect of technique II is to make the production of foodgrains import-intensive. It makes the country dependent upon the Western industrialized countries; particularly when the Western world is not very helpful. The concept of "self reliance", therefore, goes through the window. The effect of such imports is also to export the effective demand, thus making the situation still worse.

Take the case of wheat, for instance, under the New Agricultural Strategy. Of the total costs per acre of wheat, fertilizers and manures account for 38.5 per cent, while capital expenses per year claim 29.5 per cent.... As such nearly all of the cultivator's expenses on fertilizer and agricultural capital equipment goes out of the country in the course of payments for imports. Let us round it off at 60 per cent, and observe that three-fifths of the cost of production of wheat under the New Agricultural Strategy finds its way out of India through import trade, leaving only Rs. 40 within the country for every Rs. 100 spent to produce the wheat. Clearly in that case there would be a deficiency of demand for wheat. All the signs of overproduction would raise their heads no matter how many millions of people are starving side by side. The market does not recognize you if your wallet is empty.[48]

Inequalities Technique II is certainly more profitable. It is also more profitable for larger farms. Thus it encourages the capitalist to increase the size of the farm. This is done by continuously buying up the small land holders. Thus the small land holders are joining the rank of wage earners. Further, the technique leads to displacement of labour; it substitutes capital for labour. Accordingly, more people get unemployed while a small number of farmers becomes richer. The inequalities of income are thus becoming wider. Virtually every commentator or thinker has already pointed to this effect. It is this contradiction in terms of inequalities that is reflected in the statement that the "green revolution leads to the red revolution".

Ecological contradictions Technique I is ecologically sound; it has adapted itself to the larger environment. Technique II, however, is ecologically unsound, and does not fit into the biological cycle.

The ecological problem arises from breaking the biological cycle. The biological cycle is broken at two ends; (i) at the level of production of inputs

(a) pesticides, and (b) inorganic fertilizers; and (ii) at the level of their disposal. Since both the inputs have to be produced industrially, they require the process of making artificial chemical compounds. To do so, first the natural (organic) chemicals have to be broken up into their constituents and then compounded together into artificial chemicals. Both these processes require large doses of energy. The use of energy is one of the sources of pollution. According to the second law of thermodynamics, the use of large doses of energy implies an increase in entropy.

Once produced, these chemicals are used in the agricultural production process. The agricultural production cycle may not, and actually does not, have the capacity to completely biodegrade or utilize these chemical compounds. A part of these chemicals, thus, seeps into the environment and leads to environmental degradation.

When pesticides are applied (the high-yielding varieties do need an application of pesticides), the most susceptible insects die, leaving the least susceptible insects to reproduce. Because natural selection[49] promotes the evolution of resistance in pesticide targets, it becomes necessary to increase the dose and frequency of spraying the pesticides. It is, thus, a process that feeds on itself. The more pesticides are used, the more they are needed. Being a self-generating process, it is like an addiction.[50] Actually, in some parts of the world, resistance to three major groups of insecticides—chlorinated hydrocarbons, organic phosphates, and carbonates— is now widespread. There are also indirect effects. One group of pesticides, the chlorinated hydrocarbons, like DDT, DDD, DDE, etc., is highly resistant to oxidation and enzymatic attack. This resistance plus insolubility in water results in their concentration at the top of the food chain which leads to the extinction of some species.

Inorganic fertilizers also have similarly harmful effects. Fertilizers (nitrates as well as phosphates) seep into water. The nitrate content of water rises, which is conducive to algae growth. Algae consume large amounts of oxygen so that the living organisms in water, like fish, die (this is what water pollution is all about.) Inorganic fertilizers "loosen" the nitrogen cycle in the soil by short-cutting certain steps. Like pesticides, the more fertilizers are used, the more they are needed. They are also addictive. Also like pesticides, fertilizers do not remain where they are applied but are dispersed in and contaminate unexpected places. Fertilizers spread through rain and underground water.

In view of the ecological contradiction, just as the productivity of technique II is large, so is the likelihood it will lead to disaster.

REFERENCES

1. In the terminology of welfare economics, wage goods may be defined as goods the consumption of which leads directly to the production of utilities. In Marxian economics, these are the "basic" goods.

2. In terms of welfare economics, the utility comes from consumption, and raw materials are not directly consumable. To become consumable, these goods have to be processed. Their utility, therefore, is contingent upon the nature and availability of the facility processing them into the consumable form.

3. Initially, the plantation economy did not produce wage goods. Over time some of these goods have become a part of general consumption. Thus, tea was formerly produced purely for export. Over 150 years, tea has entered the consumption of every household.

4. The planting of tea in India and Ceylon, rubber in Malaysia, cocoa in Ghana, to take only a few examples, was enforced by the ruling English government for export to England.

5. Actually, there are three additional ways as well; namely, (i) beg, (ii) borrow, and (iii) steal. (i) In the international arena, begging is rarely possible. There is hardly any nation that gives away these goods for charity. Some propagandists (prestigious professors can also be, and many times are, propagandists) of Western countries have generated a myth, by the use of such terms as "aid", "grants", etc., that the Western countries are giving away these goods to the poor countries. In reality such charity is only a myth and the poor countries pay through their noses via political influence. Thus, in 1966 when India suffered a serious shortage of these goods, as a result of underproduction due to two very bad droughts, the US government was able to force three policy changes; (a) devaluation, (b) liberalization of trade restrictions, and (c) permission to the US Corporations to produce fertilizers in the private sectors, in exchange for the "aid" in foodgrains. (ii) Borrowing is simply trade over time. It is thus, another form of trade. (iii) Stealing is done only by militarily strong countries. Unfortunately, poor countries are also militarily weak.

6. This is only a simplifying assumption.

7. More generally, we may ask the question: is $A = \sum_{i=1}^{n} A_i$? where A_i refers to the amount of production of the ith commodity. For example, $A_1 = $ rice; $A_2 = $ wheat; $A_9 = $ gram; $A_{11} = $ sugarcane; $A_{13} = $ cotton; $A_{16} = $ tea; etc.

8. More generally, $pA = \sum_{i=1}^{n} P_i A_i$; where p_i refers to the price of the ith commodity. For example, $p_1 = $ price per ton of rice; $p_2 = $ price per ton of wheat; $p_9 = $ price per ton of gram; $p_{11} = $ price per ton of sugarcane; $p_{13} = $ price per bale of 180 kilograms $p_{16} = $ price per ton of tea, etc.

9. In the general case, $A = \sum_{i=1}^{n} c_i A_i$; $c_i = (P_{i/p})$; $(i = 1, \ldots n)$. Since p is only a fictional number, it is legitimate to divide by P.

10. It is suggested that the reader should analyse the implications of this condition.

11. National income is also a fictional quantity and it is quite possible that National Income may be increasing while people feel more miserable. Some observers think that such a situation is already taking place in the USA.

12. It is suggested that the reader should find for himself the weighting scheme used in the determination of the index for "total output" in Table 5.3.

13. The general case follows from the equation: $$L = \sum_{i=1}^{n} L_i$$ where L and L_i refer to total labour used in all agriculture and total labour used in the production of commodity A_i respectively. Thus $n = L/A$ and $n_i = L_i/A_i$. It is suggested that the reader should develop some other methods to determine c_i so that the meanings of the weighting can be fully appreciated.

14. K. N. Raj, "Food Shortage: Failure of a Policy", *Times of India*, 20 January 1966, p. 8. In this connection also see M.L. Dantwala, "Food Policy; Misplaced Criticism", *Times of India*, 10 February 1966, p. 8; and Romesh Diwan, "The Debate on Food in India; Some Relevant Variables",

Economic and Political Weekly, 31 December 1966, pp. 849–856.

15. Romesh Diwan, "Debate on Food", p. 851.
16. These data are collected by the National Sample Survey in its various rounds.
17. V. M. Dandekar and Nilakantha Rath, "Poverty in India", *Economic and Political Weekly,* 2 January 1971, pp. 25–48, and 9 January 1971, pp. 100–146.
18. Ibid., p. 29.
19. The reader is requested to analyse Table 5.4 in order to understand and appreciate the gravity of this conclusion. In this connection also see Ranjit Sau, "Poverty in India, A Comment", *Economic and Political Weekly,* 20 March 1971; "The New Economics" *Economic and Political Weekly,* Special number 1972, pp. 1571–1580; and Romesh Diwan, "Planning for the Poor", *Economic and Political Weekly,* 21 August 1971, pp. 1809–1814.
20. Romesh Diwan, "The Debate on Food in India; Some Relevant Variables", *Economic and Political Weekly,* 31 December 1966, pp. 849–856. More precisely, the analysis is couched in terms of a dual economic system.
21. It is suggested that the reader should question this assertion and prove or disprove it by defining certain criteria and testing it with the actual production data.
22. One of the reasons why some of the agricultural crops cannot be grown in Britain, Sweden, etc., is the lack of sunshine.
23. Some argue that computers may be a substitute for mental energy. However, there is a lot of controversy on this issue.
24. A reader fascinated with some forms of algebra may work out these combinations. The questions is as follows: there are 7 inputs and these have $n_1, n_2, n_3, n_4, n_5, n_6, n_7$ forms. A combination of the 7 inputs generates a technique. How many techniques are there?
25. It may be pointed out that the effect of a change in technique is not only to change the input combination but also to change the physical qualities of the output.
26. When they talk of the "green revolution" in literature it is this method they have in mind.
27. This is the form associated with the Cobb-Douglas production function.
28. I am indebted to Professor Radha Sinha for elucidating the argument from this graph.
29. Professor Radha Sinha has not yet published his paper in which he has made this argument. He has very kindly allowed me to quote him.
30. Theodore W. Schultz, *Transforming Traditional Agriculture* (Chicago: The University of Chicago Press, 1964).
31. Interestingly, it is this question that separates the classical from the neoclassical economists. Classical economists believed in the importance of institutions. Neoclassicals believe that the institutions hardly play any role.
32. It is suggested that the reader should analyse the various principles in these systems and apply these to a concrete situation. For example, does sharecropping involve capitalistic or feudalistic modes of production?

Again, is the cooperative movement, particularly cooperative farming, a capitalistic or a socialistic institution?
33. It will be noticed that the term *zamindar* is made up of *zamin*—land and *dar*—possess. Thus *zamindar* is the person who possesses the land; the lord of the land.
34. The princely states in India, perhaps, had similar serf-like tenants.
35. For an understanding of the Zamindari System in India, See Romesh Dutt, *Economic History of India,* vols. I and II (London: Oxford University Press, 1903). These volumes were written around 1900 and Romesh Dutt represented the interests of the landlords. The books analyse, inter alia, the economic impact of the various forms of the Zamindari System—Permanent Settlement versus Temporary Settlement.
36. This distinction is very important and needs to be clearly understood.
37. Feudalism is not only a mode of production but also a way of life. For a lucid expression of this idea see Satyajit Ray's film, "Jalsaghar"—"Music Room".
38. Eugene Genovese has convincingly argued that the US Civil War can be explained by the institution of slavery (another way of saying landlordism). Productivity by the slave-owning white landlords in the South was so low that they could compete with the North only by acquiring more land; hence the Civil War. See Eugene D. Genovese, *The Political Economy of Slavery* (New York: Random House, 1965).
39. Ernest Mandel, *Marxist Economic Theory,* vol. I (New York: Monthly Review Press, 1969), p. 126.
40. Ibid., pp. 119–120.
41. It is not necessary that the capitalist be rich or his land holding large. The owner could be a small capitalist as well. The important thing is that the owner behaves like a capitalist.
42. We refer here only to the "legitimate" methods of making a profit. There are other methods, like plundering, looting, stealing, etc., which are used quite commonly. Once one decides to make profits, there is nothing sacrosanct about a particular method. In this case, the ends fully justify the means.
43. There is a growing school of thought that argues that many of the poor countries devote a comparatively large part of their resources to satisfy the demand of the rich countries and far less resources to satisfy the needs of the people of the poor countries.
44. There are quite a few varieties of this system. Basically these were determined by the method of payment of the land revenue. Still, in these systems, land ownership vested in the person or family who actually carried on the production.
45. Ashok Rudra, Majid and Talib of the Agriculture Centre of the University of Delhi conducted research in capitalistic farming in Punjab. Some of the results of this research are contained in Ashok Rudra, "Big Farmers of Punjab", *Economic and Political Weekly,* 27 December 1969.

46. Ranjit Sau, "Resource Allocation in Indian Agriculture", *Economic and Political Weekly Review of Agriculture,* 25 September 1971.

47. Martin H. Billings and Arjan Singh, "Mechanisation and Rural Employment", *Economic and Political Weekly,* 27 June 1970.

48. Ranjit Sau, "The New Economics", *Economic and Political Weekly,* Special Annual Number 1972, p. 1575.

49. This is based on the Darwinian principle of survival of the fittest.

50. मरज बड़ता गया जूँ जूँ दवा की : With each dose of medicine the sickness increased.

6

Agrarian Structure and Land Reforms in India

J. S. UPPAL

"Agrarian structure" covers the institutional framework of agriculture, and it includes distribution of ownership of land, forms of land tenure, and pattern of agricultural employment. Ownership of land refers to property rights: private or public or cooperative ownership, the question of ownership of land—the major means of production in agricultural economies like India—is crucial from the point of view of the political structure of the society (e.g., capitalistic or socialistic), concentration of political and economic power, and also from the point of view of economic incentives for work effort and risk taking. Land tenure refers to the possession of rights to the use of land. People holding different kinds of rights in the use of land vary between the two extremes of owner operators and landless agricultural labourers. Between these extremes are cooperative cultivators, share croppers, *bergadars, panniyals,* etc., and numerous combinations of these groupings. The tenure arrangements influence the efficiency with which inputs are used and they also affect the degree of uncertainty encountered in the operation

of a farm. The pattern of employment indicates the arrangement used to employ agricultural workers (e.g., share cropping, serfdom, wage-paid labour). The institutional framework deals essentially with the man behind the plough and thus, the right type of framework is a necessary and highly desirable condition for socio-economic development.

Land reform in a broader and philosophical sense covers improvements of all facets of institutional arrangements mentioned above. In the operational sense, land reform measures entail:

1. Land redistribution or distributive measures: abolition of intermediaries and absentee landlords, transfer of ownership of landholdings, already under peasant cultivation, from landowners to peasants. The change in ownership involves two phases: (i) taking over the land with or without exemptions and compensation, and (ii) distribution involving terms of ownership rights to be conferred and size of the holding to be allocated.

2. Tenancy arrangements: regulation of rent; security of tenure for tenants; ceiling and floor levels on land holdings, and

3. Agrarian reorganization including consolidation of small holdings and prevention of their subdivision and fragmention.

The needs for land reform involve social, economic and political considerations. The necessity for land reforms is essentially due to various shortcomings in the agrarian structure of underdeveloped societies, leading to intractable problems of rural poverty. The literature on economic development in general, and agricultural development of underdeveloped economies in particular, abounds in justifications of the need for land reforms. The following quote from an early United Nations document sums up the case for land reforms quite well:

> Among the features of the agrarian structure which have most serious effects are the uneconomic size of farms, the maldistribution of land ownership with concentration of large estates insufficiently utilized and the landlessness of a large part of the rural population; the fragmentation of holdings; the high rents and the insecurity of tenure characteristic of many tenancy systems; indebtedness and lack of adequate credit facilities for the small farmer; absence of settled title to land and water...; and in general an unsatisfactory set of incentives for rising and sustained agricultural production.[1]

Certainly in India, uneconomic size of farms, maldistribution of land ownership, insecurity of tenure conditions and high rents, characterize the rural society. Harold Mann believes that "the crucial obstacle to [rural progress] was the social one, the institutional framework of Indian agriculture... the fundamental obstacle to the taking up of improvements by the peasant was not technical or narrowly agricultural. It was rather a question of the very foundation of village economy and society".[2] These remarks seem to put more blame on "institutional" than on "technical" factors for the backwardness of the agrarian structure in India.

The objectives of land reforms have been succintly stated by the Indian Planning Commission:

Land Reforms... have two specific objects. The first is to remove such impediments to increase in agricultural production as arise from the agrarian structure inherited from the past. This should help to create conditions for evolving as speedily as possible an agricultural economy with high levels of efficiency and productivity. The second object, which is closely related to the first, is to eliminate all elements of exploitation and social injustice within the agrarian system, to provide security for the tiller of soil and assure equality of status and opportunity to all sections of the rural population.

These objectives are broad and comprehensive enough to cover all facets of the land reforms outlined earlier. Land reforms are viewed as means towards achieving equity, efficiency, and productivity in the Indian rural sector. In this chapter we will outline the land tenure system in India, and land reforms legislation, and then evaluate the various reform measures from the theoretical point of view. Lastly we will assess the implementation of land reform legislation, and its impact on various aspects of the Indian economy.

Land Systems in India

The land tenure systems during the pre-British period were static in character. The systems developed by the British were not greatly conducive to economic growth. The changes introduced aimed at maximizing the revenue flow to the government to the utter neglect of the interests of the peasantry and the economy.

During the pre-independence period, there were essentially three types of tenure: (i) the *zamindari*, (ii) the *mahalwari*, and (iii) the *ryotwari*.

At the beginning of British influence in India, the East India Company, and later the representatives of the Crown, had to deal with the landed interests. The Company was confronted with long-established customs and usages. The land-revenue system prevailing at that time dated far back to the days of the Hindu kings prior to Moghul rule. Under the system, the king was entitled to one-sixth of the gross produce. In the later days of the Moghul Empire, some reforms such as the form of cadastral survey was introduced. The option of payment of revenue in kind or cash was left to the cultivator. Later on, collective assessments were introduced. Settlements were made with the provincial chief or any person in authority, for a fixed annual revenue and the imperial share was raised to 50 per cent of the produce. The obvious result was oppression of the cultivators, who were forced to pay exorbitant rates. The East India Company continued the system by assigning the collection of land revenue to the *zamindars* and chiefs in the provinces of Bengal, Bihar, and Orissa.

During Warren Hastings' period, Temporary Settlements were tried but with disastrous results. Lord Cornwallis introduced the Permanent Settlement in Bengal. Under this system, the *zamindars* who were only the agents of Government, were declared full proprietors of the areas where they collected land revenue. The land revenue assessment was fixed at 10/11ths of what the *zamindar* collected as rent from the cultivators, the balance going to the *zamindars* as remuneration. The system gave an open hand to the *zamindars* and landlords to extract the highest possible rents from the cultivators. They became in effect a parasitic class with only this interest.

The system of Permanent Settlement was extended to Banaras, North Madras and certain parts of South Madras Presidency. It then ran into difficulties and was therefore given up in favour of the *ryotwari* system.

Two noticeable phenomena constituted the outgrowth of the Permanent Settlement. First, the *zamindars* enriched themselves by collecting exorbitant rents, thereby impoverishing the peasants, second, the owner cultivators were reduced to tenants.

The *mahalwari* or Joint Village system was first adopted in Agra and Oudh and later extended to Punjab in the early 1800's. Under this system, individual villages were considered units in themselves. Joint ownership of property was recognized. The villages or *mahals* were settled with directly. The primary liability of

paying land revenue was generally assigned to a co-sharer of standing (called by different names, e.g., *namberdar* in Punjab) in the village. The state's share varied between 40 and 70 per cent of the rental. In spite of the joint character of the village, and the method of payment of land revenue, the system led to the break-up of the old village community and the growth of individualistic attitudes in the cultivators.

The *ryotwari* system was introduced in Madras by Thomas Monroe in 1772, and was later extended to Bombay. Under this system, the land holder was held responsible for paying the land revenue to Government. There were no intermediaries between the cultivator and Government. Under the *ryotwari* system, the lands were heritable, transferable and alienable without the sanction of Government. Failure to pay land revenue would result in forfeiture of this right. The powers of discretion given the Settlement Officer, coupled with the possibility of periodical enhancement of land revenue, deprived the system of benefits that would have otherwise accrued to the proprietor. Moreover, the claim of the State led to the destruction of the collective basis of village organization and life.

Land Reforms in India

The Abolition of the Zamindari System
Strong sentiments against the *zamindari* system had already developed before Independence. In 1928, the All India Congress Committee declared that the abolition of landlordism must occupy a prominent place in our programme"[4]. Absentee landlords were accused of being oppressive, and in general the high rents obtained from the tenants were frittered away on conspicuous consumption, rather than used for capital formation. In the absence of any State interference, absentee owners exploited the actual tillers by indulging in rack-renting, evictions, *begar* (service without payment). Abolition of the *zamindari* system, to be replaced by a system of "land to the tiller," became a part of the national movement for political and economic independence from alien rule.

After Independence, high priority was given to the abolition of intermediary tenures (*zamindars*). Accordingly, every state enacted its own legislation to abolish this tenure system with payment of compensation. Basically, the law provided for the State take-over of the estates of *zamindars* on payment of compensation, and offering ownership to cultivators on payment of fixed sums. The process of legislative actions commencing in 1948, was completed in 1954, by which time most states had adopted the necessary legislation. During this interim period of 6 years, *Zamindari* Abolition Acts were challenged in the High Courts and later taken to the Supreme Court for adjudication. The Supreme Court, while upholding the rights of the state legislatures to take over lands for public purposes, ruled that the question of the adequacy of compensation was a justiciable issue. A constitutional amendment to meet the ruling of the Supreme Court was effected, and also the laws already passed regarding the rates of the method of payment of compensation were revised. However, during the six-year period of confusion, the *zamindars* not only extracted more compensation for the expropriated rights, they also resorted to steps such as resuming personal cultivation, eviction of tenants by force or social pressure, and parcelling of the estates to obviate the law.

What are the results of the abolition of the *zamindari* system? According to the Fifth Five-Year Plan "...about 20 million tenants are estimated to have come into direct contact with the State".[5] As a result of conferment of rights, more than 3 million tenants and share croppers acquired ownership rights over a total cultivated area of 6.22 million acres. This is described as a "great achievement, a kind of silent revolution", which helped India's infant democracy and enhanced the process of nation-building. Some critics, however, point out the staggering amount of compensation involved Rs. 670 crores of which Rs. 275 crores was actually paid. Discussing the overall effect of the abolition of the *zamindari* system, Lawrence A. Veit remarks:

... even though this brought the government into closer contact with a great many tillers of

the soil, the devolution of wealth did not proceed very far. The losses were borne by a tiny number of landlords, who through various loopholes, continued to hold large estates. The benefits accrued to a larger, but still very limited, number of farmers. On the balance, the lowest echelons of society such as share croppers and day labourers neither gained nor lost from these rounds of land reform.[6]

The abolition of *zamindari* has, in this way, created a more broadly-based and powerful rural elite. Daniel Thorner has described this process in two states, Uttar Pradesh and Maharashtra:

The UP *Zamindari* Abolition Act has provided for a new hierarchy of tenure holders in place of the old one—at the top are the *bhumidars*, below them the *sirdars*, and still further down the *assomis*. At the bottom of the heap remain the mass of crop sharers, and landless labourers. The *zamindars* have disappeared but these same persons have been confirmed as landholders....For the great bulk of peasantry who were classified as *sirdars*, the rent remains exactly the same.[7]

The Bombay legislation has not created a new hierarchy on the land but simply preserved the old one: viz., landlords, permanent tenants, protected tenants, and the ordinary tenants. Below them persist the same large mass of crop sharers and landless labourers. ...[8]

Khusro, in his study on the economic effects of abolition of *zamindari* and land reforms in Hyderabad,[9] found large-scale evictions of tenants. He found that in ex-jagir areas, out of every hundred protected tenants created in 1951, only 45.39 retained their protected status by the beginning of 1955. Another 12.42 per cent had purchased the land and became owners, 2.58 per cent had been evicted under the laws, and 17.38 per cent of the protected tenants voluntarily surrendered their rights. Apart from so-called voluntary surrenders, as many as 22.14 per cent were illegally evicted. Additional tenancy reform legislation had to be passed to prevent these massive evictions.

Tenancy Reforms
The sad social and economic plight of tenants and also their sheer numbers call

for serious and concerted efforts for improvement of their lot. Broadly speaking, tenants can be divided into (i) tenants at will, (ii) sub-tenants, and (iii) occupancy or permanent tenants. While occupancy tenants enjoy fixity and security for rent and can receive reimbursement for improvement made on the land, the other categories, especially tenants-at-will, continue to suffer from serious disabilities. They are subject to ruthless exploitation, periodic enhancement of rent, eviction on any pretext. A high proportion of these tenants belong to the lower castes and backward social classes. They are, thus, in an extremely weak position to deal with land owners who are in a comparatively stronger position. Tenants constitute 12.7 per cent of the total agricultural population, and tenants' households constitute 23.6 per cent of the total cultivating households in India. The percentage of area leased out forms 20 per cent of the total cultivated area, though this ratio varies in the states, ranging from 27.0 in the Punjab to 6.7 per cent in Madhya Pradesh.

What should the appropriate public policy objectives in dealing with tenancy problems of insecurity of tenure, and excessive rent charged, be from a theoretical point of view? The basic function of tenancy is to allow two parties, landowners and tenants, to combine their inputs into a single producing unit. Economic theory tells us that for maximizing net revenue an owner-operator will carry production to the point where the value of marginal product is equal to the price of the inputs. In tenant–land owner arrangements, each party is utilizing inputs belonging to the other. If each party considers the inputs contributed by the other party to have zero price (as is generally the case), there will be a tendency to use the other party's inputs up to the point where the value of the marginal product is zero. The landowner would tend to push the use of the tenant's labour to the point of zero marginal product. The tenant, on the other hand, considers the price of land to be zero while for the landowner, it is his important investment. The tenant, in that case, will have an incentive to use the additional land as long

as the value of its marginal product of land is greater than zero. The tenancy arrangement, thus, creates a conflict of interests. Another case of conflicting interests is the degree of certainty of tenure for tenants. Insecurity of tenure is frequently pointed out as a major problem in tenancy arrangements. Uncertainty is said to prevent cultivating tenants from making long-term plans for improvements on land and methods of cultivation. Recent legislation has been aimed at protecting tenants. In some countries (especially in Europe) security of tenure has been increased to a degree which resembles ownership. Landlords have been reduced to little more than rent receivers, much as though they were mortgage holders in the property. It is interesting that this type of feeling also exists among landowners in India,[10] and the resultant hesitancy on their part in renting their holdings. This high degree of security for tenants can be criticised as favouring misallocation of resources. If the landlord is to fulfil his role in the agricultural economy as an active partner, he should enjoy security for his investment, in land and other fixed investments. This, in turn, would require less security for tenants. This conflict in interests should be resolved by carefully weighing the relative priority given to objectives such as equity and efficiency. There are several other important considerations affecting tenant–land owner arrangements such as fixed rent versus rent varying with output, length of tenure and the question of compensating tenants for capital improvements.[11] Khusro has provided a theoretical basis for the empirical findings in India that "where there is no cost-sharing by the landlord, acre for acre, the tenant-farmers invest less per acre than owner-farmers and hence produce less per acre too".[12] It can be shown by equating marginal revenue and marginal cost curves for a one-half share rental arrangement, that if landlord and tenant share variable costs in the same proportion as they share the returns from the farm, ʼoptimum use of the inputs is the same as for an owner-operated farm.

The various states of India have enacted tenancy reform legislation to protect the weaker position of tenants of different categories as outlined above. These measures pertain to (1) regulation of rent, (2) security of tenure, and (3) conferment of ownership on tenants.

1. Regulation of rents. Maximum rent payable by a tenant is not to exceed a fixed proportion of the crop of value thereof. This proportion varies in different states, ranging from one-sixth of the gross produce in Gujarat, Maharashtra and Rajasthan, to 33.3–40 per cent in Tamil Nadu. Generally rents are paid in kind, which is perhaps a legacy of the barter and subsistence economy. In Maharashtra, tenants can get their crop-share rents commuted into cash rents irrespective of the landlords' wishes. The Planning Commission, India, proposes to reduce the maximum proportion of rent to one-fourth or one-fifth of the gross produce in the states with presently higher permissible ratios. The Planning Commission has also recommended that "produce rents, which are difficult to enforce should be abolished and replaced by fixed cash rents so that the uncertainties arising out of annual fluctuations in rents may be eliminated and the tiller assured of the full benefits of his investment".[13]

2. Security of Tenure. Legislation providing for security of tenure has been enacted in all states with variations in detail of different provisions for eviction, definition of personal cultivation, etc. Basic elements in the state laws are:

(a) Evictions: A tenant can be evicted only on the basis of legal provision. Generally, a cultivator can be evicted on the following grounds: failure to pay rent, failing to cultivate land, use of land rendering it unfit for cultivation, area held being in excess of the permissible limit. It has also been provided that if a tenant is evicted, such land should be leased to other cultivating tenants.

(b) Resumption of self-cultivation: Landowners can resume land for self-cultivation, but there is an upper limit (family-holding size) beyond which they cannot resume land. Again, details differ in different states, but in most, the cultivator must be left with a minimum of land beyond which only the

owner can resume cultivation.

The definition of self-cultivation is vague, with the result that, according to the Indian Planning Commission, "in many cases lands may have been resumed ostensibly on grounds of personal cultivation, but are cultivated through arrangements lacking some of the essential elements of personal cultivation".[14] Thus under the guise of "personal cultivation", evictions took place on a massive scale. The term "self-cultivation" needs rigorous definition and it is suggested that "personal labour" by the owner should be considered an essential element of "self-cultivation".

Another problem regarding security of tenure is that quite often the tenancy arrangement is made on an oral informal basis, and thus the tenant can face ejectment and be forced to pay rent higher than the prescribed limit, without having any resort to legal protection. "Voluntary surrenders of land by tenants is another device commonly used by landowners to disguise the forceable eviction of tenants. The Fifth Five-Year Plan is aware of this malpractice and it asserts that "...there were large-scale ejectments through the device of 'voluntary surrenders', many tenancies have been converted into *Nawkarnamas,* and crop-sharing arrangements remain largely oral and informal. Thus the objectives of tenancy reform still remain to be attained".[15]

3. Conferring Right of Ownership. Since the achievement of Peasant Proprietorship is the cornerstone of India's land policy, the states have enacted legislation to enable tenant cultivators to become owners of lands on which the landowners cannot resume ownership, on payment of specified compensation (fixed price or multiple of rent, etc.). According to the Planning Commission's estimates, about 3 million tenants and share-croppers have been able to acquire ownership of more than 7 million acres of land under this provision.

Ceiling on Land Holdings
An important part of land reforms relates to the fixation of a ceiling or an upper limit on land holdings and also, by implication defining a "floor" level or lower limit on land holding. There are two elements

here: one is related to the fixation of ceiling above which nobody can hold land, and this will be applicable to future holders as well; the second is concerned with acquisition of surplus land from holdings above the ceiling, for distribution among farmers and landless labourers to bring them up to ceiling level. The object is two-fold: both to reduce the size of land-holding of big landowners, and also to increase the size of holdings of small culti-vators. There are great variations among different states in details about (i) unit of application, (ii) maximum limit, and (iii) exemptions.

Uptil 1972, ceiling legislation largely treated the individual landholder as the unit of application. This enabled larger families to keep large amounts of land, e.g., a family of five in Andhra Pradesh could keep $300 \times 5 = 1,500$ acres of land. On the recommendation of the Central Land Reforms Committee (1971), the basis of fixation of ceiling has since been adopted as family which is defined as consisting of husband, wife and children with a special provision for larger families (with more than 5 children), to hold land in excess of the ceiling at specified amounts.

Maximum Limit Prior to 1972, the ceiling level had a wider range, e.g., 27–324 acres in Andhra Pradesh; 22-336 acres in Rajasthan; 30–80 acres in Punjab and Haryana. After 1972, the upper limits of the ceiling were lowered and the range was narrowed. Generally speaking, the range of ceiling was fixed at 10–18 acres for land which had assured water supply and yielded at least two crops. The acreage is adjusted with reference to irrigation facilities and cropping pattern. As stated earlier, the unit of application was a family holding— defined as a piece of land sufficient to yield Rs. 1,200 of net farm income per year with some adjustments for variation in family size, and the minimum or basic holding was to be one-third of the family holding. The ceiling would be 3 times the family holding. Households with land above the ceiling were to surrender the excess land, with compensation (equal to some multiple of rent). The surplus land would be allotted to landless families or to those with less than a basic holding.

In the per-1972 legislation, there were a large numbr of exemptions, e.g., 20 types in Uttar Pradesh, 17 in Kerala, 13 in Punjab, and these fell into three categories: (i) transfer among family members, since the individual was a unit of application; (ii) *benami* transfers, and (iii) transfers for specific considerations, e.g., area under orchards, model farms. This large number of exemptions led to massive amounts of transfer. Thus, as the Fifth Five-Year Plan admits "... the results achieved have been meagre due to the high ceiling level, large number of exemptions from the law, mala fide transfers and partitions and poor implementation". Uptil 1974, only about one million hectares of land had been declared surplus and about 0.53 million hectares of land had been distri-buted to landless agricultural workers and small farm holders. It is distressing that in some states, Bihar, Karnataka, and Orissa, no land was declared surplus on the imposition of ceiling legislation.[17] Provision for exemptions has been tightened since 1972 and they are now only permitted for specified purposes such as (i) plantations of tea, coffee, rubber, cardamom, and cocoa; (ii) land held by industrial or commercial undertakings; and (iii) sugar-cane factories which are permitted to retain an area not exceeding 100 acres. Despite the restrictiveness of legislation, its implementation is still far from satisfactory.

As pointed out earlier, imposition of ceilings on land holdings is a crucial instru-ment of land policy in India to achieve the goals of equity, social justice and efficiency. We will now discuss the relationship between land reforms, parti-cularly ceilings, and the above objectives of land policy:

Land Ceilings and Productivity
The relationship between ceilings on land holdings and productivity has a direct bearing on economic development. There is a popular misconception that since the imposition of ceilings reduces the size of bigger farms, the output would be adversely affected because smaller farms cannot practise economies of scale and have no access to investment funds. The view that there exists a highly positive relationship

between the size of farm holding and agricultural productivity, is based on misinterpretation of Western agriculture, especially of farm management studies in USA, Australia, and Canada: economies with land-abundant and labour-scarce factor endowment situation. The problem is totally different in overpopulated underdeveloped economies like India where almost all production factors (e.g., capital, land) except labour, are limiting. In such economies, the marginal cost of labour approaches zero (or even negative), suggesting that there may be a positive social value in employing additional labour to the point of its zero marginal product. With high unemployment and underemployment in Indian agriculture being further accentuated with increasing population, labour will, from the social standpoint, continue to be a non-cost element at any forseeable levels of increased agricultural productivity. Thus, in contrast to the highly developed economies, the criterion of the relative efficiency of Indian farms of different sizes must be viewed in terms of returns to nonlabour resources. In other words, in Indian agriculture, gross value product *per acre*, above variable cost, would be the most relevant measure of efficiency against net-income per unit of labour under American conditions.

Several empirical studies on the relative productivity of different size farms in India have shown an inverse relationship between the size of farm and value of output per acre. Using data developed by the Farm Management Research Centres in India for different states, Erving Long has computed gross output per acre on different sizes of farm and his results clearly show that the gross output per acre decreases with increase in farm sizes.[18] This conclusion also remains unchanged when he relates size of farm to gross value of product above variable cost. On the basis of an elaborate statistical analysis of the Farm Management Studies data for the period 1954–55 to 1955–56, Khusro reaches the following conclusions on the relationship between farm size and productivity: "If acreage is taken at its (uncorrected) face value, then as acreage increases, gross output per acre decreases;

if acreage is corrected with an index of fertility—gross output per corrected acre remains constant as farm size increases."[19] Later, similar studies using 1960's data by Vashishtha and Saini do not show any major changes in the relative efficiency and productivity of farms of varying size.[20] From these results, Khusro reaches an important conclusion: " ... there is nothing to choose between large farms and small farms in respect to cost efficiency and productivity; that Indian agriculture is typically a scene of constant return to scale; and the ceilings are size-neutral". If the per acre productivity is relatively greater on smaller farms than the larger ones, and if the former are greater in number (as is certainly the case in India), reducing the size of larger farms through imposition of ceilings may in fact increase the overall productivity and economic development.

This raises an important related question: should there be a minimum size of holding or "floor level" holding? Though the Indian Planning Commission's panel on land reforms uses the term "family holding" (explained in an earlier section), and also the term "basic holding" (minimum size holding) is mentioned in the land reform legislation, the proposed limits on upper and lower sizes have not been worked out by any rigorous analysis of farm data. Evidently, the determination of size of economic holding has to take into consideration various factors such as fertility of soil, methods of cultivation, and nature of crops. Recently Khusro has done a rigorous analysis of Farm Management Studies data and come up with useful estimates on the sizes of the "minimum feasible" and "optimum" holdings. He computes the "minimum size holdings" separately for "plough unit" (holding size below which a single pair of bullocks remain underemployed) at 7.5 acres; "work unit" (holding size below which family labour will be underemployed with the prevailing techniques) at 7.5 acres; and finally "income unit" (holding size below which the adequate business income of Rs. 12,000 per farm will not accrue to the farming family) at 15 acres. Khusro reconciles the three different minima of bullock, work and income norms, on the basis of present realities and future patterns of the Indian rural sector and suggests 5 acres as the minimum level, which he regards as "a dividing line between incentives and disincentives and between efficiency and disability". According to Khusro, "it will presumably be an objective of land policy to fix floors for the landless and marginal farmers at not much less than 5 acres."[22] Applying this "minimum holding size" to the ownership of holdings data published by the National Sample Survey, Khusro estimates that while 68.7 per cent of all land-operating households have an area less than 5 acres each, only 16.7 per cent of total owned acreage is subject to size disabilities.[23] These are very significant results for the formulation of a meaningful land policy.

Impact on Investment
Even if the land redistribution programme is implemented, the level of farm productivity will ultimately be determined by the levels of capital formation and farm investments. What will the investment behaviour of the small farm operators be? Conventional wisdom suggests that on small farms the capital invested per acre will be smaller than on larger farms on account of the higher propensity to consume of the small-farm holders and also of their inability to borrow funds from financial institutions. It is, perhaps, in connection with this view that Raj Krishna suggests active encouragement from Government for private rural savings.[24] The problem of low rate of capital formation by small farm operators could be somewhat solved by credit obtained from financial institutions, especially the nationalized banks and cooperative societies. But, as pointed out by Lawrence Veit,[25] the recent record of financial institutions in this respect has been rather disappointing. For example, in 1973, a report on the operations of credit societies in Maharashtra showed how difficult it is to help weaker members of the rural society.[26] An analysis of one crop season in West Bengal during 1971–72 shows that the nationalized banks financed only 111 share croppers in the state.[27] However, there is still real potential for using financial-institution credit to help small farm operators to finance their investment needs.

Land reforms have an important impact on the growth of social capital, and particularly human capital. The experience[28] of other countries with successful land reforms, e.g., Taiwan and Japan, show that land reform has impacts on investments in local services—education, health, recreation, transport, welfare, etc. A landlord-dominated economy usually provides for a separate system of these services to serve only the elite. Farm families, following land reform, used a substantial part of their increased incomes to educate their children. To the extent land reforms in India contribute to the growth of essential human capital, the overall results will be beneficial to the society at large.

Impact on Distribution of Income
Amelioration of the lot of weaker sections of the Indian rural society, through achieving better distribution of income, is a recurring theme of agrarian policy in India. To what extent, will the imposition of ceilings on land ownership reduce income and wealth inequalities, and reduce poverty? On the basis of careful analysis of land reform legislation and its implementation within the context of the hard realities of the Indian rural economy, Dandekar and Rath believe that "however simple it may appear, it is futile to try to resolve the problem of rural poverty, in an over-populated land, by redistribution of land which is in short supply....[29]

The major reasons listed for this view are: (i) Much of the land to be surrendered will be of inferior quality, and has more chance of being improved as a part of large profitable farms. (ii) Lowering of the ceiling will not be politically acceptable, and if imposed will be sabotaged in more than one way. (iii) Small landholders receiving surplus land from the redistribution plan will not have access to new inputs, and thus they will not be able to take advantage of the recent technological advances in agriculture. As we shall discuss in the next section, there has been strong opposition from landed interests to the ceiling legislation. Lawrence Veit quotes reports that to defy legislation, land owners resorted to "...a variety of evasive measures, some of them harmful to production. Among the more extraordinary steps taken by landowners were the dismantling of tube wells in order to be certain that their land could not be double-cropped and was not therefore subject to expropriation."[30]

Chaudhri, however, disagrees with the Dandekar and Rath thesis stated above. On the basis of the estimated effects of establishing a 2.5 acre floor and a 7.5 acre ceiling on operational holdings in West Bengal, and using data from the National Sample Survey 1960–61, Chaudhri asserts that it is feasible to reduce inequality and increase output by redistributing land.[31] He maintains that ceiling legislation would create an egalitarian land distribution pattern, which would induce more intensive land-use increasing both employment and output. In our view, the question of promoting income equality and reducing poverty among the weaker sections in the rural sector needs further research.

It will, however, be pertinent to indicate the experience of other countries on this issue. Peter Dorner, analysing the experience of land reforms and impact on income distribution in Egypt, Taiwan, Bolivia and Chile, reaches the conclusion that "large-scale land reforms result in substantial income transfers to the poorer rural classes—the farm workers and cultivators.... They show increased participation in the money economy following such income transfers."[32]

But, as Dorner points out, this favourable outcome from land reforms depends on strong government support in "providing yield-increasing inputs, improving roads and transport systems, building up marketing and storage facilities, improved credit systems for reaching the countryside, etc".[33] The experience of other countries should thus be followed in formulating an integrated land reform policy which should not stop merely at redistributing land, but should go further in helping small-farm operators to increase productivity and employment, for realizing the ultimate goal of more equal distribution of income and wealth.

An Overall Appraisal of Land Reforms

A recent statement from the Task Force on Agrarian Relations appointed by the Planning Commission, sums up the general ineffectiveness of the land reform in India to date:

> The overall assessment has to be that programmes of land reform adopted since independence have failed to bring about the required change in the agrarian structure.[34]

Unfortunately, the achievements from various land reform measures have fallen far short of the target. Commenting on the implementation of various measures, the Task Force further remarks:

> In no sphere of public policy in our country since Independence has the hiatus between precept and practice, between policy pronouncements and actual execution, been as great as in the domain of land reforms.[35]

We have already mentioned the outcome of various land reform measures: large-scale eviction of tenants; growing informal-tenancy arrangements; lack of implementation of ceiling legislation. Why the land reform measures have been so largely ineffective, is a much-debated question in the country. From a survey of the literature, we can classify the different reasons advanced, into the following categories: (1) loopholes and deficiencies in legislation, (2) faulty administration, and (3) political and social factors.

Loopholes
We have already mentioned various loopholes which made the measures inoperative. Some are discovered in the normal course by legal interpretations, but it is tragic that, as Pranab Bardhan claims, "laws were frequently enacted with deliberate loopholes and tell-tale exemptions designed to induce fictitious transfers of land to close and distant relatives..."[36]

Implementation
As already noted, when it came to actual implementation of legislative measures, mostly well-intentioned, they were defied

rather than observed. To a great extent, the local bureaucracy given charge of implementation, was, to quote Bardhan again, "largely indifferent, occasionally corrupt, and biased in favour of rural oligarchy".[37] The Task Force on Land Reforms elaborates on this point further:

> The attitude of the bureaucracy towards the implemention of land reforms is generally lukewarm, and often apathetic. This is, of course, inevitable because, as in the case of men who yield political power, those in the higher echelons of administration also are substantial landowners. The village functionaries like *patwaris* are invariably petty landowners. They are also under the sway of big landowners ...As a matter of fact there have been cases where administrators who tried to implement land reform laws honestly and efficiently were hastily transferred elsewhere.[38]

This alliance between the bureaucracy and landowners is, according to Dandekar,[39] the principal cause of India's policy failures. The landed interests wield strong political power. As John Mellor remarks:

> Today landowners with over five acres of land comprise over one-third of the rural population and occupy over three-quarters of land. Since, together with the upper half of the small farmer group, they wield considerably more than half the provincial political power, they are in a strong position either to block or evade effectively any change in rights to land.[40]

This strong landed-interests lobby affects the political will, and the Task Force on Land Reforms finds[41] this an important cause of non-implementation of land reform legislation.

Political and Social Factors
There is something in our political and social environment that enables the bureaucracy to collaborate illegally with the landed interests, and as a result the weaker sections of our rural society are helpless in getting their grievances against powerful and well-connected landowners redressed. Myrdal calls India a soft state, in which radical reforms are difficult to implement. Whatever radicalism we profess seems a set of empty political slogans, in which the masses have lost confidence. "To win back the credibility among the masses", according to Minhas, "the planners must translate political slogans into realistic radicalism".[42]

The weaker social and political position of the poor peasants also contributes to their helplessness and economic plight. Except in a few scattered pockets, practically all over the country the poor peasants and agricultural labourers are passive, unorganized, and inarticulate. They do not constitute any homogeneous social or economic group. To remedy the situation, the Task Force recommends "a certain degree of politicalisation of poor peasantry on militant lines".[43]

Joshi attributes another cause for the ineffectiveness of land reforms: "During the past twenty-five years, land reforms have not assumed the form of a gigantic revolutionary upheaval as in China...."[44] It is difficult to generate a revolutionary upheaval in a democratic society where lobby groups with conflicting interests operate to change public opinion in their favour. It is, however, true that in India during the last two decades we have not succeeded in creating a climate in which our professed radical land-reform measures could be implemented.

What we need is political will to deal with the "implementation crisis". For this we need a committed government cadre which will frustrate the alliances of vested interests, for the good of the Indian nation as a whole.

REFERENCES

1. United Nations, *Land Reform: Defects in Agrarian Structure as Obstacles to Economic Development*, (New York: Department of Economic Affairs, 1951), quoted in Lawrence A. Veit, *India's Second Revolution* (McGraw-Hill, 1976), p. 243.

2. Harold H. Mann, *The Social Framework of Agriculture* (Bombay: Vora and Co., 1967), p. xxvii.
3. Government of India, Planning Commission, *The Third Five-Year Plan* (New Delhi, 1956) p. 220.

4. *Report of the Congress Agrarian Committee*, quoted in C.B. Mamoria, *Agricultural Problems of India* (Allahabad: Kitab Mahal, 1966), p. 430.
5. Government of India, Planning Commission, *Draft Fifth Five-Year Plan, 1974–79* (New Delhi), p. 42.
6. Lawrence A. Veit, *India's Second Revolution* (New York: McGraw-Hill, 1976), p. 245.
7. Daniel Thorner, *Agrarian Prospect in India* (Delhi: Delhi University Press, 1956), pp. 25, 28.
8. Ibid., pp. 25, 28.
9. A.M. Khusro, *Economic and Social Effects of Abolition of Jagirdari and Land Reforms in Hyderabad* (Hyderabad: Osmania University Press, 1958), pp. 41–48.
10. J.S. Uppal, "Implementation of Land Reform Legislation in India—A Study of the Two Villages in Punjab", *Asian Survey*, vol. IX, no. 5, May 1969, pp. 359 and 372; and J.S. Uppal, "Attitudes of Farm Families Towards Land Reforms in Some Punjab Villages", *Journal of Developing Areas*, vol. IV, no. 1, October 1969, pp. 59–68.
11. For an excellent treatment of this subject see C.E. Bishop and W.D. Toussaint, *Agricultural Economic Analysis* (New York: John Wiley, 1958), ch. 14.
12. A.M. Khusro, *Economics of Land Reform and Farm Size in India* (Delhi: Macmillan, 1973), p. 27.
13. Government of India, Planning Commission, *Draft Fourth Five-Year Plan*, New Delhi, p. 130.
14. Government of India, Planning Commission, *Progress of Land Reforms* (New Delhi, 1963), p. 10.
15. *Draft Fifth Five-Year Plan*, p. 43.
16. Ibid., p. 43.
17. Ruddar Datt and K.P.M. Sundharam, *Indian Economy* (Delhi: S. Chand, 1976), pp. 349–350.
18. Ervin Long, *The Economic Basis of Land Reform in Underdeveloped Economies*, in Tara Shukla (ed), *Economics of Underdeveloped Agriculture* (Bombay: Vora and Co., 1969), pp. 287–288.
19. Khusro, "Economics of Land Reform", p. 128.
20. Quoted in Khusro, "Economics of Land Reform", p. xii.
21. Khusro, "Economics of Land Reform", pp. 44–73.
22. Ibid., p. xix.
23. Ibid, p. 78.
24. Raj Krishna, "Some Aspects of Land Reform and Economic Development in India", in Walter Froehlick (ed), *Land Tenure, Industrialization and Social Stability* (Milwaukee: The Marquette University Press, 1961), p. 236.
25. Veit, *India's Second Revolution*, p. 251.
26. Ibid.
27. Ibid.
28. Peter Dorner, *Land Reform and Economic Development* (Penguin Books, 1972), p. 130.
29. V.M. Dandekar and N. Rath, "Poverty in India", *Economic and Political Weekly*, vol. VI, no. 2, 9 January 1971, p. 121.
30. Veit, *India's Second Revolution*, p. 247.
31. D.P. Chaudhri, "New Technologies and Income Distribution in Agriculture", in David Lehmann (ed), *Peasants, Landlords and Government* (New York: Holmes and Meier, 1974), p. 169.
32. Peter Dorner, *Land Reform and Economic Development*, p. 90.
33. Ibid., p. 91.
34. Government of India, Planning Commission, *Report of the Task Force on Agrarian Relations* (New Delhi, 1973), pp. 8–9.
35. Ibid, p. 9.
36. Pranab Bardhan, "Some Country Experience: India", in Hollis Chenery et al., *Redistribution with Growth* (London: Oxford University Press, 1974), p.256.
37. Ibid.
38. *Task Force on Agrarian Relations*, p. 8.
39. V.M. Dandekar, "Next Step on the Socialist Path", *Economic and Political Weekly*, vol. 7, no. 31, August 1972, pp. 1553–1558.
40. John Mellor, *The New Economics of Growth* (Ithaca: Cornell University Press, 1976), p.105.
41. *Task Force on Agrarian Relations*, pp. 25–26.
42. B.S. Minhas, *Planning and the Poor* (New Delhi: S. Chand and Co., 1974), p. xvii.
43. *Task Force on Agrarian Relations*, p. 25.
44. P.C. Joshi, *Land Reforms in India* (Bombay: Allied Publishers, 1975), p. 99.

7

Basic and Large-Scale Industries in India

BALWIR SINGH CHEEMA

One of the major factors which kept India from making significant economic progress before Independence was the slow pace of industrialization. The process of industrialization, defined broadly, means the organization of production based on the principles of specialization, and division of labour among enterprises as well as within them, necessitated by as well as resulting in the application of new technology and mechanical and electrical energy with a view to maximizing returns and minimizing the per unit cost of production.[1]

Thus defined, the process of industrialization requires accumulation of capital for the creation of productive capacity and the building of social and economic overhead capital. In this sense, industrialization represents an approach which seeks to develop all sectors of the economy. In fact, in the case of the developed countries like the USA, Japan, Australia, Canada, New Zealand, the UK, Germany, France, and other European countries, it is very difficult to draw distinctions between the agricultural and industrial sectors of the economy on the basis of the usual indicators such as: investment and productivity per worker, the degree of specialization and division of labour, sophistication of marketing and management techniques, the use of mechanical and electric power, and the application of science and technology. Viewed in this sense, one may find more similarities between the agricultural sector of the developed economies and the organized industrial sector of the underdeveloped economies, than between the agricultural sectors of these two types of economies. Furthermore, one can make a strong case that the process of industrialization, thus defined, must first take place in agriculture to some minimum level in order to generate sufficient surplus, both in terms of manpower and capital needed, to develop industry and guarantee sufficient demand for its products. In this respect one can cite the experiences of the UK and the US in the eighteenth and nineteenth centuries. There are the interesting cases of New Zealand and Australia where the agricultural sector, even after the attainment of a high level of economic development, continues to play a dominant role. However, on the basis of these arguments, it will be wrong to advocate that the developing economies should concentrate exclusively on modernizing their agriculture to the neglect of establishing industries, in their quest for economic development. In recommending the establishment of organized large-scale industries in India, we cannot deny either the mutual dependence of agricultural and industrial development, or the importance of the agricultural sector for the national economy. Our purpose is simply to point out that the industrial sector has to play an important role in the economic development of India, and in the long run it has to assume the role of the dominant sector, especially in view of the present and potential size of the market for industrial products and the availability of raw materials and abundant labour.

The following are some of the basic objectives often cited for development of the industrial sector: First, to provide gainful employment for the backlog of underemployed and unemployed manpower in the agricultural sector, estimated at approximately 30 per cent of the total labour force in India,[2] and for the increasing number of new entrants to the labour force. The addition to the labour force between 1974 and 1986 is estimated at about 65 million.[3] Second, to increase the per capita productivity for raising the living standards of the poor masses, and to generate sufficient savings for capital formation. Third, to improve the balance of payments situation of the Indian economy by producing goods for import substitution and increasing exports. These objectives have been affirmed by the Indian Planning Commission in the five-year plans. The emphasis placed on the development of the industrial sector, and within the industrial sector, on "the basic heavy industries for the manufacture of producer goods to strengthen the foundations of economic independence",[4] as stated by the late Professor Mahalanobis in his *Draft Plan-Frame* for the Second Five-Year Plan, has remained unchanged. This emphasis on the development of the large scale and organized industrial sector in the case of India is justifiable not only on the basis of the historical experience of

developed economies, but also because of the basic economic facts which characterize the Indian economy at present.

The industrial sector in general, and the basic industries in particular, failed to grow in relative importance in the economy in spite of the ample availability of natural resources to support a sizable industrial advance, early development of the transportation system, and the fairly early start made in establishing consumer goods industries like cotton textiles, jute, and paper, around the middle of the nineteenth century. The major reason for this lack of industrial development up to 1947 was the dominance by an alien power, whose main objective was to utilize India as a supplier of raw materials to feed its growing industries and as a market for its manufactured goods.

In England, due to industrialization, a gradual change from mercantilistic ideology, based on protectionism and geared to the goal of having a surplus balance of payments, to free enterprise was made around the middle of the eighteenth century. This change proved disastrous to Indian industrial development. In the beginning, Indian exports of handicrafts, which competed successfully with the products of UK, were discouraged by the British. The production of goods like fine muslins, brocades, inlaid arms, for which India was known throughout the world, declined with the gradual decline in power of the native Indian rulers and their retinues who were their major patrons. Wherever the handicraft industries survived, the quality of their products deteriorated sharply for several reasons, including the tendency on the part of the Indian elite to copy Western designs, and the desire on the part of manufacturers to cater to the tastes of the masses in England. The ban on carrying of arms eliminated, to a great extent, the need for arms; and this led to the demise of cottage industries producing weapons like swords and shields of excellent quality and workmanship.[6] Later, when the Indian market was flooded with foreign goods, the products of Indian manufacturers were no match, in price and quality, for the products of British industry. The advantage enjoyed by Indian manufacturers in the local market was progressively cut down because of the decline in transportation costs, and of the safety and speed with which British products could be carried to Indian markets as a result of the development of railways and steamships. The marketable surplus of agricultural products which could, under favourable circumstances, be used to finance industrial growth, declined due to the increase in population and the failure of agricultural productivity to increase. The gifts, exactions, and tributes received by the East India Company and its officials, monies spent on numerous battles to subjugate powerful Indian princely states, and the military expeditions into Afghanistan, Persia, and Tibet in order to protect and strengthen British interests financed by general revenues, hindered the formation of capital. Further, the "home charges" (which included interest in the management of debt and annuities on account of railways and irrigation works; payments due in connection with civil departments in India; army and marine charges, including pensions and gratuities; payments for stores purchased in India; and furlough allowances) amounting to about 20 million pounds annually before the First World War and almost double the amount thereafter, were a tremendous drain of capital to England, which could hardly be justified on the grounds of advantages derived by India.[7]

However, in spite of these difficulties, a beginning in the establishment of the organized industry was made in the latter half of the nineteenth century. The process of industrialization picked up greater momentum in the first half of this century because of changes in the British attitude due to the Independence movement, and also as a consequence of the natural protection afforded to the Indian industries during the First and Second World War years, when the supply of foreign manufactured products to India was cut off. However, the real growth of the industrial sector—specially of the basic industries—started after Independence, with the advent of economic planning.

The index of industrial production rose from 100 in 1950–51 to 194 in 1960–61. In the first four years of the Third Plan, industrial production rose rapidly. The increase in industrial output (1960 as base) was 8.2 per cent in 1961–62, 9.6 per cent in 1962–63, 9.2 per cent in 1963–64 and 8.8 per cent in 1964–65. In 1965–66 the rate of increase declined to 5.3 per cent and fell from there to 0.2 per cent in 1966–67 and 0.5 per cent in 1967–68. Industrial production, however, recovered sharply in 1968–69 with a rise of 6.2 per cent. The increase in industrial production during the Fourth Plan years was: 7.3 per cent (1969–70); 3.1 per cent (1970–71); 3.3 per cent (1971–72); and 4.4 per cent (1972–73). The index of industrial production actually showed a decline in 1973–74, the last year of the Fourth Plan.[8] In 1974–75, the first year of the Fifth Plan, it recorded an increase of only 2.5 per cent. The progress made in industrial production during approximately the last ten years, therefore, does not compare favourably with the average growth rate of about 8 per cent achieved up to the mid-sixties. During the Fourth Plan, in comparison, industrial production grew annually only at the rate of 3.9 per cent.[9]

In this chapter we will make a brief survey of some major and key Indian industries. This is necessary in order to develop a clear understanding of the rapidly changing industrial scene and its significance in the growth of the Indian economy; and to determine the impact of the industrial strategy adopted quite early during the planning era to develop a broadly-based capital-goods industry which could in time meet the needs of widely diversified consumer goods industries. In the concluding section of this chapter an attempt will be made to evaluate the impact of the industrial strategy and the progress made towards the future growth of the Indian economy.

Iron and Steel Industry

In spite of the growing importance of aluminium and synthetic materials as substitutes, steel is still considered an indispensable basic input for industrialization. With the development of the iron and steel industry, a tremendous demand may be expected for such primary products as iron ore, coal, manganese, limestone, and refractory materials, of which India has considerable deposits, and social overhead capital in the form of cheap transportation and trained labour force. It, of course, satisfies the need for iron and steel for development of engineering, transportation, defence, and construction industries. This process is known as backward and forward linkages in the economic development process. The development of industries with large backward and forward linkages is generally considered to create a favourable climate for the industrial development of an economy.[10] Rightly, therefore, the Planning Commission has given the steel industry prime importance in the development of basic industry. This is reflected in the fact that up to the end of 1970–71, nearly a third of the total investment made in public sector undertakings was in steel.[11] During the Fourth Plan, investment in the iron and steel industry amounted to Rs. 867 crores out of a total outlay of Rs. 2,700 crores in the public sector on industry.[12] An overall investment of Rs. 1,622 crores is planned for the steel industry in the Fifth Five-Year Plan.[13]

The production of carbon steel in India can be traced to about 2,000 B.C., but the foundations of the modern iron and steel industry were only laid in 1907, when the Tata Iron and Steel Co. Ltd., which up to the Second World War was one of the biggest in the world, was started by Jamshedji Nusserwanji Tata at Jamshedpur. In the next fifty years, in spite of this comparatively early and successful start, availability of raw materials and their favourable location, and expanding demand, the industry failed to make any significant progress. During the interwar years, subsidized continental steel was dumped in India and steel prices fell sharply. The small protective duty granted from 1924 proved inadequate. Between 1939 and 1947, steel production in India remained at about a million tonnes, whereas the demand for steel had increased quite rapidly. Further, the steel industry faced the problem of replacing worn-out equipment, some of which had been operated for over thirty years without any major modernization. The Iron and Steel Panel, headed by Sir Padamji Ginwalla, recommended in 1946 the establishment by Government of two integrated steel plants with an initial ingot capacity of half a million tonnes each, in case the private sector failed to do so. Provision of an investment of Rs. 80 crores, of which Rs. 30 crores was to be incurred during the First Plan for the establishment of a new steel plant,[14] was made, but no tangible steps were taken for the establishment of any new plant.

It was during the Second and Third Plan period, 1956–66, or about fifty years after the establishment of Tata's large-scale integrated steel mill, that the three steel plants at Rourkela, Bhilai, and Durgapur were established in the public sector. The expansion and modernization of the Tata Iron and Steel Company and the Indian Iron and Steel Company was also undertaken during the period. Initially, the three steel plants in the public sector had a capacity of a million tonnes each, but because of the subsequent expansion of the Rourkela steel plant to 1.8 million tonnes, the Durgapur steel plant to 1.6 million tonnes, and the Bhilai steel plant to 2.5 million tonnes, the total steel-producing capacity increased from roughly 1.5 million before 1947 to 10.6 million tonnes, and of saleable steel to 8.9 million tonnes in 1973–74. The Fifth Plan provides for expanding the capacity of the Bhilai and Bokaro steel mills to 4 and 4.75 million tonnes respectively, and significant progress in establishing three new steel mills. The Salem (Tamil Nadu) plant will have a capacity of 1.95 million tonnes and the Vijayanagar (Karnataka) and Visakhapatnam (Andhra Pradesh) plants a capacity of 2 million tonnes each. For 1978–79, the targets for steel ingot capacity and finished steel capacity are set at 15.15 and 11.7 million tonnes respectively.[15]

With the nationalization of the Indian Iron and Steel Company in July 1976, the steel mills in the public sector now account for a little over 81 per cent of the total rated ingot capacity. The only large integrated steel mill left in the private sector is the Tata Iron and Steel Company with an installed capacity of 2 million ingot tonnes (Table 7.1). In

Table 7.1. Capacity and Output of Integrated Steel Mills
(million tonnes)

| Plant | Rated Capacity | | Actual Production of Ingot steel 1973–74 |
	Ingot Steel	Saleable Steel	
Public Sector			
Bhilai	2.50	1.97	1.89
Durgapur	1.60	1.24	78
Rourkela	1.80	1.23	1.08
Bokaro	1.70	1.37	97[a]
IISCO	1.00	80	NA
TISCO	2.00	1.50	NA
Total	10.60	8.11	5.8[b]

[a]Figure represents pig iron produced up to 31 March 1974.

[b]Figure represents total domestic steel production in 1973–74.

SOURCE: *India: A Reference Annual*—1975, pp. 230–232.

addition to the large integrated steel mills, there are a large number of small secondary steel producers which produced 1.64 million tonnes of finished steel in 1972–73. Actual production of finished steel rose from 1.0 million tonnes in 1950–51 to 2.4 million tonnes in 1960–61, against the Second Plan target of 4.5 million tonnes. Again, in 1965–66, the last year of the Third Plan, only 4.5 million tonnes of finished steel was produced against the targeted 6.8 million tonnes. At the end of the Fourth Plan in 1973–74, only 4.6 million tonnes of finished steel was produced though installed capacity had increased to 9.4 million tonnes. During 1975–76 because of the general recovery of the economy and adoption of stringent measures, the actual production of saleable steel rose to 5.78 million tonnes and is expected to reach 6.47 million tonnes in 1976–77.[16]

The total domestic demand for finished steel, which was 5.8 million tonnes in 1973–74 is expected to increase to 10 million tonnes in 1978–79. In order to meet this increased demand during the Fifth Plan the capacity of Bhilai will be raised from 2.5 million tonnes to 4.0 million ingot tonnes, and of Bokaro from 1.7 million tonnes to 4.75 million tonnes. The integrated steel plants are expected to contribute about 8.8 million tonnes of finished steel, and electric arc furnaces and rerollers an additional 0.6 million tonnes, making a total of 9.4 million tonnes by 1978–79.[17]

Steel Authority of India, Ltd. (SAIL) was established in 1973 to coordinate the development of the iron and steel industry in both the public and private sectors. SAIL owns all the shares in the public sector corporations connected with steel and associated industries, and acts as the nominee of public sector financial institutions which hold shares in private sector steel companies and associated input industries. Management of the public-sector steel plants is vested in the state-owned Hindustan Steel Ltd., a subsidiary of SAIL. Metallurgical and Engineering Consultants (India) Ltd., another subsidiary of SAIL, was established in 1973 to provide consultancy and engineering services in the field of iron and steel. This centralization of authority in the hands of SAIL is expected to result in an overall improvement in the performance of the steel industry which in the past has worked substantially below the rated capacity.

Since the beginning of the Second Plan, India has acquired considerable indigenous know-how, and the industrial potential to build steel plants without foreign help. Nearly 67 per cent of the supplies of equipment needed to establish the Bokaro steel mill has been obtained from within the country. Not only is this a great achievement in itself, but it has also opened the way to the future industrialization of India, and has reduced its dependence on foreign countries. Except for specialized steel, the industry is now able to meet the expanding domestic demand for steel, and has emerged as the largest foreign-exchange earner in the nontraditional exports sector. The exports value of iron and steel as a proportion of total exports value has increased from Rs. 8.7 crores in 1960–61 to Rs. 77.2 crores in 1969–70. In 1970–71 and 1971–72 it declined sharply to Rs. 67.2 and Rs. 25.6 crores respectively, mainly due to growth in internal demand and decline in output.[18] The targeted export of steel for 1976–77 is 1.5 lakh tonnes of which 1.0 lakh tonnes had already been exported by August 1976.[19]

The steel industry accounted for 51.3 and 40.62 per cent of total investment in public-sector undertakings in 1962–63 and 1965–66. From 1968–69 to 1972–73 it absorbed roughly one-third of the total investment in public-sector undertakings.[20] In spite of this massive investment in plan after plan, it has failed to meet the targeted capacity levels and full utilization of the installed capacity, due to poor management and availability of complementary input. It is hoped that the new centralized control of the industry vested with SAIL will improve the future performance of the steel industry.

Aluminium and Nonferrous metals

Aluminium is the youngest, but quite an important, nonferrous metallurgical industry in India. During the past decade, a phenomenal expansion in both the production and consumption of aluminium has been registered. This has been possible because of the availability of adequate quantities of bauxite deposits in India and the large increase in the production of electricity. The rapid development of the aluminium industry can also be attributed to the relative scarcity of other nonferrous metals like copper, and to the ease with which aluminium could be substituted for them. Because of its versatility, aluminium has found many new uses, leading to rapid expansion in its demand. The output increased from 18.3 thousand tonnes in 1960–61 to 181.5 thousand tonnes in 1971–72.[21] The Fifth Plan target for 1978–79 is set at 370,000 tonnes.[22] Aluminium production in 1972–73 amounted to 175 thousand tonnes. During the Fifth Plan, adequate expansion in the aluminium production capacity will be undertaken to meet the domestic

demand which is estimated to be 370,000 tonnes by 1978–79. Additional production will be achieved through the completion of the public sector Korba plant with a production capacity of 100,000 tonnes. The capacity of the Ratnagari plant will be increased by 50,000 tonnes in the early years of the Sixth Plan.[23]

The production of copper, zinc, lead and other nonferrous metals is severely restricted because of the limited availability of raw materials within the country. The Fourth Plan provided for an increase in installed capacity of copper from 9,600 to 47,500 tonnes, zinc from 18,000 tonnes to 36,000 tonnes and lead from 20,000 tonnes to 40,000 tonnes. Due to the delay in the execution of various projects, however, none of these targets were fulfilled. Fifth Plan targets for installed capacity for 1978–79 in respect of copper, zinc and lead respectively, are 57,000, 100,000, and 20,000 tonnes.[24]

Engineering and Machine Tool Industries

Next to the establishment of the steel industry, priority was given to the engineering industries. The inspiration for this came perhaps from Prime Minister Nehru's slogan, Build Machines, Build India, and this has been amply justified by subsequent events. The investment in the engineering industry in 1970 was estimated at over Rs. 2,000 crores with an annual production capacity of Rs. 2,500 to 3,000 crores. There were about 4,500 manufacturing units, employing 1.4 million.[25] This represents an annual growth-rate of 12 per cent for the years between 1950 and 1970.[26] As a result of this rapid advance, engineering industries are now mostly able to meet the domestic demand for consumer as well as capital goods; they have also succeeded, to some extent, in selling their wares in foreign markets. From a mere Rs. 24 crores in 1964–65, the exports of engineering goods increased in 1971–72 to 118 crores[27] and are expected to reach a level of Rs. 400 crores in 1978–79, the final year of the Fourth Plan.[28]

In spite of this rapid growth of the engineering industries, imports of machinery, components and spares constitute the single largest group of imports, amounting to approximately 25 per cent of the total imports. Dependence on imports has been the major inhibiting factor in accelerating the pace of development and the effort at self reliance. The Fifth Plan, therefore, envisages the expansion of the value of output of engineering industries from the estimated level of Rs. 2,700 crores to Rs. 5,200 crores in 1978–79.[29] This expansion is to be accomplished by: first, fuller utilization of capacity; second, by diversification of production; third, by filling in the gaps in machine-building capacity; and fourth, by expanding design and development capabilities. For fuller utilization of capacity, the somewhat erratic situation of the past in which periods of inadequate orders were followed by excessive bunching of orders, necessitating importation of equipment which could be produced domestically, will have to be avoided.

Machine-Tool Industry
A good indicator of the extent of the scientific and economic advance made by an economy and its potential for further growth is the size and sophistication achieved by its machine-tool industry. The machine-tool industry in India was started during the Second World War and it grew rapidly during 1939–45 with government assistance, which became essential due to lack of foreign supplies to meet the increased domestic demand. After the war the production of machine tools fell and no real headway was made in developing the industry until 1 March 1953, when the management and control of the machine-tool factory near Bangalore, established during the war as the result of an agreement between the Government of India and a Swiss firm, was taken over by the Hindustan Machine Tools Ltd. Since then, in order to increase and diversify the production of machine tools, Hindustan Machine Tools Ltd. has built half-a dozen new plants. In addition to producing over 30 different types of machine tools, it produces watches. The value of production of Hindustan Machine Tools Ltd. during 1973–74 amounted to Rs. 404 million, as against 312 million in 1972–73.[30] Further, several other large

concerns, such as the Machine Tool Corporation of India Ltd., Praga Tools Ltd., National Tools Ltd., and the National Instrument Factory, have been started. In July 1965, the Central Machine Tool Institute for designing training, standardization, prototype manufacture, research documentation, etc., started functioning at Bangalore. Simultaneously, several large- and small-scale firms were established in the private sector for the production of machine tools. The public and the private sector enterprises at present are producing all kinds of lathes, milling machines, radial drills, grinders, milling, shaping, and planing machines, pneumatic hammers and tools, and various kinds of special machines. The production of machine tools increased from Rs. 70 million in 1960–61 to 294 million in 1965–66. However, though the capacity to produce machine tools was more than doubled from Rs. 300 million to Rs. 610 million between 1965–66 and 1968–69, actual output declined from Rs. 294 million to Rs. 247 million in 1968–69,[31] due to the general slowdown in industrial activity. During 1969–73, a partial recovery was made and machine tools worth Rs. 550 million were produced in 1971–72, and worth Rs. 626 million in 1972–73.[32] In 1973–74, the machine tool industry had an estimated capacity of Rs. 950 million, and production of Rs. 650. In the Fifth Plan, target capacity of Rs. 1,600 million and production of Rs. 1,300 is provided for the machine tool industry, representing a 68.4 per cent increase in capacity and 100 per cent increase in output over 1973–74.[33]

Electrical Engineering Industries
At the time of gaining independence, the electrical engineering industry was small in size and produced mainly light bulbs and small household appliances like electric fans, heaters, irons, radios, for domestic use, and small electric transformers and motors for industrial use. Even these were made primarily by assembling imported components. In line with the dual strategy of rapidly increasing the electric generating capacity of the country for industrial, agricultural, and domestic use, and of making India

self-reliant, it was essential that the domestic production of generators, turbines, transformers, circuit breakers, etc., for the production and distribution of electricity be undertaken with the utmost speed.

As a result of Plan provisions and their implementation, generating capacity has increased from 2.3 million kw at the beginning of the First Plan to 18.5 kw in 1973–74.[34] Over 50 per cent of India's population now derives the benefits of electricity, as against only 2.5 per cent in 1947.[35] By March 1973, the per capita consumption of electricity had risen to 96.6 kwh from 38 kwh in 1960–61.[36] The Fifth Plan envisages the addition of 16.55 million kw of new generating capacity, which will increase the effective generating capacity to 33 million kw at the end of the Fifth Plan, after allowing for the retiring of old and obsolete capacity of about 1 million kw.[37] Along with this increase in the generating capacity of electricity, the heavy-electrical industry in India has been able to develop a measure of self-reliance in the designing, technology, and manufacture of a wide range of equipment for the generation and distribution of electricity.

The development of the heavy electrical industry has been mainly in the public sector. During the Second and Third Plan periods, Heavy Electricals (India) Ltd. (HEIL), and Bharat Heavy Electricals Ltd. (BHEL) were established. The output of heavy electrical equipment in the public sector increased from Rs. 103 crores in 1971–72 to Rs. 218 crores in 1973–74.[38] In addition to the main power-generating equipment, these public enterprises produce capacitors, rectifiers, industrial boilers and turbines, compressors used in fertilizer and chemical industries, high-pressure valves, and a wide range of heavy electric machines. India has also started producing equipment for atomic-powered generating plants, and has successfully exported power-generating and distribution equipment.

On the basis of the progress made thus far, "India needs no longer to import thermal or hydro-electric power equipment for the projects that are to to come up in the Fifth Five-Year Plan period".[39] How-ever, in spite of this rapid expansion and optimism, according to Dr. K.L. Rao, then Minister of Irrigation and Power, "The current [1972] shortage of power, was 1 million kw without taking into consideration the suppressed demand for power in rural and urban areas which makes the current shortage of power in reality much greater".[40] On the basis of the demand and supply trends in 1972, the Indian Institute of Public Opinion had estimated that by 1973–74 the shortage of power would amount to about 4 million kw, representing approximately 25 per cent of the total power requirements in the country. The current power shortage should be significantly higher as, against the target capacity of 23 million kw for 1973–74, actually attained capacity was estimated at only 18.87 kw.[41] If these estimates are correct, then even if the most optimistic projections regarding indigenous capacity to produce power-generating and distribution equipment come true, India will have to depend on imported equipment, to some extent at least, in the near future. The power-shortage crisis from which India has been suffering in recent years can be eased by more efficient use of electricity. Indian thermal stations, for instance, generate about 3,740 kwh of energy per kw of installed generating capacity, as against 4,700 kwh and 5,625 kwh respectively in the USA and Japan. Losses in transmission and distribution are about 20 per cent as against about only 6 to 13 per cent in most European countries.[42]

In the case of the light electrical engineering industry, significant progress has been made in the private sector. In addition to meeting the rapidly increasing internal demand for most electrical goods, such as fans, radios, electric heaters, irons, etc., Indian manufacturers have been successful in selling electrical goods, in increasing quantities, to the Middle Eastern, African, and East Asian countries.

Production figures for selected electrical engineering industries are given in Table 7.2. This will give some idea regarding their rapid growth.

Industrial and Mechanical Engineering Industries
Over the past 20 years, India has developed

Table 7.2. Production in Selected Electrical Engineering Industries

Industry (unit)	1950–51	1955–56	1960–61	1965–66	1968–69	1973–74 Estimated		1978–79 Target	
						Capacity	Production	Capacity	Production
Heavy electrical equipment									
Turbines, hydro (million kw)	—	—	—	—	0.1	1.4	0.53	1.7	1.4
Turbines, thermal (million kw)	—	—	—	—	0.4	2.7	1.7	2.9	2.2
Power boilers (million kw)	—	—	—	—	0.4	—	1.1	3.5	2.5
Power transformers (million kvs.)	0.18	0.62	1.4	5.7	8.3	18.3	12.5	30	20
Electric cables and wires									
(i) Aluminium conductors ('000 tonnes)[a]	1.7	9.4	23.6	40.6	62.5	104	85	200	170
(ii) Bare copper conductors ('000 tonnes)	5.0	8.7	10.1	3.1	—	900	600	1250	9000
Electric motors (million h.p.)	0.1	0.27	0.73	1.8	2.63	5.45	3.6	6.5	5.8
Electric fans (lakhs)	2.0	2.9	10.6	13.6	14.8	30.0	26.3	44.0	40.0
Electric lamps (millions)	14	25	48.5	72.1	96.8	—	137.8	218.0	207.0

[a] Decline in the production of bare copper conductors since 1960-61 is due to the rapid increase in the use of aluminium conductors.

SOURCE: 1. *Fourth Five-Year Plan*, p. 334
2. *India: A Reference Annual—1971-72*, p. 352
3. *Economic Survey, 1972-73*, p. 112
4. *Draft Fifth Five-Year Plan*, p. 157

a heavy and light mechanical engineering industry of a diversified character. Even a simple, but comprehensive, listing of the engineering goods presently made in India is not an easy task. The purpose of the following discussion, therefore, is to highlight some of the salient features of their development and to point out the significance of their growth in the changing industrial scene in India. The estimated and target capacity, and production figures for selected industrial machinery industries are given in Table 7.3. The output of chemical plant and pharmaceutical equipment, printing, rubber, paper and pulp,

the last year of the First Plan (1955–56), the Second Plan (1960–61), and the Third Plan (1965–66), 1968–69, and the last year of the Fourth Plan (1973–74), and capacity and production target figures for 1978–79 are given in Table 7.4 in respect of a sample of mechanical engineering industries. For lack of rupee values the figures are quantity figures which are not comparable from year to year because of product size and quality changes. For instance, instead of the steam locomotives produced in the 1950's, diesel and electric locomotives are being produced now in India.

Table 7.3. Output and Planned Targets for Selected Industrial Machinery Industries
(Rupees in millions)

Industry	1965–66 Production	1968–69 Production	1973–74 (estimated) Capacity	1973–74 (estimated) Production	1978–79 (target) Capacity	1978–79 (target) Production
1. Chemical plant and pharmaceutical equipment (including heavy fabricated machinery)	74	133	762	300	1150	800
2. Printing machinery	—	1	25	15	160	110
3. Rubber machinery	1.4	1.7	122	50	250	180a
4. Paper and pulp machinery	16.8	27	130	100	450	360a
5. Machine tools	294	247	950	650	1600	1370
6. Coal and other mining machinery	30.6	48	290	120	350	240
7. Cotton textile machinery	216	138	500	350	800	560
8. Cement machinery	49	81.8	260	50	400	280a
9. Sugar machinery	77	118	230	200	450	400a
Total	758.8	795.5	3,269	1,835	5,610	4,300

aExcluding standard bought-out items.

SOURCE: *Draft Fifth Five-Year Plan*, p. 156.

machine tools, coal and other mining, cotton textiles, cement, and sugar machinery, increased by 130.6 per cent, from Rs. 795.5 crores to Rs. 1.835 crores during the Fourth Plan. It is targeted to increase further by Rs. 134.33 per cent, to Rs. 4,300 crores by the end of the Fifth Plan in 1978–79. An increase in the production of heavy metallurgical machinery is planned to increase from 30,000 tonnes to 75,000 tonnes during the Fifth Plan, representing an increase of 150 per cent. Actual production figures for 1950–51,

In the field of rail and road transport and communications, virtual self-sufficiency in the supply of equipment and rolling stock (including diesel and electric locomotives) has been realized since 1951. Shipyards for building ships for the merchant marine as well as the Indian navy have been set up. The capacity to produce automobiles, especially commercial vehicles, has increased to such an extent that in this regard India has become self-sufficient. Manufacturing of construction, mining, and agricultural

Table 7.4. Production in Selected Mechanical Engineering Industries

Industry (unit)	1950-51	1955-56	1960-61	1965-66	1968-69	1973-74 (Estimated)		1978-79 (Target)	
						Capacity	Production	Capacity	Production
Machine tools^a	3.4	7.9	70.0	294.3	247	950	650	1600	1370
Shipbuilding^b	—	—	—	28.3	18.7	100	46	475	475
Railway wagons^c	2.9	15.3	8.2	23.5	16.48	30.8	13	45	30
Locomotives^d	7	179	272	233	135	—	249	—	362
Agricultural tractors^e	—	—	—	6.3	15	47	40	125	80
Power tillers^e	—	—	—	—	0.5	36	2	36	20
Crawler tractors^d	—	—	—	—	—	340	325	600	490
Dumpers and scrapers^d	—	—	—	—	—	520	320	650	590
Automobiles (total)^e	16.5	25.3	55.0	60.1	79.2	120.8	90	205	170
Commercial vehicles^e	8.6	9.9	28.4	35.3	35.6	73.4	48	140	110
Passenger cars, etc.^e	7.9	15.4	26.6	24.8	37.3	47.4	42	65	60
Motorcycles, scooters and mopeds^e	—	0.9	19.4	40.7	85.6	200	184	700	570

^a Rs. millions
^b '000 GKT
^c Thousands
^d Units

SOURCE: 1. *Draft Fifth Five-Year Plan*, pp. 156-158
2. *India: A Reference Annual*—1967, p. 289
3. Government of India, Planning Commission, Statistics aud Snrveys Division, *Basic Statistics Relating to the Indian Economy 1950-51 to 1968-69* (New Delhi, December 1969)

machinery has been taken up in significant quantities. Considerable progress has been made in establishing defence industries, including the manufacture of military vehicles, tanks, aeroplanes, heavy guns, and small arms and ammunition. The production of sewing machines, bicycles, motorcycles, and scooters, and all types of household electrical and mechanical gadgets has increased many-fold. It will be seen from the foregoing review that the development of the engineering industries has made India nearly self-sufficient in many respects and this has also made it possible for India to export her engineering goods in increasing quantities.

Textile Industry

Long before the advent of the British, India was known for its cotton textiles. The industry was ruined by the British in order to afford Lancashire a vast market in India for its rapidly growing production of cotton textile goods. The destruction of the Indian textile industry was so ruthless that Lord Bentinck, the then Governor-General of India, commented on the plight of cotton textile workers in 1834, "the misery hardly finds a parallel in the history of commerce. The bones of the cotton-weavers are bleaching the plains of India".[43] However, in a matter of only two decades, by 1854, the cotton textile industry regained a firm footing around Bombay. This was possible because of the availability of indigenous cotton, a large domestic market, cheap supply of labour, and the humid climate. From the beginning, the entrepreneurship and capital invested in the cotton textile industry have been Indian. The second half of the nineteenth century also witnessed the growth of the jute and woollen industries. The rayon, nylon, and other synthetic textile industries were started only after the Second World War, and they are still of minor importance compared to the cotton and jute industries, but have become almost as important as the woollen industry. From the outset, the textile industries assumed prime importance in the industrial sector of the economy in terms of employment generated, contribution made to the gross

national product, and export trade.

Cotton Textile Industry
The growth of the cotton textile industry between 1879–80 and 1968–69 is shown in Table 7.5.

Table 7.5. Growth of Cotton Textile Industry (1879-80 to 1972) and 1978–79 Targets

Year	Number of Spindles (thousands)	Number of Looms (thousands)	Mill Production	
			Yarn (kg)	Piece Goods (million metres)
1879–80	14.80	13.3	—	—
1889–90	29.35	22.1	—	—
1890	48.41	40.5	260	54
1911	60.95	85.8	283	121
1921	72.78	1,33.5	312	1,315
1931	90.78	1,75.2	421	2,456
1941	100.26	2,00.0	603	3,445
1947	103.54	2,03.0	597	3,509
1950–51	—	—	534	3,401
1960–61	157.00	2,04.0	873	4,649
1968–69	177.50	2,09.0	959	4,297
1972	182.00	2,08.0	792	4,224
1978–79 (Target)			1270	5,200

SOURCE: 1. *India: A Reference Annual*, 1966, p. 294.

2. *India: A Reference Annual*, 1975, p. 228.

3. *Draft Fifth Five-Year Plan*, p. 158.

In 1947, as a consequence of partition, of a total of 423 cotton mills India got 409 and Pakistan only 14.[44] By December 1972, the number of textile mills had increased to 674 of which 384 were spinning and 290 composite mills. All these together had an installed capacity of 18.2 million spindles and 208 thousand looms.[45] The production of cotton yarn increased from 534 million kg. in 1950–51 to 1,000 million kgs, and that of cotton cloth (mill sector) from 3.401 million metres to 4,200 million metres in 1973–74.[46] Export of cotton manufactures amounted to Rs. 126.71 crores in 1972–73.[47] In 1973, the industry provided employment directly to 9.5 lakh workers, about one-fifth of the entire labour force of 46 lakh workers employed by registered factories, employing 50 or more workers with the aid of power, or 100 or more workers without the aid of power.[48] However, this increased production of cotton textiles has failed to keep up with the increased demand caused by increase in population and improvements in living standards. This had an upward pressure on prices. In spite of the considerable expansion of the cotton textile industry and the efforts made to resolve the major problems confronting it at the time of Independence, it cannot be said that the industry, as a whole, is in a healthy state.

The industry is still heavily concentrated around Bombay, where 60 per cent of the existing spindles and looms are installed. The industry grew there at first because of the following advantages: the required humid climate; early development of major ports of entry and railway centres, which provided easy access to the cotton-growing areas, to South African coal, initially used as a source of power, and to Lancashire and other industrial centres of the world, from where textile machinery, chemicals, and engineers were imported. The textile industry can now be located with equal advantage either close to the cotton-growing areas or to the markets for textile products. Minimization of transportation costs, as a result of double savings on freight, is achieved by locating the industry in the middle of the cotton-growing areas with large markets for textile goods. As cotton is grown over large areas of India, the cotton textile industry would be better located away from the centres of concentration, such as Bombay, where wages are comparatively high.

Since Independence, the cotton textile industry has suffered from shortage of cotton, specially of the long-staple variety, which is needed for producing fine and superfine cloth. The shortage of imported long-staple cotton has been increasing rapidly with consumer demand shifting in favour of fine and superfine cloth. Periodically, this chronic shortage becomes a critical one, whether because of adverse weather conditions leading to a drop in domestic output, or because of decline in imports due to balance of payments difficulties, or because of an increase in the international price of cotton. The production of cotton increased from 3 million bales in 1950–51 to 6.6 million bales in 1971–72, but it has failed to keep pace with the increase in demand. In 1972–73, because of widespread drought in the country, shortage of power, and fertilizers, cotton production amounted to only 5.5 million bales.[49] In India cotton is at present grown mostly in unirrigated areas, where the average yield per acre is only 32.85 kg, and this is also subject to extreme variations due to variations in rainfall. Compared to this, 112.5 kg per acre is grown in irrigated areas.[50] These yields are very low compared to the per acre yield of approximately over 500 kgs in USA and USSR. To stabilize and increase the domestic output of cotton, it is, therefore, necessary not only to increase the area under cultivation, but also to increase irrigation facilities. The necessity for extending irrigation is further indicated by the gradual shift in demand from short and medium-staple to long-staple cotton, required for making the finer grades of cotton textiles. Long-staple cotton requires greater use of fertilizers, insecticides, and irrigation. The Fifth Plan provides for raising the production of cotton from 6.5 to 8 million bales annually, and increasing the area under cotton cultivation from 7.8 to 8.6 million hectares.[51] However, to overcome the shortage of cotton in years of bad crops and high international prices, it is essential to create a buffer stock in order to stabilize availability of cotton to mills from year to year.

Shortage of cotton in bad years forces the mills to operate below capacity. This leads, on the one hand, to higher costs per unit, as fixed costs have to be spread over smaller output, and, on the other hand, to a lower demand for textiles because of the decline in agricultural incomes. In recent years, power shortages have also frequently forced the textile mills to work considerably below their installed capacity. Further, the advantage of lower labour costs is lost to a very large extent because many of the mills are too small to enjoy fully economies of scale. Many mills have obsolete or worn-out machinery. The percentage of automatic looms to total looms is only 8.3 in India against 100 in the USA, 77.5 in Japan, 55.6 in Germany and 22.8 in Britain.[52] According to the Bombay Mill Owners' Association, nearly 90 per cent of the machinery in the Bombay mills is over 25 years old.[53]

On 1 November 1972, Government took over the management of 46 sick mills and brought them under the management of the National Textile Corporation. The National Textile Corporation now has management responsibility for 100 mills. Rs. 55 crores are allocated under the Fifth Plan to support the activities of the National Textile Corporation in this respect.[54] The Fifth Plan, like the Fourth Plan, lays stress on the fuller utilization of the existing capacity, and modernization of the mills. At present, the replacement demand for textile machinery cannot be satisfied by over 200 indigenous producers. The country has, therefore, to depend on imported machinery to the extent of almost Rs. 20 crores annually.[55] The domestic production of cotton textile machinery should be increased and until this has been done, its import from abroad should be permitted. The Fifth Plan provides for an increase in the production of cotton textile machinery from the estimated production level of Rs. 500 million in 1973–74 to Rs. 560 million in 1978–79.[56]

Jute Industry

From the beginning, the jute industry has been localized in West Bengal in a narrow belt, approximately 60 miles long and two miles wide, on both sides of the Hooghly River in the Greater Calcutta area. It employs roughly 7 per cent of the industrial labour force and is a major earner of foreign exchange.[57] In 1947, after Partition, India got all the jute mills and East Pakistan (now Bangladesh) most of the jute-growing areas. In 1965, there were 97 jute mills with a total employment of 2.71 lakhs and fixed capital of Rs. 56.06 crores. The output of jute goods increased from 10.52 lakh tonnes in 1947 to 13.99 lakh tonnes in 1965–66, and then declined

to 10.88 lakh tonnes in 1968–69,[58] because of the general slow-down of the economy between 1966–68. In 1971–72, 11.29 lakh tonnes of jute goods were produced. Production of jute goods in 1973–74, however, was only 10.74 lakh tonnes, compared to 12.11 lakh tonnes in 1972–73.[59] The attempts made until now to make India self-sufficient in terms of jute have met with only modest success in spite of the increase in production from 3.3 million bales in 1950–51 to 5.7 million bales in 1971–72. Because of the bad crop year, jute output dropped to 5 million bales in 1972–73.[60] The Fifth Five-Year Plan target for 1978–79 is set at 6.5 million bales against the estimated output of 5.6 million bales in 1973–74.[61] India still has to depend on large imports of jute.

The jute industry suffers from the same kind of problem as the cotton textile industry, such as obsolete and worn-out machinery, dependence on imported jute, especially of the finer qualities, and scarcity of power. As jute can be imported only from Bangladesh, imports of jute have in the past been greatly affected by political considerations, which has affected the jute industry adversely. In addition to such acute problems, during the last twenty years, the industry has had perhaps more labour difficulties than any other industry in India. This is partly due to its being located in Greater Calcutta which is prone to labour trouble. The competition facing Indian jute goods in the international market from other producers of jute goods and from substitutes such as synthetic products has also been increasing with time. For the healthy growth of the industry, the pace of rationalization— organizing production into economically viable units of production equipped with modern machinery—should be increased and a vigorous research programme to find new uses for jute, and to develop new jute products, be undertaken.

In April 1971 the Jute Corporation of India Ltd. was established. It is responsible for such activities as price support, commercial and buffer stock operations and also import and export of raw jute. Considerable progress has been made in modernizing the jute industry since 1955. Special emphasis has been placed on the

installation of high-speed machines and of broad looms for the manufacture of carpet backing, to take advantage of the expanding US market for carpet backing. Exports of jute manufactures rose from Rs. 1,128 million in 1950–51 to Rs. 2,490 million in 1966–67, and declined steadily to Rs. 1,892 million by 1970–71. They rose to Rs. 2,633 crores in 1971–72[62] but have shown a decline since then, mainly because of increasing competition from Bangladesh, the other major exporter of jute goods.

Chemical and Petrochemical Industries

Development of a basic chemical industry forms an indispensable link in the industrial and agricultural development process of an economy. The increasing use of chemical fertilizers and insecticides in agriculture, of dyes, acids, alkalis, and other chemicals, by various industries and the increase in demand for paints, varnishes, building materials, soap and detergents, drugs and pharmaceuticals, etc., on the part of consumers, has led to a rapid increase in the demand for basic chemicals. India is not well endowed with basic raw materials needed for the development of a heavy chemical industry. Sulphur, the basic raw material used in the production of sulphuric acid, which in turn is used in the production of other acids and a wide variety of chemical compounds, is not found in India, and has to be imported from the USA, Japan, and Italy. In spite of the scarcity of indigenous raw materials, the chemical and petrochemical industries have grown fairly satisfactorily during the last two decades.

Heavy Chemicals

The term heavy chemicals is generally applied to chemicals like sulphuric acid, soda ash (sodium carbonate) and caustic soda (sodium hydroxide), which can be produced on a large scale at a relatively low cost and are extensively used as raw materials by various industries. The production figures, indicating a phenomenal growth in the case of important heavy chemicals for selected years from 1950–51, and capacity and output figures for 1968–69 and 1973–74 along with target capacity

and output figures for 1978–79, the last years of the Fifth Plan, are given in Table 7.6.

Table 7.6. Production in Selected Heavy Chemical Industries

	Caustic Soda ('000 tonnes)	Soda Ash ('000 tonnes)	Sulphuric Acid ('000 tonnes)
1950–51	12	45	101
1955–56	36	82	167
1960–61	101	152.0	368
1965–66	218	331.0	662
1968–69			
Capacity	400	430	1,900
Output	304	405	1,038
1973–74 (Estimated)			
Capacity	518	618	2,225
Output	450	500	1,400
1978–79 (Target)			
Capacity	1,000	1,100	4,000
Output	785	880	3,200

SOURCE: 1. *Fourth Five-Year Plan*, pp. 334–335.
2. *Economic Survey*, 1972–73, p. 113.
3. *Draft Fifth Five-Year Plan*, p. 157.

The increase in production of caustic soda by the electrolytic process has resulted in a considerable increase in the production of chlorine, a byproduct. The demand for heavy chemicals as a result of the general expansion of the economy has outstripped the increase in supply in the past, and consequently the import of chemicals went on increasing. The index number of chemical and chemical products, with 1960 as base, stood at 301.9 in 1973, representing an annual increase of 9 per cent.[63] During the Fourth Plan, output of caustic soda increased from 304 thousand tonnes to 450 thousand tonnes, an increase of 48 per cent. Soda ash production increased by 23.4 per cent from 405 thousand tonnes to 500 thousand tonnes, and production of sulphuric acid increased by 34.9 per cent from 1,038 thousand tonnes to 1,400 thousand tonnes. Between 1966–67 and 1968–69, the imports of various chemical elements and compounds amounted, on the average, to

Rs. 71.37 crores per year as against Rs. 37.64 crores per year during 1960–61 to 1962–63.[64] Increase in the production of sulphuric acid has necessitated increasing imports of sulphur. Between 1966–67 and 1968–69, the average import of sulphur amounted to Rs. 22.38 crores. In 1972–73, the imports of chemical elements and compounds, which had been steadily increasing since 1950–51, amounted to Rs. 91.38 crores.[65] In order to reduce this increasing pressure on the country's

in Tamil Nadu, the fertilizer industry had its real start as a major industry in India with the establishment of the Sindri Fertilizer Factory on 31 October 1951. Since then, as a result of the establishment of a large number of fertilizer factories, both in the public and private sectors, production of fertilizers has increased rapidly. Table 7.7 gives figures on the rapid growth in the domestic production, installed capacity, and imports of fertilizers since 1951.

Table 7.7.   Production of Fertilizers and Pesticides

	Domestic Production			Imports
	Fertilizers Nitrogenous* (in terms of N)	Phosphatic (in terms of P_2O_5)	Pesticides	Fertilizers Crude (Rs. Lakhs) and Manufactured
1950–51	9	9	—	1,235
1955–56	80	12	—	224
1960–61	101	53	8	1,213
1965–66	232	123	13	4,482
1968–69				
Capacity	1,024	421	34	—
Production	541	210	19	15,019
1973–74 (Estimated)				
Capacity	2,284	560	28.0	—
Production	1,060	317	21.8	NA
1978–79 (Target)				
Capacity	6,000	1,715	39.2	—
Production	4,000	1,250	33.0	NA

NA = Not Available.

SOURCE: 1. *Fourth Five-Year Plan*, p. 300.

2. Government of India, Planning Commission, *Basic Statistics Relating to the Indian Economy*, 1950–51 to 1968–69 (New Delhi, 1971) pp. 76–77.

3. *India: A Reference Annual*, 1975, p. 236.

4. *Draft Fifth Five-Year Plan*, p. 157.

scarce foreign exchange resources, greater use of pyrites and byproduct smelter gases should be made in the production of sulphuric acid, and the pace of development of the chemical industry should be increased further by the expansion of installed capacity and its fuller utilization.

Fertilizer Industry

In spite of the fact that the first factory to produce superphosphate on a commercial scale was established in 1906 at Ranipet

In 1973, there were over 50 factories in operation as against 9 in 1950.[66] Production of nitrogenous fertilizers in 1973–74 amounted to 10.60 lakh tonnes as against 9 thousand tonnes in 1950–51, and P_2O_5 increased to 3.17 lakh tonnes from 9 thousand tonnes during the same period. During the Fourth Plan, the production of nitrogenous fertilizers increased by 96 per cent and that of phosphatic fertilizers by 51 per cent. This was achieved partly through the erection of new plants, partly through the expansion of existing ones, and partly through efforts made to ensure uninterrupted supply of power to fertilizer plants, and adequate wagons for the movement of raw materials and finished products. In spite of this increased production between 1950–51 and 1973–74, the need for fertilizer imports continued to grow because of the continuously increasing use of fertilizer by Indian farmers. In view of this increased demand and greater determination on the part of India to become self-sufficient in food, the Fifth Plan lays great emphasis on the production of fertilizers. The Fifth Plan envisages an increase in nitrogenous fertilizer capacity by 163 per cent and output by 227 per cent, and of phosphatic fertilizer capacity by 206 per cent and output by 294 per cent.

Pharmaceuticals, Petrochemicals and Plastics

The drug and pharmaceutical industries have made good progress since 1950. In 1948, the drugs and pharmaceuticals produced in India amounted to Rs. 12 crores. The value of drugs and pharmaceuticals produced by large- and medium-scale firms during 1970 amounted to roughly Rs. 250 crores as against Rs. 225 crores in 1969.[67] In 1973–74 their output increased further to Rs. 350 crores.[68] India produces different kinds of surgical instruments, antibiotics, and other drugs including a variety of synthetic hormones. In spite of this growth, India had to import medicinal and pharmaceutical products worth Rs. 17.50 crores in 1968–69,[69] as against Rs. 9.97 crores in 1950–51. This upward trend in imports has continued because of the enormous expansion in medical and hospital facilities in the country.

The first petrochemical complex was commissioned at Trombay in 1966 by the Union Carbide India Ltd., for the manufacture of menthol. Two more petrochemical complexes of the Union Carbide India Ltd., and National Organic Chemicals Ltd., started production in 1967 and 1968 respectively. The Indian Petrochemicals Corporation Ltd. was established in 1969 to start petrochemical complexes around

the public sector oil refineries. A provision of Rs. 284 crores has been made in the Fifth Plan for the completion of the petrochemical projects already under execution.[70] The Fifth Plan does not provide for the start of any new large petrochemical projects. Since 1966 the production of plastics, synthetic fibre, and rubber, has been growing rapidly. Plastics production amounted to 122 thousand tonnes in 1973 as against 114 thousand tonnes in 1972. Synthetic fibre production amounted to 26.4 thousand tonnes, an increase of 17 per cent over 1972. Production of synthetic rubber, however, declined to 20.9 thousand tonnes in 1973 from 32.3 thousand tonnes in 1972.[71]

Sugar Industry

The sugar industry ranks second among the major agro-industries in India. Besides employing over 2.3 lakh workers, the industry sustains about 2.5 million agriculturists. Excise duty on sugar is a major source of revenue for the Union Government. In addition, since 1960–61 the country has been able to earn much-needed foreign exchange by exporting sugar.

For centuries before the beginning of the modern sugar-mill industry with the establishment of the first sugar mill in Bihar in 1903, the sugar industry had existed as an important cottage industry. The grant of protection in 1931 gave the sugar industry a great impetus and India became self-sufficient with regard to sugar before the Second World War. The number of operating sugar mills rose to 137 by 1937 and sugar output rose to almost a million tonnes. Figures indicating the rapid progress made by the sugar industry from 1950–51 to 1973–74 and the target capacity and output figures for 1978–79 laid down in the Fifth Plan are given in Table 7.8.

It is envisaged that the area under sugarcane cultivation, which increased from 1.71 million hectares to an estimated 2.8 million hectares in 1973–74, will increase to 3.2 million hectares in 1978–79.[72] The Fifth Plan envisages that of a total output of 170 million tonnes of sugarcane, 89.2 million tonnes (52.5 per cent) will go into *gur* and *khandsari* production, 20.5 million

Table 7.8. Supply and Demand for Sugar
(million tonnes)

	Production[a]	Domestic Consumption	Exports
1950–51[a]	1.12	1.10	0.06
1955–56	1.89	1.97	0.07
1960–61	3.03	2.13	0.25
1965–66	3.54	2.79	0.39
1969–70	4.26	3.26	0.22
1973–74	4.30	2.68	0.22
1970–79 (target)	5.70	—	—

[a]Up to 1966–67 the sugar year was November–October and later on it was changed to October–September.

SOURCE: 1. *Draft Fifth Five-Year Plan*, p. 158.
2. *India, A Reference Annual*, 1957, 1974, 1975.

tonnes (12 per cent) for seed and chewing, and the balance of 60.3 million tonnes (27 per cent) only for the manufacture of sugar. The 5.7 million tonne target for sugar, after allowing for per capita internal consumption of 8.68 kgs, will leave a margin of half-a-million tonnes for building a buffer stock to ensure price stability, and for export.[73]

In the past, the production of sugar has varied greatly from year to year. The incentives provided through the raising of the minimum price of sugarcane and the maximum price of sugar in 1951, led to a very rapid expansion in production and to the end of sugar rationing. Subsequently, to discourage sugarcane production, the cane prices were lowered. This policy had the desired result but the derationing of sugar had led to higher demand for sugar, resulting in higher sugar prices and its importation. Imports of sugar in 1955–56 amounted to 70,000 tonnes. In 1954, Government again adopted the policy of protection and raised the minimum price of sugar, as a result of which the output of sugar increased rapidly and India was once again able to export sugar. The sugar controls of 1957–58 again adversely affected the production of sugar, but the incentives provided by Government once again led to a rapid expansion of sugar production, to 3.03 million tonnes in 1960–61. From 1960–61, sugar production has increased steadily because of much more consistent policies pursued by Government to encourage sugar production. However, year-to-year output has continued to fluctuate, mainly due to fluctuations in sugarcane production, due to the vagaries of monsoons, and the prices of *gur* and *khandsari*. They are not only good substitutes for sugar, but compete for available sugarcane supplies, the basic raw material for the production of all three. In bad crop years, the prices of *gur* and *khandsari* tend to rise faster than sugar prices in the absence of controls. Due to greater demand pressure, a larger proportion of sugarcane is used for their production, which leaves a smaller percentage of a smaller crop for sugar production.

The sugarcane yield per hectare in the case of India is only 48 tonnes, compared to 198.59 tonnes in Hawaii, 96.86 tonnes in UAR and 75.86 tonnes in Indonesia.[74] Furthermore, the sucrose recovery rate is lower in India compared to other leading sugar-producing countries. In spite of lower labour costs, Indian sugar, therefore, is faced with tough competition in the international market. From the beginning, sugarcane growing and the sugar industry have been concentrated in the subtropical-climate states of Uttar Pradesh, Bihar, and Punjab. Together, they grow about 54 per cent of the sugarcane whereas Maharashtra, Tamil Nadu, and Andhra Pradesh, with higher sugarcane yields and sucrose recovery rates, due to their tropical climate, account for roughly 27 per cent of sugarcane production. Sugar mills tend to be located close to sugarcane-growing areas to avoid the excessive loss of sucrose which results if it is not crushed within 24 hours of cutting. So far, the shifting of sugarcane growing to the high-yield areas has been slow due to the competing demand for land to grow other cash crops like ground nuts, cotton, chillies, and tobacco, and for lack of irrigation facilities. Irrigation facilities should be provided to facilitate the relocation of the sugar industry in tropical areas in the long run. Meanwhile, the sugarcane yield should be raised by encouraging the use of better agricultural techniques and better seeds. The sugar industry is a seasonal industry, and its activity is confined to the sugarcane harvesting season—primarily during the winter months of November to March. The greater length of the harvesting season in the tropical areas in the South will also make it possible for the sugar industry to work for longer periods during the year, resulting in greater use of plant and equipment.

The three main by-products of sugar are *bagassee,* which the sugar mills use as fuel and which is also used in the manufacture of paper pulp and cardboard, press mud, and molasses. Molasses is used in the manufactue of alcohol and power alcohol, aconitic and acetic acid, chemicals and tobacco, and from press mud, wax is extracted. The Fifth Plan emphasises fuller use of these by-products. Diversification of the raw material base with the production of beet sugar is contemplated during the Fifth Plan.

Since Independence, there has been a remarkable expansion of the sugar industry in the cooperative sector. In 1972–73, 87 of the 228 working sugar mills were in the cooperative sector, and produced 37.5 per cent of the sugar output.[75] In 1970 a Commission of Enquiry on the sugar industry was appointed to study in depth the working of the industry in the context of demands for its nationalization. In April 1974 the Commission recommended the nationalization of sugar mills except for those in the cooperative sector. However, half of the members of the Commission, including its Chairman, Mr. Bhargava, stated that Government should take over the sugar mills only if they failed to convert themselves into public limited concerns by a specified period of time.

Cement Industry

Production of cement in the country started at Madras in 1904. By 1926 cement production had increased to 6 lakh tonnes. In 1925, at the recommendation of the tariff board, cement was granted protection. The Indian Cement Manufacturers Association was formed in 1927 to secure closer cooperation among cement manufacturers. The Cement Mar-

keting Company was formed in 1930 for organizing sale of cement and extending marketing facilities. The ACC established in 1936 brought all the cement companies under common management, with the exception of one or two small companies. In 1938, the Dalmia Jain group was organized. The centralization of ownership and control in the hands of these two groups has led to the financial and administrative integration of different cement factories, the extent of which has no equal in the history of private industry in India. The ACC and Dalmia groups, barring short periods of time, have cooperated with each other in matters of marketing and pricing policies.

In 1974 there were 51 cement factories in India, only 9 of which were in the public sector, with an installed capacity of about 20 million tonnes.[76] Total production of cement in 1973–74 was 14.7 million tonnes, compared to 2.7 million tonnes in 1950–51. Figures detailing the development of the industry from 1950–51 to 1973–74 along with the Fifth Plan capacity and output targets are given in Table 7.9.

Table 7.9. Growth of Cement Industry
(million tonnes)

Year	Capacity	Production	Capacity Utilization (percentage)
1950–51	3.3	2.7	82
1955–56	4.9	4.6	94
1960–61	9.4	7.9	84
1965–66	11.6	10.8	93
1970–71	17.3	14.3	83
1971–72	19.4	15.0	77
1972–73	19.5	15.5	79
1973–74	19.8	14.7	74
1978–79 (target)	29.0	25.0	86

SOURCE: 1. *India, A Reference Annual,* 1957 and 1965.
2. *Draft Fifth Five-Year Plan.*

Limestone, coal, clay, and gypsum are the principal raw materials used in the manufacture of cement. The location of the industry is determined by the availability of limestone, as almost 1.6 tonnes of limestone is required to produce a tonne of cement, and the proximity to large centres of demand because of the heavy cost of transporting cement. · Good quality limestone is available in almost all parts of India, and as a result, cement factories are well distributed throughout India. New cement factories, especially, are being located as close as possible to the large demand centres for cement, taking into account availability of limestone, to minimize transportation costs.

From 1950–51 to 1970–71 the cement capacity rose steadily from 3.3 million tonnes to 17.3 million tonnes, and cement production from 2.7 million tonnes to 14.3 million tonnes. During the Fourth Plan period, because of the general slackening of the growth of the economy, the growth in the installed capacity slowed down, and in 1973–74, only 14.7 million tonnes of cement were produced as against 14.3 million tonnes in 1970–71. The Fifth Plan, by means of expanding the installed capacity to 25 million tonnes and its better utilization, envisages an output of 25 million tonnes in 1970–79. Of the planned additional capacity of 9.2 million tonnes, the private sector will contribute 3 to 4 million tonnes and the balance of 5.2 to 6.2 million tonnes will take place in the public sector.[77]

The demand for cement has been growing rapidly because of the quickening pace of building roads, dams, and other public works projects, and housing construction in the private sector, since 1950–51. The unrealistic regulation of distribution of cement through the permit system has been primarily responsible for the existence of the black market, which has enriched the unscrupulous, and denied the cement producers a fair return. A better distribution system will have to be devised to encourage investment by the private sector in the cement industry. By encouraging the production of slag cement from slag, a by-product of the steel industry, which is inferior to the standard portland cement but can be used for housing construction and other minor projects, the demand pressure for cement can be considerably eased. Some progress in this direction has already been made.

India has already taken up the manufacture of asbestos cement for the manufacture of roofing materials and pipe accessories.

Paper and Paper Board, and Newsprint Industry

Production of machine-made paper started with the establishment of the Bally Paper Mills near Calcutta in 1870. In 1925, protection was afforded to the industry, as a result of which it grew rapidly. In 1950–51, 116 thousand tonnes of paper and paper board were produced in India.[78] Newsprint manufacturing in India started with the establishment of the National Newsprint and Paper Mills Ltd., which went into production in 1955. The increase in production of paper and paper board and newsprint from 1950–51 along with Fifth Plan targets, is detailed in Table 7.10.

Table 7.10. Growth of Paper Industry

(thousand tonnes)

	Paper and Paper Board	Newsprint
1950–51	116	—
1955–56	190	3
1960–61	350	23.0
1965–66	558	30.3
1968–69	646.6	31
1973–74 (Estimated)		
Capacity	1025	75
Output	830	43
1978–79 (Target)		
Capacity	1400	205
Output	1200	151

SOURCE: 1. *India, Reference Annual*, 1957 and 1965, p. 226.

2. *Draft Fifth Five-Year Plan*, pp. 157, 158.

In the past, the paper industry had been overly concentrated around Calcutta because of its easy access to coal, areas producing *sabi* and *bhabar* grasses and bamboo, its large supply of water, and the availability of needed port facilities for handling the imported wood pulp from Canada and Finland that is required for the manufacture of finer qualities of paper. Since 1951 a better spread of the industry has been obtained by locating new paper mills in other parts of the country. The increasing production of paper and newsprint in the private sector has been unable to keep pace with increasing demand, resulting from increase in population and literacy; as a result, India still has to import large quantities of paper and newsprint, and wood pulp for their manufacture. Hindustan Paper Corporation Ltd., a public sector undertaking, was, therefore, set up in 1970 to establish pulp and paper projects in the country. In the Fifth Plan, output targets of 1.2 million tonnes for paper and paper board, representing an increase of 45 per cent over the estimated output of 830 thousand tonnes in 1973–74, and for newsprint of 151 thousand tonnes, representing an increase of 251 per cent over the estimated production of 43 thousand tonnes in 1973–74, are provided.

Overall Evaluation of Industrial Growth Since 1955–56

1955–56, the year just before the beginning of the Second Plan, is selected as the starting point for evaluating the growth of the Indian industry because only in the Second Plan was development of the industrial sector given top priority. Again, it was only after 1955–56 that key industries such as iron and steel, aluminium, machine tools, heavy electrical and mechanical engineering, and heavy inorganic chemicals were established, and they started changing the industrial scene in India. The general index of industrial production which stood at 72.7[79] in 1955–56 (base 1960=100), climbed to 200.6 in 1973[80] and showed a further increase of 2.5 per cent in 1974–75.[81] Investment in public sector undertakings, which derive their finances in the form of equity capital and loans from the Central Government, amounted to Rs. 872 crores during the Second Plan (1956–57 to 1960–61), Rs. 1,462 crores in the Third Plan (1961–62 to 1965–66), Rs. 1,061 crores in the three annual plan years (1966–67 to 1968–69) and Rs. 1,669 crores during the first four years of the Fourth Plan (1969–70 to 1972–73). More than

anything else, this rapid growth of investment in Central Government undertakings, which had grown to 113 by 31 March 1973, has been responsible for establishment of heavy industry and its diversification.[82]

During the ten years from 1961 to 1970, basic industries, incorporating mining and quarrying, heavy inorganic chemicals, cement, basic metals, and electricity, registered an annual growth of 8.3 per cent; capital goods industries, incorporating industrial machinery, railway equipment, and motor vehicles, an annual growth of 8.4 per cent; intermediate goods industries, an annual growth of 4.5 per cent; and consumer goods, the lowest annual growth rate of only 3.2 per cent.[83] The overall annual growth of the industrial sector amounted to 6.1 per cent during this period.

The industrial sector for the first five years from 1961 to 1965 registered an annual growth rate of about 9 per cent as against only 3.4 per cent during the five years from 1966 to 1970. This was because of the general slowdown of the economy in 1966 when industrial production actually declined by 1.5 per cent. However, this downward trend was reversed in 1968.[84] Installed capacity registered a slightly higher increase of 6.4 per cent, from 1961 to 1970, compared to 6.1 per cent in industrial production. Consequently, the level of utilization of the potential installed capacity fell from 87.7 per cent in 1960 to 80.4 per cent in 1970.[86] The level of potential-utilization ratio declined in the case of basic industries from 84.6 to 83.9, in the case of capital goods from 76.8 to 59.2, in the case of intermediate goods from 89.9 to 79.5, and in the case of consumer goods from 90.3 in 1960 to 86.2 in 1970.[87]

The growth-rate of industrial production declined sharply from 7.5 per cent in 1969 to 3.1 per cent in 1970 and to 2.9 per cent in 1971. This prolonged and sharp decline in the growth rate of industrial production was interrupted briefly in 1972 when it amounted to approximately 7 per cent.[88] In 1973–74 industrial production actually registered a slight decline. Capacity in major industries during the Fourth Plan grew at only 3.8 per cent and the average growth rate of industrial production amounted to only 3.9 per cent.[89]

The major factors responsible for this slowdown were the same as in most other previous periods of industrial slowdowns since Independence. The shortage of raw materials, especially in the case of cotton and jute, adversely affected industrial performance. Shortage of steel—due to the decline in steel production, and the lack of demand for railway wagons—and of capital goods in general, adversely affected the utilization of existing installed capacity, particularly in the engineering industries. Capacity constraints, imposed by Government in important industries like paper, caustic soda, soda ash, and other heavy chemicals, limited the growth rates of these industries which, in turn, adversely affected the performance of other industries. Industrial labour and management disputes also took their toll.

Since 1975, however, the economy has come out of this prolonged period of stagnation. The industrial output, especially in agro-based industries, benefited greatly from the record output of 116 million tonnes of foodgrains and the general increase in output of commercial crops in 1975–76.[90] A substantial acceleration in the rate of growth of industrial production has taken place since the second quarter of 1975–76, and was estimated to have reached 8 per cent in January–March 1976.[91] Power generation from existing thermal plants increased by about 13 per cent during 1975–76.[92] Freight-traffic on the Indian Railways registered an increase of 10 to 11 per cent and was estimated at about 220 million tonnes. For the first time, the demand for freight cars is being met currently and in full.[93] The index of industrial production is estimated to show an increase of about 4.5 per cent during 1975–76.[94] This revival in industrial growth has been led by the public sector which recorded an increase of 15.7 per cent in 1975–76.[95]

Conclusion and Future Outlook

The overall performance of the industrial sector since 1950–51, though not specta-

cular, has been impressive. Steel and power plants, modern factories for making machine tools, locomotives, ships, pharmaceuticals, and petrochemicals have been built and made operational. All this successfully and unequivocally demonstrates India's ability to use modern technology. Technical and managerial know-how has developed to such an extent that India is now in a position to plan and build large hydroelectric projects, modern steel plants, ships, locomotives, jet planes, industrial machines, and the sophisticated tools required to make all these. The economy has developed a considerable degree of self-reliance, and this can be utilized successfully to foster a much more rapid growth of the industrial sector, which is still relatively small, during the second half of the seventies. The progress which the Green Revolution has made since the middle sixties, first in the wheat-growing areas, such as Punjab and Haryana, and now in the rice-growing areas, especially in Andhra Pradesh and Tamil Nadu, has led to an enormous increase in the demand for fertilizers and agricultural implements. Very soon the increased demand for industrial consumer goods, which has already been felt in Punjab and Haryana, is likely to create a powerful and new chain of demand for industrial products all over India. Thus, the industrial sector of the economy, already out of its infancy, is poised for a take-off in the next decade. For the full exploitation of this newly created potential, it is essential that measures be taken to eliminate the factors which not only hindered, in the past, a more rapid growth of the industrial sector but even imposed periodically-formidable obstacles to maintaining the steady rate of industrial growth achieved in the first half of the sixties.

The criticism that there has been excessive investment in heavy industry, power generation, and transportation, which could not be justified on the basis of the high capital-output ratio and the long gestation period seems unwarranted, considering the frequent shortages of steel, cement, electricity, and transportation facilities, which often forced sizable segments of the industrial sector to work below capacity, and have now become chronic. In providing for the future development of such heavy industries, the Planning Commission should act more boldly and with greater imagination, rather than be slavishly guided by the future projections of their demand based on current trends. It is not being suggested here that in the planning their future growth, demand considerations should be ignored. Rather, what is intended is to point out that, if errors in the estimation of the demand for them cannot be avoided because of the long gestation periods involved, then errors of overestimation should be preferable to those of underestimation. On the basis of past experience, not only are the chances of overestimation small but, even if made, they are likely to prove less expensive than those of underestimation.

The reorganization and rationalization of traditional industries, such as those of cotton, jute, cement, and sugar to name only a few, should be emphasised further. Uneconomic units should be closed, and obsolete and worn-out equipment should be replaced to lower the cost of production and to give their products a competitive edge in the domestic as well as international makets. The labour unions, which have developed a comparatively greater amount of strength in India at considerably lower levels of economic development than was historically achieved by labour unions in the industrially advanced nations of today, have successfully resisted rationalization with the help of politicians both in and out of power. There is a strong need for education of all concerned, for steady development cannot be maintained without making the most efficient use of capital and without increasing the productivity of labour. In order to make more intensive use of capital equipment, multiple shifts, wherever possible, should be instituted. This has generally been resisted by labour thus far.

Greater consistency in industrial development should be planned by the simultaneous development of mutually consistent industrial projects. This can be done by proper coordination of decisions on the demand and supply sides. A flexible but effective organization should be built at the Central Government level to resolve bottlenecks which may be difficult to foresee and hard to avoid. For achieving the optimum rates of industrial growth it will be essential to revamp the managerial cadres both in the public as well as in the private sector and to streamline the decision-making processes. In the public sector, most of the time the ultimate decision-making power is vested in the top echelons of the bureaucratic hierarchy in Central Ministries rather than in the plant managers on the spot. The people occupying these positions are trained to be conservative in their approach and cannot afford to be daring and independent because their decisions are always subject to review by the minister in charge, the cabinet, and utimately, parliament. In this kind of environment, survival rather than the exercising of initiative, becomes the objective, as the best paid positions go to those who manage to survive the longest. When the decision affects more than one ministry, as is quite often the case, simple survival can be assured merely by leaving the ultimate decisions to others. This sort of administrative set-up in the past has resulted in very costly delays in starting important key industrial projects.

Private sector enterprises are not immune to the inadequacies of government machinery in these respects, for most decisions made by them cannot be implemented without the sanction of the needed licence, foreign exchange permit, or even a loan. Especially since the nationalization of the large commercial banks, the dependence of the private sector on public sector financial institutions for financing medium- and large-scale projects has increased. Because of the dual role of capitalist-cum-entrepreneur played by the managing agents under the managing agency system, there is a greater concentration of decision-making authority at the top even in the private sector in India, than in most Western economies. The prevalent system has, therefore, to be changed, as ultimately nothing affects the rate of industrial growth more than the quality of those who occupy the top entrepreneurial and managerial positions. Though India has a large number of people with the capabilities and qualities demanded of top managers and entrepreneurs, it has still to demonstrate the ability to create the environment and the institutional set-up which will enable them to flourish. This has been realized for some time now and some steps have already been taken, especially in the private sector, to delegate a greater amount of authority to middle management. The degree of success achieved in these respects will determine the destiny of the Indian industries.

REFERENCES

1. Harry G. Johnson, *Economic Policies towards Less Developed Countries* (New York: Praeger, 1968), pp. 45–46.
2. Government of India, Planning Commission, *The First Five-Year Plan*, 1951–56 (New Delhi, 1952), p. 652.
3. Government of India, Planning Commission, *Draft Fifth Five-Year Plan*, 1974–79, Vol. I, (New Delhi, 1973), p. 3.
4. Government of India, *The Second Five-Year Plan: The Framework* (New Delhi: Ministry of Information and Broadcasting, Publications Division, December 1955), p. 13.
5. R. Palme Dutt, *The Problem of India* (New York: International Publishers, 1943). See chapters VI and VII for an interesting study of the role of British imperialism in Indian economic development.
6. D.R. Gadgil, *Industrial Evolution in India in Recent Times* (London and New York: Oxford University Press, 1954), p. 38.
7. Vera Anstey, *The Economic Development of India* (London: Longmans, Green and Co., 1931), pp. 509–511. Also see R. Palme Dutt, *The Problem of India* (New York: International Publishers, 1943), pp. 45–70.
8. Government of India, Ministry of Information and Broadcasting, Publications Division, *India: A Reference Annual*, 1975 (Delhi, 1975), pp. 221–222.
9. Information Service of India, Washington D.C., *India News*, 27 August 1976, p. 3.
10. Albert O. Hirschman, *The Strategy of Economic Development* (New Haven: Yale University Press, 1958), p. 100.
11. Information Service of India, Washington, D.C., "Public Sector Undertakings", *India News*, 14 April 1972, p. 3.
12. *Draft Fifth Five-Year Plan*, Vol. II p. 132.
13. Ibid., p. 140.
14. *First Five-Year Plan*, p. 438.
15. *Draft Fifth Five-Year Plan*, Vol. II, pp. 141, 156.
16. *India News*, 8 October 1976, p. 2.
17. *Draft Fifth Five-Year Plan*, Vol. II, p. 141.
18. Government of India, *Economic Survey: 1972–73* New Delhi, 1974. pp. 73 and 163.
19. *India News*, 8 October 1976, p. 2.
20. *India: A Reference Annual*, 1975, p. 223.
21. *Economic Survey: 1972–73*, p. 110.
22. *Draft Fifth Five-Year Plan*, Vol. II, p. 156.
23. Ibid., p. 142.
24. Ibid.
25. K. Easwaran, "Exports and the Engineering Industry", *Blue Supplement to Monthly Commentary on Indian Economic Conditions*, Vol. 12, No. 1 (August 1970), p. 9.
26. Ibid.
27. Ibid.
28. *Draft Fifth Five-Year Plan*, Vol. II, p. 143.
29. Ibid.
30. *India: A Reference Annual*, 1975, p. 234.
31. *Fourth Five-Year Plan*, p. 299.
32. *India: A Reference Annual*, 1975, p. 225.
33. *Draft Fifth Five-Year Plan*, p. 156.
34. *India: A Reference Annual*, 1975, p. 206.
35. *India News*, 22 September 1972, p. 2.
36. *India: A Reference Annual*, 1975, p. 206.
37. *Draft Fifth Five-Year Plan*, Vol. II, p. 118.
38. Ibid., p. 143.
39. Indian Institute of Public Opinion, "Planning for Power: The Crisis Ahead", *Blue Supplement to the Monthly Commentary on Indian Economic Conditions*, Vol. 13, No. 10 (May 1972), p. 1.
40. Ibid., p. iii.
41. *Draft Fifth Five-Year Plan*, Vol. II, p. 118.
42. *Monthly Commentary on Indian Economic Conditions*, May 1972, p. iii.
43. Jawaharlal Nehru, *The Discovery of India* (New York: Anchor Books, Doubleday & Company, 1960), p. 211.
44. M.R. Chaudhuri, *Indian Industries Development and Location* (New Delhi: Oxford & IBH Publishing Co., 1970), p. 356.
45. *India: A Reference Annual*, 1975, p. 228.
46. Ibid., p. 158.
47. Ibid., p. 257.
48. Ibid., p. 214.
49. *India: A Reference Annual*, 1975, p. 165.
50. Dubey, R.N. and Balbir Singh, *Economic Geography of India* (Allahabad: Kitab Mahal, 1971), p. 235.
51. *Draft Fifth Five-Year Plan*, Vol. II, p. 7.
52. Chaudhuri, *Indian Industries Development and Location*, p. 169.
53. Dubey and Singh, *Economic Geography of India*, p. 472.
54. *Draft Fifth Five-Year Plan*, Vol. II, p. 149.
55. Chaudhuri, *Indian Industries Development and Location*, p. 169.
56. *Draft Fifth Five-Year Plan*, Vol. II, p. 149.
57. Chaudhuri, *Indian Industries Development and Location*, p. 171.
58. *Draft Fifth Five-Year Plan*, p. 158.
59. *India: A Reference Annual*, 1975, p. 228.
60. Ibid., p. 194.
61. *Draft Fifth Five-Year Plan*, Vol. I, p. 38.

62. *India: A Reference Annual*, 1975, p. 270.
63. *India: A Reference Annual*, 1975, p. 227.
64. Government of India, *Basic Statistics, Relating to the Indian Economy*, 1950–51 to 1968–69 (New Delhi: Manager of Publications, 1971), pp. 76–77.
65. *India: A Reference Annual*, 1975, p. 260.
66. *India: A Reference Annual*, 1975, p. 238.
67. Government of India, *India: 1972–73* (New Delhi Manager of Publications, 1973), p. 368.
68. *India: A Reference Annual*, 1975, p. 235.
69. *Basic Statistics Relating to the Indian Economy*, p. 79.
70. *Draft Fifth Five-Year Plan*, p. 146.
71. *India: A Reference Annual*, 1975, p. 236.
72. *Draft Fifth Five-Year Plan*, p. 22
73. Ibid.
74. Ibid.
75. *India: A Reference Annual*, 1975, p. 239.
76. *India: A Reference Annual*, 1975, pp. 228, 229.
77. *Draft Fifth Five-Year Plan*, p. 148.
78. *India: A Reference Annual*, 1975, p. 226.

BIBLIOGRAPHY

1. Bhagwati, J. and Desai, P.: *India, Planning for Industrialization.* New York. Oxford University Press, 1970.
2. Chaudhuri, M.R.: *Indian Industries Development and Location.* New Delhi. Oxford and IBH Publishing Co., 1970.
3. Gadgil, D.R.: *Industrial Evolution in India in Recent Times.* London. Oxford University Press, 1954.
4. Government of India, Planning Commission: *Fourth Five-Year Plan, 1969–74* (New Delhi 1970).
5. Government of India, Planning Commission: *Draft Fifth Five-Year Plan,* 1974–79, Vol. II, New Delhi, 1974.
6. Government of India, Administrative Reform Commission: *Report of the Study Team on Public Sector Undertakings.* New Delhi, 1967.
7. Streeten, Paul: *The Crisis of Indian Planning.* London. Oxford University Press, 1968.

8

Small-Scale and Cottage Industries in India

RAMSINH ASHER

Mahatma Gandhi emphasised the enlargement and strengthening of cottage industries as an effective strategy to eradicate the grievous poverty in India. Like other productive activities, cottage industries too increase the production of consumable goods, but at the same time by creating widespread work opportunities, these industries distribute the ability to consume the nation's output more evenly throughout the population. Gandhi was not against modern technology, but in his calculus deconcentration of economic and political power and promotion of human dignity through economic self-sufficiency ranked high above mere productive efficiency.

While retaining a mildly sympathetic attitude towards the development of cottage industries, the Indian Planning Commission embarked upon a strategy of first achieving rapid economic growth through the introduction of modern mass-scale technology, and then turning to resolve the poverty problem through a redistribution of the increased output. It was recognized that introduction of modern technology was essential for any nation that was to become a part of the modern community of nations. If modern technology brought a concentration of economic power, it was not feared by our planners because such concentration was to be increasingly in the public sector. Besides, the Planning Commission's strategy emerged primarily not so much from its concern for equal distribution of income, or for decentralization of economic power, but rather from its zeal for India to become an economically independent nation with the modern industrial technology which had by-passed the colonial countries. The industrial revolution has permitted industrialized nations to sustain rapidly-growing populations at rising standards of living with the help of mass-scale production technology. India decided to follow the path of this success story and adopted the policy of rapid industrialization as the sure remedy for economic stagnation.

However, in the advanced countries, industrialization was gradual, and was accompanied by (i) the opening-up of large land masses with virtually un-utilized and abundant resources, and also by (ii) the opening-up of vast markets in the colonial countries. Rising populations and gradually increasing productive capacity resulting from the application of new techniques were readily absorbed in these new frontiers. In contrast, for some of the newly developing countries there is no possibility of territorial expansion to settle their increasing populations, nor are there any unused resources and un-saturated markets waiting to be exploited. Furthermore, historically the develop-ment as well as the introduction of large-scale production technology was a gradual one in the advanced nations, permitting the technologically displaced workers sufficient time for relocation. The rate of labour displacement caused by capital-intensive technology was much slower then, compared to today. Today, for instance, an American worker in manufacturing works with an average of $ 30,000 worth of capital equipment, and produces six to eight times as much output as his counterpart did some 70 years ago.[1] It is obviously the task of some generations to develop such productive capabilities. But if that much machinery somehow "materializes" in a developing country tomorrow, its initial impact would be to make millions unemployed, until some retrain to operate and service the machinery; and much later, some more retrain to be absorbed in all the complicated processes of producing such machinery, provided that this is well within the limits set by resource availability, markets, technical and orga-nizational know-how, and the environ-mental constraints. This seems to be the way employment can increase with modern technology. Its potential rate of employ-ment creation is at best slow, and depends on the fulfilment of many strenuous con-ditions. The process is most likely to generate labour surpluses at a faster rate than it generates employment. Thus, if poverty is the emergent issue, moderniza-tion is not likely to be the most direct solution.

Our post-Independence record of industrialization has been impressive, but so has been the incidence of unemployment

Table 8.1

Year	Labour Force (crores)	Unemployment (crores)	(percentage)
1951	14.5	0.25	2
1956	15.4	0.50	3
1961	16.6	0.80	5
1966	18.3	1.15	6
1971	20.6	1.55	8

SOURCE: Wilfred Malenbaum, *Modern India's Economy* (Columbus, Ohio: Charles E. Merrill, 1971), p. 109.

as shown by Table 8.1.

Tracing this rise in unemployment to the population explosion—a large popula-tion base and the death-rate falling faster than the birth-rate—Indian planners launched the world's first nation-wide population-control programme. Demogra-phers tell us that a reduction in death rate is relatively easy to accomplish, but any downward adjustment in birth rate is essentially a long-run phenomenon, and is also believed to be a function of evenly increasing per capita real incomes. Once again, the rationale for population control policy is unimpleachable, but inasmuch as a drastic reduction in birth rates is a long-run phenomenon, the policy has little potential for solving the immediate prob-lems of unemployment and poverty. In fact, it can be argued that the two major policy choices of our planners, namely the introduction of modern industrial technology, and the reduction in birth rates, are two of the inevitable trends of our time which would come about even in the absence of planning. Through plan-ning, India has sought to accelerate their coming. On the other hand, even where the most modern technology is in use, and where population pressure is not an immediate problem, poverty and unem-ployment continue to exist. For example, in 1975, over 8 per cent of the US labour force was unemployed, and about 13 per cent of Americans had incomes below the poverty line. Thus, even when there are sufficient pressures for modernization and favourable conditions for population con-trol, eradication of poverty and reduction of unemployment is not automatic. These goals call for some rigorously planned action, even in countries which have long ago acquired the ability to eliminate poverty and unemployment. It is in this context that we must turn to a primarily employment-oriented rather than a primarily productive-efficiency-oriented policy alternative of developing cottage and small-scale industries. As will be shown below, this alternative may be a viable one, and more pertinent as well as efficient for India's special circumstances.

After a brief comparison of the small-scale and cottage industries with those in some other countries, we shall discuss some theoretical issues to formulate the rationale and to provide some criteria for evaluating the performance of these industries. Next, we shall review the measures taken during the four five-year plans, and examine the problems of our small-scale and cottage industries in some detail. Finally we shall return to the issue of the appropriate industrial policy and evaluate the prospects of the small-scale and cottage industries in India.

Small-Scale Industry—A Comparison

The pre-Independence Indian economy can be characterized by two features:

(i) The predominance of agriculture and the relative smallness of the manufacturing sector. In 1911, as well as in 1951, agriculture provided a livelihood to around 70 per cent of the population, while only about 10 per cent derived their livelihood from manufacturing.[2] The agricultural sector contributed about 50 per cent of the net national income and 70 per cent of the total employment in 1911 as well as in 1951. In contrast, the manufacturing sector contributed about 14 per cent of the net national income in 1911, and 17 per cent in 1951.

(ii) Not only was the Indian manufacturing sector small, it was dominated by the cottage and small-scale industries. The 1911 census estimated that for each worker employed in factories, there were roughly 11 workers employed in the cottage and small-scale industries. The figures for 1951 still showed a four-to-one ratio in favour of the cottage and small-scale industries. For a comparison, let

us look at the role small-scale industry plays in some other economies.

The manufacturing sector in the USA was already well developed by 1951. Yet, over 90 per cent of all manufacturing establishments in 1954 were small, employing up to 10 workers each. In total, these enterprises accounted for 25 per cent of the manufacturing employment, and 22 per cent of the output of all manufacturing establishments.[3] Thus in an economy dominated by large-scale technology, there were still certain functions which the small firms could perform efficiently.

The relative abundance of capital and shortage of labour has pushed the labour-saving technology as far as it would go in the US, whereas in Japan labour was a relatively abundant resource until recently. A manufacturing enterprise employing up to 300 workers is classified as small in Japan, provided that it uses labour-intensive techniques. This condition is indirectly enforced by putting a ceiling on the amount of capital a small enterprise can employ. This ceiling of 5 crore yen or about Rs. 11 lakh for 300 workers, is quite small by modern standards. It restricts the application of capital to about Rs. 3,600 per worker, compared to over Rs. 225,000 of capital applied on the average per US worker.

On the basis of labour productivity alone, it is estimated that a worker in a small enterprise of up to 10 employees is only 25 per cent as productive as his counterpart in a large enterprise of over 1,000 employees in Japan. In contrast, a small-enterprise worker is 73 per cent as productive in the UK and 70 per cent as productive in USA as his counterpart in a large enterprise in his respective country.[4] This difference in the relative productivity of the Japanese small-industry worker can be traced to at least two factors. The first of course is the amount of capital employed per worker, and the second is the type of technology in use.

For any given technology, there is a combination of labour and capital which can produce a certain output most efficiently. Adding more capital than needed for the most efficient production would reduce the marginal efficiency of capital, unless the scale of production is increased as well. Similarly, adding more labour than required for optimum efficiency under a given technique, would reduce the marginal productivity of labour, unless the amount of capital employed increases as well. Japan had abundant labour once. The technique selected then for the small enterprise was at its most efficient when a small amount of capital and relatively large amount of labour were combined. For small enterprises employing up to 10 workers that technique was compatible with only a very small amount of capital. However, in recent years more and more capital has become available, while labour in Japan has become scarcer. Even small firms have increased the amounts of capital employed per worker. If capital equipment suited to large-scale technology is somehow subdivided among small enterprises as in the case of power looms for village weavers, the resulting production may well be less efficient than that in either a large firm using large-scale production techniques and a small firm using a technique suited for that scale of operation. If adding labour increases the productivity of a small enterprise, then we can conclude that the enterprise does not have a technique which is efficient as small scale, but has a technique more suited to large-scale operation, which has been applied to an enterprise with an artificially-restricted size. To increase productivity in such circumstances, the number of workers should be increased, making it possible to exploit the economies of large scale made available by modern technology. Alternatively, an appropriate technique must be developed which combines capital with labour efficiently, even when the number of workers per enterprise is low. Depending on specific lines of production, either of these developments might occur in Japan as they seem to have occurred in USA and the UK. Then the differences in labour productivity of small and large enterprises would be reduced in Japan also. However, these productivity differences do not reduce the significance of the small-scale industry in Japan, where the small enterprises produced about 48 per cent of the product, employed over 70 per cent of the workers in private industries, and accounted for over 50 per cent of the total exports in the manufacturing sector in 1966.[5] From a comparative-efficiency viewpoint, Japanese small enterprises successfully competed in export markets in those lines of production which in the industrialized countries are generally characterized by large-scale production.

In contrast, cottage industries, which predominated in the Indian manufacturing sector, used traditional techniques which were mainly labour intensive, and produced traditional consumption goods for local markets using locally available resources. The Japanese and the American small enterprises had to be efficient to survive among modern industrial giants, either as competitors or as auxiliaries, whereas our cottage industries and our modern industry fell into two distinct compartments, each drawing its resources from different sources, each catering to different markets, and each using the techniques of two different generations. In the light of this dualism, neither the policies, nor the efficiency criteria of the advanced economies readily apply to our industrial sector in general.

On the other hand, as Dhar and Lydall have pointed out, most of our factories, small or large, are not part of the traditional sector, and hence the criteria of efficiency applicable to the modern sector should apply to our small factories too.[6] They emphasised efficiency in the use of scarce resource capital to be more important than the ability to absorb the surplus resource labour. On the basis of their finding that large factories seem to use capital more efficiently than small ones, they argue against preferential treatment and subsidies for small factories. Although their plea for efficiency in the management of small enterprises cannot be disputed, their finding regarding the relative efficiency of large factories in their use of capital is disputable on the basis of our somewhat cursory analysis below. Besides, just as isolating labour efficiency alone as a criterion for comparing small and large enterprises is insufficient, so is concentrating on the efficiency of capital alone. We must look into all the aspects of efficiency in the larger context of the availability and use of all the economic resources.

Some Theoretical Considerations

Theoretically, two interconnected issues must be raised in determining the appropriate policy towards small-scale industry. The first issue concerns the size of the enterprise and the second concerns the choice of technique. The size of an enterprise is conveniently measured by its rate of output, which can be increased by increasing the quantities of one or more inputs. When we apply increasing numbers of workers to a fixed plant facility,

Part of these economies of large-scale stem from both internal and external financial, technical and managerial advantages of concentrated production facilities.

And yet, there is no reason to conclude that every large-scale operation necessarily has lower costs of production per unit than a small-scale plant. Figure 8.1 shows for instance, that 100 units per week can be produced at an average cost of Rs. 2 per unit at the small-scale plant *C* but at Rs. 9 per unit at the large-scale plan *K*.

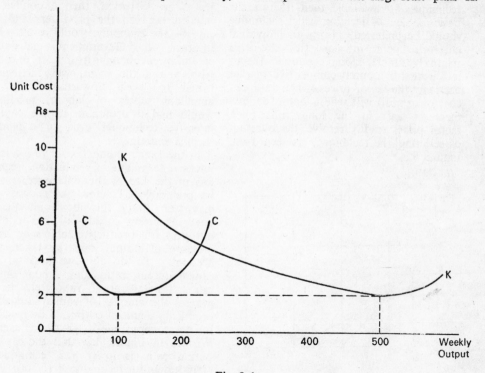

Fig. 8.1

the productivity of the inputs will increase and the average cost of production will decrease up to a point beyond which the law of diminishing returns will operate and the average cost of production will rise. The range of output over which the average cost declines is related to the scale of operations which can be enlarged by increasing both labour and capital. Average costs continue to decline over a much wider range of output for a large-scale plant than for a small-scale plant.

The costs of producing 500 units at plant *K* and 100 at size *C* plants can be the same, as illustrated in this hypothetical case, or they may be more or less, according to the cost data from which the curves are drawn. The position of these curves depends on (i) the technologically determined quantities of resources which must be combined as inputs to produce any given quantity of output; (ii) the prices of these inputs which depend on (a) the resource endowment, and (b) the

150

process of pricing whether market determined or administratively decided; and (iii) in the long run, the internal as well as the externl economies and diseconomies of scale.

The second issue concerns the choice of technique. Some goods can be produced by using either a large input of capital with a small input of labour, or a large input of labour with a small input of capital. The former technique may be called capital-intensive and the latter labour-intensive. If such alternative techniques are available, then there is the basic problem of deciding which technique should be preferred. From an individual enterprise point of view this choice is relatively simple. Microeconomic theory tells us that in a purely competitive market economy the factor prices (wage rate and cost of capital) will reflect factor endowment at least in the long run. Such factor prices readily resolve the question of selecting the technique, as seen from Figure 8.2.

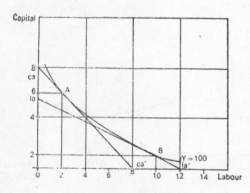

Fig. 8.2

Suppose the same output $y=100$ can be produced by using various combinations of labour and capital in conjunction with a given constant quantity of all other factors of production. Then each such factor combination represents a different technique of production. Technique A in Figure 8.2 is capital intensive (capital/labour ratio is 6/2) while technique B is labour intensive (capital/labour ratio is 1/10). If the prices of one unit of capital and labour are the same (line ca—ca'),

then Figure 8.2 shows that technique A will be chosen. On the other hand, if the factor prices are indicated by line la—la' then technique B will be selected. If the factor prices reflect the factor endowment, then for a labour surplus economy factor prices are likely to be la—la' and labour-intensive technique B will be selected by the entrepreneur. Labour employment would be high and the interests of the entrepreneurs and the society would coincide.

However, if for some reason the factor prices are distorted, then a conflict of interest between the producers and the rest of the economy would result. For instance, if Government subsidized capital by encouraging its imports or otherwise, and if the wages were artificially raised to levels unwarranted by an abundant supply of labour, producers would find it profitable to use capital-intensive techniques even in a labour-surplus economy.[7]

In the Indian context, a highly labour-intensive technique of production, regardless of the size of the enterprise, would be preferable if factor prices are not distorted. But is this choice an efficient one? Professor Reddaway has pointed out that for productive efficiency some measure of output must be taken into account.[8] To do this we look at the capital–output ratio and labour–output ratio. Capital–output ratio tells us in general the amount of capital needed in producing a unit of output. Lower values for these ratios mean greater efficiency. We see in Figure 8.2 that the capital–output ratio is lower for technique B (1/100) than for technique A (6/100) while labour–output ratio for B (10/100) is higher than for A (2/100). Technique A is more efficient in its use of labour but less efficient in its use of capital compared to technique B. For a labour-surplus economy technique B is preferable because it uses scarce capital more efficiently and utilizes labour more fully although somewhat less efficiently. If the social costs of labour unemployment are internalized to production costs, technique B would emerge as the undisputable choice.

Our theoretical discussion so far has been

partial because it has not taken into account other factors of production and considerations on the demand side.[9] Production needs raw materials, short-term financial capital, entrepreneurship, some social overheads and economic infrastructure, besides labour and capital. When selecting among techniques on efficiency grounds, we must consider all these factors. It can be readily seen that production with simpler techniques and on a smaller scale can be easily organized with locally available resources and a fairly low level of development of other factors such as a politically stable government, high degree of law and order, well-developed market mechanism with availability and mobility of various grades of human and material resources, developed financial institutions, transport and communications, etc., without which modern large-scale production cannot be achieved. In comparing the efficincy of traditional production techniques with modern ones we must take into account the costs of all of these—a fairly difficult and rarely attempted task.

Efficiency Analysis of the Indian Industrial Sector

The Indian industrial sector can be divided into two categories. The first includes the medium- and large-scale manufacturing enterprises which have a capital investment of Rs. 5 lakhs or more (Rs. 7.5 lakhs since 1966) in plant and machinery excluding building and land. The second includes small-scale manufacturing industries with fixed assets of less than the above limit. According to one estimate, large enterprises contributed Rs. 824 crores to the 1959–60 national income, compared to the Rs. 898 crore estimated contribution of small enterprises.[10] This somewhat larger contribution of the small enterprise sector can be broken up further into two categories. Small enterprises registered as factories (i.e., those employing more than 10 persons and using power, or employing 20 or more persons without using power), contributed Rs. 112 crores, while the share of the nonfactory producers was estimated at Rs. 786 crores.[11]

The nonfactory producers include the traditional crafts of potters, blacksmiths, carpenters, leather tanners, handloom workers, sericulturists, and other crafts. This subsector provides full- or part-time self-employment to a large proportion of the rural population. It is believed that this subsector requires a small amount of capital inputs, and offers a large employment potential. The subsector draws upon local agro-based resources for raw materials and produces generally for the local markets, at some places on better terms.

Figures for enterprises registered as factories are more readily available than those for the nonfactory subsector. For statistical purposes the registered factories are subdivided into two sectors. The "census sector" consists of all factories employing 100 or more workers (including factories with 50 or more workers using power), and the "sample sector" covers factories employing 20–99 workers without, and 10–49 workers with, the aid of power. Roughly 20 per cent of all registered factories belong to the census sector.

The number of factories in the census

Table 8.2
(in croes of rupees)

	1960			1970		
	Total	Small Scale	Percentage	Total	Small Scale	Percentage
Number of factories	7,839	5,421	69	13,280	8,663	65
Fixed capital	1,289	73	6	11,106	846	8
Gross output	3,100	518	17	11,399	1,481	13
Value added	854	111	13	2,878	298	10
Employment (lakhs)	28	7	25	43	9	21

SOURCE: *Annual Survey of Industries,* 1960 (*p.* 1) and 1970 (*p.* 12), (Calcutta: Central Statistical Organization), 1963 and 1974.

sector increased from 7,839 in 1960 to 13,280 in 1970. Small-scale factories with less than Rs. 5 lakhs in fixed capital accounted for 69 per cent of the census sector in 1960, and 65 per cent in 1970 when factories with up to Rs. 7.5 lakhs were classified as small scale. Table 8.2 shows the relative importance of small-scale factories.

These figures show that with a smaller share in capital, the small-scale factories provided proportionately greater employment and generated more output and value-added. Data for three intermediate years permit comparison among small-scale factories with less than Rs. 5 lakhs in fixed assets, medium-scale factories with Rs. 5–25 lakhs of fixed assets, and large-scale factories with over Rs. 25 lakhs in fixed assets in terms of their outputs, and their input proportions, from Appendix Table 8.1.

Several questions can be asked, and tentatively answered, on the basis of these data. It can be readily seen from Appendix Table 8.1 that more than 90 per cent of the factories are small-scale, but in aggregate, these factories own a little less than 7 per cent of the fixed capital of all the factories combined, employ about 33 per cent of the factory workers, produce 28 per cent of the gross factory output, and contribute about 19 per cent to value added by manufacture. In contrast, the large-scale factories possess over 86 per cent of the fixed capital of the manufacturing sector, employing about 50 per cent of the factory workers, producing 54 per cent of the total factory output, and contributing even a larger percentage—almost 65 per cent—in terms of value added by manufacture. The relative importance of the size of the factories can be seen from Appendix Table 8.2.

Appendix Table 8.2 shows a fairly close association between the asset size on the one hand, and employment and output on the other. The larger the factory in terms of fixed capital, the more workers it employs, the more output (in money terms) it produces, and contributes more in terms of value added. But, this cannot be interpreted to indicate that a larger-size factory essentially is more efficient. For instance, the average large-scale factory takes about 350 times

as much capital as a small-scale factory $(228.6 \div 0.65)$, but employs only 40 times more people $(1,486 \div 36)$, produces 54 times as much gross output $(244.5 \div 4.6)$, and only 90 times as much value added $(72.2 \div 0.8)$ compared to a small-scale factory. Now if it were desirable to produce as much as possible in the fewest number of factories regardless of cost or efficiency (some of the factors which may favour and encourage the concentration of fixed assets in a few industrial enterprises are technology, desire for monopoly control of the market, and a misconception that large size is always more efficient), one would conclude that large-scale factories should be preferred. But if other criteria, such as (i) most economical use of the scarce factor capital, (ii) maximum productivity of labour, or (iii) maximum employment, etc., were to be considered, quite a different picture would emerge.

Before leaving Appendix Table 8.2, however, it should be noted that between 1963 and 1964 the average size of the fixed assets of all types of factories has increased, with a Rs. 22 lakh or almost 11 per cent increase for a typical large-scale factory, and a Rs. 4,000 or about 6 per cent increase in the assets of a typical small-scale factory. The 11 per cent increase in capital employed in an average large factory is accompanied by a decrease in employment, a less than 2 per cent increase in average output, and a negligible increase in value added, while the 6 per cent increase in the capital in an average small factory is accompanied by an almost 3 per cent increase in employment along with 15 per cent increase in output and value added. Caution must be exercised in jumping to any conclusion from this analysis. The observations are too close really to warrant any conclusions on the incremental changes of the type considered. For instance, new investments in large-scale factories may drive up the average capital assets per factory considerably, without increasing employment and output significantly during the initial gestation period. However, if a series of observations over a period of 5 to 10 years indicates similar results, then one may conclude statistically that small-scale factories are more efficient. Even then, nothing is said about the interindustry relationship. Small factories could very well be more productive because of the fact that the large factories supply some inputs directly or buy the products of the small factories, or they indirectly provide what are known as the external economies.

To examine efficiency in the use of capital and labour one can recast the data in Appendix Table 8.1 in terms of output per worker and output per rupee's worth of capital for the three types of factory. Appendix Table 8.3 shows capital, gross output and value added per employee, and Appendix Table 8.4 gives figures on employment, output and value added per rupee's worth of fixed capital. Appendix Table 8.3 shows that in 1964 an average worker in a large-scale factory worked with fixed assets worth Rs. 15,400 or more than 8 times those available to a worker in a small factory, and contributed Rs. 4,870 to value added (a rough measure of labour productivity), or more than twice that of a small factory worker. Clearly the average worker in the large factory needed 8 times as much fixed capital to be only twice as productive as his counterpart in the small factory.

The marginal productivity of capital per worker may be estimated roughly by comparing the figures for 1964 with those for 1963. An increase in fixed capital per worker of Rs. 63, or about 3.6 per cent ($63 \div 1,757$) is accompanied by an increase in value added per worker of Rs. 78 or about 3.7 per cent ($78 \div 2,072$) for the small-scale factory. A much larger increase in fixed capital per worker of Rs. 2,014 or over 15 per cent ($2,014 \div 13,386$) in large factories is accompanied by an increase in value added per worker of only Rs. 215 or 4.5 per cent ($215 \div 4,655$). This indicates that the additional fixed investment per worker in the small-scale factory leads to a larger increase in labour productivity than in the large-scale factory. This conclusion is justifiable even when comparison is made between marginal labour productivities over the period 1960–65. This simple statistical analysis suggests that additional capital investment in smaller factories is likely to yield a larger increase in labour productivity.

Appendix Table 8.4 shows the average labour–capital ratio, the gross output and value added per rupee's worth of fixed capital by size of factory. It clearly indicates that the small-scale factory combines the largest number of workers with a rupee's worth of fixed capital; that a rupee-worth of fixed assets produces almost 7 times an output in small compared to large factories, and that the value added by a rupee-worth of fixed investment in small factories is at least three times as large as that for a large factory. On the basis of 1964 figures, it may be concluded that additional investment should be made only in small-scale factories and not in the large ones. But such a conclusion disregards important factors which can explain the records in a way more meaningful for policy than that suggested by a mere comparison of the ratios. For instance, we must take into account the rate of utilization of fixed assets, the degree of special subsidization enjoyed by small factories, the effects of the difference in fiscal and other regulations applicable to the factory types, and so on. One may very well ask, what good then is a statistical analysis of this sort? If the record, extended over a period of years, confirms the conclusions of our tentative analysis, at least we could then clearly spot the area which must be investigated, and if little can be done about the problem areas (e.g., increasing utilization of capacity), one may invest in small-scale factories, although large-scale ones, when working at full capacity, may theoretically be more efficient. The usefulness of such aggregate analysis is admittedly limited, and more industry-by-industry analysis needs to be done to formulate appropriate policy.[12] However, if these indices of efficiency retain their pattern over a period of time, criteria for policy formulation can be developed from them.

Cottage Industry in India's Industrial Policy

The importance of the cottage industry in India was acknowledged by Dadabhoy Naoroji as early as at the turn of this century. Mahatma Gandhi's movement clearly laid its policy priorities on village uplift in *sarvodaya*. Eminent economists like G.D.H. Cole recognzied the propriety of Gandhiji's spinning wheel as the effective means to attain universal economic independence and prosperity.[13]

So immense was the impact of his ideology that the plan for economic development put forward by a group of Indian industrialists, which was to be dubbed a bourgeois plan later on,[14] had left the production of consumer goods explicitly to the traditional rural-based decentralized cottage industry, confining the modern industrial sector to large-scale capital and intermediate goods production. This was specifically suggested in view of the widespread unemployment problem, and with a view to distributing both the effort and the fruits of economic development among as large a number of people as possible. In the light of the modern–traditional type dualism that characterized the Indian economic structure, the Bombay Plan, although opposed to state ownership and socialism in essence, seems to have recognized the responsibility for the uplift of the rural masses through cottage industries.

The Industrial Policy Resolution of 1948 reiterated the importance of cottage industries and the small enterprises. While the major thrust of this policy resolution was to lay guidelines for the future growth of modern industry in the public sector, the fear of nationalization, which the private sector claimed it created, was spared so far as the cottage and small-scale industries were concerned. If anything, this subsector was to receive preferential treatment.

The next significant policy statement came in response to the report of the Village and Small-Scale Industries Committee (Karve Committee) in 1955. The Karve Committee's proposals were three-pronged: (i) to avoid, as far as possible, further technological unemployment in traditional village industries; (ii) to provide for greater employment opportunities through different village and small industries; and (iii) to provide the basis for a decentralized society with progressive economic development at a fairly rapid rate.[15]

The Committee's conception of the industrial structure was that the positive pattern of industrial activity that should gradually emerge is that of a group of villages having its natural industrial and urban centre. These small urban centres will be related to big ones. Thus a pyramid of industry broad-based on a progressive rural economy will be built up.[16]

The community development programmes which began in 1952 had already emphasised the employment aspect. By the end of the Second Five-Year Plan, the rural-action programme using local labour in more intensive agriculture, rural industry, or construction, had spread almost nationwide. The negative influence of the modern industry upon employment in competing cottage and small-scale industry was to be contained by restrictions imposed on the modernization and "rationalization" of large-scale industry. Production quotas were even imposed at one time on textile mills, while subsidies were given to small-scale producers.

Towards the end of the Second Plan, the International Perspective Planning Team made a plea for the use of the micro-efficiency criteria in policies pertaining to the small industries. This emphasis on efficiency orientation is reflected in other influential writings, such as Dhar and Lydall's book. At this stage, the planners seem to have combined the Karve Committee emphasis on employment creation and the other opinion emphasising efficient use of capital. Increasingly, policy began emphasising only those labour-intensive activities that were more complementary and less competitive with modern and capital-intensive ventures. Following the recommendations of the Second International Perspective Planning Team sponsored by the Ford Foundation in 1963, the Third Plan accorded preferential treatment to urban-based small industries, such as the sewing machine, bicycle, metal processing, etc. But, contrary to the warnings against geographical decentralization made in that Team's report, the Third Plan also promoted industrial estates and rural electrification in a big way. The Plan stressed decentralized development. Some 25 lakh new jobs were expected to be created in the rural areas. The significant policy change since 1966 can be inferred from the reclassification of factories and a re-definition of small-scale factories as those with less than Rs. 7.5 lakhs in fixed capital. This definition in effect broadens the scope of activities which would be assisted by various governmental programmes. The impact of the Second International Team's efficiency orientation was echoed in the report of the Khadi and Village Industries Committee (Asoka Mehta Committee) which extended this emphasis on pro-ductive efficiency to *khadi* and handloom industries where employment for rural masses had been the policy aim so far.

These changes in policy direction are reflected in the Fourth Plan objectives, as will be seen presently.

Cottage and Small-Scale Industries in the Five-Year Plans

The industrial policy gets a more precise form in the planned outlays on investment in industry and other sectors. Investment in the industrial sector has been considered a key to rapid economic development. Accordingly, new investment has been made mostly in the large-scale modern industry, as seen from Appendix Table 8.5.

The share of the cottage and small industries has been small—5 per cent in the First Plan—and has declined to 3.4 per cent in the Fourth Plan. Another significant feature of the Plan provisions for the small industries is that a large part of the investment in this subsector has been left to the private sector.

The small outlays of the First Plan were devoted to laying the organizational foundation for the future development of the small-scale sector. During the First Plan, a network of various all-India boards, such as the Khadi and Village Industries Board, the Handloom Board and the Sericulture Board were established. Also, four regional Small Industries Service Institutes (SISI) were set up to provide technical assistance to small enterprises. At the same time, the National Small Industries Corporation to market small-scale industries' products was set up. During the Second Plan, 60 Industrial Estates were set up, and the SISIs were

spread to all the States, with 42 Extension Centres.

The Third Plan proposed to achieve the following policy objectives with regard to the small industries: (i) increased labour productivity, (ii) making available insti-tutional finance, subsidies, sales rebates, sheltered markets; (iii) encouraging the spread of small industry to rural areas and small towns, and progressively making it an ancillary type industry to large-scale industry; and (iv) organizing artisans and craftsmen on a cooperative basis. The total public sector outlays on small and village industries during the Third Plan was to be Rs. 264 crores (Rs. 150 in net investments and Rs. 114 on current outlay). The actual public sector outlays for the Third Plan were Rs. 236 crores. However, an additional Rs. 144 crores was also spent during the inter-plan period of 1966–69.

The Fourth Plan reviews the develop-ment of the village and small industries over the period 1961–69.[17] The highlights of the review are given in Appendix Table 8.6. While most of the value figures are in current prices and inflate the actual progress, some at least of the plan objectives seem to have been met. The village crafts have been organized into cooperatives, and a much larger number of small units have come under the purview of the SIDs.

In a few cases the progress of small industries has been remarkable. Hand-loom and powerloom cloth production rose from around 200 crore metres or about 30 per cent of the total production of cloth in 1960, to over 300 crore metres or 40 per cent of total cloth production in 1965, and to over 350 crore metres, almost 45 per cent of cloth production, in 1968. *Khadi* production increased from 5.4 crore square metres in 1960–61 to 8.5 crore square metres in 1965–66, but declined to 6.2 crore square metres in 1969–70.[18]

Between 1960 and 1965, the employment in small factories alone has increased by 8.6 lakhs, from 6.7 lakhs to 15.3 lakhs, while that in medium and large-scale factories together has increased only by 9.4 lakhs, from 21.3 lakhs to 30.7 lakhs (Appendix Table 8.1). It is conceivable that some of the workers now employed in the small-scale factories were previously in the unorganized village or household industries sector, and this increase may reflect a mere organizational change rather than the creation of new employment. However, the figures seem to indicate some progress in achieving the labour-intensivity employment orientation recommended by the Karve Committee. So far as the productivity objective is concerned, Appendix Table 8.3 indicates that value added per worker increased from Rs. 1,657 in 1960 to Rs. 2,352 in 1965, or a 42 per cent increase for the small factory, while it increased from Rs. 3,816 in 1960 to Rs. 5,221 in 1965, a 36 per cent increase, for the large-scale factory. In absolute terms, labour productivity in large industry is greater, but as seen earlier it is at the cost of a more than proportionate rise in capital intensity. Our analysis of the marginal ratios has already shown that in the context of a capital-short economy, the small-scale industry has shown a preferable record. A reduction in the allotment of Plan outlays to village and small industries can clearly be questioned on the basis of the actual performance of these sectors.

The Problems of the Cottage and Small-Scale Industry

While the bulk of the modern small-scale industry in India is a post-Independence phenomenon, the problems it faces are also peculiar to the rapidly changing economic scenario of the planning years. Scarce resources, such as imported raw materials, and finances for the initial investment and working capital, do not readily flow to small and relatively unknown entrepreneurs. Rapid technological development has led to a universal increase in the rate of obsolescence of machinery. The shifts in policy emphasis between capital-intensive and labour-intensive technologies in the modern industrial sector only add an element of uncertainty to the problem of obsolescence.

New production on a decentralized basis calls for creating new markets. If these are decentralized local markets, the problem may be somewhat milder. If

not, a new distributive organization would be required, which will mobilize final products from decentralized producer to central markets. Decentralized production not intended for local consumption certainly presupposes a well-developed market organization. Furthermore, the production itself calls for dissemination of technical information, development of entrepreneurial abilities, and provision of certain basic facilities such as transport, power, and water. These problems, and the measures taken to solve them, should be examined to evaluate the future prospects of this sector.

Financing and Credit Facilities

Smaller units constitute the largest proportion of new business, and of business failures in most economies. The shortage of internal financing makes them particularly vulnerable to market fluctuations. This instability in its turn makes them a poor credit risk.

It was recognized during the early years of planning that in the absence of a proper money market for short-term financing of the working capital needs of the small firm, and in the face of the inadequacy of capital markets to finance the long-term investment needs of the small firm, Government would have to take measures geared to meet the financial needs of these industries.

In 1960, a Credit Guarantee Scheme was introduced by the Reserve Bank of India. Under this scheme, the Bank guaranteed the repayment of advances made to small enterprises, up to Rs. 2 lakhs per enterprise. The number of applicants for the Guarantee Scheme went up from 2,285 in 1961–62 to 32,923 in 1968–69. The amount of loans sanctioned increased from Rs. 76 crores in 1961–62 to Rs. 163 crores in 1968–69.

The State Bank of India, in conjunction with the Reserve Bank, has endeavoured to coordinate various measures to finance small industry. The State Bank itself has advanced Rs. 69 crores to over 12,000 applicants to finance expansion and modernization, and to provide for working capital.

Various state departments of industries

have advanced to small-scale industries Rs. 13 crores in the Second Plan, and Rs. 17 crores in the Third Plan under the State Aid to Industries Act.

Commercial banks had also participated in lending the amount of Rs. 28 crores in 1960, and Rs. 90 crores in 1966 to small industrial enterprises. After nationalization in July 1969, the 14 major banks formulated special schemes for financing small-scale projects. By March 1970, these 14 banks had sanctioned a credit limit in excess of Rs. 390 crores to over 37,000 small units.

Besides these measures, financial assistance was provided by the National and State Small Industries Corporation, and the Industrial Cooperatives to some extent.

Raw Material Availability
One of the reasons given by the 1963 International Team for the relative inefficiency of the small enterprise was that scarce raw materials, particularly imported ones, were allocated more favourably to the large industries by Government. The small units' interests were to be represented by the State and National Small Industries Corporations. However, the Fourth Plan had expected regular and adequate supplies of imported and scarce indigenous raw materials, at least to those units producing priority items.[19]

Problems of Marketing
Quality variations in the product, and inability to compete with large-scale producers who enjoy marketing economies of scale clearly call for some organized effort to ensure quality, and assist in bringing the product of the small industry to the attention and proximity of the consumer. The National Small Industries Corporation has been active in this field since 1955. The Corporation acts on behalf of small enterprises in bringing them Government orders and stimulating exports of the output of small enterprises.

There are 17 State Small Industries Corporations for the purpose of distributing scarce raw materials, supplying machinery on a hire-purchase basis, and rendering marketing assistance. The National Small Industries Corporation has supplied machinery, both imported

and indigenous: imported machinery worth Rs. 206 crores, and Rs. 15 crores of indigenous origin, as of 1969. Also, in 1969, 18,223 small-scale enterprises were registered with the NSIC for participation in the Government Stores Purchase Programme. As of the same year, 24,284 Government supply contracts valued at Rs. 161.2 crores have been secured by the NSIC for small enterprises.

Technical Assistance
The shortage of trained and experienced technical and supervisory personnel, and the employment orientation in selecting the technique of production in the earlier years, have left the small-scale industries technologically backward. The agency which implements the policy to alleviate this problem is the Central Small Industries Development Organization (CSIDO). The CSIDO, through its Service Institutes and Extension Centres, provides a staff of technically qualified people who advise small industries on technical matters.

In more recent years the thinking of the planners in response to the International Team's recommendations seems to have moved in favour of modern technology, quality control and general efficiency orientation.

As of 1968, the various CSIDO agencies have made available management training to 22,000 persons, completed 252 In-Plant Studies, 150 Industry Analysis Reports, and 272 Industry Prospect Sheets.[20]

The Fourth Plan and the Future

The Fourth Plan envisaged the modernization of production techniques for the village and small-scale industries, to improve the quality of their products, and to make the enterprises viable and self-sufficient. This emphasis on efficiency emerged from the recommendations of the Ashoka Mehta Committee. In this connection it should be noted that traditional village industries have the inherent advantage of providing widespread employment. They require protection from labour-displacing modern technology if employment is a priority goal. From this perspective, modernizing the village industries seems to be a misdirected effort. Unlike its predecessors, the Fourth Plan omitted any mention of employment as an objective in connection with the small-scale and village industries. The Plan's employment potential was expected to be derived from large-scale manufacturing, agriculture, construction and such,[21] with two exceptions: (a) a "crash scheme for rural employment" which was not tied in with small-scale and cottage industries; and (b) a small gesture towards dispersing industries to industrially-backward districts.

With respect to the crash scheme, a Reserve Bank study in 1976 notes that the scheme anticipated the provision of 20,000 man-days' work per lakh rupees spent, but actually provided over 25,000 man-days' work per lakh rupees spent

to competition or perish, while on the other, the National Development Council decides to offer concessions to lure modern industry to areas which were not found suited for industrial development. Artificially-induced industry and employment in such districts would require continuous subsidization, a misallocation of scarce resources from a long-run perspective; but more importantly, if such inducement is needed, why not channel it through the traditional type local-based labour-intensive industries rather than through industry which will depend on outside resources and markets? During the Fourth Plan period the village and small-scale industry was underemphasised not only in terms of planned outlays but also in terms of actual spending as seen below:

	Village and Small Industries	Modern Industries
	(Rs. in crores)	
Fourth Plan outlays as set out in the Plan	154	1,812
Actual expenditures, first three years	79	1,473

SOURCE: *The Fourth Plan: Mid-term Appraisal*, 1971, vol. II, pp. 150–153.

outside the Plan during the first three years.[22] This has led to a revision in the outlay for this scheme, from Rs. 40 crores spent outside the Plan since 1971–72, to Rs. 100 crores within the Plan to be spent within the Plan during its last two years.[23] However, the Reserve Bank study also notes that only a few of the Permanent Assets such as roads, dams, wells, gardens, etc., produced under this scheme met the quality and durability expectations. It was more a temporary relief measure than a permanent employment scheme.

The five-crore-rupee scheme for concessions, etc., to disperse industry to industrially-backward districts seems to run counter to the efficiency orientation of the Ashoka Mehta Committee recommendations. On the one hand, the traditional industries with a viable economic base and demonstrated potential for employment, are called upon by the Committee's plea for efficiency to face up

It may be that one reason for de-emphasising the traditional industry is the excess capacity in the mass-producing modern industry which can be more fully utilized by encouraging ancillary industries with forward and backward linkages with the modern sector. It is ironical that at the end of a twenty-year period of planned investment in heavy industries we find ourselves facing the problem of underutilized industrial capacity and unemployed and underemployed labour. This makes us more and more irreversibly committed to modern technology, which was shown to be essentially a slow absorber of labour. Unless a priority commitment is made to the goal of full employment and an even distribution of well-being, we shall continue to find excuses to reinforce our efforts to push large-scale industrialization—a task relatively easy to plan—with hopes that some day in future, employment opportunities in such industries will reach down to the village level. Until then, the more urgent and difficult task of planning decentralized development will go begging for imaginative and innovative approaches. A decentralized rural-based development suited to our economy has few precedents in advanced countries, whose experience we have extensively used to determine our approaches to industrialization and whose rationale we exclusively use to evaluate our alternatives. It seems that we must develop our own unique policy criteria if we want employment-oriented decentralized development.

REFERENCES

1. Campbell R. McConnell, *Economics*, 6th ed. (New York: McGraw-Hill, 1975), pp. 612–13.
2. Kedarnath Prasad, *Technological Choice under Development Planning* (Bombay: Popular Prakashan, 1968), p. 3.
3. M.C. Shetty, *Small-Scale and Household Industries in a Developing Economy* (Bombay: Asia Publishing House, 1968), p. 13.
4. Ram K. Vepa, *Small Industries in the Seventies* (London: Vikas, 1971), p. 55.
5. Ibid.
6. P.N. Dhar and H.F. Lydall, *The Role of Small Enterprises in Indian Economic Development* (Bombay: Asia Publishing House, 1961), pp. 11–19.
7. Foreign enterprises in India are reputed to pay much higher salaries and wages than the market rates, while often bringing in cheaply bought plants and equipment enjoying special investment rebates and depreciation allowances which make capital costs low. Predictably, they find capital-intensive techniques more profitable in a labour-surplus economy.
8. W.B. Reddaway, *The Development of the Indian Economy* (London: George Allen & Unwin, 1962), pp. 71–78.
9. For an excellent theoretical discussion of the subject see A.K. Sen, *Choice of Technique* (Oxford: Blackwell, 1968).
10. S.L. Sharma, "Small-Scale Industries in India—Case for Modernization", *Small Industries Bulletin for Asia and the Far East*, no. 1, January 1963, p. 126.
11. Ibid.
12. One such study is by B. Subba Rao and V.G. Kalkundrikar entitled "A Comparative Study of the Economies of High-Capital-Cost and Low-Capital-Cost Technologies: The Manufactures of Cycle Gear Cases", *Small Industries Bulletin for Asia and the Far East*, no. 6, 1968, pp. 107–109.
13. P.A. Wadia and K.T. Merchant, *Our Economic Problem* (Bombay: Vora and Co., 1957), p. 695.
14. R. Das Gupta, *Problems of Economic Transition* (Calcutta: Nation Publishers, 1970), p. 51.
15. Government of India, *Report of the Village and Small-Scale Industries Committee* (New Delhi, 1955), p. 22.
16. Ibid.
17. Government of India, Planning Commission, *Fourth Five-Year Plan, 1969–74* (New Delhi), pp. 284–95.
18. Government of India, Planning Commission *The Fourth Plan: Mid-Term Appraisal*, Vol. II New Delhi, 1971), pp. 147–48.
19. *Fourth Five-Year Plan*, p. 290.
20. Government of India, Small-Scale Industries Development Organization, *Development Commissioner's Report for 1968–69* (New Delhi, 1970), pp. 2–3.
21. *Fourth Five Year Plan*, pp. 20–21.
22. *Reserve Bank of India Bulletin*, April 1976, quoted by Rohit Dave, "Rural Employment", in *Khadi Patrika*, vol. II, no. 126, July 1976, p. 8.
23. *The Fourth Plan: Mid-Term Appraisal*, vol. II, p. 69.

BIBLIOGRAPHY

1. All India Khadi and Village Industries Board: *Planning for Full Employment*. Bombay, 1954.
2. Dhar, P.N. and H.F. Lydall: *The Role of Small Enterprises in Indian Economic Development* Bombay. Asia Publishing House, 1961.
3. International Perspective Planning Team : *Development of Small-Scale Industries in India: Prospects, Problems and Policies*. Delhi. Govt. of India Press, 1963.
4. Mehta, Vaikunth L.: *Decentralized Economic Development*. Bombay. Gramodaya, 1964.
5. Mitra, Lalit K.: *Employment and Output in Small Enterprises in India*. Calcutta. Bookland, 1967.
6. Prasad, Kedarnath: *Technological Choice Under Developmental Planning*. Bombay. Popular Prakashan, 1963.
7. Vepa, Ram K.: *Small Industries in the Seventies*. London. Vikas Publications, 1971.
8. Schumacher, E.F.: *Small is Beautiful, Economics as if People Mattered*. New York. Harper and Row, 1973.

9. Sen, Amartya K.: *Choice of Techniques: An Aspect of the Theory of Planned Economic Development* 3rd ed. Oxford. Blackwell, 1968.

10. Ranis, G.: *The Industrial Efficiency and Economic Growth: A Case Study of Karachi.* Monographs in Economics of Development, No. 5. Karachi. Institute of Development and Economics. Inter Services Press, 1961.

APPENDIX

Table 8.1. Capital, Employment and Output Estimates for Indian Factory Sector by Value of Fixed Capital[a]

Year	Small-scale factories with fixed assets of Rs. 5 lakhs or less	Per cent	Medium-scale factories with fixed assets of Rs. 5–25 lakhs	Per cent	Large-scale factories with fixed assets of over Rs. 25 lakhs	Per cent	Total, all factories including those with leased or rented fixed assets
Number of factories							
1960	5,421	64.0	1,560†	19.0	858[b]	10.0	8,391
1963	41,851	91.5	2,063†	4.5	1,293[b]	2.8	45,757
1964	41,877	90.5	2,286†	4.9	1,499[b]	3.3	46,268
1965	43,657	90.1	2,477†	5.1	1,679[b]	3.5	48,456
Fixed capital (crores of Rs.)							
1960	73	5.0	176	14.0	1,040	81.0	1,289
1963	257	8.1	232	7.3	2,672	84.6	3,161
1964	274	6.9	260	6.6	3,427	86.5	3,961
1965	308	6.4	276	5.7	4,248	87.9	4,832
Persons employed (lakhs)							
1960	6.7	23.0	6.7	23.0	14.7	51.0	29
1963	15.0	34.8	7.1	15.7	20.0	47.5	42
1964	15.0	33.2	7.0	15.7	22.0	49.1	45
1965	15.3	32.5	6.8	14.5	23.9	51.0	47
Gross output (crores of Rs.)							
1960	518	16.0	745	24.0	1,837	58.0	3,151
1963	1,681	28.9	950	16.3	3,125	53.8	5,811
1964	1,917	28.5	1,075	16.0	3,665	54.4	6,730
1965	2,014	26.5	1,172	15.4	4,341	57.2	7,596
Value added by manufacture (crores of Rs.)							
1960	111	13.0	182	21.0	561	65.0	864
1963	302	20.4	217	14.9	929	63.6	1,460
1964	323	19.4	246	14.7	1,083	64.9	1,669
1965	360	19.1	260	13.8	1,248	66.3	1,883

[a]Ratios in subsequent tables are based on rounded figures while figures in Table 1 are rounded.

[b]Does not include factories taking fixed assets on lease or rent basis.

Source: Government of India, *Annual Survey of Industries* (Calcutta: Central Statistical Organization, 1965, 1966, 1968 and 1969) Table 1.

Table 8.2.   Average Capital, Employment and Output Estimates for Indian Factories
by Value of Fixed Capital, 1963-1964
(Rs. in lakhs)

	Year	Small-scale factories	Medium-scale factories	Large-scale factories
Average fixed capital per factory	1963	0.61	11.2	206.7
	1964	0.65	11.4	228.6
Persons employed average per factory	1963	35	319	1544
	1964	36	311	1484
Gross output per factory	1963	4.0	46.0	241.7
	1964	4.6	47.0	244.5
Average value added per factory	1963	0.7	10.5	71.5
	1964	0.8	10.8	72.2

SOURCE: Table 8.1.

Table 8.3.   Average Fixed Capital, and Value Added per Employee 1960, 1963, 1964 and 1965
(in Rs.)

	Year	Small factories	Medium factories	Large factories
Fixed capital per employee	1960	1,089	2,666	7,075
	1963	1,757	3,521	13,386
	1964	1,820	3,660	15,400
	1965	2,013	4,059	17,757
Gross output per employee	1960	7,731	11,288	12,496
	1963	11,206	13,571	15,625
	1964	12,780	15,357	16,659
	1965	13,163	17,235	18,163
Value added per employee	1960	1,657	2,757	3,814
	1963	2,072	3,299	4,655
	1964	2,150	3,460	4,870
	1965	2,353	3,823	5,221

SOURCE: Table 8.1.

Table 8.4.   Average Employment, Output and Value Added per Rupee Worth of Fixed
Capital by Factory Size, 1960, 1963, 1964, 1965
(in Rs.)

	Year	Small-scale factories	Medium-scale factories	Large-scale factories
Persons employed per rupee worth of fixed capital	1960	0.00092	0.00038	0.00014
	1963	0.00058	0.00030	0.00008
	1964	0.00054	0.00027	0.00006
	1965	0.00049	0.00025	0.00005
Gross output per rupee worth of fixed capital	1960	7.09	4.23	1.76
	1963	6.54	4.09	1.16
	1964	6.99	4.13	1.07
	1965	6.54	4.25	1.02
Value added per rupee worth of fixed capital	1960	Rs. 1.534	Rs. 1.03	Rs. 0.53
	1963	1.179	0.94	0.34
	1964	1.178	0.95	0.32
	1965	2.169	0.94	0.29

SOURCE: Table 8.1.

Table 8.5. Net Investment in the Industries and Total Investment
in the Five-Year Plans

	First Plan 1951–55		Second Plan 1956–60		Third Plan 1961–65		Fourth Plan 1969–74	
	Crore Rs.	%	Crore Rs.	%	Crore Rs.	%	Crore Rs.	%
Small-scale and cottage industries	175	5	270	5	425	4	746	3
Public sector	25	(15)	120	(45)	150	(35)	185	(25)
Private sector	150	(85)	150	(55)	270	(65)	560	(75)
Large-scale industry including power	865	23	1,810	29	3,632	35	7,821	35
Public sector	380	(44)	1,190	(66)	2,532	(73)	5,747	(73)
Private sector	485	(56)	620	(34)	11,000	(27)	2,064	(27)
Total net investment	3,500	100	6,200	100	10,400	100	22,635	100
Public sector	1,850	(53)	3,800	(61)	6,300	(62)	13,655	(60)
Private sector	1,650	(47)	2,400	(39)	4,100	(38)	8,980	(40)

SOURCE: Various five-year plan documents.

Table 8.6. Development of the Village and Small Industries, 1961–69

	1960–61	1968–69
Number of small units registered with the State Industries Directorates (SID)	36,000[a]	140,000
Value of machines supplied on hire-purchase terms	Rs 1.8 crores	Rs 4.5 crores
Value of purchases by Central Government Department from small industries	Rs 6.5 crores	Rs 28.6 crores
Number of industrial cooperatives including handloom, handicrafts, and processing societies	37,000	51,000
Membership in these Cooperatives	29.2 lakhs	38.8 lakhs
Value of sales by Cooperatives	Rs 111.9 crores	331.9 crores

[a]1962 figures.

Part Four

ECONOMIC POLICY

9

Industrial Policy of India: The Nature and Growth of the Public Sector

U. SANKAR

Framework for Industrial Policy

The type of economic system which a country chooses to realize its conception of socioeconomic optimum, depends upon goals of policy such as allocative efficiency, distributive equity and other considerations. A well-known theorem in welfare economics, based solely on the criterion of static allocative efficiency, states that given a number of ideal conditions, a decentralized economic system motivated by self-interest and guided by price signals would be compatible with a coherent disposition of economic resources that could be regarded as superior to a large class of possible alternative economic systems.[1] The ideal conditions are violated in the presence of market imperfections, economies of scale leading to natural monopoly, externalities in production, and consumption, and public goods. These violations mean the failure of a more or less idealized system of price-market institutions to sustain desirable activities or to stop undesirable activities.[2] Samuelson[3] has shown that no decentralized system can serve to determine optimally the levels of public goods such as defense, parks, and many social services. Under imperfect competition, price is above marginal cost. Externalities in production cause divergences between social and private marginal costs (benefits). Hence governmental intervention is desirable to achieve secondbest solutions.

Countries such as the USA, Japan, Great Britain and West Germany, which rely heavily on the market system for resource allocation, have many public policies to deal with different types of market failures. The US relies on anti-trust laws to curb restrictive business policies such as collusion and price discrimination, monopolization and mergers.[4] Japan has adopted measures such as antimonopoly legislation, anti-pollution regulation and consumer protection rules to guarantee the fair conduct of business.[5] In public utilities such as electricity, telephone, gas, water and sewage systems, where one firm can serve a market at a lower cost than two or more firms, a country may choose private ownership with regulation, or public ownership. In the US, except for TVA and some local utilities, most utilities are privately owned and are subject to detailed regulation by regulatory commissions. These commissions determine utility rates, taking into account costs of providing services to yield a fair rate of return on invested capital. Great Britain, France, Italy and many countries prefer public ownership of utilities.

Public enterprises are also common in finance, insurance, manufacturing and distribution in many Western countries.[6] In France, the Bank of France, the four largest commercial banks, the 34 largest insurance companies and the Renault works are publicly owned. The French government also participates in mixed companies in a number of different fields: aviation, shipping, films, broadcasting, news service, chemicals, and petroleum. Public enterprise is quite extensive in Italy, covering large banks, railways airlines, the telephone, telegraph, radio, and television system, cinema studios, coal mines, and the petroleum industry.

Besides static efficiency and equity considerations, a developing economy may favour public enterprises to assure an adequate level of social infrastructural investment, to attain a desirable level and distribution of collective consumption goods, and to organize industry where private action is considered inadequate. Many developing economies have adopted some form of a mixed economic system in which private and public enterprises coexist with various degrees of state intervention.

In India, the Directive Principles of State Policy, enunciated in the constitution, provide general guidelines for the government's social and economic policies. These principles were given a more precise direction when Parliament adopted, in December 1954, the socialist pattern of society as the objective of social and economic policy. The socialist pattern of society means that the basic criterion for determining lines of advance must not

be private profit, but social gain, and that the pattern of economic development and the structure of socioeconomic relations should be so planned that they result not only in increases in national income but also in greater equality in income and wealth.

The basic framework for the government's industrial policy is provided by the Industrial Policy Resolution of 30 April 1956.[7] This Resolution stresses that a large and growing public sector is essential in order to achieve the socialist ideal, and rapid development. It emphasises that private enterprises would have to fit into the framework of the economic and social policy of the state and remain subject to various regulations. It also underlines the need for prevention of private monopolies and the concentration of economic power in the private sector; the role of cottage, village and samll-scale industries in economic development; and the need for balanced industrial development.

Section 2 deals with the role of the state in the development of different industries. Section 3 reviews the methods used for regulating the private sector and examines their effectiveness. Section 4 deals with problems relating to planning, initiation and management of public enterprises. Section 5 contains concluding remarks.

Role of the State in Industrial Development

The first formal enunciation of the relative roles of the public and private sectors in industrial development was made in the Industrial Policy Resolution (IPR), 6 April 1948. This Resolution stated that any improvement in the economic conditions of the country required an increase in national wealth and not just a mere redistribution of existing wealth. It recognized a progressively active role for the state in the development of industries, but admitted that, under existing conditions, "the mechanism and resources of the state may not permit it to function forthwith in industry as widely as may be desirable". This Resolution classified industries into four categories.

The first category covered arms and

ammunitions, atomic energy, and rail transport. The Central Government was to have monopoly in these industries.

The second category covered coal, mineral oils, iron and steel, and the manufacture of aircraft and of telecommunications equipment. "Except where, in the national interest, the state itself finds it necessary to secure the cooperation of private enterprise", the State was to have exclusive access to the setting-up of new undertakings in this category. All existing private enterprises in this category would be free to develop for a period of ten years during which they would be allowed all facilities for efficient working and reasonable expansion. At the end of this period, Government would review the situation and if the State decided to acquire any existing undertaking, it would provide compensation on a "fair and equitable basis".

The third category covered 18 industries: automobiles, tractors, prime movers, electrical engineering, heavy machinery, machine tools, heavy chemicals, fertilizers, electrochemical industries, rubber manufactures, power and industrial alcohol, cotton and woollen textiles, cement, paper, salt, sugar, air and sea transport, minerals, and defense industries. Government felt that for industries in this category, planning and regulation were essential in the national interest.

The fourth category, covering the remainder of the field, was left' open to private enterprise, but the state would progressively participate and "would not hesitate to intervene whenever the progress of private enterprise was unsatisfactory."

The Resolution also contained promises of assistance to the private sector. The removal of transport bottlenecks, the facilitation of the import of essential raw materials, the imposition of tariffs to prevent unfair foreign competition, and the adjustment of taxation to encourage productive investment were specified as governmental responsibilities.

The declaration of the Government's industrial policy within less than eight months after Independence had helped to remove some of the uncertainties facing industrialists as to the role of the public sector and the attitude of Government

towards the private setor. The announcement that existing undertakings in the second category would not be nationalized for a period of ten years, and the promise that if Government chose to acquire any existing undertaking at the end of the period, it would pay "fair and equitable compensation" provided a healthy atmosphere for new investments in the private sector.

It appears that the four-fold classification of industries was based more on pragmatic than on ideological considerations. Despite the well-known socialist leanings of the government, public utilities (with the exception of railways) and heavy industries such as heavy engineering, heavy chemicals and machine tools were listed only in the third or the fourth category.

Hanson rightly points out that at that time Government was more interested in the control of private enterprises than in the public-private balance.[8] The Resolution clearly expressed Government's belief that administrative guidance, promotion and control were essential in the national interest. Three years later, the Industries (Development and Regulation) Act was passed to provide Government with the means of implementing the Resolution.

In December 1954, Parliament adopted the socialist pattern of society as the objective of social and economic policy. This led to the adoption of the Second Industrial Policy Resolution in April 1956. This Resolution continues to govern Government's policies for achieving the socialist pattern of society. It stresses that realization of the objectives of the socialist pattern of society and planned rapid development require that all industries of basic and strategic importance, Public utility services, and other industries which require investment on a scale which only the State could provide, have to be in the public sector. It classifies industries into three categories, having regard to the part which the State would play in each of them.

The first category consists of 17 industries whose future development would be the exclusive responsibility of the State. These industries are: (1) arms and ammunition, (2) atomic energy, (3) railways, (4) air transport, (5) iron and steel, (6) heavy castings and forgings of iron and steel, (7) heavy plant and machinery, (8) heavy electrical plant, (9) aircraft, (10) shipbuilding, (11) coal and lignite, (12) mineral oils, (13) mining of iron ore, manganese ore, chrome ore, gypsum, sulphur, gold and diamonds, (14) mining and processing of copper, lead, zinc, tin. molybdenum, and wolfram, (15) minerals specified in the Schedule to the Atomic Energy Order, 1956, (16) telephones and telephone cables, telegraphs, and wireless apparatus (excluding radio receiving sets), and (17) generation and distribution of electricity.

Of these, the first four are to be governmental monopolies. All new units in the remaining 13 industries would be established by the State. However, this does not preclude "the expansion of the existing privately owned units", or the possibility of the State's securing "the cooperation of private enterprise in the establishment of new units" when the national interests so require.

The second category consists of 12 industries in which the State would increasingly establish new enterprises, without denying the private sector its opportunities. These industries are: (1) all other minerals except minor minerals, (2) aluminium and other nonferrous metals not included in the first category, (3) machine tools, (2) ferro-alloys and tool steels, (5) basic intermediate products required by the chemical industries, (6) antibiotics and other essential drugs, (7) fertilizers, (8) synthetic rubber, (9) carbonization of coal, (10) chemical pulp, (11) road transport, and (12) sea transport.

The third category covers all the remaining industries, whose future development would, in general, be left to the initiative and enterprise of the private sector. While reaffirming the right of the State to start any industry, the Resolution stresses that the State's main role would be to facilitate and encourage the development of these industries, by the adoption of appropriate fiscal measures, and the provision of services and financial assistance. Private enterprises in these industries would have to fit into the

"framework of the economic and social policy of the State" and remain subject to various Government legislations.

The division of industries into three categories does not mean that they are being placed in watertight compartments. It is possible for privately-owned units in appropriate cases to provide an item falling within schedule A for meeting their own requirements or as by-products. Heavy industries in the public sector may obtain some of their requirements of lighter components from the private sector while the private sector in turn would rely for many of its needs on the public sector.

The Resolution allows central and state governments to have equity participation either directly or through their corporations with private parties. Since 1971, some Government-run financial institutions have converted their loans to private sector units into equity capital. Government plans to use this type of joint sector unit as a device to go into partnership with new and medium entrepreneurs in order to guide them in developing a priority industry. According to a policy statement[9] issued on 2 February 1973, the joint sector will not be permitted to be used for the entry of larger industrial houses (with assets of Rs. 20 crores or more), dominant undertakings and foreign companies in industries in which they are otherwise precluded on their own. Government would ensure for itself an effective role in guiding policies, management and operations. With respect to cottage and village and small-scale industries, the 1956 Resolution states that Government will continue its policy of helping them by "restricting the volume of production in the large-scale sector, by differential taxation, or by direct subsidies". It also promises financial facilities and provision of technical facilities via industrial estates and rural community workshops.

The influence of the 1956 Resolution on the Second Five-Year Plan and subsequent plans was great. The authors of the Second Plan wrote that, if development was to proceed at the pace envisaged and was to contribute effectively to the attainment of the larger social ends in view, "the public sector must grow not only absolutely but also relatively to the private sector". This was indeed the case. The share of public sector investment in total investment was raised from 46.4 per cent in the first Plan to 54.6 per cent in the Second Plan and to more than 60 per cent in later plans.

Implicit in the Second Resolution and in the minds of the authors of the Second and later Plans was the assumption that public enterprises contributed not only to the attainment of the socialist ideal but also to rapid development. Both the Resolution and the Planning Commission contemplated that public enterprises would help to augment the revenues of the State and provide resources for further development in fresh fields.

Hanson illustrates the tension between ideology and empiricism in the allocation decisions of coal, oil and steel industries.[10] It may be of interest here to provide one example. The Second Plan postulated an increase in coal production from 38 million tons in 1955 to 60 million tons in 1961. The question was how to allocate the additional 22 million tons between the two sectors. At that time coal production in the public sector was only 4.5 million tons. The Commission did not consider the relative cost of producing coal nor the ability of the two sectors in achieving their targets, but simply referred to the Industrial Policy Resolution of 1948 and said that additional production should be raised to the maximum possible extent in the public sector. Accordingly, it allocated an additional production of 12 million tons for the public sector and 10 million tons for the private sector. By 1959, the public sector showed an increase of only 2.2 million tons while the private sector showed an increase of 6.8 million tons. The Commission attributed the shortfall in the public sector to the difficulties in setting up new coal mines. The Third Plan provided for an increase of 37 million tons—20 million tons in the public sector and 17 million in the private sector. By the time of Mid-Term Appraisal (November 1963), the public sector had increased its production by little more than 1 million tons, while the private sector had increased its production by more than 7 million.

Regulation of the Private Sector

The IPR of 1948, as we have seen, had forecast legislation for the control of enterprises in the private sector. The Industries (Development and Regulation) Act[11] was passed in 1951 with the following objectives:
1. the regulation of industrial investment and production according to plan priorities and targets;
2. the avoidance of monopoly and prevention of concentration of ownership of industries;
3. the protection of small industries against undue competition from large-scale industries; and
4. the balanced economic development of the different regions in the country so as to reduce disparities in levels of development.

The Act was to be applied to 37 (later extended to 70) scheduled industries. In order to pursue the objectives, the Act provided that:
1. every existing undertaking covered by the schedule had to register itself with the Central Government, and no new undertaking could be established, nor any existing undertaking substantially extended without prior procurement of a license from the Central Government;
2. Government had the power to order a full and complete investigation if it had cause to believe that (a) there had been a substantial reduction in the volume of production or a marked deterioration in the quality of the articles produced, or a rise in the price, where there appeared to be no justification for such a fall, deterioration, or rise, or (b) the management of the undertaking was being detrimental to the public interest; and at the conclusion of the investigation, Government might, if necessary, take over its management, directly or through an appointed management;
3. Government had the power to publish orders for securing equitable distribution and availability at fair prices of any article or class of articles relatable to any scheduled industry;

4. by order, Government could establish Development Councils, one for each industry or group of industries, to perform functions such as production-targeting, the setting of efficiency norms, improvements in the utilization of marketing arrangements, and the promotion of standardization, trading, research, and productivity.

Hazari rightly points out that "the major assumption implicit in the Act is that growth and allocation of resources should be looked after wholly or mainly by administrative guidance, promotion and control, and hardly at all by the market mechanism".[12]

In addition to the inspectorial clauses of this Act, the Companies Act of 1956 provided enough powers to Government to regulate the internal organization of private enterprises. The two main objectives of the Companies Act were (1) to prevent dishonest practices in the formation and operation of companies, and (2) to limit opportunities for effecting under concentration of economic power. The Act, together with its amending Acts, Hanson remarks, "constitutes one of the most detailed and stringent codes of business legislation to be found anywhere in the world".[13]

The Essential Commodities Act of 1955 authorized Government to regulate or prohibit the production and control the supply, distribution, and price of certain enumerated commodities and of any other commodities which, by order, may be declared "essential".

It is extremely difficult to evaluate the total effect on the private sector of all these controls. While some of the stringent regulations over the internal organization of enterprises might have dampened entrepreneurial initiative, there is some evidence to show that these regulations have reduced corrupt practices in the formation of companies, and provided some degree of protection to the ordinary shareholder and thereby encouraged investment in equities. From an economic point of view, far more controversial are the powers over the licensing and regulation of industrial investments and control over prices and distribution of commodities. In view of the importance of licensing and price and distribution controls, we shall review the working of these controls and evaluate their effectiveness.

Industrial Licensing

The purpose of the licensing system was to provide for Central Government control over the location, expansion and setting-up of private industrial undertakings with a view, inter alia, to channelling investments in accordance with plan priorities and targets. An (Interministerial) Licensing Committee was set up in September 1952 to operate within the framework of the Industries Act. To assist this committee in making technoeconomic evaluation of the applications, the Directorate General of Technical Development (DGTD) was also set up. Up to 1964 all actual and proposed industrial undertakings employing more than Rs. 10 lakhs in value, had been subject to industrial licensing.

In addition to the approval of the Licensing Committee, a prospective investor might require licenses from other committees as well. If he wished to raise capital from the public he had to procure a license from the Comptroller of Capital Issues; if he needed foreign exchange, he must get the approval of the Capital Goods Committee; if he needed foreign collaboration, he must obtain the consent of the Foreign Agreements Committee.

The working of the licensing system during the Second and Third Plans revealed a number of deficiencies in the system. The Licensing Committee was supposed to regulate investments in the scheduled industries in accordance with plan priorities and targets. While the Planning Commission provided specific expansion programmes for the scheduled industries, indicating actual rated capacity and production at the beginning of the plan periods, it did not provide phasing of the targets to give guidance to the Committee. Hazari points out that "no attempt has been made to synchronize or adjust the pace of licensing and revocation to the actual trends in capacity and output in relation to emerging demand".[14] In the absence of adequate guidance from the Planning Commission, the Committee frequently relied upon various ad hoc criteria.

Bhagwati and Desai and the Mathur

Team on the working of the DGTD have drawn attention to the poor quality of the technoeconomic work done by the Directorate; Bhagwati and Desai point out that "there is no evidence of any studies having been carried out by the DGTD of the optimal size, time-phasing and location of industrial unit",[15] in order to guide the Committee in its deliberations.

The licensing system was also deficient in a procedural matter. The procedure in general was to issue licences on a first-come first-served basis. This enabled the bigger industrial houses to put in for licences more readily because they were better informed. These houses also preempted licensable capacity in many industries as a means of barring the entry of newcomers into these industries. Analysing data relating to applications and approvals to certain industrial houses, Hazari comments that the data justify "the presumption that multiple applications for the same product and for a wide, very wide indeed, variety of products are meant to foreclose licensable capacity. This appears to be particularly true of Birla applications".[16]

The Swaminathan Committee on Industries Development Procedures drew attention to undue delays in the processing of applications. The licensing rules required that an application must be decided upon in three months, but in practice, the average time taken for case disposal was about six months. The Swaminathan Committee attributed the delays to the enormous workload of the Licensing Committee and recommended delicensing a number of industries.

In May 1966, Government, acting on the recommendations of the Swaminathan Committee, delicensed 11 industries. By November 1966, 42 industries were delicensed. Government also raised the exemption limit for licensing from Rs. 10 lakhs of investment in February 1960 to Rs. 25 lakhs in January 1964 and up to Rs. 1 crore in February 1970. This exemption will not apply to larger industrial houses and to dominant undertakings (as defined in the Monopolies and Restrictive Trade Practices [MRPT] Act of 1969) and to existing licensed or registered undertakings having fixed assets exceeding Rs. 5 crores.

In a press note released on 31 October 1973, Government announced a streamlined system for the issue of industrial licenses. The essential objective of the new system will be to issue various clearances within defined time targets. Letters of intent, foreign collaboration approvals, and capital goods clearances are proposed to be issued within 90 days of receipt of application in each case. In MRPT cases it is proposed to give clearance within 150 days.

It is hoped that these modifications will not only simplify the task of the Licensing Committee by reducing its workload, but also enable it to make a careful appraisal of the applications. We feel that instead of providing a general exemption limit of Rs. 1 crore for all industries, Government should set different limits or different industries based on considerations such as economies of scale.

Price and Distribution Controls

As we have stated before, the Industries Act of 1951 and the Essential Commodities Act of 1956 provided the Central Government with powers to regulate the production, distribution, and price of certain enumerated commodities. Such powers were exercised by Government over a wide range of commodities: iron and steel (production, distribution, and prices), nonferrous metals (distribution, and prices), cement (distribution, and prices), coal (distribution, prices, and movement), fertilizers (distribution, and prices), cotton textiles (production, and distribution), paper (distribution), sugar (production, and supply), and motor cars (distribution). In addition, some sort of controls, formal or informal, were exercised over a number of manufactured items.

Two important factors motivated this direct regulation of distribution and prices. The most important factor was the desire to prevent inflation. Until 1963, the country had experienced shortages in many commodities and it was felt that these controls would ease inflationary pressures in the economy. Another motivating factor for direct regulation was the desire to ensure allocation of adequate amounts to priority sectors at some reasonable price. This was true of controls over steel and cement.

The working of various price and distribution controls indicates that in many cases the controls were ineffective and in certain circumstances produced "undesirable effects". The Raj Committee Report on the working of steel distribution shows that priorities were not clearly defined and allocations were chaotic. The Committee also points out that price control enabled the private-sector users to buy steel at controlled prices, but it did not require them to price their outputs in such a way as to pass on the benefits to final users.

In 1963, Government freed 16 commodities from price and distribution control. Subsequently, control on iron and steel, coal, fertilizers and cement was relaxed.

The recent shifts in policies towards delicensing of industries and relaxation of controls over distribution and prices, mark an important change in the attitude of Government towards the private sector. In the fifties, Government and the Planning Commission emphasised the defects of the market mechanism and suggested that governmental control and guidance over industry were essential for rapid development. Our experience with various controls over the last 20 years has taught us that direct regulation of the economic system by administrative control, promotion and guidance is also deficient in many respects. In this connection, the following quotation from the Fourth Five-Year Plan is of interest:

> The existing industrial structure has led generally to a high level of costs and the present system does not appear to have prevented concentration. In some cases industry has been inappropriately sited and some desirable adjustments in regional locations have not taken place.... Fixation of targets, licensing and some price and allocation controls seem to have affected the care with which entrepreneurs should weigh the long-term prospects of their investment decision.... Sheltered conditions created in part by the operation of existing controls appear to have reduced cost consciousness among entrepreneurs.[17]

Economic Performance of Public Enterprises

Government provided the following

arguments for the establishment of enterprises in the public sector:

1. A number of basic industries which require large investments and extensive collaboration with foreign firms or governments and which could be undertaken only on the assurance of future prospects, with no immediate gain in sight, would not normally be started if reliance was to be placed entirely on the private sector. Here the implicit assumption is that even with appropriate fiscal and other incentives, private enterprises would not volunteer to undertake such projects.

2. In the case of industries where, for technological reasons the plants have to be large, requiring big investments, by organizing them in the public sector undue concentration of economic and industrial power in private hands can be prevented. It is well known that, in the presence of significant economies of scale, the free market does not produce the best results. Economic efficiency considerations, therefore, require some form of governmental regulation or public ownership. In the US, firms in electric power, natural gas, telephone and some other industries are being regulated by federal and state regulatory commissions. France, Great Britain and some other countries have preferred public ownership.

3. Public enterprises would work towards the attainment of "social gain" and thereby help to create the type of social order envisaged in the "socialist pattern of society". This argument presumes that decision-making units in public enterprises have the knowledge and ability to devise socially optimal rules for allocation and pricing and that these rules could be enforced.

4. Rapid expansion of public enterprises would materially contribute to increasing public savings for investment, making it possible thereby to increase the rate of growth.

The first two arguments are valid in the Indian context. At the time of Independence, all planning groups including the authors of the Bombay Plan, agreed that the State had to play an active role in setting up heavy industries and public utilities. The third and fourth arguments depend crucially on the assumption that Government could play the role of investor and entrepreneur more efficiently than firms in the private sector. Our experience in planning and running public enterprises over the last two decades casts doubts on the validity of this assumption.

Since 1955, there has been a large expansion of the public sector in a wide range of activities, covering fields as varied as mining and manufacturing, generation and distribution of electric power, construction, transport and communications, irrigation, banking and insurance, trade, social services, etc. Undertakings in electricity and road transport are primarily owned by states. Railways, posts and telegraphs, and a few undertakings like the Chittaranjan Locomotives and Perambur Coach Factory are run as departmental concerns by the Central Government. The industrial and commercial undertakings of the Central Government are run by government companies or public corporations.

In view of the importance of the industrial and commercial undertakings of the Central Government in total investment, our analysis is confined to this group alone. The growth of investment in this group from plan to plan is given in Table 9.1. Of the 129 undertakings at the end of March 1975, 9 were still under construction. Table 9.2 gives a sectorwise distribution of completed investments. Eighty-two per cent of the total investment was in production enterprises and 18 per cent in service enterprises.

Economic problems of the public enterprises may be grouped under two broad heads: problems related to planning and construction of projects and problems related to the working of undertakings.

Problems Related to Planning and Construction of Projects
The Report of the Study Team on Public Sector Undertakings cited the following deficiencies in the planning of projects:

1. lack of detailed analysis on scope and pattern of product mix
2. selection of site based on inadequate soil investigation
3. omission and understatement of several elements of the project

Table 9.1. Growth of Investment in Public Enterprises

(Central Government Undertakings other than Departmental Projects)

Period	Total Investment (Rs. crores)	No. of Units
At commencement of First Plan	29	5
At commencement of Second Plan	81	21
At commencement of Third Plan	953	48
At end of Third Plan	2,415	74
At commencement of Fourth Plan	3,902	85
At end of Fourth Plan	6,237	122
As on 3/31/1975	7,261	129

SOURCE: Government of India *Annual Report on the Working of Industrial and Commercial Undertakings of the Central Government*, 1974–75 (New Delhi, 1976).

4. lack of proper assessment of demand for the products, and
5. incomplete analysis of commercial profitability and economic forecasts.

Despite the emphasis on "social objectives", the Planning Commission or the Bureau of Public Enterprises has not developed guidelines that clearly define the social criteria and the methodology for project evaluation from the standpoint of social profitability. Bhagwati and Desai note that a careful scrutiny of methods adopted to plan for the projects "underlines the extremely poor quality in general of the work, both from a technical viewpoint and even more so from the point of view of economic cost and benefit analysis".[18] As an example, they provide the case of Heavy Electricals Limited at Bhopal. According to them, Ian Little, a British economist, found that the actual figures of costs included in the blueprints showed that, even if all expectations about capacity utilization and efficiency of operations were to be fulfilled, the project would yield only 2.7 per cent. A later estimate by Little

Table 9.2. Sectorwise Distribution of Total Investment in Public
Sector Enterprises

	At the end of 1974–75	
	Rs. crores	%
Production Enterprises		
Steel	2,218	30.5
Minerals and metals	1,025	14.1
Petroleum	435	6.0
Chemicals and pharmaceuticals	1,066	14.7
Heavy engineering	692	9.5
Medium and light engineering	168	2.3
Transportation equipment	270	3.7
Consumer goods	83	1.1
Agro-based enterprises	9	0.1
Total	5,966	82.0
Service Enterprises		
Trading and marketing services	316	4.4
Transportation services	640	8.8
Contracts and construction services	23	0.3
Industrial development and technical consulting services	4	0.1
Development of small industries	37	0.6
Tourist services	18	0.3
Financial services	170	2.3
Rehabilitation of sick industries	87	1.2
Total	1,295	18.0
Grand Total	7,261	100.0

of the returns on the project by evaluating inputs and outputs at international prices (presumably to take into account correct opportunity costs) showed that the real return in the blueprint project was still dismal.

The *Draft Fourth Five-Year Plan* admits that many projects have taken a longer time to complete than was initially anticipated. The fertilizer industry provides an example. Table 9.3 provides a comparison of the normal time schedule needed for completion of fertilizer plants under Indian conditions and the time actually taken for completion of projects. On an average, the actual time taken exceeded the estimated by time by 18 months. The important contributing factors for the delays appear to be inadequate project preparation, difficulties

in getting foreign aid, and bureaucratic red tape.

In many undertakings, the differences between original cost estimates and final construction expenditures were very large. Table 9.4 compares the original estimate and the final cost for some selected enterprises. In the case of steel, the final cost was about 80 per cent higher than the original estimate.

Problems Related to the Working of the Public Enterprises
Annual Reports on the working of industrial and commercial undertakings of the Central Government provide (1) the ratio of gross profit (before interest and tax) to capital employed, and (2) the ratio of net profit (after interest and tax) to equity as profitability measures for

Table 9.3. Comparison of Estimated and Actual Time Schedules in the
Construction of Fertilizer Plants

(in months)

	Normal Time Schedule Estimated by UN Fertilizer Mission	Approximate Time Actually Taken in India
1. Preliminary analysis, project report, initial decision to proceed with the project.	4–5	5–7
2. Preparation of tenders, preliminary process and specifications.	3–4	3–4
3. Contractor's project bid, review of bids and official decision to construct plant.	4–8	12–20
4. Ordering construction, erection to completion and start-up.	24–30	32–40
Total	35–47	52–71

SOURCE: Government of India, Administrative Reforms Commission, *Report of the Study Team on Public Sector Undertakings,* (New Delhi, June 1967), p. 84.

Table 9.4. Comparison of Original Estimates and Actual Expenditures in the
Construction of Selected Public Enterprises

(rupees in crores)

	Original Estimate	Actual/ Anticipated Expenditures	Percentage Increase
Durgapur Steel Plant	115.00	205.25	78
Rourkela Steel Plant	128.00	230.40	80
Bhilai Steel Plant	110.00	202.34	83
Heavy Engineering Corporation Ltd.	125.95	206.50	64
Heavy Electricals Ltd., Bhopal	35.25	49.30	40
Fertilizer Corporation of India Ltd.			
(i) Trombay Unit	24.34	33.40	37
(ii) Nangal Unit	20.90	31.20	49
Hindusthan Antibiotics Ltd.			
(i) Pimpri Unit	1.15	1.59	38
(ii) Penicillin Expansion	0.45	0.61	36
(iii) Streptomycin Unit	1.73	2.08	20
Gauhati Refinery	13.06	14.51	11

SOURCE: *Public Sector Undertakings,* p. 84.

running concerns. There are some problems in using these measures to appraise the performance of public enterprises. First, they are expected to maximize "social gain" and not money profit. Second, their operations are subject to a number of constraints imposed by administrators. Third, public enterprises get preference over private enterprises in the provision of such facilities as land and construction materials, and get loans from Government at concessional rates. Fourth, a high value of one of these ratios might indicate monopoly power rather than economic efficiency.

Despite these limitations, we use these measures as crude indicators of the financial performance of the public enterprises. It is worth noting that Government and the Planning Commission have emphasised on several occasions that public enterprises have to provide

are given in Table 9.5. Rate of return on equity capital was either negative or very low. For 1974–75, 81 enterprises earned a total net profit of Rs. 322 crores while 39 enterprises had a loss of Rs. 139 crores. Bokaro Steel, Neyveli Lignite Corporation, Bharat Coking Coal and Coal Mining Authority had each a net loss of Rs. 10 crores or more in 1974–75. Nearly three-fifths of the net loss was incurred by six concerns in the minerals and metals group.

Purely commercial considerations, and the expectation that the public enterprises have to contribute to national savings, would make the performance far from satisfactory. It appears that three factors —organizational inefficiency, low utilization of capacity, and price policy—have contributed to low rates of return in many undertakings.

The study team on Public Sector Under-

Table 9.5.   Profitability of Public Enterprises
(Rupees in crores)

	1970–71	1971–72	1972–73	1973–74	1974–75
Capital employed	3,754	4,018	4,756	5,256	6,627
Gross profit	146	169	245	272	559
Gross profit as per cent of capital employed	3.9	4.3	5.1	5.2	8.4
Equity	2,290	2,742	2,954	3,310	3,770
Net profit	—3	—19	18	64	184
Net profit as per cent of equity	loss	loss	0.6	1.9	4.9

SOURCE: Government of India, *Report on Industrial and Commercial Undertakings,* 1974–75.

not only an adequate depreciation and return on capital but also the necessary surplus for future expansion. The *Draft Fourth Plan* suggested that public enterprises must yield not less than an 11 to 12 per cent rate of return on invested capital. The *Fifth Plan* states that in order for the public sector to perform its due role in economic development, it must not only fulfil physical targets, but also contribute to national savings commensurately with its size.

The overall performance of the running concerns for the years 1970–71 to 1974–75

takings of the Administrative Reforms Committee pointed out defects in the form of organization and personnel management. It argued that the company form was not suitable for industrial and commercial concerns and recommended public corporation form. It also pointed out the need for improvement in managerial and operational efficiency.

On the basis of the recommendations of the Administrative Reforms Committee, Government circulated a memorandum[9] in March 1969 outlining the measures to be taken for improving the working and profitability of public undertakings. To improve the utilization of capacity in the steel and engineering industries, it suggested diversification of products, promotion of exports, and better coordination among public enterprises. To improve managerial and operation efficiency, Government announced that (1) more financial and administrative powers would be delegated to enable management to function with greater autonomy; (2) it would assist the enterprises to secure suitable managerial talent; (3) new measures would be taken and guidelines laid down for improving management techniques in project preparation, economy in construction, financial management, inventory controls, and price policies; and (4) an effective machinery for periodical review and appraisal of their performances would be developed.

The Bureau of Public Enterprises is providing an analysis based on the recommendations of the Committee on Public Undertakings, of the state of capacity utilization in public manufacturing enterprises from 1972–73. Of 84 units studied in 1973–74, 45 recorded capacity utilization rates more than 75 per cent, 23 between 50 per cent and 16 less than 50 per cent. Groupwise analysis shows that the ratio is the highest in the transportation and petroleum groups, and the lowest in the heavy engineering group where six out of nine running units showed less than 50 per cent utilization rates. Design defects and inadequacies of equipment, power shortages, disturbed labour conditions, low productivity, and inadequate demand are cited as reasons for low utilization. Some attempts are being made to improve labour productivity by providing incentives, and to improve operating efficiency of employees by better training. Preliminary results[20] for 1974–75 showed some improvement in capacity utilization rates.

An important contributing factor for the negative or low positive rate of return on capital in steel was that until May 1967 the price of steel was fixed by Government. It is now evident that the underpricing of steel has not served any social purpose. The Raj Committee pointed out that in many cases steel underpricing merely resulted in increasing the profits of some concerns in the private sector and did not benefit the users of the end-products of steel. In October 1973, Government approved a dual pricing policy. According to this policy, steel would be sold to the priority sector at reduced prices and to compensate for the losses involved in these sales, higher prices would be charged for other uses. This involves cross-subsidization and the full implications of this policy are not analysed.

In 1968, Government laid down two guidelines. For enterprises which produce goods and services in competition with other domestic producers, the products will be governed by the prevailing market prices. For enterprises which operate under monopolistic or semi-monopolistic conditions, the landed cost of comparable imported goods would be the normal ceiling. A survey of the actual pricing methods adopted by 23 concerns in the 1973–74 *Annual Report* shows that many enterprises are operating in areas where there is a system of formal or informal price control on regulation, and price policy shows considerable variation from product to product.

Concluding Remarks

India has preferred a socialist pattern of society as the objective of social and economic policy. Her economic policy has multiple goals such as allocative efficiency, equity, regional balance and social justice. The Industrial Policy Resolution of 1956, the Industries (Development and Regulation) Act of 1956, together with many policy statements, provide the means for implementation of these goals.

India's experience in industrial licensing, regulation and public ownership over the last 25 years has taught some valuable lessons. It is now obvious that direct regulation of the economic system by administrative control and guidelines also imposes many costs on business and consumers. As noted by the authors of the *Draft Fourth Plan*, the existing industrial structure has generally led to "a high level of costs and that the present system does not appear to have prevented concentration". Further, sheltered conditions created in part by the operations of various regulations have reduced competitive pressures and weakened the motivation on the part of both private and public managers to achieve their goals. Recent attempts to streamline the licensing procedures and to raise the exemption limit for industrial licensing are steps in the right direction.

We feel that, at the present stage of development, industrial planning and regulation are necessary for some strategic industries. Given the objective of a socialist pattern of society, regulation of larger industrial houses and dominant undertakings as defined in the MRTP Act may be necessary to avoid further concentration of economic power. In other sectors, particularly in schedule C industries as defined in the 1956 Resolution, it is desirable to strengthen the operation of the market by promoting competition.

We have a growing public sector in our economy. Many public enterprises are in the infrastructural industries supplying basic inputs such as coal, steel, minerals, metals and heavy equipment. Now that the public sector has come to occupy an important position in some vital fields, with a total investment of over Rs. 7,000

crores in Central Government undertakings alone, the performance of this sector is crucial in meeting plan targets to achieve rapid economic growth.

Government cites overcapitalization, construction delays, low rate of capacity utilization, poor maintenance, and low productivity as reasons for poor performance. Attempts have been made to understand the causes of low capacity utilization and low labour productivity. Some steps are currently being taken to improve capacity utilization rates and labour productivity.

There is growing concern[21] that public enterprises must provide not only an adequate return on capital but also contribute surpluses for future expansion. We agree with the Administrative Reform Committee that unless there are clear and overriding reasons of public interest, public enterprises should aim at earning a reasonable rate of return on invested capital. Given the objective of an enterprise and a target rate of return, it is possible to devise a rational pricing policy. The contribution of French economists[22] in devising optimal policies for investment and pricing of publicly-managed firms would be some relevance to India.

REFERENCES

1. A rigorous proof of the theorem is in K.J. Arrow and F.H. Hahn, *General Competitive Analysis* (San Francisco: Holden-Day, 1971).
2. See, for example, F.M. Bator, "The Anatomy of Market Failure", *Quarterly Journal of Economics*, August 1958.
3. P.A. Samuelson, "The Pure Theory of Public Expenditure", *Review of Economics and Statistics*, November 1954.
4. See C. Wilcox and W.G. Shepherd, *Public Policies Towards Business* (Homewood, Illinois: Irwin, 1975).
5. See O.E.C.D. publication, *Japanese Industrial Policy*.
6. For details, see Wilcox and Shepherd, *Public Policies*; and J. Margolis and H. Guitton, *Public Economics*, (MacMillan, 1969).
7. This Resolution is reproduced as Appendix 1 in Government of India, *Guidelines for Industries* 1975-76, New Delhi.
8. A.H. Hanson, *The Process of Planning* (London: Oxford University Press, 1966) p. 452.
9. This statement is reproduced as Appendix 2 in *Guidelines for Industries* 1975-76.
10. Hanson, *Process of Planning*, pp. 465-76.
11. The Provisions of this Act are given in Chapter 2 in *Guidelines for Industries*, 1975-76.
12. R.K. Hazari, *Industrial Planning and Licensing Policy* (New Delhi: Government of India, Planning Commission, 1967), p. 17.
13. Hanson, *Process of Planning*, p. 486.
14. Hazari, *Industrial Planning*, p. 18.
15. J. Bhagwati and P. Desai, *India: Planning for Industrialization* (New York: Oxford University Press, 1970), p. 255.
16. Hazari, *Industrial Planning*, p. 7-8.
17. Government of India, Planning Commission, *Fourth Five-Year Plan* (New Delhi,), p. 27.
18. Bhagwati and Desai, *India: Planning for Industrialization*, p. 158.
19. This memorandum is reproduced in *Eastern Economist*, vol. 50, 14 March 1969.
20. A summary for the year 1974-75 is given in *Eastern Economist*, vol. 67, no. 16, 16 April 1976.
21. This concern is also evident in many Western

countries. For example, in a *White Paper on the Economic and Financial Objectives of the Nationalized Industries,* published in November 1967, the British Government suggested a target rate of return of 8 per cent.

22. For a survey of the literature, see J.H. Dreze, "Some Postwar Contributions of French Economists to Theory and Public Policy, with Special Emphasis on Problems of Resource Allocation", *American Economic Review,* June 1964. See also Margolis and Guitton, *Public Economics.*

BIBLIOGRAPHY

Bhagwati, J. and Desai, P.: *India—Planning for Industrialization.* New York. Oxford University Press, 1970.

Government of India: Administrative Reforms Commission. *Report of the Study Team on Public Sector Undertakings.* New Delhi, June 1967.

———, Planning Commission: *Second Five-Year Plan.* New Delhi.

———: *Third Five-Year Plan.* New Delhi.

———: *Fourth Five-Year Plan.* New Delhi.

———: Department of Industrial Development: *Guidelines for Industries* 1975–76. New Delhi, 1976.

———: Bureau of Public Enterprises. *Annual Reports on the Working of Industrial and Commercial Undertakings of the Central Government.* New Delhi.

Hanson, A.H.: *The Process of Planning.* London. Oxford University Press, 1966.

Hazari, R.K.: *Industrial Planning and Licensing Policy.* Government of India. Planning Commission. New Delhi, 1967.

Margolis, J. and Guitton H. (eds.): *Public Economics.* MacMillan, 1969.

Ramanadham, V.V. (ed.): *The Working of the Public Sector.* Bombay. Allied Publishers, 1965.

Wilcox, C. and Shepherd W.G.: *Public Policies toward Business.* Homewood, Illinois. Irwin, 1975.

10

Elements of Gandhian Economics: Their Relevance to India's Economic Problems

ROMESH DIWAN

> Today the cities dominate and drain the villages so that they are crumbling to ruin. My *khadi* mentality tells me that cities must subserve villages when that domination goes. Exploiting of villages is itself organized violence. If we want *swaraj* to be built on non-violence we will have to give the villages their proper place... To serve our villages is to establish *swaraj*. Everything else is an idle dream.[1]
>
> MAHATMA GANDHI

The 1940's and 1950's were years of formal decolonization. During these years many erstwhile colonies achieved political independence. These newly independent governments consciously pursued policies of development. We can now witness some of the results of such development: by and large, the efforts, in spite of their magnitude and even when successful, have followed a path that has led to the intensification, instead of solution, of the problems of poverty, unemployment and inequality. We thus find that after successful operation of these policies, the number and percentage of the population that is poor and unemployed has substantially increased. One explanation of this phenomenon is that the development strategy has been misguided, in the sense that it has tried to solve a different problem.

The solution to the problems of poverty, inequality, and unemployment requires a completely different strategy. Such a strategy is implied in the writings of Mahatma Gandhi. The elements of this strategy involve the provision of opportunities for "self-defined" work, encouragement of production of "use values", and strengthening of the small organizational structures that are not based on the principle of pure exchange. The production of "use values" and "self-defined work" go together; certainly in the initial stages when these are most needed. There already exist, in these countries, small organizational structures that provide "grants" and "income transfers" without quid pro quo The joint family and village are excellent examples of such institutions. Some of these structures are intact, others need repair and still others need overhauling. It must be added and emphasised that strengthening such structures is a positive developmental activity that takes us forward and not backward.

Nature of Development in India

There are various ways of examining development processes. Some refer to GNP estimates, index numbers of production of various industrial goods, etc. We suggest that we look into the effects of development in terms of human beings, i.e., increase and decrease in their suffering. A measure of the suffering of people is the magnitude of poverty and unemployment. It is now recognized that the development effort in India has not been successful when viewed from the point of view of the poor. The development process in other countries, Pakistan, Bangladesh, Nepal, Ceylon, is quite similar to that in India.[3] The results are also similar.

Our proposition is that development efforts over the last 28 years in India have not helped the poor. They have led actually to greater poverty. The proposition implies that the process of development was predicated precisely to help the poor. One may argue that development in India never had such a purpose. In that case, to argue that development did not help the poor would be illogical. There is, however, ample proof to the effect that one of the main goals of economic and development policy has always been to remove poverty. Even the Constitution embodies such a purpose, and the Indian society has fully accepted this purpose. So much so, that in the 1960's when the development process had taken enough time, virtually all the political parties spoke of this purpose, and the Congress party invented the slogan,

garibi hatao.[4] Thus it is both logical and legitimate to ask if the development effort did or did not help the poor.

There is now ample evidence, statistical and otherwise, that development has not helped the poor.[5] Some researchers and authors make a stronger statement: that development in India has harmed the poor. Thus, the studies of Diwan (1971), Rath and Dandekar (1971), Minhas (1968, 74), Bardhan (1973), Srinivasan and Bardhan (1974) show that the magnitude of poverty is very large. Bardhan (1973) estimates that "the percentage of rural people below the minimum level of living has significantly gone up from 38 per cent in 1960–61 to 54 per cent in 1968–69. In absolute numbers, this means a rise from about 135 million to about 230 million rural people below the minimum level between 1960–61 and 1968–69".[6] Poverty is defined at the minimal level, the capacity to obtain 2,000 calories of food a day and nothing else, not even a piece of cloth. The reason for this increase in the size of poverty lies in inflation, by which the prices of things consumed by the poor have increased at a much faster level than the general price level and the prices of commodities consumed by the rich. Since there is hardly a difference between the consumption of the poor in the rural areas and the urban areas, a similar rise in the size of the poor is also taking place among the urban people. The total poor, thus, would form around 60–70 per cent of the whole population;[7] and this is an increase from 42 per cent in 1960–61.

The size of and change in poverty is a summary statistic. It catches the total impact of the development process. We can judge this effect from two other aspects: increase in unemployment and increase in income inequalities. The data on unemployment are not easily available,[8] and there are various estimates. Raj Krishna (1972) has estimated that in 1971 there were as many as 30 million people unemployed and severally and moderately underemployed. Even the Committee on unemployment estimates: "In our view, therefore, the estimates of unemployed should include the persons who are wholly unemployed as well as those who have worked for less than 14 hours a week. On the whole, therefore, we are inclined to the view that the likely number of unemployed persons in 1971 may reasonably be taken as 18.7 million."[9] And this committee, by all standards a conservative one, is biassed towards underestimating. Also 1971 was a non-recessionary year. Compare this estimate with the estimate at the beginning of the Third Five-Year Plan. It was estimated then that there were 9 million unemployed. Thus unemployment has literally doubled over the decade, giving a rate of growth of 10 per cent a year.

As regards income inequalities, there is now sufficient evidence on the following facts:

1. The number of poor has increased both in size and proportion of population.

2. The number of unemployed has increased, again both in size and proportion.

3. The wages of rural workers have not increased in real terms. Similarly, the real wages of industrial workers have not increased.

4. The prices of goods consumed by the lower 70 per cent of the society have increased much faster than the general price level.[10]

5. The real income of the economy has increased, even if marginally.

The effect of these facts is, and has to be, to increase income inequalities. There is now ample evidence on this fact via measures of income inequality.[11]

Philosophy of Industrialization Development

The philosophy underlying the development strategy (in spite of its lofty ideals), is based on two propositions: (1) Development can be defined as an increase in GNP per capita.[12] Since GNP per capita is a ratio, it involves two quantities, GNP and population. The proposition implies maximization of GNP and minimization of population. (2) Once production has taken place, it can always be distributed easily and equally.[13] The distributions can be ensured by such fiscal policies as selective taxes and subsidies.

In view of these two propositions,

maximization of the rate of growth of GNP becomes the key strategy. Some further subpropositions follow.

1. Since GNP is the aggregate of the quantities produced, more precisely value-added, its rate of growth will be maximized if the goods produced are (a) those that can be produced on a large scale, and (b) those that command high prices.[14] If one accepts the generally-held view that industry obeys the law of increasing returns to scale and agriculture that of diminishing returns to scale, the subproposition (a) would imply the introduction, extension and acceleration of the industrial modes of production. This effect is further accentuated if we add the further proviso that production on a large scale leads to economies of scale. Since the prices of those goods are high which are (i) luxury goods, (ii) goods that are imported, and (iii) goods whose cost of production is high, subproposition (b) would suggest the extension of production to these types of goods.

2. Methods that lead to production on a large scale or the production of luxury, high-cost and imported goods, are the methods generally prevalent in the developed countries. Historically, they are resource-, capital-, energy-, and skill-intensive. These methods have also high labour productivity. Since efficiency has been defined in terms of labour productivity, these methods are sold as highly efficient. Since these methods of production are already in existence and use, in developed countries, the development strategy provides a strong argument for the import of such goods, and techniques, from the developed countries.

3. Since imports are possible only, and only if, the importing country has foreign currency resources, the strategy suggests the following policies: (a) export as much as it can to these countries. Export-oriented production, thus, becomes equally important; (b) obtain as much foreign aid or capital as possible. This leads to the policies of formulating programmes acceptable to the aid-giving country, or relaxing production relations that suit the investor of capital.

A variant of such policies has been and is prevalent in all the South Asian countries. Since the leverage to production comes from investment, the objectives of maximizing the rate of growth of GNP translates into policies for investment. Thus the five-year plans in all the countries in South Asia have followed the practice of increasing the level of investment in every plan. Further, an increasing proportion of this investment has been concentrated in providing overheads that facilitate industrial production. Investment in agriculture has also been directed to the capitalization of agricultural production.[15]

Fallacies of Industrialization Development Strategy

As we have noticed in the previous section, when judged from the point of view of the people, this strategy has failed, because of a number of fallacies it contains.

1. The interesting thing about the strategy is that there is hardly any consideration given to either the needs of the people, particularly poor people, or their employment. It is not accidental that references to people and employment are indirect.[16] In the words of Minhas, "in spite of a number of references in the plans to the employment problem, the creation of employment opportunities was seen more or less as an adjunct to or a by-product of the development strategy".[17]

2. The proposition that distribution will take care of itself, or can be easily taken care of, does not stand analysis. If the production structure produces luxury goods such as refrigerators, airconditioners, automobiles, expensive houses, etc., how would the government or any market system distribute these to poor people who need food, clothing and shelter? Once goods-not-needed by the poor are produced, there is no mechanism that can distribute them to the poor. In other words, a production system also implies a distribution system. Production of luxury goods, at least in the initial stages of development, implies a denial of goods to the poor.

3. It is because of the increase in poverty, unemployment, and income inequality, in recent years and as a result of development, that some development

economists have started to ask: What is the meaning of development?[18] This question arises from the asymmetry of the relationship between poverty and GNP. It is true that if the GNP of a number of poor people living not as a cohesive social unit but as individuals, is measured, their GNP per capita will be low. However, its converse does not follow. In other words, if the GNP per capita of a group is low, it does not follow that the group is composed of poor people or people who suffer from poverty. This asymmetry arises from the methods of GNP estimation. GNP is incapable of evaluating a highly cohesive social group which is predominantly non-exchange oriented.

4. The effect of industrialization is to introduce exchange relations, and destroy structures where the relations are not defined by exchange. Since GNP methodology is based on, and biassed towards, exchange relations, industrialization is automatically associated with increases in GNP. Yet in real fact, the introduction of exchange relations between persons is not an improvement but a deterioration in the conditions of the poor.

Gandhian Development Strategy

We have argued, and demonstrated, that the existing industrialization development strategy is, at best, misguided. It is, therefore, necessary to define an alternative development strategy. To do so, we must recognize the existing facts and state the objectives of development. In the context of India and even of other developing countries, one could list the following stylized facts:

1. A very, very large part, approximately 80–90 per cent, of the population lives in rural areas and villages.

2. A sufficiently large part, more than 60–70 per cent, of the population is poor. In other words, its income is very low; less than one rupee a day.

3. A substantial part of the working population has little or no paid work. To put it in another form, a very large number of the working people are either unemployed or underemployed.

The objectives of development are to

provide work and income to these people within the villages.

In developing the alternative strategy, we must learn from the failures of the existing industrialization strategy. Two lessons are worth pointing out: one, the existing industrialization strategy provides an impetus (a) for the working people in the villages, and hence their dependents, to leave the village and move to the shanties and ghettos of towns and cities, and (b) for the producers to produce goods and services for the needs of the towns and cities. The self-sufficiency and advantages of village life are reduced, and eventually villages become functionless and even dependent. However, the towns and cities cannot absorb the large population of the villages.

The basic problem of development, as Gandhi saw it, is the provision of "work opportunities" and "use values". The people at large in these countries do not have resources to obtain "use values" for their physical and social needs. Their only resource, by and large, is their own body labour. The problem, however, is that these people are not able to transform this body labour into "use values". In the last analysis, the purpose of development strategy is to facilitate such a transformation. This paper deals with some of the elements in this problem.

Transformation implies two states: the existing state and the desired state. One can write about the existing state of the Indian economy or about its desired state. The development process so far has defined "the desired state" as the state when a society is properly industrialized. The USA of today provides an approximation of this desired state, call it State I. There are two problems about this desired State I: one, it is virtually impossible of achievement; it is a mirage. The reason is that the resources needed to attain even half of US material product per capita in India just do not exist. This desired State I, thus, is a will-o'-the-wisp. Two, even if one does get to achieve this desired State I, it is not worth the sacrifice. These days, there is a lot of questioning whether the quality of life in countries like the USA is good enough, and there is even a small movement towards decentralized

small societies in the USA. In view of these two problems, it is necessary to define the development process differently, aiming at another desired state: State II. This is the state that Mahatma Gandhi visualized and articulated. What follows are some of the elements in this State II.

Work

What "work" is depends upon who defines it. If the "work" is defined by the person "working" or the family (an extended family), or a neighbour[19] (in the human sense), the concept of work is going to be fundamentally different from how it is defined by a "master", "capitalist", "stranger", etc. There are thus two categories of "work": (i) "work" defined by self or "self-defined work"—family or neighbour-defined work is close to this category, and (ii) "work" defined by a stranger—landlord/master-, capitalist-, bureaucrat-defined work lies in this category. The nature of work in these two categories is very different.

"Self-defined work" is non-alienating and has little disutility. It is basically pleasant, with some hard and unpleasant moments. It is not very "productive" in the neoclassical, GNP/labour-ratio, sense. Part of the production of such work is not amenable to measurement via GNP methodology and conventions. It is, perhaps, no accident that a large part of such work, e.g., voluntary work, housework, etc., is excluded from GNP estimates. There is little conflict in this work. The person who "works" has a complete, or a very large, say on what "work" has to be.

"Stranger-defined work" on the other hand is very different. In the neoclassical sense, it is the most productive, though not always.[20] Some forms of "stranger-defined work" are more productive than others. One can categorize it into three different forms: (i) pure slavery (serfdom, bonded labour are all a form of slavery), (ii) share-cropper, and (iii) wage labour under the capitalistic system.[21] It is argued that as one moves from (i) to (iii) the productivity of labour, defined a là neoclassical economics, also increases. It is productive simply because the stranger who defines "work" considers only that activity work which brings direct benefit not to the worker but to the stranger. The GNP methodology has been devised to estimate and measure exactly this type of work. One can recognize this bias in the GNP methodology clearly if one considers the same work done under two different forms. Thus some work done voluntarily by a housewife is not estimated. However, if it is done "involuntarily" by a paid servant, it is counted in GNP. Part of the reason why "stranger-defined work" is considered more productive lies in the bias[22] of the GNP methodology.

On the other hand, "stranger-defined work" has many disadvantages. First, it creates a situation of conflict between the person who defines work and the one who actually works. This is an important source of inhumanity in the system and institutions that encourage "stranger-defined work". Two, from this conflict follows what has come to be known as "alienation". Weisskopf (1973) considers alienation as the difference between one's potentialities and the actualization of these potentialities.[23] The alienation in this work arises from two sources: (a) the feeling of exploitation, and (b) the lack of capacities to actualize one's potentialities. Alienation in the Western industrialized societies is increasing at such a high rate that it causes serious concern. Galbraith argues that the motivation of pecuniary gain works no longer and has to be substituted by "identification". Three, this "work" must have disutility. Contrary to "self-defined work", "stranger-defined work" only has pleasant moments. The norm is discipline, routine, and drudgery which have to be inhumanly forced.

The concept of employment is based on "stranger-defined work".

The various employment policies in underdeveloped countries have failed to generate enough "stranger-defined work".[24] Schumacher (1973) is very right when he states, "poor countries slip—and are pushed—into the adoption of production methods and consumption standards which destroy the possibilities of self-reliance and self-help. The results are unintentional neocolonialism and hopelessness for the poor".[25]

The solution of this part of the problem, therefore, lies in the encouragement of opportunities for "self-defined work".

Production and Distribution of "Use Values"

Our next question relates to the "obtaining of use values" by a person. This question involves two issues: (i) production of "use values" and (ii) sharing or distribution of these "use values" We take up these issues one by one.

Production of "use values" immediately raises the definitional question: what are "use values"? The neoclassical, even a variant of Marxian,[26] economic theory defines output as a commodity or service which has "utility" for its consumer. This definition does not distinguish between a necessity that is essential for survival and a luxury that satisfies only a non-basic want. On the other hand, classical economics made the distinction between "basic" and "nonbasic" goods. By "use values" we wish to define only "basic" goods that are necessary for a person's and society's survival. To make the point clear, we can divide the total output between "use values" and "exchange values" or between "basic" goods and "non basic" goods. There will always be a certain amount of arbitrariness in such a classification. The classification will be affected by time, production modes, etc. Thus, some commodities may have been "non basic" at some time and become "basic" at another. Tea in India is a good example. Some 200 years ago, tea was not a "basic" commodity. Today it is. Another way of defining "basic" goods or "use values" is to consider which section of the society consumes them. We consider those goods "basic" or having "use values" which are consumed by 99 per cent of the members of a society. Thus, in the case of India, foodgrains, wheat, rice, pulses, milk, oil, vegetables, tea, fruit, fish, sugar, salt, spices, *pan*, clothing, mud bricks, timber, etc., are the "basic" goods. These are the goods that have "use values". The issue of production of "use values", thus, boils down to the production of such goods.

Translated into the current terminology

of economics, production of "use values", as defined above, poses two questions: (i) composition of output, and (ii) magnitude of output particularly the magnitude of that part of output which relates to "basic goods". In the economic literature, this issue of composition of output is never discussed. It is only socialists and social thinkers like George Bernard Shaw who raise these questions. There is a very famous quotation from Shaw to the effect that society needs carpenters, cooks, plumbers, doctors; while the capitalistic system provides prostitutes, pimps, police, alcoholics, etc. In other words, in a capitalistic society the composition of output is heavily weighted against "basic goods". Similarly, the "industrialism" school argues that "the present industrial system is dynamically unstable. It is organized for indefinite expansion and the concurrent unlimited creation of new needs, which in an industrial environment soon become basic needs".[27] In other words, the industrial system does not produce "use values" to satisfy the needs but instead creates the needs to conform to what it produces.

The question relating to the magnitude of the production of "use values" leads to methods, modes and techniques of production. In the last analysis, all production originates from "work".

We assert that "self-defined work" is more suited to the production of "use values" or "basic goods", and "stranger-defined work" to that of "non basic" or "exchange values". In an industrial or industrializing system, there is a preponderance of "exchange values" and hence "stranger-defined work" is very important. Yet the basic problem of poverty is not the lack of production of "exchange values" but that of "use values". The solution to the problem of poverty, therefore, lies in the encouragement or development of opportunities for "self-defined work" since it also produces "use values".

Our next issue is the sharing and distribution of the "use values". In an organizational structure where a person who works for himself and where this work produces "use values", the problem of distribution does not arise. The person obtains "use values" in the process of "work". However, production of "use values" is rarely an individual activity. It is basically a group activity. The person who works in the "self-defined work" sense has to belong to a group, a family, a village, etc. The "use values" are produced jointly. It is virtually impossible to ascertain the particular contribution of a particular person in this production system. One should recognize the importance of this fact. Logically, it may be possible to ascertain the contribution of a person (even though empirically it may be an impossible task). Also, no person is indispensable in this production effort. Yet it does not follow from these two propositions that the particular contribution of a particular person can be ascertained. The problem becomes all the more complicated if one recognizes that the production process produces not only "material use values" but also "non-material use values". For example, if a person tends an old sick person, this person does not contribute to the "material use values". Similarly, a person who simply talks to and entertains by talking, persons working in the fields, also contributes by relieving the unpleasantness of the work. This is not to suggest that there are no rip-offs in such a system as well, but these certainly are minimal.

Sharing of the "use values" produced jointly, therefore, has to be defined on some other basis. The most acceptable basis, which is founded in empirical observation, is that of need and equity. It is also a humane system because one cannot have a "self-defined work" without a family or a neighbour. The distribution by equity and need between neighbours and/or members of a family cannot be unjust (no doubt there are always exceptions), because the relationships at all levels are fundamentally human.

The above system is contrasted with a production process in which production comes from "stranger-defined work". In such a system, unless there is some arrangement made to share production of "use values" among persons who for one reason or another cannot or do not work, the problem of poverty and inhumanity remains. The "industrialism" in the poor countries bears testimony to it. The basic evidence from a large number of underdeveloped countries is that this is not a solution to their problems.

Self-Sufficient Village

Once it is recognized that the objectives of development can be achieved only by the provision of opportunities for self-defined work, then the question of institutions becomes an important one. One of the most important of such institutions is the Indian village. It is no accident that Mahatma Gandhi emphasised the need to strengthen the village structure. "Village" is an amorphous term and it stands for at least two well-defined concepts. A great deal of confusion has arisen from not distinguishing between them. Let us, therefore, clarify these two concepts.

Village concept one, is the village as Gandhi seemed to have understood it. We shall call it the Gandhian concept of a village: decentralized village for short. (This is basically an ideal village particularly in the late twentieth century. It actually existed perhaps, one thousand years ago when Indian civilization was at its height). This village is small, with a population of 500–5,000, 1–5 miles in area. It is self-sufficient in the sense that it produces all the "use values" that persons living in the village desire and need. It allows the villagers sufficient leisure, so that they can be, and are, creative.[28] Both, economic and political power are shared equally. One can go into this in greater detail, but for our purpose here, it should suffice.

Village concept two is the village as it is commonly understood in India today, the late twentieth century. It is not self-sufficient. Quite often, economic and political power is in the hands of one or two families. It does not produce use values for all the persons in the village. Instead, it produces exchange values for the town or city nearby. The only relationship of this village concept two with the decentralized village is in terms of geographical area, and size of population. We shall call concept two "periphery village"; a village which is basically on the periphery of the city or town. It does not have to be peripheral in only the geographical sense: a village, far, far away from the city, say 150 miles away, which produces goods by and large for the market in the city, is in our sense a periphery village.

There are, obviously, differences between a decentralized village and a periphery village. The morality, modes of production, social relations, mental outlook of villagers, etc., in these two are quite different, even opposed. The Gandhian or decentralized village is resilient and very strong. The Vietnamese defense against US military power is the best testimonial to this resilience. The fact that the Chinese commune system has been an important factor in solving the problem of poverty among such a large population is evidence of its potential.

In the debate on the development of villages, the protagonists of industrialization have used the periphery village concept to denounce the decentralized village. They have thus condemned it by giving it names like "primitive", "backward", etc. Yet there is nothing primitive and backward about a decentralized village. On the contrary, this may perhaps be the only hope of mankind in the future.[30]

The decentralized village is an institution, par excellence, for providing opportunities for self-defined work.

Joint-Family System

Another equally important and relevant institution in this context is the much censured joint family system. Like the village, the joint family system is also an old institution. With our present day values, where everything old is condemned, the joint family system has not fared any better. Standard textbooks on Indian economics and the Indian economy always devote a chapter or a section to the joint family system. By and large, the thesis in these textbooks is that the joint family system is not suited to development: "In the context of a subsistence economy, the joint family system does have both social and economic utility but in the context of economic growth it may not be appropriate".[31] The arguments offered in favour of this contention are that joint family system inhibits initiative and mobility, and encourages population growth.

This argument is, unfortunately, based on a misconception. The objective of development implied in this argument is very different from the objective we have set in this paper. The strategy of development implied by it is industrialization and its concomitant, stranger-defined work, production of exchange values, etc. After all, how does mobility help the production of use values? How can a joint family sap the initiative to produce use values? The idea that the joint family system encourages population growth is bunkum: there is no relationship between economic and social security and an increase in birth rate. On the contrary, the relationship may be just the reverse. This is the contention of affluent lands and the effect of economic growth. Yet we admit, the joint family is a hindrance to stranger-defined work.

Once again, there are concepts of the joint family quite similar to the village concepts. There is the concept of the joint family in the environment of a decentralized village. Here the joint family is "convivial". On the other hand, the joint family in a peripheral village has all sorts of problems: envy, greed, etc., among the members of the family.

Science and Technology

The very mention of the village arouses, in some quarters, the idea of a "back-to-the-woods" and primitive life. The major element of this idea about primitiveness is felt in terms of science and technology. The general perception is that science and technology are modern and that they flourish in towns and cities. It is argued that technology is complex and requires a large scale of operation which cannot be obtained at the village level. This argument, however, is fallacious and is based on myths rather than on science, scholarship or facts.[32]

The development and strengthening of the decentralized village requires an advanced knowledge of science and suffi-

ciently complex technology. A few examples will illustrate this statement. In Indian agriculture, there is need for the production of such goods as wheat, rice, foodgrains, vegetables, etc. Not only is there a need for production but also a need for increase in production.[33] To increase agricultural production one needs some new inputs such as fertilizers. Now fertilizers are generally produced on a large scale by centralized large-scale production techniques. However, to make the village self-sufficient, it will be necessary to produce fertilizers in the village. The real scientific task is therefore to devise a method to produce fertilizers from the resources available in the village. The technical task is to produce these in the village itself. As Reddy (1975) has shown, it is possible to produce fertilizers from cowdung (biogas plant) in a small production unit. Such a production unit will use only the resources of the village, and it can be set up in the village itself. It will use a small number of persons in the village. This is what the "alternative", or "appropriate' technology is all about. This "appropriate" technology is actually an "advance" on existing technology. In his own words, "the general conclusion is that 'alternative technologies' are certain to be 'advanced technologies', if the 'advanced' character of a technology is to be judged not from the trivial criterion of scale but from the sophistication of the scientific and engineering thinking that goes into it".[34] The choice of technology, however, will depend upon the nature of the development strategy, the rules of the game, and the type of society the development process generates.[35]

Similarly, we can take the case of use and production of energy. It is now recognized that the development strategy being followed at present is energy-intensive.[36] Yet it is a mistaken strategy, since it utilizes energy sources that are scarce and expensive, ignoring energy sources that are abundant, such as the sun and wind. Production and use of energy can also be dichotomized, at the risk of simplification, into two groups: (i) decentralized form of production and use, and (ii) centralized form. Large power plants, electricity generating systems, etc., are basically centralized.

A village cannot produce or maintain a Bhakra dam, or an atomic power plant. One needs towns and cities for these. However, a very large part of the energy utilized from these large centralized-producing plants is for comparatively simpler tasks, in terms of raising the temperature. The American Physical Society has now done a study and suggested that the use of electricity, produced at 1,000° F and above, for such tasks as space heating at temperatures of 80° F or so is rather inefficient. They define efficiency in terms of the second law of thermodynamics. Barry Commoner has argued persuasively that the second law efficiencies are generally high if the production of energy is decentralized.[37] For example, if a house produces heat from the sun to heat the house, the efficiency is very high indeed. From the second law efficiency point of view, decentralized forms of producing and using energy become very efficient indeed. These technologies also lead to the further strengthening of the village.

REFERENCES

1. M.K. Gandhi, *Rebuilding our Villages* (Ahmedabad: Navjivan, 1952), p. 3.
2. The moment one uses the term "village" there is a tendency to denounce it as backward, even though in USA the most modern communities and groupings are called villages and attempt to recreate the humanity and freedom of the village.
3. "Underdevelopment is also a state of mind, and understanding it as a state of mind, or as form of consciousness, is the critical problem." Ivan Illich, *Deschooling Society* (New York: Harper and Row, 1970).
4. A mood of competitive radicalism descended on the political scene in 1970. Almost all political parties were now vying with each other for establishing their radical credentials. Even the Rightist groups (in terms of the old-fashioned definition) were busy putting on a radical plumage. This development was a manifestation of the sociopolitical compulsions of our situation and most of the forward-looking elements in our national life, particularly the poorer and the weaker sections, welcomed it." B.S. Minhas, *Radicalism and Demagogy*, II, *The Overseas Hindustan Times*, New Delhi, 30 May 1974.
5. The deficiencies of the development process, particularly in terms of the effect on the poor is, to quote Suresh Desai, "In sum, the present development strategy has resulted in accentuating inequalities of income and wealth, in increasing unemployment, in creating a balance of payment crisis, in increasing dependence on foreign countries, in misdirection of educational and R&D efforts, in the use of inflation as a strategy to place the burden of development on those least capable of bearing it, and in the development of state power that is being used for the benefit of politically and economically entrenched powerful classes. The new economy and society that has emerged in the last twenty-eight years of developmental effort has been perceived, rightly or wrongly, as controlled and operated by the con men, bunko artists, speculators, wheeler-dealers, and corrupt bureaucrats and politicians who are merely interested in making a quick buck. The masses have come to perceive the emerging inequalities as a result of fraud, misinformation, illegal actions, and favouritisms and having no relation to technological or organizational efficiency or to equity or social weal." S. Desai, "Whither India? A Gandhian Alternative", in Romesh Diwan (ed.), *Issues in the Indian Economy* (Albany, New York: Association of the Indian Economics Studies, 1976), p. 38.
6. K. Pranab Bardhan, "On the Incidence of Poverty in Rural India of the Sixties", *Economic and Political Weekly*, Annual Number, 1973, p. 245–254.
7. These are my own rough estimates based on rough data on prices, urban incomes, etc.
8. It is a distressing commentary on the ideology of this particular type of development that even after 28 years the country has no clear ideas about the size and composition of unemployment. An excuse is made, from committee to committee, that the conceptual problems are serious. Yet these conceptual problems are far less serious and far less numerous than those in the estimation of GNP. The estimates on GNP are nevertheless made religiously. The problem is of priorities and not of proficiencies.
9. Government of India, *Report of the Committee on Unemployment* (New Delhi: Manager of Publications), May 1973, p. 55.
10. Ranjit Sau shows that "the market for industrial consumption goods in India is, in a sense, shrinking: the percentage of per capita consumer expenditure spent on industrial goods is declining over the years, rather sharply in rural India and mildly in urban. Among various fractile groups of population, the ones at the bottom are increasingly withdrawing from the market for industrial consumer goods." Sau, "Some Aspects of Intersectoral Resource Flow", *Economic and Political Weekly*, Vol. 9, Nos

32–34, pp. 1277–84.

11. Gini ratio is generally considered a measure of income inequality. Recent studies show that this ratio has increased over time, implying an increase in income inequalities.

12. Dazzled by the high living standards of the developed countries and convinced that real life begins at $ 1,000 or thereabout, they [underdeveloped countries] decide to go after high growth rates in GNP in their mad chase after certain magic figures of average per capita incomes".

13. This argument is reduced in a simple form to a common home simile, namely, the important thing is to increase the size of the cake (or pie) and not how to slice it. Note, slicing a cake is the simplest of all possible activities.

14. Since value added is different from the value of the output, the argument will hold so long as value added is a linear function of the value of the output. Unless the value added and value of output are inversely related, even a nonlinear relationship will not change the direction of the effect of the value of output on GNP. The exact maximum, will no doubt, be affected.

15. Some economists argue that agricultural production under the "green revolution" is basically of the nature of industrial production. The "green revolution" is basically a capitalistic and capital-intensive method of production. These arguments are discussed in detail in Romesh Diwan, "Green Revolution in India: A Second Look", paper presented at the New York State Conference on Asian Studies, Cornell University, Ithaca, October 19–20, 1974 (mimeographed).

16. In more recent publications there is a direct reference to poverty, unemployment, etc., but fiscal and economic policies as well as investment programmes do not bear any relation to these references.

17. B.S. Minhas, Planning and the Poor (New Delhi: S. Chand, 1974) p. 3. This is true not only for India but a large number of other countries. Thus Haq makes these comments: "The employment objective, in short, has been the step-child of planning, and it has been assumed, far too readily, that high rates of growth will ensure full employment as well. But what if they don't? A sustained 6 per cent rate of growth in Pakistan in the 1960's led to rising unemployment, particularly in East Pakistan". Mahbub-ul-Haq, "Employment in the 1970's: A New Perspective", International Development Review, Vol. 13, No. 4, 1971.

18. One must recognize that the concept of employment and unemployment, as presently understood, is defined in terms of industrialization.

19. Two conditions define a neighbour: one, geographical proximity, not exactly next door but within a reasonable distance; and two, existence of a human relationship, i.e., that the two share in each other's sorrow and happiness.

20. It has been argued cogently and proved empirically that the productivity and efficiency of labour by slaves was far lower than that under capitalistic production. See Genovese (1965). This, however, does not disprove the statement that "stranger-defined work" is more productive in the neoclassical sense of the term. The radical economists do not recognize or analyse this fact. Part of their difficulties arise from ignoring it completely.

21. J.K. Galbraith in The New Industrial Estate (Boston: Houghton Mifflin, 1965), classifies these three categories into two: (i) and (ii) under "compulsion", and (iii) under "pecuniary gain". His classification is based on motivation. Incidentally, he argues that these two sources of motivation, compulsion, and pecuniary gain are becoming obsolete in the new industrial state. What is needed is "identification" and "adaptation". These are the motives associated with "self-defined work".

22. It is this bias that is partly responsible for the divergence of GNP from actual or true welfare.

23. Walter Weisskopf distinguishes between social and existential alienation. "What constitutes existential alienation is that man can only actualize certain selected potentialities and must necessarily sacrifice others which are also within the limit of his personality. He could actualize them, but having made a choice he has sacrified them. This is alienation because he thus becomes alienated from some of his own potentialities. The conclusion is that alienation cannot be completely eliminated. Being human is being alienated." A condition of antimony arises between the human traits and propensities which society permits to become real and actual, and potentialities which are neglected, suppressed and repressed... This situation is the social root of alienation". Walter Weisskopf, Alienation and Economics (New York: E.F. Dulton, 1973), pp. 25, 32.

24. There is now ample evidence that the development strategies in the developing countries have failed to generate employment. See Huq, Employment in the 1970's, Minhas, Planning and the Poor, Myrdal, Asian Drama. As a matter of fact, the industrialization strategy generates more unemployment by destroying the existing integrated social structure.

25. Schumacher, Small is Beautiful, p. 184.

26. The use-value of a commodity depends on the totality of its physical qualities, which determine its utility. The existence of this use-value is an indispensable condition for the appearance of an exchange value; nobody will accept in exchange for his own product a commodity which has no utility, no use-value, for any one." Mandel (1968) p. 64. In this sense, even narcotics have "use-values".

27. Illich, Tools for Conviviality, p. 49. Perennial Library Edition, "Industrialism" is like an addictive drug; the more you take the more you need it.

28. "When our villages are fully developed there will be no dearth in them of men with a high degree of skill and artistic talent. There will be village poets, village artists, village archi-tects, linguists, and research workers. In short, there will be nothing in life worth having which will not be had in the villages. Today the villages are dung heaps. Tomorrow they will be like tiny gardens of Eden where dwell highly intelligent folk whom no one can deceive or exploit." Mahatma Gandhi quoted by Narayan, in *Relevance of Gandhian Economics*, p. 69.

29. S. Radhakrishnan does not find anything primitive in a village. Thus he writes: "Going back to villages is not to become primitive. It is the only way to keep up a mode of existence that is instinctive to India, that supplied her once with a purpose, a faith and a meaning. It is the only way to keep our species civilized. India of the peasant and rustic life, of village communities, of forest hermitage and spiritual retreats has taught the world many great lessons but has wronged no man, has injured no land and sought no domination over others." Quoted in Narayan, *Relevance of Gandhian Economics*, p. 153.

30. See Heilbroner, *Business Civilization in Decline*, It is interesting to note that while the villages have stood the tests of time, city civilizations have come and gone. In the Indian continent itself, Mahenjo Daro is an excellent example. Here is a city with an inhabitation of 100,000 persons in those early days. Yet so little is known of why and how this civilization died, while the village has continued.

31. Datt and Sundharam, *Indian Economy*, p. 162.

32. Paulo Freire describes the need and purpose of myths to maintain an oppressive system; and industrialism is an oppressive and violent system: "it is necessary for the oppressor to approach the people in order, via subjugation, to keep them passive. This approximation however, does not involve being with the people, or require true communication. It is established by the oppressor's depositing myths indispensable to the preservation of the status quo." Freire, *Pedagogy of the Oppressed*, p. 135.

33. See Diwan, *Agriculture in India*.

34. Reddy, *Alternative Technology: Viewpoint from India*, p. 337. In this paper, he actually gives details of two methods of producing fertilizers and shows that by virtually all criteria, the village technology is not only appropriate but preferable. He calls them income-inequality-reducing technologies.

35. See Diwan, *Gandhi and Modernization of Modes of Production*. It is also being recog-nized now that imitation of western technology is not helpful. For the case of the Green Revolution, see Diwan, *Green Revolution in India*.

36. Diwan, *Green Revolution in India*.

37. Commoner, *The Poverty of Power*.

BIBLIOGRAPHY

Amin, Samir: *Accumulation on a World Scale*. Vols. 1 and 2. New York. Monthly Review Press, 1974.

Bardhan, Pranab, K.: "On the Incidence of Poverty in Rural India of the Sixties". *Economic and Political Weekly*. Annual Number 1973, pp. 245–254.

Bhargava, Ashok: "A Critical Look at India's Development Strategy". In Romesh Diwan (ed.) *Issues in Indian Economy*. Albany, New York. Indian Economic Studies Association, 1976, pp. 1–16.

Commoner, Barry (ed.): *The Poverty of Power*. New York. Knopf, 1976.

Dandekar, V.M. and Rath, N.: *Poverty in India*. Poona. Indian School of Political Economy, 1971.

Datt, Ruddar and Sundaram, K.P.M.: *Indian Economy*, 8th edn. New Delhi. S. Chand, 1972.

Desai, Suresh A.: "Whither India? A Gandhian Alternative". In Romesh Diwan (ed.) *Issues in Indian Economy*. 1976, pp. 33–45.

Diwan, Romesh: "Planning for the Poor". *Economic and Political Weekly* Vol. VI. 21 August 1971, pp. 1809–1814.

————: "Plannostructure and Poverty in India". Paper presented at the New York State Conference on Asian Studies. New Platz, 1973 (mimeographed).

————: "Plannostructure and Garibi Hatao", Paper presented at India Forum, Chicago, 10 February 1974 and at South Asia Seminar, University of Chicago, 12 February 1974 (mimeographed).

————: "Green Revolution in India: A Second Look." Paper presented at the New York State Conference on Asian Studies, Cornell University, Ithaca, 19–20 October 1974 (mimeographed).

————: "Gandhi and Modernization of Modes of Production". Paper presented at the Conference on South Asia. Oshkosh, Wisconsin, 15–16 November 1974.

————: "Agriculture in India: Problems and Prospects," in J. Uppal (ed.) *India's Economic Problems*. New Delhi. Tata McGraw-Hill. 1975, pp. 45–63.

————: "Energy Implications of the Indian Economic Development in 1960's". Paper presented at the Annual Meeting of the Association for Asian Studies, March 24–26 1975. San Francisco; and at the 4th Wisconsin Conference on South Asia, Madison Wisconsin, November 7–8 1975 (mimeographed).

————: "Development, Education and the Poor: Context of South Asia". Paper presented at the International Conference on Adult Education and Development, Dares Salaam, Tanganyika, 21–27 June 1976.

———: "Conceptual Issues in Employment and Unemployment" (mimeographed).

———: "Small is Beautiful in India". In Diwan (ed.) *Issues in Indian Economy*, pp. 45–62.

———: "Diwan (ed.) *Issues in the Indian Economy*.

———: "Some Elements in Gandhian Theory of Development". Paper presented at CASAS 1976, Meetings in Quebec City, Canada (mimeographed).

Fanan, Frantz: *The Wretched of the Earth*. New York. Grove Press, 1966.

Freire, Paulo: *Pedagogy of the Oppressed*. New York. The Seabury Press, 1970.

Galbraith, John Kenneth: *The New Industrial Estate*. Boston. Houghton Mifflin, 1965.

Gandhi, M.K.: *Economic and Industrial Life and Relations* Vol. II. Ahmedabad. Navjivan, 1957.

———: *Rebuilding our Villages*. Ahmedabad. Navjivan, 1952.

Genovese, Eugene D.: *The Political Economy of Slavery*. New York. Random House, 1965.

Government of India. Ministry of Labour and Rehabilitation: *Report of the Committee on Unemployment*. New Delhi, 1973.

Haq, Mahbub-ul: "Employment in the 1970's: A New Perspective". *International Development Review* Vol. 13, No. 4. 1971, pp. 9–13.

———: "The Crisis in Development Strategies". Paper presented at the International Development Conference Washington, D.C., 1972 (mimeographed).

Heilbroner, Robert L.: *Business Civilization in Decline*. New York. W.W. Norton, 1976.

Illich, Ivan: *Celebration of Awareness*. New York. Doubleday, 1969.

———: *DeSchooling Society*. New York. Harper & Row, 1970.

———: *Tools for Conviviality*. New York. Harper & Row, 1973.

Mandel, Ernest. *Marxist Economic Theory*. 2 vols. New York. Monthly Review Press, 1968.

Minhas, B.S.: *Planning and the Poor*. New Delhi. S. Chand, 1974.

Myrdal, G: *Asian Drama*. New York. Pantheon Press, 1968.

Narayan, Shriman: *Relevance of Gandhian Economics*. Ahmedabad. Navjivan, 1970.

Raj Krishna: "Unemployment in India". *Economic and Political Weekly* Vol. 8, No. 10. 3 March 1973.

Reddy, A.K.N.: "Alternative Technology: A Viewpoint from India". *Social Studies of Science* Vol. 5, No. 3. 1975, pp. 331–342.

Sau, Ranjit K: *Indian Economic Growth: Constraints and Prospects*. New Delhi. Orient Longman, 1973.

———: "Some Aspects of Intersectoral Resource Flow". *Economic and Political Weekly*, Special Number Vol. 9, Nos 32-34, 1974, pp. 1277-1284.

Schumacher, E.F.: *Small is Beautiful: Economics as if People Mattered*. New York. Harper & Row, 1973.

Seers, Dudley: "The Meaning of Development". *International Development Review* vol. II, No. 4, 1969, pp. 2–6.

———: "Economic Development: Objectives and Obstacles". Paper presented at the Research Conference on the Lessons of China's Development Experience for the Developing Countries. San Juan, Puerto Rico. January 21–February 2, 1976 (mimeographed).

Sen, Amartya K.: *Employment, Technology and Development*. New York. Oxford University Press, 1975.

Weisskopf, Walter A.: *Alienation and Economics*. New York. E.F. Dutton, 1973.

Part Five

THE LABOUR SECTOR

11

Economics of Agricultural Labour in India

SURENDRA N. KULSHRESHTHA
AND
J.S. UPPAL

Human resources in an economy constitute a significant input in the production process of goods and services. The study of human resources—their quality, and problems—is, thus, of immense importance for manpower planning in both developing as well as developed economies. Knowledge of this sector is even more crucial for the rural economy of India where techniques of production are highly labour-intensive. Agriculture is the major sector of the Indian economy, employing about 72 per cent of the total work force and contributing about 42 per cent of the total national income.

The primary objective of this chapter is to analyse theoretically the agricultural labour situation and also some of its major problems, and offer suggestions for improvements.

Agricultural Labour in India—A Historical Perspective

Indian agriculture has been traditionally managed in the form of a very large number of tiny owner-operated farm units; each tiny unit further fragmented into a number of small pieces. The structure of the industry does approach atomistic competition in the conventional sense. In spite of the large number of farm units, there is a tendency towards concentration of production. From an analysis of the land resource base[1] in India during 1961, a very uneven-size distribution is noticed. About three-fourths of all farm holdings constitute only 30 per cent of the total cultivated area, whereas the top 4.6 per cent of the holdings occupy 29.7 of the total acreage. The pattern is also shown by the Lorenz curve in Figure 11.1, which clearly indicates highly unequal distribution. The further away the line OaA is from the 45° line of equality, the higher is the concentration coefficient, and greater inequality.

According to the First Agricultural Labourer's Enquiry Committee[2], an agricultural labourer is defined as a person

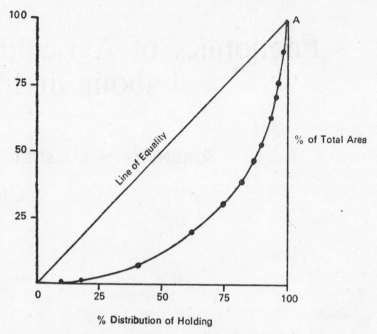

Fig. 11.1 Lorenz curve showing size distribution of agricultural holdings
in India, 1961–62

who for more than half the total number of days on which he actually works during the year, is engaged in agricultural operations as a hired worker. The definition of agricultural labour force includes these, plus all the operators of agricultural holdings.

The agricultural labour force during 1971 comprised 188.4 million workers, which constituted 72.0 per cent of the total labour force in the country. The proportion of agricultural labourers to total labour force varies from state to state. For example, in Kerala this proportion is only 38 per cent, whereas in Madhya Pradesh it is as high as 79 per cent.[3] Historically, the predominance of Indian agriculture in providing gainful employment[4] has not declined. Data in Table 11.1 show that the agricultural labour force as proportion of the total work force has increased since 1900. It may also be noted from Table 11.2 that during the period 1961–71 the number of farm operators decreased while the hired labour increased.

Table 11.1. Labour Force in Agriculture, India, 1900–71

Year	Percentage of Workers Engaged in Agriculture to Total
1900	62.5
1911	67.8
1921	68.5
1931	66.4
1951	69.0
1961	69.5
1971	72.0

SOURCE: 1. *Census of India*, 1961, Series I, Paper I, 1962.

2. *Census of India*, 1971, Series I, Paper I, 1972.

It may also be noted that as farms grow in size the dependence on hired labour resources grows (Figure 11.2).

The labour force in rural India consists of persons of varying ages, ranging from below 14 to over 60 years. The partici-

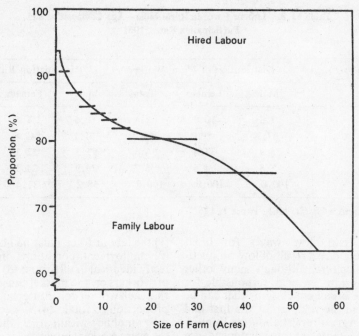

Fig. 11.2   Proportion of hired to family labour on farms by size
SOURCE: Data obtained from Kalra, p. 2.

Table 11.2.   Change in Agricultural Labour Force, 1961–72, India
(in millions)

Type of Worker	Total Number		Percentage to Total		Percentage Change
	1961	1971	1961	1971	(1961–71)
Operators	99.5	78.2	52.8	43.3	−9.5
Hired Labour	31.5	47.5	16.7	26.3	+9.6
Total	131.0	125.7	69.5	69.6	+0.1

SOURCE: 1. *Census of India*, 1961, Paper I, 1962.
2. *Census of India*, 1971, Series I, 1972.

pation rates vary substantially with different age groups and sexes. (Table 11.3). Participation by workers below the age of 14 in the labour force is rather unusual in developing economies like India. Compared to some of the Western developed countries, at least two marked differences can be noted: first, the labour force in India has a relatively high proportion of people under 34 years of age[5], secondly, participation rates in India for male labour are significantly below those in Canada or the USA. In the US, partici-pation rates for male workers of all ages for 1961 were estimated at 79.7 per cent, as against only 57.7 per cent in India.[6] A part of the explanation may lie in the inclusion of workers below 14 years of age in these figures, who expectedly have a very low participation rate. However, the explanation of low participation may also lie in the low opportunity for jobs, prevalence of particular work ethics, and low opportunity cost of being unemployed. Another serious problem facing hired agricultural workers is the low level of

Table 11.3. Labour Force in Rural India—Age Composition and
Participation Rates, 1961

(Per cent)

Age Groups (Years)	Distribution of Rural Workers			Participation Rates In		
	Male	Female	Total	Male	Female	Total
0–14	7.6	10.0	8.4	10.6	7.6	9.2
15–34	47.7	51.0	48.8	91.1	49.8	70.3
35–59	36.8	34.4	36.0	97.5	52.3	76.0
60+	7.8	4.6	6.7	79.9	24.3	52.0
All Ages	100.0	100.0	100.0	58.2	31.4	45.1

SOURCE: *Census of India*, 1961, Paper I, 1962.

wages. In part, low wages for hired workers are a direct result of low productivity in agriculture, although many other factors may also be held responsible for them. The broad conclusions that can be derived from the findings of the first and the second Agricultural Labourers Enquiry Committee reports are: greater dependence of agricultural labour families on wage employment, a tendency of widening wage differentials between male and female, and a general decline in wage levels.

In this section we have briefly reviewed some aspects of the economics of labour in Indian agriculture. An analysis of these aspects would facilitate understanding of the basic problems facing the rural work force in India.

Agricultural Labour Market—
A Theoretical Expose

In theoretical economics, the term "market" refers to the set of buyers and sellers existing for a homogeneous factor of production, good or service. It does not generally refer to any specific geographic area. In reality, however, the entire industry in a country seldom constitutes a single labour-market area. Rather, one can make distinctions on the basis of geographic regions, and occupational patterns. Such distinctions become necessary since the characteristics of a perfect labour market can very seldom be satisfied by a country as large and diverse as India. According to Peitchinis[7], a perfect labour market must possess the following characteristics:

(1) the labour force must be homogeneous; (2) employment conditions must be perfectly identical in all forms; (3) the number of workers on the market must be so large that each worker constitutes an infinitesimal proportion to total; (4) workers should be fully mobile within the labour market; (5) every worker should seek to improve his economic position; and (6) every employer should seek out the worker who will accept the lowest possible wages, and always be ready to replace any one of his workers who refuses to accept that rate, with another worker who offers his services. If there were a perfect market, there would be only one wage, and an employer could hire any number of workers at that market rate. The two basic forces which bring about a change in the market wage rate are the supply for labour, and demand for labour, as shown in Figure 11.3. Given that at a point in time, demand and supply for labour are in equilibrium with a market wage of OW units, if for some reason supply exceeds demand, the wage rate is expected to fall. (This fall is shown from OW to OW_1). Conversely, if demand for labour exceeds for a given supply, the wage rate must go up. An increase in demand from DD' to $D_1D'_1$, given a supply of labour at Oq_1, should lead to an increase in the wages (from the previous equilibrium) by WW_2 units. This mechanism will operate indefinitely in any economic system if a perfect market exists. Imperfections in the labour market are universal and agriculture in India is by no means an exception. Some of the major

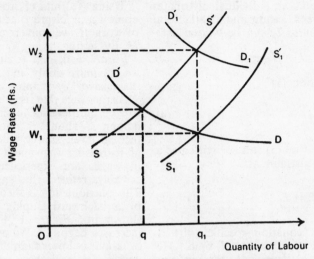

Fig. 11.3 Equilibrium in a perfect labour market

imperfections in labour markets are: absence of a homogeneous service, lack of mobility due to cultural, food and language barriers, lack of communication or knowledge, emigration of workers, and so on. In order to understand the market mechanism, concepts of market supply and demand should be developed further.

Supply of Labour
In common terminology, the term "supply of labour" denotes the number of people able and willing to work. A more satisfactory measure would be the amount of productive work people are able and willing to put in at various levels of wage rates. The term "productive" has been used to denote productive of the means of production, and of durable sources of enjoyment.[8] Any form of physical and mental exertion with the objective of production of goods and services (whether immediate or ultimate) is included in labour. This definition includes all types of workers: hired workers, self-employed workers, employees and unpaid workers.

The size of the labour force in any economic system is determined by factors affecting the population in offering their services. A distinction must therefore be made between the potential labour force and actual labour force. Potential labour force includes all those individuals in the civilian population who are over a certain age.[9] Actual labour force is composed of that portion of the potential labour force which is able and willing to work. The participation of the population in the labour force is determined by a number of factors, such as age group and sex; compulsory retirement; unemployment rate in appropriate age, sex, and occupational category; family disposable income.

A labour supply function for an economy (or individual) can be derived from the utility function for the individual. An equilibrium in employment is reached when the marginal utility of wages is identically equal to the marginal disutility of labour or work. The utility function therefore denotes a person's choice between leisure and work at a given wage rate.

Let utility be denoted by U, hours of leisure by L, and hours of work by H, and wage rate by ω. Total wage income of the individual (I) is:

$$I = H\omega \qquad (1)$$

and his utility from leisure and wage income can be expressed as:

$$U = \phi \, (I, L) \qquad (2)$$

Assuming that an individual distributes his time between leisure and work, total number of hours, T, can be written as:

$$T = L + H \qquad (3)$$

From equation (1)

$$H = \frac{I}{\omega} \qquad (4)$$

Therefore equation (3) can be written as a time-budget constraint as:

$$T = L + \frac{I}{\omega} \qquad (5)$$

This budget equation specifies how a person should spend his total time. He has a choice between not earning any income (or purchasing leisure at T units), or earning an income. Maximizing his utility in (2) subject to time-budget constraint (5), a solution for hours of work can be obtained.

Assuming that the utility function is of a Cobb-Douglas type:

$$U = K \, I^{\alpha} \, L^{\beta} \qquad (6)$$

where K, α, β are constants, such that $K > 0, 0 < \alpha < 1, 0 < \beta < 1$.

Using (3) and (5) to express wage income I and leisure L as functions of hours of work H, we convert utility in terms of H. By setting $dU/dH = 0$, and testing $d^2U/dH^2 < 0$, we maximize utility and solve for H as a function of wage rate.

As the wage rate rises, on an average up to a certain level of income the supply of labour, H, should increase. At a certain income level, supply will not respond to an increasing wage and if further increases in wages are experienced, it may conceivably reduce the supply of labour. This phenomenon is theoretically denoted by a backward sloping supply curve as shown in Figure 11.4. As wage rate increases beyond OW_3 units, the quantity of labour is lower than the maximum OH_3 units. The hypothesis of negative-sloping supply curve has been empirically tested by Winston[10] using 29 countries' cross-sectional data.

Demand for Labour
Concept of Derived Demand Demand for a factor of production in industry is a derived demand. It is derived on the basis of:
1. demand for the final good,
2. nature of the production function (as dictated by technology), and,

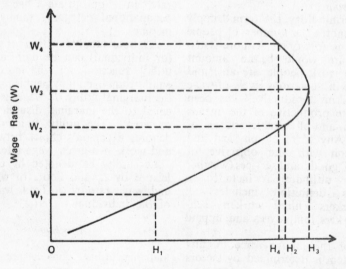

Fig. 11.4 A backward-sloping supply curve of labour

3. relative factor prices.

One may be given a production function denoting multiproducts and multi-inputs of a firm in the following form:

$$Q(Y_1,\ldots, Y_p; L, X_1,\ldots,X_{k-1})= 0 \tag{7}$$

where $Y_i \geq 0$ are products $(i = 1,\ldots, p)$
$X_j \geq 0$ are inputs of nonlabour factors $(j = 1,\ldots,k - 1)$
$L \geq 0$ is labour input

Simplifying the analysis to assume a single product function, such that

$$Y = f [L, X_1,\ldots X_{k-1}] \tag{7.1}$$

and assuming that P_y is the unit price of output, P_L is price per unit of labour, and P_j is price per unit of jth input, we can develop the profit function of the firm as follows.

Denote profit as π,
where

$$\pi = TR - TC \tag{8}$$

TR = total revenue, and
TC = total cost

$$\pi = [f(L, X_1,\ldots,X_{k-1})]P_y$$
$$- \sum_{j=1}^{k=1} P_j x_j - P_L L \tag{8.1}$$

Profit is maximized where the marginal net return from the application of an input is zero. This is obtained by taking the first derivative of equation (8.1) and setting it to zero, and then testing if second-order condition is satisfied.[11] The first-order derivatives are:

$$\frac{\partial \pi}{\partial L} = \frac{\partial Y}{\partial L} \cdot P_Y - P_L = 0$$

$$\frac{\partial \pi}{\partial x_1} = \frac{\partial Y}{\partial X_1} \cdot P_Y - P_{x_1} = 0$$

$$\vdots$$

$$\frac{\partial \pi}{\partial X_{k-1}} = \frac{\partial Y}{\partial X_{k-1}} \cdot P_Y - P_{x_{k-1}} = 0$$

From equation (9) equilibrium condition is obtained as follows:

$$\frac{\left(\frac{\partial Y}{\partial L} \cdot P_Y\right)}{P_1} = \frac{\left(\frac{\partial Y}{\partial X_1} \cdot P_Y\right)}{P_{x_l}} = \ldots$$
$$= \frac{\left(\frac{\partial Y}{\partial X_{k-1}} \cdot P_Y\right)}{P_{x_{k-1}}} \tag{10}$$

For the multiproduct firm, equation (10) would be extended to equation (11).

$$\frac{\left(\frac{\partial Y_1}{\partial L} \cdot P_{Y_1}\right)}{P_L} = \ldots = \frac{\left(\frac{\partial Y_2}{\partial L} \cdot P_{Y_2}\right)}{P_L} = \ldots$$
$$= \frac{\left(\frac{\partial Y_P}{\partial L} \cdot P_{Y_p}\right)}{P_L} \tag{11}$$

The equilibrium condition can also be shown diagramatically in Figure 11.5.

In order to simplify presentation, a case of a firm producing a single product and employing only one input—labour—is assumed. Total value product (TVP), marginal value product (MVP), and average value product (AVP) for labour are shown. Equilibrium demand for labour is obtained at the point

$$MVP_{labour} = MFC_{labour} \tag{12}$$

or

$$P_y \cdot \frac{\partial Y}{\partial L} = P_L \tag{12.1}$$

as shown in equation (10).

Concept of Unemployment and Disguised Underemployment According to Pigou[12], in a perfect labour market involuntary unemployment is not possible if the wage structure is responsive to changes in the demand for labour. It is assumed here that if supply of labour exceeds demand, wage rates will drop sufficiently to create extra employment, until the economy reaches full employment. However, in realistic models of an economy it is very seldom that one reaches a zero level of unemployment, and hence full employment is defined in terms of some minimum level of unemployment. There are at least five types of unemployment which are present. These are:

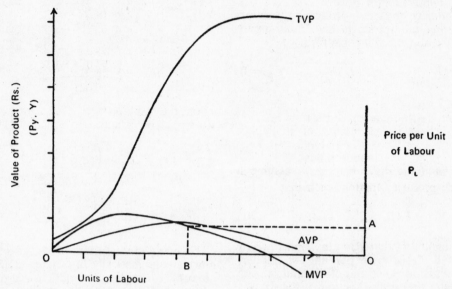

Fig. 11.5   Derived demand for labour for a single product—single factor firm

1. cyclical unemployment, caused by contractions in the economic activity;
2. frictional unemployment which is attributed to movement of workers between jobs, industries and regions;
3. structural unemployment, caused by an imbalance in the structure of the economy and occupational structure of the labour force;
4. technological unemployment brought about by changes in the production process; and
5. seasonal unemployment, which can be attributed to fluctuations in both demand, and production process within a calendar year.

In addition to various types of unemployment, a developing country suffers from very serious problems of underemployment and disguised underemployment. Underemployment exists if workers are prepared to offer their services even at wage rates below bare subsistence level. Disguised underemployment prevails in a situation when withdrawal of a certain quantity of labour does not diminish total output of the sector. Diagrammatically the situation is depicted in Figure 11.6. Given a subsistence wage level of OW_s the level of labour employment should be OA units. However, if supply of labour

is OD and all are being employed, then there are AB units of underemployment and BD units of disguised underemployment.

In this section we have developed a theoretical analysis of the labour market, which will be useful in analysing problems of agricultural labour in India in the next section.

Problems of Agricultural Labour

A comprehensive discussion of all the problems facing agricultural labour in India is beyond the scope of ·this chapter. Instead, only a few major problems will be described briefly. These are:

1. low labour-productivity in agriculture;
2. underemployment and surplus manpower;
3. landless labour and mechanization of agriculture; and
4. low standards of living.

Low Productivity of Agricultural Labour
Productivity of a factor input can be viewed in terms of intertemporal, interregion, interfirm, interindustry, and international differences. When one analyses the agricultural labour productivity in India,

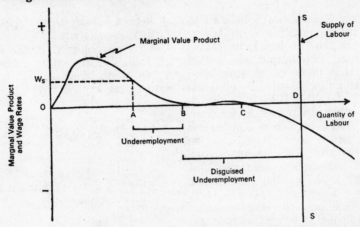

Fig. 11.6 Underemployment and disguised underemployment in agriculture

one faces the insurmountable problem of lack of data and their comparability. This is not to say that appropriate data do not exist or are not collected. The series of farm management studies sponsored by the Government of India contained comprehensive data but most of it is published in the form of averages, thereby rendering much of its use in analysis difficult.

Earnings of Agricultural Workers: An Interindustrial Comparison Data available on average wages, number of workers, and duration of employment in various industries are very scanty. Consequently, earnings per worker were approximated, using gross domestic production, as shown in Table 11.4. An

average worker in agriculture had a gross earning of Rs. 501 per year, compared to an amount of Rs. 3952 in construction industry, or Rs. 2,320 in manufacturing. Earnings in the nonfarm sector are as much as six times the level earned by an average agricultural worker. A great deal of caution must however, be exercised in interpreting these productivity differences. Since the gross earnings are a result of all factors of production—land, labour, capital, and management—a clearcut comparison of labour earnings per se cannot be made, unless these figures are adjusted for the share of other factors of production.

International Comparison of Agricultural Labour Productivity Information gathered in the studies carried out by Hayami[13] and

Table 11.4.   Relative Earnings of Workers by Industries, India, 1960–61

Industry	Gross Domestic Production (in Billion Rs.)	Labour Force (Million)	Gross Output Per Worker (Rs.)	Index Ag=100
Agriculture	65.70	131.0	501.5	100
Forestry, mining Etc.	3.95	5.2	759.6	152
Manufacturing	18.56	8.0	2320.0	463
Construction	6.20	2.1	2952.3	590
Trade and communications	13.01	7.6	1711.8	3 2
Transportation	5.69	3.0	1896.7	379
Other	20.55	21.0	662.9	132
Total	133.66	188.4	709.4	142

SOURCE: Calculated from data on the Gross National Product and Labour Force from various publications of Census of India, 1961 and National Income Accounts, 1960.

by Hayami and Ruttan has been used to illustrate the comparative farm labour productivity in the US and India (Table 11.5). Average farm output per worker (in comparable units of measurement) in India was estimated at 2.2 units, as against 96.2 for the US. In addition, the use of other inputs such as fertilizer, machinery, and land (on a comparable per worker basis) were much lower in India than in the US. These factors, along with education, research and development were used to explain the productivity differential (Table 11.6). A lack of fertilizer and land resources together explained the next 41 per cent differential. The evidence presented here tends to show the comparatively low productivity of agricultural labour in India. Theoretically, this may be interpreted as an indication of misallocation of labour resources in the Indian economy.

A Regional Analysis of Agricultural Labour Productivity

Using data collected in the Government of India's Farm Management studies[15], a regression analysis of the following nature was applied[16]

where

$$\frac{O}{A} = f\left[\frac{L}{A}, \frac{NL}{A}, D_1{}^L, D_2{}^L, D_3{}^L, D_4{}^L,\right.$$

$$\left. S_1{}^D, S_2{}^D, S_3{}^D\right] \quad (13)$$

O/A = gross output per acre

L/A = labour cost per acres

NL/A = nonlabour cost per acre

$D_1{}^L - D_4{}^L$ = location binary variable.[17] (One each for Madhya Pradesh, Tamil Nadu, Punjab, and UP respectively)

$S_1{}^D - S_3{}^D$ = size of farm binary variable (one for each size of farm; < 5 acres, 5—10 acres, and 10—20 acres)

Table 11.5. Comparative Farm Output and Inputs Per Male Worker, India and USA, Average 1957–62

Particular	Unit	USA	India
Farm output	Wheat Units/Worker	96.20	2.22
Fertilizer	Mill. Tons/Worker	2.1300	0.0038
Machinery	Horse Power/Worker	45.9000	0.0077
Agricultural land	Hectare/Worker	129.70	1.99
Literacy ratio	Per cent	97.0	18.0
No. of graduates	Per 10,000 workers	22.8	0.4

SOURCE: Compiled from the results reported by Y. Hayami, "Agricultural Gap among Selected Countries".

Table 11.6. Contributions of Various Factors to the Difference Between Farm Output Per Worker in USA and India

Factor	Contribution (Per cent)
Fertilizer	21.0
Machinery	15.0
Land	20.0
Education	38.0
Research, development and extension	10.0
Residual	4.0
Total	100.0

SOURCE: Hayami, "Agricultural Gap among Selected Countries". p. 573.

Two variations of equation (13) were estimated, one in linear form using all the variables specified, and the other bringing L/A in nonlinear form[18] and deleting NL/A variable. The results obtained are shown in Appendix 11.2.

Mean elasticity of agricultural labour use was estimated at 0.4906 using a log function implying that a 1 per cent change in labour cost per acre will increase the gross output by 0.49 per cent. Labour productivity functions can be developed for each of the five regions, by appropriate adjustments[19] in equation (A.1), as shown in Table 11.7. Average gross output per acre was higher in UP and Punjab, and was lowest in West Bengal as estimated by the author in Table 11.7.

Table 11.7. Regional Labour Productivity Relations

Province	Intercept	Regression Coefficient for	
		L_A	NL_A
M.P.	71.71	0.318	0.770
Tamil Nadu	83.78	0.318	0.770
Punjab	99.86	0.318	0.770
U.P.	152.61	0.318	0.770
W. Bengal	62.64	0.318	0.770

From equation (A.2) one can also derive conclusions as to the relative (per acre) labour productivity on farms of various sizes. The regression coefficients with respect to the three size binary variables indicate that average labour productivity per acre is highest on smaller farms (0–5 acres) and consistently declines except for a moderate rise for farms of over 50 acres. This rise may be interpreted to be a result of superior technology applied by these farms, relative to smaller size units.

A discussion of regional agricultural labour productivity will be incomplete without a discussion of the implications of the Green Revolution in Indian agriculture. The Green Revolution is a term which is collectively used for a number of programmes such as:

1. increase in the area under high-yielding cereal varieties;
2. increased use of nitrogeneous and other fertilizers;
3. increase in improved irrigation and drainage facilities; and
4. better extension efforts to improve cultural practices.

The success of the Green Revolution varies from crop to crop, and from state to state. For example, in the case of wheat, increase in yield per hectare in 1968–69 over the earlier year in Punjab, was 16.6 per cent, in Bihar 32.6 per cent, in Maharashtra 21.3 per cent, as against an all-India gain of only 5.9 per cent.[20] Recognizing that not all this gain in yields can be attributed to a differential rate of adoption of the programme implied in GR, implications of such changes for agricultural labour productivity are significant. An accelerated rate of adoption of the GR programme would inevitably mean an improved level of economic performance by the human resources in agriculture of that region. However, a differential rate of adoption in some states would have far-reaching implications. These include: (1) a larger surplus of cereals, and increasing inequality in cereal production, thereby causing a decline in prices unless a free movement of grain across borders is secured; (2) increased burden on marketing and transportation systems and need for improved facilities; (3) wide interregional disparity in agricultural incomes, resulting in social and political problems.

Underemployment and Surplus Manpower in Indian Agriculture

In this section, a review of various estimates of underemployment in Indian agriculture is presented; no attempt is made to make new estimates because of inadequate data. Data limitation is a major problem in computing meaningful estimates. Similar conclusions were drawn by a Committee of experts on preparing estimates on unemployment:

...The data available for estimating unemployment and underemployment in the past have not been adequate and...the conclusions based on them were, therefore, unavoidably subject to an unknown margin of error. Some of the limitations are inherent in the socioeconomic conditions of our country and can not be wholly overcome by the conceptual refinements or improvements in the technique of estimation.[21]

Three studies dealing with disguised underemployment in agriculture using whatever available data are reviewed. These are by Majumdar[22], Uppal[23], and Mathur[24]. Majumdar's study focussed on two facets of underemployment—seasonal and disguised. Disguised underemployment was estimated for the Bombay-Karnataka region using an arbitrary unit: standard cultivated holdings. No adjustments were made for differences in capital, fertility, and irrigation on various farms. The major conclusion of the study was that "roughly about 71 per cent of the farmers are affected by disguised unemployment".[25]

Uppal[26] estimated the disguised underemployment in Punjab agriculture to be 8.41 per cent of the toal labour force, using a standard quantity of labour. This quantity was defined as the minimum number of labour inputs required to produce the existing output, with other factors remaining the same.

Mathur[27] estimated disguised underemployment using the following relationship:

$$D(U) = \sum_{i=1}^{n} \frac{(E-d)_i \times (p \times T)_i}{100}$$

where

$D(U)$ = disguised underemployment,

$(E-d)_i$ = surplus manpower per acre on size group i

and $\frac{(p \times T)_i}{100}$ = actual cultivated area in size group i.

The estimates of $(E-d)$ were made by using a standard man–land ratio, which was not defined in any meaningful way. Mathur[28] estimated disguised underemployment at 33.1 per cent of rural working force in West Bengal, 4.8 per cent in Punjab and 8.8 per cent in UP. Although all these estimates vary in magnitude, they do in general, support the hypothesis of surplus manpower in Indian agriculture—a resource which can effectively be used for nonfarm alternatives.

Landless Labour and Mechanization of Farms

In the 1971 Census, landless labourers were estimated at 47.5 million. This labour constituted 26.3 per cent of the total agricultural labour supply in 1971—a significant part of the industry. One of the major problems faced by this sector is that of high seasonal variations in the employment pattern particularly for those whose contractual agreements are not for the entire season. Opportunities in the nonfarm sector of the economy are meagre for two basic reasons: one there is in general a lack of employment potential;[29] two, the skills required for the jobs available are beyond the capability of unskilled farm workers.

Related to the question of hired help, is the issue of mechanization of Indian agriculture. It is obvious that mechanization at the level of some Western developed countries is neither feasible nor desirable. The labour that this would further displace would accentuate the already serious problem of underemployment and unemployment not only in agriculture but in the entire economy. In addition, an average farm unit consisting of a tiny fragmented holding cannot effectively and efficiently utilize machine power, except under the assumption of joint (cooperative) ownership. However, if the concept of mechanization is applied to the use of improved implements and machinery as appropriate for Indian agricultural conditions, there may be some merits in such a programme. It may even out some of the seasonal fluctuations by reducing labour demand at peak time for agricultural operations; it may reduce the losses in crop production by more timely operations; it may tend to move agriculture from the noncommercial diversified industry to a commercial specialized industry.

Low Standard of Living

As a direct consequence of low productivity, underemployment in agriculture, and lack of opportunities in the nonfarm sector, the standard of living of most agricultural families is lower than that enjoyed elsewhere. In addition, there is a wide degree of regional difference in farm income per person—a variable which determines the level of living a family may maintain. This is a direct result of the productivity per worker, as shown in figure 11.7. Interregional productivity differentials exist because of differences in resource quality, use and management, and also because of lack of mobility of workers due to social, cultural and dietary differences. Differences in the technology for farm production are also a very important determinant of labour productivity differentials.

All these problems of agricultural labour essentially stem from the same basic problem—the problem of farm resource

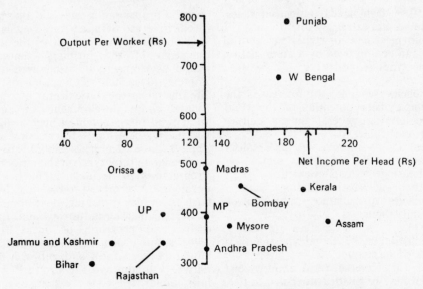

Fig. 11.7 Relationship between net income and productivity, States

use, and therefore an effort should be made to find a common set of solutions to these problems.

Programme to Improve Agricultural Labour Situation in India

The immediate cause of mounting unemployment in India and many other developing countries is the inability of the land to provide employment for the growing population. One very important development in India—the Green Revolution— has raised a series of questions about rural employment which have not been fully answered, and more research in this area is indicated.

Since the problems of agricultural labour are so diverse among regions, and within a region among farms of various size-groups, no single uniform policy is going to be a panacea. For employment policies to be more effective, they should be integrated with general economic development plans. The unsatisfactory rate of employment growth in the development process, together with inadequacies in the present state of planning would justify according a higher priority to employment creation in development planning, and working out appropriate policies to achieve it.[30]

The Planning Commission in the Second Five-Year Plan envisaged improving labour conditions through development of agriculture. The same philosophy was extended through the Third Five-Year Plan. The Third Plan proposed to improve the conditions of the agricultural labour force through improvements in irrigation, soil conservation programmes, and through development of cottage industries. In the Fourth Five-Year Plan, the Commission acknowledged that the benefits of development had not reached the bulk of hired agricultural workers to any appreciable extent. The Plan therefore intended to concentrate on small but potentially viable farms through developing minor irrigation, agricultural credit, and animal husbandry.[31]

The conditions of hired agricultural workers can be improved through an increase in the level of employment and conditions of work, and through an improvement in the wage level. To secure the latter, the Minimum Wages Act of 1948 was passed. The level of wages varies from state to state, and is in general very low. For example, in Punjab, the minimum wage level is between Rs. 1.00 and 2.50; in Tamil Nadu between Rs. 0.75 and 1.25; in West Bengal between Rs. 1.50 and 2.25; and in UP between Rs. 1.00

and 1.50.[32]   Compared to industrial wages, these wages are extremely low.

Employment level of rural agricultural labour can be improved by a combination of three types of policy:

1. policies tending to increase the employment potential of the rural economy in general and agriculture in particular;
2. policies to improve labour employment in the nonfarm sector by choosing a capital-extensive and labour-intensive technology; and
3. policies to facilitate migration of rural labour.

A discussion on the second type of policy is provided in chapter 12.

Policies to increase rural employment potential may be divided further into two broad types: those for increasing labour-use in agriculture, and those aimed at rural development. Programmes to increase agricultural labour-use may take a variety of strategies. These would include programmes aimed at improving the technical efficiency of labour-resource use and information for optimum decision-making. Training of workers for particular types of operations and research-cum-development of general agricultural problems should constitute a major strategy.

General rural development can make a very effective strategy for rural employ-ment, if proper emphasis is laid on making productive use of underemployed labour, and on raising the incomes of the poorer segments of the farming community. Rural development is being used in this context to include all sectors of rural life, including the agricultural production sector. Since development of agricultural production potential may be limited (by the physical limits to resource availability), more emphasis should be laid on nonagricultural type rural development. Programmes to be included in this are: development of other productive activities such as forestry or fishing, development of viable small-scale industries and handicrafts, and provision of local capital construction projects. Allocation of labour between farm and off-farm alternatives will improve the productivity of farm labour, reduce the extent of under-employment, and provide a reserve of labour resources for future industrialization.[33]

The other type of policy which would improve productivity in agriculture includes those programmes which tend to increase the rate of outmigration of agricultural workers. These programmes include knowledge of work opportunities in various regions, proper job-counselling, assistance in moving from one area to another, and so on. Attempts should also be made to reduce the institutional barriers for interregional migration of workers.

REFERENCES

1. It is recognized that the size of holding is a measure of production potential under the rigid assumption of homogeneous quality, identical technology, comparable product mix, and homogeneous set of other factors of production. Given that such a situation very seldom exists the conclusions based on land holding distribution alone would be of limited value.
2. Government of India, Ministry of Labour, *Agricultural Labour in India,* Report of the First Enquiry, New Delhi, 1952.
3. Figures are based on estimates of the Government of India, *Report of the Second Agricultural Labour Enquiry Committee,* 1956–57 (New Delhi, 1960); and Government of India, *Census of India,* 1961, Paper I of 1962 (New Delhi, 1962); *Census of India,* 1971, Series I, India, Paper I of 1971, Supplement (New Delhi, 1971).
4. The term "gainful" should be interpreted with a great deal of caution. Concept of gainful employment in occupations with a great deal of self-employed labour resources cannot preclude the possibility of a few being underemployed.
5. A relatively lower proportion of workers over 34 years of age may be a result of the relatively shorter production life of an individual, and also as a result of the deliberate policy of some institutions for early retirements in order to create more jobs.
6. For details of these figures see Appendix Table 11.1

7. S.G. Peitchinis, *The Economics of Labor* (New York: McGraw-Hill, 1965), p. 43.
8. For more discussion, see A. Marshall, *Principles of Economics* (London: MacMillan, 1926), p. 56.
9. Legal age is determined by the legislative and institutional regulations regarding eligibility for employment.
10. G.C. Winston, "An International Comparison of Income and Hours of Work", *Review of Economics and Statistics*, Vol. 48, February 1966.
11. The second order condition is satisfied when $\frac{\partial \pi}{\partial L} < 0$, $\frac{\partial \pi}{\partial X_1} < 0$, ... and so on.
12. A.C. Pigou, *A Theory of Employment* (London: MacMillan, 1933), p. 252.
13. Y. Hayami, "Sources of Agricultural Gap Among Selected Countries", *American Journal of Agricultural Economics*, Vol. 51, No. 3, 1969.
14. Y. Hayami and V.W. Ruttan, "Agricultural Productivity Differences Among Countries", *American Economic Review*, Vol. LX, No. 5, December 1970.
15. Government of India, Ministry of Food and Agriculture, *Studies in the Economics of Farm Management* (Delhi, 1955–56), for Madhya Pradesh, Madras, Punjab, Uttar Pradesh, and West Bengal.
16. A cross-section of data for the provinces of Madhya Pradesh, Madras, Punjab, Uttar Pradesh, and West Bengal was used.
17. A binary variable is one which only takes value 0 and 1, depending upon whether a certain event takes place or not.
18. The nonlinear forms were $(L/A)^2$ and $(L/A)^3$
19. Regional functions are derived as follows: setting $D_1 L = 1$ and other binary variables to zero, function for M.P. is derived, similarly when $D_2 L$, $D_3 L$, $D_4 L$ are set to one, functions for Madras, Punjab, and U.P. are estimated. When all the binary variables are zero, the function for West Bengal is obtained.
20. Data obtained from Government of India, Directorate of Economics and Statistics, *Indian Agriculture in Brief*, 10th ed. (New

Delhi, 1974).
21. Planning Commission, Government of India, *Fourth Five Year Plan*, New Delhi, 1969–74.
22. N.A. Majumdar, *Some Problems of Under-employment* (Bombay: Popular Book Depot, 1961).
23. J.S. Uppal, "Measurement of Disguised Underemployment in Punjab Agriculture", *Canadian Journal of Economics and Political Science*, vol. XXXIII, November 1967; and J.S. Uppal, *Disguised Unemployment in an Underdeveloped Economy* (Bombay: Asia Publishing House, 1971).
24. A. Mathur, "The Anatomy of Disguised Unemployment", *Oxford Economic Papers* (New Series), Vol. 16, No. 2, July 1964.
25. Majumdar, *Problems of Underemployment*, p. 208.
26. Uppal, "Disguised Underemployment in Punjab Agriculture" and *Disguised Unemployment in an Underdeveloped Economy*.
27. Mathur, "Disguised Unemployment".
28. Ibid., p. 186.
29. The backlog of unemployed labour during the 1966–71 period was estimated at 13.5 million workers. See *Fourth Five-Year Plan*. The All India Agricultural Labour Enquiry of 1956–57 shows that male agricultural labourers obtained an average of 222 days of employment per person per year. Sixty-eight of the days of unemployment were attributed to "want of work".
30. For further details, see ILO, *The World Employment Programme* (Geneva: International Labour Office, 1969).
31. Government of India, Planning Commission, *Fourth Plan Draft Outline* (New Delhi, 1964).
32. C.B. Mamoria, *Agricultural Problems in India*, 6th ed. (Allahabad: Kitab Mahal, 1969), p. 348.
33. For further details on the optimizing criterion to allocate labour on part-time farms, see J.E. Lee, "Allocating Farm Resources between Farm and Nonfarm Uses", *Journal of Farm Economics*, Vol. 47, No. 1, February, 1965.

BIBLIOGRAPHY

Bachmura, F.T.: "Under-employment in Relationship to Macro-Economic Policy". *Indian Journal of Agricultural Economics* Vol. XIX, Nos 3 & 4, July–December 1964.

Galenson, W. (ed.): *Essays on Employment*. Geneva. International Labour Office, 1971.

I.L.O.: *The World Employment Programme*. Geneva. International Labour Office, 1969.

Kao, C.H.C., K.R. Anschel and C.K. Eicher: "Disguised Unemployment in Agriculture: A Survey". C.K. Eicher and L.W. Witt (ed.) *Agriculture in Economic Development*. Bombay. Vora and Co., 1970.

Kulshreshtha, S.N.: "Measuring the Relative Income of Farm Labour 1941–61". *Canadian Journal of Agricultural Economics* vol. 17, No. 1, 1967.

Majumdar, N.A.: *Some Problems of Under-employment*. Bombay. Popular Book Depot, 1961.

Mehmet, O.: "Disguised Unemployment and Agricultural Development". *Canadian Journal of Agricultural Economics* vol. 19, No. 1. July 1971.

Mellor, J.W. and R.D. Stevens: "The Average and Marginal Product of Farm Labour in Undeveloped Economies". *Journal of Farm*

Economics Vol. XXXVIII, No. 3. August 1956.

Ornati, O.A.: *Jobs and Workers in India*. The Institute of International Industrial and Labour Relations. Cornell University, 1955.

Peitchinis, S.G.: *The Economics of Labour*. Toronto. McGraw-Hill, 1965.

Rao, R.M.M.: "Unemployment and the Demand for Leisure". *Indian Journal of Agricultural Economics* Vol. XXI, No. 1. January–March 1966.

Uppal, J.S.: *Disguised Unemployment in an Underdeveloped Economy*. Bombay. Asia, 1973.

APPENDIX I

Table 11.1.   Age Distribution of Labour in India and Selected Countries

Country	Year	Per Cent Distribution in Age Groups				
		0–14	15–34	35–64	65+	All
India	1961	7.67	49.32	36.51[a]	6.50[b]	100.00
Canada	1961	0.20	44.05	52.05	3.70	100.00
USA	1960	0.30	38.73	56.31	4.66	100.00
Japan	1955	0.21	52.37	43.18	4.24	100.00

[a]Belongs to 35–59 age group

[b]Belongs to 60+ age group

SOURCE: 1. *Census of India*, 1961,1971.

2. Government of Canada, *Census of Canada*, 1961 (Ottawa, 1962).

3. US Government, *Statistical Abstract*, 1967 (Washington D.C., 1967).

APPENDIX II

The estimated equations for the gross output per acre[1]:

I.
$$\frac{Q}{A} = 62.64 + 0.318^b \frac{L}{A} + 0.770^a \frac{NL}{A} + 9.07 D\frac{L}{1} + 21.14^b D\frac{L}{2} + 37.22 D\frac{L}{3} + 87.97 D\frac{L}{4}$$

$$+ 23.51^b S\frac{D}{1} + 17.61^b S\frac{D}{2} - 9.67 S\frac{D}{3}$$

$$R^2 = 0.930^a \qquad Se = 15.83 \qquad dW = 2.17 \tag{A.1}$$

II.
$$\frac{O}{A} = -48.06 + 8.63^a \frac{L}{A} - 0.120^a \left(\frac{L}{A}\right)^2 + 0.0005^b \left(\frac{L}{A}\right)^3 + 5.93 D\frac{L}{1} + 37.04^b D\frac{L}{2}$$

$$+ 16.06 D\frac{L}{3} + 70.08^a D\frac{L}{4} + 23.82^a S\frac{D}{1} + 10.38 S\frac{D}{2} - 12.16 S\frac{D}{3}$$

$$R^2 = 0.949 \qquad Se = 13.72 \qquad dW = 1.84 \tag{A.2}$$

Both the functions explained over 93 per cent of variations in gross output per acre, and no tendency of autocorrelation was apparent.

[a]Significant at 1 per cent level.

[b]Significant at 5 per cent level.

[1]Due to limitation of space, standard error of estimates are not provided.

Table 11.2.   Labour Force Participation Rates in India and Selected Countries
(percentage)

Age Group (Years)	Sex	India	Canada (1961)	USA (1960)
0–14	M	9.45	—	—
	F	6.62	—	—
15–34	M	89.52	82.00	83.50
	F	43.78	35.70	37.30
35–59	M	97.07	90.70[a]	93.00[a]
	F	47.62	30.40	43.80
60+	M	76.83	28.70[b]	32.20[b]
	F	22.38	6.70	10.50
All ages	M	57.70	77.70	79.70
	F	28.02	29.50	36.10

[a]Belongs to 35–64 age group.

[b]Belongs to 65+ age group.

SOURCE: As for Appendix Table 11.1.

12

The Unemployment Problem in India

J. S. UPPAL

Unemployment constitutes a serious economic, social, and political problem for the Indian economy. Regarding its economic aspect, the existence of large numbers of unemployed means a tragic waste of human resources and the resultant deprivation of society of the goods and services the unemployed could produce. Socially, the unemployed become alienated against the social order, from frustration, and anger against the system that cannot provide them with work. If unemployment persists for very long, the disillusioned unemployed will be a potential source of danger to the political stability of the society as they are prone to be attracted to subversive elements in society. The recent Naxalite movement in India and youth unrest in Sri Lanka are some indications of political instability resulting from the serious unemployment problem in South Asia.

Unemployment is, however, a worldwide phenomenon, existing both in the developed as well as in underdeveloped countries. During the post second war period, the unemployment rate in the US has ranged from 3 to 9 per cent of the total labour force. During 1953–54, the annual average unemployment figure touched a height of 10 per cent. At the time of writing (December 1976) the rate of unemployment in the US is 9.0 per cent.

The concept of unemployment however, is not simple one. The meaning of any particular unemployment rate depends on the way unemployment is defined and measured and on the sources and composition of unemployment. In the US,[1] persons are classified by the US Department of labour as unemployed if they were not employed during the survey week, but were available for work and had made a specific effort to find a job at some time within the preceding four weeks, or if they were waiting either to report to a new job within 30 days, or to be recalled to a job from which they had been laid off. The measured magnitude of unemployment would thus change with different definitions of the terms used and the manner in which the questionnaire on the state of employment is administered. According to the *Economic Report of the President* (1975) the change in definition of unemployment introduced in 1967, stipulating that the unemployed should include those seeking work at any time during the preceding four-week period rather than the previously implied one week period, increased the measured unemployment rate, especially of women. Unemployment may be classified into various categories according to the major causes and duration of the phenomenon. Some unemployment is cyclical; that is, it is associated with fluctuations in the business cycle. During a downturn in economic activity, unemployment rises, accompanying the general decline in business activity. Other unemployment may be frictional: arising as a byproduct of normal economic changes, e.g., the closing of some firms, and changing production techniques within firms. Frictional unemployment may also arise from personal factors such as completion of school, or of service in the Armed Forces, preference for a different job environment or geographical area, etc. The unemployment arising out of imperfect market adjustments as a result of some barriers to mobility of resources, e.g., unemployment among blacks in urban ghettoes in the US or unemployment among scheduled castes in a slum area, is referred to as structural unemployment. Seasonal unemployment arises from seasonal fluctuations in the demand and supply of labour. The nature of some production processes such as agriculture and construction, and of some consumption, e.g., visiting hill-stations and holiday resorts in summer and ski resorts in winter, can create seasonal fluctuations in employment and unemployment. In terms of the duration of unemployment, the phenomenon can be classified into short-term seasonal and frictional, short-term structural and cyclical, and long-term chronic. The causes of all these categories of unemployment, except the last one, are obvious. In advanced developed economies, long-term chronic unemployment is generally due to the lack of effective aggregate demand relative to aggregate supply in the Keynesian sense. Aggregate demand may fall short of aggregate supply from inadequate consumption expenditure, which increases at a declining rate with increase in income and/or private investment. The unemployment resulting from the deficiency of aggregate demand can usually be reduced by appropriate fiscal and monetary policies.

The following important aspects of unemployment in the developed countries should be kept in mind to understand the difference in employment patterns in developing countries like India. In almost all categories of unemployment, unemployed persons are conscious of their state. They are either looking for work or have a job from which they are temporarily absent. Their state of unemployment can be described as "open" or "visible" unemployment. Further, most workers in developed countries are "hired" workers as against the self-employed and unpaid workers in family enterprises. Assuming the employers to be profit maximizers, it can be safely inferred that the wages of the hired labour approximate to its marginal productivity. In the US, the ratio of self-employed or unpaid family workers to the total labour force is about 10 per cent.[2] This extent of self-employment is important from the point of view of the measured magnitude of unemployment in a particular country because self-employed persons and unpaid workers in family enterprises (mainly agricultural farms) are seldom reported as "unemployed". Also, in most developed countries the workers classified as unemployed are supported by some form of social security benefits during the duration of their unemployment, and to that extent the state of unemployment becomes less painful to them.

Any discussion on the nature and magnitude of unemployment in India should take into account her socioeconomic structure. India's is essentially a rural economy with about 85 per cent of the labour force employed in agriculture. In agriculture and also in nonagricultural small-scale and cottage industries, the unit of operation is the traditional joint or extended-family system. In these family-operated farms and nonfarm enterprises, members of the family are associated in varying degrees with production activities on the farm; farm work by its very nature makes the entire system and technique of production adapt itself to the abundance of farm workers. The earnings of all members are thrown into a pool from which they are drawn to meet the common needs of the family. In short, in family enterprises the members share both the work and family earnings.

Some important implications of this dominant traditional family system for employment patterns in India may be noted. Each family member shares the farm work and has a definite role, recognized by all members of the society, to justify a share of the family product. The individual member's role may not involve "full-time work" or any "product" in the conventional sense. What is interesting about these situations is that the individual member, and for that matter the other members of the family, feels that he is employed, though he may be contributing nothing or less than what he receives as his share from the total family output. Should such a family member be considered "employed" or "unemployed"? Applying the definition of "unemployed" explained earlier, he should be characterized as employed since he is "not seeking work", but from an economic point of view, he is like the unemployed since he is not contributing anything or is contributing less than his marginal product, i.e., his contribution to the family's total output. This pattern of unemployment is referred to as "disguised unemployment" or "hidden unemployment" in the literature on economic development.[3] Since the disguised unemployed labour with zero marginal product can be removed from agriculture for productive employment elsewhere without loss of total farm output it is also called a potential source of "capital formation". It is rightly believed that the proper utilization of this disguised unemployed or surplus labour can contribute to the economic growth of underdeveloped countries. As we will note later, according to various estimates, in India the magnitude of disguised unemployment is enormous, and growing. We must however point out that the phenomenon of unemployment cannot be precisely explained by the theoretical concepts and terminology developed in the Western world explained above. For instance, we will not be able to identify the "unemployed" on family farms by applying the concept with its attributes: "seeking work", "made specific efforts to

find job", "waiting to report for a new job", since the family workers, though unemployed from an economic point of view, do in fact consider themselves to be "employed". Thus if we apply the concept "unemployment" to the Indian agricultural economy it will give us the ridiculous result of near full-employment condition. For instance, defining the unemployed as those persons who were not engaged in work but "were seeking work", the census data collected in India in 1961, estimated unemployment at 1 per cent of the rural labour force. This is an absurd estimate, and as Sen remarks, "...these figures are low enough to put many advanced countries to shame..."[4] Such estimates do point out the limitations of applying Western theoretical concepts to South Asian economies including India. After examining several studies of employment and underemployment done in South Asia using those theoretical concepts, Gunnar Myrdal remarked:

> In general these studies have led [us] to ask the kind of questions Western economists would wish to investigate in their own countries. At the same time, however, it is often acknowledged that Western categories cannot be transferred intact to a South Asian environment.... The orientation of these studies—fully as much as the errors in their execution —lies at the root of the problem.[5]

A Committee of Experts on unemployment Estimates appointed by the Government of India, after a thorough review of unemployment conditions in India with the use of Western theoretical concepts, concluded:

> It is now realized that the concept as adopted in developed economies is unsuitable for an economy like ours with its preponderance of self-employment and production within household enterprises.[6]

In view of the difficulties involved in applying Western concepts to Indian conditions, the Committee of Experts stated: "In our complex economy, the character of the labour force, employment and unemployment is too heterogenous to justify aggregation into single-dimensional magnitudes".[7] They proposed to give up this practice.

Thus, we must exercise caution in interpreting the estimates made in various studies. However, some estimates on the extent of unemployment and under-development are required in order to plan for fuller employment in economic development plans. It is our contention that the concept of unemployment as developed in Western advanced countries is appropriate in the urban nonagricultural sector, while we need to formulate different criteria to estimate unemployment in the rural sector in view of the peculiarities of the Indian economy. The nature and extent of unemployment in India can, thus, be classified as follows.

Urban Unemployment

Open unemployment and underemployment: These are similar to "involuntary unemployment" in Western developed countries. Workers are conscious of their state of unemployment and are looking for work. Urban unemployment in India mostly falls into this category. It may be further classified into (1) unemployment among educated persons, or educated unemployment; and (2) other urban unemployment, i.e., among labourers and industrial workers. The classification is essential to stress the seriousness of the growth in educated unemployment in India. For an educated person not to find a job after all the hopes and dreams built during the period of acquiring education, results in a great deal of disillusionment and frustration. The educated unemployed are vocal, and can spread dissatisfaction and cynicism about the political and economic structure. They are susceptible to revolutionary ideas aiming at the destruction of the economic and political order which cannot provide them with work.

Rural Unemployment

Disguised or Hidden Unemployment and Underemployment

Here, the workers are visibly active but underutilized. Most workers on family farms in rural sectors fall into this category. As already explained, the rural workers, members of the joint or extended family system,

work on the family farms sharing work and income. Since these workers consider themselves employed, they do not look for work. The extent of this unemployment can be analysed from "production" or "time" approaches. From the "production approach", a worker is "disguised unemployed" if his marginal product (equal to worker's contribution to total family farm income) is less than its average product or income (share in family output). In the case of zero marginal product, the situation can be called one of "disguised unemployment". In this case, the withdrawal of workers from farms will not reduce the total output. The situation, with the marginal product being positive but less than the average product, can be described as "disguised underemployment". In this case, the withdrawal of workers will reduce the total farm output to the extent of their marginal product. From the point of view of "time", we arbitrarily fix a certain number of hours (say 40 hours per week) as constituting full employment. Disguised employment or underemployment is, then, indicated by the number of hours the workers are actually working against the time norm of full employment.

To some extent our classification of "open unemployment" as urban and "disguised unemployment" as rural is arbitrarily made, for convenience. We should be aware that disguised unemployment may also exist in urban sectors in cases where business firms are organized and operated on a family basis, or that in private as well as in government offices, many people are employed on a full-time basis even though the services they render may actually require less than full time.

An interesting illustration of disguised unemployment in urban areas is provided by Ronald Ridker:

> The street-corner vendor of shoe strings may sit at his stall for fourteen hours and sell only a few pairs. The semi-redundant messenger in an office may spend most of his day waiting for a message to deliver or an order to get his superior's tea.[8]

What is the relationship between the "open unemployed" in urban areas and "disguised unemployed" in the rural sector? Edgar Edwards has pointed out an interesting relationship:

It appears, however, that the most visible dimension of the underutilization of labour in developing countries, namely, open unemployment in the modern sector, is but the tip of an iceberg resting on a stratum of underemployed outside the modern sector, both obscuring larger numbers of others who are visibly active, as in education or civil service, but really underutilized.[9]

On the basis of this relationship, Edward contends that:

Efforts to clear away the visible portion of the iceberg may simply motivate other layers to emerge: for example, efforts to provide jobs for the unemployed in urban areas may simply entice others from the countryside to take their places.

Any meaningful employment policy, as Edwards rightly points out, "...must be one which pervades the entire economy".[10] What has been happening in the Indian economy, as in other developing countries, is that emphasis has been placed on creation of job opportunities in urban areas through industrialization and creating government jobs. This has not eased the urban unemployment situation simply because there has been a corresponding shift of unemployed and underemployed from the rural to the urban areas.

Having pointed out the nature of unemployment and underemployment within the context of the socioeconomic structure of India, we must now take note of the extent and major causes of the phenomenon. We also mention some important strategies adopted to reduce unemployment in different categories.

Urban Unemployment

Urban unemployment, although a serious economic and social problem fraught with political dangers, remains largely unmeasured in quantitative terms. Besides the conceptual difficulties already pointed out, the statistical information in this area is grossly inadequate. This explains why the results of different studies are so varied. For India, the estimates on overall urban unemployment have been provided by the Planning Commission, the Ministry of Labour and Employment, the Central Statistical Organization (a government research organization), and a few individual studies. These estimates are summarised in Table 12.1.

As regards educated unemployment, Bhardwaj estimated that at the end of the Second Five-Year Plan (1960–61), of a total of approximately 6.45 million educated people, around 1 million (or 15.5 per cent) were unemployed.[11] According

Table 12.1.   Estimates on the Volume of Urban Unemployment in India

Source	Reference Period	Urban Unemployment (in millions)	Urban Unemployment as Proportion of Total Labour Force
B.N. Datar	March 1951	2.5–3.0	12.00
National Sample Survey and Employment Exchange Data	Sept. 1953	2.4	11.00
Second Five-Year Plan	March 1956	2.5	10.0
Wilfred Malenbaum	March 1956	2.5	10.0
National Sample Survey and Employment Exchange Data	May 1956	3.4	13.6
R.C. Bhardwaj	March 1951	2.5	11.4
	March 1956	3.4	13.5
	March 1961	4.5	15.5

SOURCE: R. C. Bhardwaj, *Employment and Unemployment in India* (New York: Humanities Press, 1969), pp. 109–126.

to the Study Group of the National Commission on Labour, unemployment among educated persons increased from 244.4 thousands in 1951 to 3,278 thousands in 1972—about a sixteen-fold increase, as shown in Table 12.2.

Table 12.2. Educated Unemployment in India
(in thousands)

Qualifications	1951	1972
Matriculation	187.0	1744
Undergraduates	30.6	932
Graduates and postgraduates	26.8	602
Total	244.4	3278

SOURCE: Compiled from the Government of India, *Report of the Committee on Unemployment* (New Delhi, 1973).

Paradoxically, unemployment is assuming serious proportions even among educated persons with technical qualifications. In 1968, 17 per cent of engineering graduates and diploma holders were unemployed. In the decade preceding 1965, the unemployed in this category were estimated at no more than 7 to 8 per cent and according to the Report of the Committee of Experts on Unemployment (1973)[12] even this appears to have been largely due to the waiting period (of no more than one year) for the bulk of new graduates before securing employment. Another disquieting development in the employment pattern of educated personnel in India during the decade 1961–72, is that persons with higher education suffer from a greater incidence of unemployment. Among the unemployed, the proportion of matriculates (completed high school) has decreased from 78.5 per cent in 1961 to 53.2 per cent in 1972. The proportion of undergraduates has increased from 12.0 to 28.4 per cent, and that of graduates and postgraduates has increased from 9.5 per cent to 18.4 per cent during this period. Clearly, the Indian economy has not developed sufficiently to absorb its increasing educated manpower; and on the part of the unemployed, there is a tendency towards overeducation in order to secure a job.

Rural Unemployment

This type of unemployment and under-employment, which generally assumes the form of disguised unemployment already discussed, plagues rural areas. The Indian Planning Commission[13] asserts that rural unemployment is the principal cause of Indian poverty and that *Garibi Hatao* (remove poverty) cannot be achieved without providing work to our unemployed rural work force.

As already pointed out, in the context of the social and economic structure, "underemployment" rather than "unemployment" is relevant in the rural sector of the Indian economy. This explains why the estimates of unemployment made by the National Sample Survey in India (NSS) in 1960–61, that 1.62 per cent of the rual population was unemployed, are considered gross underestimates. Underemployment includes (1) underemployment from sharing work on farms owned and operated by joint families and (2) seasonal unemployment. The NSS has provided some estimates on the extent of underemployment. Persons working less than 28 hours per week were considered severely underemployed and those working between 29 and 42 hours as moderately underemployed. Estimates of severe underemployment in Indian agriculture are given in Table 12.3.

Table 12.3. Percentage of Employed Males and Females Working for 28 Hours or Less in Indian Agriculture

Year	Males	Females
1958–59	5.78	8.94
1959–60	5.46	9.08
1960–61	3.34	6.55
1961–62	3.96	5.89

SOURCE: Planning Commission, Government of India, *Report of the Committee of Experts on Unemployment Estimates* (New Delhi, 1970), p. 10.

Interestingly there has been a decline in the percentage of the "severely under-employed" from 14.72 per cent in 1958–59 to 9.85 per cent in 1961–62. It may be either the result of additional work opportunities created in the rural areas under the Five-Year Plans or due to a change in statistical coverage and methods applied. In its Mid-Term Appraisal of the Fourth Plan issued in February 1972, the Indian Planning Commission remarked, "the incidence of seasonal unemployment and underemployment remains as heavy as before. It is, perhaps, heavier than before except in some parts of the country where the Green Revolution has achieved significant success".[14]

The Indian peasantry continues to depend for work on the vagaries of nature:

> The period of complete inactivity in each agricultural region varies with the nature and variety of crops and cropping pattern. Broadly speaking, Indian cultivator is unoccupied anywhere from 4 to 6 months in a year except in places where he has undertaken the cultivation of wet crops or where he grows more than one crop from the same soil in a year, while the cultivator's womenfolk are unoccupied for an even longer part of the year.[15]

Since the area under double-cropping is only 14 per cent of the total cultivated area, this enforced idleness caused by seasonal factors afflicts the vast majority of the Indian rural work force.

The extent of underemployment among the agricultural labourers in India was estimated by the First and Second Agricultural Labour Enquiry Committees in 1950–51 and 1955–56 respectively. The seriousness of underemployment is indicated by the following figures:[16]

1. Casual adult male workers were employed, on an average, for wages for 200 days in 1950–51 and for 197 days during 1956–57. They were self-employed for 75 days in 1950–51 and for 40 days in 1956–57. Thus, they were without work for 90 days and 128 days during 1950–51 and 1956–57 respectively.
2. Casual adult female workers were employed on wages for 134 days during 1950–51 and for 141 days during 1956–57.

As regards "disguised unemployment" or "surplus labour", several estimates have been made by different writers. Tarlok Singh[17] estimated in 1945 that 21 or 22 million persons, out of the working population of 99 to 103 million (i.e., 33–55 per cent of the total population), were surplus in British India. Shakuntala Mehra[18] estimated the surplus labour at 17.1 per cent of the agricultural work force on an all-India basis. Uppal[19] estimated disguised unemployment in Punjab agriculture at 8.41 per cent of the total rural work force for the year 1956–57. On the smaller-size holdings (e.g., on farms less than 10 acres in size) more than one-fifth of the labour force was surplus.

Some Major Causes of Unemployment

Employment problems in India can be traced to the following factors:

1. rapid population growth and increase in labour force;
2. use of inappropriate technology—distortion of factor prices; and
3. inappropriate educational systems and attitudes towards work.

The most important cause of unemployment is, of course, the population explosion, which in turn, causes an increase in the labour force. In Chapter I, we have examined the nature and main causes of the phenomenon of the population explosion in India. During the decade 1960–70, the Indian population increased by 2.45 per cent per year, causing an increase in the labour force by 1.9 per cent. It may be noted that the growth rate of the labour force is increasing over time. This is explained both by the increase in population and also by some sociological changes, e.g., higher participation rate, particularly of women, in the labour force; weakening joint-family systems especially in urban areas; encouraging more family members to seek employment. These sociological changes are due mainly to the spread of educational facilities and development of mass media. The increasing population is accentuating the unemployment problem in both the urban and rural sectors. In rural sectors, agriculture is becoming more crowded without the corresponding increase in productivity. In India, between 1961–73, the agricultural yield per acre increased annually by the compound growth rate of 1.24 per cent annual increase in the rural population.[20] Indian agriculture is, thus, becoming a reservoir of ever-increasing underemployed and surplus population. Increase in urban employment is also caused by a persistent trend towards urbanization. In the past, overcrowding, insanitary conditions, and unemployment in urban centres have discouraged rural folk from leaving their families and migrating to cities. but recent developments like worsening unemployment conditions in rural areas, increase in rural debt, lack of rural industries to provide alternative sources of employment and low incomes and wages, have had a "push" effect, causing rural–urban migration.

The increasing population and labour force against inadequate supplies of capital inputs, would make the Indian economy labour-abundant and capital-scarce economies. If the forces of demand and supply of labour and capital were operating freely, the relative prices of these two factors of production would induce a profit-maximizing entrepreneur to use "labour intensive" or "capital extensive" technologies, i.e., the techniques of production which will use relatively more labour and less capital. Interestingly enough, the technologies used in many sectors do not correspond to the prevailing factor-endowment situations. According to Jyotirmoy Bosu, a member of the Committee of Unemployment in India, "In their drive of maximum profit, the capitalists constantly resort to rationalization, market manipulation and other labour-saving devices and thus, the process of replacing of human labour by machine and other artificial methods is a continuous one." The Bhagwati Committee on Unemployment has advised against the fast introduction of mechanization to prevent the displacement of labour, accentuating further the serious problem of unemployment in the economy.

Why should capital-intensive technology be used in a labour-abundant economy? The main explanation seems to be that the technologies used are highly capital-intensive, imported from the advanced Western economies, and geared to their factor endowment situation. An important reason for using capital-intensive technology is the existence of distortion of factor prices, i.e., the market prices of factors such as capital, foreign exchange, and labour, do not reflect their true equilibrium prices based on the factor-endowment situations. A number of factors, e.g., fixation of minimum wages, tended to raise the price of labour (wage rate). For instance, the wage rates in urban industrial sectors are, on the average, 3–4 times the wage rates prevailing in the rural areas. Several factors tend to reduce the price of capital, e.g., grant of import licences to industrialists to import capital goods at official foreign exchange rates, which were considerably overvalued. This is tantamount to subsidizing imported capital goods for industrialists. Various tax advantages, such as liberal accelerated depreciation allowances also served as incentive for use of capital. These steps raise the market price of labour and lower the market price of capital from their equilibrium levels (shadow prices). These distortions and biases in factor prices do affect the employment situation adversely. In the absence of such distortions, more labour would have been hired, thus easing the employment situation somewhat.

The deterioration in the unemployment rate among educated persons is partly explained by the massive increase in educational facilities provided in India as a part of economic planning. The massive increase in enrolments in Indian educational institutions is illustrated by Table 12.4.

To provide employment for the fast-increasing number of educated persons is an extremely difficult task. In other words the deteriorating unemployment rate among educated persons is due to the big increase in their numbers, beyond the ability of the economy to absorb them.

Strategies for Improving Employment

Provision of employment opportunities to millions of unemployed and underemployed in India is in itself a stupendous task and will require substantial changes

Table 12.4.   Students Attending Educational Institutions in India

	1950	1974	Percentage Increase
1. Number of students in classes VI–VII (in millions)	3.12	17.65	466
Percentage thereof to total population, age group 11–14.	12.7	41.3	
2. Number of students in classes IX–XI/XII (in millions)	1.22	9.85	707
Percentage thereof to total population, age group 14–17	5.3	24.0	
3. Number of students at the university stage (in millions)	0.36	2.77	669
Percentage thereof to total population, age group 17–23	0.8	3.8	

SOURCE: Government of India, Ministry of Information and Broadcasting, *India: A Reference Annual,* 1974, p. 63.

in the economic policies pursued in the past. In this section we shall mention some of the crucial policies for alleviating the unemployment problem in the economy.

Population Control
Control of the population explosion confronting South Asia economies is fundamental to any attempt to provide work opportunities for the swelling labour force. The Indian Government is aware of the gravity of fast-increasing numbers, and has included population planning programmes as an integral part of its development plans. Unfortunately, the major achievement of these programmes until now has been only in creating awareness of the problem, rather than adoption of family planning measures. We have already discussed the population problem in Chapter I. Any failure to check increasing population will accentuate the unemployment problem further.

Removal of Factor Price Distortions
Careful analysis of the market versus Shadow prices of factors is essential in formulating appropriate technology for efficiency and greater employment in any economy. As already discussed, in the Indian economy characterized by a labour abundant and capital-scarce factor endowment situation, the existence of factor price distortions has led to the adoption of inappropriate capital-intensive techniques. A diminution of this distortion will expand employment opportunities. Current policies which discriminate in favour of capital, policies such as provision of depreciation

allowances and other tax advantages, grant of import licences at lower foreign exchange rates, should be revised. Appropriate wage policies will have to be adopted to ensure that wages do not get out of line with labour productivity.

From the purely economic-efficiency point of view, while an underdeveloped economy, with labour abundance and capital shortage, should choose technologies characterized by higher labour–output and lower capital–output ratios, it should not entail any loss of output. Otherwise the objective of employment creation will come into conflict with income generation or economic growth. For achieving the criterion of economic efficiency, the crucial variables are factor and product prices in competitive markets. There is, however, a school of thought which emphasises the objective of employment creation by suggesting the need to take into account the social cost of unemployment and the social benefits of providing work opportunities in determining the pertinent techniques of production:

Special care has to be taken in those countries which have a large surplus of unskilled labour, for in such circumstances, money wages will not reflect the real cost of rising labour. In these circumstances, capital is not productive if it is used to do what labour could do equally well, given the level of wages. Such investments may be highly profitable to capitalists but they are unprofitable to the community as a whole since they add to unemployment but not to output.[21]

Mahatma Gandhi made a strong case for

using highly labour-intensive techniques of production (cottage industries and handicrafts) on the basis of the high social costs of capital-intensive labour-displacing technology, and the social benefits derived from providing meaningful work opportunities to workers, specially in rural areas. During the early stages of development, the People's Republic of China sacrificed economic efficiency to labour-absorption, by using labour-intensive techniques for the production of normally highly capital-intensive products such as iron and steel. The question of choice of technology is, however, quite complex and needs careful consideration. The main objective of employment policy is to strike a balance between the objectives of greater employment and greater output.

Reform of the Educational System
The purpose of the Indian educational system has not been to develop human resources but rather, in the words of Gunnar Myrdal, "to train clerks, minor officials, and low-level administrative personnel for government and business".[22] Such an educational system results in serious waste of scarce educational resources because people "are not merely being insufficiently educated, they are miseducated on a huge scale".[23]

The reform of the educational system should start with achieving a proper balance in the skill structure and manpower needs of the countries. In other words, education should be made responsive to the specific requirements of the nation. It must have relevance to future work and life, and should provide adequate preparation for productive employment. The system should produce a cadre of skilled manpower for the development needs of the country. It should no longer turn out scores of "educated" persons who remain mostly unemployed or unemployable. The reformed educational system will inculcate certain basic values so that a worker, irrespective of the nature and location of work, is honoured; social prestige will be determined by one's contribution to the needs of the society rather than by holding wealth and political power. Ideally, education should create initiative,

self-reliance, and an urge for creativity, so that an educated person is able to find work on his own or be self-employed, rather than depend on the Government to hire him.

These reforms may read like a list of dreams and pious hopes but they are essential for the economic development of South Asia. Attempts to provide jobs for the fast-increasing number of educated persons on a permanent basis will fail until the education system is linked more effectively with the demands of social and economic development.

Reform of the educational system would require long-term attention. The Indian Planning Commission[24] has proposed the following schemes for speedy generation of employment opportunities for the educated unemployed:

1. intensification of research and development in identified priority areas;
2. formulation of a shelf of projects from which choices could be made for inclusion in the Fifth Plan;
3. acceleration of construction activities; and
4. assistance to technically qualified persons for setting up small-scale industries.

The Planning Commission recognizes the fact that "the lasting solution...must, eventually, be found in greatly intensified tempo of growth. In this context, a sharp set-up in the rate of investment and industrial expansion particularly in areas that have a high employment potential is essential".[25]

More Rural Jobs Through Work Programmes
Historically, the absorption of surplus rural manpower has followed a definite pattern of development in the presently advanced countries during their phase, of economic development. In a predominantly agricultural economy, farm productivity increases; fewer people are required on land to produce needed agricultural commodities; a process of industrialization emerges; the surplus population in the rural sector is absorbed in the expanding urban industrial centres; and, finally, the urban industrial centres and rural areas become complementary to each other in economic expansion. The Indian

economy, unfortunately, cannot follow this path of development. The urban industrial sector has not developed sufficiently to absorb the surplus rural population. In fact, the cities have not been able even to provide employment to the new entrants to their labour force resulting from the natural increase in urban population. Serious overcrowding and unemployment characterize most Indian cities. Solution for rural unemployment, thus, lies in the overall development of the economies in the long run, and through undertaking rural work programmes to create employment for the existing unemployed in the short run. Creation of works programmes is also an integral part of the Indian five-year plans. In the words of Indian Planning Commission:

...the rural works programme has a vital contribution to make, both towards relief of unemployment and underemployment and assuring of minimum earnings and towards acceleration of the pace of agricultural and rural development.[26]

To face the deteriorating unemployment position, the Government of India has recently introduced some "crash programmes"[27] for the rural sector. The main programmes are:

1. Crash Scheme for Rural Employment (1971–75): the scheme was aimed at rapidly expanding employment in rural areas, by hiring rural labour for labour-intensive public works.
2. Marginal Farmers and Agricultural Labour Scheme: specifically aimed at providing employment opportunities to underemployed "marginal farmers"

and "agricultural labourers" by providing subsidized credit support for agricultural and subsidiary occupations like diary, poultry, fishery, horticulture operations, etc.
3. Small Farmers Development Agency: This programme was aimed at "small but potentially viable farmers" and its objectives include "making available to them farm inputs, including credit, to enable them to participate in available technology and practise intensive agriculture and diversify their activities".

Despite these crash programmes and provisions for employment opportunities in development plans, the employment position in some countries—specifically India and Bangladesh—has deteriorated further. This raises the important issue of the implementation of planned policies. The Indian development plans are full of planned policies and ambitious targets, but the achievement in most cases falls severely short of target. This wide performance gap not only leads to an acute sense of national frustration but also makes the plans nothing more than "paper plans" and "wishful thinking". Feelings are so strong on the performance gap that two members of the Government of India, Committee on Unemployment, have recently proposed "penal action" against those who are held responsible for the nonimplementation of employment programmes. Mr. Basu, one of the members of the Committee commented, "It is not enough to recognize in theory the necessity for tackling the problem of unemployment. It is also necessary to translate this theory into action."

REFERENCES

1. For discussions of concepts and the problems of measuring of unemployment, see Betty G. Fishman and Leo Fishman, *Employment, Unemployment and Economic Growth* (New York: Thomas Y. Crowell, 1969); Seymour L. Wolfbein, *Employment and Unemployment in the United States* (Chicago: Science Research Associates, 1964); and US Government, *Economic Report of the President* (Washington, D.C., 1975).

2. US Government, *Economic Report of the President* (Washington, D.C., 1975), pp. 86–102.
3. For details, see J.S. Uppal, *Disguised Unemployment in an Underdeveloped Economy* (New York: Asia Publishing House, 1973).
4. Amartya Sen, *Employment Technology and Development* (Oxford: Clarendon Press, 1975), p. 119.
5. Gunnar Myrdal, *Asian Drama* (New York:

Pantheon, 1968), p. 2221.

6. Government of India, Planning Commission, *Report of the Committee of Experts on Unemployment Estimates* (New Delhi: 1970), p. 30.

7. Ibid., p. 31.

8. Ridker, "Employment and Unemployment in Near East and South Asian Countries", in Ridker, and Lubell (ed.), *Employment Problems of the Near East and South Asia* (New Delhi: Vikas, 1974), p. 359.

9. Edgar O. Edwards, *Employment in Developing Nations* (New York: Columbia University Press, 1974), p. 10.

10. Ibid., p. 100.

11. Bhardwaj, *Employment and Unemployment in India*, p. 83.

12. Compiled from Government of India, *Report of Committee on Unemployment.*

13. Planning Commission, Government of India, *Towards an Approach to the Fifth Plan* (New Delhi, 1972), pp. 5–6.

14. Government of India, Planning Commission, *The Fourth Plan Mid-Term Appraisal* (New Delhi, 1973), p. 47.

15. C.B. Mamoria, *Agricultural Problems of India* (Allahabad: Kitab Mahal, 1966), p. 727.

16. Quoted in Mamoria, *Agricultural Problems*, p. 728.

17. Tarlok Singh, *Poverty and Social Change* (Bombay: Oxford University Press, 1945), p. 136.

18. Shakuntala Mehra, "Surplus Labour in Indian Agriculture", *Indian Economic Review*, April 1966, p. 112.

19. J.S. Uppal, "Measurement of Disguised Unemployment in Punjab Agriculture", *The Canadian Journal of Economics*, Vol. 33, No. 4, November 1967, pp. 590–96.

20. Government of india, Ministry of Food and Agriculture, *Indian Agriculture in Brief* (New Delhi, 1975), p. 120.

21. W.A. Lewis, *The Theory of Economic Growth* (London: George Allen and Unwin, 1955), p. 356.

22. Gunnar Myrdal, *Asian Drama: An Inquiry into the Poverty of Nations,* (New York; Pantheon Books, 1968), Vol. III, p. 1647.

23. Ibid., p. 1649.

24. Planning Commission, Government of India, *The Fourth Plan: Mid-term Appraisal* (New Delhi: February 1972), pp. 44–45.

25. Ibid., pp. 45–46.

26. Government of India, Planning Commission, *Fourth Five-Year Plan: A Draft Outline* (New Delhi, 1968), p. 111.

27. For details, see Sen, *Employment Technology and Development*, pp. 135–145.

Part Six

SOME FINANCIAL ASPECTS

13

Capital Formation in India

BALWIR SINGH CHEEMA

Since its establishment in March 1950, the Indian Planning Commission has regarded capital formation as one of the major objectives of the five-year plans. This emphasis by the planners on capital formation stems from two basic considerations. First, periods of take-off have always been characterized by an increase in the rate of capital formation, irrespective of differences in the social and political conditions and institutions.[1] Second, in the growth models, great importance is attached to the rate of capital formation.

In this connection, one cannot ignore the impact of the Harrod-Domar growth model[2] on the thinking of Indian planners. According to Harrod-Domar, the rate of growth is*

$$G = s \, X \, \sigma$$

where $G =$ the rate of growth of output, defined as the ratio of the increase in income to total income in a given period $(\triangle Y/Y)$;

$s =$ saving expressed as a proportion of income (S/Y);

and $\sigma =$ the incremental output capital ratio, IOCR, $(\triangle Y/\triangle(K))$.

The rate of growth minus the population rate equals the growth rate in per capita income.

The model is based on the behavioural assumptions that saving depends on the level of income, and that investment depends on the rate of growth of income. The level of investment plays a dual role in determining the rate of growth. Not only does it generate income, the precise extent of which is determined by the value of the multiplier*, but it enlarges the capa-

---

*Assuming that in the case of India because of substantial unemployed labour, both skilled and unskilled, the potential aggregate supply is directly proportional to the capital stock available. That is supply $= Y_s = \sigma K$. Assuming further constant output to capital ratio in the short run, the addition made to income or the growth in the potential supply during any time period will be $= \triangle Y_s = \sigma \triangle K$. Since change in capital stock during any period is net investment we can rewrite the above equation as

$$\triangle Y_s = \sigma I.$$

Under equilibrium conditions investment and saving must equal substituting saving $s\,Y (s =$ propensity to save) for I in the above equation

$$\triangle Y = \sigma s Y$$
$$G = \frac{\triangle Y}{Y} = s\sigma$$

---

*In a closed economy aggregate demand Y_D is the sum of consumption C and autonomous investment I.

Demand $= Y_D = C + I$
$$= a + bY + I$$

$a =$ autonomous consumption,

and $b =$ marginal propensity to consume

Since aggregate spending is identical to aggregate income, the equilibrium level of aggregate demand is city of an economy to produce, the magnitude of which is determined by the incremental output capital ratio (IOCR). one may ignore lags in the working of the multiplier and the accelerator in a simplified model, but their significance in the formulation of economic plans and their effective implementation can hardly be overestimated. Thus, given the values of s, the ratio of saving to income, and IOCR, one can easily calculate the rate of growth —or, in case a certain target rate of growth is adopted, given the IOCR, one can easily calculate the saving effort needed to realize the target growth rate on the basis of the Harrod-Domar growth equation.

The postulate that the level of saving is determined by the level of income finds considerable support among development economists who support the theory of vicious circles.[3] However, economic planners, for practical reasons, cannot accept it without qualification as it precludes the possibility of economic development based on domestic saving. Furthermore, it cannot be upheld historically.[*]

$$Y_D = \frac{1}{1-b}(a + I)$$

or $$Y_D = \frac{1}{s}(a + I)$$

$$\frac{1}{s} = \text{multiplier}$$

The change in aggregate demand resulting from a change in investment amounts to

$$\triangle Y_D = \frac{1}{s} \triangle I$$

The change in investment times the simple multiplier.

[*]According to Professor Lewis, "No nation is so poor that it could not save 12 per cent of its national income if it wanted to;... least of all can those nations plead poverty as an excuse for not saving, in which 40 per cent or so of the national income is squandered by the top 10 per cent of income receivers". Arthur W. Lewis, *The Theory of Economic Growth* (Homewood, Ill.: Richard D. Irwin, 1955), p. 236. According to national sample survey conducted between July 1967 and June 1968, in India the top 10 per cent of households were responsible for 23.61 per cent of consumption against 28.36 per cent by the bottom 50 per cent. In urban areas the differences in consumption among the rich and the poor were slightly greater than in the rural areas. See Government of India, Planning Commission, *Fourth Five-Year Plan* (New Delhi, 1970), p. 36.

For instance, in 1965 the proportions of income saved and invested in China and Japan (33.2 and 35.2 per cent respectively) were almost one and a half times those of the USA and the UK (20 and 19.3 per cent respectively). By comparison, the per capita income of China was dismally low and that of Japan was roughly half of the UK and one fourth of the USA.[4] As against the investment rate of 25.2 per cent in China in 1965–66, the rate of investment in India amounted to only 13.4 per cent, of which 2.3 per cent[5] represented foreign investment, even though per capita income in India was not substantially lower than in China. Therefore, in addition to the level of income, the proportion saved and made available for investment must be influenced by psychological and institutional factors. Distribution of income, social customs and habits, the rate and direction in which the distribution of income and price levels change, and the degree of effectiveness with which government, banking and other financial institutions mobilize savings are some of the factors which play an important role in determining the rate of saving attained. Thus, without giving serious consideration to these factors, no economic plan can be realistically formulated and successfully implemented.

Along with the saving ratio, the IOCR has been the most important variable in determining the growth rate. In spite of the seeming simplicity of the IOCR, the difficulties involved in its empirical measurement tend to make it appear to be a very crude concept.[6] Nevertheless, theoretically it is a higly useful measure for estimating the need for investment over a period of time to achieve the target rate of growth.

Countries with high growth-rates have, without exception, low IOCR's. This shows that a high growth-rate is not only the function of saving and investment ratio but also of how effectively additional capital is used. Economic efficiency in the use of capital can only be maintained if other complementary factors of production like land, labour, technical know-how, and entrepreneurship can be mobilized simultaneously to meet the demands of the optimum production function. In mathematical terms, this means that the IOCR has to be treated as a total derivative. For determining the value of IOCR the supply of all factors of production, except capital, is treated as a variable. The growth of per capita income further depends on the growth-rate of population and is indirectly related to it.

Long-Term Capital Formation Plan of India

Every five-year plan has laid down the long-term strategy to achieve the minimum rate of capital formation considered necessary to transform the economy into a self-reliant one in a matter of about two decades. Thus, the First Five-Year Plan in 1952 envisaged that the average proportion of income saved and invested could be raised from 5 per cent to 20 per cent by 1968–69, by maintaining the marginal propensity to save at 20 per cent up to 1955–56 and 50 per cent thereafter.[7] The existing per capita income was considered to be too low to be tapped for additional saving. If this strategy had worked, the rate of saving as a proportion of income would have risen to 7 per cent by 1955–56, 11 per cent by 1960–61, and 20 per cent by 1967–68. On the basis of a projected capital-output ratio (the inverse of IOCR) of 3.0, it was considered possible to attain a growth rate of 6.25 per cent in national income by 1967–68. As the population growth-rate was assumed to be 1.25 per cent this would have meant an annual increase of roughly 5 per cent in per capita income. In Table 13.1, figures regarding the planned and actual performance of the Indian economy are given to evaluate the long-term Indian planning strategy.

Because of fuller utilization of installed capacity, and favourable weather conditions which resulted in bumper crops, the saving and investment targets were met during the First Plan period of 1951–56. National income registered an increase of 3.4 per cent against the target of 2.1 per cent. The capital-output ratio turned out to be 2.1 against the anticipated 3.0. Because of the initial success, the capital-output ratio estimates were revised downwards to 2.3 for 1956–61 and to 2.6 for 1961–66.[8] These projections proved to be quite low in view of the actually realized capital-output ratio of 3.0 and 5.5 respectively during the Second and Third Plan periods. At this point, too, the Second Five-Year Plan, with much larger investment targets, was adopted. Moreover, in the allocation of investment, emphasis was shifted to the development of heavy industry wherein the capital-output ratio is generally considered to be much higher. The Second Plan can at best be considered a qualified success. In spite of the difficulties of inflationary pressure, mounting deficits in the balance of payments and delay in the execution of key projects experienced during the Second Plan, the Planning Commission did not compromise on the long-term objectives laid down in the First and Second Plans in the formulation of the Third Five-Year Plan. Instead, emphasis was placed on the need for still greater effort to regain the ground lost during 1956–61. Again, during the Third Plan, specially in its last two years, the economy failed to make any headway in raising the savings ratio or in improving the capital-output ratio. National income grew only at 2.5 per cent annually against the 5.4 per cent provided in the Third Plan. Coupled with an increase in population of approximately 2.4 per cent, this meant an increase in per capita income of only about one-tenth of 1 per cent. One can blame the poor performance on the two wars with China and Pakistan, in 1962 and 1965 respectively, and on bad weather. However, this does not alter the fact that measured in terms of the crucial economic variables referred to above, the Indian economy failed to make significant progress. This led to a holiday in planning of three years, though the annual plans adopted during 1966–69 continued to follow the investment strategy laid down in the Fourth Five-Year Plan draft. Only the investment target of 14 per cent was nearly fulfilled during the Third Plan. This was made possible principally because of a large increase in foreign investment Table 13.2. Domestic savings, after touching a high of 10.8 per cent in 1965–66, declined to 8.0 per cent during 1966–67 and 1967–68. In

Table 13.1. Planned vs Actual Growth of Domestic and Foreign Saving, Investment and National Income Growth Rate and Capital Output Ratio

	Domestic Saving (as percentage of national income)		Foreign Saving (as percentage of national income)		Investment (as percentage of national income)		Average Annual (national income growth rate)		Incremental (capital-output ratio)	
	Planned	Actual	Planned	Actual	Planned	Actual	Planned	Actual	Estimated	Actual
First Plan										
1951–52 (Base Year)	—	5.0	—	—	5.0	—	—	—	—	—
1955–56 (Final Year)	7.0	7.3	0.2	0.3	7.0	7.3	2.1	3.4	3.0	2.1a
Second Plan										
1960–61 (Final Year)	9.7	8.5	1.0	2.5	10.7	11.0	4.6	3.7	2.3	3.0a
Third Plan										
1965–66 (Final Year)	11.5	10.8	2.5	2.3	13.1	13.1	5.4	2.5	2.6	5.5a
Annual Plan Years										
1966–67	—	8.0	3.2	3.2	—	11.2	—	1.5	—	7.5
1967–68	—	8.0	2.7	2.7	—	10.7	—	9.2	—	11.63
1968–69	—	8.4	2.5	1.1	—	9.5	—	2.4	—	3.96
Fourth Plan										
1973–74 (Final Year)	12.2	10.0	1.3	1.5	14.5	—	—	—	2.0	7.25
Fifth Plan										
1975–76	—	14.5	—	1.5	—	16.0	—	4.3	—	3.72
1978–79 (target)	15.7	—	.6	—	—	16.3	—	5.5	—	—

SOURCE: 1. *The Five-Year Plans.*

2. *India News,* 24 September 1976, p. 2; and 8 October 1976, p. 1.

aBlue *Supplement to the Monthly Commentary on Indian Economic Conditions* (New Delhi: Indian Institute of Public Opinion), Vol. XIII, No. 5, December 1971, p. VIII B.

Against these figures which are calculated on the basis of acutal average annual national income growth-rate and the investment rate, the Planning Commission figure for the first three five-year plans is 2.4 and 3.7 per cent for the Fourth Five-Year Plan. See pp. 44-45 of *Fourth Five-Year Plan* and page 27 of *Draft Fifth Five-Year Plan.*

Table 13.2. Rate of Investment and Saving as a Percentage of National Income
(1950–51 to 1973–74 in India)

Year	Internal Saving				Foreign Investment 5	Total Investment 4+5=6
	Household (1)	Corporate (2)	Government (3)	Total 1+2+3=4		
First Plan						
(1951–52 to 1955–56)	4.9	0.5	1.2	6.5	0.4	6.9
Second Plan						
(1956–57 to 1960–61)	6.5	0.4	1.6	8.5	2.9	11.4
Third Plan						
1961–62				8.9	2.2	11.1
1962–63	6.3[a]	0.7[a]	2.5[a]	9.6	2.4	12.0
1963–64	8.1	0.8	3.1	12.0	2.0	14.0
1964–65	7.6	0.4	2.7	10.7	2.2	12.9
1965–66	7.2	0.4	3.2	10.8	2.3	13.1
Annual Plan Years						
1966–67	5.7	0.5	1.8	8.0	3.2	11.2
1967–68	6.8	0.2	1.0	8.0	2.7	10.7
1968–69	6.2	0.2	2.0	8.4	1.1	9.5
Fourth Plan						
1969–70	5.9	0.4	2.2	8.5	0.8	9.3
1970–71	7.3	0.6	2.2	10.1	1.3	11.4
1971–72	8.9	0.6	2.0	11.4	1.4	12.8
1972–73	8.8	0.3	1.9	11.0	0.8	11.8
1973–74	8.0	0.3	1.7	10.0	1.5	11.5
Fifth Plan						
1975–76	—	—	—	14.5	1.5	16.0

[a]Average figures for 1961–62 and 1962–63.

SOURCE: 1. Indian Institute of Public Opinion, *Blue Supplement to the Monthly Commentary of Indian Economic Conditions*, Vol. XIII, No. 5, December 1971, p. 11.

2. *The Fifth Five-Year Plan.*

3. Ruddar Datt, *Indian Economy* (New Delhi: S. Chand, 1974) p. 102.

1968–69, when the Fourth Five-Year Plan was finally adopted, the domestic savings ratio made a partial recovery to 8.4 per cent, but it was still below the average level of 8.5 per cent attained during the Second Plan. After 1968–69 the saving ratio improved considerably. Because of the general improvement of the economic situation, the rate of saving of 14.5 per cent and an investment rate of 16.0 per cent were achieved in 1975–76.

According to Professor Rostow, the rate of productive investment must rise from less than 5 per cent to over 10 per cent of net national product for the economy to take off.[9] During 1968–69 and 1969–70,

the net investment fell short of this minimum of 10 per cent. The situation would have been made difficult if foreign aid had not been forthcoming. However, because of India's strained political relations with the US, the biggest contributor of foreign aid to India in the past, the flow of foreign aid had declined considerably after 1967–68. It is likely to decline further in the future. As a result, India will have to rely increasingly on domestic resources for economic development.

After almost a quarter-century of experience in economic planning, and increasing difficulties experienced in its execution since 1962–63, the Fifth Five-Year Plan was formulated. Again, it was to function in terms of the estimates of capital-output ratio and target saving rates, deemed necessary to make the economy self-reliant, after taking into account the projected population-growth rates. The target ratios of net domestic savings to national income by sectors for 1978–79 are given in Table 13.3.

Achievement of a higher saving ratio of 20 per cent by 1985–86 will involve the following measures: first, the public disposable income as a ratio of GNP must increase from 14.7 per cent in 1973–74 to 20.7 per cent in 1985–86; second, the ratio of public saving to public disposable income must increase from 19 per cent in 1973–74 to 39.6 per cent in 1985–86; third, for the economy as a whole marginal rate of savings of about 26 per cent in the Fifth Plan of 28 per cent thereafter must be achieved,[10] fourth the economy must grow at the postulated rate of 5.5 per cent during the Fifth Plan, 6 per cent in the Sixth Plan, and 6.2 per cent thereafter.[11]

The long-term projected rate of investment between 18 to 20 per cent, which the Indian planners have upheld so tenaciously, is justifiable, since it exceeds the minimum rate of investment needed to prevent the per capita income from falling in the face of population growth-rate of 2.03 per cent for 1971–76, 1.68 per cent in 1976–81 and 1.37 per cent in 1981–86.[12] If one examines the projected rate on the basis of the feasibility criteria, one is likely to come up with widely divergent answers. Theoretically, the maximum feasible rate of investment can be considered to involve saving of all income above the subsistence level (though it is difficult to define the level of subsistence in absolute terms). However, in view of the rapid increase in population, the longevity of the life span, and the relatively greater increase in per capita income than the increase in savings during the last two decades, one can safely say that domestic savings thus far generated have fallen considerably short of the maximum feasible. Considering, on the other hand, the political structure of India and the willingness on the part of different sections of Indian society to abstain from present consumption in order to assure a higher standard of living in the future, and in view of past experience, one can say with little hesitation that the savings stipulated in the Plan are far in excess of the maximum feasible. Judging from the demonstrated ability of the central and state governments to impose this magnitude of sacrifice by imposing additional taxation and keeping government expenditures from rising, before the declaration of emergency and the adoption of the Prime Minister's Twenty Point economic programme, one comes to a similar conclusion. Examining the stipulated rate of investment on the basis of absorptive capacity criterion defined in terms of the availability of natural resources, infrastructure, skilled and unskilled labour, one can say that very largely the Indian economy can profitably utilize this level of investment. However, it badly lacks the essential ingredients of devoted and skilled administrators and entrepreneurs.

Mobilization of Saving for Capital Formation

For attaining the investment ratio of 18–20 per cent, the Indian planners have laid emphasis on the mobilization of domestic savings. Three essential steps are involved in increasing the rate of capital formation. First, the volume of real savings must increase. This can be accomplished by diverting some of inputs from the production of consumption goods, or by making greater use of inputs without a corresponding increase in consumption. Second, real savings must be channelled from actual savers to investors with the help of financial intermediaries. Third, through proper demand management a corresponding change in gross national expenditures in favour of investment goods must take place to match the increased capacity to produce investment goods. This is essential not only for the effective utilization of capacity of investment-goods producing industries but to avoid excessive demand being placed on consumer goods industries, resulting in an increase in consumer goods prices. In seeking to determine the reasons for India's failure to mobilize savings and to increase the rate of capital formation

Table 13.3. Sectoral Distribution of Saving

Sector/Subsector	1973–74			1978–79			1978–79 increase over 1973–74	
	Rs. Crores	As a Percentage of National Income	As a Percentage of Total Saving	Rs. Crores	As a Percentage of National Income	As a Percentage of Total Saving	Rs. Crores	As a Percentage
1. Public sector	1,393	2.8	20.11	4,096	6.0	36.80	2,703	3.2
(a) Government	759	1.5	10.96	2,460	3.6	22.10	1,701	2.1
(b) Autonomous Public Undertakings	634	1.3	9.16	1,636	2.4	14.70	1,002	1.1
2. Private Savings	4,743	9.4	68.52	6,612	9.7	59.40	1,869	0.3
(a) Households	4,024	8.0	58.13	5,581	8.2	50.14	1,557	0.2
(b) Cooperative	50	0.1	.72	68	0.1	.61	18	—
(c) Corporate	669	1.3	9.66	962	1.4	8.65	294	0.1
3. Total Domestic Savings	6,136	12.2	88.64	10,708	15.7	96.20	4,572	3.5
4. Foreign Savings	786	1·5	11.36	422	0.6	3.79	−364	−0.9
Total Savings	6.922	13.7	100.00	11,130	16.3	100.00	4.208	2.6

SOURCE: *Draft Fifth Five-Year Plan*, pp. 11–13, and 41–52.

during the four five-year plans, these essential steps in the process of capital formation must be kept in mind. Further, as conditions for generating savings differ in the household, corporate, and government sectors, their study can best be undertaken separately.

Savings to be generated by various sectors of the economy to meet the investment targets of Rs. 31,400 crores in the public sector and Rs. 16,161 crores in the private sector are detailed in Table 13.4.

Table 13.4. Sources of Funds for Investment in the Fifth Five-Year Plan (1974–75 to 1978–79)

	Rs. in Crores	Percentage of Total
Public Sector		
(a) Public Sector Saving	14,907	31.3
(b) Public Sector Draft on Private Saving	14,062	29.6
(c) Draft on Foreign Saving	2,431	5.1
1. Total Public Sector Investment	31,400	66.00
Private Sector		
(a) Household Saving	10,216	21.5
(b) Corporate Saving	5,261	11.1
(c) Cooperative	684	1.4
2. Total Private Sector Investment	16,161	34.0
Total Investment 1 and 2	47,561	100.00

SOURCE: *Draft Fifth Five-Year Plan*, Vol. I, Chapter, 5.

Household Sector Savings

Household savings, comprising direct investment and net acquisition of financial assets, currently account for about two-thirds of total domestic saving. The total net domestic saving as a percentage of GNP is expected to grow from 8 per cent in 1973–74 to 8.2 per cent in 1978–79. This improvement of 0.2 per cent is planned to be achieved in spite of the anticipated decline in household disposable income from 83.9 per cent of GNP in 1973–74 to 80.3 per cent in 1978–79. This will involve a rise in the average rate of household saving from

9.5 per cent of houshold disposable income in 1973–74 to 10.2 per cent in 1978–79. The marginal rate of household saving works out to 12.6 per cent. This increase in household savings should be feasible if the planned average compound rate of increase of 5.3 per cent in household disposable income is achieved. This increased rate of saving will allow for a 4.6 per cent annual increases in consumption.[13]

Separate savings figures for rural and urban households are available only up to 1962–63, and are given in Table 13.5. The rural household savings figure as a percentage of national income between 1951–52 to 1962–63 declined slightly from 1.6 per cent to 1.5 per cent. There is little reason to believe that the rural household savings ratio has changed substantially since 1962–63. On the other hand urban household savings grew from 3.4 per cent in the First Plan to 5.0 per cent during the Second Plan. After reaching the all-time high of 8.1 per cent in 1963–64, because of the general slackening of the economy between 1965–66 and 1966–67, household savings declined to 5.7 per cent in 1966–67. They recovered to 6.8 per cent in 1967–68 but to the difficulties experienced by the economy in 1968–69 and 1969–70 they declined again to 5.9 per cent in 1969–70.

The urban household savings ratio has increased substantially, though in the past it used to fluctuate considerably. The share of rural household saving in the total household saving, had declined from 32 per cent during the First Plan to 23.81 per cent between 1961–62 and 1962–63. In general, the present • household saving and national income ratio in India compares quite favourably with that in developed economies. The US for instance had, between 1967–1971, a personal savings to national-income ratio of 6.15.[14]

In the household sector, the number of rural households is proportionately very large, as about 79 per cent of India's population still lives in villages.[15] Population belonging to the lowest three deciles in terms of income consists to a large extent of people living in agroclimatic conditions.[16] Between 1951–52 and 1961–62,

Table 13.5.   Household Saving as a Percentage of National Income and Total Domestic Saving

	Net Domestic Saving	House-hold Saving	Rural House-hold Saving	Urban House-hold Saving	Household Saving as Percentage of Domestic Saving	Rural Household Saving as Percentage of Total Household Saving	Urban household Saving as a Percentage of Total Household Saving
First Plan	6.6	5.0	1.6	3.4	75.75	32.00	68.00
Second Plan	8.5	6.6	1.6	5.0	77.65	24.24	75.76
1961–62 to 1962–63	9.5	6.3	1.5	4.8	66.32	23.81	76.19

SOURCE: Kuan-I Chen and J.S. Uppal, *Comparative Development of India and China* (New York: The Free Press, 1971), pp. 229–41, from D.R. Khathkhate and K.L. Deshpande, "Estimates of Saving and Investment in the Indian Economy: 1950–51 to 1962–63", *Reserve Bank of India Bulletin*, March 1965, pp. 314–333.

rural households received slightly less than 50 per cent of the total household income.[17] Relatively more rapid growth of income in large-scale manufacturing and mining, as compared to the agricultural and allied sectors, since 1960–61 has further reduced the share of the rural household sector in the total household income.[18] The income of rural households, therefore, is comparatively low, and the gap between the rural and the urban household incomes is widening.

In the rural sector the very rich, who have the greatest capacity to save, get most of their income from rent on land. Traditionally they belong to classes who have had close ties with the governing class. They find to lead a life of luxury and often try to maintain their political influence and social image by spending lavishly on marriages and other social and religious ceremonies. By living frugally, the small landholders and landless labourers may be able to save small amounts in good crop years, but in bad years they are forced to spend more than their income. Over a period of years they are, therefore, unable to generate much saving. The very high degree of their indebtedness to money-lenders makes this evident. A very high ratio of defaulted loans to cooperative societies in rural areas further confirms this observation.

Further, most of the income earned by rural households is earned from agriculture or activities closely related to agriculture.

Income is generally received in terms of goods and services rather than in cash, and most of the income generated by the household is self-consumed. A large portion of the household saving is invested directly by the household in land and buildings, which does not add to productive capacity. Moreover, farmers as well as such rural artisans as cobblers, barbers, weavers, carpenters and blacksmiths think of their job as a way of life rather than a means of earning a livelihood. As a result, production in the rural sector is rarely organized on business principles. Rural households generally do not clearly understand the significance of the link between savings and capital formation.

Finally, in the rural sector many transactions are made on the basis of barter. Even when the transactions are in terms of money most of them are made with the shopkeeper who also acts as a banker and moneylender. It is generally observed that monetization of an economy along with the creation of financial and monetary institutions has a positive influence on the rate of saving. Because of these features, up to now, the saving generated by rural households compared to urban households has been small. This is especially apparent when such figures are compared to the contribution made by the agricultural sector to total investment during the initial stages of economic development, in some of the developed economies of today.

There has been a tendency among the Indian planners and development economists in general to underestimate the actual and potential saving of rural households, in view of the very low levels of productivity, and in turn to attribute the low levels of saving and investment to it, on the basis of the vicious circle theory of Nurkse. In contrasts, the hypothesis relating low investment in agriculture to the constancy of the state of arts or stagnant technology has been given very little attention up to now.[19] This hypothesis seems more plausible in the context of the recent experience in India, especially in the Punjab and other wheat-growing areas, where the investment and saving picture in the agricultural sector has been radically changed in a matter of a few years, by the Green Revolution. Even on the basis of the earlier findings of the National Sample Survey and Rural Credit Survey covering the entire country, it has been estimated that in case of the agricultural sector the gross savings-income ratio is over 12 per cent, excluding direct investment. Allowing for noncash savings and after taking into account repair, maintenance and depreciation, the net cash savings-income ratio works out to be over 8 per cent.[20] This compares quite favourably with the savings in urban and industrial centres.

Urban households because of their comparatively higher incomes (in contrast with rural households) have a greater potential for saving. Certainly the conditions for the generation of savings and for their mobilization are more favourable in urban areas. The literacy ratio and degree of monetization, for instance, are much greater. Professionals and persons belonging to the capitalist and entrepreneurial classes tend to live in urban areas where there is a greater concentration of business opportunities, and educational and civic amenities. These classes, a great portion of whose income consists of profits and interest, generally tend to save a greater portion at the same levels of income, than landlords in rural areas.[21] In general, economic development in the countries of Western Europe and North America was accompanied by the gradual emergence of a new class of entrepreneurs

and a gradual erosion of the political and economic strength of the landed aristocracy. However, higher savings out of profits are unlikely to be generated in India because of the deliberate choice made to create a socialist pattern of society, and not to tolerate great concentrations of wealth as well as income. The continued enlargement of the public sector and comparatively higher rates of taxation at a relatively early stage of economic development have also affected adversely the growth of profits and savings out of them in the private sector of the economy.

In urban areas a great preponderance of middle class salaried employees and skilled wage-earners are employed by the government and organized industry. They enjoy comparatively high levels of income because the increase in the development rate has generated a relatively greater demand for educated and skilled labour. However, this growing urban middle class is unable to save a large amount of its income because of the pressure felt by it to spend a large proportion of the income on children's education and on "keeping up with the Jones'es". The impact of the demonstration effect on their consumption levels is also comparatively great. The income of unskilled labourers is not only close to subsistence level, but they are unable to save for the same general reasons as farmers in the rural areas.

In view of the democratic nature of the Indian society and government, the final choice regarding the extent of saving, through voluntary restraint from consumption, is made by the households. In order to encourage households to save India must, therefore, encourage by propaganda the desire to save. Second, the Indian government must provide incentives to save by providing sufficient returns in real terms on savings. Up to now the returns on savings, especially on small savings, have been very low because of the deliberate policy pursued by the government to keep the interest rates low. A low interest-rate policy is considered essential to keep the cost of public debt within reasonable limits and to encourage investment in the private sector. A comparatively high rate of inflation in the past, however, has rapidly eroded the real value of monetary assets. This has further curtailed returns on savings in real terms. Third, for the mobilization of household savings the government must provide conveniently located facilities for banking savings. The service at these facilities should be prompt and courteous.

Even before the start of economic planning, the Government of India was aware of this problem. This awareness grew further with the inception of the economic planning era, as it was forced to mobilize greater amounts of household savings for financing capital projects within the public sector. The public sector draft on private savings to finance public sector investment will equal Rs. 14,062 crores an amount almost equal to the public sector's own saving of Rs. 14,907 crores, (See Table 13.4). In order to meet this need a vast network of organizations consisting of primary cooperative societies, district and central cooperative banks, land mortgage banks, post-office savings banks, commercial joint-stock banks, industrial and agricultural finance and development corporations, the State Bank of India (till 30 June 1955, the Imperial Bank of India), Agricultural Refinance Corporation (ARC), Industrial Finance Corporation, National Industrial Development Corporation, Industrial Development Bank of India, and Investment trusts and Unit trusts have been created. The role of the Reserve Bank of India, which sits at the apex of these banking and financial institutions to meet their need for financing, supervision, and training of personnel, has grown each year. In harnessing small savings, the Government further depends on the National Life Insurance Corporation of India and provident and pension funds both in the private as well as in the public sector. After the nationalization of the 14 big commercial banks in July 1969, new branches (especially in rural areas) have been opened at an unprecedented rate. As a result, deposits of all scheduled commercial banks stood at Rs. 10,454 crores on 31 May 1974 as against Rs. 4,646 crores on 30 June 1969—an increase of over 125 per cent. Bank deposits in 1973 increased by 17.5 per cent.[22] The quality of service at the financial and banking institutions has deteriorated after

nationalization, however, because of increased red tape.

Institutional arrangements to harness the potential growth in agricultural income into saving and investment have been created, but these are still highly inadequate and inefficient. The most important of these institutions is the agricultural credit cooperative. It has a three-tier credit structure, consisting of cooperative banks at the state level, central cooperative banks at the district level, and primary agricultural credit societies at the village level. The basic weakness of the cooperative credit system is the non-viability of a large number of primary agricultural societies because of inefficiency and poor book-keeping. These deficiencies can be ascribed partly to lack of education on the part of members, and partly to lack of honest, well-trained, and conscientious administrators. In spite of the programmes of rationalization and consolidation which resulted in the decline in the number of primary agricultural credit societies from 212,000 to 171,800 between 1960–61 and 1967–68,[23] the situation did not improve much. As a result of further reorganization leading to consolidation and amalgamation, the number of primary agricultural societies is provisionally estimated at 157,775 in 1972–73, with a membership of 34.4 crores and share capital of 237 crores.[24] However, it seems that like the many previous attempts to reform cooperative societies, present attempts to rationalize them had not been successful prior to the declaration of Emergency. Overdue loans, which have been consistently rising since 1951–52, amounted to Rs. 376 crores in 1971–72. However, the provisional figure for 1972–73 shows a decline to 364 crores.[25] An enormous amount of mismanagement and inefficiency also exists in the district and central cooperative banks.

Comparatively speaking, the situation in urban areas (where household savings are mainly channelled for industrial development through the joint-stock commercial banks, post-office savings banks, investment and unit trusts, etc.) is much better because of greater literacy, better maintenance of records, less participation of local interest in management, and comparative absence of political pressure. However, here too the situation has been slowly deteriorating and, on the basis of the very sketchy and incomplete evidence available so far, nationalization of the large commercial banks has not helped the situation as much as was initially expected.

In spite of these shortcomings, household savings have continued to grow and have provided the needed financing for investment in the public as well as the corporate sectors of the economy. The compulsory deposit scheme started in July 1974 for compulsory deposits on a graded scale in the case of incomes of Rs. 150,000 and above, and the scheme of impounding additional incomes through compulsory deposit, both in relation to income tax payers in the higher brackets and to additional dearness allowance, by adding an element of forced saving, is likely to improve the household saving ratio. The increasingly greater emphasis on more equitable distribution of wealth and income is likely to affect household savings adversely, because in general the propensity to consume among lower-income brackets is comparatively higher.

Corporate Saving
Economic development is made possible by the rapid expansion of the capitalist sector at the expense of the subsistence sector. The capitalist sector which can be private, public, or partly private and partly public, employs reproducible capital and wage labour for profit making. Capitalists have been distinguished from other classes by their passion for saving and productive investment. Along with the growth of the capitalist sector, the corporate form of business organization emerged, without which it would have been difficult to raise and accumulate the capital needed for large-scale production. Well before the Second World War, privately owned corporations started generating an increasing proportion of savings internally, by retaining a greater and greater percentage of their growing profits to finance investment in the free market economies. For instance, in the US during the 1960's, corporate saving accounted for roughly 8.83 per cent of the national income.[26] In the Soviet Union and other communist

countries, on the contrary, the ownership of the means of production as well as the responsibility to generate savings has been vested in the hands of the State.

In India the Government, in line with its objective of establishing a socialist pattern of society based on equitable distribution of income and wealth, has assumed the major responsibility for development of the capitalist sector. Under the Industrial Policy Resolution of 1956,[27] the private sector has been given a minor but important role in enlarging the capitalist sector. With the passage of time as a result of the nationalization of insurance companies and large commercial banks, the passage of the Monopolies and Restrictive Trade Policies Act of 1969, the Industrial Licensing Policy of 1970, and the new Industrial policy announced on 2 February 1973, the role of the private sector has been limited further. In view of this, the private corporate sector is unlikely to play the same role in the expansion of the capitalist sector and the generation of saving, as has been played traditionally by the corporate sector in the free-enterprise developing economies. The raising of equity capital for expansion, because of the nationalization of large commercial banks and insurance companies and the increase in the public sector draft on private savings, has become more difficult. In spite of these limitations, the corporate sector has registered a considerable growth since 1951, as indicated by the increase in the paid-up capital of the private joint-stock companies, from Rs. 208.9 crores to Rs. 3,534 crores in 1974. The number of private joint-stock companies increased from 15,964 to 31,160 during the same period.[28]

Because of the relative smallness of the corporate sector of the Indian economy, its share in the national savings has been small. During the First Plan period it amounted to 0.5 per cent of national income and constituted 8 per cent of total domestic savings. It declined slightly during the Second Plan but in 1963–64 reached a peak of 0.8 per cent of national income, representing 6.7 per cent of total saving. Thereafter it declined sharply and in 1967–68 amounted to only 0.2 per cent of national income, representing 2.5 per cent of total savings. By 1970–71 it had increased again to 0.6 per cent of the national income, constituting 6.0 per cent of the total saving. In 1972–73 and 1973–74 it again declined to 0.3 per cent of national income (Table 13.2). This lack of growth of the share of corporate savings in total savings and as a percentage of national income, can mainly be attributed to the relatively faster growth of the public and noncorporate sectors (largely representing agriculture and small-scale industry) of the Indian economy. The large fluctuations in corporate savings are attributed to its extreme sensitivity to fluctuations in profits and national income. Some of the other important reasons which have adversely affected the growth of corporate savings are discussed below.

The ability of the corporate sector to generate profits in a developing economy, is directly related to its ability to pay wages close to the subsistence wage. This is made possible because of the presence of a large pool of unemployed labour in the subsistence sector. In India the capitalist sector has been unable to take full advantage of the situation because of the development of strong and well-organized labour unions, comparatively early on the way to economic development. Under strong labour-union pressure the real wages, instead of remaining at subsistence levels, have registered a significant increase since 1951. Corporate profits have, therefore, failed to increase rapidly partly due to the upward pressure on the real wages of the growing labour force employed in the corporate sector.

Corporate income-tax rates in India possess a certain degree of progressivity as corporations are taxed at different rates according to their class (distinction is made on the basis of ownership, private or public, and foreign or domestic), priority being given to various industries on the basis of their significance in economic development and size. The surtax imposed on corporate profits as a super profits tax since 1964 along with the penal tax (levied on closely held companies, with the intention of checking tax evasion by the rich through company formations), add further to the progressive nature of corporate income-tax. Justification of a progressive tax is generally based on the principle of ability to pay, but the principle is considered to be relevant only in the case of individuals. In the case of corporate income tax, the progressiveness of the tax simply penalizes efficiency, especially where the extent of corporate profits is determined by relative efficiency rather than on the monopoly power exercised. It is very difficult to measure the direction and the extent to which the incidence of corporate income tax is shifted, since the results of the studies made in this connection differ widely.[29] However, to the extent corporate income tax has affected retentions, corporate saving has been adversely affected.

In view of these difficulties and on the basis of past experience it can be safely concluded that the target of 1.4 per cent of national income for corporate saving, laid down in the Fifth Plan for 1978–79, is not likely to be reached. For achievement of target corporate saving, some substantial changes in the overall role assigned to the private sector in the Indian economy will have to be made. Even major tax concessions by way of tax holiday in the case of certain types of new investment projects, larger depreciation allowances, and more favourable treatment given to export industries, as in the past, are not likely to affect corporate saving significantly.

Government Saving

In view of the general inadequacy of household and corporate savings to meet the needs of rapid growth in capital formation, economic planners in India have acknowledged, from the beginning, the urgent necessity of enlarging public saving. The basic weakness in this connection has been that the government sector has very few resources of its own, by way of surpluses, to finance investment. Public saving, like individual saving, depends upon the relative levels of revenues and expenditures. Public saving can, therefore, only be increased by widening the gap between government revenues and government expenditures. Government income can be increased by either raising the ratio of tax revenue to national income, or by increasing the income of the factors of production owned by the government. Government expenditures can be lowered by reducing government consumption expenditures or by curtailing government subsidies paid to the private sector.

In 1950–51, the ratio of tax revenue to national income was 6.6 per cent. Between 1951–52 and 1965–66, it rose rapidly and reached a peak of 14.2 per cent in 1965–66, the last year of the Third Plan. In spite of their rapid increase, the tax ratios in India amounted to about half to one-third of the developed economies and remained considerably below the tax ratios of some developing economies.[30] By 1967–68, because of the general slowing down of the Indian economy after 1965–66, it had declined to 12.2 per cent. With resumption of economic growth after 1967–68, it had again increased to 12.8 per cent by 1970–71. The public disposable income as a percentage of GNP was estimated at 14.7 per cent in 1973–74. It is projected to increase to 20.7 per cent by 1985–86. Meanwhile the ratio of public savings to public disposable income is projected to increase from 19 per cent in 1973–74 to 39.6 per cent in 1985–86.[31] Public savings as a ratio of GNP are estimated to increase from 2.8 per cent in 1973–74 to 6.0 per cent in 1985–86. Of the projected improvement of 3.5 per cent in the overall rate of savings the contribution of public saving is put at 3.2 per cent. (See Table 13.3).

The income elasticity of taxes as a whole, between 1953–55 and 1966–68 in India was 2.4.[32] This meant that every increase of 1 per cent in national income resulted in a 2.4 per cent increase, on the average, in tax revenues. High income-elasticity of taxes, as a whole, causes the tax ratio to increase as income goes up. It can, therefore, be considered as a reasonably good indicator of the effort being made to raise the tax ratio. The high income-elasticity of taxes in India and the success achieved in raising the tax ratio can be attributed to the following factors: first, both individual and corporate income taxes have been made increasingly progressive. This has meant that as individual and corporate incomes have risen, a relatively greater proportion has been paid in taxes. The progressive nature of direct taxes and

high income-elasticity of taxes in general in India has also been mainly responsible for the drop in the tax ratio in years of economic slowdown in the past. Second, during the last two decades, new taxes have been levied and the existing taxes have been increased or made more progressive. Third, the tax structure has been changed to incorporate more taxes on production and internal transactions with high income-elasticity.[33] In spite of this considerable increase in the tax ratio since 1950–51 among the underdeveloped countries the Indian tax effort to raise revenue during the last two decades is ranked about average.[34]

There are a number of reasons for the present low tax ratio in India and for the problems encountered in trying to raise it. Perhaps the most important of these is the low per capita income in India, even when compared to most developing economies. Among democratic countries, where the choice to abstain from consumption is made voluntarily, much greater emphasis has been placed by India on the equitable distribution of income and wealth. This commitment to establish a socialistic pattern of society has resulted in a great reluctance to tax directly a very large proportion of the population at the lower end of income distribution.[35] The lower-income classes also largely escape the payment of indirect taxes, since necessities, on which most of their income is spent, are generally exempt from such taxes. However, in the case of India where the vast majority of people live in abject poverty it is futile to expect a very small sprinkling of the rich and middle-income people to generate enough savings (forced or voluntary) for capital formation. The poor, because of their low income, rising aspirations and the operation of the demonstration effect, have a propensity to consume of almost equal to 1. It is, therefore, imperative for the success of the savings effort to force, by the imposition of direct taxes, a large number of people in low-income brackets to refrain from consumption. Usually it is easier to tax exports and imports. However, because of the sheer size of the Indian economy, its dependence on foreign trade is comparatively small. India's annual imports and exports constitute only about 10 per cent of the gross domestic product. In spite of the fact that the Indian economy is relatively less open, taxes on international trade from 1953 to 1955 and 1966 to 1968 generated 25 per cent and 17.8 per cent, respectively, of the total tax revenues.[36] The comparatively low literacy and monetization ratios along with the lack of efficient tax administration no doubt makes the task of raising tax revenues more difficult.[37]

The agricultural sector relative to the mining and manufacturing sector in India is large, in comparison to developed economies.[38] Low levels of literacy, monetization, and incomes among agriculturists make taxing the agricultural sector very difficult. Agricultural incomes, therefore, remain lightly taxed. Relatively more rapid growth of the agricultural sector and other lightly taxed sectors of the Indian economy has been partly responsible for the comparative drop in the overall tax ratio since 1965–66.[39]

The taxing of agricultural incomes is made more difficult because the power to tax agricultural incomes is given to the states under the Constitution of India. Most of the states, including those where agricultural productivity and incomes have risen sharply as a result of the adoption of Green Revolution technology, are reluctant to tax agricultural incomes for political reasons. A majority of the states, therefore, have no or very low agricultural income-tax. The incidence of agricultural income tax has, in fact, always been less than a rupee per hectare.[40] Agriculturists also largely escape the burden of indirect taxes, as a large proportion of the consumption of agricultural households consists of their own produce. The tax contribution of the agricultural sector, up to now, has not only been small, but since 1950–51 the intersectoral inequity in tax burdens has increased further in favour of the agricultural sector.[41]

The Government of India, over the last two decades, has been consistently pursuing the policy of expanding the public sector in order to raise the income of Government-owned factors of production. As a result of this emphasis on investment in the public sector its share in reproducible

tangible wealth has increased steadily.[42] Roughly, over half the actual outlay in the public sector in the past has been in large-scale capital-intensive industrial projects, as they have been considered to generate large surpluses for future investment. Nevertheless, the public sector's contribution to total savings has remained disappointingly small. Autonomous public undertakings contribution to total savings was estimated at only 1.4 per cent in 1973–74 and is targeted at 1.1 per cent in the Fifth Plan for 1978–79 (Table 13.3).

Public consumption expenditures and the subsidies paid to the private sector, on the other hand, have risen more rapidly than anticipated. This has been mainly due to the rapid rise in prices since 1950–51. The long-term increase in prices has been caused in part by the large annual budgetary deficits undertaken to meet investment targets, and in part by the failure to achieve the planned increase in gross national product based on the estimates of capital-output ratio. Concern over employment, especially among the university-educated white-collar workers in urban areas, has resulted in disproportionate expansion of employment in the public sector. There has also been a rapid increase in the health, education, sanitary, and welfare and relief services rendered by the Government. Defence expenditures have increased rapidly, especially since 1962, due to tensions with China and Pakistan.

The increase in public consumption expenditures in the past may have been justified and even unavoidable; nevertheless, this does not negate the fact that, in spite of the considerable increase in the share of the public sector in national income and reproducible tangible wealth, its relative contribution to national savings has not increased significantly. Unless this trend is reversed, any additions in government revenues will only replace private consumption by public consumption, and will adversely affect private saving. The greater emphasis placed on the utilization of economic policy to attain more equitable personal and regional distribution of income and wealth in general in order to eliminate poverty (*Garibi hatao*) in the Draft Fifth Five-Year

Plan (1974–79), is likely to make it more difficult to check the rise in public consumption expenditures

Conclusion

Increase in the savings ratio is a necessary condition for more rapid capital formation. In free-enterprise economies the necessary incentive for saving and the mobilization and investment of savings have been primarily provided by the opportunity to make profits and to get rich. In communist countries, on the other hand, people have been forced· to forego present consumption in order to meet the investment needs of the economy. Acknowledging the need for investment, as well as realizing the improbability of its being realized purely through the market mechanism, India has been trying to raise the rate of investment by following a middle-of-the-road policy. In order to preserve the democratic nature of the society and the right to property (within broadly accepted limits), the decision to save has been left primarily with individual households. However, the responsibility to invest has been increasingly shifted to the public sector. An important justification given for enlarging the size of public sector investment has been that increase in the relative size of the public sector will in time lead to an increase in its share of total savings. Besides, public saving adds to the collective wealth and income of the community (which will grow further with every successive round of saving and investment) that is considered essential for building a society based on a socialistic pattern.

In spite of the failure to achieve planned targets, considerable progress has been made in raising the level of savings. Between 1951–52 and 1963–64 the net domestic savings to national income ratio increased from 6.5 per cent to 12 per cent. By 1967–68, it had nosedived to 8 per cent. This reversal in trend was caused primarily by a sharp decline in government saving, from a high of 3.1 per cent in 1963–64 to a low of 1 per cent in 1967–68. Since 1967–68 the net domestic saving ratio has resumed its upward trend and was estimated at 14.5 per cent in 1975–76,

the highest since the beginning of the Fourth Five-Year Plan.

Household saving has grown considerably, in the face of almost insurmountable difficulties posed by low levels of income, education, and monetization. This has been made possible through education and infusion of national fervour by the adoption of plans and plan targets, as a result of which perhaps an average household has become more conscious of the fact that the saving habit is not only a personal virtue, but also helps in strengthening the national economy by making investment possible. A network of financial and monetary institutions for the mobilization of household saving has been created. The effectiveness and efficiency of these institutions, however, still leaves much to be desired. In the past, the returns on household saving in real terms have been very modest because of the government policy of keeping interest rates low, and the rapid decline in the real value of monetary assets due to inflation. Returns in real terms on household saving, therefore, need improvement.

Corporate saving in India, unlike corporate saving in free enterprise economies, is likely to remain relatively small because of the limited role assigned to the private sector under the industrial policy adopted by India. Progressivity of corporate income tax has discouraged efficiency and the presence of strong labour unions has adversely affected the corporate sector's ability to make profits. In spite of the serious limitations placed on the sphere of activity of the private sector and the mushrooming of government red tape, which the private sector has to confront daily in conforming to government regulations, the performance of the private corporate sector up to now has been remarkable. This fact, along with the importance of the profit motive and individual initiative, considered essential for economic development under a democratic set-up, needs greater recognition.

The main cause for India's inability to attain the target-saving ratio in the past, has been the incapacity of the public sector to generate adequate saving. As far as raising the public sector's income is concerned, India has been fairly successful.

The ratio of tax revenues to gross national product has been almost doubled. In tapping private sector saving for public sector investment, the Government has been increasingly successful, as evidenced by the rapid growth in the public-sector draft on private saving. The share of the public sector in the reproducible tangible wealth of the country has increased rapidly. Besides, the contribution of public sector enterprises to gross national product has increased. Nonetheless, because of the increase in public sector consumption, delays and the high cost of building public sector projects, and their inefficient operation, the government sector has so far failed to generate the necessary savings. The flow of foreign aid, which had largely enabled India to bridge the gap between investment targets and domestic saving in the past, has declined sharply and the outlook regarding the future flow of foreign aid remains bleak. The need to make the economy self-reliant has therefore become more urgent. The responsibility of meeting the challenge to generate sufficient savings to match investment targets has increasingly come to rest with the public sector, because of the rapid increase in its relative importance in the economy. The provision for rapidly increasing public savings in the Fourth and Fifth Plans was a clear recognition of this responsibility of the public sector by the Planning Commission. In spite of this correct reading of the situation at the beginning of the Fourth Plan, very little progress was made during the Fourth Plan in raising government saving. As a result, the crisis of saving, which has existed for so long, remains unabated in the Indian economy.

REFERENCES

1. Government of India, Planning Commission, *The First Five-Year Plan* (New Delhi, 1952), p. 13.
2. R.F. Harrod, *Economic Essays*, Essay 14 (London: Macmillan, 1952); "Second Essay in Dynamic Theory", *Economic Journal*, vol. LXIXI (June 1960), pp. 277–93. Also see E.D. Domar, *Essays in the Theory of Economic Growth* (Oxford: Oxford University Press, 1957). For more detailed discussion of Harrod-Domar model and its limitations see G.R.D. Allen, *Macro-Economic Theory: A Mathematical Treatment* (New York: Macmillan, 1968), pp. 197–219; and Warren L. Smith, *Macroeconomics* (Homewood, Ill.: Richard D. Irwin, 1970), pp. 391–428.
3. R. Nurkse, *Problems of Capital Formation in Underdeveloped Countries* (Oxford: Basil Blackwell, 1953), p. 5.
4. A. Maddison, *Economic Growth in Japan and the U.S.S.R.* (New York: W.W. Norton 1969), p. xix. Also see William W. Hollister, *Trends in Capital Formation in Communist China*, reproduced by Kuan-I. Chen, and J. S. Uppal, *Comparative Development of India and China* (New York: The Free Press, 1971), pp. 242–254. The figures are actually investment figures but because of the very low component of foreign investment in these countries they are also considered to be equal to domestic saving.
5. Indian Institute of Public Opinion, *Blue Supplement to the Monthly Commentary on Indian Economic Conditions*, vol. XIII, No. 5, December 1971, p. 11.
6. Everett E. Hagen, *The Economics of Development* (Homewood, Ill: Richard D. Irwin, 1968), pp. 185–187.
7. Government of India, Planning Commission, *The First Five-Year Plan* (New Delhi, 1952), pp. 20–23.
8. Government of India, Planning Commission, *Second Five-Year Plan* (New Delhi, 1956), p. 11.
9. W.W. Rostow, *The Stages of Economic Growth* (Cambridge: Cambridge Univesity Press, 1963), p. 39.
10. Government of India, Planning Commission, *Draft Fifth Five-Year Plan*, vol. I (New Delhi, 1973), p. 13.
11. Ibid., p. 7.
12. Ibid., p. 2.
13. *Draft Fifth Five-Year Plan*, vol. I, p. 48.
14. US Government, *Economic Report of the President: Transmitted to the Congress, January 1973* (Washington, D.C.: 1973), pp. 211–216.
15. *Draft Fifth Five-Year Plan*, vol. I, p. 2.
16. Ibid., p. 22.
17. Kuan-I Chen and J.S. Uppal, *Comparative Development of India and China* (New York: The Free Press, 1971), p. 239. Figure computed on the basis of the rural and urban household saving figures given as a ratio of national income.
18. Ibid., *Fourth Five-Year Plan*, p. 6, also see *Draft Fifth Five-Year Plan*, p. 22.
19. T. W. Schultz, *Transforming Traditional Agriculture* (New Haven: Yale University Press, 1964), p. 84.
20. P.G.K. Panikar, *Rural Savings in India* (Bombay: Somaiya, 1970), p. 163.
21. W. Arthur Lewis, *The Theory of Economic Growth* (Homewood, Ill.: Richard D. Irwin, 1955), p. 226.
22. Government of India, Ministry of Informa-

tion and Broadcasting, *India: A Reference Annual*, 1975 (New Delhi, 1975), p. 147.
23. *Fourth Five-Year Plan*, p. 217.
24. *India: A Reference Annual*, 1975, p. 195.
25. Ibid.
26. *Economic Report of the President: 1973*, p. 211. The saving figure has been computed on the basis of corporate profits and inventory valuation adjustment minus dividend figures for 1960–69.
27. *Second Five-Year Plan*, pp. 43–50.
28. *India: A Reference Annual*, 1975, p. 150.
29. Ved P. Gandhi, *Some Aspects of India's Tax Structure: An Economic Analysis* (Bombay: Vora, 1970), p. 141.
30. Raja C. Chelliah, "Trends in Taxation in Developing Countries", *I.M.F. Staff Papers*, vol. XVII, no. 2, July 1971, pp. 302–303, also see Jorgen R. Lotz and Mors Elliott, "Measuring 'Tax Effort' in Developing Countries," *I.M.F. Staff Papers*, vol. XIV, no. 3, November 1967, p. 479.
31. *Draft Fifth Five-Year Plan*, vol. I, p. 13.
32. Chelliah, *Taxation Trends*, p. 265. Income elasticity of taxes$=\Delta T/T \div \Delta Y/Y$, where T and Y stand for taxes and gross national product. Income elasticity of taxes at 2.4 in the case of India was the highest among the 27 developing countries considered by Prof. Chelliah.
33. Ibid. Between 1953–55 and 1966–68 income elasticity of major categories of taxes according to Professor Chelliah were: Income taxes 1.7, taxes on production and internal transactions 4.1, import taxes 1.8 and taxes on international trade 1.5.
34. Lotz and Morss, *'Tax Effort' in Developing Countries*, pp. 494–495, also see Roy W. Bahl, "A Regression Approach to Tax Export and Tax Ratio Analysis", *I.M.F. Staff Papers*, vol. XVII, No. 3, November 1971, p. 596. Among 52 countries considered by Lotz and Morss, India was ranked 21 and was grouped among average tax effort countries after taking into account the difference in the per capita gross national product and exports and imports. In terms of taxable capacity India was ranked 41 among the 49 countries considered by Bahl.
35. In 1963–64, less than a million persons paid income tax. Because of the consistently declining effective tax ratio for the low and middle-income classes and a simultaneous shift in the (pre-tax) income distribution in their favour, the average burden of income tax has declined since 1950–51. See Gandhi, *India's Tax Structure*, p. 29.
36. Chelliah, *Taxation Trends*, p. 270.
37. Because of the laxity of tax administration, the tax arrears of those tax payers owing Rs. one million or more alone totalled to Rs. 890 million on 1 December 1968: Chelliah, *Taxation Trends*, p. 31.
38. Empirical studies point out that the share of agricultural income has a significant negative correlation to the tax ratio, whereas the mining and manufacturing incomes bear a significant positive correlation to tax ratio. Bahl, "Regression Approach to Tax Export", p. 605.
39. *The Fourth Plan: Mid-Term Appraisal*, pp. 11, 25. During the first two years of the Fourth Plan, 52 per cent of the additions to real national income accrued to the agricultural sector. The share of national income accruing to agriculture, measured in current prices, has been still greater, because of the above average increase in agricultural prices since 1960–61.
40. Gandhi, *India's Tax Structure*, p. 141.
41. Ibid., pp. 131–37. In 1952–53, in the income bracket of Rs. 1,200 to Rs. 1,800, urban households paid 5 per cent of their income in taxes against 3.2 per cent paid by the rural households, and in the income bracket of Rs. 1,800 to Rs. 3,600 the taxes paid by them amounted to 5 per cent and 3.6 respectively. Due to the increased importance in the Indian tax structure of the indirect taxes, which fall primarily on monetized urban consumption, it is felt that relatively the burden of taxes on rural incomes has declined further.
42. In 1965–66, 35 per cent of the entire reproducible wealth was owned by the public sector and was estimated to rise to 43 per cent as a result of the implementation of the Fourth Plan. See Planning Commission, Government of India, *Fourth Five-Year Plan: A Draft Outline* (New Delhi, August 1966), p. 42.

BIBLIOGRAPHY

Bhagwati, Jagdish N.: *Indian Planning for Industrialization and Trade Policies since* 1951. London. Oxford University Press, 1970.

Eckaus, Richard S. and Kirit S. Parikh: *Planning and Growth: Multisectoral, Intertemporal Models Applied to India*. Cambridge, Massachusetts. The M.I.T. Press, 1968.

Government of India, Planning Commission: *Draft Fifth Five-Year Plan*, Vol. I. New Delhi, 1973.

Panikar, P.G.K.: *Rural Savings in India*. Somaiya. Bombay, 1970.

Patel, V.G.: *An Analysis of Plan Implementation in India*. Ahmedabad Balgovind Prakashan, 1969.

Shenoy, B.R.: *Indian Economic Policy*. Bombay, Popular Prakashan, 1968.

Singh, Tarlok: *Towards an Integrated Society*. New Delhi. Orient Longmans, 1969.

Solow, Robert W.: *Growth Theory*. Oxford. Oxford University Press, 1970.

Streeten, Paul: *The Crisis of Indian Planning*.

London. Oxford University Press, 1968.

Kuan-I Chen and Uppal, J.S.: *Comparative Development of India and China.* New York.

The Free Press, 1971.

Uppal J.S.: *Economic Development in South Asia.* New York. St. Martin's Press, 1977.

14

Banking in India

V. S. CHITRE

Elementary Theory of Finance and Financial Intermediation

The institutions of money, finance, and financial intermediation are fundamental to the working of a modern economy. The use of money allows the separation, in time and space, of the act of purchase from the act of sale, thus avoiding the necessity of the double coincidence of wants, and thereby reduces the associated exchange costs in the form of search, storage, and transportation. The possibility of lending and borrowing, or finance, makes it possible to transfer the command over resources or consumption goods and services in the economy for a specified period, and enables the economic units to increase their asset holding and production operations or their consumption, beyond the limits of their present net worth, that is, beyond the limits of their present level of accumulated savings. Since such loan transactions enable a transfer of resources to those who expect to use these resources to produce a larger value, than those who originally possessed the command over the resources expect to produce themselves, and since the possibility of loan transactions allows the

economic units to rearrange their consumption plans so as to maximize their satisfaction, we can say that the loan transaction or finance increases the full employment equilibrium real wealth of the community relative to its current real income, given the technology and time-and-risk preferences in the community. This is called the *asset transmutation effect* in the theory of finance.[1]

The possibility of lending and borrowing also raises the full-employment equilibrium ratio of saving and investment to current income in the economy, given the technology and the time-and-risk preferences in the community. That the possibility of borrowing raises the ratio of full employment equilibrium investment to community's income is easy to see. Production units can now supplement the financing of their investment out of their own resources (by raising the price of their product, if necessary), by borrowing from other economic units. Also, as the return on investment is increased when resources can be transferred by loan transactions to economic units with higher marginal productivity of capital, and when pooling of small savings can result in the exploitation of economies of large-scale production,

Banking in India 249

the total investment is certain to increase. Furthermore, loan transactions make it possible to transfer resources from economic units with higher risk aversion to those with lower risk aversion, resulting in an increase in total investment in the community.

The same factors which increase the total investment when borrowing and lending are possible, also lead to an increase in the community's propensity to save. The possibility of lending induces a larger saving out of a given current income because a positive interest can be earned on the amount saved and lent. If borrowing and lending are not possible, the only way by which an economic unit can allocate its wealth between current consumption and future consumption is by holding its saving in the form of idle cash (when prices are expected to be stable or to decline), or in the form of unperishable goods (when prices are expected to rise), until it is to be used for acquiring consumption goods. In this case the saving earns no interest (except insofar as prices change). Now if lending of current surplus funds at positive interest is permitted, current consumption becomes that much more expensive relative to future consumption and is discouraged. If the increase in income or wealth implied by a positive interest rate does not lead to an excessively strong (normal) income-or-wealth effect on current consumption, saving out of current income will increase.

The ratio of saving and investment to current income is increased further by the possibility of introducing a variety of financial instruments. For example, the possibility of using a debt claim (i.e., a claim on a specified stream of money sums) or an equity claim (i.e., a claim on a specified share of a productive unit's profits and losses) makes it further possible to meet the risk—and liquidity-requirements of the surplus and the deficit spending units more exactly, thereby inducing them to increase their saving-investment activity.

The effect of the possibility of financing on the full-employment equilibrium ratio of saving and investment to current income is called the *intermediation effect*.[2] Because of the presence of financial instruments, economic units are enabled to hold the productive assets indirectly through the holding of financial instruments. In the process, the saving and investment in the economy relative to the economy's current income are increased as described above.

Financial intermediation further magnifies the effects of finance, viz., the asset transmutation effect and the intermediation effect. Just as the intermediary of financial instrument makes it possible to hold productive assets indirectly by holding financial assets, a financial intermediary enables economic units to hold financial assets indirectly by holding other financial assets. Financial intermediaries are enterprises which interpose themselves between the ultimate borrowers and the ultimate lenders by holding primary or direct securities, i.e., financial claims of the ultimate borrower with the funds acquired by issuing secondary or indirect securities, i.e., financial claims against themselves.

Financial intermediation becomes profitable for several reasons.[3] The fundamental reason is the presence of economies of scale in lending and borrowing operations which arise on account of (1) the lumpy nature of the costs of lending and borrowing operations including especially those for acquiring the relevant information, and (2) the possibility of reducing the risk of the total operation through pooling of independent risks.

Given that a typical surplus-spending unit's surplus funds are relatively small, it cannot diversify its portfolio of direct financial securities because of the large fixed transactions costs of making each individual financial transaction. Consequently, its portfolio is subject to considerable risk. A financial intermediary, on the other hand, can pool together funds from a large number of surplus units and operate on a scale at which it can achieve a vastly increased degree of diversification and hence a substantially reduced risk on the total portfolio of its holding of direct securities for any given level of transaction costs. The total risk on a well-diversified portfolio is lower because first, the capital values of different types of direct securities (for example, corporate bonds and ordinary shares) may move in the opposite directions, unless there is strong positive correlation between them, and reduce the possibility of a major loss (and also gain) of capital value of the portfolio.

Thus the individual surplus units with relatively small savings would normally prefer holding a claim on a diversified portfolio through a financial intermediary to risking their entire savings through the purchase of a very narrow range of direct securities. Furthermore, whereas individual surplus units may not have the time, resources, or the inclination required for a continual acquisition and analysis of the relevant information regarding the credit-worthiness of the various borrowers, financial intermediaries specializing in this business and operating on a substantial scale can find it profitable to devote resources to acquire the regular information and expertise required for the purpose.

Another important fact which financial intermediaries exploit in their operations is that, although the probability distribution and the time profile of an individual economic unit's net claims made on the financial intermediary are likely to be unstable and difficult to predict, the total net claims of a large group of economic units on a financial intermediary tend to be stable and predictable. Also, the total claims on the financial intermediary sought to be realized by economic units over a given interval of time tend to be only a fraction of the total claims held by them against the intermediary at any given moment of time. This enables the financial intermediary to hold primary securities having a somewhat longer maturity period compared to that of the secondary securities offered by it to the surplus units.

Furthermore, financial intermediaries realize major savings in the cost of collecting and analysing relevant information regarding the liquidity requirements of the ultimate lenders and the credit requirement and the credit worthiness of the ultimate borrowers, by specializing in certain restricted types of primary and secondary securities. Although this marginally restricts the scope for diversification, the savings in information costs and the administration of borrower and lender accounts of specialized types is sufficient in such cases to compensate the intermediary for any increase in risk; and diversification within the class of the special type of securities is possible to a considerable extent. This kind of product differentiation also limits, although it does not eliminate, the extent of competition from other financial intermediaries. To strengthen the effect of this kind of product differentiation each type of financial intermediary also tries to provide to its customers a variety of ancillary services, especially attractive to its customers who form a somewhat more homogeneous group on account of the intermediary's specialization in the selected types of primary and/or secondary securities (e.g., tax and investment consultancy service, provision of broker's services, provision of the payments and remittance mechanism, etc.)

Finally, very often, financial intermediaries of specific types get the advantage of government action to reduce the intermediary's risks (for example, through deposit insurance for commercial banks and re-financing facilities for many financial intermediaries) and to protect them from excessive competition.

In these different ways, financial intermediaries greatly strengthen both the asset transmutation effect and the intermediation effect in the economy. The result is that, due to the presence and development of financial intermediaries (1) ultimate borrowers are able to secure loans involving a given risk and maturity at lower interest rates, the liquidity of the secondary securities held by the ultimate lenders is substantially increased, and they are able to obtain a higher yield for a given degree of liquidity of these securities held by them; (2) the transactions costs actually borne by both the ultimate lenders and the ultimate borrowers are substantially reduced; and (3) the maturity pattern of debt in the society corresponds more closely to the preferences of the ultimate borrowers and lenders.

Financial Development and Economic Growth

The connection between financial technology and economic growth is of central relevance to the present paper. We shall discuss this point in some detail here.

As we have seen, financial intermediation (or any financial innovation, for that matter) increases the rates of saving and investment in the economy and makes resources available to those economic units for whom their marginal productivity is higher and who are less averse to risk-taking. The growth of financial intermediaries (and improvement of financial technology in general) therefore plays a vital role in the process of economic growth.

Another important way in which financial intermediation crucially affects the pattern of economic growth in a country, is by influencing the pattern of the use of funds in the economy. Financing of capital expenditures (or even consumer expenditure in some cases) by financial intermediaries may differ in "form, durability, industry, location or any other characteristic",[4] or in type of the user of funds, from what the pattern of capital (or consumer) expenditures would be in the absence of indirect financing. An allocation effect pointed out by R.W. Goldsmith, and particularly relevant to our study of banking in India, is that financial intermediation tends to

> increase the share of capital expenditures made by business enterprises and governments on large projects and to reduce the share of small projects by households. This will, of course, increase the share of the types of structures and equipment and of industries in which large projects are of above average importance and will reduce the share of other types and of other industries.[5]

The reallocation of funds by financial intermediaries is greatly influenced by the economic structure of the country, the size and character of the financial intermediaries, and particularly by the regulation of financial intermediaries by the government. These factors are especially important in determining the share of government, housing, agriculture, large and small business enterprises, agrobased and export industries, consumer durables and foreign borrowers in capital expenditures.[6]

B.J. Moore has best summarised how the lack of an appropriate financial technology hampers economic development:

> In underdeveloped countries savers typically prefer to accumulate tangible assets, for example real estate, precious metals, inventories, jewellery, and foreign exchange, in place of domestic primary and secondary financial assets. This reflects in part traditional experience with inflation, expropriation and default, and in part prejudice, uncertainty and the absence of information. But most importantly it reflects a primitive financial technology. Such wealth-forms represent "low-priority" investment for purposes of growth, yet investors in "high priority" capital projects may be unable to issue primary debt to finance their deficits on terms acceptable to such savers.[7]

With a rudimentary financial system, the requirement of financial balance during the process of economic growth forces one or more of the following readjustments:

1. lower and less efficient programme of capital formation, in the absence of government action;
2. dependence on internal financing of investment programmes by public or private enterprises;
3. government promotion of financial development.

An overview of the economic and financial development of India also shows the aptness of Moore's suggestive observations.

This question of the relation between financial development and economic growth has been examined with great thoroughness by R.W. Goldsmith in his *Financial Structure and Economic Development*. He constructs two related summary measures of the overall financial structure of any economy, first, a ratio of the flow of aggregate new issues during a year to the flow of the gross national product of the economy during the year (called the Aggregate New Issue Ratio or ANIR); and second, a ratio of the stock of all financial assets in the economy on a given date to the stock of all tangible assets or wealth in the economy (excluding human wealth) on the same date (called the Financial Interrelations Ratio, or FIR). FIR may be considered a measure of the overall financial development of the country upto a given date; ANIR may be considered to be a measure of the overall financial activity in the country during a given year. Goldsmith has also developed a number of sectoral and other measures to describe important detailed aspects of the financial structure of the economy, such as the ratio of new issues by nonfinancial sectors to financial intermediaries to the total new issues by nonfinancial sectors (approximately also equal to the ratio of net issues (i.e., gross issues less retirements) by financial inter-mediaries to nonfinancial sectors to the total net issues by the nonfinancial sectors). This ratio has been called the financial intermediation ratio. Similar ratios for any type of financial intermediary such as the banking sector as a whole, or for commercial banks, can also be constructed. Goldsmith has examined the relation of these and other financial ratios to per capita gross national product and to the rate of growth of per capita national product, with the help of data for 35 countries and available time series data of selected countries. His main finding is that the relationship between the measures of financial structure and measures of economic growth is positive but quite loose. The cause and effect relation between financial development and economic growth is difficult to esta-blish empirically, and the mechanism through which financial development might cause economic growth is extremely complex and difficult to verify empirically.

The FIR generally tends to increase over time with an increase in the per capita national product of the country (except for periods of high inflation when FIR tends to fall rapidly), eventually tending to level off. In a cross-section comparison of the FIR for different countries, it is again found that countries with low levels of per capita national product have low levels of FIR, whereas countries with high levels of per capita national product generally have high levels of FIR. India with a per capita national income in 1958 of 67 dollars (at 1958 prices) had an FIR of 0.35 in 1963, whereas the FIR for Great Britain with per capita income of 1085 dollars in 1958 at current prices was 1.71, and that for USA with a per capita income of 2361 dollars in 1958 at current prices was 1.23. Japan with a medium level of per capita income of 285 dollars had an exceptionally high FIR of 1.75, whereas USSR with a some-what high per capita income had an exceptionally low FIR of 0.36. The exceptionally high level of FIR for Japan is due to the very high level of ANIR (0.63, ascompared to 0.20 for USA, 0.21 for Great Britain and 0.07 for India, the highest in the world), representing a high level of borrowing and lending activity compared to national product in that country in recent years. (The high level of FIR for Great Britain compared to that for USA, in spite of the similar value of their ANIR (or the flow ratio) is largely due to the high ratio of income to real wealth in Great Britain compared to the US). The excep-tionally low level of FIR for USSR is due to the low level of ANIR for USSR, representing the minor role played by external financing and financial inter-mediation in that country. (Since the government carries the major responsi-bility for the saving and investment plan the scope for finance as interpreted in the present paper is quite limited in that country.)

These figures for FIR can be better appreciated by keeping in mind the simple considerations that if all the tangible assets in the economy are financed entirely out of own financing, the FIR will be zero, and if all the tangible assets in the economy are financed entirely by the issue of primary securities, the FIR will be equal to unity; whereas if they are entirely financed indirectly through financial intermediaries, the FIR will take the maximum value of 2.[8]

If FIR is correlated with per capita national product, ANIR and especially its component representing the net issues of the nonfinancial sectors, is correlated with the rate of growth of the country's per capita national product; the other major component of ANIR, consisting of the net issues of the financial sector is correlated with per capita national product, increasing with it upto a point but tapering off around a level of 0.10 for high income countries. The relationship between ANIR and the growth-rate of per capita national product is discernible but not close. The reason for this must be that a high ANIR implies a high level of direct and indirect borrowing and lending activity, and hence presumably a high level of saving and investment activity as argued above, but a high level of saving and investment activity does not necessarily require a high level of borrowing and lending activity and a high ANIR. Clearly the possibility of financing economic growth through internal resources of private and public enterprises and/or through taxation and government investment always exists.

Commercial Banks and Economic Growth

So far we have been discussing the relationship of financial intermediation in general (or financial innovation for that matter) with economic growth. Needless to say our discussion also applies to the narrower question of the relationship between growth of banking and economic growth in a country. We shall in this section make a few specific observations on this narrower subject of the relationship between banking and economic growth.

An important finding from the Goldsmith study on the role of commercial (deposit) banks during the process of economic growth is worth noting here. It has been observed by Goldsmith that although the share of commercial banks in the net issues of all financial institutions has generally remained high (around 40 per cent), taking all nonsocialist countries together, it has tended to increase in the early stages of economic growth, and later declined to a level of 35 per cent as other financial institutions grew. Also, the share of commercial banks in the net issues of financial institutions for less developed nonsocialist

countries has remained substantially higher than that for the developed nonsocialist countries; even for the less developed nonsocialist countries as a group, this share has declined considerably with economic growth (from about 71 per cent during 1881–1900 to about 48 per cent during 1949–63).[9]

For India, the net issues of financial institutions as a percentage of GNP has increased from 0.41 during 1901–13 to 1.71 during 1930–38 to 3.45 during 1949–63. Compared to India, the net issues of financial institutions as a percentage of GNP for the period 1949–63 for Great Britain has been 8.56, for USA 9.57, and for Japan 16.68. The net issues of commercial banks as percentage of GNP for India has increased from 0.20 during 1930–38 to 1.01 during 1949–63. By implication, the share of commercial banks in the net issues of financial institutions for India has increased from 11.6 per cent in 1930–38 to 29.2 per cent in 1949–63.

According to the data on financial flows in the Indian economy published by the Reserve Bank of India, the total gross annual lending/borrowing in the Indian economy increased from Rs. 1,763 crores in 1961–62 to Rs. 5,151 crores in 1970–71.[10] Total gross annual lending/borrowing in the Indian economy increased from 11 per cent of GNP at current prices in 1961–62 to a little over 13 per cent of GNP at current prices in 1970–71, thus indicating an increase in the total financial activity in the country during the past decade.[11] Of this, gross borrowing of the financial sector increased from 4 per cent of GNP at current prices in 1961–62 to 5.8 per cent of GNP at current prices in 1970–71, indicating a moderate increase in the financial intermediation in the country during the decade. The commercial banks' share of the total gross borrowing increased substantially from 12.87 per cent in 1961–62 to 18.27 per cent in 1970–71. The corresponding share of cooperative banks and credit societies also increased from 4.47 per cent in 1961–62 to 5.45 per cent in 1970–71.

The main distinguishing characteristic of commercial banks is that the bulk of the secondary securities issued by them (i.e., the banks' liabilities), consists of widely accepted means of payments. From the point of view of their role in the process of economic growth this fact has some important implications. First and foremost, a smoothly-functioning payments and remittance mechanism is an essential prerequisite for economic growth, and banks, whether of the modern, joint stock variety or of the indigenous variety, perform this crucial function. Secondly, since the secondary securities of commercial banks consist of means of payments, or its closest substitutes such as time deposits (or savings and fixed deposits in India) they provide the most effective mechanism of mobilizing the temporary surpluses of households, businesses and government to cover the short-term deficits of businesses and government. That is, even though taking the year as a whole, the rate of net saving is low, it is possible that during some part of the year the rate of saving is quite high, and these savings can be channelized through the banking mechanism to finance short-term investments during the same period. As the secondary securities issued by the commercial banks are generally acceptable as means of payments, even funds awaiting expenditure (as well as temporarily surplus funds) may be held in the form of bank deposits. Thus only a negligible or no loss of liquidity, and generally no post-ponement of current consumption is involved on the part of the lender-depositor of a commercial bank. Lending to a commercial bank generally involves what B.J. Moore referes to as "convenience" waiting. This implies that even when the national income and aggregate saving are low, some short-term investment is possible because of the presence of commercial banks. Hence the particularly important role played by commercial banks in mobilizing savings in the early stages of economic development of the country. As economic growth takes place, other financial institutions expand and aggregate savings increase simulta-neously, leading to a decline in the relative importance of commercial banks. Thrift institutions such as cooperative banks, small-savings schemes, etc., insurance organizations and mortgage banks play an important role in this second stage.

From this discussion about commercial banks, the reader might get the impression that since the commercial banks mobilize only temporarily surplus funds, they can make only short-term investment or investment in working capital. As a general statement, however, this would be a misleading proposition. For example, in the above example, commercial banks can make fresh loans for longer term than one year if they can induce their depositors to hold their increased deposits with them for a longer period than one year, i.e., if they can induce the depositors to increase their rate of saving for the year as a whole, or if they can be assured adequate re-finance from the Central Bank.

Early History of the Indian Banking System

The beginning of banking on modern lines in India dates back to 1806 when the Bank of Calcutta was established. By the East India Company Charter of 1809, this bank was converted into a Presidency Bank, renamed the Bank of Bengal with 20 per cent of its share capital supplied by the Company, and empowered with a right of note issue. Two other Presidency banks, the Bank of Bombay and the Bank of Madras were established under the Charters of 1840 and 1843 with a similar support from the East India Company and a similar right of note issue. The three Presidency banks continued to possess the right of note issue until 1862 when this right was taken over by the Government of India. The Government of India also withdrew financial support to the share capital of the Presidency banks in 1876. The Presidency banks were later amalgamated in 1921 to form the Imperial Bank of India, which acted as a quasi-Central bank until the establishment of the Reserve Bank of India, and operated as a bankers' bank and a banker to Government, providing remittance and clearance facilities to banks and the public, and undertaking a statutory obligation for a programme of branch expansion. The Imperial Bank was taken over by the Government of India in 1955 and set up as the State Bank of India, with special responsibilities for the development of rural branches and the provision of agricultural credit.

In 1870, there were in all 8 commercial banks of which there were 5 Indian joint stock banks (including the 3 Presidency banks) and 3 exchange banks which had their head office outside India and which financed the bulk of the country's foreign trade. The total deposits of the commercial banks were Rs. 12.49 crores, of which Rs. 11.83 crores were deposits with the Presidency banks and Rs. 0.52 crores deposits with the Exchange banks.[12]

By 1935, the Indian banking system had developed considerably. There were in existence by then, 101 Indian joint-stock banks and 17 exchange banks, 12,054 cooperative societies and 12,926 post office savings banks. The total deposits of all commercial banks (including the Exchange banks) had grown by 1935 to Rs. 245.01 crores (of which Rs.76.18 crores were the deposits with the Exchange Banks). In the same year the total deposits with cooperative societies amounted to Rs. 46.94 crores, and deposits with the post office savings banks amounted to Rs. 67.25 crores.[13]

The year 1935 is a landmark in the history of Indian banking. In that year, the Reserve Bank of India was established to act as the Central Bank in India. Although the Reserve Bank was constituted as a shareholders' bank with the Government holding only 4.5 per cent of its shares, the Act incorporated statutory provisions to safeguard the public interest. The Reserve Bank of India was nationalized in 1949 and the Government acquired all the shares of the Bank.

Besides the traditional functions of a Central Bank, namely, acting as a note-issuing authority, bankers' bank and banker to Government, the Reserve Bank of India has been made responsible for the supervision and regulation of banking, and for the promotion and development of a suitable financial infrastructure in the country.

Structural Changes in the Indian Banking System Since Independence

The period since Independence saw a rapid and varied development of banking in India, in terms of the magnitude and the pattern of deposit mobilization by banks, the magnitude and the character of credit dispersal by banks, the extent and nature of banking services, and in terms of a variety of institutional changes designed to strengthen the operation of banking in India and/or aiming at adapting the banking system to the special needs of the country's economic development.

The most striking change which the Indian banking system underwent over the years was a substantial reduction in the number of banking companies, through a process of mergers and amalgamations among banks actively initiated and encouraged by the Reserve Bank of India, with the object of weeding out financially weak banking units. The number of banks declined from 566 at the end of June 1951 to 83 at the end of June 1974.[14] The number of scheduled banks[15] declined from 92 in 1951 to 70 in 1968 and then increased to 74 in 1974, but the truly remarkable decline in the number of banks was in respect of the nonscheduled banks, viz., from 474 in 1951 to 9 in 1974 (figures for end of June for each year), indicating a decrease in the number of banks which could be considered to be financially less sound and of a suboptimal size. The reduction in the number of banks, however, did not constitute a curtailment in the extent of banking services available. Indeed, the number of banking offices in India increased fourfold, from 4,151 in 1951 to 16,936 in 1974 (and fivefold to 21,220 in 1976).[16] The population per banking office declined from 87,000 in 1951 to 32,000 in 1974 (and 26,000 in 1976). There has been a deliberate extension of banking services to hitherto unbanked centres and to rural areas (centres with a population less than 10,000).[17]

Another important development was that as the Indian banks increased their banking operations, the relative importance of foreign banks in the overall banking business in the country declined. Although the number of foreign banks in the country declined only slightly from 15 in 1951 to 14 in 1974, the share of deposits with foreign banks in total bank deposits declined from 19.22 per cent in December 1951 to 6.75 per cent in December 1974. The share of foreign banks' advances in the total bank advances fell even more rapidly, from 28 per cent in December 1951 to 6.5 per cent in December 1974.

Over the years, the deposits mobilized and the credit disbursed by commercial banks have both grown quite rapidly. The total deposits (i.e., demand and time deposits) with commercial banks in India (including the Indian scheduled banks, foreign banks, nonscheduled banks), increased from Rs. 832.14 crores in 1951 to Rs. 11,605.4 crores in 1974, representing an annual compound growth-rate of 12.12 per cent. Over the same period, commercial bank advances (including loans, cash credits and overdrafts and bills discounted and purchased), increased at a slightly faster rate, from Rs. 542.96 crores in 1951 to Rs. 8,004.59 crores in 1974, or by 12.43 per cent per year, compounded every year. As the advances-to-deposit ratio of the banks so increased, from 65.2 percent in 1951 to 68.9 per cent in 1974, they squeezed their cash-reserves to deposits ratio, which fell from 11.1 per cent in 1951 to 6.9 per cent in 1974. (If the banks' balances with other banks on the current account are included in their total cash, the cash-to-deposit ratio shows a decline from 12.9 per cent in 1951 to 8.2 per cent in 1974.) The banks also reduced investments in Government and other securities: their ratio to total deposits from 40.7 per cent in 1951 to 33.4 per cent in 1974. The decline in the banks' investment ratio was of course limited on account of the liquidity requirement stipulated by the Reserve Bank of India (which stood at 25 per cent of total demand and time liabilities upto 1964, and has since been increased upto 33 per cent in 1974). The cash reserve ratio of the banks now appears to have stabilized at between 6 and 7 per cent It therefore seems as though the future increase in bank advances would depend more than before on the increase in bank deposits and Reserve Bank credit to scheduled banks.

As the total bank advances increased, the character of these advances also tended to alter somewhat. These changes mainly consisted of a change in the average period of bank loan, a change in the pattern of bank advances by purpose and by security, and an emphasis on different types of bank advances. The average period of bank advances tended to increase over the priod, especially by the "rolling over" of the banks' short-term loans from year to year.[19] According to a Reserve Bank survey of commercial bank advances conducted in April 1962, 14 per cent of the banks' outstanding advances to industry were medium-term advances, and of these, 42 per cent represented short-term credit rolled over more than one year. Loans originally sanctioned for a period exceeding one year amounted to about 8 per cent of banks' total outstanding advances in April 1962. However this percentage had not changed even by March 1968. No data is available in the March 1968 survey of bank advances regarding the magnitude of short-term bank-credit rolled over.[20]

What is more important, the pattern of bank advances has changed considerably over the years. The share of bank credit going to industry has increased substantially, from 34 per cent in March 1951 to 64.3 per cent in March 1967; while over this period, the share of bank credit going to commerce has declined from 36 per cent to 19.4 per cent, that of bank credit going to the financial sector has declined from 12.7 per cent to 3.6 per cent, and that of bank credit going to the personal sector has declined from 6.8 per cent to 4.2 per cent. The share of agriculture in the total bank credit remained roughly constant around 2 per cent over the period.[21] With the deliberate encouragement given ·to the provision of bank credit to agriculture, small-scale industry, exports and other priority sectors, this trend has been somewhat reversed in the years since the adoption of the policy of Social Control of banks in January 1968; this reversal of the trend being further intensified after the nationalization of 14 major banks in July 1969. The share of scheduled commercial bank credit going to agriculture and allied activities which stood at 2.2 per cent at the end of March 1968, had already risen to 5.2 per cent in June

1969, and it increased farther to 8.9 per cent by the end of June 1974. Correspondingly, the share of industry in the total bank credit which had risen to 65 per cent by the end of March 1968 went down to 58.4 per cent by the end of June 1974. Between June 1969 and June 1974, the share of small scale industries in the total bank credit going to industry increased from 6.9 per cent to 12.6 per cent.[22]

Along with the pattern of commercial bank credit, the commercial bank deposits also show a change in character, in terms of the shifting proportions of current deposits, savings deposits and fixed deposits; in terms of the ownership of deposits; and in terms of the regional and the rural-urban distribution of bank deposits.

Indeed some of the changes in the pattern of bank advances must be traceable to changes in the pattern of bank deposits. The increase in term lending by banks, if only through rolling over short-term credit, and also perhaps the increase in the banks' overall credit-to-deposit ratio should have been made possible due to the increase in the proportion of time deposits (i.e., fixed deposits plus a part of the savings deposits) in their total deposits. Between the last Friday of December 1951 to December 1974, the share of time deposits in the commercial bank total deposits increased from 37 per cent to about 59 per cent.

Of the total demand and time deposits of commercial banks, the share of business deposits fell from 35.2 per cent in December 1951 to 22.9 per cent in March 1968, while that of the personal sector increased correspondingly from 46.5 per cent in December 1951 to 57.3 per cent in March 1968. As the personal sector holds a considerably larger proportion of its total deposits in the form of fixed deposits (34.0 per cent in December 1951 and 51.9 per cent in March 1968) than the business sector (22.1 per cent in December 1951 and 34.5 per cent in March 1968), this has naturally also resulted in an increase in the share of fixed deposits in total deposits. The share of fixed deposits in the total deposits further increased as both the personal and the business sectors showed an increasing preference for fixed deposits over time.[23]

The change in the regional and the rural-urban distribution of bank advances and bank deposits which particularly came about in the wake of the nationalization of major scheduled banks, has been discussed in the following section on the nationalization of banks.

Institutional Changes Affecting the Indian Banking System

Over the years since Independence, the banking system in India has been subjected to many institutional changes designed to adapt it to the special requirements of its economic development. Some of these, such as the establishment of the Deposit Insurance Corporation in January (which by 1970 covered deposits of upto Rs. 10,000 per depositor and now, since 1976, covers deposits of upto Rs. 20,000 per depositor and which by 1968 also covered the deposits in the state cooperative banks, central cooperative banks and primary cooperative banks with paid-up capital and reserves larger than Rs. 1 lakh).[24] The expansion of bank offices into rural and semi-urban areas, the general strengthening of banks through mergers and amalgamations, building up of the banks, capital reserves through transfer of a part of their profits (especially upto 1963) undoubtedly led to an increased proportion of saving flowing through the banking sector, and perhaps also to a strengthening of the public's savings habits. Similarly, the purpose of the Bill Market Scheme introduced in 1951 was to permit banks to secure accommodation from the Reserve Bank against their cash credits, overdrafts and advances by enabling them to convert these into usance promissory notes; and, therefore, it really increased the liquidity of bank advances from the point of view of the banks, and aided the smooth functioning of the banking system. This probably influenced the total flow of credit from banks more than its pattern. The new Bill Market Scheme, initiated in November 1970, introduced the re-discounting of trade bills evidencing sale of goods. This measure may be expected to lead to an increase in bank credit extended through purchase or discounting of bills relative to cash credits which have thus far been more common, and apart from this change in the pattern of bank credit, it would have a more significant effect on the overall quantum of bank credit. However, apart from these few measures which probably increased the banks' willingness to extend credit, most of the other institutional changes affecting the Indian banking system have been primarily designed to influence the purposewise pattern of bank credit. The majority of important institutional changes were designed towards directing the flow of credit through banks to socially-desired channels.

Prior to nationalization of the major scheduled banks, the Reserve Bank's policy towards promotion of agricultural credit was in terms of providing substantial re-finance at concessional interest rates for credit to agriculture, especially by cooperative banks, but also by commercial banks.[25] In 1956, the Reserve Bank established two funds, viz., the National Agricultural Credit (Long Term Operations) Fund and the National Agricultural Credit (Stabilization) Fund. The former was set up with a view to providing medium- and long-term finance to the state cooperative banks and to the Central Land Mortgage banks, either directly or through loans to the State Governments for this purpose. The latter fund was meant for converting the short-term borrowings of the State Cooperative banks from the Reserve Bank, into medium-term credit when the repayment of these loans became impossible on account of widespread drought, floods, famines, etc. The total amount to the credit of the National Agricultural Credit (Long Term Operations) Fund by end-June 1975 was Rs. 334.00 crores. Loans amounting to Rs. 53.8 crores were made out of this Fund during 1974–75, and the loans from this Fund outstanding in June 1975 were Rs. 171.3 crores. Total amount to the credit of the National Agricultural Credit (Stabilization) Fund by end-June 1975 was Rs. 140 crores. Depending upon the climatic conditions in the country, the amount of loan extended from this Fund fluctuates from year to year. In 1974–75, the amount of loan

from this Fund was as high as Rs. 106.9 crores as against Rs. 22.5 crores in the previous year.[26] A major step in the promotion of investment credit for agriculture was the setting up in 1963 of the Agricultural Re-finance Corporation as a subsidiary of the Reserve Bank. Obtaining funds by issuing debentures guaranteed by the Central Government; or by borrowing on a short-term basis from the Reserve Bank of India or the Central Government or by accepting term deposits from Central and State Governments local authorities, the State cooperative banks, central land development banks, the scheduled commercial banks, etc.; or by raising a foreign currency loan, it provides re-finance on a medium-term or long-term basis to agricultural investment schemes financed by land development banks, state cooperative banks, scheduled commercial banks and State Governments. The cumulative number of schemes receiving assistance from Agricultural Re-finance Corporation till 1974–75 rose to 2,053, involving a financial outlay of Rs. 1,007.2 crores; of this amount, its own commitment was Rs. 877.4 crores.[27] In July 1969, the All India Rural Credit Review Committee recommended that efforts relating to the provision of agricultural credit should not be concentrated on the cooperative banks alone and that the commercial banks also, especially the nationalized banks, should vigorously and intensively take up the responsibility of providing agricultural credit. Following this change of emphasis, the commercial banks have stepped up their credit to agricultural and allied activities substantially, a point already made. It must be emphasised that the bulk of agricultural credit still comes from the cooperative and land development banks. In 1973–74 as in 1968–69, 64 per cent of total credit for agricultural and allied activities came from the cooperative and land development banks; between 1968–69 and 1973–74, the share of commercial banks in the total credit for agricultural and allied activities increased from 12 per cent to 20 per cent, while that of Government went down from 25 per cent to 16 per cent.[28]

As pointed out earlier, credit to industry, both short-term and medium-term (even if by simply rolling over short-term credit), formed a major part of commercial bank credit in India (being as high as 58.4 per cent of total bank credit in June 1974, as indicated earlier). Re-finance for this has been available to banks from the Reserve Bank in the form of purchase and re-discounting of commercial bills held by the banks, and in the form of loans and advances against Government securities and other eligible paper. Apart from the re-finance from the Reserve Bank which strictly is not available for medium-term purposes, re-finance for short-to-medium term industrial credit has been available to commercial banks from the Industrial Development Bank of India, which was established in 1964 with a view to strengthening the provision of medium-term industrial credit in India either through the banks or directly, and which later in 1976 was made into an independent apex institution for this kind of credit. IDBI outstanding advances to scheduled banks, state cooperative banks and other financial institutions stood at Rs. 93.65 crores at the end of June 1974, which represented 19.1 per cent of IDBI's total assets, 21.4 per cent of the commercial banks' total term credit to industry, and 18.8 per cent of the commercial banks' total export credit to industry at that time.[29]

Export credit has received special attention from the Reserve Bank, the Industrial Development Bank of India, and the Government of India, over a long period of time. Export credit forms a fair proportion of commercial bank credit to industry, being 10.6 per cent of it in June 1974.[30] Apart from a ceiling on the interest rate on export credit by banks (compensated partly by a Government of India subsidy of $1\frac{1}{2}$ per cent to banks against their export credit, the provision of re-finance to commercial banks at concessional interest rates by the Reserve Bank of India for short-term export credit and by IDBI for medium-term export credit, and the exemption of commercial bank export credit by the Reserve Bank of India from measures of credit control), promotion of export credit by commercial banks has benefited from financial innovations promoted for this purpose. A noteworthy institutional change in this context is the setting up of the Export Risks Insurance Corporation in 1957 which offered insurance to exporters against default on the part of foreign importers for various reasons. In 1964, this Corporation was renamed the Export Credit and Guarantee Corporation and its functions increased to include providing guarantees to banks for export credit extended by them, in addition to extending insurance to exporters as before. The value of risk covered during the year 1974–75 was Rs. 2,113 crores, of which the value of shipments covered under the policies amounted to Rs. 359 crores (or 10.7 per cent of India's exports during the year), and financial guarantees amounted to Rs. 1,753 crores (or $3\frac{1}{2}$ times the commercial bank export credit to industry in June 1974).[31]

The risk of default had prevented the growth of bank credit to small industrial units. To protect banks against this risk, a Credit Guarantee Organization was set up in July 1960 which guarantees credit by banks and other financial institutions to small industrial units, upto 75 per cent of the amount defaulted. Guarantee cover can be purchased by the credit institutions at a fee of 1/10 per cent per year on the total limits sanctioned (on outstanding credit in the case of term loans) to eligible borrowers, without applying for guarantees against individual credit limits. Originally, the scheme applied mainly to small units involved in manufacturing, processing and preservation of goods. In January 1971, the Reserve Bank promoted a new public limited company called the Credit Guarantee Corporation of India Limited, with an expanded credit guarantee scheme covering transport operators, retail traders, self-employed persons, professionals, other business enterprises, and small farmers as well. In December 1974, the total credit facilities guaranteed by the Credit Guarantee Corporation amounted to Rs. 530 crores or about 40 per cent of scheduled commercial bank credit to small industry and other priority sectors at that time.[32, 33]

Social Control and Nationalization of Major Commercial Banks

The institutional change which most profoundly affected banking in India was the introduction of social control over banks in December 1967 and later, the nationalization of major scheduled commercial banks on 19 July 1969.

Major deficiencies of the commercial banking system in India which provided economic justification for nationalization of major commercial banks were:

1. the dominance of the banks' policies by a small number of large business houses, who contributed equity capital amounting only to a small fraction of the banks' total resources;

2. the inadequate flow of bank credit into socially desirable channels in spite of the various schemes initiated by the Reserve Bank for this purpose; and

3. the unbalanced expansion of banking facilities, with little or quite inadequate growth of banking in the less developed parts of the country and in rural areas, despite the dent made in this problem by the branch expansion programme of the State Bank of India. In addition, there was also the political-economic reason for the nationalization of banks, namely acquiring direct control over their huge investible resources for financing public sector investments and for regulating their flow into the various private sector lines. This was the idea of controlling the "commanding heights" of the economy.

Monopoly control of banks by large business houses naturally meant that credit flowed into industrial units favoured by them and credit flow into other channels was inhibited. Even if the monopoly control of banks had not existed, the vastly unequal regional distribution of industries and the unequal distribution of wealth and production-risk among potential borrowing units would necessitate the institution of various credit-guarantee schemes or other ways of subsidising credit to backward regions or weaker sections. Monopoly ownership of credit institutions by large business houses only makes it more iniquitous for the state to be subsidising credit institutions. (It is for this reason that a reliance on social control of banks would

have eventually been unacceptable). Furthermore, even in the absence of monopoly control of financial intermediaries, they can still be expected to channelize investible funds to areas and sectors with high marginal productivity and low risk (from their point of view). These areas and sectors may not necessarily represent investment allocations with the highest social rates of return, or may not represent investment allocations required to fulfil objectives of society other than that of maximizing total production or its growth rate—objectives such as changing the distribution of incomes and wealth, or achieving a balanced regional development, or promoting employment-intensive industrial development.

What has been the performance of banking after nationalization of the major banks?

First, a few facts relating to this question may be mentioned here briefly:[34]

1. The share of priority sectors consisting of agriculture, small-scale industry, exports and other priority sectors (i.e., retail trade, small business, professionals and self-employed and education) in total credit (excluding food advances), of the scheduled commercial banks increased from 22.3 per cent in June 1969 to 37.8 per cent in December 1975. Public sector banks whose credit to priority sectors was 23.2 per cent of their total credit in June 1969, have channelized 40.8 per cent of their credit in December 1975 to priority sectors. During this period, the priority sector advances of public sector banks grew at the compound rate of 27.08 per cent per year whereas those of private sector banks grew at the compound rate of 13.77 per cent per year.

2. Scheduled commercial banks' credit to the public sector has increased from 8.6 per cent of their total credit in June 1968, to 18.3 per cent of their total credit in June 1975.

3. The share of bank advances disbursed in rural areas (i.e., centres with a population of less than 10,000) to total advances by scheduled commercial banks has increased from 1.5 per cent in June 1969 to 5.9 per cent in June 1975; that of semi-urban areas (or centres with a

population of between 10,000 to 100,000) has increased from 11.3 per cent in June 1969 to 15.0 per cent in June 1975. The share of metropolitan centres (i.e., of centres with a population of 1 million and above) in bank advances has dropped from 67.2 per cent to 55.0 per cent during the same period.

4. The share of rural areas in the total deposits of scheduled commercial banks has increased from 3.1 per cent in June 1969 to 8.1 per cent in June 1975. The share of semi-urban and urban areas has changed marginally. The share of the metropolitan areas has come down slightly from 49.0 per cent to 45.0 per cent during this period. Thus there has been considerable deposit mobilization in the rural areas since the nationalization of banks.

5. Considering the percentage distribution of the scheduled commercial bank deposits by states between December-end 1968 and December-end 1974, the share of Maharashtra, Gujarat and the Union Territories (including Delhi) went down respectively from 24.8 to 21.6 per cent, from 8.5 to 7.4 per cent, and from 11.5 to 10.9 per cent. The percentage share of total deposits for Andhra Pradesh, Bihar, and Tamil Nadu showed moderate increases, while those of other states showed marginal changes. As Maharashtra, Gujarat, and the Union Territories rank among the five states with the highest per capita Net Domestic Product in 1968–69, we could conclude that there was some trend towards mobilizing deposits in the relatively less developed states, although this trend might simply be a reflection of relatively increased deposit mobilization in the nonmetropolitan centres.

6. The distribution of bank credit by states showed a more significant change between December-end 1968 and December-end 1974 than did the distribution of deposits. The shares of Maharashtra, West Bengal and Union Territories (including Delhi) in total credit by scheduled commercial banks declined substantially, from 31.2 to 26.8 per cent in the case of Maharashtra, from 21.2 to 15.3 per cent in the case of West Bengal, and from 9.1 to 8.5 per cent in the Union Territories. All the other states showed increases in

their shares of total credit extended by scheduled commercial banks in India. In particular, states such as Andhra Pradesh, Karnataka, and Uttar Pradesh showed significant increases. Again there is some indication of increased credit flowing to low income states although, especially as in the case of West Bengal, this might just be a sign of relatively larger credit flowing to nonmetropolitan centres.

7. There has been a phenomenal increase in the number of branch offices of the scheduled commercial banks since June 1969. The number of commercial bank branch offices increased from 8,262 to 21,220 between June 1969 and June 1976, or at an average rate of about 1,850 bank offices per year. Compared with this, between December 1961 and June 1969, bank offices expanded at the average rate of less than 435 bank offices per year.

8. The average number of population per bank office came down progressively from 65,000 (1961 Census) in June 1969 to 26,000 (1971 Census) at the end of June 1976. There has been an even more marked decline in the population per bank office for a large number of relatively less-developed states, for example, Assam, Bihar, Jammu and Kashmir, Madhya Pradesh, Nagaland, Orissa, Tripura, and Uttar Pradesh.

9. Great emphasis was laid on the expansion of bank offices in rural centres. Of the total commercial bank offices in India, in December 1964, only 10.37 per cent were in rural areas.[35] The proportion of bank offices in the rural areas had increased to 22.1 per cent upto June 1969. In June 1974, 36.4 per cent of all commercial bank offices in India were located in the rural areas. In June 1976, this percentage declined marginally to 36.2. We can state from this that although the growth of rural branches of commercial banks was already significant in the years just before nationalization of banks, it was greatly stepped up during the years immediately after nationalization, but now appears to be slowing down relatively. According to the Reserve Bank's Annual Report for 1975–76, this decline is attributable mainly to the fact that a large number of rural centres with

reasonable banking potential were already covered by the banks' branches.

10. There was particular emphasis on opening bank branches in hitherto un-banked centres. The number of offices opened in unbanked centres was 46.8 per cent of the total increase in bank offices between July 1969 and June 1976.

In the wake of the trend towards greater regional balance in the development of banking, and a greater flow of credit into priority sectors, a few important questions relating to the working of public sector banks in India should be given some consideration.

Have priority sector loans increased the default risk of public sector banks? Has nationalization of banks made them indifferent to cost considerations and operational efficiency? Has there been an over-expansion of commercial bank branches in general, and of commercial bank branches in rural and unbanked centres, in the sense that the increase in costs entailed by this branch expansion programme greatly cuts into the banks' profits? Finally and more generally, how can we ensure the financial soundness of nationalized banks while their operation is directed towards meeting socially deter-mined objectives?

There is not much information available on the recoveries of priority sector loans. The Credit Guarantee Corporation which insures commercial banks' credit to small industries (and recently, to the remaining priority sectors including agriculture but excluding exports), had guaranteed credit facilities for an amount of Rs. 636.13 crores as on the last Friday of June 1975, while the claims under the Guarantee scheme upto April 1976 came to Rs. 1.27 crores. Considering that the Credit Guarantee Corporation undertakes to reimburse 75 per cent of the amount of guaranteed credit which is defaulted, the default rate on these loans appears to be about 1/4 per cent.[36]

Considering the cost and efficiency aspects of Indian banks since nationaliza-tion,[37] we find that between December 1969 and December 1973, establishment expenses (which include salaries and allowances of employees), and the other working expenses increased, both relative to the number of bank offices and to the number of bank employees, as well as relative to total deposits and total bank credit. Establishment expenses per bank employee increased from Rs. 6,400 per year in December 1969 to Rs. 9,200 per year in December 1973, or by 43.7 per cent. Over the same period (between 1969–70 to 1973–74), the All-India Consumer Price Index Number for Urban Non-manual Employees increased from 167 to 221, or by 32.3 per cent. The number of employees per bank office fell from 25 in December 1969 to 20 in December 1973. However, since between these dates, the share of rural branches in the total number of commercial bank branches increased from around 22 per cent to around 32 per cent, and since the number of employees in a typical rural branch may be expected to be substantially less than 20 (the average number of employees per bank office in December 1973), it follows that the number of employees per bank office in urban centres must have increased considerably over this period. Similarly, bonus as percentage of total profits as well as bonus per employee have both increased considerably in recent years, when the ratio of capital and reserves to total deposits for the banking system has reached the precariously low level of 1.3 per cent (in 1973), and there is an urgent need to strengthen the reserve base of the banks by transferring a larger share of profits for this purpose.

We conclude by making a few general suggestions as to how the nationalized banks might increase their financial soundness. First, it is undesirable to think that the risks taken by the nation-alized banks in providing increased flow of credit to the priority sectors, or any increased costs due to rural expansion of bank offices which mobilize smaller depo-sits per bank office (whether the establish-ment and other working expenses of rural branches are correspondingly lower is not known due to lack of separate cost data for rural branches) will somehow be covered by the general revenues of the State. But it is necessary to build up adequate reserves for covering these risks and losses, so that the burden on the general exchequer is exactly known and properly provided for. Furthermore, it is necessary to keep this burden to the minimum through a business-like management of banking units. In order to achieve this, banks may be instructed to fulfil pre-specified targets in respect of socially desirable credit and branch expansion programmes, selecting from among them those with the lowest overall risk to the bank (incurring the lowest cost associated with these selected programmes and building up a special reserve fund or joining a suitable credit guarantee or insurance scheme to cover this risk). For the remainder of the business, each bank should follow a policy of maximizing the rate of return on its capital, consistent with bearing an overall risk on this business in tune with its capital and reserves position (and over time, adjusting the capital and reserves position to enable it to take a desired level of risk). Finally, there is need for some organization, perhaps on the lines of the National Credit Council, which would continuously evaluate the targets set for the nationalized banks in terms of their relationship with the ultimate social objectives of achieving greater production, more equitable distribution of income and wealth, more balanced regional development, and increased employment.

REFERENCES

1. See B.J. Moore, *Introduction to the Theory of Finance* (New York: The Free Press, 1968), p. 17.
2. Ibid., p. 16.
3. Ibid., pp. 98–100; and L.W. Chandler, *The Economics of Money and Banking* (Harper & Row: New York, 1969), pp. 65–68.
4. R.W. Goldsmith, *Financial Structure and Economic Development* (Yale University Press, 1969), p. 395.
5. Ibid., p. 399.
6. Ibid.
7. Moore, *Theory of Finance*, p. 103.
8. Ibid., p. 106.
9. Goldsmith, *Financial Structure and Economic Development*, p. 264.
10. *Reserve Bank of India Bulletin,* March 1965, July 1969 and August 1975. The figures for 1961–62 and 1970–71 presented in this paragraph are based on disaggregated flow of funds tables being compiled by Mr. S.B. Swami from the original Reserve Bank of India data.
11. These figures, the reader will notice, correspond to the Aggregate New Issue Ratio discussed above. Goldsmith's estimate for ANIR for India was 7 per cent for 1963. The difference is mainly due to the difference in the treatment of the rest of the world sector in Goldsmith. Goldsmith uses the net foreign balance on the current account, or the net borrowing by the rest of the world, in the sense of the difference between the net acquisition of foreign issues (i.e., gross issues less retirement) by domestic units and the net acquisition of domestic issues by foreign units, whereas the figure in the text uses only the net acquisition of foreign issues by domestic units. See Goldsmith, *Financial Structure and Economic Development*, p. 74.
12. Moore, *Theory of Finance*, p. 171.
13. The figures in this and the next paragraph are taken from the Reserve Bank of India, *Banking and Monetary Statistics*, vol. I, Bombay, various years.
14. Government of India, *The Report of the Banking Commission* (New Delhi, 1972), p. 34, and Government of India, *India, 1976* (New Delhi, 1976). Apart from these, the data presented in this section have been taken from various issues of *Reserve Bank of India Monthly Bulletin,* Bombay and of Reserve Bank of India, *Report on Currency and Finance*, Bombay. Specific references are given only where it is considered necessary.
15. A scheduled bank is a banking company, or since 1966, a State Cooperative Bank, with paid-up capital and reserves of an aggregate value not less than Rs. 5 lakhs, included by the Reserve Bank of India in the second schedule to the Reserve Bank of India Act on being satisfied that the bank's operations are not being carried in a manner detrimental to the interests of its depositors. The scheduled banks are entitled to the facility of obtaining accommodation from the Reserve Bank of India.
16. Reserve Bank of India, *Annual Report and Trend and Progress of Banking in India,* 1975–76 (Bombay, 1976), pp. 47–48. Figures are at the end of June of each year.
17. Reserve Bank of India, *Annual Report and Trend and Progress of Banking in India,* 1975–76, p. 45.
18. Including investments in Government and other approved securities for Indian and foreign scheduled commercial banks and only the investment in Government securities for nonscheduled banks. Compiled from *Reserve Bank of India Bulletin* 1952 (Bombay, 1953) and *Banking Statistics, Basic Statis-*

tical Returns (Bombay, December 1974).

19. S.K. Basu, *A Review of Current Banking Theory and Practice* (Calcutta: Macmillan, 1971), pp. 283–86.

20. Reserve Bank of India, *Annual Report of the Trend and Progress of Banking in India*, 1902, p. 33.

21. *Reserve Bank of India Bulletin* (Bombay, Decembr 1968.

22. Reserve Bank of India, *Report on Currency and Finance*, 1974–75 (Bombay, 1975).

23. Reserve Bank of India, *Report on Currency and Finance*, 1951–52 (Bombay, 1952), pp. 188–89; and *Reserve Bank of India Bulletin*, March 1970 (Bombay, 1970), pp. 389–402.

24. *Reserve Bank of India Working and Functions* (Bombay, 1970), pp. 90–91.

25. It may be noted here that the Reserve Bank of India provides substantial short term accommodation through its normal rediscounting and the "lander of the last resort" credit facilities to cooperative banks as well as to the scheduled commercial banks for financing bona fide trade transactions relating to agricultural commodities (as for other commodities) and for financing seasonal agricultural operations or the marketing of crops.

26. Reserve Bank of India, *Report on Currency and Finance*, 1974–75. .

27. Reserve Bank of India, *Report on Currency and Finance*, 1974–75.

28. S.L. Shetty, "Deployment of Commercial Bank and Other Institutional Credit", *Economic and Political Weekly*, vol. 11, no. 19, 8 May 1976.

29. Reserve Bank of India, *Report on Currency and Finance* 1973-74 and Shetty, "Development of Commercial Bank Credit", p. 704.

30. Shetty, Development of Commercial Bank Credit".

31. Reserve Bank of India, *Report on Currency and Finance*, 1975–76.

32. Reserve Bank of India, *Annual Report* 1975–76, and *Report on Currency and Finance* 1975–76.

33. In a recent article, V.M. Dandekar has argued that all short-term agricultural loans to small farmers by cooperative banks be required to be covered on a compulsory basis by a crop insurance for the amount of loan to be obtained by the borrower, premium for the insurance being deductible by the lending institution at the time of making the loan. He suggests that the scheme could be extended later on to all farmers, to medium and long-term agricultural loans and to agricultural loans made by commercial banks and the state governments. Dandekar has criticised the present arrangement for covering the default risk on agricultural credit through the Credit Guarantee Scheme and the present facilities for converting short-term agricultural loans into medium-term loans in the event of a crop failure (and for the writing off of these loans in the event of successive crop failures) as being inadequate for mobilizing funds on the scale required to cover the considerable risk arising out of the year-to-year fluctuation of agricultural production. See V.M. Dandekar, "Crop Insurance in India", *Economic and Political Weekly*, vol. XI, no. 26, 26 June 1976, pp. A61–A80.

34. Data used in this section are drawn from Reserve Bank of India, *Report on Currency and Finance*, 1975–76, vol. I (Bombay); and Reserve Bank of India, *Statistical Tables Relating to Banks in India* (Bombay, 1969 and 1974). The figures mentioned for June 1975 are provisional.

35. The figures for December 1964 have been worked out from the indexes of banking offices presented in M. Tyagarajan, "Expansion of Commercial Banking, An Assessment", *Economic and Political Weekly*, vol. 10, no. 47, 22 November 1975, pp. 1819–24. The December 1964 percentages are for the last Friday (and not for the last day) of the month. Other percentages are at the end of each month.

36. See Reserve Bank of India, *Report on Currency and Finance*, 1975–76, vol. I, pp. 106–07. However, data on Credit Guarantee Scheme for Small Scale Industries presented in Statement 42 in Vol. II of the same report indicates that the amount of advances under default at the end of June 1976 (Rs. 60 crores) was 3.47 per cent of Guarantees outstanding (Rs. 1726 crores) at the end of June 1975. It has not been possible to mesh the two sets of data. It might also be noted here that the bad and doubtful debts as proportion of total outstanding debt amounted in 1973–74 to 0.60 per cent for the State Cooperative banks, 4.92 per cent for the Central Cooperative banks and 0.74 per cent for Primary Agricultural Credit Cooperatives; the corresponding figures for overdues were 5.79 per cent, 31.03 per cent and 42.01 per cent respectively.

37. The discussion in this paragraph is based on M. Tyagarajan, "Impact of Expansion on Banks' Earnings, Expenses and Profits", *Economic and Political Weekly*, vol. 10, no. 48, 29 November 1975, pp. 1841-47.

15

Inflation and Economic Growth in India

G. C. DORAI

The rapid and persistent decline in the purchasing power of money poses a serious challenge to the economic stability and maintenance of social order in many countries today. While random disturbances emanating from unexpected and infrequent events such as crop failures or wars do affect the value of a nation's monetary unit, such inflationary influences appear to be historical curiosities in the modern world. During the last decade, there has been a continuous and accelerating erosion of the purchasing power of money throughout the world. This includes the currencies of developing countries like India, as well as those of advanced industrial countries like the US. Thus the value of the US dollar declined from a base of 100 in 1965 to 59 in 1975, and the Indian rupee fell from 100 to 42 during the same period.[1] The value of a monetary unit or its purchasing power is defined as the reciprocal of the consumer price index. The median rate of depreciation for industrial developed nations as a group was 4.4 per cent between 1965–70, and this rate roughly doubled to 8.5 per cent for

the years 1970–75. Though the less-developed country group experienced a median rate of decline of only 4.2 per cent for the former 5-year period, their rate of depreciation for the recent quinquennium was 10.3 per cent. Within this broad spectrum, there were wide variations in the rates of depreciation experienced by individual countries. For example, the annual rates of depreciation varied between 5.8 per cent for West Germany and 11.5 per cent for Britain during 1970–75. For the developing country group, the rate ranged between 5.4 per cent for Venezuela and 67.5 per cent for Chile. The rupee's annual rate of depreciation for the period 1965–70 was 6.4, and averaged 10.4 per cent during the 1970–75 period. It should be pointed out that since consumer price indices do not typically reflect the full extent of decline in the value of domestic currencies owing to various forms of formal or informal price controls on consumer goods and services, or subsidised distribution programmes of essential commodities in many countries, the price inflation reflected in these numbers underestimates the true decline in purchasing power. What is apparent is that there has been a marked trend towards accelerating rates of inflation, with scores of countries registering double-digit inflation during the seventies.

Though inflation appears to be a common phenomenon throughout the world, the mechanisms causing the inflationary process and the consequences thereof, vary widely from one country to another. As in other areas of economic analysis, there are different theoretical explanations for the causes of inflation. The impact of inflation on macroeconomic variables such as production, employment, economic growth and balance of payments depends on the nature and characteristics of the inflationary process. During the last quarter-century, India has witnessed differential rates of inflation and economic growth. Our study brings into focus the relationship between movements in the aggregate price level and the growth performance of the Indian economy.

The analysis is divided into five parts. A succinct review of some theories of inflation is provided in the first. Since no single theoretical explanation can fit the actual experience of a particular country because of differences in the economic, social and political framework within which the inflationary process operates, there are compelling arguments for an eclectic approach to the problem. Apart from differences in the causal factors, the economic policy instruments available to deal with inflation, and their efficacy, differ from one country to another. Such constraints account for the relative success or otherwise of anti-inflationary policies pursued by different countries at different times.

There is considerable controversy among economists about the role of inflation in generating or retarding economic growth. Besides examining the relationship between the rates of change in the general price level and growth in output experienced by some countries, in the second section we examine the arguments for and against using inflation as a deliberate instrument for accelerating capital formation and economic development. This historical perspective provides a background for the understanding of India's own efforts at promoting rapid economic development by stepping up the rate of investment through deficit financing.

In the third section, the longest and most descriptive part of this essay, a detailed analysis of trends in prices and output during the years 1951–76 is provided. The 25 years covered by the study is divided for convenience into 5-year periods, coinciding with the various five-year plans. This facilitates exposition, and enables us to compare the performance of the successive plans with respect to the movement of various production and price indices. In the subsequent section, the price policy pursued by the Indian government to moderate rising inflationary pressures is discussed. The final section provides a summary of the study, and concludes with some observations which seem relevant in dealing with inflation in a developing economy.

I

Theoretical Considerations: An Overview

Inflation occurs when the aggregate price level rises. Starting from a position of equilibrium between aggregate demand and supply, if the rate of increase of monetary demand exceeds that of the growth-rate of production (excluding imports), an imbalance is introduced into the system. Such excess money demand manifests itself in a rising price level for goods and services. When an economy has large, unused productive potential, increases in money demand can be translated into higher levels of output and employment without increases in the aggregate price level. Modern income and employment theory draws attention to the possibility of raising the level of resource utilization in an economy by management of aggregate demand. While demand management policies can contribute to a higher rate of capital and labour-force utilization in the short run, such manipulation of aggregate demand may also sow the seeds of inflationary pressures. Recent experience in countries such as the US and Britain shows the limitations of expansionary fiscal and monetary policies to bring about full employment without inflation. While the old "Quantity Theory" approach emphasised the key role of the money supply in explaining the relationship between money and prices in the long run; recent research and thinking on the subject of inflation emphasise the structural features of an economic system as the main contributory cause of the inflationary process.

Assume, for example, that a government, concerned with socially unacceptable rates of unemployment, resorts to budgetary policy to stimulate aggregate demand. Increases in government expenditures, or sizeable tax cuts designed to increase private consumer spending, result in cumulative budget deficits. The financing of these deficits through expansion of bank credit increases the quantity of money. Budgetary stimulation without expansion of the quantity of money would increase the market rates of interest on loanable funds. This would nullify the expansionary budgetary policy if private investment spending is adversely affected by rising interest rates. In any case the increased demand for money brought about by a higher level of economic activity would create a liquidity shortage and push up interest rates, with adverse consequences on private consumer and investment spending, unless the central bank accommodates the expansionary fiscal policy by increasing the quantity of money. Thus, monetary policy is seen to be the handmaiden of fiscal policy in the task of economic expansion. As the level of national income rises, the price level starts to creep up. Although in the initial stages of economic expansion, output and employment respond to the fiscal-monetary stimulus, inelasticities and rigidities in the economic system begin to slow down the recovery as it gathers momentum. As the economy's unused resources are used up, shortages of materials and supply bottlenecks in certain key sectors begin to emerge, pushing up their relative prices. Due to the downward rigidities in wages and prices characteristic of modern industrial societies, the rapidly growing sectors of the economy experience upward pressures on prices without a corresponding fall in prices in other lagging sectors. As the

nation approaches full employment, larger and larger quantities of money may be needed to achieve a given rate of increase in output and employment. This process of monetary expansion creates inflationary expectations throughout the economy.

Although one can visualize a reduction in the budget deficit resulting from increased tax receipts and reduced levels of government spending, the inflationary expectations built up during the process of expansion become difficult to contain. One of the key elements in the inflationary process is the behaviour of labour unions with respect to real wages. If money wage-rates increase faster than the rate of overall productivity growth in the economy (and this seems to happen in periods of rapid economic expansion), unit labour costs begin to rise rapidly, putting further upward pressure on prices. Thus wages and prices begin to chase each other in an upward spiral.

Though for analytical purposes, one may label the forces initiating the inflationary process as "demand pull" or "cost push" monetary expansion plays a crucial role in the inflationary drama. In the ultimate analysis, unless there is a slowdown in the rate of growth of the money supply relative to real output, any anti-inflationary policy can have only limited success. The real dilemma faced by macroeconomic policymakers in today's world is the conflict between the objectives of full employment and price stability. Attempts to mitigate or contain the inflationary effects of fiscal and monetary stimulus through measures such as incomes policies, wage and price controls, exchange rate changes and other types of interventionist policies fail to remedy the situation. They suppress the real forces behind the inflationary pressures in the short run, and exacerbate the basic imbalances between aggregate demand and real output.

The Inflationary Process in India: A Digression

In order to understand the trend in prices in India during the last two-and-a-half decades, it is necessary to analyse broadly some of the features of the Indian economy which make it inflation prone. The analysis of inflation generally applicable to a developed industrial country like the US or UK needs to be modified to take account of the nature and characteristics of a developing economy such as India's. Most of the Keynesian-type analyses of inflation in which the overall pressure of aggregate demand pulls prices up in the face of full utilization of available resources, or the monetarist-type theories which seek to explain inflation by correlating the quantity of money in the economy with the availability of goods and services, are not readily applicable in the context of a developing economy. On the contrary, the explanation for persistent inflationary trends has to be sought in the nature of the development process itself. Accordingly, we shall show a model of inflationary behaviour taking explicit account of the changing structure of the Indian economy during the five-year plans, and in terms of the various aggregate economic variables which influence price behaviour.

Understanding the causes and process of inflation is crucial in order to moderate and control its more undesirable consequences. Although inflation is almost always accompanied by an increase in the quantity of money, the latter may be a consequence, rather than the proximate cause, of the rise in prices. The monetary authorities or the commercial banking system may respond passively to the additional demand for money generated by the inflationary spiral. Assume for example, an autonomous decline in the quantity of agricultural output resulting from unfavourable weather conditions, or a slowdown in the relative growth of output in the primary producing sector. Given the existing demand for agricultural products as final consumption goods, or exports, or as inputs for the growing industrial sector, there will be a rise in the relative price of the primary products, in the absence of sizeable imports or compensatory sales from buffer stocks (if any). As the agricultural sector constitutes a significant proportion of total net national product, the general price level will begin to rise. The price index rises not only because of the direct rise in the price of agricultural wage goods, but indirectly,

because the cost of farm goods used as inputs in industry has risen, and consequently the price of manufactured goods increases too. To the extent that consumers increase their demand for manufactured products as incomes rise, their cost of living goes up further. Certain industrial products used as inputs in other user industries go up in price, and those sectors find their costs and prices rising simultaneously. In short, a mechanism causing an inflationary process is readily apparent. If workers now clamour for higher money wages to maintain their real income and living standards, wages would have to be increased further, thus providing additional fuel to the accelerating rise in prices. Assuming all industries maintain their initial profit margins, mark-ups will continue to ensure a rising price index throughout the economy. Under these conditions, the monetary authorities would have to increase the quantity of money to satisfy the additional need for means of payment. Otherwise unemployment or a liquidity crisis will ensue. Thus we find that the quantity of money may respond passively to the inflationary spiral, rather than cause that process initially. In this situation ensue, controlling the quantity of money will not result in the disappearance of the "real" phenomena which are the underlying cause of inflation.

The Need for Balanced Growth

One of the most important causes of inflation in India as well as other developing countries is to be found in the inability of the agricultural sector to expand its output in relation to the growth of demand. It is well known that the income elasticity of demand for food is high at low levels of per capita income. It has been estimated that the average income elasticity for India is[2] in the neighbourhood of 0.63. If population grows at an average rate of 2–2.5 per cent per year as in fact happened in India during the fifties and sixties, and if per capita income grows at 3 per cent or thereabouts (as planned), the growth of demand for food may be expected to be roughly rising at 3.8–4.4 per cent annually. The minimum annual rate of expansion of foodgrains must therefore be in this range, unless the country has recourse to, or wants to import, a sizeable quantity of foodstuffs.

The output of commercial crops such as cotton, jute, tea, oilseeds and other agricultural raw materials must also increase commensurate with the need for them as industrial inputs (as determined by the country's input-output structure), or as exports. Otherwise, shortages of these commodities are bound to develop, leading to a gradual and persistent increase in their relative prices, as well as short-falls in the achievement of plan targets set for industry and export performance. This results in overall inflationary pressures. Exports may suffer because of inadequate supplies or because the pressure of "home demand" and a ready and ever-growing domestic market leave exporters with little incentive to seek foreign markets. India's competitiveness in these commodities also suffers as a consequence. As a result, the country's capacity to import is reduced, foreign exchange earnings fail to grow adequately and overall shortages of essential imports ensue. In addition, imports of these very commodities (food and agricultural raw materials which are produced domestically) may be required to meet the domestic needs of an expanding population and growing industry. But this means diversion of foreign exchange from other uses which suffer in consequence.

This theoretical model explains, in large part, the achievements as well as failures observed in the Indian Government's concern with maintenance of price stability during the course of the five-year plans. More important, it helps to identify the real causes and consequences of inflationary pressures in India. Many other relevant factors such as fiscal and monetary development, cumulative budget deficits, increasing outlay on nondevelopmental expenditures in excess of planned magnitudes, defence spending (especially since 1962), and the overall industrialization policy and performance, affect price trends in the economy. These will now be examined.

II

Inflationary Financing of Investment: Pros and Cons

We shall now briefly examine the case for and against inflation as a stimulant to economic growth, since this will help us understand India's recent inflationary experience in proper perspective. It is interesting that India provides us with a real-world example of government-engineered capital formation in a democracy, using many of the techniques advocated by a generation of planners and development economists, including inflationary methods of financing economic development. Also, governmental policies and actions during the plan periods to control the rise in prices, can be related to the concern with the consequences of inflation.

There are two distinct schools of thought among economists about the efficacy of inflation in generating capital formation and rapid economic development. According to the pro-inflationist school, forced savings brought about through deliberate deficit financing of investment programmes is a swift method of mobilizing resources for development.[3] It is also argued by some that "a slow and steady rate of inflation provides a most powerful aid to the attainment of a steady rate of economic progress".[4] The theoretical argument for inflation as an engine of growth is based on the assumption that (1) in an underdeveloped country, voluntary saving and investment ratios are too low; (2) the tax system is too inelastic to generate the needed investible resources for the public sector; and (3) in the face of supply bottlenecks and institutional rigidities, the private sector's incentives for raising the ratio of investment to national income are limited. Real capital formation is also hampered by lack of mobility of resources. Private capital markets are undeveloped, and financial institutions as vehicles for transferring savings of rural households and other surplus units (savers) to urban industry or other deficit units (investors) are inadequate or imperfect. It is further argued that the market mechanism does not adequately reflect social priorities, and that there exists a large potential for real investment and capital formation by transferring surplus labour from the agricultural sector to modern industry— the urban or capitalist sector. In these circumstances, it is possible to accelerate economic growth by a deliberate policy of credit creation, bidding away resources for real investment and capital formation, thus raising the rate of saving in the economy. Thus, inflation is considered as an alternative to increased taxation, which is administratively difficult or politically painful. Inflationary financing of investment can break the barriers of the "vicious circle of poverty and unemployment", provided it is done judiciously, and suitable projects with low gestation periods are chosen for the investment programme. In this view, inflation is a "growing pain" and is a lesser evil than stagnation or perpetual poverty. In fact inflation is inevitable for growth: it is beneficial and desirable; its long-run benefits far outweigh the short-run costs. It is a self-liquidating process, because, if undertaken in appropriate doses, the fruits of investment projects begin to flow through the pipelines with the minimum time-lag.

The opponents of this approach emphasise the undesirable and harmful consequences of inflation.[5] It is pointed out that inflation is a highly discriminatory and inequitable form of tax, imposing intolerable burdens on the poorer sections of the community, leading to social tensions and political instability. Groups with fixed incomes (government employees, retired pensioners, rentiers, wage-earners with limited bargaining power, bond holders and other saving units) bear the burden of inflation, as the purchasing power of their contractual incomes shrinks in value. The real value of savings is eroded by inflation. The incentives to save and invest get distorted, as people try to protect their savings by seeking forms of investment which appreciate in value over time, rather than in terms of calculations of current returns or socially desirable forms. Speculation abounds with the rising price level. Time and effort are invested in bidding up property values. If the inflationary spiral gathers momentum, expectations are generated which result in

eventual loss of confidence in money, and when this happens, the monetary mechanism may break down. The longer inflation lasts, the greater the distortions that it creates. It is difficult to contain the rate of inflation within narrow limits, and it soon gets out of hand. As the internal value of the monetary unit declines, balance of payments difficulties begin to pile up. The currency becomes overvalued under a regime of fixed exchange rates, and exports get priced out of foreign markets. Imports increase as foreign goods become relatively cheaper to buy. Foreign exchange reserves are lost, and capital inflows decline as foreign investors lose confidence in the currency. Government and the monetary authorities are unable to control the deteriorating situation, as they find that they have killed the "goose that lays the golden egg". In sum, forced saving is a self-destructive process, because inflation soon gets out of hand, and whatever short-run benefits it provides for stepping up the rate of capital formation prove illusory in the long run. Thus, according to this view, the real-resource costs of inflation on the development process far outweigh its advantages.

Inflation and Growth: The Historical Evidence

This debate can now be put in historical perspective by assessing the efficacy of inflation in generating or retarding economic growth in other countries.

There have been several empirical studies dealing with the relationship between inflation and growth.[6] A number of statistical studies have been made to document the evidence from historical country case studies on whether inflation helps or hampers the process of development. Unfortunately, the results are not clear-cut or conclusive. In some countries, (profit) inflation resulted in redistributing income towards the capitalist sector which has a high propensity to save, thus aiding investment, capital formation and economic growth. Thus, according to Rostow, "In Britain of the 1790's, the United States of the 1850's and Japan of the 1870's, capital formation was aided by price inflation, which shifted resources from consumption to profits".[7] However, in an extensive empirical study, Geoffrey Maynard has reported[8] that the rapid growth that took place in the US during the 1870's and early 1880's was associated with periods of rising as well as falling prices. High rates of growth were observed in the late nineties and early 1900's when prices were rising, but the decade before the First World War witnessed very rapid rates of inflation with slow growth. He has also shown that during the greater part of the nineteeth century, prices were regularly falling in the UK, and yet this period was characterized by rapid growth of national income as well as per capita output. After 1895, prices began to rise almost continuously, but during this period, the growth of the economy was slower than in the preceding 40 years.

Japan and the USSR both experienced government-sponsored growth through inflationary means. In Japan, inflation did not retard growth, as evidenced by almost continuous inflation coupled with the spectacular growth of the economy since the 1870's, as well as in the recent post-war years.

Russian economic growth and industrialization in the 1930s was accompanied by severe inflationary pressures. In fact the cost of living of urban workers increased more than 650 per cent over a decade. Money wages rose much less, and the worker's real wages fell by one-half! But there is no doubt that a high rate of capital formation and rapid growth of the economy took place during this decade.

Looking at more recent historical evidence from the less developed countries, the experience of many Latin American nations during 1946-76 show no clear correlation between rates of inflation and economic growth.[9] In some of these countries, high rates of inflation retarded growth; yet in others, rates of growth above the average were achieved simultaneously with severe inflationary pressures. Nor did the absence of inflation or relative price stability in some of these countries necessarily promote growth. In fact, different patterns of overall price trends have been observed with high as well as

low rates to economic growth, or even retardation and stagnation. Brazil's experiment with indexing shows that high rates of growth coupled with rapid increases in the price level are possible, as participants in economic transactions can learn to adjust their behaviour.

We can summarise this discussion by saying that there is some evidence for the view that rates of inflation in excess of 10 per cent per year are inimical to growth, whereas rates between 3 to 10 per cent do not seem to influence growth very much either way. The acceptable or tolerable rate of inflation seems to be a matter of getting used to, as Brazil's experience with indexing during the last two decades has demonstrated.

III

Price Trends in India During 1951-76

The inflationary trends in the Indian economy under the impact of the five-year plans can best be studied by looking at the behaviour of prices during each plan period. Although this procedure is somewhat arbitrary, it will help us understand how the general and sectoral price levels reacted to the overall imbalance between aggregate demand and supply under the impact of rising development outlays. The ratio of investment to net national product was progressively increased under the plans with a view to stepping up the rate of capital formation. Domestic savings available (household, corporate, and governmental savings) to finance the investment programmes were inadequate. The saving and investment ratios were:

	First Plan	Second Plan	Third Plan	Fourth Plan
I/NI %	7.4	10.2	12.8	12.49
S/NI %	5.7	8.1	9.8	11.15

Some of the factors that have a direct influence on the price level would be:
1. the overall size of the investment outlays;
2. the strategy of planning and sectoral

allocation of investment;
3. availability of external aid (or foreign exchange reserves);
4. methods of financing the gap between investment and savings; and
5. success of plans in achieving the targets set.

Given the size of the investment programme and the expenditure multiplier dictated by spending propensities, aggregate demand measured in money terms would rise. The increase in the supply of goods and services available to satisfy the additional demand generated, would be a function of the productive capacity created by the investment as defined by the marginal capital output ratio. Such parameters as the capital-employment ratio, the gestation period of the investments chosen, and the productivity of the resources employed, would determine whether or not aggregate demand and supply are in balance. In order to avoid a rise in the general price level, the supply of wage goods (especially food products and manufactured consumer goods) must keep pace with the spending pattern of income recipients.

As has been discussed earlier, the most important criterion for price stability (or alternatively, to prevent an excessive or socially unacceptable rate of inflation) is that there must be a rough overall balance between the output of the agricultural sector and the industrial sector's demand for it. Also, since economic development implies urbanization and monetization of the economy, the primary sector must produce enough food not only to satisfy its own increasing demand consistent with the income elasticity of farmers, but to meet the requirements of the urban workers engaged in various investment projects. The behaviour of the marketed surplus of agricultural produce is thus an important determinant of the trend of food prices.

Deflationary Growth During the First Plan: 1951–56

The general price level during the First Plan period rose remarkably little because of the tremendous success in the production of agricultural commodities. The Plan outlays were modest in relation to the size of the economy. Investment in

agricultural projects was emphasised, and thanks to favourable weather conditions, the index of agricultural production over the Plan period increased 22.2 per cent, or at an average annual rate of 4.2 per cent. The per capita net availability of food increased from 13.92 ounces per day at the beginning of the Plan to 15.19 ounces towards the end of 1956. Table 15.1 shows the changes in the indices of agricultural production.

Table 15.1. Changes in Indices of Agricultural Production

	First Plan	Second Plan	Third Plan
All commodities	22.2	21.7	−7.4
	(4.2)	(4.3)	(−1.1)
Foodgrains	27.4	18.9	−11.5
	(5.3)	(4.0)	(−1.9)
Other agricultural commodities	13.2	27.3	−0.1
	(2.8)	(5.1)	(−0.3)

NOTE: Figures in brackets represent annual rates of increase in output.

SOURCE: *Reserve Bank of India Bulletin*, June 1967, p. 747.

The wholesale price index for food articles during the 5-year period 1951–56 declined 23.0 per cent. The general Wholesale Price Index (WPI) for all commodities declined −17.3 per cent. In fact, the terms of trade turned against agriculture. The ratio of the index of agricultural prices to nonagricultural prices, which stood at 114.3 in 1950–51, declined to 90.1 in 1955–56. The all-India Consumer Price Index (CPI 1949=100) which stood at 101 in 1951, fell 5 points to 96 in 1956.

Several factors account for the stability (or decline) of the price level during the years 1951–56. While the planners had anticipated an incremental capital output ratio of 3.1, the actual ratio turned out to be only 2.4. The growth of net national product at constant prices increased 18 per cent during the period, exceeding the growth of net national expenditures at market prices (6 per cent).[10] Many of the crucial targets for production were achieved and in some cases, exceeded planned magnitudes. It is interesting that the actual monetary outlay of Rs. 1,960 crores was only 82 per cent of the Plan provision of Rs. 2,378 crores for the public sector. In sum, in contrast to the later plan periods, the First Plan period turned to be one of relative price stability, and indeed this may be termed "deflationary" growth.

Growth with Inflation: the Second Plan Years (1956–61)
In contrast to the deflationary price trends observed during the First Plan period, economic growth during the second half of the decade was accompanied by inflationary trends. The general index of wholesale prices (1952–53=100) which stood at 92.5 at the end of the last year of the First Plan, rose to 124.9 towards the end of the Second Plan period. The all-India working class CPI (1949=100) rose from 96 in 1955–56 to 124 in 1960–61. The overall trend in some of the sectoral indices may be observed from Table 15.2.

commercial crops, leading to large year-to-year variations in the price index. The rapid industrial expansion planned during this period added to the pace of developmental expenditures. Actual outlays in the public sector amounted to Rs. 4,672 crores, about 2½ times greater than in the First Plan period. The growth of net national expenditures at market prices rose 44 per cent or at about 7.6 per cent per year, whereas the growth in output at constant prices was one-half of this rate (22 or 4.7 per cent per year). This gap between aggregate monetary demand and supply resulted in a rise of 35 per cent in the WPI during the period, in contrast to the 17 per cent decline registered in the First Plan. The actual increment of gross domestic product at a ratio of planned magnitude was 0.86, as the incremental capital-output ratio turned out to be 2.9 instead of the planned figure of 2.3.

Since the Plan emphasised industrialization, the outlays on building up heavy

Table 15.2. Index Numbers of Wholesale Prices: Main Groups. Base: 1952–53=100

Groups	Weights	1955–56	1960–61	%Variation in	
				First Plan	Second Plan
All commodities	1000	92.5	124.9	−17.3	35.0
Food articles	504	86.6	120.0	−23.0	38.6
Liquor and tobacco	21	81.0	109.9	−17.8	35.7
Fuel, power, light and lubricants	30	95.2	120.0	2.8	26.1
Industrial raw materials	155	99.0	145.4	−24.3	46.9
Manufactures	290	99.7	123.9	− 3.4	24.3
Intermediate products	41	100.1	130.6	−10.9	30.5
Finished products	249	99.6	122.8	− 2.2	23.3

SOURCE: *Reserve Bank of India Bulletin*, June 1967, p. 767.

It will be seen that most of the rise in the index was accounted for by the increase in agriculture-based commodities: food products and industrial raw materials, which rose 38.6 and 47 per cent respectively. The overall WPI rose 35 per cent during the period, at an average annual rate of 5.9 per cent. Although the annual rate of growth of agricultural production (4.1 per cent) during the period was roughly equal to that attained in the preceding one, there were considerable, erratic, fluctuations in the output of

industry in the public sector increased ten-fold over the period. In fact, actual expenditures ran ahead of plan by 18 per cent. It was the output of heavy industry or the capital goods sector that grew most rapidly: an annual growth rate of 11.2 per cent vis-a-vis consumer goods output which grew at 3.5 per cent per year. The employment and money income generated by the public sector during the Plan period rose 37 and 44 per cent respectively. The relative shortage of consumer goods available to satisfy the added demand resulted in an upward pressure on most consumer goods prices. There was a 33 per cent increase in the CPI for food items alone during the period, reflecting the great shortage of cereals, whose price rose 7.5 per cent per year. The increase would have been still higher without large imports, which were roughly 20 million tons over the five-year period. Cereal imports in the final year of the Plan constituted almost 16 per cent of total imports in terms of value. Thus infla-

income at 1960–61 prices grew at only 2.6 per cent; taking into account the growth of population at a rate of 2.3 per cent per year, per capita income grew at a meagre rate of 0.3 per cent per year.

In fact most of the growth that took place during this period was due to industrial expansion. The index of agricultural production at the end of the Plan period was below what it was at the beginning. Table 15.3 brings out some of the important features of the period.

Table 15.3. Index Numbers of Agricultural Production, 1949–50=100

	Weight	1960/1	1961/2	1962/3	1963/4	1964/5	1965/6
Foodgrains	66.9	137.1	140.3	133.6	136.5	150.8	121.3
Nonfood	33.1	152.6	153.9	151.6	156.5	176.7	157.0
All commodities	100.0	142.2	144.8	139.6	143.1	159.4	133.1

SOURCE: *Economic Survey*, 1970–71, p. 82.

tionary pressures were somewhat mitigated.

Although there were shortages of staple commodities, industrial raw materials and consumer goods, the general index of industrial production increased from base year 1956 = 100 to 133 by 1960–61, or at an average annual rate of growth of 5.9 per cent. The net national product (1950–51 = 100) grew at an average rate of 3.9 per cent annually over the Plan period and, as we shall see, the rate of inflation was considerably lower than that during the Third Plan.

Rapid Inflation and Slow Growth: Third Plan (1961–66)
Compared to the two previous Plan periods, the rate of inflation during the years 1961–66 was much higher, while the growth rate of the economy was considerably less. Inflation became rampant so that several special measures had to be taken by the Government to control prices. (These are discussed in later section). Indeed, a accelerating inflation necessitated revision of various indices to a new base with 1960–61 as the starting point, to make comparison with other years meaningful. Money national income grew at an annual rate of 9.2 per cent during the 5-year period, but real

Except for the bumper-crop year of 1964–65, there was relatively little progress in agricultural production from the beginning of the Plan period. In fact, taking the 5-year period as a whole, the rate of growth of production was negative— 0.9 per cent. The poor record of agriculture permeated the economy with undesirable consequences. The single most important cause of the failure of the Plan was the inability of agricultural production to expand as envisaged. The planners had targeted for a foodgrain output of 101.6 million tons by 1965–66; however the actual output turned out to be only 72.0 million tons. This was, in large part, the consequence of the disastrous fall in output during 1965–66.

As a result of the shortfall in agricultural output, the index number of wholesale prices for agricultural commodities rose 42 per cent during the 5-year period (1961–62 = 100 to 142 in the final Plan year of 1965–66). The terms of trade moved consistently in favour of agriculture year after year, though this trend failed to bring about any expansion of output. during the First Plan period, the relative price changes had been in the opposite direction. Indeed, agricultural prices throughout the sixties continued their upward climb: they almost doubled in a decade! The consequences of this shift of relative prices for the growth of the economy, as well as for overall price stability, were very unfortunate.

Besides the poor performance of agriculture, several other factors contributed to the extraordinary rise in the price of goods and services during this period.

The first year of the Plan started with war with China, and the last year ended with the war with Pakistan. During this period, defence outlays were increased from Rs. 281 crores in 1960–61 to Rs.884 crores by 1965–66, a 3-fold rise in 5 years. Defence outlays have continued to increase since then, year after year, and in 1970–71 were estimated to be Rs. 1,152 crores.

Both public and private investment during the Plan period were stepped up substantially, compared to the earlier Plans. The public sector's actual outlay of Rs. 8,608 crores was more than Rs. 1,000 crores in excess of the planned figure of Rs. 7,500 crores. This increase was necessitated by the rise in prices that occurred during the Plan, in order to carry out the physical targets for investment. We should point out that the increased public sector outlays during the 5-year period exceeded the total outlay of the First and Second Plans combined, by more than Rs. 2,000 crores. An investment programme of this magnitude was bound to create some inflationary pressures in the economy (especially in the market for consumer goods and services) even during normal periods, because the proportion of total investment devoted to the creation of capital goods (heavy industry, electric power generation and mining) was to be 35 as against 29 per cent in the Second and 23 per cent in the First Plans.

Although the Plan had visualized deficit financing of the order of only Rs. 550 crores, the actual magnitude turned out to be almost twice that figure: Rs. 1,133 crores. The relevant figures for the Plans are given in Table 15.4.

As pointed out earlier, inflationary financing of economic development results in a rapid increase in the price level unless the economy has an elastic supply of wage goods available to satisfy the added consumer demand. While deficit financing during the First and Second Plans could be

Table 15.4. Deficit Financing during Five-Year Plan. Annual Averages—Current Prices

	Plan	Actual	Total
First Plan	58	69	345
Second Plan	220	191	955
Third Plan	110	227	1135
Annual Plans	104	227	682
Fourth Plan	170	213	1066

SOURCE: 1. Wilfred   Malenbaum,   *Modern India's Economy* (Columbus, Ohio: Merrill, 1971) p. 103.

2. Reserve Bank of India, *Report on Currency and Finance 1974–1975* (Bombay, 1975), p. 94.

undertaken with relative ease because of the increasing supply of consumer goods (rapid increase in foodgrain production during the First Plan and use of foreign-exchange reserves to finance imports during the Second Plan), the inflationary pressures that it created during the Third Plan period were difficult to contain. The overall aggregate demand created was too large in relation to the economy's capacity to satisfy that demand without a very rapid rise in prices.

The growth of output of consumer goods, which had lagged behind other industrial-output growth during the Second Plan, continued to increase slowly during 1961–66. A study of the percentage change in index numbers of industrial production revealed that the lowest rate of expansion was in respect of consumer goods. It is also of interest to note that high-income consumer goods (cars, refrigerators, air-conditioners) grew much more rapidly than the middle-income class (cycles, fans, sewing machines) or mass consumption goods (soap, kerosene, textiles). The output of the former grew during the 15-year period (1951–65) about 100 per cent, whereas the latter grew less than 50 per cent.

The rise in prices accelerated during the last two years of the Third Plan, because the gap between expenditures and output-growth widened considerably (in part due to increased defence expenditures), compared with the first 3 years. The growth in expenditures at market prices was 50 per cent over the 5-year period, whereas output at constant prices grew only 14 per cent.

It has been estimated that annual payrolls in the public sector alone increased 100 per cent over the Third Plan period, from Rs. 615 crores in 1960–61 to Rs. 1,232 crores in 1965–66. This is an annual growth-rate of 15 per cent, compared to 7.7 and 4.8 per cent for the earlier Plans.[11] The country did not or could not produce sufficient consumer goods to absorb the demand generated by such expenditures.

India's attempt at rapid industrialization by emphasising the building-up of basic heavy industries, capital goods and import-replacing types, added to the severe inflationary pressures that started at the beginning of the sixties. The aim during these years was to increase the nation's productive capacity. It became apparent as the Plan progressed, and especially during the latter half of the decade, that capacity creation did not necessarily result in capacity *utilization*. Shortage for foreign exchange, industrial raw materials, lagging demand from user industries and the poor performance of agriculture in two successive years (1965–67) added to the strain on the economy.

As a result of inflation, India's competitiveness in foreign markets suffered throughout 1960–67. Although the volume of exports rose during the Plan period, export performance in general was below expectation. In this respect, the following quotation is of considerable interest.[12]

An interesting recent analysis of Indian export performance by Professor Benjamin Cohen has shown that while imports from all sources of India's traditional exports by North America, Europe and Japan increased in value during the period 1960 to 1967 by 19 per cent, those from Indian declined by 3 per cent. On the other hand, Pakistan's share rose by 13 per cent. If India-had remained as competitive as in 1960—Professor Cohen argues— she could at least have added some 23 per cent to her traditional exports. Such an increase would have eliminated about 30 per cent of the 1968/9 trade gap.

Thus we find that (1) failure of the

agricultural sector to expand production to meet the economy's rising demand; (2) large defence outlays; (3) expenditures in excess of planned magnitudes deficit-financed by large-scale borrowings from the Reserve Bank; and (4) heavy industrialization not matched by a corresponding flow of consumer-goods production, were the primary causes of the rise in the price level during the Third Plan period. The rate of inflation was especially severe during the last two years. The price of food articles rose 22 per cent in 1965–66 alone, and the price of finished goods by 7.4 per cent. The overall rise in the food price index for the 5-year period was 48.4 per cent and the rise in the general price index was 36 per cent. Unlike the First and Second Plan periods, however, the Third Plan period was characterized by very slow growth during the first two years, followed by higher growth during the next two years, and negative growth in the final year. The annual growth rates of income were: 2.5, 1.7, 4.9, 7.6 and –4.2 per cent. As pointed out earlier, real growth in net national product for the 5-year period amounted to 2.6 per cent per year.

We shall now discuss the salient features of growth and inflation during the next decade, 1966–76.

Annual Plans, 1966–69
The Fourth Five-Year Plan, which was supposed to have started in the year 1966, was postponed until 1969. The interim period, 1966–69, was marked by the so-called Annual Plans, drawn up and implemented on an ad hoc basis. During this period, the economy experienced a recession coupled with severe inflationary pressures. The shortfall in agricultural output during two consecutive years, 1965–67, adversely affected the economy's performance not only during those two years, but subsequently. The Index of Agricultural Production for these years may be seen in Table 15.5.

Consequently the rate of increase in food prices in each of these two years was almost 20 per cent, a rate which adversely affected not only the living standards of most people, but contributed to increasing wage pressures, and cost inflation throughout

Table 15.5. Index Numbers of Agricultural
Production 1961-62=100

Year	Foodgrains	Non-Foodgrains	All Commodities
1960–61	102.1	103.8	102.7
1965–66	89.9	107.1	95.8
1966–67	91.9	103.7	95.9
1967–68	117.1	115.6	116.6
1968–69	115.7	113.2	114.8
1969–70	123.5	120.5	122.5
1970–71	133.9	126.6	131.4
1971–72	132.0	128.9	130.9
1972–73	121.2	118.9	120.4
1973–74	131.5	137.1	133.4
1974–75	125.6	136.5	129.3

SOURCE: *Economic Survey*, 1975–76, p. 62.

the economy. Rice and wheat prices during the year 1967–68 temporarily reached unheard-of levels: 208 and 186 respectively (1952–53:100). Only the large imports under PL 480 helped ease the food situation in the country. Total imports during the years 1965–68 amounted to 26 million tons, and averaged 7 to 10 million tons of foodgrains annually. The all-India CPI for urban non-manual workers (1960=100) which stood at 132 in 1965–66 rose to 146 in 1966–67 and 159 the following year. The rate of increase was somewhat moderated in the next two years, due mainly to increasing availability of foodgrains, as well as government procurement and distribution through fair price shops throughout the urban areas. Some of the indices reflecting the performance of the Indian economy are shown in Table 15.6.

It is significant that despite the slow growth of industrial production in the year 1967–68, national income grew rapidly. In part, this rapid growth was no more than a recovery to the absolute level of national income attained in 1964–65. Net National Product (at 1960–61 prices) in 1964–65 was Rs. 15,885 crores and had fallen to Rs. 15,082 crores in 1965–66, and Rs. 15,240 crores in 1966–67. It reached Rs. 16,494 crores in 1967–68 (see Table 15.8). This was due to the relatively large increase in agricultural production, which had fallen in the two previous years below the level attained in 1964–65. The increased output of agricultural goods had a favourable effect on wholesale prices, especially the following year, and helped to moderate the rise in the price level.

The rate of growth of money supply during these years ranged between 8-11 per cent per year. Repeated budget deficits incurred by Central and State governments resulted in large-scale borrowings from the Reserve Bank, and contributed to the rapid increase in money supply with the public. Nondevelopmental outlays (mainly defence expenditures) had climbed very rapidly during the years 1967–71 (Table 15.7). Almost one-third of the nondevelopmental (or government consumption) outlays were accounted for by defence expenditures. Because real growth in the economy during these years was very limited, inflationary pressures gathered momentum, fuelled by increased money supply generated by deficit financing. Between the years 1965 and 1969, population growth was sufficient to absorb the growth in national product with very

Table 15.6. Selected Economic Indicators
(Percentage change over previous year)

	1966–67	67–68	68–69	69–70	70–71	71–72	72–73	73–74	74–75	75–76
National income at constant prices	1.0	8.2	3.0	6.5	5.2	1.8	−1.5	5.0	0.2	5.5
Agricultural production	−1.1	22.4	−1.0	6.7	7.3	−0.4	−8.0	10.8	−3.1	8.0
Industrial production	0.3	0.5	6.7	7.4	3.0	3.3	4.4	−0.2	2.5	4.5
Wholesale prices	13.9	11.6	−1.1	3.7	5.5	4.0	9.9	22.7	23.1	−2.4
Money supply	8.3	9.1	8.1	10.8	11.2	13.1	15.9	15.4	6.9	7.5

SOURCE: *Economic Survey*, 1970–71 and 1975–76.

Table 15.7. **Budgetary Transactions of the Central and State Governments**
(Rs. Crores)

	1967–68	1968–69	1969–70	1970–71	1971–72	1972–73	1973–74	1974–75
Developmental outlays	3,676	3,937	4,408	4,697	5,710	6,695	6,864	9,403
Nondevelopmental outlay	2,772	2,890	3,266	3,249	4,358	4,561	5,380	6,321
TOTAL	6,448	6,827	7,674	7,946	10,068	11,256	12,244	15,724
Current receipts	4,516	4,943	5,405	6,023	7,009	8,075	8,986	11,562
GAP	1,932	1,884	2,269	1,923	3,059	3,181	3,258	4,162
Financed by: Capital Receipts	1,675	1,571	1,967	1,512	2,321	2,329	2,715	3,620
Overall budgetary Deficit	257	313	302	411	738	852	543	542

SOURCE: *Economic Survey*, 1970–71 and 1975–76.

little margin left for increase in per capita income. It was only during the years 1969–70 and 1970–71 that national income grew more rapidly than did population. Per capita consumption in 1968–69 was not significantly higher than the level attained in 1960–61!

The rate of growth of industrial production during these years was also slow: in fact, in 1966–67, it was negative. Even the production of capital goods, which had continuously increased throughout the previous plans at a very rapid rate year after year, barely rose, except in 1970. The overall rate of industrial expansion was considerably slower than that achieved uptil 1965.

Fourth Five-Year Plan (1969–74)
In 1969–70 the Fourth Plan was officially inaugurated. The performance of the economy during the first two years of the Plan was a modest improvement over the three preceding years. Although overall agricultural production continued to advance, the output of commercial crops, as mentioned earlier, changed erratically (Table 15.5). The production of foodgrains increased by about 8 per cent in 1970–71 with a favourable influence on food prices and India's balance of payments, which had been severely strained during the preceding five years by the large imports needed to feed a rapidly growing population.

As we have seen, since the middle of the Third Plan period, the general price level has continued to advance at a rapid rate, with accelerating food prices. It soon became apparent that such increases in the cost of living were intolerable, and several policies were initiated by the Government to moderate the price advance. These actions and their results will be reviewed in a later section.

Although an economic recovery began during the closing years of the decade, shortages of key industrial raw materials like jute, cotton, and oilseeds continued to push prices up rapidly. The index for raw material prices, which stood at 170.6 in November 1969, rose to 201.2 in June 1970, and climbed to 206.5 in January 1971, a rise of 20 per cent in annual terms. Costs and prices throughout the economy continued to increase. The all-India working classs CPI rose 5.1 per cent in 1970–71.

In order to provide an overall perspective concerning the trends of prices and output during these years, we have shown in Table 15.8 some statistics on net national product measured in current as well as constant rupees. As will be seen, NNP measured in current prices rose about 55 per cent from Rs. 31,770 crores in 1969–70 to Rs. 49,148 crores in 1973–74, the final year of the Fourth Plan. Measured in constant rupees of 1960–61 purchasing power, however, there was a meagre 11 per cent growth during the entire Fourth Plan period, from Rs. 18,092 crores to Rs. 20,034 during this 5-year period. In other words, the increase in the overall price level exaggerated the growth of output by a factor several times greater than the real growth-rate. The divergence between money and real NNP has become greater and greater over the years, reflecting the phenomenal increase in the price index. Thus while the index of NNP in current rupees rose from about 217 to 371 during the 5-year period, the real magnitudes changed from 128 to 151. Measured in per capita terms, the growth of income was insignificant, as shown in the last column of Table 15.8. In aggregate real terms, the overall growth of NNP during the entire Fourth Plan period averaged 3.3 per cent per year vis-a-vis 2.6 per cent during the Third Plan.

"stagflation" of the economy was a disastrous decline in agricultural production. The lackluster performance of agriculture from 1970–71 crippled the Plan targets for industrial production as well. The index of agricultural production (revised series) which stood at 131.4 in 1970–71 fell during the next two years, and did not recover until the final year of the Fourth Plan. The two intervening years were characterized by relative stagnation of the economy, accompanied by rapid inflation.

While agricultural production declined due to unfavourable weather conditions as well as the failure of the Green Revolution to register any substantial improvement in productivity, industrial production was hampered by lack of power, transport, shortage of raw materials and various intermediate inputs such as steel, coal,

Table 15.8. Net National Product (Aggregate and per capita)
1960–61 to 1974–75

Year	Net National Product (Rs. crores)		Net National Product Per Capita		Index Numbers of NNP		Index Numbers of Per capita NNP	
	Current	1960–61	Current	1960–61	Current	1960–61	Current	1960–61
1960–61	13,263	13.263	305.6	305.6	100.0	100.0	100.0	100.0
1961–62	13,987	13,729	315.0	309.2	105.5	103.5	103.1	101.2
1962–63	14,795	13,993	325.9	308.2	111.6	105.5	106.6	100.9
1963–64	16,977	14,771	365.8	318.3	128.0	111.4	819.7	104.2
1964–65	20,001	15,885	422.0	335.1	150.8	119.8	138.1	109.7
1965–66	20,636	15,082	425.5	311.0	155.6	113.7	139.2	101.8
1966–67	23,883	14,240	482.5	307.9	180.1	114.9	157.9	100.8
1967–68	28,102	16,494	555.4	326.0	211.9	124.4	181.7	106.7
1968–69	28,729	16,991	554.6	328.0	216.6	128.1	181.5	107.3
1969–70	31,770	18,092	600.6	342.0	239.5	136.4	196.5	111.9
1970–71	34,476	19,033	637.3	351.8	259.9	143.5	208.5	115.1
1971–72	36,535	19,367	660.7	350.2	275.5	146.0	216.2	114.6
1972–73	39,573	19,077	700.4	337.6	298.4	143.8	229.2	110.5
1973–74	49,148	20,034	851.8	347.2	370.6	151.0	278.7	113.6
1974–75	60,120	20,075	1,022.4	341.4	453.3	151.4	334.6	111.7

SOURCE: *Economic Survey*, 1975–76.

What were the main factors responsible for this unflattering performance of the economy? In addition to a rapid rate of increase in the money supply, averaging between 10 to 16 per cent per year, large budget deficits and stepped-up nondevelopmental expenditures (see Table 15.7), the main contributing factor for the

cement, etc. Towards the closing years of the Plan period, wholesale prices rose very rapidly indeed: 19.2 per cent in 1973 and 27.3 per cent in 1974. It is significant that half the price increase was due to "food" articles. The trend in output of foodgrains during the seventies is shown below:

Production of Foodgrains

Year	Millions of tons
1970–71	108.4
1971–72	105.2
1972–73	97.0
1973–74	104.7
1974–75	101.1
1975–76	118.0

Thus it can be seen that the continuous decline in production of foodgrains during most of the Fourth Plan years had an adverse effect on the economy.

Since agro-industries account for about 45 per cent of total industrial production in the Indian economy, the erratic output growth of the commercial crops sector (which provides inputs to these industries) impeded the overall performance of the economy.

According to the *Economic Survey* 1974–75, since "73 per cent of cultivated area remains under food crops, a shift in acreage to commercial crops is predicated on a significant rise in productivity of food. Unfortunately, despite the addition of 7.1 million hectares under irrigation during the Fourth Plan, and a three-and-a-half fold increase in acreage under high yielding varieties of rice", no substantial addition to output has been registered in the last four years. The main response for the shortfall in production, even though the target for area under cultivation was over-fulfilled, were: inadequate water and fertilizers, and failure of the high-yielding technology to increase productivity. Unless these problems are speedily resolved, it seems that the Indian economy's overall output growth will continue to be stifled by the primary producing sector.

Turning now to industrial production, the average growth-rate of this sector was only 3.9 per cent during the Fourth Plan period, vis-a-vis 8 per cent during the years 1956–64. The performance of consumer goods industries (which are directly dependent on agriculture-based inputs) was especially poor. Since the industrial sector provides the bulk of government revenues (agricultural incomes are tax-exempt), the slowdown in its growth had unfavourable consequences for public

sector savings and investment. The decline in government receipts, coupled with the requirement for maintaining non-developmental outlays (such as drought relief, defence spending, dearness allowance, increments to civil servants, and expenditures on social services) resulted in large budget deficits (Table 15.7). As pointed out earlier, money supply with the public increased at a rapid rate (10 to 16 per cent per year), and the increase in effective demand coupled with the slow growth of output resulted in severe inflationary pressures. These factors contributed to the continuous erosion of the purchasing power of the rupee mentioned at the beginning of this essay.

Another salient feature of this period was that capacity creation in the public sector was slowed down considerably due to shortage of governmental savings, escalation in costs resulting from rapid inflation, and monumental delays in the execution of construction projects. There were critical shortages of inputs such as electric power (which grew roughly 6.4 per cent per year vis-a-vis the target growth rate of 10.7 per cent during the Plan), coal, cement, transport, and steel. It is reported that steel capacity use declined from 71 per cent in 1968–69 to 57 per cent in 1973–74, and output of finished steel declined during the Fourth Plan period at 1 per cent per year.[14] Poor operating efficiency of various public sector undertakings contributed to cost inflation throughout the economy.

The achievements of the Fourth Plan may be summarised by stating that real national income grew at a rate slightly higher (3.3 per cent) than during the Third Plan period, while per capita income grew at an annual rate of 1.2 per cent. Without a sustained increase in agricultural production, which continued to be hampered by adverse weather conditions as well as lack of dynamism in productivity growth, the Indian economy exhibited weaknesses in several sectors. Real private savings did not increase significantly due to the slow growth of national income, while governmental savings failed to expand as planned due to the lag in output of the industrial sector. Inflationary expectations built up during these years became hard to contain. Both the wholesale price index and the consumer price index registered very large increases, reflecting the underlying imbalance between aggregate demand and supply in the economy.

Fifth Plan and Declaration of Emergency: 1974-76

The first year of the Fifth Plan witnessed the sharpest rate of increase in prices recorded in postwar years. The WPI which stood at 283.6 during 1973-74, rose to 307 during 1974-75, while the all-India CPI rose to an all-time peak of 335 in October 1974. The year 1974-75 was one of the most difficult periods in India's recent history. As can be seen from Table 15.8, while NNP measured in current prices registered an increase of 22.3 per cent over the previous year, the real growth in output was an insignificant 0.2 per cent: in per capita terms, NNP declined from 113.6 in 1973-74 to 111.7 during 1974-75. The year 1974-75 was the most inflationary in the memory of most people in India today. This unprecedented inflation was triggered off by a sharp decline in foodgrain production. As mentioned in the discussion of the Fourth Plan period, foodgrain output continued to decline during those years, and the index for 1974-75 was 129.3 compared to 131.4 for 1970-71. This was primarily responsible for the phenomenal increase in prices during the year.

Table 15.9. **Dollar Value of Selected Imports**

(in millions of dollars)

Item	1973-74	1974-75	% increase
Food	537.4	867.9	61.4
Petroleum	630.0	1,310.0	106.5
Fertilizers	257.8	656.7	154.8
Iron and steel	283.6	474.2	67.3
Nonferrous metals	159.4	202 3	26.9
Newsprint	22.0	50.0	143.0

SOURCE: Government of India, Ministry of Information and Broadcasting, *India's War Against Inflation* (New Delhi, January 1976).

Inflation and stagnation proceeded simultaneously during the first year of the Fifth Plan. Apart from the debilitating effect of crop failures, the nation experienced an unprecedented decline in the living standards of most people due to the steep increase in the cost of imports of petroleum, food and other raw materials. Due to the worldwide shortage of staple materials during 1974, India experienced a sharp fall in its commodity terms of trade. In addition to the internally-generated demand inflation, rising prices of imported inputs contributed to cost inflation as well. The increased cost of imports may be seen from Table 15.9 in which the dollar value of imports during 1974-75 are compared with those of the preceding year.

Alarmed by the steep rise in prices throughout the economy, the Government of India took a series of anti-inflationary measures on a "war footing". Severe restrictive fiscal and monetary measures were instituted to reduce governmental spending and the growth of money incomes. Firstly, the rate of increase in the money supply was slowed down to 6.9 per cent during the year, which was the lowest level in fourteen years! Nondevelopmental outlays were cut drastically, and the budgetary deficit was reduced by 50 per cent. Special measures were introduced to keep down private money incomes and to mobilize savings throughout the urban sector. These included:

1. Compulsory Deposits of Additional Emoluments and Dearness Allowances of 18 million Government employees designed to hold down Disposable Incomes (450 crores)
2. Restriction of dividend payments (60 crores)
3. Compulsory Deposit Scheme for all income-tax payers whose annual incomes exceed Rs. 15,000 (50 crores)
4. New excise duties to raise additional taxes (136 crores)
5. Tax of 7 per cent on *interest earned* by commercial banks (25 crores)
6. Increased railway fares and freights to reduce the growing deficit in the Railways Budget (140 crores)

These and other measures designed to raise government revenues were expected to add approximately Rs. 1,000 crores to the budgetary resources of the Government during 1974–75.

In addition to fiscal and monetary policy measures, several changes were instituted to bring about relative price stability in the economy. These were primarily designed to reduce incentives for hoarding inventories, tax evasion, and conspicuous consumption. More stringent enforcement of antimonopoly and restrictive trade practices, promotion of effective competition in commodity markets, restraint on wages and austerity in governmental spending supplemented the restrictive fiscal-monetary policy. As a result of these, the price level did in fact begin to decline from October 1974. The consumer price index fell from 335 in October 1974 to 321 in March 1975, and the wholesale price index declined by 7.4 per cent during the same period.

This declining trend in the general price index was aided by resumption of agricultural-output growth in 1975. Foodgrains production in 1975 was estimated to be 110–113 million tons, which was about 12 per cent above the output of 1974. National income during the year 1975–76 grew at about 5.5 per cent compared to 0.2 per cent in the preceding year. According to the *Economic Survey* 1975–76, "price stability is likely to be accompanied by a substantial improvement in the overall rate of growth of the economy in 1975–76".[15]

The Declaration of National Emergency in June 1975 seemed to have softened the inflationary trends by giving special powers to the Government, designed to crack down on "anti-social" economic activities. Restoration of civic discipline appear to have helped the economy by raising production and productivity. It has been reported[16] that 26 million man-days were lost in 1974 due to various industrial strikes. To the extent that hoarding of commodities (especially consumer goods like foodgrains, sugar, edible oils, etc.), has been typical of the Indian economy in the last few years, this practice resulted in rising prices in the open market, as well as help create inflationary expectations among producers and consumers. Many of the programmes designed to curb

black-market activity, hoarding, tax evasion and other "economic abuses" certainly augured well for the success of the antiinflationary policy. In the long run, however, the best hope for price stability lies in the ability of the economy to raise productivity growth by stepping up the rate of real investment. Unless the agricultural sector continues to grow at a significantly higher rate than in the last few years, the Indian economy cannot achieve sustained rates of higher economic growth. This central theme has been amply demonstrated by our detailed examination of the inflationary trends experienced in India during the last 25 years.

The restoration of industrial peace as well as relaxation of various administrative and foreign trade controls during the Emergency period, did help raise industrial production substantially during 1975–77. Industrial production growth during these two years was roughly 6 and 10 per cent. The orientation of economic policy in the direction of freer markets as well as adoption of lower marginal tax rates designed to encourage savings, investment and production, helped to restore investor confidence. Despite such pro-capitalist policies, however, industrial growth during these two years was erratic. While there was a significant expansion in public sector output (notably steel), many consumer goods industries were suffering from excess capacity and unsold inventories on the one hand, and reduced availability of industrial raw materials (cotton, oilseeds, jute) on the other. The decline in agricultural production during 1976–77 was primarily responsible for the unprecedented shortage of raw cotton and oilseeds and the steep increase in the prices of these inputs. Thus, while the bumper crop of 1975–76 helped to contain inflationary pressures on the food front, the overall trend in prices during 1976–77 has been upward.

The Indian economy was in better health in March 1977 than at the time when Emergency was imposed in June 1975. Many favourable statistical indicators such as food production, industrial growth, an adequate level (about 18 million tons) of foodgrains reserves, large foreign exchange (about 3500 crores) reserves, and higher savings/investment ratios attest to this. Yet one can point out that some of these results were the result of pure luck, or of exogeneous circumstances which had nothing to do with Authoritarian Rule. Indeed it is possible to argue that the major claims made for the accomplishments of the regime, i.e. (1) restoration of some semblance of price stability by controlling runaway inflation, (2) reversal of industrial and agricultural stagnation, and (3) building of reasonably large buffer stocks of foodgrains and foreign exchange reserves, would have been possible, and perhaps inevitable, given the favourable weather conditions, buoyancy in demand for exports which has prevailed in the last two years, and large inward remittances of foreign exchange. One should also remember that India had attained high levels of growth with relative price stability during the first Five-Year Plan period, as well as during intermittent years in the 1960s.

It is possible to step up an economy's rate of growth in real output or employment for short periods of time by using fiscal and monetary expansion. Temporary wage and price controls can attain price stability by suppressing inflationary pressures. Favourable exogeneous shocks such as increased foreign demand for exports, sudden and unanticipated resource discoveries or exceptionally good weather conditions, can help a country to attain short-run spurts in real output and higher per capita incomes. But long-term, continuous, sustainable improvements in the economic well-being of a people depend on pursuit of responsible economic policies. In addition, other determinants of economic growth include: increases in factor productivity, sustainable high rates of savings/investment, technological progress, political and social conditions favouring entrepreneurship and individual initiative, freedom for market participation through just competition and an innate desire for improvement in living standards. To the extent that these factors are prevalent in the Indian economic scene, long-run economic growth is possible and certain. There are many signs that the long-run prospects for the economy are good.

The 21 months of Emergency Rule have not altered fundamental economic institutions, or the aspirations of the people.

IV

Price Policy During the Five-Year Plans: Rationale and Execution

Indian planners have laid great stress on the need for price stability during the process of economic development. From the very inception of the five-year plans, there seemed to be recognition of the distorting consequences of inflation, as evidenced by successive plan documents as well as other government publications and official pronouncements.[17]

The function of the price system in a market economy as a signalling device, providing incentives for substitution in production and consumption choices, and as a regulating mechanism for directing the allocation of resources, was very well recognized by Government. At the same time, the authorities did not hesitate to intervene in the market process whenever it was considered that such intervention was called for:

1. to moderate the inequality of income distribution brought about by natural monopolies or contrived scarcities;

2. to alter the market-determined prices of goods and services to attain equity (which really meant assuring some minimum availability of essential goods to poorer sections of society);

3. to indicate directions in which resources should be rechannelled, whenever the market-determined investment and allocation decisions conflicted with the socially-perceived Plan priorities.

We have seen that rapid inflation began to emerge in the Indian economy during the middle of the Third Plan period. The prices of essential consumer goods (especially foodgrains, textiles, sugar, kerosene and vegetable oils) and industrial raw materials, started their steep upward climb during 1963–64. It soon became apparent that some kind of overall control of prices as well as other administrative measures, were required to ensure implementation of Plan projects, to prevent profiteering and to ensure equitable distribution of available supplies of critical items. Until 1963–64, Government did not consider it necessary to institute formal price controls, rationing,procurement, and direct distribution policies in respect of foodgrains, although prices of some mass consumption goods such as textiles, sugar, etc., were under constant Government review; and production of several goods and services were regulated by licensing, allocation of foreign exchange, and capital-issues control. Many commodities included in the WPI were already "regulated". By the year 1966, about two-thirds of the items included in the WPI were price-regulated through statutory or informal controls, licensing requirements and the like, in order to softenthe inflationary impact of ever-increasing scarcities. As a consequence, inflation was suppressed, and the actual price indices did not adequately reflect the extent of inflationary pressures in the economy.

However the main anti-inflationary thrust of governmental policies in recent years was directed at controlling food prices, which were rising at an average rate of 20 per cent per year in the past decade. Large imports under PL 480 programmes, forced procurement from farmers, opening up of fair-price shops in urban areas for distribution at controlled prices, prohibition of interstate movement of foodgrains (so as to facilitate government procurement from surplus areas at low prices) and increasing government domination of wholesale trading in foodgrains, were among the policies adopted by the authorities. A loose rationing system, covering 240 million people through 140,00 fair-price shops was in effect to assure minimum supplies of foodgrains at subsidised prices, costing over Rs. 100 crores annnally.

These and other policies pursued by the Government did not always meet with the desired results. Several critics have pointed out the distorting consequences and dis-incentives caused by these policies, which, they have convincingly argued, have held back agricultural progress and dampened local production.[18] Price controls, rationing and subsidised distribution of food are only short-run solutions to the problem of insufficient supplies in an expanding economy. Since the demand curve for food cannot be shifted back to the left, and since price controls or subsidies are nonequilibrating devices in the long run, the only sensible solution is to seek ways and means to produce more, or shift the supply curve to the right. Nor are continuous and ever-increasing imports possible or desirable. They have been a heavy drain on India's foreign exchange earnings throughout the sixties and seventies. Food imports as a percentage of total consumption during the last year of the first three plans were: 2.3, 4.6 and 14.4 per cent. During the years 1965–66 to 1968–69, cereal imports alone have contributed as much as 18 to 32 per cent of the value of imports (though under PL 480 auspices). Although food imports become inevitable during disaster crop years such as 1965–66, continued dependence on foreign sources of food supply do not augur well for the economy in the long run.

This fact has been recognized by the planners. A number of reforms are now under way to reorient policies designed to encourage agricultural production. (These are matters demanding separate treatment and have been discussed elsewhere in this book).

A comprehensive price policy, covering the prices of factors of production, producer as well as consumer goods, cannot long remain operationally efficient. Regulating the prices of innumerable inputs and outputs throughout the economy, even in a centrally planned system, becomes an almost impossible task. It creates its own distorting influences, adversely affecting private incentives; breeds corruption, creates black markets, reduces allocative efficiency by causing administrative delays and proliferating bureaucratic control. There seemed to be a danger that the Indian planning machinery was moving in this direction during the early sixties; but there are certain indications that official policy has veered towards less control and greater freedom for free market forces to prevail in recent years. There are deep and continuing conflicts between diverse social and economic objectives. These will have to be recognized and resolved.

V

Concluding Comments: Implications of the Analysis

The most important cause of inflation in a developing country like India is the inadequate growth of the agricultural sector during a period of rapid industrialization. Unless the primary sector is able to generate adequate supplies of food and raw materials needed for an expanding industrial development programme, severe and prolonged inflation will result. Although the failure of agricultural output to expand can be compensated by imports, this results in a foreign exchange crisis because (1) rapidly growing industry needs imports of capital equipment and industrial raw materials locally unavailable; (2) exports of agricultural commodities is the main source of foreign exchange earnings; and (3) there seem to be limits beyond which foreign aid or private capital flows cannot be depended upon.

During the period of the first decade of planning in India, the average growth-rate of the economy was higher than that experienced subsequently. The annual rate of inflation during the First and Second Plan periods was moderate. In fact, growth during the First Plan was deflationary.

Rapid population growth, coupled with the deteriorating and uneven performance of the agricultural sector resulted in a high degree of inflation during the sixties. Several other factors such as (1) increasing budget deficits, (2) rising defence expenditures, (3) rapid monetary expansion to finance the shortfall between outlays and tax receipts, and (4) emphasis on building up of heavy industries and the associated capital-intensity of investment plans, helped fuel the inflationary pressures.

The Reserve Bank of India played a passive role in the expansion of money supply. Ever-increasing government expenditure plans, which were not adequately matched by domestic savings, foreign aid or tax receipts, had to be deficit-financed by Reserve Bank credit. Fiscal rather than monetary policy was responsible for inflationary pressures. In these circumstances, control of the money supply alone would not have helped to bring about price stability.

Inflation did not necessarily promote or retard growth. A rapid and prolonged inflation in excess of what society can tolerate hampers economic growth, but only because adequate growth fails to take place. What is needed is growth-inducing policies and programmes to control inflation. If agricultural and consumer-goods output expansion can be accelerated, inflationary pressures can be held in check.

Many developing and developed countries have experienced rapid inflation during the course of economic development. In most developed countries, the rate of inflation has averaged 3 to 25 per cent in recent years. In developing countries, it has ranged from 2 to 400 per cent. The mechanisms causing inflation, and its impact, depend on particular circumstances. The instruments needed for control of inflation differ too.

During the seventies, the rate of inflation in India accelerated due to the failure of agricultural production to expand as planned. Real savings and investment suffered as a result of stagnation of industrial production. Governmental policies in the last two years have brought about relative stability on the price front, though favourable weather conditions still seem to be the pre-condition for any sustained advance in economic expansion.

With the resumption of agricultural-output growth since 1975, there is clear evidence that inflationary pressures are receding. But it is too early to predict that inflation has been conquered. The renewed emphasis accorded to agriculture in the Fifth Plan and determined efforts to salvage the Green Revolution may help to accelerate economic growth with acceptable rates of inflation in the present decade.

REFERENCES

1. First National City Bank, *Monthly Economic Letter* (New York, September 1976), p. 14.
2. Economic Commission for Asia and the Far East, *Economic Survey*, Bangkok, 1964, p. 123.
3. Arthur Lewis, "Economic Development with Unlimited Supplies of Labour", *The Manchester School*, May 1954 reprinted in A.N. Agarwala and S.P. Singh (eds.), *The Economics of Underdevelopment* (Bombay: Oxford University Press), 1963.
4. A.P. Thirlwall and C.A. Brown, "Inflation and Growth: The International Evidence", *Banca Nazionale del Lavoro Quarterly*, vol. 14, no. 98, September 1971.
5. S. Mookerjee, "Financial Stability and Planning", *Finance and Development*, vol. 9, no. 1, March 1972, p. 5.
6. U. Tun Wai, "The Relation Between Inflation and Economic Development: A Statistical Inductive Study", *IMF Staff Papers*, vol. 7, no. 3, October 1959; R.J. Bhatia, "Inflation, Deflation and Economic Development", *IMF Staff Papers*, vol. 8, no. 3, November 1960; and Graeme Dorrance, "Inflation and Growth: The Statistical Evidence", *IMF Staff Papers*, vol. 13, no.

7, March 1966.
7. W.W. Rostow, *The Economist*, 15 August 1959, reported in Thirwall and Brown, *Inflation and Growth*.
8. Geoffrey Maynard, *Economic Development and the Price Level* (London: Macmillan, 1963) pp. 117–23.
9. Thirwall and Brown, "Inflation ond growth". See also Committee for Economic Development, *How Low Income Countries Can Raise Their Own Growth* (Washington, DC: September 1966), pp. 23–46.
10. *Reserve Bank of India Bulletin* (Bombay, June 1967), p. 746.
11. Ibid., p. 750.
12. Austin Robinson, "Economic Progress in India", *The Three Banks Review*, March 1970, p. 27.
13. *Economic Survey*, 1974–75 (Government of India: New Delhi), p. 7.
14. *Economic Survey*, p. 13.
15. *Economic Survey*, 1975–76, p. 1.
16. *Economic Survey*, 1974–75, p. 16.
17. L.K. Jha, "Price Policy in a Developing Economy", *RBI Bulletin*, April 1968.

BIBLIOGRAPHY AND SELECTED READING LIST

J.N. Bhagwati, and S. Chakravarty: "Contributions to Indian Economic Analysis: A Survey". *American Economic Review* (Supplement). September 1969, pp. 29–66.
R.J. Bhatia: "Inflation, Deflation and Economic Development". *IMF Staff Papers*, October 1959.
Committee for Economic Development: *How Low Income Countries Can Advance Their Own Growth*. Washington. September 1966, pp. 23–46.
Graeme Dorrance: "Inflation and Growth: The Statistical Evidence". *IMF Staff Papers*, November 1960.
L.K. Jha: "Price Policy in a Developing Economy". *Reserve Bank of India Bulletin*, April 1968.
A.M. Khusro: "The Pricing of Food in India". *Quarterly Journal of Economics*. May 1967, pp. 271–86.
Arthur Lewis: "Economic Development with Unlimited Supplies of Labour". *The Manchester School*, May 1954. (Reprinted in

A.N. Agarwala and S.P. Singh (eds) *The Economics of Underdevelopment*. New York. Oxford University Press, 1963, pp. 400–49.
Geoffrey Maynard: *The Price Level and Economic Development*. London. Macmillan, 1963.
S. Mookerjee: "Financial Stability and Planning". *Finance and Development*. March 1972, pp. 2–9.
Austin Robinson: "Economic Progress in India". *The Three Banks Review*. March 1970, pp. 5–34.
A.P. Thirlwall and C.A. Brown: "Inflation and Growth: The International Evidence". *Banca Nazionale del Lavoro Quarterly*. September 1971.
N.K. Velayudhan: "Price Trends During the Three Plan Periods". *Reserve Bank of India Bulletin*. June 1967, pp. 740–66.
U Tun Wai: "The Relation Between Inflation and Economic Development: A Statistical Inductive Study". *IMF Staff Papers*, October 1959.

16

Black Money and the Indian Economy

RAM L. CHUGH

India has faced the problem of black money since the Second World War, but it assumed serious proportions in the last decade. At present, the problem is indeed a very grave one, threatening the social and economic stability of the country. While the exact holdings of black money are not known, they are believed to constitute a massive sum, and to be growing at a rapid rate. It is estimated nearly 10 per cent of the national income goes "black" every year. Put differently, nearly Rs. 1,500 to Rs. 2,000 crores worth of black income is created every year. As we shall see, the proliferation of black money at such an alarming rate has serious consequences for the Indian economy. The Direct Taxes Enquiry Committee (the Wanchoo Committee), appointed by the Government of India in 1970 to investigate the problems of black money and tax evasion, made the following observations:

In our country tax evasion and black money have now reached a stage which can only be described as a menace to the economy and a challenge to the fulfilment of the avowed objectives of distributive justice and setting up of an egalitarian society. The effects of "black money" on the economy of the country cannot but be described as disastrous.... Today, the country is seriously handicapped in its endeavour to march forward, when the resources needed for development are not forthcoming for the reason that business is carried on in the "black"... It is therefore no exaggeration to say that black money is like a cancerous growth in the country's economy which, if not checked in time, is sure to lead to its ruination.

The main objective of this chapter is to provide an overall understanding of the black money problem. We shall examine the definition of black. money, its magnitude, and the effects which it has on the Indian economy. We shall also examine the causes which lead to its creation and suggest methods to check its growth.

It should perhaps be pointed out that the problems of black money and tax evasion are not unique to India. These problem exist in almost every country of the world both developed and underdeveloped.[2] But the incidence of these illegal activities is reported to be much greater among the developing countries which can ill afford them because of the very tasks of economic development facing them.

Definition of Black Money

At the outset let us be clear as to what the term black money denotes. Even though the term is widely used in India, there is a lot of confusion about its meaning. Some people regard holdings of currency notes obtained primarily by illegal means as black money. Others take a much broader view and argue that in addition to the possession of illegal currency, black money should include investments in gold, jewellery, precious stones, real estate, and other business assets over and above those shown in the books of accounts for tax purposes. Other usages of the term lie somewhere between these two extreme. The Wanchoo Committee, instead of providing a clear definition, seems to have combined all the existing usages of black money and has given a definition which is all-embracing. According to the Committee, "the term black money is generally used to denote unaccounted money or concealed income and/or wealth as well as money involved in transactions wholly or partly suppressed".[3] The term black money thus is used to denote all types of illegal gains both financial and real, whether made in the current year or in the past.

The basic confusion in the Committee's use of the term and in those of others, is that no distinction is made between black money as wealth and black money as income. At present, the term refers to both. The terms income and wealth, even though closely related, are not identical in meaning. Wealth is a stock concept and refers to the accumulation of financial and real assets at a given point in time. Income, on the other hand, is a flow concept and refers to earnings made over a period of time, usually a year. The distinction between black money as income and black money as wealth is

important not only for measuring black money and in analysing its effects on the economy, but also for making policy recommendations for controlling it. The controlling of black income would require a set of policy tools different from those required for the unearthing of black wealth. In our discussions, we would use the term black income to include all illegal earnings and gains obtained through tax evasion and clandestine operations and through performing illegal services over a one-year period. Black income not spent in the current period but saved and invested would constitute black wealth. Thus, for example, when a public official accepts a bribe for granting a licence or a permit, he is earning black income. Similarly when a trader sells a controlled commodity at a price above the legal one and does not show this in his returns, he is earning black income. When a person sells a piece of property at a price higher than what is actually shown in the official records, he is earning black income. When an exporter underinvoices the exports and keeps the money abroad or brings it back by selling the foreign exchange in the black market, he is also earning black income. Such examples can be multiplied. One common feature of income earned through such methods is that these are kept secret and hidden from the tax authorities. Black income according to the Wanchoo Committee is a kind of "tainted" income. It has a stigma attached to it.

The term black money came to be frequently used in India during World War II, and was applied to earnings primarily made through black market transactions. India had to impose severe controls on several essential commodities during the war. But these controls were often violated by unscrupulous businessmen and traders who hoarded the commodities and sold them later in the black market. Consequently, huge profits were made by them and these earnings also escaped the tax net; since such profits were obtained illegally, they were kept hidden from the tax authorities. With the passage of time, the term black money has come to acquire a much broader meaning and now refers to the earnings and gains (financial and real) made primarily through violation of legal provisions and regulations.

Sources of Black Income

There are several causes for the creation of black income, but the two considered the most important are: the existence of extremely high marginal rates of taxation, considered confiscatory by many experts, which leave no incentive for saving and investment; and the economy of shortages with a multiplicity of controls and regulations which induce businessmen, traders, and middlemen to manipulate them for their benefit. Other causes, such as the prevalence of corruption, red tapism,' and the lack of social obligation on the part of both the business community and public officials, are to a great extent the byproducts of these two major causes. We shall examine these causes more carefully.

High Rates of Direct Taxation

The existence of extremely high rates of taxation on personal and corporate incomes appears to be one of the major causes of tax evasion, and generation of black income. The rate structure of direct taxation in India is one of the highest in the world. Until recently, the marginal rate on income tax alone was as high as 97.75 per cent. This indeed is an expropriatory level of taxation. And to assume that most people who fall in this income range would not be tempted to conceal their incomes to evade taxes is unrealistic. The Wanchoo Committee which has conducted an intensive study of this problem, has concluded that:

> The implication of 97.75 per cent income tax is that it is more profitable at a certain level of income to evade tax on Rs. 30 than to earn honestly Rs. 1,000. We will not be surprised that placed in such a situation it would be difficult for a person to resist the temptation to evade taxes. And, so long as the marginal rates of taxation are confiscatory it would be difficult to convince the public that tax evasion is anti-social.[4]

Economy of Shortages, Controls and Regulation

Like most developing countries, the Indian economy is a highly regulated one. The prices of several consumer goods (such as rice, wheat flour, vegetable ghee, and kerosene oil) and industrial raw materials (such as cement, steel and chemicals) are fixed and their distribution regulated. And, through various import and export controls, the foreign-exchange market is highly regulated and so is the allocation of foreign-exchange earnings. Similarly, the Government has instituted a battery of regulations to obtain a licence for starting an industry. From time to time, the Government has also imposed quotas and other quantitative restrictions on the production and distribution of several commodities in the country. All these and other regulations are designed to bring about a socially desirable production and distribution of essential commodities, and for diverting resources to areas of priorities consistent with the objectives of planned economic development.

Despite the government's good intentions, these controls have not been effectively implemented and, according to many observers[5] have failed to meet their objectives. These controls and regulations have been blatantly violated by businessmen, traders and even by government servants for their private gain. The basic motivation for violating the price and distribution controls is the high margin of profit between the controlled prices and the market clearing prices. Since the prices of most essential goods are fixed at below their market clearing prices, this leads to shortages and excess demand. Businessmen and distributors who obtain the supplies of controlled items through quota allotments, find the wide margin (between the controlled prices and the actual market prices) extremely alluring. Margins as high as 100 per cent have been reported for many of these commodities. To exploit the profitable situation, businessmen have been known to sell part of the stocks of such commodities in the black market. Such markets have been reported to flourish in most controlled items. It is the earning through such illegal operations which constitutes black income. As the Government imposed more controls and regulations to achieve the desired resource allocation for meeting the goals of five-year plans, it, in fact, kept increasing the scope for earning black income. To earn these illegal incomes, businessmen and traders manipulate the regulations and often bribe public officials to obtain quota allotments, and law enforcement agencies to hush them up. Thus, with the expansion of controls, the black market and corruption also increased which, in turn, generated black income.

Incomes earned through black market operations and through violation of other regulations escape the tax net as well because these are not revealed to the tax authorities for fear of severe penalties. It is argued that the intention of the tax evader in this case may not be the evasion of taxes but rather the clandestine operation itself which he is then forced to keep hidden from the tax authorities. Thus, the opportunity for earning black income is provided by the multiplicity of controls and regulations ineffectively implemented. It has often been argued that if the economy was less regulated and the price mechanism was allowed to operate freely, black income of this magnitude would not be generated. N.A. Palkhivala, an expert on taxation and constitutional law, also attributes the creation of black income mainly to these causes. He says: "The honour of enthroning black money must be divided equally between our industrial policy which believes in perpetuating shortages and our fiscal policy which believes in putting a strain on public integrity which it cannot bear".[6]

Method of Estimating Black Income

Estimates of black income generated primarily through tax evasion are available in the Wanchoo Committee Report. The Committee used the Kaldor method with some modifications to take into account the structural changes in the Indian economy. The estimation procedure involves looking at the national income data during a year and estimating how much of it would have gone into tax returns if no evasion had taken place and then comparing it with the income actually subjected to tax. The estimation procedure involves the following

steps:

1. The national income data is broken up into agricultural and nonagricultural income. Since agricultural income is not subjected to tax, attention is focused on national income originating in the non-agricultural sector. Income in the non-agricultural sector originates from several sources, such as mining and quarrying, manufacturing, and transportation, etc.

2. Income from each nonagricultural source is identified and is then broken up into its salary and nonsalary components. It is assumed that salary incomes are generally fully reported for taxation, and attention is, therefore, confined to non-salary income for possible tax evasion.

3. The whole of nonsalary income is not subjected to tax. An estimate is made of the proportion that is. Each sector is assigned a weight for determining the assessable nonsalary income (i.e., above the exemption limit).

4. The estimates of assessable non-salary income are compared with the income actually reported for tax purposes for that year. From this, the estimate of the tax-evaded income is made.

5. Given the estimates of tax-evaded income and the existing tax rates, an estimate of tax revenue lost by the Government is then made.

The method used by the Wanchoo Committee for estimating the assessable nonsalary income for the financial year 1961–62, is summarised in Table 16.1. Column 4 in the Table indicates the weights assigned to each sectoral income for estimating the proportion of nonsalary income above the exemption limit. These weights vary from 50 per cent for income grouped under the head Miscellaneous to 100 per cent for the income from Banking and Insurance and Public Administration and Defence. The assessable nonsalary income for 1961–62 was estimated at Rs. 2,686 crores. The income actually reported for tax purposes for that year was Rs. 1,875 crores. Hence the tax-evaded income for 1961–62 was Rs. 811 crores. By applying the ratio of evaded income to the assessable nonsalary income of 1961–62 to the assessable nonsalary income of 1965–66, the Committee estimated that the tax-evaded income for 1965–66 was about

Table 16.1. Sector-Wise Distribution of Assessable Nonsalary Income for 1961–62

Assessment year 1962–63

(Rs. Crores)

| Sectors | National Income | | Assumed Pro-portion of Non-salary Income Above Exemp-tion Limit (percentage) | Assessable Nonsalary Income |
	Total Salary Income	Non-salary Income		
1	2	3	4	5
1. Mining and quarring	60	89	60	53
2. Manufacturing^a	1,247	1,523	60	914
3. Railways and Communications	286	67	—	—
4. Other Transport	151	151	60	91
5. Trade, Hotels and Restaurants	278	1111	70	777
6. Banking & Insurance	134	49	100	49
7. Public Administration & Defence	475	118	100	118
8. Miscellaneous^b	—	1,369	50	684
Total	2,631	4,477	—	2,686
9. Agriculture	1,030	6,025		
Grand Total	3,661	10,502		
Nonsalary income of financial year 1961–62 which was actually assessed to tax				1,875

^{a}Includes large scale, small scale, construction, electricity, gas, water supply, etc.

^{b}Includes real estate, ownership and other services.

SOURCE: *The Wanchoo Committee Report*, p. 7.

Rs. 1,216 crores. The estimates of the nonsalary income for 1965–66 are given in Table 16.2. The Committee made some further "adjustments"[7] in these estimates to arrive at the final figures of the tax-evaded income. The final estimates show that the tax-evaded income was Rs. 700 crores for 1961–62, Rs. 1,000 crores for 1965–66, and Rs. 1,400 crores for 1968–69. From these estimates, it appears that nearly 30 per cent of the assessable nonsalary income escapes taxation every year.

Dr. D.K. Rangnekar, a member of the committee, considers these estimates to be on the low side and feels that the actual magnitude of tax-evaded income is much higher. In a dissenting note to the Committee *Report*, he says: "The magnitude of the tax-evaded income or "black" income is underestimated in the main report. This is so mainly because of the arbitrary assumptions behind them. The estimates would change if the assumptions

and arbitrary multipliers changed".[8] Rangnekar has provided his own estimates of black money which are based on a detailed analysis of expenditure statistics for the different sectors of the economy. According to his estimates, the tax-evaded income for 1961–62 was Rs. 1,150 crores, compared to the Committee's estimates of Rs. 811 crores. For 1965–66, Rangnekar's estimate was Rs. 2,350 crores as against the Committee's estimate of Rs. 1,216 crores. Rangnekar's estimate of the tax-evaded income for 1968–69 was Rs. 2,833 crores.

There is a significant difference between the Committee's estimates of tax-evaded incomes and those of Rangnekar's. The Committee used the earning approach for making its estimates whereas Rangnekar used the expenditure approach. It is difficult to determine which approach is the more reliable.[9] By the very definition of black income and the very nature of these transactions, there are no reliable

Table 16.2. **Sector-Wise Distribution of Assessable Nonsalary Income for 1965–66**
Assessment Year 1966–67
(Rs. Crores)

Sectors	National Income		Assumed Pro-portion of Non-salary Income Above Exemp-tion Limit (percentage)	Assessable Nonsalary Income
	Total Salary Income	Non-salary Income		
1	2	3	4	5
1. Mining and Quarrying	94	140	60	84
2. Manufacturing*a*	1,890	2,310	60	1,386
3. Railways and Communication	416	97	—	—
4. Other Transport	223	222	60	133
5. Trade, Hotels and Restaurants	445	1,784	70	1,249
6. Banking and Insurance	245	90	100	90
7. Public Administration and Defence	1,040	260	100	260
8. Miscellaneous*b*	—	1,651	50	825
Total	4,353	6,554	—	4,027
9. Agriculture	1,575	8,271		
Grand Total	5,928	14,825		

*a*Includes large scale, small scale, construction, electricity, gas, water-supply, etc.

*b*Includes real estate, ownership and other services.

Source: Government of India, Ministry of Finance, *Direct Taxes Enquiry Committee, Final Report* (New Delhi, December 1971).

or verifiable data on the subject. There is however, no doubt of the magnitude of black wealth and that it is growing at at a rapid rate. The figure most often quoted is that nearly 10 per cent of the national income goes "black" every year.

Effects of Black Income on the Economy

Black income has come to exert a strong power in the economy. It has given rise to what the Wanchoo Committee calls the "parallel" or the "black" money economy in India. The black money economy operates side by side with the "open" or the "official" economy; while the latter is subject to the controls of monetary and fiscal policies the former seems to be immune to it. It in fact defies almost every kind of discipline and regulation and operates with a momentum of its own. It has been estimated that the total money value of transactions con-

ducted in the black money economy in 1968–69 was of the order of Rs. 7,000 crores, which represents 1/5 of the total.[10] Although estimates for later years are not available, unofficial reports indicate evidence of further growth in the value of such transactions.

The black money economy is often blamed for thwarting the developmental and stabilization efforts of the Government by (1) encouraging various types of pro-hibited economic activities, such as black-marketing, racketeering, adulteration, and smuggling of foreign goods; (2) creating artificial scarcities of essential commodities through speculation and hoarding; (3) altering the distribution of income in favour of the rich; and (4) diverting scarce resources to areas considered socially undesirable. In other words, by blatantly violating the existing economic regulations, the black economy undermines the very process of economic planning and development. To understand fully the serious implications which the black money economy has for price stability, economic growth, and distribution of income, it is essential that we examine the pattern of consumption, saving, and investment of black income.

Loss of Tax Revenue

The direct result of the creation of black income is, of course, the loss of tax revenue to the Government. Based on the Wanchoo Committee's estimates, and applying an average tax rate of 33 per cent, the estimated tax revenue loss for the years 1961–62, 65–66, and 68–69 would be Rs. 233 crores, 333 crores, and 470 crores. Tax evasion in reality involves the transfer of control over the use of the tax-evaded funds from the Government to the tax evader. The expenditure pattern of the tax-evaded funds has serious economic consequences: to the extent they are spent on current consumption rather than paid to the Government as taxes, there is a reduction of aggregate savings, which retards the rate of growth. The total loss of tax revenue over the last 20 years would probably exceed the quantum of deficit financing incurred. In addition to losing revenue, the Government also ends up spending a lot of its time and energy enforcing tax laws and apprehending tax evaders.

Distribution of Income

By eroding the progressivity of tax rates, tax evasion undermines the equity concept of taxation and leads to greater income-inequality and concentration of wealth. Available estimates indicate that tax-evaded income has been growing faster than national income. Tax evasion thus breeds further evasion, which widens the gap between the rich and the poor even further. Tax evasion makes it difficult to achieve the declared policy objectives of distributive justice, and the establishing of an egalitarian society.

Consumption, Savings, and Investment of Black Income

Black income like "white" income is partly consumed and partly saved and invested. Unlike white income which can be saved

and invested in several forms openly and legally, black income has limited options available to it. For example, savings out of black income may not be deposited in a regular commercial bank or invested in Government securities for fear of being detected. Because of this, a greater proportion of black income is likely to be consumed rather than saved and invested. Since black income is cheap money because it does not suffer reduction through taxation and is generally concentrated in the hands of people who are already well-off, the consumption pattern out of black income is likely to be biased towards luxury goods and extravagant living. For instance, lavish and wasteful expenditure on weddings and other festivities has been attributed to the availability of black earnings. This consumption pattern has adverse effects on the growth possibilities of the country because it causes the diversion of scarce resources into sectors which are primarily devoted to producing goods and services for satisfying these needs. The adverse effects of this consumption pattern are further accentuated through the demonstration effect which it has on the rest of society. Since this expenditure pattern supports a pattern of production and investment which uses resources considered socially more valuable, it in effect retards the process of economic growth.

The consumption pattern of the black-income elite also includes demand for foreign goods, such as tape recorders, cameras, cosmetics, appliances, and synthetic fabrics. There is a general craze for imported goods, especially among the black-income "elite". Perhaps there is a strong desire among these people to differentiate their living standards from those of the rest of the people, and one way to accomplish this is through the possession of foreign goods. Since there are severe restrictions on the import of non-essential goods, a large-scale smuggling operation exists to meet this demand. Every year smuggled goods worth crores of rupees are caught by the Anti-Smuggling Squads: smuggled goods caught in Bombay during September 1973–January 1974 were valued at Rs. 64 crores.[11] The magnitude of smuggling must be very great. Payment for these goods is made through illicit foreign funds.

Black income not consumed but saved and accumulated constitutes black wealth. As indicated before, savings out of black income can take only limited forms. The most common forms in which black savings are generally held, are: cash; gold and precious stones; foreign bank deposits; inventories build-up; residential and commercial property; and investment in business and industry. All these savings are kept hidden and are not shown in the regular books of accounts.

Black savings held in the form of currency are noninflationary because that much currency gets sterilized. Government can supply currency equivalents to that amount without worrying about its inflationary consequences. However, as we shall see, hoarded currency is a potential threat to the economy because it provides its holder with a readily available stock of black liquidity.

Black savings held in the form of gold and precious stones are generally inflationary because of the increased demand for such metals. Given the favourable price differential, they also encourage the smuggling of gold and other metals into the country. Black savings held in this form lead to immobilization of investible funds, and to the extent these savings are used to buy the smuggled-in gold and precious stones, they create leakages into the foreign sector.

Similarly, when part of the black savings are transferred abroad as deposits in foreign banks (e.g., Swiss banks), through illegal channels, this leakage is further intensified. The smuggling-in of consumer durable goods, gold and precious stones, and the illicit transfer of funds abroad are a severe drain on scarce domestic resources, and worsen the country's balance-of-payments position. The payment for these transactions is made through fraudulent invoice practices in foreign trade through other illegal deals in the foreign-exchange market. It is estimated that India loses around Rs. 300 crores worth of foreign exchange annually through such illicit transfers.[12] The loss of foreign exchange of this magnitude seriously affects the country's capacity to import capital and other essential goods for economic development, and weakens the external value of the rupee.

Residential and commercial property is yet another means of investing black savings. The method used for investing in real estate is by making part of the payment of the total value of the land or building in "white" (for the purpose of recording the transaction officially) and part in "black". The ratio of payments between "white" and "black" is agreed upon between the buyer and seller. Sometimes the ratios of "white" and "black" payments for real-estate deals are widely quoted, as the Wanchoo Committee found out during its investigations. For example, the Committee found that the commonly quoted ratio in Bombay was 60 to 40, i.e., 60 per cent of the total value of the deal had to be paid in "white" and 40 per cent in "black".[13] Because a part of the purchase price is paid in "black", it results in the undervaluation of the property which, in turn, leads to loss of wealth and property tax for the Government. Because of inflation, investment in real estate has become attractive. This has resulted in the skyrocketing of prices and rents for land and other real estate, especially in big cities like Bombay and Delhi.

Part of black savings are invested in business activities, primarily through understating the true value of capital equipment and other business assets. It is sometimes argued that the availability of black savings has stimulated the growth of small and medium business enterprises in the country. Since black investment generates more black income, it has given rise to a new class of entrepreneurs or black-income elite. The temptation to evade taxes and to become rich quickly provides the necessary motivating force. Since black money helps promote entrepreneurship and industrial growth, some people would regard this aspect as a positive contribution to the process of economic growth. Economic benefits notwithstanding, growth through tax evasion and clandestine operations is undoubtedly socially and morally undesirable.

Investment of black savings, whatever form it takes, is always concealed and is generally recorded in the "number two" account. For the purposes of tax evasion and conducting illegal operations, businessmen in general maintain two sets of accounts. One set contains records of business transactions which are open, legal, and subject to tax. The other set, often referred to as the "number two" account, contains business dealings which are kept hidden from the tax authorities. Sometimes well-paid professional accountants and even tax consultants are hired to prepare the number two account.

Black Savings, Black Liquidity and Monetary Policy

Black savings are also used for the financing of inventory hoardings of essential consumer goods and sensitive industrial raw materials. Scarcity conditions provide hoarders and speculators with an opportunity for making lucrative gains by hoarding such commodities and selling them later at a considerable margin of "black" profit. Working capital needed for the financing of inventory build-ups is provided by the availability of black liquidity. Current and past black savings held in the form of currency and in other readily cashable assets like gold and precious stones, constitute black liquidity. It is the existence of vast amounts of black liquidity which provides the necessary finance for all kinds of illegal operations, including the stock-piling of essential goods, and thereby poses a severe threat to the price and other economic stabilization programmes of the government.

Black liquidity, by becoming an alternative source of finance, often conflicts with the credit-rationing policies of the monetary authority. Whenever the monetary authority wants to pursue a tight money policy or a policy of selective credit control, the availability of black liquidity can frustrate these policies by making funds available to those areas. Recent shortages of essential commodities such as sugar, edible oil, and foodgrains, have been attributed to the availability of these funds to speculators and hoarders in contravention of the directives of the monetary authorities. According to Rangnekar:

Massive concealed money income moved, python-like, now in foodgrains trade, now in edible oils, now in raw materials, in soap, matches and what have you. Black money and uncanny instinct for windfall gains combined to play havoc with supply of sensitive goods and also with finance controls. Black money has become an alternative source of finance for all speculative operations.

Black liquidity thus defies the monetary authority and renders its restrictive credit policy almost ineffective.

Corruption and Bureaucracy The fact that economic regulations are violated and the black money economy functions actively, indicates that the laws and economic regulations are not enforced effectively. The large-scale corruption prevalent among the public officials responsible for executing these laws is considered one of the major causes of this. The implementation of economic regulations gives Government officials a vast amount of discretionary power for granting (or denying) licences, quota permits, foreign-exchange allocations, and entitlement to various controlled items. But the very existence of acute scarcity conditions for most of the controlled commodities provides unprecedented opportunities for bribery and corruption, and the temptation to misuse this power. Businessmen and traders seeking entitlement to various restricted commodities are often eager to bribe the concerned official to obtain such allocations because they know that they can sell these commodities in the black market at a very handsome profit. Since the public officials who have this discretionary power are often low-paid functionaries, they find that this black income (earned by accepting bribes) supplements their incomes to a considerable degree. The perpetuation of existing controls and the imposition of new ones, thus is in the interest of the officials. Consequently, the black-money economy and corruption become self-reinforcing and flourish together.

Graft and corruption have become so widespread that for the performance of what is considered their normal official duties, many officials have to be paid. For example, in order to speed up the process of obtaining various permits, quotas, and other allocations, it has become necessary for businessmen to pay what the Santhanam Committee calls "speed money" to civil servants. Black income lubricates the wheels of the slow-moving governmental machinery. Inordinate delays in completing various administrative procedures are not uncommon. According to a recent study, "The average time taken for the issue of an industrial licence (from the date of application) which was 93 days in 1970, increased to 176 days in 1971 and to 291 days in 1972".[15]

The foregoing discussion has brought out the adverse effects which black income has on the economy. These effects have been summarized in Chart 16.1. It must be recognized that black income is illegal because the economic activities which give rise to it are prohibited by law. It is, however, possible that some laws regulating economic activities may be politically motivated and designed to serve vested interests rather than have a sound economic rationale. It is also possible that while formulating an economic regulation, Government may not fully recognize all the causes underlying an economic problem and also it may not fully appreciate all the effects which the regulation would have on the economy. Because of this, some economic regulations may be poorly designed and have undesirable effects. Thus, to the extent that black economic activities make the government re-evaluate the structure of economic regulations for adequacy and rationality, they do serve a useful purpose.

Measures for Reducing the Creation of Black Income

Reforming the Tax Structure and Its Enforcement

Tax evasion, which is one of the major sources of black income, has been attributed primarily to the existence of exorbitantly high marginal rates of taxation. But it should be recognized that tax evasion is a function not only of the level and degree of progressivity of tax rates but also of the degree to which the tax laws are actually enforced. Tax evasion is an illegal economic activity and the person who participates in it takes the risk of being caught and punished. If we assume that the tax evader is rational and is interested in maximizing his expected profits, he would engage in tax evasion only if the expected gain from it exceeds the expected loss. Expected gain from tax evasion equals the amount of tax evaded times the probability of being able to get away with it. Expected loss, on the other hand, equals the penalty he would have to bear (if caught and convicted) times the probability of getting caught. Through an effective and rigorous tax-enforcement policy, the Government can increase the probability of the tax evader being apprehended and convicted. And, through suitably devising the severity of the punishment imposed (penalties), the Government can raise the "expected cost" of tax evasion, and thereby make it less profitable. But the policy of vigorous enforcement is not without cost to the society because its implementation requires a considerable amount of resources. However, the cost of tax enforcement should be viewed in relation to the tax revenue expected through such an enforcement policy. In order to formulate a suitable tax enforcement policy, it is essential that the Government weigh the extra cost of the tax administration against the tax revenue expected. It should push the enforcement policy only up to that point where the additional cost of tax enforcement equals the tax revenue generated[16]. In a situation where the extra cost of tax enforcement is smaller than the tax revenue, it would be desirable to strengthen the enforcement policy further. Conversely, if the extra cost exceeds the extra tax revenue, it would be unwise to pursue the policy any further. Under the circumstances, it may be desirable to modify the rate structure of taxation suitably to reduce the incentive for evasion.

Thus, the Government can attack the problem of tax evasion not only through investing more resources in a stringent tax-enforcement policy but also through the manipulation of tax rates. It has been

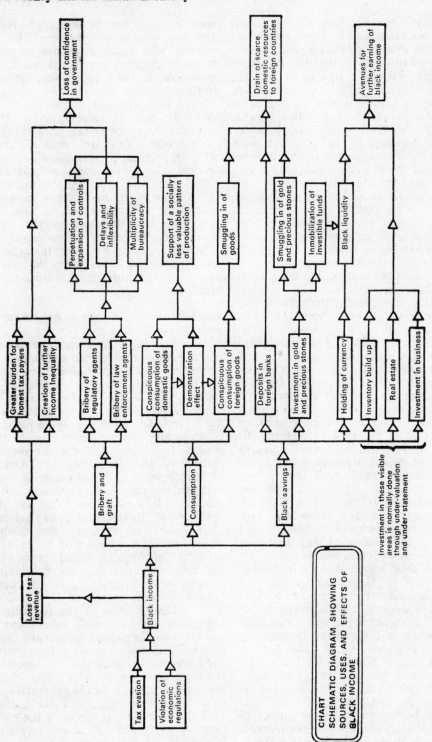

CHART
SCHEMATIC DIAGRAM SHOWING
SOURCES, USES, AND EFFECTS OF
BLACK INCOME

Chart 16.1

generally observed that tax structures based on extremely high marginal rates make tax evasion profitable, and governments often find it difficult to divert "enough" resources to enforce the tax laws effectively.[17] The existence of tax evasion, in effect, reduces the degree of progressivity of the tax rates. Consequently, the Government may have to choose between a tax structure with relatively high marginal rates but enforced somewhat ineffectively (thus giving rise to tax evasion) and a tax structure with relatively low rates but enforced effectively, that brought in the same revenue. Those people who are hardened tax evaders may prefer the former structure of taxation, but in general, most people would prefer the latter.

To combat tax evasion and the generation of black income in India, the Wanchoo Committee recommended the reduction of the marginal tax rates from the 97.74 per cent level to 75 per cent. The Committee also called for the strengthening of the tax administration, and recommended a strong and vigorous enforcement of tax laws. The Government of India has already accepted most of these recommendations. The marginal tax rates on income were reduced to 77 per cent in the 1974–75 budget. To give some edge to the tax enforcement machinery, the Government has made several changes and amendments in the existing tax laws. These changes are now embodied in the 1975 Taxation (Amendment) law and make new provisions for disclosure of incomes, higher penalties, and increased jail sentences for the convicted tax evaders.

It has been argued that the reduction of tax rates to 77 per cent would not reduce the incidence of tax evasion because the cost of evasion in India is very low.[18] In fact, it is argued that it would even lead to a decline in tax revenue because the honest tax payers would now pay at reduced rates. Whether the new tax rate structure accompanied with more effective enforcement would succeed in reducing the incidence of tax evasion, will not be known for some time. If the magnitude of tax evasion is not reduced significantly despite the stringent enforce-

ment policy, it may be desirable to reduce the tax rates even further. The tax evaders who find tax evasion profitable at the 77 per cent rate would not find it profitable if the rates were reduced further. In fact, the tax rates rising to 77 per cent are still considered to be relatively high by some experts. Most countries have income-tax rates rising to 50 per cent. Thus, to deal effectively with the problem of tax evasion and black income, the Government will have to experiment with reducing the tax rates still further.[19] It should also be added that a tax structure based on relatively low rates that brought in the same revenue as the tax structure based on relatively high rates because of tax evasion, may be preferred both from the equity and income-distribution aspects of taxation.

Rationalization of Economic Regulations and Controls

Rationalization of the structure of economic regulations through the elimination of unwanted and ineffectively enforced controls, would help considerably in reducing the scope for the creation of black income. As discussed before, the Indian economy relies heavily on physical controls and direct intervention in the market for bringing about the desired pattern of resource allocation. Almost all important economic activities are regulated in one form or other. But most of the studies conducted on the working of these regulations indicate their failure in achieving the desired objectives. It is argued that by creating artificial scarcities, delays, and bottlenecks, and inflexibilities in the decision-making process, most of these regulations have slowed down the process of development. This is because most of the regulations are poorly designed, badly administered, and are often formulated without any clear rationale and consideration of the adverse consequences on economic performance. Bhagwati and Desai, who have done painstaking research on the industrial and trade policies pursued by India during 1951–68, indicate that many of the controls were adopted in an arbitrary and haphazard manner. And, after carefully analysing the working of various price and distribution controls, Bhagwati and Desai conclude that most of these controls "were ill-advised and formed a part of the general economic philosophy of direct intervention without careful examination of direct efficiency and of efficiency vis-a-vis alternative ways of achieving the given objectives".[20] A case in point is the fixing of prices for intermediate products like cement and steel. The price of cement was effectively controlled at the point of production but not at the point of final sale. The result was that while the consumer often paid the black market price, the producer of the cement got only the controlled price. The excess profit was kept by the distributor as black income or it was shared with the officials granting the cement quota. In the process, this income also escaped the tax net. Price control in such a situation neither benefited the consumer nor provided the necessary incentive to the producer for expanding production. If the price of cement had not been regulated, the excess profit would have gone to the producer and part of it to the government as tax revenue.[21]

The effectiveness of various regulations on foreign trade during the 20-year period 1951–71, and their ultimate impact on the performance of the Indian economy have also been studied in depth by Bhagwati and Srinivasan. The following summarises their findings:

India's foreign trade regime, in conjunction with domestic licensing policies in the industrial sector, led to economic inefficiencies and impaired her economic performance. This conclusion follows not merely from the static analysis but also from our analysis of growth effects. The policy framework was detrimental, on balance, to the growth of the economy by adversely influencing export performance, by wasteful inter-industrial and inter-firm allocation of resources, by permitting and encouraging expansion of excess capacity and by blunting competition and hence the incentive for cost consciousness and quality improvement.[22]

The foregoing discussion, though not a complete review of the working of all economic regulations, does suggest the need for a critical evaluation of the existing economic regulations. Economic regulations devoid of any clear rationale and others which have outlived their usefulness, should be discarded. Economic regulations which are essential and promote the interests of the society as a whole, should be retained and implemented effectively. It may be worthwhile to compare the expected cost of enforcing an economic regulation with its expected benefits. While doing this, it is essential to take into account both the direct and indirect costs and benefits which the regulation would have on the economy. Implementation of any regulation requires valuable resources and something would have to be given up in the process. Thus, a society has to weigh carefully the expected benefits and costs of implementing a regulation. If the implementation is too expensive, it may be worthwhile to examine alternative methods of achieving the given objectives. Other methods, such as monetary and fiscal policies, and positive discretionary controls, may prove to be equally effective in achieving the desired results.

Removal of nonessential controls and regulations would release administrative resources which can then be used elsewhere for socially more productive purposes. Similarly, it would free the energy not devoted to hiding illegal economic activity. It would also reduce the scope for generation of black income and, thus, bring in more tax revenue for the Government. And, more important, the relaxation of controls would bring about more efficient allocation of resources.

Unearthing Black Wealth

The measures discussed above deal primarily with the problem of black income and not with the unearthing of black wealth. As we have already indicated, black wealth, especially when held in readily cashable assets, poses a serious threat to the stability of the economy. Several methods, such as demonetization, voluntary disclosure schemes, and searches and seizures, have been tried to unearth black wealth. But the results of these efforts have never been encouraging and the problem persists unabated. Demonetization, which was tried in 1949, does not find much favour now because of the extreme difficulties in implementing it. The voluntary disclosure scheme has been tried several times but the wealth disclosed constituted a very tiny sum. The method of searches and seizures has been used quite frequently but the amount of black wealth seized has been insignificant. For example, during the period 1964 to 1971, 1,447 searches and seizures were conducted, of which 1,418 were successful; the value of black assets seized amounted to the tiny sum of Rs. 7 crores. The Wanchoo Committee advised against the voluntary disclosure scheme because it felt that it almost sanctifies the earning of black wealth. The Committee recommended strengthening the settlement machinery, and using the method of searches and seizures more frequently and effectively. The Government of India, however, experimented again with the voluntary disclosure scheme which was announced in October 1975, and called it the "last" chance. It gave three months' time for people to disclose their black incomes and hoarded black wealth. Because of the incentives offered, the scheme was much more successful than was anticipated. The amount disclosed was nearly Rs. 1,600 crores, which far exceeded the total amount disclosed for all the three schemes tried earlier, which had been Rs. 267 crores. Even though the scheme was considered a success it barely "touched the tip of the iceberg".[23] When the annual generation of black income is estimated at around Rs. 2,000 crores, the accumulated stock of black wealth over many years must constitute a formidable sum.

The major reason for efforts in the unearthing of black wealth being abortive appears to be the continued existence of unlimited opportunities for earning black income. Black wealth is needed for earning black income. In order to deal with the problem of black wealth effectively, it is essential to direct efforts towards eliminating the "sources" which give rise to black earning.[24] Once the root causes of black income are eradicated, black wealth would not be a potential threat to the economy. It would either lie idle or attempts would be made to convert it into "white".

In closing, it should be pointed out that the problems of black income and black wealth exist in almost every society, though in varying degrees. From the experience of other countries, it appears that it is almost impossible to wipe out completely all the causes of black income. But what can be done is minimize the scope for the generation of black income.

REFERENCES

1. Government of India, *Direct Taxes Enquiry Committee: Final Report* (New Delhi: Government of India Press, 1972), pp. 5–6.
2. Illegal economic activities plague almost every country. Even some of the socialist countries suffer from them. But when the incidence of these activities gets to be unmanageable and threatens the functioning of the economy (as in most developing countries including India), it becomes essential to take effective measures to counteract them. For a discussion of some of these activities in the United Sates, see Clarke Thurston and John J. Tigue, Jr., *Dirty Money* (New York: Simon and Schuster, 1975); and Timothy B. Schellhardt, "Stiffer Sentences for Price-Fixers?", *The Wall Street Journal*, 17 December 1976. For black market activities in Burma, see Barry Kramer, "Burma's Black Market Bustles With Activity as Economy Stagnates", *The Wall Street Journal,* 3 August 1976. Billy J. Dudley, "Bogged Down in Speed Money", *FAO Review*, vol. 6, September–October 1973, pp. 26–29; and Herbert H. Werlin, "The Consequences of Corruption: The Ghanaian Experience", *Political Science Quarterly*, vol. 88, no. 1, March 1973, pp. 71–85, contain discussion of some of these activities among African countries.
3. *Direct Taxes Enquiry Committee Report*, p. 4.
4. *Direct Taxes Enquiry Committee Report*, p. 7.
5. For a critical analysis of the working of various economic regulations, see Jagdish N. Bhagwati and Padma Desai, *India : Planning for Industrialization* (London:

Oxford University Press, 1970), and S. Sen, Smuggling, Exchange Controls and Indian Economy", *Economic and Political Weekly,* February 1975, Annual Number, pp. 205–216.

6. N.A. Palkhivala, "If I Were the Finance Minister", *The Illustrated Weekly of India,* 12 March 1972, p. 13.

7. These adjustments are made to take into account various expenses and other allowances considered nontaxable. See *Direct Taxes Enquiry Committee Report,* p. 8.

8. *Direct Taxes Enquiry Committee Report,* p. 249.

9. The Committee's method of estimating tax-evaded income and black income does appear to suffer from several weaknesses. Firstly, the weights assigned to various sectors for estimating assessable nonsalary income above the exemption limit seem arbitrary and no justification is provided for choosing those weights. Secondly, the assumption that salary incomes are generally fully reported for taxation may not be true in reality, especially for the employees in large corporations. Finally, the Committee perhaps treats black income as equivalent to tax-evaded income. While tax evasion is a prime source of black income, it can also be created through other means as well, such as through the payments of "speed" money and "hush" money (bribes). The giver and receiver of such monies may not be within the taxable range. Because of these weaknesses, it is possible that the Committee's estimates are on the low side but that does not automatically make Rangnekar's estimates more reliable. Considerable research needs to be done before a definite judgement can be made.

10. *Direct Taxes Enquiry Committee Report,* p. 6.

11. D.K. Rangnekar, "Inflation, Taxation, and Black Money", *The Economic Times Annual* 1974, Bombay p. 55.

12. Meena Gupta and M.J.K. Thavaraj, "Tax Evasion and Development", *The Economic Times Annual*, 1974, Bombay, p. 63.

13. *Direct Taxes Enquiry Committee Report,* p. 5.

14. Rangnekar, Inflation, Taxation, and Black Money", p. 54.

15. Dilip Thakore, "The Causes and Effects of Corruption", *Quest,* vol. 58, November-December 1973, p. 38.

16. In the calculation of the extra revenue ex-pected, one should also include the amount received through penalties.

17. See John F. Due, *Government Finance: Economics of the Public Sector* (Homewood, Illinois: Irwin, 1968), especially ch. 15.

18. See A.K. Dasgupta, "Tax Concession as a Remedy", *Economic and Political Weekly,* vol. 9, 1 June 1974, 875–76.

19. Reduction in the marginal tax rates may be confined to the top brackets.

20. Bhagwati and Desai, *India: Planning for Industrialization,* p. 278.

21. For a discussion of the working of steel controls, see Government of India, Ministry of Steel and Heavy Industries, *Report of Steel Control* (New Delhi: Government of India Press, 1963).

22. Jagdish N. Bhagwati and T.N. Srinivasan, *Foreign Trade Regimes and Economic Development: India* (New York: National Bureau of Economic Research, 1975), p. 245. References to different parts of the book in this quotation have been omitted.

23. *Economic and Political Weekly,* vol. 11, 27 March 1976, p. 487.

24. Recently, the Government of India took several steps to reduce the incidence of illegal economic activities. The adoption of the Taxation (Amendment) Act of 1975 designed to discourage tax evasion has already been referred to. The degree of success which the voluntary disclosure scheme achieved can be partly attributed to the new determination which the government showed in dealing with these problems. Through the Conservation of Foreign Exchange and Prevention of Smuggling Activities Act (COFEPOSA) of 1974, the Government took several measures to deal effectively with the problems of smuggling and foreign exchange racketeering. The Government took measures to tone up the administration by weeding out the employees who had links with persons involved in smuggling or the foreign exchange racket. Under the Essential Commodities Act, the Government took drastic steps against black marketeers, speculators and hoarders. The Government liberalized the Industrial Licensing Policy by exempting certain medium-sized industries from the normal industrial licensing procedures. For a discussion of these measures, see Government of India, Ministry of Information and Broadcasting, *India: A Reference Annual,* 1976 (New Delhi: Government of India, Publications Division, 1976).

Part Seven

PUBLIC FINANCE

17

Taxation and Economic Development in India

JAMES CUTT

Objectives of Taxation Policy under Planned Economic Development

The financing of economic development is primarily a "bootstraps" operation. Developing countries must to a very large extent finance internally their development programmes. The primary means of internal financing available to such countries is taxation.

It is the object of this paper to examine the role of taxation policy, as one of a set of public policy instruments, in furthering the attainment of the objectives of planned economic development. The explicit context for the examination and evaluation of taxation policy must therefore be the specification of the objectives of taxation policy in the context of planned economic development, the objective set reflecting the objectives of planned development articulated in the series of five-year plans.

The appropriate set of taxation policy objectives may be derived from the articulation of broad planning objectives, and may be subsumed under three major heads : Growth, Equity and Stabilization.

Growth: The growth objective may be defined as the attainment of *the rate and pattern* of growth of national income considered desirable in terms of planning objectives. In the context of the central planning objective to improve living standards as quickly as possible, taxation policy must be designed to *increase the rate of growth of national income in aggregate terms*, but also to *transform the pattern of national income growth* in accordance with planning priorities.

In order to promote an increase in the rate of growth of national income, taxation policy must serve to increase the proportion of national income directed to developmental spending, defined as the aggregate of investment spending in the private sector, and investment spending plus consumption spending of a developmental nature in the public sector. The division of public expenditures into developmental and nondevelopmental is now made annually in the Economic Survey which precedes the Union budget, and the broader concept of developmental or growth-oriented spending which this statistical classification facilitates, underlines the contribution to economic growth of a considerable proportion of public spending which though formally classified as of a consumption nature is, in fact, directly growth-promoting in nature.

With respect to the private sector, the growth objective of taxation policy may be couched in both negative and positive terms. On the one hand, taxation policy for increased public revenue must be so designed as to minimize the opportunity cost of increased revenue in terms of private savings (and therefore investment) foregone. On the other hand, and more positively, the tax system must incorporate a set of incentives designed to promote directly an *increased savings ratio* in the private sector.

In sum, the aspect of the growth objective relating to the rate rather than the pattern of economic growth may be defined as the maximization of the incremental ratio of developmental spending to national income, in effect, substituting $\triangle [Y - (C_h + C_{gn})]/\triangle Y$, for the traditional $\triangle S/\triangle Y$, where Y is national income, S is saving, C_h and C_{gn} are, respectively, household consumption and public consumption expenditure of a nondevelopmental nature, and $\triangle$ indicates an increment in the variable.

The maximization of the ratio of incremental developmental spending to national income will, of course, be constrained by the extent to which increases in household consumption and public sector nondevelopmental spending can be limited; the degree of restraint on increases in household consumption will reflect a compromise between the maximum possible rate of economic growth and the desire to improve living standards in the short run—in effect, an acutely difficult generational tradeoff.

The policy of providing incentives to private sector saving and investment, and, possibly, to work of certain kinds, constitutes an active policy of fiscal dirigism. The principle of neutrality, whereby the tax system seeks to avoid interference in the private allocation of resources, is defensible in a developed

economy, but, it may be argued, is of little relevance to the problem of economic development, where optimum resource allocation may not unreasonably be defined as that allocation specified as desirable in the national plan.

In addition to a system of incentives to save, invest and work, it may be argued that the tax system in developing countries should be designed to promote the desired use of resources by taxing in terms of "potential" resource use. This principle is of great importance in agriculture, where the tax base may be defined as "average potential output", and in the case of wealth taxation, where the net wealth tax effectively taxes on an assumed average rate of return on capital, penalizing, respectively, the inefficient farmer on the one hand, and the hoarder and the conservative investor on the other.

The concept of a policy of fiscal dirigism implies not only that growth be maximized —subject to the constraint indicated above—in an aggregate sense, but that the *pattern* of growth be modified so as to conform as closely as possible to the pattern of resource allocation specified in the national plan.

The equity objective may be broadly defined to include a basic *principle* of taxation policy and a major *objective* of taxation policy in developing countries. The principle is that of horizontal equity, and requires the equal treatment of tax-paying units in similar circumstances. Although in this broad sense unexceptionable, the principle may be construed in a literal way to require tax neutrality, and may thus be redefined in the planning context to require the avoidance of non-neutral or unequal treatment of tax-paying units in similar circumstances except insofar as such non-neutral treatment reflects deliberate fiscal dirigism, i.e., intended inequalities of treatment intended to induce behaviour of the sort considered desirable under planning objectives.

The second, more controversial, aspect of equity is the objective of redistribution —the moderation of inequalities of income, wealth and opportunity through the use of taxation policy. The redistribution objective originates in the Indian Constitution and has been re-affirmed in each of the five-year plans. Perhaps its most eloquent articulation was by the Taxation Enquiry Commission:

> We can no longer afford to leave the problem of equality to the automatic functioning of economic and social forces... The demand that the instrument of taxation should be used as a means of bringing about a redistribution of income more in consonance with social justice cannot be kept in abeyance.[2]

The specification of the redistribution objective, i.e., the actual degree of income and wealth equality toward which the tax system—in conjunction with the expenditure side of the budget—should aspire, will reflect the political consensus at any given time as to the desirable state of income and wealth distribution. Although the precise magnitude of the degree of equality is not specified in the planning literature, the evidence on the existing degree of inequality and attitudes to that inequality suggest unequivocally that, at least in directional terms, taxation policy be employed to diminish inequalities further.[3]

Although there is seldom disagreement on the principle of horizontal equity, it is frequently argued that a redistributive tax policy designed to promote the objective of vertical equity will conflict with the objective of promoting private sector growth, and that, accordingly, the vertical equity objective be relegated to the status of a long-term aspiration. There is no question that a redistributive tax policy which retards growth will be self-defeating, and it may be argued that the necessary reconciliation between private sector growth and vertical equity objectives can be approached by the introduction of the principle of "functionalism" into the tax structure. Such a principle would provide for concessionary treatment, within an overall progressive tax system, for income or wealth used for priority investment purposes. In this manner, "functional" inequalities would be tolerated, while nonfunctional inequalities—inequalities of consumption in the case of income tax, and inequalities of unproductive wealth in the case of wealth taxation—would be moderated.

The question of reducing unemployment and underemployment may be subsumed in developing countries under the growth objective. The *stabilization* objective may therefore be defined essentially as the prevention of inflationary price increases. The body of evidence suggests that a rate of price increase beyond a rather low maximum—certainly not higher than 5 per cent per year —retards the rate and distorts the pattern of growth, and worsens the redistributive problem.

It is, of course, important in a growing economy to permit price increases in growing sectors in order to attract resources to these areas. Since equivalent price reductions in declining areas are unlikely, some upward pressure on the general price level may be expected as a result of what may be referred to as "functional" instability. Inflationary price increases, unlike functional price increases, tend to be cumulative and pervasive in nature. It is equally important to ensure that measures to promote stability do not conflict with the growth objective. To this end, the functional exemptions and concessions referred to above under the vertical equity objective will serve to ensure that reductions in aggregate spending are primarily at the expense of consumption spending rather than investment spending.

An Overview of the Indian Tax System

Federal Finance
The Indian Constitution provides for the division of tax powers between the State and the Union. The division closely follows that established by the Government of India Act (1935). Local authorities are considered to fall under the aegis of their respective State governments and thus have no explicit share in the allocation of tax powers. Under the quasifederal character of the Constitution, fairly wide powers are vested in the States, but residual tax powers belong to the Union.

The Constitution also provides for the distribution of certain revenues between the Union and the States through the agency of a Finance Commission which reports at five-year intervals on the state of federal finance and makes recommendations for changes in the distributional arrangements. The relevant sections of the Constitution are Articles 268, 269, 270, and 275.

In practice, funds allocated to the States by the Finance Commission have amounted to only 25 per cent of the total Union allocation to the States in the planning period. The balance of revenue transfers has fallen under the aegis of the Planning Commission which makes loans and grants to the States for sanctioned Plan expenditure, and the Ministry of Finance, which provides grants-in-aid of non-Plan expenditure where it is considered that such expenditures are of national significance.

The rather complex system of federal finance in India is examined in detail elsewhere in this volume.

Tax Revenue of the Union and State Governments, 1950–51 to 1973–74
General Survey of Revenue Sources The division of Union tax revenue into constituent items over the planning period is presented in Table 17.1, Appendix 17.1: tax revenue accruing to the States over the same period is set out in Table 17.2, Appendix 17.1.

The tax revenues of the Union Government are mainly derived from three heads: taxes on income, both personal and corporate, customs duties, and Union excise duties.

In 1950–51, the year before the beginning of the First Plan, net receipts from these three heads accounted for 35.01, 44.0, and 18.92 per cent respectively, of Union tax revenue. Corresponding proportions in 1973–74 are 20.44, 25.57 and 50 per cent. Comparing the First and Fourth Plans, taxes on income provided 29.7 per cent of Union tax revenue over the First Plan as a whole, and 20.34 per cent over the Fourth Plan. Corresponding figures for customs revenue were 43.6 and 23.43 per cent and for Union excise duties, 22.9 and 52.87 per cent.

The remarkable increase in revenue from Union excise duties is accounted for by the extension of coverage to a wide range of commodities, increased consumption, and rate increases. The Report of the Central Excise Reorganization Committee indica-

ted that over the period 1953–54 to 1961–62, the most important factor was rate increases, accounting for 57.8 per cent of the overall increases in excise tax revenue of Rs. 3,310 million. Increased consumption accounted for 19.7 per cent, and additional coverage for 21.3 per cent.[4]

Taxes on income have formed a relatively stable proportion of Union tax revenue over the planning period to date, in spite of the increasing States' share in personal tax. It is apparent, however, that the maintenance of this proportion is in large measure the result of the rapid increase in revenue from corporation income tax. Revenue from this latter source has moved from 32.2 per cent of net Union revenue from income tax in 1950–51 to 73.24 per cent in 1973–74; viewed as a proportion of gross income tax revenue—before deduction of the States' share—corporation tax revenue has moved from 23.3 to 43.90 per cent over the same period. The greatest relative decline has taken place in revenue from customs, from 44 per cent of Union tax revenue in 1950–51 to 25.57 per cent in 1973–74.

The tax revenues of the State governments are derived mainly from their share of Union income tax and excise duties, land revenue, the tax on stamps and transactions, the State excise on alcoholic liquor, and variety of commercial taxes including the general sales tax, the tax on motor spirit, the entertainment tax, the tax on motor vehicles and electricity duties.

The States' share of Union income tax has increased from Rs. 526.5 million in 1951–52 to Rs. 5,228 million in 1973–74, but the relative significance of this source as a percentage of total States' revenue has dropped from 18.7 to 15.08 per cent. This decline in relative significance has occurred despite the trend towards increasing allocation of income tax revenue to the States—from 50 per cent in 1951 to 66.66 per cent in 1961 and 75 per cent in 1965—and reflects, first, the relatively slow growth of personal income tax revenue to the Union, and second, the more rapid growth of alternative sources of States' revenue, in particular the general sales tax.

The contribution of Union excise revenue to States' revenue began on the recommendation of the First Finance Commission in April 1952 and has grown rapidly; this source provides 18.12 per cent total States' revenue in 1973–74. This is accounted for by the great expansion of Union excise duties and by the trend towards increasing States' share in their revenues.

Land revenue has declined over the planning period as a proportion of total States' revenue, from 17.1 per cent in 1951–52 to 4.53 per cent in 1973–74. The relative decline of land revenue is even more apparent if the 1938–39 percentage (45 per cent of total revenue of the then nine provinces) is also considered.

Direct to Indirect Tax Ratio Taxes listed in Tables 17.1 and 17.2 under the headings of "taxes on income and wealth" and "taxes on property and capital transactions" will be regarded as direct; "taxes on commodities and services" will be regarded as indirect; this classification adopts the simple "basis of assessment" criterion, whereby taxes levied on the receipt of income are termed direct and taxes levied on expenditure are termed indirect. The Expenditure tax is included under the direct tax head.

Direct taxes as a proportion of total (Union+States) tax revenue have fallen from 41.0 per cent in 1951–52 to 23.61 per cent in 1973–74. Although the present Indian ratio is comparable to that in other developing countries, the diminishing relative significance of direct tax revenue in India runs contrary to a general correlation between the direct to indirect tax ratio and per capita income.

Tax Burden or Sacrifice in India The simplest measure of tax burden sacrifice in a national sense is that of the *ratio of tax revenue to national income*. Table 17.1, Appendix 17.2, presents this information for twenty selected countries between 1950–64. The tax to income ratio, expressed as a percentage has almost doubled for India over this period. In this limited sense then, the national tax burden may be assumed to have doubled. The concept of burden or sacrifice is,

however, most meaningful in a relative sense, and India emerges very poorly from the comparison. India, indeed, ranks eighteenth out of twenty. Does it therefore follow, in some sense, that India is making a lesser tax sacrifice than almost all the other countries selected?

Tax sacrifice may best be considered as a measure of the relative importance to the citizens of the resources given up to government in countries at different levels of income, and must relate taxes to some index of "ability-to-pay". A meaningful index of tax sacrifice must, therefore, incorporate per capita income as well as national income.

Several indices incorporating per capita income have been proposed.[5] The index proposed by Richard Bird takes taxes as a percentage of disposable income, all as a percentage of per capita domestic product.[6]

A further refinement of tax to income ratio analysis provides insight into the changing tax burdens over the planning period. In Table 17.5, Appendix 17.1, tax revenue and national income figures are set out for the planning period until 1964–65. The tax to income ratio, here interpreted as the average tax rate in the year in question, is calculated for gross Union tax collections, net Union revenue plus State revenue, and State tax collections (i.e., State revenue minus Union transfers). The marginal tax rate on increments in income between years may be obtained from the national income and tax revenue data, and is set out for all three categories in column eleven.

The average tax rate rises steadily from 1959–60 on, the larger part of the increase being accounted for by Union tax collections. A measure of the increasing tax burden imposed by both levels of government in India is the marginal rates of tax imposed in the period after 1959–60. For total tax revenue, the average of the final six marginal rates (column six) is 19.3 per cent; for Union gross collections the average is 27.6 per cent, and for State collections, 8.3 per cent. The inference may again be drawn that the resource mobilization efforts particularly of the Union Government, and the corresponding tax burden on at least the nonagricultural sector, have been not inconsiderable —certainly far greater than the *prima facie* inference suggested by the comparative tax to income ratios.

Major Indian Taxes: A Brief Appraisal

Personal Income Tax
Under the Indian personal income tax, the various sources of income are not taxed separately, as would be the case under a "schedular" income tax, but are aggregated on a "global" basis. Elements of a schedular system persist, however, in the exemption of agricultural income and the concessionary treatment afforded capital gains. Tax is levied at progressive rates on the total income of all individuals, joint Hindu families, unregistered firms, and other associations of persons; total income for tax purposes is reduced by certain exemptions and deductions and tax liability is further diminished by a set of tax assets based on the taxpayer's family status.

The rates of basic income tax on all noncorporate assessees rise progressively from a zero rate on taxable incomes up to Rs. 5,000, to 85 per cent on incomes above Rs. 200,000. A union surcharge is also levied as a percentage of the basic tax; the rate of surcharge is 10 per cent on taxable income up to Rs. 15,000, and 15 per cent on income above Rs. 15,000. Figure 17.1 illustrates marginal income tax rates on different levels of income.

Accretions to capital value—other than in the case of agricultural land outside urban areas and disposal of house property by small house-owners—are subject to tax under the personal income tax. Short-term gains —where the asset is held for less than twelve months—are fully incorporated in income for tax purposes. Long-term gains are subject to tax at concessionary rates.

In developed countries the progressive personal income tax is generally an elastic and productive revenue source; is an extremely flexible fiscal device, in that a variety of forms of selectivity, discrimination, etc., can be introduced into the tax if so desired; tends to be the most useful tax instrument in stabilization policy, in terms of both built-in stabilization and as a discretionary stabilization

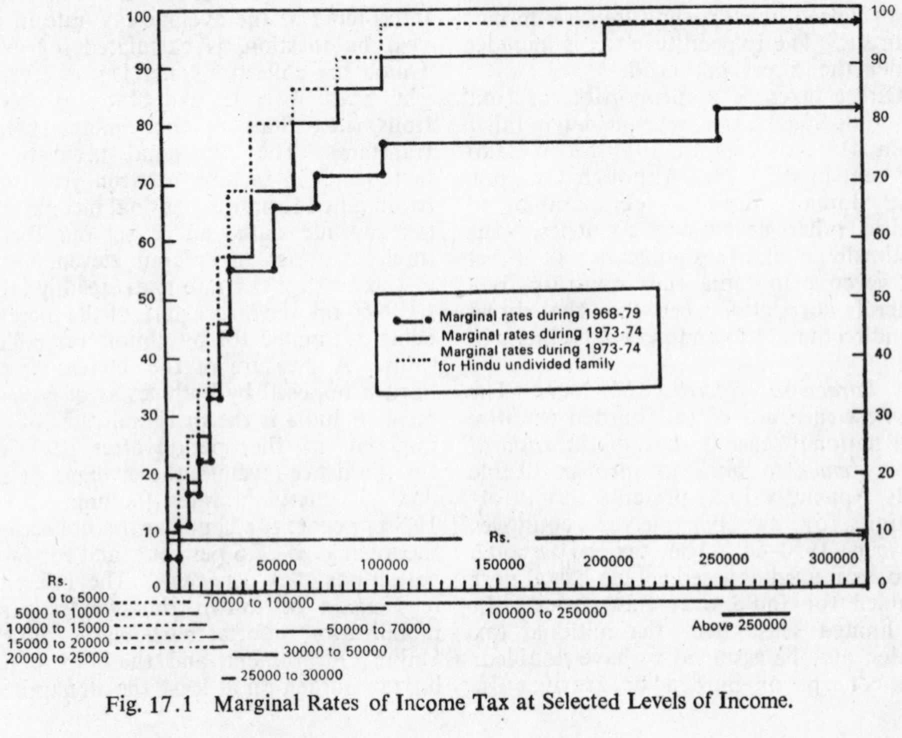

Fig. 17.1 Marginal Rates of Income Tax at Selected Levels of Income.

device; and, finally, by dint of its progressivity, is considered the most appropriate tax instrument for the pursuit of vertical equity.

In developing countries, on the other hand, the personal income tax generally has a very limited coverage, frequently is inapplicable to the agricultural sector —for either constitutional or administrative reasons—and tends to be subject to widespread avoidance and evasion. For these reasons, the personal income tax generally plays a less significant role in the tax structure than in developed countries.

The Indian case provides a classic illustration of the relative inadequacy of the personal income tax as a source of public revenue, and as a tool of stabilization and redistribution.

Although the number of assessees under the personal income tax in India has tripled from the figure of just under 500,000 at the inception of the Second Five-Year Plan, the coverage of the tax is still limited to a very small proportion of the total population, and the disappointing revenue productivity of the tax largely reflects this inadequate coverage. Taking elasticity of tax revenue as the annual compound rate of growth of tax revenue, the average elasticity of personal income-tax revenue from the beginning of the Second Five-Year Plan to 1973–74 comes to 3.7, as against an average for Union tax collections as a whole, of 9.66. Defining the income elasticity of tax revenue as the ratio of the percentage in tax revenue to the percentage change in national income, the performance of the personal income tax is again disappointing, the income elasticity of personal income tax revenue emerging as 0.55 as against 1.4 for Union tax collections as a whole.

Revenue productivity may be increased by widening the definition of the tax base, increasing tax rates and/or lowering exemptions, and by ensuring that all those assessees intended to be covered are so covered up to full intended liability. Under the first of these heads, reform may be approached in a piecemeal fashion by moving to the inclusion of agricultural incomes within the tax base—such a move would require the cooperation of the State governments in view of the present consti-

tutional exclusion of the Union from the taxation of agricultural income—and by the correction of a variety of loopholes such as the existing privileged treatment of Hindu undivided families, or might be approached in a grander, if more administratively formidable, fashion, by moving to the definition of a comprehensive tax base essentially as consumption plus increase in net worth. This latter definition would bring all forms of receipts, both in cash and in kind, within the tax base.

Under the second head, the trend in India over the planning period has been toward the provision of relatively more generous exemptions (or equivalent tax credits), and this approach, although commendable in administrative terms, is one of the major reasons for the relatively slow growth of coverage and revenue productivity. This is particularly true in the light of the rather sharp increases in rate progressivity over the middle income ranges in the 1970–71 Union Budget, which effectively makes the rate structure the most progressive of the major developing countries and relatively harsh even in comparison to the sharpest progressive rate structures in developed countries.

Under the last head, what is required is a set of measures to diminish the chronic problem of tax evasion. Although there is some controversy over the magnitude of evasion, there is unanimity on the seriousness of the problem.[7] Many approaches to the dilemma of evasion have suggested[8], the most intriguing remaining the completely self-checking tax return advocated by Professor Kaldor[9].

The suggested broader tax base combined with the recent increases in rate progressivity should increase the built-in stabilizing effectiveness of the personal income tax and enhance its effectiveness as a discretionary stabilization instrument. The changes should also improve the performance of the tax as a means to the reduction of inequalities of income distribution.

The question that remains is whether these changes can be achieved without a serious tradeoff against the second aspect of the growth objective—the effect of private sector saving and investment.

The growth of "functionalism" or the favourable treatment for tax purposes of income saved and invested in certain ways, has progressed piecemeal in India over the last three or four Union budgets, the 1970–71 budget extending the list of preferential treatment at the same time as it sharply increased tax rates. The case remains, however, for a systematic programme of functional exemptions and preferences, and by development of provisions for generous loss-offset for risk investment, and for a scheme of averaging for tax purposes.

Taxation of Agricultural Income
As an extension of the principle of horizontal equity, it seems a not unreasonable principle of taxation to require intersectoral balance in the tax system. There are several historical cases—particularly in pre-revolutionary Russia and Meiji Japan—where intersectoral imbalance was deliberately used as an instrument of development, the agricultural sector being required essentially to finance industrial growth. The problem in many contemporary developing countries is quite the reverse. For a variety of reasons—often largely administrative—the relative tax burden on the agricultural sector tends to be light, the heavier tax burden falling on the more rapidly growing urban, industrial sector. India is a classic example of this problem.

Despite like still predominant role of the agricultural sector in national income and the high and increasing rate of government expenditure on agriculture over the planning period, resource mobilization from the agricultural sector—whether in the form of voluntary savings or taxation—has been relatively low and inelastic. Such limited evidence as is available on indirect tax burdens[10] suggests a lower relative burden and a diminishing relative share in the rural as against the urban sector. More precise evidence is available on the direct tax burden borne by agricultural incomes. Agricultural income is exempt from Union income tax but is subject to tax by a number of Indian States—significantly a diminishing number over the planning period. Although nominally progressive, agricultural income tax

revenue has been relatively inelastic, constituting approximately 8 per cent of total State tax revenue throughout the planning period. The more important direct tax on agriculture is land taxation, and the record is one of stagnancy, inflexibility, and diminishing relative burden. Revenue from land taxation has fallen from 73 per cent of State tax revenue in 1918–19 to 4.5 per cent in 1973–74 and revenue forecasts suggest a further relative decline. Mitra summarises:

> ...The tax complex of the country is made up of two disparate fiscal systems. In the agricultural sector, barely 4 per cent of the aggregate income flows out to the state in the form of taxation. Outside agriculture, on the other hand, the government's tax claims are in the neighbourhood of 10 per cent. The current average tax revenue for the nation as a whole—about 8 per cent of national income—tells only part of the story and conceals the significant reality of two parallel tax structures.[11]

The growth-objective of taxation in the agricultural sector may be defined in two parts. First, a reformed tax system should seek to siphon off an increasing proportion of the increases in agricultural income consequent on the programme of public investment in agriculture; the system should provide, in short, a productive and elastic source of revenue. Second, not only must the resource mobilization role of taxation of agriculture be carried out with the passive qualification of minimum adverse consequences, but taxation must be so fashioned as to complement positively the expenditure programmes designed to increase agricultural productivity.

The case for reform on the grounds of resource mobilization is reinforced by considerations of the need to develop a fiscal tool to mitigate inequalities of income in the agricultural sector, and to contribute to the stabilization objective.

The theoretically most effective means of combining the tax objectives of increased and elastic revenue productivity, diminished inequalities, and enhanced flexibility and consequent stabilizing effectiveness, with the provision of a comprehensive assortment of incentives, allowances and exemptions designed to promote agricultural productivity, would be a progressive agricultural income tax based on ascertained net income—supported by the necessary accounting records—with a series of specific exemptions and allowances for reinvestment, land improvement, etc. But the history of attempts to levy tax on agricultural incomes is sufficiently discouraging to suggest that the agricultural income tax approach be seen as a long-run aspiration to be arrived at after several stages of reform. The only practicable procedure at present would seem to be the reform of the land tax base to accord with some notion of, at least, *presumptive* income or output, the long-run intention being the transition from land taxation to agricultural-income taxation and the integration of the latter with the Union income tax. To fulfil the three major tax objectives, a revised land-tax system would have to be determined on a standardized base, to be flexible in response to changes in prices and output; be capable of personalization in terms of the individual circumstances of the taxpayer, and be adaptable to a comprehensive series of incentive and disincentive devices designed to promote agricultural productivity.

Given the necessary standardization of land classification procedures, the first essential step in the reform of Indian land taxation would seem to be the definition of a standardized tax base which is sufficiently flexible to fulfil the specified requirements. Such a base would have to correspond in some predetermined manner with *presumptive* net income or output. Concern over the effect of taxation on agricultural productivity suggests, further, that presumptive income be defined not in terms of *actual output* but in terms of *productive capacity*, or the output which the land should yield if managed with average efficiency. The tax would thus be based on *potential* output in relation to some regional average. Thus the inefficient farmer whose production is less than the average for the region and/or for the type of land concerned, would be penalized, whereas the efficient farmer would be correspondingly encouraged; the tax would also promote the transfer

of land from inefficient to efficient hands and would penalize heavily underutilization, absentee ownership, etc.

The tax might be made *progressive* in terms of land holdings, though remaining proportional in terms of potential output for any given land size. In this way not only is the vertical equity criterion satisfied but there would be a sharp inducement to either the utilization of large land holdings —which are most likely to be held idle— or to the breakup of such large holdings into smaller units which would presumably be worked more efficiently. Allowance under the productive capacity criterion would have to be made for reduction or remission of land revenue in the event of extensive crop failure.

Tax yield under a reformed tax structure would clearly have to be responsive to price and production changes. What would appear most appropriate would be, say, a five-yearly reassessment of regional average rated capacity to take account of growing conditions and price changes. Such adjustment of norms would seem unlikely to have serious incentive implications, inasmuch as the adjustments would be regional rather than individual. Effectively, the marginal tax rate on output would remain zero for an individual farmer, but would be positive for farmers, in the aggregate.

The proposed structure might be further refined to take account of the personal circumstances of assessees, to incorporate a variety of additional incentive devices, to distinguish the liability of landlords and tenants, and to reflect the process of land reform.

Other Direct Taxes
Wealth Tax   A tax on net wealth has been in operation in India since 1957 and is levied annually on the taxable net wealth of individuals and Hindu Undivided Families. In a series of reforms beginning in the 1968–69 Union Budget, and culminating in the corresponding 1971–72 Budget, the rate structure of the tax was made more progressive and the rate maximum raised to a quite remarkable 8 per cent on taxable wealth over Rs. 1.5 million. Additional wealth tax on urban real property reaches a rate maximum of

7 per cent on property valued above Rs. 1 million. The generous exemption structure has also been truncated—the removal of jewellery being the most important of the changes—and, perhaps most remarkable of all, agricultural wealth has been brought within the purview of the Wealth Tax Act.

An annual tax on net wealth of the form taken by the Indian net wealth tax prior to the recent reforms is envisaged more in the nature of an additional income tax on income from capital than as a tax on capital itself. As such the tax is generally not a major revenue source, but is important for the redistributive objective as essentially a surtax on income tax, and has an interesting investment incentive effect inasmuch as the tax is directed to an assumed average rate of return on capital and thus provides an incentive to high-yield risk investment, and a disincentive to hoarding and conservative investment. The structure of the tax now in force in India—if that structure is administratively enforceable—bears much more resemblance to a capital levy or a genuine tax on capital, inasmuch as the average rate of wealth tax liability seems likely to exceed the average rate of return on all forms of taxable wealth. The new tax will certainly be more effective than the old in the diminution of inequalities of wealth and income, will yield more revenue, and will, in principle, provide a sharply increased incentive to high-yield risk investment. The question is whether the effects will all be positive, i.e., whether the new rates will be, in effect, confiscatory, acting to diminish private investment in the aggregate, and to promote evasion and capital flight.

Expenditure Tax A tax on expenditure was first levied in the 1958–59 Union Budget, and, other than in the two fiscal years, 1962–63 and 1963–64, persisted till its abolition in the 1966–67 Budget. Prior to abolition, the tax was levied annually on expenditure incurred by individuals and Hindu Undivided Families. A basic exempt expenditure allowance of Rs. 30,000 was superimposed on an initial income level exemption of Rs. 36,000. A broad range of expenditure was exempt from tax, and tax rates on taxable expenditure were

graduated to a maximum of 20 per cent.

The abolition of the tax was justified by its relatively low revenue productivity and its administrative awkwardness. It is arguable, however, that a really effective expenditure tax was never tried, and that a dramatically widened tax base—to be attained largely by the removal of income exemption and the reduction of expenditure exemptions—and more severe rate structure would have been necessary to make the tax an effective fiscal tool with respect to the major tax objectives.

The role of an expenditure tax in a development context has several dimensions; first, the tax serves to curtail the extent to which increases in income are directed to conspicuous consumption instead of saving, to diminish consumption inequalities, to assist in limiting consumption in an inflationary situation, and, finally in the context of major income-tax reform, to act as an integral part of a self-checking personal direct tax return.

Gift and Estate Taxation Estate Tax in India became payable on the capital value of property passing on the death of any person on or after 15 October 1953, in accordance with the provisions of the Estate Duty Act of that year. The definition of taxable property transfers has been widened to encompass such transfers as gifts made in contemplation of death or within a short period before death. Above a minimum exemption level of Rs. 50,000, tax rates are graduated reaching a maximum of 85 per cent. A limited group of assets is tax exempt.

The estate tax has been complemented by a tax on inter vivos gifts since 1958. Graduated tax rates are imposed on transfers above a minimum exemption level of Rs. 5,000 by individuals, Hindu Undivided Families and associations of individuals. The range of exempt assets is considerably wider than under the estate tax, and the rate and exemption structures differ. The first Rs. 50,000 of the value of an estate passing at death is exempt, whereas the annual gift exemption is limited to Rs. 5,000—reduced from Rs. 10,000 in the 1971–72 Budget. The differences between the two rate structures were considerably reduced in the 1971–72

Budget, where gift tax rates were sharply increased, and the maximum rate of gift tax is now 75 per cent on gifts over Rs. 2 million —as against the maximum rate of estate tax on the corresponding slab of 85 per cent.

The existing estate and gift taxes in India and in developing countries generally —indeed, also in most developed countries —have not proved to be productive revenue sources, and would appear to have made little contribution to the diminution of inequalities of opportunity between generations. Within the standard structure of separate estate and gift taxes, the most effective reform would be the complete integration of gift and estate taxation into one transfer tax levied on a cumulative basis, and the use of an overall sharply progressive rate structure in the transfer tax. More liberal tax payment procedures and preferential tax treatment for "functional" assets would serve to moderate any adverse effects of the proposed changes on the private sector.

The optimal reform on both equity and revenue grounds would be of a more radical nature, and would go beyond such variants as the accessions tax to suggest the full incorporation of all gratuitous transfers—whether testamentary or inter vivos—in the cumulated taxable income of the recipient.

Corporation Income Tax Corporations are regarded as separate entities for income tax purposes in India, and have been subject to income tax since 1860. Corporations are classified for tax purposes into four major categories, three covering domestic and one foreign corporations. The corporate tax rate structure is complex. Total corporation income—exclusive of a wide range of exempt receipts and deductible expenditures—is subject, according to its place in the four-group classification, to proportional tax rates of between 45 and 70 per cent. Additional taxes imposed on corporations include a capital gains tax to which all corporations are subject, and a surtax imposed at a rate of 25 per cent—reduced from 35 per cent in the 1968–69 Union Budget— on all corporations the total income of which exceeds 10 per cent of the capital base, or Rs. 200,000, whichever is higher.

A penalty tax on distributed profits in the case of public corporations was abolished in the 1968–69 Union Budget.

For many developing countries corporation income taxation is a more important revenue source than personal income taxation. In India, the corporation income tax has proved to be a relatively elastic and productive revenue source. Further, a separate, nonintegrated corporation tax contributes to vertical equity— on the assumption that at least a portion of the tax is borne by capital owners—by taxing dividends and curtailing stock appreciation, and by dint of broad coverage and elasticity, is of great significance in automatic and discretionary stabilization policy.

The major disadvantage of the corporation tax is that it probably reduces funds for investment more than any other tax. However, this effect may be moderated by the introduction of extended loss-offset provisions, and the use of selective accelerated depreciation (the latter is to be preferred to the frequently suggested alternative of replacement cost depreciation).

The proposal to integrate either fully or partially the personal and corporation income taxes has merit only on grounds of horizontal equity, and would considerably reduce the contribution of the corporate income tax to revenue productivity, vertical equity and stabilization.

Major Indirect Taxes
Indirect taxes (taxes on commodities and transactions) are imposed in India by the Union Government and by all of the States. The Union Government levies a sales tax on interstate sales, manufacturers' and producers' excise taxes, and import and export duties; the States levy general sales or purchase taxes, excise taxes on alcoholic beverages and drugs, entertainment taxes, electricity duties, and taxes on sales or purchases of specific commodities. The most important indirect measures—in terms of their contribution to revenue— are Union customs duties, Union and State excise duties, and State sales taxes. (a) *Union Customs Duties*: The Union Government levies import and export duties under its constitutional allocation of tax powers; revenue from the former is

much greater than from the latter.

The import tariff was rationalized in the 1965–66 Union Budget, and most of the duties across a wide range of commodities are now ad valorem, although some of the ad valorem duties are made specific by fixing the tariff values of the commodities to which they apply. Prior to devaluation in 1966, the basic rate of duty was 60 per cent on most intermediate goods and raw materials (other than primary raw materials), and 40 per cent on machinery and primary raw materials. Rates were much higher on consumer goods, generally 100 per cent, but ranged as high as 200 per cent. Following devaluation, the revised rates are generally 27.5 per cent on machinery and primary raw materials, 50 per cent on other raw materials, 60 per cent on processed materials and intermediate goods, and 100 per cent (unchanged) on consumers' goods.

Revenue from export duties had diminished to insignificance by 1965–66, and it would be accurate to suggest that the export duty in India had been virtually replaced by the export subsidy. Devaluation in 1966 altered the situation, and export duties were imposed on a group of twelve commodities. Eleven of the duties were specific and one ad valorem. As might have been expected, the export duty on these commodities has been reduced and in some cases eliminated in subsequent budgets, and revenue from export duties seems likely again to diminish to insignificance by the end of the Fourth Plan.

(b) *Union Excise Duties* : An excise tax is best seen as a true commodity tax, rather than as a transactions tax, since it is essentially imposed on the production of a commodity, and collected at the factory, rather than on the actual sale of the commodity. In this sense, an excise tax is distinct from a retail sales tax, the latter being strictly a transactions tax. Both taxes are, of course, intended to be shifted forward to consumers and are therefore ultimately incident on consumption.

Union excise duties are imposed under the Constitutional provision which reserves to the Union Government the exclusive power to impose excise taxes on tobacco and all other goods manufactured or produced in India, except alcoholic beverages and narcotics, the taxation of which is reserved to the States. The imposition and collection of the duties are governed by the Central Excises and Salt Act of 1944, as amended from time to time. The first excise duty in India was levied in 1894, and the device was extended to a wider range of articles in the 1930s, during World War II, and, particularly following the recommendations of the Taxation Equiry Commission in 1953–54. Revenue is derived from a broad range of commodities. Although the larger part of the set of rates remains specific, Union Budgets since the end of the Third Five-Year Plan have moved increasingly toward the use of ad valorem rates, both in the treatment of new commodities and in the modification of tax rates on previously taxed commodities. Excise duties are levied at the manufacturing stage, and the basic duties are supplemented by *additional* and *special* excise duties and by a small group of *benefit excises*.

(c) *State Excise Duties* State Governments are empowered to levy excise taxes solely on alcoholic liquors for human consumption, and on opium, Indian hemp, and other narcotics. Excise taxes on medicinal and toilet preparations containing alcohol or narcotics are imposed by the Union Government but are collected by and accrue entirely to the States. Opium, Indian hemp, and other narcotics are subject to excise tax at varying rates in all States which have not prohibited their sale.

(d) *State Sales Taxes* A sales tax, as distinct from an excise tax, is a true transactions tax, and, further, is generally imposed at a uniform rate on the sale of a wide range of goods and services. A *universal* or *general* sales tax would cover the sale of all goods and services; a *selective* sales tax covers only specified or selected goods and services. In practice, most sales taxes are not general but exhibit varying degrees of selectivity; this is true of all the sales taxes levied by the Indian States. Another broad distinction made in India is between a sales tax proper and a *purchase tax*. A tax assessed on the aggregate sales of a registered dealer and collected from that dealer, is called a sales tax. If, on the other hand, the tax is assessed on the aggregate of a dealer's purchases, irrespective of his sales, it is referred to as a purchase tax. The sales tax is levied only on dealers, whereas the purchase tax is occasionally levied directly on consumers in the case of conspicuous articles of consumption.

A sales tax on motor fuel and lubricants was first levied in Madhya Pradesh in 1938 and the first general sales tax was introduced in Madras in 1939. Presently all the States levy a sales tax in one form or another. The Constitution, as adopted in 1950, gave the States exclusive power to impose taxes on the sales of all goods except newspapers. Services are excluded from the ambit of sales taxes.

The various sales taxes differ widely in their intended incidence and operation. In each system the most important characteristic is the point or points between production and retail sale at which the tax is levied, since this affects the qualifications of tax payers, the classes of goods subject to the tax, rates of tax, and administrative procedures. The evolution and character of the sales tax system in each state has been conditioned by economic structure, financial needs, and adaptation to constitutional amendment.

In general terms, States which are characterized by substantial urban trade and significant industrial and manufacturing activities have tended to adopt a single-point tax imposed at only one point between production of goods and their sale to a consumer, and usually on a limited group of dealers. In these states, a relatively high rate of tax is imposed on taxable sales and a large number of essential goods and basic raw materials are usually exempt. The incidence of a single-point tax is closely controlled, in accordance with the largely urban commercial economy in which it operates. States with predominantly rural economies, on the other hand, have generally adopted multipoint sales taxes, imposed on every sale between production of the goods and their sale to the ultimate consumer. Since the incidence of such taxes is not controlled—so that the number of occasions on which different products are

assessed before the retail level may vary considerably—the rates of tax are relatively low, exemptions are few, and most dealers are subject to the tax.

The rates at which the State sales taxes are levied depend on whether the tax is a single-point or a multipoint tax and on the nature of the goods sold. The rates applicable to each sale under single-point systems are generally higher than under multipoint systems, although the total of taxes imposed from producer to consumer under a multipoint system may be as high as the tax under a single-point system. Exemptions and concessionary rates vary widely between States. So-called "luxury" goods, such as motor cars, radios, electric appliances, watches and cosmetics are taxed at higher rates than other goods in most States.

The major group of indirect taxes is of great and increasing importance in the aggregate of Union and State tax revenue. From around 50 per cent of total (Union+State) tax revenue at the beginning period, revenue from the four major tax heads constituted over 70 per cent of the total in the 1971–72 budgets. Union excises are the most important revenue source, followed by Union customs duties, State sales taxes and State excises.

The annual compound rate of growth of customs revenue from 1955–56 to 1973–74 has averaged 10.5 per cent; the income elasticity of customs revenue over the same period was 1.096. The development context, with its requirements of foreign exchange and capital goods imports, suggests that revenue from customs will continue to decline relatively, and, possibly, absolutely.

The annual compound rate of growth of Union excise revenue from 1955–56 to 1973–74 averaged 12.1 per cent; the income elasticity of Union excise revenue over the same period was 1.7. The general conversion to ad valorem rates should increase the elasticity of excise tax revenue, and the possibility of increased revenue from rate increases and base widening is demonstrated annually in the Union Budgets. An interesting possibility which has not yet been tried is the formal planning of excise tax rates and base definitions on the basis of estimates of income elasticity of demand for groups of commodities.

The relevance of State excises emerged strongly in the Third Plan period with the apparent disintegration of prohibition. From the beginning of the Third Plan until 1973–74, the annual compound rate of growth of State excise tax revenue was a robust 13.25 per cent, and the income elasticity an equally impressive 1.6. The tradeoff between revenue and prohibition is self-evident.

The annual compound rate of growth of State sales tax revenue from 1955–56 to 1973–74 was 11.13 per cent; income elasticity was 1.8. The possibility of increased revenue from rate increases— and indeed also base widening, since services are generally excluded from State sales tax bases—is so apparent that it seems certain that this form of tax will be one of the main revenue growth-points throughout the 1970s.

In examining the contribution of indirect taxes to equity, the basic premise will be that indirect taxes are completely shifted forward and are borne by consumers in proportion to consumption expenditures on the taxed goods. On the basis of this assumption and further estimates of consumer demand patterns classified by income groups, the definition of indirect tax bases and rate structures can be designed to conform in principle to an intended distribution of burden by income groups. Such evidence as is available on the distribution of indirect taxes by income groups in India confirm[5], not only that the burden of indirect taxes is progressive but has become more sharply progressive.[12] Clearly the introduction of universal food exemptions under the State sales taxes and the gearing of Union excise rates to estimates of income elasticity could serve to further improve the progressivity of indirect tax devices in India, or at least to offset the regressive impact of the State excises in liquor and tobacco.

With respect, finally, to stabilization, the significance of indirect taxation lies in reducing consumption through an initial once-for-all increase in the price of the taxed commodity. Indirect taxation is particularly significant in the growth context in India in that, at least directly, the dimin-

ution in demand is purely at the expense of consumption rather than investment. The potential stabilizing effectiveness of a mode of taxation is a function of the size of tax revenue in relation to national income, movement of tax revenue in the same direction as national income changes, and the degree of responsiveness of tax revenue to changes in national income.

A measure of built-in flexibility—change in tax revenue other than from budget changes, over change in national income—comes to 0.055 for the aggregate of customs revenue, Union excises, and State sales taxes, over the period 1955–56 to 1973–74, indicating that the change in revenue from the major indirect taxes constituted 5.5 per cent of the change in national income over the same period. The most important of the indirect taxes is, of course, Union excises, the increased revenue from which constituted 3.3 per cent of the change in national income. The changes in customs revenue and State sales taxes were both 1.1 per cent.

Given the relatively high flexibility coefficient, and the fact that a large proportion of the flexibility of Union excises is the consequence of heightened rates and, to a lesser extent, coverage, it follows that indirect taxation in India offers an effective tool of both discretionary and automatic stabilization. A system of import duties, sales taxes and excise taxes set up to maximize responsiveness to income changes, with increased rates and coverage geared to movements in wholesale or consumer prices by a predetermined statutory automatic formula (formula flexibility), would offer increased effectiveness as a means of correcting inflationary price trends.

Summary and Conclusions

Important questions pertaining to the principles of federal finance and the adaption of the Indian tax system to the peculiar cultural and institutional context were omitted in the preceding brief overview. Three broad, general issues of principle may, however, be considered to have emerged.

First, the role of taxation policy as an instrument of planned economic development can only be determined and evaluated in terms of the specification of a set of policy objectives. Further, the objective set can be meaningful only if the component objectives are operationally defined, and if the relationship between the component objectives, whether of conflict or complementarity, is clearly articulated.

Second, in terms primarily of resource mobilization and horizontal equity, a major deficiency in the Indian tax system lies in the problem of intersectoral imbalance, i.e., in the relatively light tax burden on the large agricultural sector.

Third, the development of the Indian tax system as a flexible, elastic policy instrument which can be effectively calibrated to objectives requires the correction of the present relative decline of major direct tax instruments.

With respect to objectives, it was argued that the objective set might be defined at the highest level of aggregation to include growth, equity and stabilization. The most acute area of conflict—for which the compromise solution of "functionalism" was suggested—was defined to lie between the desire to increase revenue productivity and diminish inequalities, on the one hand, and the desire to encourage private saving and investment, on the other.

With respect to intersectoral imbalance, a major overhaul of the agricultural taxation system was suggested, the first step in the reform involving the redefinition of the land tax base in terms of average potential output.

With respect to the direct tax to indirect tax ratio, it was argued that the major scope for increased revenue productivity and increased effectiveness under the equity and stabilization objectives lay in the reform of personal direct taxation. It was argued, in particular, that the personal income tax and estate and gift taxes should be reformed by base widening and the extension of coverage. It was acknowledged, however, that indirect taxation, particularly Union excise taxes and State sales taxes, had provided a remarkably elastic and productive revenue instrument which could be reformed both in terms of tax bases and rates in order to increase its stabilizing effectiveness and its contribution to vertical equity.

REFERENCES

1. J. Cutt, *Taxation and Economic Development in India* (New York: Praeger, 1969).
2. Government of India, *Report of the Taxation Enquiry Commission* vol. I (New Delhi: Ministry of Finance, 1953–54) p. 145.
3. Cutt, *Taxation and Economic Development*, Chapter 2.
4. Government of India, *Report of the Central Excise Reorganization Committee* (New Delhi: Manager of Publications, 1963), p. 68.
5. See, for instance, H. Frank, "Measuring State Tax Burdens", *National Tax Journal* XII, June 1959, pp. 179–85; and R. Bird, "A Note on Tax Sacrifice Comparisons", *National Tax Journal* XVII, 1964, pp. 303–08.
6. $[(T/Y - T)\ 100 \div Y/P]\ 100$
   where T = tax revenue, Y = Gross National Product and P = Population. Bird uses Gross National Product in the first ratio, and Gross Domestic Product in the second.

   The same convention has been followed in the present work.
7. *Report of the Direct Taxes Administration Enquiry Commission*, 1958 (Delhi: Manager of Publications, 1960), pp. 146–188.
8. Cutt, *Taxation and Economic Development* Chapter 11.
9. N. Kaldor, *Tax Reform in India* (New Delhi: Government of India, Ministry of Finance, 1958).
10. Government of India, Ministry of Finance, *Incidence of Indirect Taxation in India,* 1958–59 (New Delhi, 1961); and *Report of the Taxation Enquiry Commission,* vol. 1.
11. Ashok Mitra, "Tax Burden on Indian Agriculture", in R. Braibanti and J. Spengler (eds), *Administration and Economic Development in India* (Durham: Duke University Press, 1963), pp. 281–303.
12. *Incidence of Indirect Taxation.*

Table 17.1   Tax Revenue as Per cent of National Income: Twenty Selected Countries, 1950–64

Country	1950			1963			1964			Ranking (1964 figures)
	Direct Tax	Indirect Tax	Total	Direct Tax	Indirect Tax	Total	Direct Tax	Indirect Tax	Total	
Australia	10.0	6.6	16.6	12.8	7.3	20.1	12.5	8.5	21.0	12
Austria	8.2	8.5	16.7	15.5	16.2	31.7	12.4	19.8	32.2	1
Belgium	8.6	12.2	20.8	9.5	14.8	24.3	9.4	14.9	24.3	6
Burma	1.8	6.2	8.0	5.1	9.8	14.9	10.8	9.9	20.7	13
Canada	9.0	7.0	16.0	10.9	7.3	18.2	10.5	7.5	18.0	15
Ceylon	3.5	10.8	14.3	5.1	9.8	14.9	5.1	16.3	21.4	11
Denmark	6.7	8.9	15.6	9.2	13.0	22.2	9.0	13.5	22.5	9a
France	7.9	16.5	24.4	7.2	18.5	25.7	7.7	19.2	26.9	5
Germany, West	10.4	11.3	21.7	14.0	14.2	28.2	15.0	14.2	29.2	2
Greece	2.9	9.6	12.5	2.9	13.2	16.1	3.0	13.5	16.5	16
India	2.4	4.2	6.6	4.0	9.5	13.5	3.8	8.8	12.6	18
Ireland	6.9	12.4	19.3	8.4	14.2	22.6	8.1	14.1	22.2	10
Italy	3.0	9.3	12.3	5.5	14.3	19.8	5.9	17.1	23.0	8
Japan	9.4	7.4	16.8	7.7	5.7	13.4	7.7	5.7	13.4	17
Netherlands	14.5	13.6	28.1	16.4	10.9	27.3	16.7	11.2	27.9	3
Norway	7.6	11.8	19.4	6.2	16.7	22.9	5.9	16.6	22.5	9a
Philippines	1.0	4.3	5.3	2.6	8.4	11.0	2.6	8.4	11.0	19
Sweden	9.9	7.8	17.7	12.5	13.0	25.5	11.0	13.0	24.0	7
U.K.	17.9	14.1	32.0	16.5	11.2	27.7	15.7	11.5	27.2	4
U.S.A.	13.2	3.4	16.6	19.1	6.1	25.2	13.9	6.7	20.6	14

aEqual ranking.

SOURCE: United Nations, *Statistical Yearbook*, 1965 (New York, 1966).

Total Third an Period	1968–69 (Actuals)	1969–70 (Actuals)	1973–74 (Actuals)	Total Fourth Plan 1969–70 to 1973–74		62–63 counts)	1963–64 (Account
						,057.7	1,284.
						952.4	1,181.
						95.7	92.
						9.4	10.
,662.4	4,837.3	5,086.6	7,960.0	30,350.0			
						,791.2	1,911.
,483.0	3,784.7	4,484.5	7,450.0	28,340.0		38.9	42.
,555.2	1,945.1	2,931.8	5,320.0	21,390.0		,200.7	1,234.
,927.8	1,839.6	1,552.7	2,130.0	6,950.0		522.1	614.
,714.4	2,997.7	2,533.9	5,830.0	23,360.0		29.7	20.
22.2	—	—	—	40.0			
						090.6	6,195.
	215.6	247.3	520.0	1,950.0		249.2	1,360.
249.1	67.4	69.4	100.0	450.0		628.1	728.
255.5	55.4	68.8	110.0	400.0		875.2	2,454.
—6.4	12.0	—0.4	—10.0	50.0		213.5	229.
505.6	111.1	156.2	360.0	1,280.0		462.9	574.
75.8	15.1	20.2	50.0	170.0			
	74.6	69.7	120.0	440.0		182.1	225.
	2.8	1.6	—	10.0		194.8	272.
						284.8	350.
,081.6	15,135.7	16.680.1	30,470.0	116,890.0		939.5	9,390.
,232.2	3,739.7	3,269.7	9,320.0	31,160.0		599.0	6,807.
302.3	1.019.3	755.7	880.0	3,990.0			
324.5	t5.9	512.9	170.0	1,640.0			
564.9	359.9	305.2	410.0	1,830.0			
,294.2	4,465.0	4,233.1	9,960.0	34,960.0			
,171.5	13,206.7	15,243.1	26,020.0	102,700.0			
,170.6	2,909.3	3,215.1	1,730.0	5,490.0			
,148.1			6,310.0	23,830.0			
,075.4	10,297.4	12,028.0	19,710.0	78,870.0			
820.4	81.8	105.2	800.0	3,060.0			
,581.0	20,188.6	22,014.0	38,950.0	149,190.0			
,981.1	26,950.0	28,230.0	50,690.0	194,810.0			

1964–65 (Accounts)	1965–66 (Accounts)	Total Third Plan Period	1968–69 (Accounts)	1969–70 (Accounts)	1973–74 (Accounts)	Total Fourth Plan (1969–70 to 1973–74)
1,352.6	1,338.9	6,077.0	2,068 6	3,100.0	5 372.0	21,872 0
1,235.9	1,231.7	5,546.0	1,945.0	2,932 0	5,228·0	21,130 0
107.3	98.8	489 0	99.3	140.0	118.0	499.0
9.4	8.4	42.0	24.3	28.0	26.0	127.0
1,978.5	1,967.1	9,135.0	2,243.3	2,264 0	3,445.0	13,141.0
67.6	67.8	256.0	55.3	70.0	112.0	395.0
1,197.9	1,119.3	5,703.0	1,139.1	1,028.0	1,570.0	5,661.0
685.5	741.1	3,027.0	1.012.9	1,126.0	1,719.0	6,877.0
27.5	38.9	149.0	36.4	40.0	44.0	208.0
6,893.1	7,871.5	30,147.0	12,768.3	14,442.0	25,861.0	98,470.0
1,272.4	1,458.0	6,146.0	2,871.7	3,252.0	6,264.0	23,846.0
845.4	963.7	3,753.0	1,590.4	1,736.0	3,537.0	12,341.0
2,950.9	3,385.7	12,297.0	4,370.9	4,908.0	11,428 0ᶜ	41,916.0
233.3	292.2	1,151.0	352.9	386.0	—	—
593.3	642.2	2,651.0	893.2	935.0	2,626.0	9,387.0
251.1	294.4	1,104.0	424.5	504.0	996.0	3,469.0
334.3	353.6	1,305.0	548.7	581.0	813.0	6,987.0
412.4	481.7	1,740.0	253.3	300.0	177.0	1,771.0
10,224.2	11,177.5	45,359.0	17,083.6	19,809.0	34,678.0	152,820.0
7,648.3	8,420.0	33,411.0	12,211.6	13,555.0	23,054.0	98,737.0

Table 17.4.   Tax Burden in Terms of Per Capita
Income, 1964

Country	Index	Ranking
Australia	3.0	11[a]
Austria	5.9	5
Belgium	2.5	13
Burma	8.4	1
Canada	2.0	14
Ceylon	4.2	9[a]
Denmark	2.7	12
France	4.8	7[a]
Germany, West	4.8	7[a]
Greece	7.9	2
India	4.2	9[a]
Ireland	4.9	6[a]
Italy	6.5	3
Japan	6.0	4
Netherlands	4.9	6[a]
Norway	4.3	8
Philippines	2.1	14
Sweden	3.4	10
UK	3.0	11[a]
USA	1.4	1

[a]Equal ranking.

SOURCE: United Nations, *Statistical Yearbook*
1965 (New York, 1966).

Table 17.5. Average and Marginal Rates of taxation over the Planning Period

Year	National Income at Current Prices	Total Union and State Tax Revenue	Gross Union Tax Collections	State Tax Collections	Average Tax Rate on (3)	Marginal Tax Rate on (3)	Average Tax Rate on (4)	Marginal Tax Rate on (4)	Average Tax Rate on (5)	Marginal Tax Rate on (5)
	Rs. Million	Rs. Million	Rs. Million	Rs. Million	Per cent	Per cent	Per cent	Per cent	Per cent	Per cent
1	2	3	4	5	6	7	8	9	10	11
1951–52	99,700	7,387	5,050	2,337	7.4	—	5.06	—	2.34	—
1952–53	98,200	6,778	4,420	2,358	6.9	—	4.50	—	2.40	—
1953–54	104,800	6,725	4,200	2,525	6.4	–0.80	4.00	–3.33	2.40	2.5
1954–55	96,100	7,204	4,560	2,644	7.5	—	4.74	—	2.76	—
1955–56	99,800	7,676	4,850	2,826	7.7	12.75	4.85	7.83	2.85	4.92
1956–57	113,100	8,904	5,730	3,174	7.9	9.23	5.06	6.61	2.84	2.62
1957–58	113,900	10,450	6,960	3,490	9.2	193.25	6.11	153.75	3.09	39.50
1958–59	126.000	10,893	7,150	3,743	8.6	3.66	5.67	1.57	2.93	2.09
1959–60	129,500	12,164	7,840	4,324	9.4	36.31	6.05	19.71	3.35	16.60
1960–61	141,400	13,504	8,770	4,734	9.6	11.26	6.05	7.81	3.35	4.45
1961–62	148,000	15,430	10,370	5,060	10.4	29.18	6.20	24.24	3.40	4.94
1962–63	154,000	18,651	12,670	5,981	12.1	53.68	7.00	38.33	3.40	3.40
1963–64	172,100	23,246	16,130	7,116	13.5	25.38	8.22	19.11	3.88	15.35
1964–65	200,100	25,988	17,980	8,008	13.0	9.79	9.37	6.60	4.13	6.27
							8.98		4.02	3.19

SOURCE: 1. Reserve Bank of India, *Report on Currency and Finance, 1965–66* (Bombay: Reserve Bank of India, 1967).

2. Government of India, *Explanatory Memorandum on the Budget of the Central Government, 1967–68* (New Delhi: Ministry of Finance, 1967).

3. Finances of State Government, 1967–68, *Reserve Bank of India Bulletin* (August 1967).

18

Federal Finance in India After Six Finance Commissions

A.T. EAPEN

Before embarking on a study of inter-governmental fiscal relations in India, a student of economics may briefly consider some of the grounds on which federal financial transfers to state and local governments may be justified. The first section of this study deals briefly with some of the important grounds which justify transfer of resources, in one form or another, from the federal government to the states in any federation. The rest of this study is concerned with an examination of Centre-State financial relations in India.

Economics of Federal Transfers to States[1]

Given the nature of political federalism, which involves a division of powers between the governments at the federal and state levels, there are several reasons which call for financial transfers from one level of government (usually the federal) to the other (usually the states). The more important among these are:

1. promotion of efficient allocation of resources in the public sector;

2. promotion of equalization of the fiscal position of the states; and
3. superiority of federal taxation which makes sharing of federal taxes a better alternative to state taxation.

Promotion of Efficient Allocation of Resources

Whenever an economic activity (production or consumption) is accompanied by beneficial or detrimental external effects (externalities) which are not valued by the market, there is likely to be an inefficient allocation of resources. This can be illustrated by public services such as public health and education, provided by a state government, which characteristically have external effects. A state S_1 may provide a certain quantity of, say, educational services at a certain price in accordance with the preference of its residents. At price P_1, the quantity of the service demanded by the residents of the state is Q_1 (Fig. 18.1). The demand curve D_{S_1} indicates that at quantity Q_1 the marginal valuation of benefits received by the residents of S_1 is exactly equal to the price P_1.

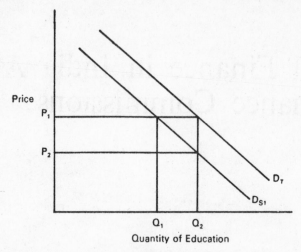

Fig. 18.1

If all the benefits from the service were received exclusively by the residents of S_1, then the quantity Q_1 would have been optimal. However, since part of the benefits from S_1s educational programme would spill over to other states (persons trained by the state S_1 may provide their services to other states), the quantity Q_1 would very likely be nonoptimal. The marginal evaluation of the total benefits including spillovers (social benefits from Q_1 of education supplied by S_1 is likely to be larger than P_1; indeed the marginal evaluation of the social benefits of any quantity of the service provided by S_1 is likely to be higher than the marginal evaluation of the benefits enjoyed by the residents of S_1. The marginal evaluation of the social benefits of various quantities of the service provided by S_1 is indicated by the curve D_T which is to the right of D_{S_1}. Thus, at price P_1, the optimal quantity of the service from the society's standpoint is Q_2, larger than Q_1. To remedy this inefficiency arising from spillovers (externalities or external effects), S_1 has to be given a unit subsidy equal to P_1P_2 as suggested by A. C. Pigou. Such a Pigouvian subsidy will induce S_1 to do what is correct by society and produce Q_2 of educational services. Since most of the public services produced by the states in a federation have spillovers or externalities, optimal allocation of resources in the public sector of the states cannot be achieved without a Pigouvian type of subsidy to them, presumably from the federal government. Thus, from the standpoint of optimal allocation of resources, a strong argument may be advanced for a federal per-unit-of-service subsidy to the states, if there are no better alternatives for internalizing the externalities in the provision of public services by the states.[2] It is important to note that the type of subsidy called for in this case is a matching open-end conditional grant, the matching ratio being governed by the proportion of benefits spilled over outside S_1. (If the proportion of spillover varies with quantity of services provided, then the matching ratio will vary with quantity).[3] Undoubtedly it is quite difficult to determine the precise matching ratio in the case of any service provided by the states; the larger the proportion of spillovers, the larger is the matching ratio. Certainly theoretical considerations buttress the position that federal matching conditional grants are in the right direction for promoting allocational efficiency, if the states do indeed provide public services in conformity with the preferences of their residents.

Promotion of Equalization of Fiscal Positions of the States

The economic resources of the constituent states of a federation may vary considerably. As a consequence, the wealthier states may be able to provide their residents with a fairly high standard of public services at relatively moderate tax efforts while the poorer states may be unable to do so even at relatively high tax effort. Increasing national concern regarding the undesirability of wide interstate differences in the standards of essential public services has led to federal financial transfers to states with a view to equalizing their fiscal capacities.

There are several possible schemes of equalization which federal finance may adopt.[4] A meaningful scheme of equalization would be to underwrite the cost of maintaining a certain minimum in the standards of all or some important public services throughout the nation, having due regard to the fiscal capacities, tax efforts, and needs of the states. The technical problems that have to be solved, before a meaningful form of federal transfers can be drawn up, include the determination of minimum standards for various public services and the indices of need, fiscal capacity, and tax effort.

Federal Taxation as an Alternative to State Taxation

Efficiency in tax administration as well as minimization of taxpayer compliance costs may require the assignment of the more income-elastic tax sources (e.g., personal income tax and corporation income tax) exclusively to the federal government. At the same time, efficiency in the provision of various public services may require that a wide range of public services be entrusted to the state and local governments which are better able to tailor them to the preferences of their citizens. This imbalance in the assignment of financial resources, on the one hand, and functional responsibilities, on the other, between the federal and state governments calls for an arrangement to share tax receipts of the federal government between it and the states.

The aforementioned grounds are some of the major reasons for federal financial transfers to the state governments. These grounds are exemplified in the scheme of federal-state financial relations that have evolved in the Indian federation

after 1947. Since that year, six Finance Commissions have attempted to resolve the emerging issues in fiscal federalism in India. We now turn to an examination of federal finance in India.

Federal Finance In India

Taxation and Borrowing: Constitutional Provisions

The Indian Constitution vests in the federal government the exclusive power to levy the following taxes:[5] customs, taxes on corporations and nonagricultural income, estate taxes on property other than agricultural land, and all excises except those on alcohol and narcotic drugs. The states have the exclusive power to levy taxes on agricultural income and estate taxes on agricultural land. The Constitution permits the states to levy sales taxes; however, they are prohibited from imposing such taxes on transactions which occur outside their boundaries or which arise in the course of interstate or international trade.[6] Furthermore, a constitutional amendment made in 1956 empowers the Indian Parliament to restrict state sales tax laws concerning goods declared to be of "special importance" in interstate trade.

The borrowing powers of the states are limited by the provisions of the Indian Constitution. The state governments have no right to borrow outside India. Furthermore, if a state is indebted to the Union (as every state is now), it may not resort to further borrowing without the prior consent of the federal government.[7]

Methods of Financial Adjustment: Constitutional Provisions

The Constitution provides for three avenues for supplementing the financial resources of state governments. These are: (1) sharing of certain federal taxes, (2) grants-in-aid, and (3) grants for public purposes. The first two are designed to be integral parts of normal federal-state financial adjustments. The architects of the Indian Federation provided for an independent statutory body, namely, a Finance Commission[8], to be appointed every quinquennium or earlier, entrusted with periodic review and resolution of federal-state fiscal problems. It was the clear intention of the fathers of the Indian Constitution that all matters pertaining to normal federal-state financial adjustments should be scrutinised by the Finance Commission, which was given a preeminent role in the resolution of problems in fiscal federalism.

The third means of financial adjustment, namely grants for public purposes (permitted under Article 282 of the Constitution), was intended to be resorted to only in emergencies. Since such grants are not envisaged as part of normal federal-state financial adjustments, they are kept outside the purview of the Finance Commission.

Although grants for public purposes under Article 282 were intended for meeting emergencies, with the advent of centralized economic planning, the federal government has chosen this avenue in order to award grants for the execution of various projects under the economic plans. These grants are made on the recommendation of the Planning Commission, which is essentially a political body. Thus, soon after the inauguration of the Indian Constitution, the Finance Commission was bypassed in the determination of a vital part of the federal-state financial adjustment mechanism.

Not only has the Finance Commission been excluded from the determination of significant aspects of fiscal federalism, but also the dominant role assigned to it in the Constitution has been progressively circumscribed. The directives to the second and third Commissions explicitly required them to take into account, among other things, the states' needs under the economic plans and their tax efforts before determining grants-in-aid of their revenues.[9] On the contrary, the fourth, fifth, and sixth Finance Commissions were directed not to take into account the states' requirements under the economic plans for determining grants-in-aid. Furthermore, by implication, they were even precluded from a study of the states' tax efforts. For example, in assessing grants-in-aid for the five years ending with the fiscal year 1978-79, the sixth Commission was directed to consider not the tax efforts of states but the revenues

available to them on the basis of levels of taxation likely to be reached at the end of the fiscal year 1973-74.[10]

The rise of the Planning Commission with wide powers over the allocation of resources between the federal and state governments has resulted in a progressive downgrading of the role of the Finance Commission. Prior to the formulation of each economic plan, the Planning Commission is expected to make an assessment of all the resources available to the federal and state governments, including additional taxation, borrowing, deficit financing, and foreign assistance. On the basis of this assessment, the Planning Commission determines the size of the national plan which is composed of subplans for the federal government and each state government. To minimize overlapping between the Planning and Finance Commissions, the latter has been restricted to the nonplan sector of state budgets. This led the Third Finance Commission to observe:

> Against this background, the role of the Finance Commission comes to be, at best, that of an agency to review the forecasts of revenue and expenditure submitted by the states and the acceptance of the revenue element of the Plan as indicated by the Planning Commission for determining the quantum of devolution and grants-in-aid to be made; and, at worst, its function is merely to undertake an arithmetic exercise of devolution, based on amounts of assistance for each state already settled by the Planning Commission, to be made under different heads on the basis of certain principles to be prescribed.[11]

Taxsharing
The Indian Constitution spells out a wide variety of federal-state arrangements in regard to taxation. These dispositions have stemmed from a desire to minimize a wide array of tax problems endemic to federal systems, such as duplicate tax administrations, double taxation, tax rivalry among states, tax evasion, excessive tax compliance costs, etc. Four types of arrangements may be readily identified:

1. taxes which are levied by the Federal Government but collected and appropriated by the states;[12]

2. taxes which are levied and collected by the federal government but assigned to the states;[13]
3. taxes which are levied and collected by the federal government but mandated to be shared with the states;[14] and
4. taxes which are levied, collected and retained by the federal government which, on its own volition, may share proceeds with the states.[15]

The Constitution enumerates the taxes that fall into each of the four groups mentioned above. However, the actual details with respect to sharing are left to the recommendations of the Finance Commissions.

The first two arrangements mentioned earlier are evidently not intended for making any financial adjustments between federal and state governments but for ensuring uniformity of taxation, minimization of tax evasion and tax compliance costs, and administrative convenience. In the first case, the taxes are collected and appropriated by the states; thus the allocation of the receipts among the various states is automatic. The taxes in this group are certain stamp duties and excises on certain medicinal and toilet preparations and a federal interstate sales tax.

In the second category, although the federal government levies and collects the taxes, it has no right to the revenues. In regard to the allocation of the receipts from these taxes among the various states, all the Finance Commissions have felt that the principles of distribution should be such as to secure, as far as possible, for each state the amount it would have collected, if it had the power to levy the taxes.[16] The only tax in this category which is levied and collected by the federal government is an estate tax on nonagricultural property.[17]

Under the third and fourth categories are respectively, federal tax on nonagricultural income and federal excises. The former is mandated to be shared with the states. The latter may be shared with the states at the discretion of the Indian Parliament.[18]

Progressively rising budgetary pressures have prompted the state governments to plead before the Finance Commissions for increasing shares of federal income tax and excises. In the case of income tax, the states have advanced two reasons for a larger share of the receipts. First, the Income Tax Act of 1959 reclassified income tax paid by companies as corporation tax, thereby excluding it altogether from sharing with states. Second, the receipts from income tax have proved to be less elastic than those from corporation income tax. Because of these two reasons, the states have felt justified in asking for a larger share of federal income tax. The Finance Commissions have responded to the states' demands by progressively increasing the states' share from 50 to 80 per cent. The last four Finance Commissions have cautioned against further increases in the states' shares of income tax, lest the federal government, which levies and collects the tax, may lose interest in the yield of the tax.[19]

In the case of federal excises, the Finance Commissions' response to the states' demands for a larger share has been to broaden the base by including more and more federal excises within the divisible pool. Although the earlier Finance Commissions restricted sharing to some selected federal excises, the later Commissions have found no justification for doing so. Moreover, if only some selected federal excises are shared, a reduction or even abolition of one of these may adversely affect the revenue position of the states. Furthermore, the larger the number of shared taxes, the greater the stability of shared revenues for state governments. Thus, all basic excises, additional excises on mineral oils, and special excises have been recommended to be included in the divisible pool. With the broadening of the base, the Finance Commissions have reduced the states' share from 40 to 20 per cent, although in absolute terms the divisible share has progressively increased.

In regard to the distribution of shared federal tax receipts among the various states, generally each state has advanced the formula which is the most beneficial to it. For the distribution of income tax, states have urged the Finance Commission to take into account one or more of the following: contribution, population, area, proportion of scheduled castes and tribes in population, etc. In the case of federal excises, the criteria put forward include population, consumption, contribution, collection, and various other indices of financial need.

The Finance Commissions have generally felt that income taxes and excises should be allocated among the states on the basis of some broad index of need, such as population. In general, the special circumstances and needs of the various states are germane only to the determination of grants-in-aid and not for the distribution of taxes shared between the Union and the states.[20]

Population is given predominant weight in the distribution of income tax; in addition, some weight is given to the respective contribution of the states to the receipts of the tax. In 1969, four relatively industrialized states alone accounted for about three-fourths of the income tax collections.[21] All the Finance Commissions except the second have been inclined to give some weight to the respective contributions of the states because of the fact that "there is all over the country a core of incomes—particularly in the range of personal and small-business incomes—which could be treated as of local origin".[22] The fifth and sixth Finance Commissions, for example, have recommended that 90 per cent of the divisible income-tax pool be distributed on the basis of population and the remainder on the basis of contribution.[23]

The population of the states is the major factor in the formula for the distribution of federal excises, too. The Finance Commissions have been reluctant to give any weight to consumption of taxed commodities in the distribution formula because it would result in considerable disadvantage to the less urbanized states which are not in a position to raise revenues from sales taxes to the same extent as the more urbanized ones. The first Finance Commission distributed the states' share of excises solely on the basis of population.[24] The subsequent Commissions, while still keeping population as the most important factor in distribution, have made some adjustments in favour of the relatively poorer states. The sixth Finance Com-

mission, for example, distributed 75 per cent of the divisible excises on the basis of population and the remainder on the basis of the relative needs of the states, as indicated by their per capita incomes.[25]

Comments on Tax Sharing The Constitution gives the right to levy tax on nonagricultural income and most excises exclusively to the federal government. The state governments have absolutely no right to impose them within their boundaries. The readiness of all Finance Commissions except the second to acknowledge the relevance of contribution in the distribution of income tax implies the recognition of the inherent right of each state to a part of the income tax contributed by it. Such a right has no constitutional basis. If a broad index of need is the appropriate basis for distribution of the proceeds of a shared tax, then there is no justification for giving any importance to contribution in the scheme for distribution.

Also it may be argued that there is no reason for giving any consideration to the special needs of states in the formula for the distribution of shared taxes. Presumably, every state is entitled to a share of federal income tax and excises irrespective of need, but grants-in-aid are awarded only to those states which have demonstrated a need for such assistance. Therefore, it seems appropriate to take into account the special needs of states for the determination of grants-in-aid rather than for the distribution of shared taxes. Moreover, if the absolute share of a state from the distributable pool of federal taxes is raised because of its special needs, the grants-in-aid received by it should be correspondingly reduced. At the margin, it should not make any significant difference whether the funds are received from shared taxes or grants-in-aid. Therefore, instead of making inadequate and haphazard provisions for the special needs of states in the formula for distribution of shared taxes, the entire problem may be systematically considered in the determination of grants-in-aid. Hence a strong case may be made for simplifying the method of distribution of shared taxes among the states on the basis of a broad index of need, such as population, leaving their special needs to be covered, if necessary, by grants-in-aid.

Furthermore, given the present formula for the distribution of shared taxes, it may be asked why contribution is not relevant for the distribution of federal excises, if it is relevant for the distribution of income tax? Likewise, if the special needs of the states are relevant for the distribution of federal excises, why are these same needs not significant for the allocation of income tax?

At present, the receipts from shared taxes add substantially to the surpluses in the nonplan budgets of several states, some of which have the highest per capita incomes in the country. The fourth Finance Commission found six states with surpluses,[26] whereas the fifth Commission found eight, and the sixth Commission found seven states with substantial surpluses.[27] Swelling the surpluses in nonplan state budgets by receipts from shared taxes leads to a reduction in the overall federal resources that are made available to support the economic plans of all states, especially the less advanced ones.[28] More importantly, however, given the prevailing undertaxation even by the wealthier states, swollen surpluses in the nonplan budgets are certainly not likely to impel the state governments to intensify tax efforts and enhance efficiency. This situation points to the need for reducing the states' shares of divisible taxes (which are now 80 per cent for federal income tax and 20 per cent for federal excises) so that large surpluses in nonplan state budgets may be avoided. Of course, such reduction should not affect the total amount payable by way of shared taxes *and* grants-in-aid to any state which currently receives grants-in-aid.

In the future, Finance Commissions may be well advised to fix the states' shares of divisible taxes and adopt schemes for their distribution with a view to avoiding large surpluses in state budgets. They may also adhere to a broad index of need, such as population, as the basis for distribution of shared taxes. By doing so, they may avoid the ritual of states pleading for larger shares of federal taxes and presenting ingenious formulae for the

allocation of shared federal levies. This would give future Commissions an opportunity to devote a greater part of their time and energy to an intensive study of state and local finance, which is indispensable for making meaningful decisions with respect to federal-state fiscal problems in general, and the sharing of federal levies and estimation of grants-in-aid in particular.

Grants-in-Aid

The first Finance Commission laid down some important principles governing the determination of grants-in-aid for states.[29] These principles have been generally endorsed by all the subsequent Commissions.[30]

The budgetary needs of a state are an important consideration for the determination of grants-in-aid; however, before assessing such needs several adjustments have to be made to the state budgets in order to make them comparable. Uniform treatment has to be accorded to the commercial and business undertakings of the state governments, the separation of their capital and revenue (current) budgets, and interest and amortization charges of their debts. Unusual and nonrecurring items of receipts and expenditures have to be eliminated from state budgets. Due allowance should be made for failure to maximize tax efforts or to perform public services efficiently. Furthermore, special consideration may be given to less advanced states for improving the standards of certain basic social services.

Although all the Finance Commissions have been in agreement about the principles governing the determination of grants-in-aid, none has so far undertaken any detailed inquiry into the tax efforts, efficiency of administration, or relative needs of various states. They have been handicapped by a serious lack of the time, resources, and statistical information necessary to make a meaningful study of state and local finance. Consequently, grants-in-aid have been based on the budgetary gaps reported by the states. This led the third Finance Commission to observe:

... We have therefore been compelled, like our own predecessors, to cover the annual budgetary gaps of all states, whether caused by normal growth of expenditure, the maintenance cost of completed schemes and mounting interest charges or even by a measure of improvidence.[31]

In order to assess grants-in-aid on a realistic basis, the Finance Commission has to determine standards for the tax effort and services provided by the state governments. On the basis of these standards, the Commission may determine the amount of resources that a state should raise on its own, the amount of resources required by the state to perform various public services at certain predetermined levels, and the amount of grants-in-aid required by it.[32] To be sure, there are no precise criteria by which standards for tax effort or public services could be measured. However, an independent statutory body, such as the Finance Commission, entrusted with the responsibility for resolution of problems in fiscal federalism, has to persevere in the construction of reasonably satisfactory standards for tax efforts and public services

Tax Efforts of States
It is practically impossible to devise objective indices for the determination of the relative tax efforts of various states.[33] What constitutes an adequate tax effort is open to debate. A comparison of the tax performance of states may be obtained by comparing their per capita tax yields. This, however, does not compare tax performance to the fiscal capacity of states.

A comparison of the actual rates of various taxes prevailing in different states would give an indication of the relative use of their tax capacity.[34] However, such a comparison should be made with caution since seemingly similar taxes may have very different bases in the different states. A variation of this method would be to test actual tax performance against the yield of a model of tax programme for the states.

A reasonably satisfactory index of the relative tax efforts of the states may be obtained by comparing their tax per-

formance to fiscal capacity. Tax performance and fiscal capacity may be respectively measured by per capita state and local tax collection, and per capita state income adjusted for federal personal income tax drain.[35]

There are several methods by which the tax efforts of states may be compared. But the first four Finance Commissions expended very little, if any, of their energy to make such comparisons. The directives to the fourth and fifth Finance Commissions implicitly precluded them from an examination of the states' relative tax efforts. In spite of this, the fifth Finance Commission made some cursory attempts to study the relative tax efforts by comparing the ratio of per capita state and local tax collection to per capita state income.[36] But the sixth Finance Commission refrained from any such attempt.[37]

There is considerable variation in the fiscal capacity, tax performance and tax efforts of the different states (see Table 17.1). Comparing the states at the extreme ends of the distribution, average per capita domestic product during 1967–70 in Punjab was well over double that of Bihar,[38] per capita tax revenues in 1971–72 in Punjab were well over three times that of Bihar; the tax efforts of Tamil Nadu—as indicated by the tax collected in 1971–72 from every Rs. 100 average state domestic product during the period 1967–70—was double that of Orissa. Tamil Nadu had the highest tax effort even though its average per capita domestic state product during 1967–70 was equal to the national average. On the average, in 1971–72 the state governments taxed away about 7 paise from every rupee of their average domestic product received during 1967–70. Many of the poorer states (e.g., Bihar, Orissa, Uttar Pradesh) indicate tax efforts well below the national average. The most blatant case of statewide undertaxation as well as interstate disparity in taxation is with respect to agricultural income, the taxation of which is exclusively reserved for the states. Comparing proceeds from land revenue and agricultural income tax in 1967–68 as a percentage of average state agricultural income during 1962–65,

Table 18.1.   Fiscal Capacity, Tax Performance and Tax Efforts of States
(In Rupees)

State	Fiscal Capacity Average State Per Capita State Domestic Product, 1967–70		Tax Performance Per Capita Tax, 1971–72		Tax Effort State Tax Collection Per Rs. 100 of State Domestic Products 1967–70	
	Amount	Index[a]	Amount	Index[a]	Amount	Index[a]
Andhra Pradesh	537	97	40	100	7.5	107
Assam	581	105	22	72	5.0	71
Bihar	409	74	23	59	5.7	81
Gujarat	667	121	56	140	8.4	120
Haryana	810	147	58	144	7.1	102
Himachal Pradesh	585	106	30	76	5.2	74
Jammu and Kashmir	426	77	25	63	5.9	84
Kerala	555	101	43	108	7.7	110
Madhya Pradesh	458	83	31	77	6.7	94
Maharashtra	686	125	66	164	9.5	136
Manipur	458	83	7	18	1.6	23
Mysore	552	100	47	119	8.6	122
Nagaland	420	76	18	44	4.2	60
Orissa	488	89	24	60	4.9	70
Punjab	940	171	77	192	8.1	116
Rajasthan	455	83	33	83	7.3	104
Tamil Nadu	558	101	57	139	10.0	142
Tripura	532	97	5	12	0.9	13
Uttar Pradesh	480	87	26	65	5.4	77
West Bangal	667	121	43	108	6.4	92

[a]Indices are based on weighted national average being equal to 100.

SOURCE: 1. *Sixth Report*, p. 161.

2. *Combined Finance and Revenue Accounts of the Union and State Governments in India for the Year 1971–72.*

the fifth Finance Commission found that it was 2.6 per cent for the relatively very low-income state of Rajasthan; it was only 0.5 per cent for the most prosperous agricultural and also highest-income state of Punjab, the same as for Bihar and Orissa, which are among the lowest-income states.[39] Andhra Pradesh, Gujarat, Madhya Pradesh, Haryana, and Punjab do not levy any tax at all on agricultural income; even in those states where the tax is levied, there is a general feeling that it is inadequately enforced.[40]

Wide variations in tax effort, gross undertaxation of the agricultural sector and rampant tax evasion appear to be chronic features of state taxation in India.[41] The Uttar Pradesh Taxation Inquiry Committee reported that in 1967–68 sales tax receipts increased by 53 per cent over the year 1965–66 without any increase in rates, but by some improvements in the administrative machinery.[42] Substantial evasion of sales tax was found also by the Kerala State Taxation Inquiry Committee.[43]

The manner of determining grants-in-aid or the states' share of receipts from federal income tax and excises has done very little, if anything, to penalize the states for their failure to maximize tax effort. On the contrary, it appears to have rewarded the states for their laxity in tax effort. This serious problem was alluded to by the third Finance Commission as follows:

> Secure in the knowledge that the annual budgetary gap would be fully covered by the devolution of Union resource and grants-in-aid, the states are tending to develop, as we have noticed, an allergy to tap resources in the rural sector on many considerations and also disinclination to make up the leeway in others.[44]

The fifth Finance Commission made some allowance for the tax effort of a state if it "appeared to be considerably lower than that of other states with similar per capita income and particularly states with similar conditions of development." However, the sixth Finance Commission did not take into account deficiency in tax effort in the determination of grants-in-aid.

Standards for Public Services None of the Finance Commissions has made any serious effort to study the standards of the public services provided by the various states or to inquire into the efficiency with which they perform various functions.

Devising standards for public services is often more difficult than devising those for tax effort. Just as in the case of tax effort, it is impossible to formulate completely satisfactory indices for the standards of public services.

The fifth Finance Commission adopted a method used by the Commonwealth Grants Commission in Australia to compare the standards of public services provided by the states. The method involves a simple comparison of per capita expenditure of various services provided by the states. Per capita expenditure as an index of the standard of public services is subject to serious qualifications. Interstate differences in per capita expenditures for any service are not necessarily indicative of the differences in the quality of that service. For example, a given quality of police protection may cost more per capita in an urbanized state than in a rural one; per capita cost of highway construction depends on the terrain of a state, and so on. Where large differences in per capita expenditures for a particular

service exist, the Finance Commission will have to investigate further in order to ascertain whether such differences are due to genuine variations in quality, inefficient administration, or other special reasons. If there are clear cases of inefficiency or extravagance, the Finance Commission should adjust the budgetary positions of the states correspondingly before determining their grants-in-aid.

There are wide variations in the 1971–72 per capita expenditures for various public services provided by the state governments, as seen from Table 18.2. The per capita expenditures[45] for all social and developmental services[46] in Kerala was more than twice that of Bihar and Uttar Pradesh.[47] The situation is similar with respect to education, for which Kerala's per capita expenditure was more than three times that of Bihar.[48] Similar variations can be seen in expenditures for medicine and public health, civil administration, tax collection, etc.

None of the earlier Finance Commissions attempted to upgrade the standards of vital public services, especially in the poorer states such as Bihar, Orissa, and Uttar Pradesh. The sixth Finance Commission, however, broke new ground in seeking to raise the standard of such services in the relatively poorer states up to the national average. In assessing the nonplan budgetary gap of the states which are to be covered by grants-in-aid, the Commissioners allowed for the necessary funds required to enhance the per capita expenditures for essential social services in the poorer states up to the national average in a period of five years.[49]

Business Undertakings and Public Debt of States Before the grants-in-aid needed by a state are ascertained, allowance has to be made not only for the tax effort and standards of public services but also for the results of their commercial undertakings and interest charges and amortization provisions for their debts. The mounting debts of the states and losses from commercial undertakings and other investments have put their budgets under severe pressure.

In assessing the budgetary needs of states, a strong case may be made for

Table 18.2. Per Capita Expenditures for Selected Public Services Provided by States, 1971–72
(In Rupees)

Per Capita Expenditures for

	Civil Administration		Tax Collection		Education		Medicine and Public Health		Total Social and Development Sources	
	Amount	Index[a]	Amount	Index[a]	Amount	Index[a]	Amount	Index[a]	Amount	Index[a]
Andhra Pradesh	9.3	99	2.4	80	15.2	92	6.4	99	32.3	95
Assam	12.3	130	2.1	70	18.6	113	6.5	101	37.5	110
Bihar	6.1	65	1.8	60	8.9	54	3.8	59	20.8	61
Gujarat	9.4	100	5.3	176	18.5	112	8.9	138	37.0	109
Haryana	9.2	98	1.7	56	20.1	122	9.0	139	41.4	122
Himachal Pradesh	18.9	200	3.5	116	38.1	231	12.2	189	79.0	232
Jammu & Kashmir	21.5	228	3.1	103	21.3	129	11.7	181	49.6	146
Kerala	7.5	78	3.3	110	31.0	188	8.8	136	51.3	151
Madhya Pradesh	7.3	77	1.9	63	13.2	80	5.6	87	28.4	83
Maharashtra	13.7	146	9.4	312	20.3	123	8.6	133	40.6	119
Manipur	43.3	459	2.2	73	46.6	283	9.9	153	71.4	210
Mysore	7.4	78	2.5	83	18.5	112	5.9	91	40.2	118
Nagaland	169.2	1794	2.8	93	63.4	385	40.0	619	159.2	468
Orissa	7.3	77	2.7	90	12.5	76	5.8	90	30.1	88
Punjab	12.8	136	2.3	76	23.1	140	8.4	130	45.9	135
Rajasthan	8.4	89	2.7	90	17.4	106	9.8	152	36.0	106
Tamil Nadu	12.1	128	2.0	66	21.0	128	3.3	128	45.3	133
Tripura	19.5	207	3.0	100	36.4	221	8.9	138	64.3	189
Uttar Pradesh	6.1	65	2.2	73	10.9	66	3.1	48	23.3	68
West Bengal	12.0	127	2.7	90	17.1	104	6.8	105	33.1	97

[a]Indices based on weighted national average being equal to 100.

SOURCE: *Combined Finance and Revenue Accounts of the Union and State Governments of India for the Year 1971–72.*

excluding all their commercial undertakings and investments on the presumption
that they should be so managed as to
produce no loss. In the event losses do
occur, the states may be expected to
cover them not by grants-in-aid from the
federal government but by their own
sacrifice. This salutary principle has not
been applied to all the business undertakings by the Finance Commissions.
The fifth Finance Commission has,
however, extended its application to
practically all commercial enterprises and
investments of state governments.[50]

On the same principle, interest charges
and amortization for public debt incurred
for business ventures may be kept out of
the current (revenue) budget altogether.
They have to be met from the revenues
from investment. However, if loan
finance is used for nonrevenue-yielding
capital expenditures, such as roads, hospi-
tals, school buildings, and flood control
projects, it may be appropriate to meet
interest cost and amortization from
revenues. In actual practice, large items
of such capital expenditures for social
overhead capital (undertaken in many
cases to fulfill projects in the economic
plans), are placed in the capital budget
which is financed by borrowing. But
with the mounting capital expenditures
financed by loans, the states have come to
feel that interest charges and amortization for such loans should be provided by
the federal government.

In assessing the needs of the states for
grants-in-aid, it appears that the earlier
Finance Commissions had allowed all
interest charges including those on debts
for commercial enterprises.[51] The fifth
Finance Commission was, however, more
discriminatory in allowing interest charges.
The Commissioners, as a rule, did not
allow any interest charges on that part
of states' debts which is utilized for
business undertakings, loans to other
parties, and unauthorized overdrafts from
the Reserve Bank of India; but interest
charges on debt incurred for expenditure
on social overhead capital (which do not
yield any revenue) were allowed subject
to certain uniform limits laid down by the
Commission.[52]

The treatment accorded to amortization of states' debts has varied from one
Commission to another. The second and
third Commissions did not allow for
amortization when such provision had to
come from shared taxes or grants-in-aid.
The fifth Commission, however, felt that
amortization for all *market* borrowings
of states should be allowed as legitimate
charges against revenue. It took the
Fifth Commission to stress the proposition
that the principle that governs the eligibility
or otherwise of interest cost as a legitimate
charge against revenue also governs
the disposition of amortization. The
Commissioners, therefore, allowed amortization only for that part of the states'
debt which was incurred for capital
expenditure of a nonrevenue-yielding
nature, subject to certain uniform
limits.[53]

Special Assistance to Low-Income States
The wide variations among states with
respect to resources and standards of
public services have been discussed earlier.
In view of this, the first Finance Commission felt that grants-in-aid should be
so designed as to bring about a certain
measure of equalization among the states.
As a modest beginning, the Commissioners
recommended special grants-in-aid for
the promotion of primary education in
eight less-advanced states.[54]

The second Finance Commission did
not, however, recommend any special
grants-in-aid for low-income states. The
Commissioners were of the opinion that
where the national and state governments
cooperated for planned economic development, priorities and provisions in the
plan itself should determine the fiscal
needs of the states for the period of the
plan. Although equalization is a valid
criterion for the assessment of grants-in-
aid, the Commissioners felt that it was the
function of the Planning Commission and
the National Development Council to
ensure equalization of the standards of
essential public services provided by the
states. Having accepted the plan as
ensuring an equitable standard in the
field of social services, there was no room
for any grants for the expansion of any
particular public service in any state, such
as the primary education grants recommen-

ded by the first Commission.[55]

The position taken by the second Finance Commission with respect to special assistance to low-income states did not, however, deter the third Commission from recommending special grants for the maintenance and construction of roads and other communications to some less advanced states.[56] But the later Commissions, except the sixth Commission, endorsed the second Commission's position and put the burden of ensuring equalization on the Planning Commission.[57] The sixth Commission, as explained earlier, allowed for the upgrading of the standards of essential social services in the poorer states.

Comments on Grants-in-aid
No Finance Commission has so far made a serious study of state and local finance with a view to a realistic determination of the grants-in-aid needed by the states. The sixth Finance Commission did not consider it worthwhile to expend any effort to evolve some criteria for determining the relative tax performance in the states. The Commissioners stated:

... But we have given up the effort on the practical consideration that the application of a formula based on relative tax effort, however designed, would place at a disadvantage some of the states faced with big gaps on non-Plan revenue accounts. To leave such gaps uncovered on the ground of their poor tax performance, however defensible on theoretical considerations, would jeopardize maintenance of essential administrative and social services for want of adequate resources. States, both advanced and backward, which have done better than average at resource mobilization might feel aggrieved that their efforts have not received recognition. But, if in the determination of the principles of Central assistance for the Plan, some weight is given for the relative efforts of the States at mobilization of revenues, as was done at the time of the formulation of the Fourth Plan, the grievance of such States would be substantially met.[58]

Thus, the Commissioners were willing to leave the determination of the relative

tax effort of the States and their weightage in Central assistance to the Planning Commission. This, however, did not preclude the Commissioners from quantifying "the requirements in financial terms of the backward states from the standpoint of progressive equalization of standards of essential administrative and social services within a definite time horizon",[59] and making provision for Central assistance to backward States whose per capita expenditure is below the all-State average to come up to that average within five years.[60] The sixth Finance Commission was willing to leave the task of progressive equalization of the standards of tax effort among the states to the Planning Commission; but it was ready and perhaps eager to take on the task of progressive equalization of the standards of essential social services among the states and make the necessary provision for Central assistance to the states! This situation exemplifies one of the significant weaknesses in federal-state financial arrangements in India—determination of federal grants-in-aid to States without due regard to their relative tax efforts. The Finance Commissions have, perhaps unwittingly, rewarded laxity and penalized severity in tax effort with consequent detrimental effects on the mobilization of resources by the States.

Modifications in Centre-State Fiscal Arrangements

After more than twenty years of experience in federal-state financial relations under the new Constitution, what possible suggestions for modification of the existing arrangements can be made? The second, third, and fourth Finance Commissions strongly felt that modifications should be made in the existing arrangements for federal-state financial adjustments.[61] The wide variations that continue to prevail in the states' tax efforts and levels of public services stress the need for a reexamination of the machinery as well as the methods adopted to deal with problems of fiscal federalism.

The mechanism of an independent statutory body, such as the Finance Commission, to deal with all evolving problems of fiscal federalism in a non-political environment is indeed worth preserving and promoting. But the rise of the Planning Commission, with wide powers over the allocation of resources in the Indian Union has almost led to a total eclipse of the Finance Commission. The relegation of the Finance Commission to the nonplan sector of the state budgets and the implicit restrictions placed on it with respect to scrutinising the tax efforts of the states have made it practically impotent. It is highly desirable to restore the Finance Commission to the preeminent status intended for it in the sphere of fiscal federalism.

In order to restore the Finance Commission to the role destined for it in the Indian Constitution, the first step would be a clear demarcation of the roles of the Planning and Finance Commissions. The Planning Commission may continue to have the responsibility for formulating the national economic plan with its constituent state plans. But the Finance Commission should have the responsibility of determining what resources the states should raise by existing and new taxation, and how much residual federal aid should be given by way of shared taxes, grants-in-aid, and loans, so that the state governments may meet the needs of their plan as well as nonplan budgets. Undoubtedly, this requires very close coordination between the Planning and Finance Commissions.

If such a demarcation between the roles of the Finance and Planning Commissions is agreed upon, it is clear that the Finance Commission, as envisaged in the Indian Constitution, cannot fulfill the responsibility placed on it. It would have to be transformed into a permanent body with an adequate research staff to undertake continuing studies of state and local finance in India. The Commission will have to determine the adequacy of the tax effort of each state; it will have to determine the efficiency with which states perform public services and manage their business undertakings. It is only

by an intensive study of state and local finance that the Finance Commission can fulfill the responsibility placed on it by the Indian Constitution. It is indeed a serious indictment of fiscal federalism in India that no earnest efforts have been made so far in this direction, even twenty-five years after the inauguration of the Indian Constitution.

It may be added that the proposed demarcation of the roles of the two Commissions would promote more effective planning as well as better mobilization of resources. The Planning Commission would be able to concentrate on physical planning as well as on ensuring an appropriate regional balance in economic development. The Finance Commission would be concerned with the fiscal aspect of the plan and nonplan budgets of states which would include a careful assessment of the resources that should be raised by every state and the additional resources that should be transferred to it in the form of shared federal taxes, grants-in-aid, loans, etc. The Finance Commission would thus be able to spur the states' efforts to improve tax performance and enhance efficiency in the provision of public services. This would promote a better mobilization as well as allocation of resources.

Lastly, it is very important to modify the existing arrangement with respect to taxation of agricultural property and income. Under the Constitution, State governments have the exclusive power to tax agricultural income and property. This is, indeed, a very serious inequity in the Indian tax structure.[62] Moreover, this had led to considerable undertaxation of the agricultural sector of the Indian economy at a stage in the economic development of the country when that sector, in fact, should be making a substantial contribution towards capital formation. The distinction between agricultural and other income should be done away with and taxation of all income should be placed in the hands of the federal government.

REFERENCES

1. For a detailed consideration of the various theoretical issues involved, see W.E. Oates, *Fiscal Federalism* (New York: Harcourt, Brace, Jovanovich, 1972); also, R.A. Musgrave and P.B. Musgrave, *Public Finance in Theory and Practice*, 2nd. ed. (New York: McGraw-Hill, 1976). Chap. 29.

2. The situation is more complex than pictured here. In a system of state governments there would be reciprocal externalities and then the subsidy to one state would depend on the subsidies to others.

3. A matching conditional grant for a service will have an income and a substitution effect which are both favourable to augmenting the provision of public sources whereas an unconditional grant has only an income effect. See James Wilde, "The Expenditure Effects of Grant-in-Aid Programs", *National Tax Journal*, vol. 68, no. 3, September 1968, pp. 340–48.

4. R.A. Musgrave, "Approaches to a Fiscal Theory of Political Federalism", in National Bureau of Economic Research, *Public Finances: Needs, Sources, and Utilization* (Princeton University Press, 1961), pp. 97–122.

5. See *Constitution of India*, Seventh Schedule (hereinafter cited as C.I.).

6. Ibid.

7. Ibid., Art. 293.

8. Ibid., Art. 280.

9. Government of India, *Report of the Finance Commission, 1957* (New Delhi, 1957), p. 2. (Hereinafter cited as *Second Report*), and *Report of the Finance Commission, 1961* (New Delhi, 1962), p. 2 (hereinafter cited as *Third Report*).

10. *Report of the Finance Commission, 1973* (New Delhi, 1973), p. 1, hereinafter cited as *Sixth Report*); also, *Report of the Finance Commission, 1969* (New Delhi, 1969), p. 2 (hereinafter cited as *Fifth Report*); and *Report of the Finance Commission, 1965* (New Delhi, 1965, pp. 1–2 (hereinafter cited as *Fourth Report*).

11. *Third Report*, p. 35.

12. *C. I.*, Art. 268.

13. Ibid., Art. 269.

14. Ibid., Art. 270.

15. Ibid., Art 272.

16. *Second Report*, pp. 51–52; *Third Report*, pp. 13–14, *Fourth Report*, p. 12; *Fifth Report*, p. 237; and *Sixth Report*, p. 25. For example, the estate tax on nonagricultural immovable property, which comes under this category, is distributed among the states in proportion to the gross value of such property assessed and located in each state.

17. A federal tax on railway passenger fares imposed in 1957 used to be in this category until 1961 when it was repealed. To compensate for the consequent loss of revenue to state governments, an ad hoc grant is made by the federal government. Moreover, as a result of an extraconstitutional arrangement, the state governments have agreed to replace their sales taxes on three widely used commodities, namely factory-made textiles, sugar and tobacco, by additional federal excises on them. The net proceeds of these excises are distributed among the states.

18. At present, receipts from wealth tax on agricultural land levied by the federal government are passed on to the states as grants-in-aid. See *Sixth Report*, Chap. 8.

19. *Third Report*, p. 17; *Fourth Report*, p. 18; *Fifth Report*, pp. 25–26; and *Sixth Report*, p. 11.

20. *First Report*, p. 75; *Second Report*, pp. 39–40 and 44; *Third Report*, pp. 17–18 and 22; *Fourth Report*, pp. 19 and 28–29; and *Fifth Report*, p. 28.

21. *Fifth Report*, p. 27.

22. *First Report*, p. 73; *Third Report*, p. 18; *Fourth Report*, p. 19; and *Fifth Report*, pp. 26–28.

23. *Sixth Report*, p. 12.

24. *First Report*, p. 82.

25. For details, see *Sixth Report*, p. 17.

26. *Fourth Report*, p. 59.

27. *Fifth Report*, p. 65; and *Sixth Report*, p. 73.

28. See Minute by Shri G. Swaminathan, *Fifth Report*, pp. 99–103.

29. *First Report*, pp. 96–97.

30. *Second Report*, p. 23; *Third Report*, pp. 28–29; *Fourth Report*, pp. 46–47; *Fifth Report*, p. 47; and *Sixth Report*, p. 67.

31. *Third Report*, p. 38.

32. The Commonwealth Grants Commission in Australia determines grants-in-aid in this manner.

33. U.S. Advisory Commission in Intergovernmental Relations, *Measuring the Fiscal Capacity and Effect of State and Local Areas* (Washington, D.C., March 1971).

34. The Commonwealth Grants Commission in Australia adopts this method to examine the states' relative tax efforts.

35. Per capita income is an inadequate index of fiscal capacity. The fiscal capacity of a state depends not only on income but also on wealth; it depends not only on income *received* but on income produced within the state. Furthermore, the index does not make any allowance for difference in the distribution of income within states. Allowing for federal income tax drain is particularly important in view of the exemption of agricultural income from federal income tax in India. Also per capita tax collection does not make any allowance for interstate shifting of state and local taxes.

36. This index does not measure the relative degree of sacrifice of income for taxes borne by the residents of different states. Various attempts have been made to develop a measure of tax burden which incorporates an element of vertical equity. See Ved P. Gandhi, *Tax Burden on Indian Agriculture*, (Cambridge, Mass: The Law School of Harvard University, 1966,) Chapter 2. See also

K.V.S. Sastri, *Federal-State Fiscal Relations in India* (Bombay: Oxford University Press), 1962, Chapter 2.

37. *Sixth Report*, p. 52.
38. Himachal Pradesh, Jammu and Kashmir, Manipur, Tripura, and Nagaland are excluded from comparison owing to their special circumstances.
37. *Fifth Report*, p. 82.
40. Ibid., p. 84. The undertaxation of the agricultural sector is all the more unjustified since a number of services are provided free or at subsidized rates to agriculturists by the federal and state governments. These services include improved seeds, fertilizers, pesticides, pumps and implements, rural electrification, agricultural credit, irrigation, etc. On the undertaxation of the agricultural sector in India, see Gandhi *Tax Burden on Indian Agriculture.*
41. See *Fifth Report*, Ch. 8; see also Government of India, Planning Commission, *Appraisal and Prospects of the Second Five-Year Plan,* (New Delhi, 1958), pp. 12 and 20; Government of India, Planning Commission, *Third Five-Year Plan Progress Report,* (New Delhi, March 1963), p. 39; and Government of India, Planning Commission, *The Third Plan: Mid-Term Appraisal* (New Delhi, November 1963), pp. 34, 105–06.
42. *Fifth Report*, p. 88.
43. Ibid.
44. *Third Report*, p. 38.
45. Himachal Pradesh, Jammu and Kashmir, Manipur, Tripura, and Nagaland are excluded from comparison owing to their special circumstances. The relatively very high figures for these states do not significantly distort the national average since their population is only 11 million out of a total of 541 million.

46. Social and developmental services are expenditures for the development of human and physical capital and include expenditures for education, public health, rural and community development, public works, etc.
47. It may be noted that Bihar had the lowest per capita domestic state product and one of the lowest tax efforts. Kerala had an above-average tax effort but a per capita domestic state domestic product about the same as national average.
48. Before a meaningful comparison of per capita expenditure for a particular service can be made, it is important that the service is defined uniformly for every state. In the case of education, even if the service is defined uniformly for every state, some of the variation in per capita expenditure may be due to variation in the proportion of school-age children actually attending school.
49. *Sixth Report*, pp. 8–9 and 47–51.
50. *Fifth Report*, p. 59.
51. *Second Report*, p. 37; *Third Report*, p. 41; and *Fourth Report* p. 51.
52. *Fifth Report*, pp. 58–59.
53. Ibid., p. 63.
54. *First Report*, pp. 103–104.
55. *Second Report*, p. 25.
56. *Third Report*, pp. 32–33
57. *Fourth Report*, pp. 48–49; and *Fifth Report*, p. 12.
58. *Sixth Report*, pp. 52–53.
59. Ibid., p. 47.
60. Ibid., p. 68.
61. *Second Report*, p. 72; *Third Report*, pp. 35–36; and *Fourth Report*, pp. 86–93.
62. See Government of India, Ministry of Finance, Department of Economic Affairs, *Report of the Taxation Inquiry Commission,* 1953–54, vol. III (New Delhi, 1955), pp. 220–36.

SUGGESTED READINGS

Adarkar, B.P.: *Principles and Problems of Federal Finance.* London. P.S. King & Son, 1933.

Bhargava, R.N.: *Union Finance in India.* New Delhi. Popular Book Services, 1956.

Bhatt, V.V.: "On The Magnitude and Allocation of Federal Assistance To The States in India: Some Rational Criteria". *Public Finance* XXIV, No. 4/1969, pp. 563–72

Birch, A.H.: *Federalism, Finance, and Social Legislation in Canada, Australia, and the United States.* London. Oxford University Press, 1955.

Clark, D.H.: *Fiscal Need and Revenue Equalization Grants.* Toronto. Canadian Tax Foundation, 1969.

Commonwealth of Australia: *Report of the Commonwealth Grants Commission (Annual).* Canbera, 1974.

Dwivedi, D.N.: "A Critique of Indian Fiscal Federalism—A Comment". *Public Finance* XXVI, No. 3/1971, pp. 498–501.

Eapen, A.T.: "A Critique of Indian Fiscal Federalism". *Public Finance* XXIV, No. 4/1969, pp. 537–57.

——: "On the Magnitude and Allocation of Federal Assistance to The States in India: Some Rational Criteria—Comment". *Public Finance* XXV, No. 3/1970, pp. 430–32.

——: "A Critique of Indian Fiscal Federalism—Reply". *Public Finance* XXVI, No. 3/1971, pp. 502–04.

Musgrave, R.A.: *The Theory of Public Finance.* New York. McGraw-Hill, 1959.

——: "Approaches to Fiscal Theory of Political Federalisms". *Public Finances: Needs, Sources, and Utilization,* A Conference of the Universities. National Bureau Committee for Economic Research. New York, 1961, pp. 97–122.

Musgrave, R.A. & Musgrave, P.B.: *Public Finance on Theory and Practice.* 2nd ed. New York. McGraw-Hill, 1976.

Oates, W.E.: *Fiscal Federalism.* New York.

Harcourt, Brace, Jovanovich, 1972.

Prest, W.: "Federal-State financial Relations in India". *Economic Record.* April 1960, pp. 191–219.

Government of India: Reports of the Finance Commission, 1952, 1957, 1961, 1965, 1969. New Delhi, Manager of Government Publications.

Sastri, K.V.S.: *Federal-State Fiscal Relations in India.* Bombay. Oxford University Press, 1962.

U.S. Advisory Commission on Intergovernmental Relations: *Measuring the Fiscal Capacity and Effort of State and Local Areas.* Washington, D.C., March 1971.

Wilde, James: "The Expenditure Effects of Grant-in-Aid Programs". *National Tax Journal.* September 1968, pp. 340–48.

Part Eight

INTERNATIONAL ECONOMIC
RELATIONS

19

Foreign Trade and Balance of Payments

JALEEL AHMAD*

Introduction

The purpose of this chapter is to highlight the important characteristics of the pattern of India's international trade and balance of payments, particularly in regard to their implications for her economic development. This is done in a framework provided by: (a) the neo-classical theory of international trade and payments; (b) the nature of structural constraints that modify the processes of continuous and smooth "transformation through trade"; (c) the overall strategy of Indian economic planning; and (d) finally, the similarity and the divergence of India's experience from the experience of today's developed, industrialized countries on the one hand, and the less developed, semi- or nonindustrialized countries on the other. The discussion attempts a clarification of the central issues involved and avoids the elaboration of their myriad ramifications. Clearly, no attempt at exhaustiveness is made. Merely quantitative and descriptive material has been kept at a minimum.

The quantitative magnitude of India's foreign trade in terms of its value, volume, and prices during 1951–75 is shown in Appendix Tables 1 and 2. The development programmes embodied in the five-year plans since 1950 gave utmost priority to the import of capital goods for capacity creation. As a result, imports rose both in absolute terms and relative to national income, particularly since 1956 and at least until 1968. On the other hand, India's export earnings from traditional commodities like jute and tea have either remained stagnant or have risen insignificantly. These differential growth rates of imports and exports have created a fundamental disequilibrium in India's balance of payments, necessitating large inflows of capital, mainly in the form of intergovernmental grants and loans. The magnitudes of various items in India's balance of payments are summarized in Appendix Table 2.

*The author wishes to thank Peter Miles for reading the draft and making valuable comments and Miss Lise Brault for secretarial assistance.

This chapter attempts to analyze systematically the major economic forces that explain the behaviour of foreign trade and balance of payments during the recent past. In particular, we discuss such critical factors as the domestic transformation difficulties, high propensity to import, limitations on demand and supply of exports, and the effect of devaluation on balance of payments.

Static and Dynamic Gains from Trade

In open economies, international trade plays an important role by providing alternative sources of demand and supply in the form of a country's exports and imports. It is through the expedient of international trade that a country specializes in the production of the goods and services for which its resource endowments are best suited, and exchanges them for other goods and services whose domestic opportunity costs are higher than prices at which they can be obtained from other countries. Thus, participation in international trade has farreaching implications for efficient utilization of domestic resources and the level of economic welfare in the country concerned. The study of the pattern of a country's international trade and the means for financing of such trade is, therefore, an integral part of the study of a country's economic development.

The important normative implication of international trade is that a relatively free trade will make a country "better off", in the sense that more goods and services will be available for consumption than under a regime of "autarky" or of a less free trade. The neoclassical trade theory usually illustrates the welfare possibilities of trade by means of a diagram such as Figure 19.1, using the production possibilities surface and the community indifference curves.[1]

The production possibilities curve TT' of a country indicates all the possible combinations of any two goods, say tractors (X) and wheat (Y), that could be produced with existing resources and technology. The production possibility curve, in turn, is derived from a "contract curve" which is the locus of all points of tangency of the isoquants and is inscribed in a box diagram whose axes represent the fixed quantities of the two factors of production, labour and capital. The two factors of production are assumed to be freely substitutable for each other and, being non-specific, are transferable from one sector to the other. The transformation curve so derived is drawn concave to the origin, implying an increasing opportunity cost of transformation of one good into the other.

The production possibility curve is combined with a set of community indifference curves which reflect the collective pattern

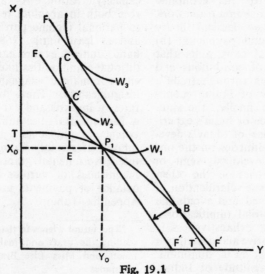

Fig. 19.1

of demand as determined by consumers' tastes and distribution of income.

In the absence of trade, resources are optimally allocated and welfare maximized at a point where a community indifference curve is tangent to the production possibilities curve. This occurs at point P in Fig. 19.1, where Y_0 of wheat and X_0 of tractors are produced and consumed. The domestic price ratio of Y and X is represented by the slope of the tangent at P.

Trade and balance of Payment

Now, trade will take place between two countries whenever the domestic price ratio differs from the price ratio prevailing in the trading-partner country. Thus, if a country faces an international price ratio (FF'), it can profitably specialize in the production of Y and exchange it for X. Production would take place at B and consumption at C. In doing so, the country would have moved to a higher community indifference curve W_3.[2]

This conclusion of the trade theory has significant implications for resource allocation in the developing economies. The productivity of domestic resources will be maximized if they are invested in line with a country's comparative advantage, and the subsequent exchange of these commodities in accordance with consumer preferences maximizes national income. It must be clearly understood, however, that the allocation analysis of trade described in the preceding paragraphs is completely *static* and reveals what the structure of foreign trade should be at a given point of time. But a country's comparative advantage undergoes a constant change in response to underlying changes in the supply and prices of production factors, technological developments, and the process of "learning by doing", and could in itself be modified by domestic economic policies otherwise desirable. There is thus no presumption in trade theory that the present comparative costs reflect long-run advantages and are not susceptible to changes in the course of time.

Given the static nature of trade theory, it does not give any guidance as to what a country should produce and export in order to increase its *dynamic* efficiency or its rate of growth.[3] This neglect of dynamic aspects in trade theory is partly a reflection of the enormous conceptual difficulties in handling the consequences of "time", and partly a reflection of the fact that noneconomic objectives undertaken for legitimate reasons frequently modify the economic ones and require different methodological tools for their analysis.

In a country where the composition of production factors and technology is rapidly changing, the production possibility curves and the domestic-cost ratios can undergo substantial changes. These purely domestic changes eventually bring about changes in the volume and composition of international trade, as well as in the terms at which a country trades with others. For example, the economic development of the United States during 1850 and 1900 caused a perceptible shift in its production possibility curve away from resource-based production, viz., agriculture, forestry and fisheries, and towards capital-based manufacturing output. During this period, the share of manufactures in the US exports almost doubled from 12.6 to 23.3 per cent of total exports.[4]

There is, therefore, no presumption that since India has in the past been exporting primary commodities, she will continue to have a static comparative disadvantage in the production of manufactures. Nevertheless, problems of adjustment are bound to arise as resources are reallocated and the economy strives to attain a new equilibrium. These structural problems take many different forms. Firstly, development theorists have argued that current market prices frequently diverge sharply from the longrun social costs and, therefore, fail to reflect "potential" costs of production.[5] The disadvantage in the export of manufactures attributed to the presently less-developed economies may consequently be more apparent than real, and may persist only as long as the price system remains a poor allocation guide.[6]

Secondly, adjustment problems may arise because in the critical short-run the domestic factors of production are nonhomogeneous, durable, and nonshiftable from one sector to the other. Once a particular structure of production is in place, capital (and labour) become specific and immobile and cannot readily be transferred from one sector to the other. A country has, therefore, little flexibility in determining the range of feasible outputs and cannot instantly and without cost adjust to a new production pattern. This problem of domestic transformation can be overcome only through a radical restructuring of economic policies designed to obtain a pattern of production and trade which is in line with the real, long-run social costs.

In developing countries like India, the static gains arising from the reallocation of existing resources may be outweighed by the impact of trade on such factors as the supply of additional resources, the savings/investment process, a fuller utilization of capacity, the extent of markets, and ultimately, the rate of economic growth. But perhaps the most critical role of foreign trade in India consists in its ability to provide capital equipment and other materials necessary for investment. Without trade, such goods may be obtainable only at prohibitive cost or, in extreme cases, not at all. This point underscores the fact that international trade comprises not only the finished products intended for the final consumer, but also factors of production in the form of equipment, semiprocessed goods, and raw materials.

International trade and economic growth interact in many different and significant ways. Rapid economic growth is usually accompanied by a high rate of growth in both exports and imports, and often by an increasing share of foreign trade in national income. Rising exports may act as a cause of economic growth by enlarging the markets and thus inducing a larger employment of domestic resources. Similarly, imports in a growing economy, in addition to being a source of vital capital goods, help to widen the consumer's choice with respect to the range of goods and services available.

In addition to these direct effects, there are other, more subtle and indirect relationships between international trade and economic growth. The cumulative effect of any change in the quantities exported and imported is transmitted to other sectors of the economy via interindustry transactions involving purchases and sales between a group of sectors. These effects depend on the intensity of input-output relations between sectors and are likely to be quite complex in a rapidly growing economy. Similarly, the "external economy" effects of domestic production in any particular sector—either through export expansion or through import substitution—singularly influence the mutual profitability of investment in related sectors. The production changes in turn favourably influence and are influenced by corresponding changes in technological knowledge.

Structural Obstacles to Transformation through Trade

International trade has traditionally occupied a relatively small part of the Indian economy as far as the quantities of her exports and imports are concerned. This is partly a reflection of the fact that large countries generally tend to be self-sufficient in producing the bulk of their supplies and trade plays only a marginal part. But it is also partly a symptom of her underdevelopment in the sense that long periods of economic stagnation and, until recently, the absence of any planned economic development, effectively reduced the demand for imports and the supply of her exports. In a state of underdevelopment, i.e., at a level of income lower than that necessary to generate self-sustaining growth or to raise living standards, an economy is likely to attain a balance of payments equilibrium, and may even have a trade surplus as did India between the two World Wars.

Small quantitative magnitudes notwithstanding, India's imports are vital to the operation and development of her economy. It is not difficult to demonstrate that, in the absence of imports of certain key raw materials and industrial components, the resulting loss in national production would be a large multiple of the cost of imports. This extreme dependence on imported supplies is a characteristic which India shares in large measure with other less developed countries and is of enormous consequence for her future development. The matter is of sufficient importance to deserve further analysis.

It is difficult to think of a developing country that does not face intolerable balance of payments problems. Oddly enough, these problems are the result of development itself. The process of development increases the demand for capital goods to a level and a rate that is beyond the production capacities of most less-developed countries. A policy of accelerated capital accumulation, therefore, requires adequate quantities of foreign exchange, to an extent that the rate of economic growth becomes dependent on the ability to finance the "development" imports.

The high propensity to import arises basically due to an internal disequilibrium connected with the structural inability to transform domestic resources into the capital goods required for development. India's immense manpower resources cannot, in the short run, be transformed into the industrial machines and equipment necessary for growth. This transformation rigidity would not in itself be a bottleneck if production functions were sufficiently flexible to allow possibilities of substitution between the domestic and imported inputs. But the dominant technological constraints give rise to a factor proportions problem, in the sense that there is little or no substitutability between domestic and imported inputs along an isoquant.[8]

Why does the problem of nonsubstitutability arise? Clearly, a primary product qualifies as a "noncompetitive" import if it cannot be produced at home and must be imported in a certain, more or less, fixed proportion to existing domestic factors. The imports of crude oil in India belong in this category. However, the nonsubstitutability with respect to capital goods—both for capacity expansion and maintenance purposes—is more subtle and less tractable. First of all the problem may arise simply because in many industrial operations there may be only a limited number of technologically feasible processes, requiring inflexible factor proportions. Production techniques that could intensively use the domestic resources are simply not available, or alternatively the international "demonstration effect"

may influence the choice of imported technology.

Secondly, nonsubstitutability may be the indirect result of the divergence between market and shadow rates of wages and foreign exchange. In India, like in other less-developed countries, the market wage rate is likely to be higher than the shadow price of labour, while the "official" rate of exchange of domestic for foreign currency may be lower than its shadow price, the latter being a function of the marginal productivity of imports in their most optimal uses. Given the dichotomy between the market and shadow prices, a profit-maximizing entrepreneur is likely to choose a factor proportion which is relatively more import-intensive and relatively less labour-intensive than is desirable from the point of view of the economy as a whole. It must be clearly understood that, while the shadow prices are relevant from a social standpoint, an individual entrepreneur's factor proportion decisions are made on the basis of the market prices of labour and foreign exchange. The problem is accentuated by the frequent tendency to maintain overvalued rates of foreign exchange, as well as by the almost universal practice of keeping low tariffs on imported capital goods, with a view to encouraging domestic capital formation. In any event, domestic production becomes relatively import-intensive and requires increasingly larger quantities of imports.

In addition, the inequalities that characterize the distribution of income in India tend to aggravate the factor proportions problem. The more skewed the income distribution, the greater the proportion of increases in demand that leaks directly or indirectly into imports. India's trade policies, directed at switching the demand for imports towards domestic substitutes as a means of conserving scarce foreign exchange, have led to just the opposite result. Import substitution policies, designed to produce domestically the consumer goods hitherto imported, often require further imports in the form of raw materials, components, and capital goods. As a consequence, the domestic production of these commodities, often involving no more than an assembly of imported components, conceals the real costs to the economy and allows the more affluent consumers to bid away scarce foreign exchange from socially more desirable production.

Limited domestic transformation possibilities and the resulting rigidity in factor proportions would not be much of a problem if the economy could generate sufficient exports to finance the imports.[9] Our earlier discussion of the welfare aspects of trade theory had implied that, as long as there are relative differences in productivities, a country can export goods in the production of which it has a comparative advantage in exchange for those in which it does not. Thus, there would seem to be no obstacle, other than inappropriate domestic expenditure and exchange policies, to the maintenance of an export level sufficient to ensure external balance. In reality however, the current structure of international trade provides no such built-in mechanism for expanding India's traditional exports.

For an economy to utilize the escape route of international trade, one will have to assume that the reciprocal foreign demand for its exports is perfectly elastic.[10] This condition is far from being fulfilled, since India's major exports are faced with either falling or slowly expanding world demand, with the result that without a drastic change in export composition, it is difficult to maintain the value of her export earnings. Almost all primary-oriented less-developed countries suffer from the combination of export concentration, export dependence, and price fluctuations.[11] Quite different problems are faced in the export of manufactures and semiprocessed goods. These problems are due partly to low absolute productivities and other production bottlenecks in the newly created industrial sector, and partly to the existence of virtually impregnable tariff and nontariff barriers on the entry of such products into the industrially-advanced countries.

In any event, significant expansion of exports of manufactures, with the possible exception of handicrafts, requires a corresponding increase in imports of essential inputs from abroad, and we are back at the original factor proportions problem.

In extreme cases, production functions may be such that input-imports for export production demand the use of more foreign exchange than the exports eventually yield, and may give rise to negative value-added.[12]

Economic Planning and Foreign Trade

The characteristic features of India's international trade are greatly conditioned by these and similar structural disabilities. The underlying constraints had become particularly acute following an articulate policy of economic development embodied in the successive five-year plans since 1950. The trade picture has since then been dominated by rapidly rising imports and virtually stagnant export earnings. It is doubtful whether any conceivable strategy of development could have substantially reduced the import requirements without seriously affecting the rate of growth. It is a matter of some controversy, however, as to whether India could have pursued a more vigorous programme for export expansion and thus avoided the large trade deficits.

Before answering this and other questios, it is worthwhile examining the undercurrents of trade policy and tracing their logical relationship to the Indian planning procedures. The Indian planning procedures, from the very start, have been concerned with the overall size of the savings/investment in public and private sectors as well as with the allocation of investment among alternative uses. The sectoral allocations, initially determined by the ad hoc availability of worthwhile projects, came to develop a tenuous relationship with the two-sector[13] and four-sector models which provided the theoretical framework for the Indian plans.[14]

The time-path of growth in these models is determined by the proportion of capital-goods output devoted to the further production of capital goods. Since the models assumed the absence of international trade, the growth rate of the economy effectively became a function of the capacity of the domestic capital-goods industry. This assumption had the effect of significantly restricting the scope of domestic transformation possibilities only to those permitted by the domestic capital goods sector, since the "closed economy" precluded an enlargement of transformation possibilities through recourse to international trade. This feature of the model has been much criticised for ignoring an important means of solving the domestic transformation problem.[15]

In any event, a major objective of Indian economic policy came to be the development of the domestic capital-goods industry by allocating a higher proportion of total investment to such sectors. This policy clearly implied the declining role of foreign trade in obtaining such goods from abroad, and envisaged an eventual independence from imports. It was thus natural that a policy of import substitution in the manufacturing sectors should come to occupy a central place. While it is quite clear that in primary-oriented economies like India, any industrial development necessarily has to take the form of import substitution, the wisdom of indiscriminate reliance on import substitution as a growth strategy may be questioned. But first let us turn to the rationale of import substitution.

Foreign Exchange Constraints and Import Substitution

The traditional justification for import substitution in India, as elsewhere, seems to have been provided by the "two gap" models of development,[16] although it has been suggested that this may have been an ex post rationalization for the development of heavy industry on other than strictly economic grounds.[17] The two-gap approach postulates limited substitution possibilities between domestic savings and foreign exchange. Given this rigidity in production function, it is stated that a high potential saving is by no means a sufficient condition for growth of national product since its (domestic savings) optimal use may be prevented by a shortage of imported inputs. By the same token, a large capacity to import may fail to stimulate growth if the requisite domestic savings do not materialize.

The critical conclusion of the model is that a developing country is likely to be faced with two structural constraints of enormous significance, viz. (1) a minimum requirement for imports to sustain a given rate of growth of GNP; and (2) an actual or a potential ceiling on export earnings which are insufficient to finance the required imports. The "foreign exchange" gap,[18] the difference between minimum required imports and total exports, is given by

$$\overline{M}_n - \overline{E}_n = M_0 + \beta (V_n - V_0) - E_0 (1+e)^n$$

where,

$M_0 =$ the observed initial level of imports
$V_0 =$ the Gross National Product in the initial year
$V_n =$ $V_0(1+r)^n$, r being the compound growth rate and n the number of years after 0
$E_0 =$ the initial level of exports
$\beta =$ the marginal rate of imports per additional unit of GNP
$e =$ rate of growth of exports.

The gap can be seen in Figure 19.2.[19] In situations where the foreign exchange gap is dominant, the existing total import capacity, i.e., $E_n = E_0 (1+e)^n$ will effectively set the upper limit to the increase in GNP.[20] Barring foreign aid, the development of the domestic capital goods industry may be the only viable solution for closing the foreign exchange gap. It must be remembered that in this model, exports are assumed to take their highest value and thus cannot eliminate the gap.

In practical terms, the United Nations had calculated the "trade gap" (including factor income payments) for India in 1962–63 to the tune of $ 950 millions in 1960 prices. On the basis of a projected growth rate of the economy of 5.0 per cent per year, the trade gap was estimated to be as high as $ 2500 millions in 1975–76.[21]

Foreign aid inflows in India have always been regarded as something one can do without in the long run when the economy is able to cope with the structural adjustments necessary for selfsustaining growth. One such adjustment can be effected through a process of import substitution whereby the continued depen-

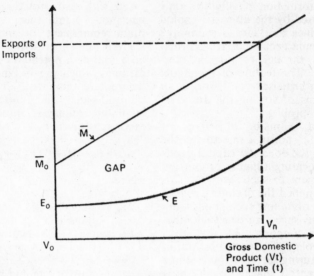

Fig. 19.2

dence on massive imports of capital goods and equipment can be reduced or eliminated.

Import substitution in open economies may be recognized when, ceteris paribus, an increase in the domestic production of a commodity results in a decline of competing imports. However, if the increase in domestic production is less than the growth of demand—both for final and intermediate consumption—imports will continue to rise and import substitution may not be obvious. Yet it is clear that import substitution has been positive in the sense that domestic production is now supplying part of the output that would have otherwise been imported. In order to overcome this difficulty, import substitution may be defined as "the difference between growth in domestic output with no change in the import ratio and the actual growth".[22] Symbolically, import substitution in the ith sector is measured as :

$$S_i = Z_i{}^2 \, (u_i{}^2 - u_i{}^1)$$

and $n_i{}^2 = X_i{}^2/Z_i{}^2, \; u_i{}^1 = X_i{}^1/Z_i{}^1,$

$Z_i = X_i + M_i$ and $X_i = D_i + W_i + E_i$

where

$X_i =$ domestic production,
$D_i =$ domestic final demand

$W_i =$ intermediate demand
$E_i =$ exports, and
$M_i =$ imports.[23]

Subscripts refer to sectors or industries and superscripts refer to time periods.[24]

Summary estimates of import substitution for the Indian economy following the above method are given in Table 19.1.[25] These estimates suggest that for the 15-year period, 1950–51 to 1965–66, import substitution accounts for roughly one-fourth of the total growth in output, and for nearly one-half of the growth of output of the capital-goods sector. This is not surprising since import substitution is an independent source of economic growth in much the same way as export expansion. Indeed, in the early stages of industrial growth, the contribution of import substitution may be the more important one. Econometric analyses of Japanese industrial growth show that import substitution, and not exports as popularly believed, accounted for nearly 40 per cent of the growth of manufacturing industry during 1914 to 1954[26]. Table 19.1 also shows that of the three broad groups of industries, import substitution in the capital goods sectors seems to be the most pronounced. The figures on import substitution and export growth in India during 1963–67 for different products

Table 19.1.   Import Substitution in the Indian Economy

	Import Substitution		
Period and Industry Group	Value (Rs. Crores)	Share in Total Growth (percentage)	Ranking in Group
1950/51–1955/56			
Consumer goods	25.27	10.4	3
Intermediate goods	46.11	47.9	2
Capital goods	65.74	54.4	1
Total	137.12	29.8	
1955/56–1960/61			
Consumer goods	90.29	16.2	1
Intermediate goods	62.63	12.1	2
Capital goods	48.18	10.9	3
Total	201.10	13.3	
1960/61–1965/66			
Consumer goods	87.99	12.2	3
Intermediate goods	152.47	20.1	2
Capital goods	376.16	38.9	1
Total	616.62	25.2	
1950/51–1965/66			
Consumer goods	163.31	10.8	3
Intermediate goods	207.79	12.6	2
Capital goods	705.30	42.0	1
Total	1076.40	22.3	

SOURCE: J. Ahmad, "Import Substitution and Structural Change in Indian Manufacturing Industry", *Journal of Development Studies*, Vol. IV, No. 3, April 1968, Tables 4–5, pp. 333–364.

Table 19.2.   Import Substitution and Export Growth: India

(millions of U.S. dollars)

ISIC Sector Description		Import Substitution	Export Growth
20	Food manufactures	−37.2	−98.7
21	Beverages	−1.7	0
22	Tobacco manufactures	0	−0.7
23	Textiles	16.9	−70.4
24	Footwear and wearing apparel	0	8.1
25	Wood and cork manufactures	0.9	0
26	Furniture	0.2	−0.5
27	Paper and paper products	15.0	2.1
28	Printing and publishing	2.3	−0.7
29	Leather and fur products	0	17.7
30	Rubber products	10.2	2.2
31	Chemical products	−106.9	5.8
32	Petroleum and coal products	117.6	−2.5
33	Non-metallic and mineral products	−9.8	39.3
34	Basic metal products	37.5	55.2
35	Metal manufactures	25.3	6.9
36	Machinery	215.2	2.6
37	Electric machinery	25.0	5.8
38	Transport machinery	−2.5	5.0
39	Miscellaneous manufactures	64.4	1.3
20–39	Total manufactures	372.3	−18.0

NOTE :   The estimates are based on 1963–67 data

SOURCE: J. Ahmad, *Import Substitution, Trade and Development*, (Connecticut: Johnson Associates Press) forthcoming.

in Table 19.2 show the relationship between these two variables.

India's experience in this regard is by no means unique; many of the less-developed countries for much the same reasons have resorted to import substitution as a development strategy. In Latin America, notably in Argentina and Brazil, import substitution has been the chief element of economic change and industrialization. India is relatively fortunate in possessing one of the important preconditions of successful import substitution—that of a large potential market. Given her vast potential consuming and producing resources, India can initiate large-scale industrialization on a number of fronts and meet the requirement of minimum efficient scale for most industries.

Although the immediate justification for import substitution was provided by the necessity to conserve foreign exchange, the Indian planners had more in mind than a mere saving of foreign exchange. Even a cursory reading of the policy documents leaves little doubt that the planners were interested in initiating structural changes of farreaching significance which could not have been possible without drastically changing the pattern of trade inherited from a long history of colonial relations with her major trading partners.

The manner in which a deficit on balance of trade is financed has important implications for the domestic economy and is, therefore, not a matter of indifference to the country concerned. The command over foreign exchange is desired not for its own sake, but to further other objectives, e.g., changes in production structure, to which it contributes by allowing increased imports. The point is that a country's objectives in acquiring foreign exchange should be kept in mind while evaluating the alternative means of earning them. The planning authorities have constantly to evaluate the impact of foreign exchange earning activities on as many economic and social parameters as possible.

Suppose that India could "earn" an equivalent amount of foreign exchange by exporting either commodity A or commodity B, or by displacing the imports of commodity C. Now, the production of commodities A, B or C is likely to have different consequences both for her domestic structure and the trading position. The production and export of commodity A, for instance, may imply a movement toward the country's long-run comparative advantage, while the export of B may tend to perpetuate a situation where potential gains from trade and other dynamic considerations are ignored. Similarly, the domestic production of C may attempt to correct an inefficient production structure resulting from past misallocation of resources. In addition, the production of the three commodities may have different implications for labour productivities, resource use, and technological progress. If so, the country can hardly remain indifferent as to the source of its foreign exchange;[27] a choice has to be made between the commodities or, most likely, an optimal output mix has to be determined. This choice inevitably forces attention on the values and weights implicit in a country's "demand function" for foreign exchange.

In India, this kind of function was never made explicit since the trade policy during the last 25 years had only a tenuous relationship with plan objectives and was itself simply a collection of ad hoc measures taken from time to time to deal with problems as they arose. Yet, it is quite clear that the policy of import substitution was embedded in the desire to create a large-scale domestic industrial structure which was expected to lead the economy to a "self-reliant and self-generating stage". It was, therefore, no accident that the Second Plan of 1956 embodied farreaching social and political goals in its allocations and its priorities. These goals and priorities have undergone only minor changes due more to expediency than to any basic rethinking.

By any reckoning, India's industrial performance during the past twenty years has been impressive. Apart from the fact that the index of industrial production has trebled since 1950, the industrial structure has achieved diversification and the depth needed for future growth. The process of import substitution has been extended both vertically and laterally to include a larger proportion of value-added in the gross value of Indian output, and the average import coefficient in most manufacturing sectors has witnessed a dramatic decline. This relative independence from imports may be seen in the illustration that in 1956, India only "assembled" motor trucks, while in 1971 it manufactured them with an import content of barely one per cent.

Import Substitution and Efficiency

India's vast potential, both as a producing and a consuming unit, leaves little doubt as to the viability of large-scale import substitution; yet, some questions may be raised about its efficiency. These questions concern not so much the supposed incompatibility of import substitution with export expansion,[28] but rather its indiscriminate extension to a wide range of sectors without regard to costs, productivities or the growth of demand. Again, India is in the company of a large number of countries which have succumbed to the temptation to import-substitute in as many lines as possible without carefully considering the role of international trade, It is certainly possible to grow bananas on the North Pole (in hot houses) but it would not be optimal to do so in view of the possibility of acquiring them through trade. Similarly even though a country may be capable of import-substituting in all sectors from A to Z, the comparative advantage from doing so may lie in only a few of them.

Little analytical work on these lines has been done in India, so that emphatic answers are hard to come by.[29] But there can be little doubt that valuable resources could have been saved if the process of import substitution had been more selective with a limited number of strategically chosen sectors and industries, where a concentration of effort and resources could have maximized the gains in efficiency. Particularly in the heavy industry sector, simultaneous development of a plethora of manufacturing activities may have deprived the economy of the advantages of large-scale production and of meeting the minimum critical thresholds. In addition, a proliferation of industries has deprived her of specialization and the eventual development of comparative advantage in selected lines. This lack of specialization can be seen in the fact that after 20 years of vigorous development of heavy industry, there are only a few lines of production in which India can claim a decided cost advantage relative to international prices.

The process of import substitution ran into a structural difficulty of another sort. As imports of most luxury consumer goods were restricted by prohibitory tariffs, the profitability of their domestic production automatically increased. If this production had required the use of only the domestic factors, the initial cut in imports would have conserved foreign exchange for "essential" uses. But their domestic production required additional imports of components and spare parts—a process which was extended to other sectors of the economy via interindustry repercussions. Hazari has estimated that for the years 1961–62 and 1963–64, the proportion of India's total imports which supported the domestic production of "luxuries" was 7.6 and 8.3 per cent res-

pectively. The corresponding figure for "necessities" was 28.7 and 32.9 per cent respectively.[30]

The above illustrates a frequently observed phenomenon in countries which rely on import substitution strategies for "saving" foreign exchange. Trade policies designed to exclude the imports of "inessential" goods automatically create incentives to channel domestic investment into their production. At the same time, since exchange rates are frequently overvalued, the cost of importing the inputs for their production is kept artificially low. This accentuates the tendency toward import intensive techniques of production, and further aggravates the factor proportions problem, discussed earlier in this chapter. India's predicament in this regard may be compared with Argentina where the intermediate import requirement per composite unit of final output were higher in 1960 than in 1953, despite considerable import substitution in the intervening years.[31] In other words, the desire to import less builds up pressures to import more—a process that may continue unabated. In the longer run, however, the cumulative direct savings of foreign exchange are likely to exceed the cumulative indirect expenditures of foreign exchange.[32]

Given a built-in incentive to domestically produce luxury goods whose imports have been curtailed, and the political pressure of the affluent to satisfy this demand, the establishment of a wide range of import-substituting consumer goods industries presumably at high opportunity costs, has been a prominent feature of the industrial landscape in India since 1955. Most of these industries catered to the demand of the affluent few for sophisticated and highly diversified products, totally out of line with the average per capita income in the country. The present structure of income distribution in India means that the demand for these products is not enough to cross the minimum threshold for exploitation of economies of scale. Moreover, the demand tends to fall off beyond a certain point, resulting in unutilized capacity and higher average costs. This same sort of demand insufficiency has plagued the Argentinian consumer goods industry during the last decade. It was estimated, for instance, that the cross-sectional income elasticity of demand for a large number of durable goods, including refrigerators, vacuum cleaners, and television sets, was below unity.[33] The remedy in both cases lies either in scrapping the domestic production of some of these goods and letting imports fulfil the demand, or in changing the structure of income distribution in a way which makes these industries viable through large increases in demand.

Indiscriminate import substitution without basic changes in income distribution inevitably leads to a slowing down, as seems to be the case currently with the industrial sector in India. Since the Indian economy was subject to excess demand initially, investment continued to grow at its maximum rate determined by the marginal savings ratio and the rate of import of capital goods. But the full capacity income seems to have caught up with potential real aggregate demand. In a large number of industrial sectors, particularly in the consumer goods sector, supply seems to have outstripped demand, with the result that investment has ceased to grow because of excess capacity. It would be instructive to draw a parallel with the experience of Brazil where a vigorous process of import substitution seems to have led to a slackening, for the same reasons. This has been explained in terms of a growing inequality in the functional distribution of income in Brazil which is directly attributable to the growth of highly protected domestic industries. During 1955–65, the growth rate of real wages per worker in the Brazilian industry was 2.8 per cent per year, while the index of industrial productivity during the same period grew at 5.0 per cent.[34] These differential growth rates suggest that the distribution of income tends to be biased against the working class and inhibits the growth of income. Indeed, the proportion of value-added in manufacturing attributable to wages, declined from 34 per cent in 1957 to 23 per cent in 1965.[35]

The point is simply that a given bundle of consumer goods may require, for their domestic production, a larger volume of imports than an alternative bundle. Thus, even if there are fixed proportions between domestic and imported inputs in each industry, it is unlikely that this proportion would be the same for all industries. Variations in product-mix will, therefore, give some flexibility in import requirements. India could significantly reduce her overall import requirements by redistributing income in favour of poorer classes who are likely to spend a greater proportion of their income on goods that require less imported inputs. It should be noted, however, that possible variations in the product-mix will be constrained by the extent to which growth must be balanced between the different sectors of the economy, for any given distribution of income.

Import and Exchange Controls

The overall import policy that has dominated the entire planning period in India is one of a fairly tight regime of import and exchange controls, which alternated with occasional periods of liberalization. The principal feature of the regime has been the allocation of permissible imports by categories, e.g., capital goods, raw materials, etc., among sectors and industries by means of an elaborate administrative machinery which was gradually evolved over a period of time.[36]

The procedures followed for allocation of foreign exchange had two ostensible criteria: (1) the principle of "essentiality", and (2) the principle of "indigenous non-availability". Thus, if an import was deemed essential and if it could be shown that there was no competing domestic production, it was permitted. In practice, however, it is not clear as to how the actual priorities were determined for industry-wise and plant-wise allocations. This is not surprising, since the large number of sectors and industries involved precluded any clear notions of priority. Bhagwati and Desai conclude "that the agencies involved in determining industry-wise allocations fell back on vague notions of 'fairness', implying pro rata allocations with reference to capacity installed or employment, or shares defined by past import allocations and similar rules of thumb without any clear rationale".[37] These simple ad hoc rules of allocation seem to have little relationship to productivity, and have probably resulted in large-scale inefficiencies in the allocation of a scarce resource. One measure of this inefficiency may be the fact that large foreign exchange resources were allocated of consumer goods industries at the expense of vital producers' goods industries.

Quota restrictions on imports, implied by the criterion of "non-availability", have meant "automatic and anticipatory" protection to all industries that qualify, regardless of relative prices in domestic and foreign markets. It has been estimated that the resulting effective rates of protection for some industries during 1960–62 were as high as 10,000 per cent.[38] Moreover, the reliance of AU allocations of foreign exchange on the level of installed capacity may have been partially responsible for underutilization of existing capacity. Insofar as import allocations under the AU licensing were directly related to the additional capacity *installation*, while the materials necessary for additional *utilization* of existing capacity must be purchased at import-premium-carrying prices, a bias in favour of creating capacity would result even when excess capacity exists.

Export Structure and Policy

Like all less-developed countries, India's export trade is heavily concentrated in a few traditional commodities. This lack of diversification is reflected in the fact that only five commodities—jute, tea, cotton textiles, vegetable oils, and tobacco—account for over 70 per cent of her total export earnings. These commodities have not only shown a poor rate of growth, but are also losing their share in the world markets.[39] Sticky export earnings in turn have seriously impaired India's capacity to import.[40] This is particularly significant when one considers the fact that the reduction in the value of her exports and of her share in world exports has occurred in a setting of rapidly rising value and volume of world trade.

This unsatisfactory performance raises the question whether India's stagnant export earnings are due to unfavourable demand conditions for her exports, or are a result of her own economic and commercial policies. Few systematic analyses are available to provide a categorical answer.[41] There is little doubt, however, that India's export commodity composition is heavily biased toward commodities whose world demand is either stagnant, as of jute, or rising only slowly, as of tea. These exports belong to the group of commodities which not only have an income elasticity of demand of below unity, but are also largely unresponsive to price changes. It is, therefore, not surprising that India is experiencing difficulty in maintaining the value of her exports. Part of the difficulty seems to be the presence of a number of competing suppliers from other parts of the world attempting to expand their exports from very low initial levels. The relative decline in India's share of world exports of tea between 1950 and 1970 is partly the result of highly competitive policies on the part of Ceylon, Indonesia, and countries in Africa wich have markedly increased their share of the world total. In a stagnant world market the gain of one country is the loss of another.

India's export policies since the 1950s have been based on two broad assumptions: (1) stagnant world demand for her major export commodities provides no optimism for any appreciable increases, and (2) in any event, it would be desirable to reduce her dependence on a few resource-based commodities, and to encourage the export of new industrial goods, particularly the products of the rapidly-growing light engineering industries.

The first assumption is immensely valid in the sense that it would have been extremely difficult, if not altogether impossible, to increase export earnings from traditional commodities where external demand factors call the tune as to the quantities sold and prices paid. This is true of export commodities of which India is a major world supplier, and hence, has to operate in an oligopolistic world market, constrained by the actions of a small number of rival producers. Under these circumstances, it is very difficult for a single producer country to increase its share of world trade, without disturbing the hierarchy of market shares and provoking retaliatory measures. Thus India could have no control over its export earnings from commodities like tea and cotton textiles, and has to abide by world demand and supply constellations determined by the combined actions of a small number of producers.[42]

In the case of other commodities, of which India is either a marginal supplier or holds a near monopoly, her domestic policies may have influenced her export earnings by influencing the volume of their production, the terms on which they are exported, and their domestic demand. All these factors seem to have played their part in making the supply of Indian exports inelastic. By far the most significant factor limiting the export growth seems to have been the growth in domestic consumption of exportables in the wake of growth of incomes and population. This phenomenon can be illustrated by the example of cotton textiles. The high income elasticity of demand for cotton textiles coupled with a high rate of population growth assures the domestic industry of a steadily rising domestic demand.[43] Certain other important exports, like vegetable oilseeds, were in demand at home in increasingly large quantities to serve as raw materials for the growing Indian vegetable-oils industry. This is also true of raw cotton and leather. Thus the conclusion is inescapable that exports in most cases have succumbed to the overwhelming pressure of competing domestic demand.[44] This is despite the fact that India has been fairly successful in holding the price line and had the mildest inflation of all developing countries in recent times.[45] Inflationary pressures were kept in check partly by increasing the domestic absorption of exportables. Undoubtedly, the maintenance of an overvalued exchange rate has created disincentives for exports, thereby raising the profitability of domestic sales.

India's experience in this regard is fairly in line with that of all other developing countries who are faced with the dilemma of maintaining a viable rate of growth of exports in the face of a rising domestic demand. In certain countries domestic demand has been restrained

by imposition of excise duties in order to keep export sales rising. In India, however, political pressures for effecting reasonable increase in consumption have always been strong. The five-year plans themselves have consistently planned for a monotonic rise in private consumption, whereas a more restrictive consumption policy would obviously have avoided the strain on balance of payments.

The second assumption, viz., the desirability of the exports of manufactures rather than those of primary commodities, is rooted in the desire to provide structural support to domestic industrialization through broadening of the markets. There can be no doubt that from the point of view of long-run efficiency, it is desirable for India to reduce her dependence on traditional commodity exports, which suffer from adverse factors on both demand and supply sides. Such a diversification could arise through the development of "new" exports of what has come to be known in India as the "engineering industries" sector.

India's record in this respect has been quite satisfactory, though by no means exceptional. The exports of a large number of newly established industries have shown rapid rates of growth, even though the absolute quantities involved are as yet quite small. Completely new lines of exports have emerged, and there is some evidence that the range of commodities entering export trade is gradually increasing. This diversification can be seen by comparing the commodity-concentration index of the engineering industries. For eighty commodity subgroups within the engineering industries, this index declined from 27.2 in 1956–58 to 17.8 in 1962–64, implying that a larger assortment of commodities is being exported.[46]

It is worth noting also that the growth in exports of manufactures has been accompanied by a growth in the domestic consumption of these commodities. Exports of manufactures seem to have been subject to the same kind of restraining influence from domestic demand noticed in the case of resource-based commodities. It is quite possible, therefore, that the growth rate of exports of manufactures would have been much higher were it not for the inelasticity of supply caused by the competition between domestic and foreign sales. Nonetheless, export performance of the industrial sector has been encouraged by the export promotion measures undertaken since the Third Five-Year Plan. These promotion measures have taken the form of "import entitlement" schemes,[47] exemption from sales and excise taxes on inputs, "drawback" of import duties on raw materials, direct tax concessions, special allocation on controlled rates of scarce inputs like iron, steel, transportation, etc. At the same time efforts were made to increase the trade in manufactures with the USSR and other socialist countries.[48]

Although exports of manufactures have now become an important feature of India's foreign trade, serious production and trade problems continue to hamper their development. Not the least of these concern the external impediments which pose a problem of "entry" of such manufactures both in the markets of the developed, industrialized, and of the less developed, semi-industrialized countries. The single most inhibiting factor against the development of exports of manufactures from the less developed countries, is the system of tariffs adopted by the industrial countries. The characteristic feature of this system is that the tariff rates on imports rise successively with the degree of product elaboration.[49] For example, tariff rates become increasingly higher as one moves from iron ore to raw steel to machine goods.[50] This tariff discrimination against products with high value-added content makes it difficult for the less developed countries to compete in the world market for manufactures. In addition, there is a bewildering array of quota restrictions and other nontariff barriers on products of existing and potential interest to the less developed countries.[51]

Potential Indian exports to the other less developed countries also present problems insofar as the process of import substitution in other countries encompasses virtually the same range of goods which India is trying to export. The case of the cotton textile industry in this respect is typical. The cotton textiles industry in practically all less developed countries is the first casualty of the domestic import substitution process, due both to the rising profitability of home production and its relative technological simplicity. The Indian cotton textiles industry which emerged after World War II as the largest among all the less developed countries has now serious rivals for supplying both the home demand and the exports.

Quite apart from the limitation on trading possibilities, the young Indian manufacturing industry has to cope with production problems of serious dimensions which prevent any significant entry into foreign markets. The world trade in manufactured goods is not simply a matter of intercountry differences in costs of production, so that the cheaper Indian costs are not sufficient to generate exports. Potential export items, particularly in the western countries, have also to meet standards of quality, homogeneity, and speed of delivery, etc., to go over the hump. These products have also to be sufficiently "differentiated" from close substitutes in the international market-place[52] in order to develop strong consumer preferences.

It is thus difficult to escape the conclusion that India's export promotion efforts are beset with serious difficulties both at home and abroad. One may even assert that the export problem could not be solved independently of the more fundamental structural problems that India has to grapple with in the early stages of her economic growth. One can maintain this general position without implying that India has done everything possible to increase her exports or that all efforts in this direction are bound to be fruitless. One could go further and claim that there may indeed be no export problem at all, but that is another story.

Balance of Payments

Having described at some length the pertinent structural features of India's foreign trade. it is now a straightforward matter to draw the balance of payment implications The "factor proportions" rigidity between domestic and foreign resources, combined with the unfavourable commodity composition of exports implies that development efforts in India have a built-in tendency to generate balance of payments pressures. These pressures, reflecting an excess demand for imports, can be eliminated only by scaling down the development effort which, in the Indian context, means abandoning the targets embodied in the five-year plans.

These pressures have resulted in a continuing deficit in India's trade balance since 1955, and in recurrent crises with respect to the means for covering such deficits. In all the years since 1956, India had an excess of imports over exports of goods and services to the tune of nearly \$ 14 billions or an average yearly deficit of \$ 900 millions. The deficit had increased dramatically in the last years of the Third Five-Year Plan, but is in a downward trend since 1968 as seen in Table 19.3. The quarterly data for 1971 estimated from IMF sources indicate that India's commodity trade is now nearly in balance.[53]

It is important to realize, however, that the deficits or surpluses on the trade balance should not, in themselves, be a cause for alarm or jubilation. This is because of the equilibrating role of the autonomous and induced capital movements between nations. While India was saddled with huge deficits on its current account balance, the capital account has shown correspondingly large inflows of capital. Capital inflows embody a "real" transfer of goods and services which increase national income and assist in capital formation. On the other hand, a balance on trade account is not necessarily a blessing, since it may signify (as it does in the contemporary Indian scene) a petering out of profitable investment opportunities due to insufficiency of demand rather than a genuine structural viability.

This relationship between trade and capital accounts is not accidental; it is characterisitc of capital-importing and capital-exporting nations. A capital-importing country must generate trade deficits in order to offset the surplus on capital account, while a capital-exporting country must have a surplus on trade account in order to balance the deficit in capital account. In other words, deficits and surpluses on trade and capital accounts are companion phenomena that offset each other so as to yield an overall balance.

The phenomenon of "real transfer" rests on the fundamental proposition that a country cannot invest, for domestic purposes, beyond the level of its own savings, except to the extent of its ability to secure investments from abroad.[54] Assuming fixed prices and no government, output Y in an open economy consists of consumption C, investment I and exports X,

$$Y = C + I + X \tag{1}$$

Similarly, income received Y, is spent on consumption of domestic goods C, on imports M, or it is saved S,

$$Y = C + M + S \tag{2}$$

Combining the two equations results in the identity:

$$I + X = S + M \tag{3}$$

and therefore,

$$S = I + (X - M) \tag{4}$$

It can be seen from (4) that

$$S \gtreqless I = X \gtreqless M = \pm FI \tag{5}$$

where FI = net foreign investment. What this means is that a country can increase domestic investment beyond the level of domestic savings to the extent that it has a deficit on merchandise account, i.e., $X < M$, or in other words, has a net foreign capital inflow, i.e., FI. If a country is willing to let its international payments position deteriorate, it can dissave, i.e., $-FI = S < I$.

It should, therefore, come as no surprise that continuous deficits on merchandise trade in India for the past fifteen years have been accompanied by large inflows of capital.[55] These capital inflows have permitted the total of domestic expenditures—"real absorption"—to, remain at a level higher than real income. This should not be construed to mean that a country can permanently live beyond its means by running trade deficits, Such deficits in the short and the intermediate run can be financed by accumulating debts to other countries. In the long run, however, an adjustment process must set in to eliminate the deficit. In practice, the limit to foreign borrowing is set by the increasing burden of debt servicing and repayment of capital to foreign lenders, which requires generation of everincreasing trade

Foreign Trade and Balance of Payments

359

Table 19.3. Balance of Payments, 1967–73

(millions of rupees)

	1967	1968	1969	1970	1971	1972	1973
A. GOODS, SERVICES and TRANSFERS	−8,407.5	−4,980.0	−1,725.0	−2,940.0	−4,792.5	−1,156.2	−4,130.8
Trade Balance	−6,457.5	−2,902.5	−60.0	−982.5	−2,790.0	516.6	−1,508.8
Service	−3,300.0	−3,397.5	−3,412.5	−3,697.5	−4,005.0	−3,796.6	−4,692.0
Transfers							
Private	1,012.5	1,200.0	1,320.0	1,215.0	1,432.5	1,556.2	1,821.6
Government	337.5	120.0	427.5	525.0	570.0	557.6	248.4
B. LONG-TERM CAPITAL	8,917.5	7,095.0	5,490.0	4,215.0	5,182.5	2,542.0	3,404.0
Private	−22.5	−127.5	−292.5	−180.0	−165.0	−16.4	−340.4
Government	8,940.0	7,222.5	4,792.5	4,035.0	5,017.5	2,525.6	3,063.6
C. SHORT-TERM CAPITAL	−712.5	−1,342.5	−997.5	−7.5	−225.0	−2,361.6	−110.4
Total A to C	−202.5	772.5	2,767.5	1,267.5	165.0	−975.8	−837.2
D. MONETARY AUTHORITIES	202.5	−772.5	−2,767.5	−1,267.5	−165.0	975.8	837.2
Monetary gold	—	—	—	127.5	—	—	—
IMF Credit	712.5	−622.5	−997.5	−1,732.5	−75.0	—	—
SDR	—	—	—	615.0	−22.5	16.4	9.2
Reserve position at IMF	—	—	—	−157.5	−412.5	—	—
Foreign exchange	−510.0	−150.0	−1,770.0	−120.0	345.0	959.4	828.0

SOURCE: International Monetary Fund, *International Financial Statistics* and *Balance of Payments Yearbook*, various years.

surpluses. The annual outflow of repatriated earnings on foreign capital in India grew to a total of $ 362 millions in 1970 from a low of 90 millions in 1960.[56] Debt-service charges account for approximately 20 per cent of her total export earnings in 1970. The problem can be postponed for a while by further borrowings to pay for the earlier debts.

The other significant constraint on India's external borrowing capacity arises due to a greatly reduced supply of foreign private capital. During the period 1950–69, India received capital inflows to the tune of Rs. 90 billions. Out of this, only Rs. 12 billions are private, direct and portfolio investments, and the rest is external assistance and loans from foreign governments and international agencies, chiefly the Aid India Consortium which includes twelve industrial countries and the World Bank group. Actually, loans constituted about 80 per cent of all nonprivate capital inflows—a circumstance which explains an increasing repayment burden. For the years 1966–69, nearly 32 per cent of fresh external assistance was used up for amortization and interest payments.

On the whole, foreign assistance "authorizations" in India have tended to correspond with the actual deficits on the current account, including the debt service and other repayments. Long-term, autonomous private capital inflows have been far less insignificant than in many other less developed countries of India's size and potential. The future prospects of high assistance levels are not promising, both from India's standpoint as well as from her donors' and the burden of adjustment for potential deficits will increasingly have to be borne by autonomous capital inflows. Eventually, however, the adjustment will have to be done through trade surpluses. An important part of the process of development is, therefore, to ensure that the sequence from a trade deficit position to one in which there is a net outflow of goods and services can be followed through smoothly.

Balance of Payments Adjustment Policies

This brings us to the question of policy instruments available to a developing country like India to bring about an equilibrium in the balance of payments. An initial difficulty arises with respect to the nature of such disequilibrium. Should one treat an *actual* deficit (or surplus) in the balance of autonomous transactions as evidence of disequilibrium, and attempt to correct it by eliminating the external assistance and other accommodating capital inflows? Or, should one define disequilibrium with respect to a *potential* deficit on the assumption of a high rate of growth, full employment, and free trade?[57] A full-scale discussion of these issues will take us afar and will raise more questions than it will solve. In the Indian context, Manmohan Singh suggests that an equilibrium in the balance of payments must be consistent with a rate of economic growth of at least 5 per cent per year, with a minimum amount of import controls to eliminate the excess demand for foreign exchange.[58]

The classical prescription for dealing with payments imbalances rests on the proposition that disequilibrium contains the seeds of its own reversal. A newly developed deficit results in a multiple reduction in income, which in turn, lowers imports (and expands exports) and may thus offset whole or part of the deficit.[59] Since this "automatic" contraction in the level of economic activity following a deficit is likely to correct the situation only partially, the governments are urged to reinforce the automatic tendencies by "expenditure-reducing" policies through fiscal and monetary means.[60]

Recent discussions have tended to put a greater reliance on "expenditure-switching" policies like devaluation to bring about balance of payments adjustments through changes in relative prices, i.e., the ratio of import prices to domestic prices. Thus the effect of devaluation of the Indian rupee is to lower the prices of goods and services produced in India relative to prices in other countries, making Indian products more competitive both at home and abroad. In other words, Indian imports become more expensive in terms of rupees, inducing a "switch" to the cheaper home-produced substitutes while Indian exports become cheaper in terms of foreign currencies in which they are brought. A devaluation, therefore, is a two-pronged remedy: it reduces imports and expands exports in a way that the total effect is in the direction of eliminating the deficit.

The condition that must prevail, if devaluation is to bring the foreign balance back into equilibrium, is that the sum of the two demand elasticities must exceed unity, and further, that the two supply elasticities must be infinite. These are known as Marshall-Lerner conditions.[61] But if the balance of payments deficits arise due to deeply rooted structural causes, the Marshall-Lerner conditions are not going to be satisfied in practice. It will be recalled that balance of payment deficits in structurally weak economies arise not so much because their prices are out of alignment with those of the rest of the world, but because of the "transformation problem" where domestic resources cannot be transformed into importables. This rigidity in production functions is reinforced by further rigidities in indirect transformation through trade, which requires that foreign demand for a country's exports be perfectly elastic. In these circumstances, devaluation may not only be irrelevant; it may even make the balance of payments worse.

This is likely to occur if the domestic demand for imports (particularly, of capital goods) is inelastic and devaluation simply raises their cost in terms of exportables. Similarly, if the foreign demand for exports is relatively inelastic— price reduction produces a less than proportionate increase in quantity demanded— the total earnings from exports decline.[62] In either case, the effect on balance of payments is to increase the deficit. The deficit can only be avoided by reduction in capital imports, which in turn, will reduce the rate of growth and further aggravate the structural problem. The remedy in this case may be worse than the disease.

Devaluation is usually urged for a country suffering simultaneously from unemployment and a deficit—a situation characteristic of India as well as of most less developed countries. It is important to realize, however, that unemployment in these countries is due to complex struc-

tural causes and not due to a lack of effective demand. Thus, devaluation, which relies on a simple price-quantity relation, cannot be expected to increase the degree of employment. Even if the unemployment is of the "effective demand" type, it is easy to see that devaluation cannot reduce it if complementary imports are reduced and exports do not increase, or increase only marginally. For devaluation to be effective, the demand elasticities must not only be greater than unity but they must be considerably greater.[63]

In any event, the "reversal factors" attendant on any policy of devaluation must be reckoned with. One such reversal factor is that devaluation leads to an increase in the domestic price level by raising the prices of imported commodities. If imports enter into the production process as inputs, a cost-price inflationary spiral may arise as the producers attempt to pass on the increases in costs to the consumers in the form of higher prices. This will wipe out the competitive gain, exports will suffer and imports will begin to rise.

The burden of the above discussion has been to show the futility of devaluation as a policy, without considering its structural context. Orthodox exchange rate adjustment solutions are not applicable without qualification under these conditions and may aggravate the problem. It is not uncommon to find a less developed country simultaneously experiencing a balance of payments deficit, inflation, unemployment and slow growth. In fact, the Indian economy, six years after the devaluation of the rupee in June 1966, closely approximated this situation.

It is obvious that the foreign exchange devaluation of 1966 (from a par value of 4.76 rupees to 7.50 rupees per US dollar) has failed to stimulate exports, since sufficient time has now passed to allow for the lags in price-quantity adjustments to work themselves out. It is also true that the net devaluation in 1966 may have been much less than the apparent one, since almost all export subsidies, chiefly the import entitlement schemes, were withdrawn with the devaluation. Thus the devaluation was largely a measure for the rationalization of the maze of administrative procedures and allocations designed to subsidize exports and implying a de facto devaluation. Indeed, it was argued then, that a devaluation can be simulated by equivalent import duties and export subsidies and was, therefore, not necessary.[64] On the other hand, it may have been necessary just for this reason—to avoid the bureaucratic delays, lack of coordination among agencies and other administrative deficiencies which such a simulation involves. In any event, the empirical questions relating to the precise manner in which devaluation would help—either through price-quantity adjustment or as part of a general rationalization—and how much devaluation was required, were not discussed either before or after the devaluation.

A detailed discussion of the complexity of devaluation in developing economies is outside the scope of this chapter. In conclusion, it must be said that the intention here is not to suggest that the alternative to devaluation is to revalue the currency or to postpone devaluation indefinitely when changes in cost structure clearly justify a change in parity. The purpose is merely to suggest that devaluation is never a substitute for necessary, and often radical changes in the structure of international trade and is not even the most important policy tool in economies suffering from structural weaknesses. It is also important that devaluation be accompanied by the appropriate subsidiary policies that are usually necessary to increase exports and reduce imports.

Bhagwati and Srinivasan in a recent analysis[65] conclude that after allowing for inevitable time-lags and other confusing factors, the performance of the 1966 "liberalization package" in India appears significantly better. The devaluation, undoubtedly aided by the presence of excess capacity in Indian industry, seems to have improved the relative profitability of foreign markets for Indian goods. Furthermore it is instructive to point out that the 1966 devaluation insofar as it replaced the earlier, ad hoc subsidization of exports, was aimed at rationalization of an inefficient and cumbersome

process. In other words, it was designed to replace an inefficient de facto devaluation by a de jure devaluation.

Conclusion

In foreign trade as in other sectors of the economy, India's emphasis since Independence in 1947 has come to rest on fundamentally different considerations from those which dominated her development experience over most of the earlier two decades. It is doubtful whether any conceivable development strategy could have reduced her heavy capital imports since 1950, without seriously impairing the total development effort. Similarly, import substitution in key sectors to an extent and degree permitted by potential domestic capabilities was inevitable, even though one may quibble about whether the transformation difficulties were as severe as implied in the plans. But one must not lose sight of the fact that in initiating import substitution processes, planners had more in mind than a mere saving on foreign exchange. The major reason has undoubtedly been the desire to reorient the country's production and trade structure in line with projected changes in demand conditions and resource availabilities.

The burden of the analysis in this chapter has been to highlight the structural features that prevent an attainment of balance of payments equilibrium. We have shown the built-in features that lead to excess demand for imports and the role of foreign demand and domestic supply elasticities that put severe limits on the growth of export earnings. The policy implications that emerge from this analysis are scattered throughout the discussion. As an overall assessment, it is quite clear that a long-run attainment of India's balance of payments presupposes a solution to the structural problem that affects her foreign trade. In any event, a balance of payments equilibrium is not desired for its own sake; a single-minded concern with balance of payments, to the exclusion of basic structural disequilibria in the foreign trade sector, is misplaced.

APPENDIX

Table 19.1. India's Imports, 1951–75
(Value, volume and prices)

Year	Value of Imports (millions of rupees)	Volume of Imports (Index, 1970=100)	Import Prices (Index, 1970=100)
1951	5,678	77	76
1952	7,167	75	77
1953	5,547	60	69
1954	8,538	67	65
1955	6,729	73	64
1956	8,215	91	65
1957	10,683	86	72
1958	8,778	73	67
1959	9,459	83	62
1960	11,083	88	66
1961	10,845	92	66
1962	11,241	99	63
1963	11,795	97	65
1964	13,694	103	66
1965	13,926	125	69
1966	17,100	123	87
1967	21,060	126	103
1968	18,823	122	97
1969	15,333	101	101
1970	15,940	100	100
1971	18,156	117	99
1972	16,978	107	101
1973	24,885	118	132
1974	40,872	124	206
1975	51,343	125	286

NOTE : Import values are CIF.

SOURCE: International Monetary Fund, *International Financial Statistics*, various years.

Table 19.2. India's Exports, 1951–75
(Value, volume and prices)

Year	Value of Exports (millions of rupees)	Volume of Exports (Index, 1970=100)	Export Prices (Index, 1970=100)
1951	7,670	63	82
1952	6,167	59	67
1953	5,312	61	58
1954	5,627	62	59
1955	6,077	69	58
1956	6,192	66	58
1957	6,565	73	60
1958	6,817	66	58
1959	6,229	70	58
1960	6,338	66	63
1961	6,607	69	64
1962	6,682	74	61
1963	7,766	83	61
1964	8,328	89	61
1965	8,031	82	65
1966	9,920	85	85
1967	12,100	82	98
1968	13,153	92	94
1969	13,754	90	101
1970	15,198	100	100
1971	15,256	101	102
1972	18,595	109	112
1973	22,591	110	136
1974	31,786	123	173
1975	36,003	136	187

NOTE : Export values are FOB.

SOURCE: International Monetary Fund, *International Financial Statistics*, various years.

REFERENCES

1. For details, the reader should consult any standard text on international trade, such as B. Sodersten, *International Economics* (New York: Harper & Row, 1970).
2. It should be noted that the welfare gains from trade arise from two distinct sources, viz., from specialization, and from exchange at price ratios different from those prevailing at home. Thus, strictly speaking, specialization is not essential for gains from trade. If we abandon the assumption of non-specificity of factors of production and their trans-ferability between sectors, we obtain a single-point production possibilities curve at P instead of the curve TT′ as before, where production and consumption before trade take place. International trade in the face of non-transferability of factors forces the production to remain at P, i.e., there is no specialization; nevertheless, consumption moves up to C′ on the higher indifference curve W_2. The country exports PE of Y in exchange for EC′ of X. The inability to transform resources reduces the gains from

trade, but it does not eliminate them.

3. A few attempts have been made to relate the static to dynamic efficiency in trade by separating the production and consumption problems of a developing economy, but the results are unsatisfactory. For a recent discussion, see Bent Hansen, *Long and Short Term Planning in the Underdeveloped Countries* (Amsterdam: North Holland Publishing Company, 1967).

4. Richard E. Lipsey, "Foreign Trade" in Lance E. Davis et al., *American Economic Growth—An Economist's History of the United States* (New York: Harper & Row, 1972), Table 14.4.

5. S. Chakravarty, "The Use of Shadow Prices in Programme Evaluation", in P.N. Rosenstein-Rodan (ed.) *Capital Formation in Economic Development* (Cambridge, Mass: M.I.T. Press, 1964), as well as his *Logic of Investment Planning* (Amsterdam: North Holland Publishing Company, 1960).

6. Keith B. Griffin, *Underdevelopment in Spanish America* (Cambridge, Mass.: M.I.T. Press, 1970), Chapter 2.

7. W.B. Reddaway. *The Development of the Indian Economy* (London: George Allen & Unwin, 1962), Chapter 3.

8. Staffan B. Linder, *Trade Policy in the Less Developed Countries* (New York: Praeger, 1967).

9. We are, at the moment, ignoring the problem of capital transfers which may serve to finance a deficit in the balance of trade. These problems are considered later in the section on balance of payments.

10. This is the well-known "small country" assumption of trade theory which means that in an atomistic world market a country can sell as much as it likes to, at an unchanged world price.

11. See, for instance, M. Michaely, "Concentration of Exports and Imports: An International Comparison", *Economic Journal*, vol. 30, no. 7, December 1958.

12. Jagdish Bhagwati and Padma Desai, *India: Planning for Industrialization* (London: Oxford University Press, 1970), have suggested the possible existence of negative value-added at international prices in such manufacturing sectors as leather goods, non-ferrous metals, iron and steel and automobiles. They caution, however, that the phenomena could have arisen because of statistical difficulties which are substantial.

13. P.C. Mahalanobis, "Some Observations on the Process of Growth of National Income", *Sankhya*, vol. 12, part 4, September 1953; and "The Approach of Operational Research to Planning in India", *Sankhya*, vol. 14, parts 1 and 2, December 1955.

14. For further details on India planning models, the reader should consult A. Ghosh, *Planning Programming and Input-Output Model* (Cambridge University Press, 1968).

15. For a recent discussion of these and other issues connected with trade and development policy, the reader is referred to Bhagwati and Desai, *India: Planning for Industrialization.*

16. There is a growing literature on the "two gap" models of development, of which the following are representative: R.I. McKinnon, "Foreign Exchange Constraints in Economic Development and Efficient Aid Allocation", *The Economic Journal* vol. 74, no. 2, June 1964; H.B. Chenery and A. Strout, "Foreign Assistance and Economic Development", *American Economic Review*, vol. 56, no. 3, September 1966; J. Vanek, *Estimating Foreign Resources for Economic Development* : *Theory, Method and a Case Study of Colombia* (New York: McGraw-Hill, 1967); and A. Martens, "The Two-Gap Theory of Development Reconsidered with Special Reference to Turkey", *European Economic Review*, Summer 1970, vol. I, no. 4.

17. Bhagwati and Desai, *India: Planning for Industrialization*, p. 236.

18. The following illustration will clarify the concept. An initial value of $M_0=2000$ and $\beta=0.15$, $V_0=10,000$, $V_n=16,289$ and $n=10$ will give the value of minimum imports $\overline{M}_n=2943$. Similarly, given $E_0=1500$, $e=0.04$, $E_n=2220$, the foreign exchange gap will equal $2943-2220=723$.

19. Since we are primarily concerned with trade problems, any discussion of savings gap is ignored in this analysis.

20. For details of this formulation, see OECD *Quantitative Models as an Aid to Development Assistance Policy* (Paris, 1967), Annex. III.

21. United Nations, *Trade Prospects and Capital Needs of Developing Countries* (New York, 1968), p. 76.

22. H. B. Chenery, "Patterns of Industrial Growth", *American Economic Review*, vol. 50, no. 3, 1960, p. 640.

23. These measures represent a simplification from a comprehensive national income model for the study of structural changes. For details, see J. Ahmad, "Import Substitution, and Structural Change in Indian Manufacturing Industry", *Journal of Development Studies*, vol. IV, no. 3, April 1968.

24. None of the possible measures of import substitution is completely free from ambiguities. The present measure is by far the most straightforward and widely accepted in literature. For a discussion of this problem, see Robert B. Sutcliffe, *Industry and Underdevelopment* (New York: Addison Wesley, 1971).

25. For alternative definitions and measurement of import substitution in India, the reader is referred to Bhagwati and Desai, *India: Planning for Industrialization*, Chapter 5. Though sensitive to the choice of measures, the orders of magnitude are roughly the same.

26. H.B. Chenery, S. Shishido and T. Watanabe, "The Pattern of Japanese Growth, 1941–1954", *Econometrica*, vol. 30, no. 1, January 1962.

27. To the extent that self-reliance and self-sufficiency in economic matters may be desir-

able objectives in themselves, a country may be reluctant to finance its balance of payment deficits through foreign capital inflows. Presumably, this reflects a desire to reduce the influence of foreign private and governmental, and sometimes international, agencies implied by the foreign borrowing.

28. On this supposed conflict, see Ian M.D. Little, Tibor Scitovsky and Maurice Scott, *Industry and Trade in Some Developing Countries* (New York: Oxford University Press, 1970).

29. Exercises of this kind in India have been limited generally to ascertaining the "saving" in foreign exchange which would result by initiating substitute domestic production, both with reference to direct and indirect inputs. If one could produce, let us say, chemical machinery worth Rs. 10 crores, the saving of foreign exchange may be greater or lesser than this amount depending upon the import intensity of such production as well as of the indirect requirements.

30. B.R. Hazari, "The Import Intensity of Consumption in India", *Indian Economic Review* vol. 2, New Series, October 1967.

31. David Felix, "The Dilemma of Import Substitution—Argentina", in Gustav F. Papanek (ed.), *Development Policy—Theory and Practice* (Harvard University Press, 1968).

32. This conclusion requires certain assumptions about the rate of investment, its import intensity and the output-capital ratios. For a comprehensive treatment of this problem, see Carlos F. Diaz-Alejandro, "On the Import Intensity of Import Substitution", *Kyklos*, vol. 18, no. 3, 1965.

33. David Felix, "Import Substitution, Argentina", offers the following explanation. The cross-sectional income elasticity tends to be high when durables are being newly acquired by upper income families. The lower half of the upper income family units in 1962 bought under 50 per cent of all refrigerators and washing machines sold, almost 40 per cent of all TV sets and about one-third of all stoves, radios, and vacuum cleaners, while the upper 25 per cent of all income recipients purchased from two-thirds to three-fourths of the automobiles sold. In total, 44 per cent of expenditures on durable goods were on automobiles alone, and another 18.6 per cent on television sets, leaving little more than one-third of total expenditures to be shared by a large number of remaining items.

34. Werner Baer and Andrea Maneschi, "Import Substitution, Stagnation and Structural Change: An Interpretation of the Brazilian Case", *The Journal of Developing Areas*, vol. 5, no. 2, January 1971.

35. Ibid.

36. The allocation has taken the form of licensing for imported capital goods and the AU ("actual user") licensing for imported inputs and raw materials.

37. Bhagwati and Desai, *India: Planning for Industrialization*, p. 290.

38. For details of this and other research into these problems, see Jagdish N. Bhagwati and Sukhamoy Chakravarty, "Contributions to Indian Economic Analysis: A Survey", *American Economic Review*, vol. LIX, no. 4, September 1969, Part 2, p. 64.

39. For example, the earnings from the export of jute manufactures declined from a value of Rs. 1.633 millions in 1952 to Rs. 1.255 millions in 1960. There was some improvement in the later 1960s, but by 1970 they had merely regained a value approximately equal to the one in 1952, viz., Rs. 1,707 millions. The export earnings from tea grew from Rs. 1,236 millions in 1960 to a mere Rs. 1,447 millions in 1970—a change of 17 per cent in ten years. Similarly there has been a reduction in India's share of world trade in these commodities. India's share of world trade in jute manufactures declined from 95 per cent in 1950–51 to 45 per cent in 1969–70. Her share of world exports of tea declined from 50 per cent to 21 per cent during the same period. These declines in individual commodity exports are in line with an overall decline of India's share of world exports from 2.0 per cent in 1950 to 0.9 per cent in 1966.

40. Export earnings financed 83 per cent of India's total imports during the First Five-Year Plan (1951–55), while this proportion fell to 56 per cent during the Second Plan period (1956–60). The percentages, of course, conceal the fact that imports had dramatically increased during the Second relative to the First Plan.

41. However, the reader is referred to the very detailed study by Manmohan Singh, *India's Export Trends and the Prospects for Self-Sustaining Growth* (Oxford: Clarendon Press, 1964).

42. For a detailed commodity-by-commodity account of these problems, the reader is referred to Singh, *India's Export Trends*.

43. The income elasticity of demand in India for cotton textiles is estimated to be 1.4, cf. B.R.M. Chatterjee, "A Statistical Study of Consumption of Cotton Textiles in India", *Monthly Abstract of Statistics*, vol. 13, no. 10, New Delhi, 1960.

44. See Benjamin Cohen, "The Stagnation of Indian Exports", *Quarterly Journal of Economics*, vol. 78, no. 4, November 1964.

45. The All-India Wholesale Price Index rose by only 6.8 per cent during the ten-year period, 1950–51 and 1960–61, while the Consumer Price Index during the same period rose roughly by 18 per cent. The degree of inflation revealed by these indices is infinitesimal compared to price rises in some of the Latin American countries, where a 30 per cent inflation in one year is not uncommon.

46. The Commodity Concentration Index is defined as $100 \sqrt{\sum \frac{x_{ij}^{3}}{x_j}}$ where x_{ij} = India's exports of sub-group i within group j, and x_j = the country's total commodity group j, cf. Bhagwati and Desai,

India: Planning for Industrialization, p. 429.

47. Import entitlement schemes are a form of hidden subsidy to exports, in so far as they entitle the eligible exporters to premium-carrying import licenses in proportion to the value of exports. The important feature of these schemes is that a specified percentage of the f.o.b. value of exports is allowed to be used for the import of raw materials and components necessary for the production of the exports or of allied products.

48. Bilateral trade and payments agreements with a limited number of countries have become a regular feature of India's foreign trade since 1959, when the five year bilateral agreement between India and the USSR came into force. These agreements provide for trade in specified commodities during a given period of time on the basis of a self-balancing monetary mechanism. The local currency balances arising out of such trade are in general not convertible into "hard" currencies.

49. Bela Balassa, *Trade Liberalization Among Industrial Countries* (New York: McGraw-Hill, 1967), pp. 180–81.

50. Consider the following example from the United States imports tariff schedule:

Commodity	Tariff Rate
(a) Iron ore	Free
(b) Pig iron	$ 1.12 per ton
(c) Bar iron	$ 20–30 per ton
(d) Machine goods	
(i) Mining machinery	27.5% ad valorem
(ii) Machine tools	30% ad valorem
(iii) Textiles machinery	40% ad valorem

51. The most organized form of non-tariff barriers is embodied in the Long Term Arrangement for Trade in Cotton Textiles, popularly known as LTA, which was negotiated under the auspices of GATT and lays down specific quota ceilings, by commodity and by destination, for the import of cotton textiles in North America and Western Europe.

52. A recent analysis suggests that the intensity of international trade in manufactures depends on the similarity of income and demand patterns. As a result, countries with broadly similar demand structures tend to trade with each other in products which are close subtitutes for each other, though sufficiently differentiated to have a slice of the world market in an oligopolistic fashion. It must be stressed that this analysis refers to only the manufactured products in international trade, and does not attempt to explain the pattern of trade in natural commodities. For details, the reader is referred to S.B. Linder, *An Essay on Trade and Transformation* (New York: John Wiley, 1961).

53. IMF, *International Financial Statistics*, vol. XXV, no. 3, March 1972. Other data based on annual *International Financial Statistics* and the *Balance of Payments Yearbook*.

54. For details, the reader should consult a standard textbook on the theory of balance of payments, e.g., B. J. Cohen, *Balance-of-Payments Policy* (Baltimore: Penguin, 1969).

55. The subject of foreign aid and foreign capital in India is discussed in chapter 20.

56. I.M.F., *Balance of Payments Yearbook*, August 1971.

57. A discussion of some of these issues is contained in a well-known paper by R.F. Kahn, "The Dollar Shortage and Devaluation", *Economia Internazionale*, vol. 3, no. 1, 1950.

58. Singh, *India's Export Trends*, p. 323.

59. Analogous reasoning would apply to a surplus situation: the multiple rise in income due to trade surplus brings about an increase in imports (and a reduction in exports) that wholly or partly offset the surplus.

60. An example is the British "stop-go" policy during the 1950s and 1960s: contractionary monetary and fiscal measures in times of deficits and expansion in times of surplus.

61. For details, see F. Machlup, "The Theory of Foreign Exchanges", and Joan Robinson, "The Foreign Exchanges"—both reprinted in American Economic Association, *Readings in the Theory of International Trade,* (Homewood, Illinois: Irwin), 1950.

62. Consider the example of India's exports of jute manufactures. Their volume increased from 746,000 metric tons in 1952 to 850,000 metric tons in 1960—a gain of 14 per cent—while their value during the same period declined from Rs. 1,600 millions to Rs. 1,100 millions—a fall of 30 per cent.

63. The question is discussed in greater detail in Keith B. Griffin, *Underdevelopment in Spanish America* (Cambridge, Mass., M.I.T. Press. 1969), Chap. 5.

64. P.M. Bardhan, "The Case Against Devaluation", *The Economic Weekly*, vol. 14, September 1962

65. Jagdish N. Bhagwati and T.N. Srinivasan, *Foreign Trade Regimes and Economic Development : India,* A Special Conference Series on Foreign Trade Regimes and Economic Develoment, volume VI (New York: Columbia University Press, 1975).

BIBLIOGRAPHY

Ahmad, J.: *Import Substitution, Trade and Development*. Johnson Associates Press. Connecticut, 1977.

———: "Import Substitution and Structural Change in Indian Manufacturing Industry". *Journal of Development Studies* Vol. iv, No. 3, April 1968.

Baer, W. and A. Maneschi:"Import Substitution, Stagnation and Structural Change: An Interpretation of the Brazilian Case". *The Journal of Developing Areas* Vol. 5, No. 2, January 1971.

Balassa, B.: *Trade Liberalization among Industrial Countries.* New York. McGraw-Hill, 1967.

Bardhan, P.K.: "The Case Against Devaluation". *The Economic Weekly* Vol. 14, September 1962.

Bhagwati, J. and S. Chakravarty: "Contributions to Indian Economic Analysis: A Survey". *American Economic Review* Vol. 49, No. 4, September 1969, Part 2.

Bhagwati J. and P. Desai: *India—Planning for Industrialization.* London. Oxford University Press, 1970.

Bhagwati, J. and T.N. Srinivasan: *Foreign Trade Regimes and Economic Development: India.* New York. Columbia University Press, 1975.

Chakravarty, S.: "The Use of Shadow Prices in Programme Evaluation". In P.N. Rosenstein-Rodan (ed.) *Capital Formation in Economic Development.* Cambridge Mass. MIT Press, 1964.

Chakravarty, S.: *Logic of Investment Planning.* Amsterdam. North Holland Publishing Company, 1960.

Chatterjee, B.R.M.: "A Statistical Study of Consumption of Cotton Textiles in India". *Monthly Abstract of Statistics* Vol. 13, No. 10. New Delhi, 1960.

Chenery, H.B. and A. Strout: "Foreign Assistance and Economic Development". *American Economic Review* Vol. 56, No. 3. September 1966.

Chenery, H.B., S. Shishido and T. Watanabe: "The Pattern of Japanese Growth, 1914–1954". *Econometrica* Vol. 30, No. 7, January 1962.

Chenery, H.B.: "Patterns of Industrial Growth". *American Economic Review* Vol. 50, No. 3, 1960.

Cohen, B.J.: *Balance of Payments Policy.* Baltimore. Penguin Modern Economics, 1969.

Cohen, B.: "The Stagnation of Indian Exports". *Quarterly Journal of Economics* Vol. 78, No. 4, November 1964.

Diaz-Alejandro, C.F.: "On the Import Intensity of Import Substitution". *Kyklos* Vol. 18, No. 3, 1965.

Felix, D.: "The Dilemma of Import Substitution—Argentina". In G.F. Papanek (ed.) *Development Policy—Theory and Practice.* Harvard University Press, 1968.

Ghosh A.: *Planning, Programming and Input-Models.* Cambridge University Press, 1968.

Griffin, K.B.: *Underdevelopment in Spanish America.* Cambridge, Mass. MIT Press, 1969.

Hansen, B.: *Long and Short-Term Planning in Under-developed Countries.* Amsterdam. North Holland Publishing Company, 1967.

Hazari, B.R.: "Import-Intensity of Consumption in India". *The Indian Economic Review* Vol. 2, New Series, October 1967.

Kahn, R.F.: "The Dollar Shortage and Devaluation". *Economia Internazionale* Vol. 3, No. 1, 1950.

Linder, S.B.: *Trade Policy in the Less Developed Countries.* New York. Praeger, 1967.

Linder, S.B.: *An Essay on Trade and Transformation.* New York. John Wiley, 1961.

Lipsey, R.E.: "Foreign Trade". In L.E. Davis et al. (eds) *American Economic Growth—An Economist's History of the United States.* New York. Harper & Row, 1972.

Little, I.M.D., T. Scitovsky and M. Scott: *Industry and Trade in Some Developing Countries.* New York. Oxford University Press, 1970.

Machlup, F.: "The Theory of Foreign Exchanges". In R.D. Irwin (ed.) *Readings in the Theory of International Trade.* Homewood, Illinois. American Economic Association, 1950.

Mckinnon, R.I.: "Foreign Exchange Constraints in Economic Development and Efficient Aid Allocation". *The Economic Journal* Vol. 74, No. 2, June 1964.

Mahalanobis, P.C.: "Some Observations on the Process of Growth of National Income". *Sankhya* Vol. 12, Part 4, September 1953.

Mahalanobis, P.C.: "The Approach of Operational Research to Planning in India". *Sankhya* Vol. 14, Parts 1 and 2, December 1955.

Martens, A.: "The Two-gap Theory of Development Reconsidered with Special Reference to Turkey". *European Economic Review.* Summer 1970, Vol. I, No. 4.

Michaely, M.: "Concentration of Exports and Imports: An International Comparison". *Economic Journal* Vol. 8, December 1958.

Organization for Economic Development and Cooperation: *Quantitative Models as an Aid to Development Assistance Policy.* Paris, 1967.

Reddaway, W.B.: *The Development of the Indian Economy.* London. George Allen & Unwin, 1962.

Robinson, J.: "The Foreign Exchanges". *Readings in the Theory of International Trade.* Homewood, Ill. American Economic Association, 1950.

Singh, M.: *India's Export Trends and the Prospects for Self-Sustained Growth.* Oxford. Clarendon Press, 1964.

Sodersten, B.: *International Economics.* New York. Harper & Row, 1970.

Sutcliffe, R.B.: *Industry and Underdevelopment.* New York. Addison Wesley, 1971.

United Nations: *Trade Prospects and Capital Needs of Developing Countries.* New York, 1968.

Vanek, J.: *Estimating Foreign Resources for Economic Development: Theory, Method and a Case Study of Colombia.* New York. McGraw-Hill, 1967.

20

Foreign Private Investment in India

V. N. BALASUBRAMANYAM

The role of foreign private investment (FPI) in the development process has been a very vigorously debated issue in recent years. The participants in the debate can be generally divided into the "benign impact" and the "malign impact" schools, to use J.N. Bhagwati's terminology. The former believe that it can not only confer all the benefits of official aid on the recipients, but also impart certain additional benefits. The foreign capital that it provides can bridge both the foreign exchange and saving gaps; and the technology that it imparts can bridge the technology gap. It can redress regional disparities and confer a host of other benefits in the form of the linkage effects which it creates, and employment opportunities which it provides, all contained in the catch-all phrase, externalities.

The case of the "malign impact school" against FPI is an amalgam of economic and political arguments. To the extremists of this school, FPI is no more than an instrument of neocolonialism; the substitution of economic for political domination. Most developing countries are jealous of their political independence, and wary of widespared foreign domination.

Admittedly, the issue of FPI is clouded by political considerations and evokes strong emotional reactions. But the case against FPI is not based entirely on political considerations. There are grounds for arguing that under certain circumstances FPI may adversely affect the balance of payments of the recipient countries, destroy instead of create employment opportunities, thwart national economic objectives and aggravate income disparities.

It is conceivable that in the absence of FPI, local capital and enterprise would have entered the fields in which foreign enterprises are active. It is also not unreasonable to argue that many developing countries would have been better off, at least for the time being, without many of the projects in which FPI has occurred. Alternatively, they might have been better off importing the products rather than producing them domestically with foreign private capital.

To make an objective assessment of the benefits and costs of FPI, one must consider these alternatives. Considering the opportunity cost of a particular project or an investment is after all basic to economic analysis. A mere listing of the pros and cons of FPI in the absence of an analytical framework within which to assess its net impact on the economy, would be a barren exercise.

Apart from the need for an analytical framework, FPI also poses a challenge to economic management. Admittedly, it is an amalgam of good and bad from the point of view of the developing countries. Its proponents claim it provides an admirable conduit for the international transfer of technology and skills. In fact the technology-transmitting ability of FPI is one of its distinguishing characteristics. But it also implies control and management of operations by foreigners. The objectives of the foreign firms and that of the recipient countries may not always coincide. Further, there is the problem of how best to transfer the maximum possible amount of resources from the foreign firms to the local economy. In short, the problem is one of maximising the "benign" impact and minimising the "malign" impact of FPI.

Recent years have seen a burgeoning of research on these issues. The application of the now well-known Little-Mirrlees technique of social benefit-cost analysis to the analysis of FPI is a major advance. Further, novel methods of foreign-enterprise participation such as licensing agreements, management contracts, and joint ventures between foreign and local firms, are being increasingly advocated. These alternatives are supposedly a means of harnessing the benefits of FPI without incurring its disadvantages. In addition, the need to strengthen the bargaining position of the developing countries vis-a-vis the multinational enterprises has been an often-rehearsed theme. In fact, effective regulation of the operations of the multinational enterprises is one of the main areas in which strident demands have been made by the developing countries in the proposed New International Economic Order.

India's experience with foreign private investment provides a case study of the analytical issues involved. This essay discusses these issues in the context of FPI in India. Since many of the problems posed by FPI are engrained in its distinguishing characteristics, we shall first discuss the nature of FPI and the factors motivating firms to go abroad.

Characteristics of Foreign Private Investment

Portfolio capital flows and direct foreign investment constitute the two main forms of foreign capital participation. Portfolio capital flows refer to the acquisition of securities by individuals or institutions issued by foreign institutions, without any associated control over, or participation in, their management.[1] Foreign direct investment differs from portfolio capital flows in that it confers on the investing entity an ability to exercise control over the decision-making process of the entity in which it invests. The investor acquires this power to exert control over operations by virtue of his owning the capital stock of the entity in which he invests in a major way. The distinguishing features of direct investment, then, are the majority ownership of capital stock by the foreign entity, and the ability to exercise control over operations which flows from it.

The ability to exercise control over decision-making immediately suggests that something more than mere flows of financial capital are involved in the case of foreign direct investment. These relate to transfers of technical and managerial skills.

A major theoretical explanation for foreign direct investment does in fact run in terms of the monopoly of technology that foreign firms possess. More generally, foreign firms possess a monopoly over advantages of production which may relate to production techniques, managerial skills, marketing expertise, or internal and external economies of scale.[2] It is the need to exploit those advantages in foreign markets that gives rise to foreign direct investment. In other words, imperfections in product and factor markets provide the impetus for foreign investment. In a world characterized by perfect competition where all firms have equal access to technology and factors of production, there would be no foreign direct investment. In any case, foreign firms would be at a disadvantage vis-a-vis local firms in terms of knowledge of local cultural, social, and economic factors. It is the possession of a monopoly over advantages that enables foreign firms to overcome these disadvantages and earn a higher rate of return.

The possession of a monopoly over advantages is, however, not a complete explanation of the foreign investment decision process. Why do firms prefer to invest and produce abroad instead of exploiting the advantages they possess by simply exploiting the product? Briefly, local production enhances the rent accruing from the monopoly over advantages. By producing abroad the firm can exploit international factor-price differentials and overcome tariff and transport cost barriers. The presence of profitable domestic markets sheltered from international competition by tariff barriers is an often-advanced explanation of FPI in developing countries. Further, nearness to markets enables the firm to undertake modifications of the product to adapt it to local conditions and tastes. This would be especially so in the case of oligopolistic industries manufacturing differentiated products.[3]

Moreover, strategic considerations may also influence oligopolistic international firms to invest abroad. Such firms may be faced with the threat of losing their traditional export markets to host-country firms operating behind tariff walls, or to third-country firms entering a protected market. In such an event, firms may decide to invest abroad on long-run market considerations even though the investment may be unprofitable in the short run. Such investment based on strategic considerations is termed "defensive investment".

Firms may also go abroad to take advantage of international factor-price differentials. In recent years such investment, especially in the Far East, has assumed significant proportions. Much of this investment, termed the Hong Kong-Puerto Rico type of investment, is for the production of labour-intensive components. The production of other parts and assembly of the firms' product takes place in the home country of firms. The electronics industry is a prime example of this type of investment. The production of such high value-added low transport-cost products has an obvious appeal to developing countries in view of their export and employment potential.

Nature and Pattern of Foreign Private Capital in India

Nearly three-quarters of the foreign capital in India on the eve of independence was British owned. As is typical of the colonial pattern of investment, it was mostly concentrated in extractive industries and processing of raw materials for export and international trade and anciliary industries. It is estimated that by mid-1948 nearly 20 per cent of the total foreign private investment was in plantations, and 38 per cent in the services sector. While tea accounted for a major proportion of the investment in plantations, trading accounted for a bulk of the investment in the services sector. Thus no more than one-fifth was invested in the manufacturing sector excluding jute.[4]

Since independence, however, significant changes have occurred in the nature and pattern of foreign private participation in India. Its area of interest, its volume and organizational pattern have all changed considerably. Over the period 1948–72, the total stocks of foreign direct investment increased more than six-fold, but portfolio capital which accounted for only 17.5 per cent of the total stock of foreign private capital in 1948, now accounts for more than 53 per cent (Table 20.1). Foreign direct investment is now heavily concentrated in the manufacturing sector, accounting for 64 per cent of the total stock of foreign direct investment in 1972 (Table 20.2). A third important organizational feature is the increasing importance of technical collaboration agreements and joint business ventures between Indian and foreign firms (Table 20.3).

Size Although portfolio capital accounts for more than 50 per cent of the total stock of foreign private capital, much of it is in the form of creditor capital consisting of suppliers' credits and loans as opposed to equity holdings (Table 20.1). The former refers to credit extended by foreign suppliers of equipment and machinery to Indian importers and the latter to ordinary shares held by foreigners in Indian commercial enterprises. The predominance of loans and suppliers' credits in the stock of

Table 20.1. Composition of Foreign Private Capital in India
(in million rupees)

Year	Direct Foreign Investment	Portfolio Capital	Equity Capital	Creditor Capital	Col. 3 as % of Col. 2	Col. 4 as % of Col. 2	Total Private Capital	Col. 4 as % of Col. 6	Col. 2 as % of Col. 6
1948	2111.0	447.0	—	—	—	—	2558.0	82.5	17.5
1961	5248.0	1526.0	—	—	—	—	6810.0	77.6	22.4
1964	5655.0	3285.0	530.0	2755.0	16.1	83.9	8940.0	63.3	36.7
1965	6119.0	3904.0	547.0	3355.0	14.0	85.9	10,023.0	61.0	39.0
1966	6282.0	4401.0	570.0	3831.0	12.9	87.0	10,683.0	58.8	41.2
1967	6920.0	7797.0	632.0	7165.0	8.1	91.9	14,717.0	47.0	53.0
1968	7101.0	8420.0	752.0	7668.0	8.9	91.1	15,521.0	45.8	54.2
1969	7377.0	8816.0	765.0	8051.0	8.7	91.3	16,193.0	45.6	54.4
1970	7354.0	9056.0	941.0	8125.0	10.4	89.6	16,410.0	44.8	55.2
1971	7673.0	9123.0	966.0	8157.0	10.6	89.4	16,796.0	45.7	54.3
1972	8149.0	9355.0	973.0	8312.0	10.4	89.6	17,504.0	46.6	53.4

SOURCE: *Reserve Bank of India Bulletins*, various issues.

portfolio capital is indicative of the growing import needs of India's manufacturing sector. Suppliers' credits have grown in importance in the flows of international capital to developing countries in general. By the end of 1971, they accounted for nearly 16 per cent of the total capital flows, including foreign aid, from the developed to the developing countries. This growth in suppliers' credits has been both a result of the export competition among the developed countries and the growing import needs of the developing countries. This form of financing, however, may have several drawbacks from the recipient's point of view. It could be an expensive form of financing. The rates of interest charged on the loans and prices charged for equipment supplied by foreign exporters may be higher than normal market prices. Such overpricing of equipment means that the real interest costs of suppliers' credits would be greater than the nominal cost. Moreover suppliers' credits are usually restricted to short-term credit. If importing countries overextend themselves in the short run, they may run into serious difficulties over debt servicing and repayments and impair their credit-worthiness. Data published by the Reserve Bank of India show in fact that gross outflows of capital, in the case of suppliers' credits and loans, have continuously risen since 1965, and for the years 1971 and 1972 outflows considerably exceeded inflows. Thus the inclusion of suppliers' credits and loans which are essentially short-term credit arrangements overstates the extent of portfolio capital stock in the Indian economy.

Although the stock of foreign direct investment has increased appreciably (Table 20.4), two important points need to be made regarding its size. First, compared to some other developing countries in the Asian region, the stock of foreign direct investment in India is not very high. Available estimates show that the stock of direct investment per capita at the end of 1967 was $ 2.5 for India, $ 11.9 for Ceylon, $ 2.8 for Pakistan, $ 65.6 for Malaysia, $ 20.9 for the Phillippines, and $ 6.0 for Thailand.[5] A more meaningful estimate of the extent of foreign direct investment would be its share in the total private capital formation in the country. Unfortunately comparable figures on this statistic are not readily available. However some indication is given by the available estimate that for the period 1961-66 the net inflows of foreign private capital into the Indian economy account for 7.5 per cent of the total investment in the private sector whereas for Malaysia this figure was around 30 per cent for the period 1960-63.[6]

The second important point to note is that much of the increase in the stock of

Table 20.2. Sectoral Distribution of Foreign Direct Investment in India

	1948		1961		1967		1969		1971		1972	
	Million Rs.	%	Million Rs.	%	Million Rs.	%	Million Rs.	%	Million Rs.	%	Million Rs.	%
Plantations	523.0	20.4	1005.0	19.0	1072.0	16.4	1225.0	16.7	1199.0	15.6	1205.0	14.8
Mining	115.0	4.5	109.0	2.1	44.0	0.7	37.0	0.5	63.0	0.8	67.0	0.8
Petroleum	223.0	8.7	1481.0	28.0	1276.0	19.5	1315.0	17.8	1158.0	15.1	1226.0	15.0
Manufacturing	710.0	27.8	1868.0	35.3	3226.0	49.0	3920.0	53.1	4857.0	63.3	5235.0	64.2
Food, Beverages and Tobacco	101.0	14.2	337.0	18.0	350.0	10.1	405.0	5.5	435.0	5.7	466.0	5.7
Textile Products	280.0	39.4	140.0	7.5	161.0	5.0	177.0	2.4	252.0	3.3	244.0	3.0
Transport Equipment	10.0	1.4	86.0	4.6	229.0	7.1	257.0	3.5	277.0	3.6	282.0	3.5
Machinery and Tools	12.0	1.7	79.0	4.3	213.0	6.3	250.0	3.4	314.0	4.1	344.0	4.2
Metals and Metal Products	80.0	11.3	267.0	14.3	495.0	15.3	612.0	8.3	733.0	9.6	812.0	10.0
Electrical Machinery	48.0	6.8	120.0	6.4	284.0	8.8	413.0	5.6	528.0	6.9	587.0	7.2
Chemicals	80.0	11.3	476.0	25.5	946.0	29.3	1158.0	15.7	1496.0	19.5	1608.0	19.7
Others	99.0	13.9	363.0	19.4	584.0	17.0	319.0	4.3	440.0	5.7	892.0	10.9
Services	988.0	38.6	821.0	15.6	929.0	14.2	880.0	12.0	396.0	5.2	416.0	5.1
Total	2559.0	100.0	5284.0	100.0	6542.0	100.0	7377.0	100.0	7673.0	100.0	8149.0	100.0

Table 20.3. Number of Collaboration Agreements Approved by the Government of India, Classified According to Countries of Participation

	1957	1958	1959	1960	1961	1962	1963	1964	1965	1966	1967	1968	1969	1970	Total
UK	17	34	52	120	126	79	70	105	60	44	50	19	34	39	849
USA	6	4	10	61	77	57	67	78	48	42	34	36	18	41	579
W. Germany	2	6	13	58	67	42	48	68	44	41	24	22	28	28	491
Japan	1	3	8	39	30	24	32	35	26	18	21	12	17	15	281
Switzerland	—	2	1	13	19	19	19	19	18	19	6	6	7	13	152
France	2	1	2	9	16	14	16	11	12	11	9	8	7	7	125
Italy	4	4	4	9	13	11	6	8	7	3	6	3	3	8	89
E. Germany	—	—	1	5	4	5	10	24	6	3	2	2	5	5	72
Sweden	1	—	1	13	—	6	1	6	3	5	8	4	2	3	53
Netherlands	1	—	—	6	10	7	4	5	2	3	4	2	3	3	50
Denmark	—	—	—	6	5	1	5	4	3	3	1	4	1	5	38
Others	47	49	56	35	37	32	22	25	15	21	17	13	9	20	414
TOTAL	81	103	150	380	403	298	298	403	242	202	182	131	135	183	3191

SOURCE: Complied by the Indian Investment Cente, New Delhi.

Table 20.4. Pattern of Direct Investment Inflows into India

(Rs. Million)

	Cash Inflow	Re-invested Earnings	No-cash Inflow	Gross Inflow
1956–61	45.0	137.0	17.0	352.0
(Annual Average)				
1963–64	40.0	98.0	141.0	279.0
1964–65	22.0	204.0	190.0	416.0
1965–66	26.0	188.0	121.0	335.0
1966–67	26.0	149.0	73.0	248.0
1967–68	38.0	182.0	88.0	308.0
1968–69	15.0	178.0	115.0	308.0
1969–70	12.0	290.0	54.0	356.0
1970–71	7.0	284.0	90.0	381.0
1971–72	12.0	339.0	25.0	376.0

SOURCE: *Reserve Bank of India Bulletins*, various issues.

foreign direct investment that has occurred in India in recent years has been on account of reinvested earnings and investment in kind. Fresh foreign inflows of capital into the country have been meagre (Table 20.4). The investments in kind are accounted for by the imports of equipment and knowhow from parent companies by foreign subsidiaries operating in India.

Sectoral Composition A significant change that has occurred in the pattern of foreign private investment in India relates to its sectoral composition. Foreign direct investment has increasingly fanned out towards the manufacturing sector and away from its traditional strongholds of the extractive and services sectors. Nearly 60 per cent of the stock of foreign direct investment is accounted for by the manufacturing sector in recent years (Table 20.2). Within the manufacturing sector, chemicals, metals and metal products, and electrical machinery have gained in importance. Significant changes have also occurred in the sources of supply of foreign private capital. Traditionally, the UK has been the major source of direct investment. Although it still leads the field, its share declined from 80 per cent in 1948 to around 62 per cent by 1972. The US investments, on the other hand, had increased from 4.2 per cent in 1948 to 19 per cent by the end of 1972. Japan and West Germany who did not figure at all in 1948 had a share of 4.5 per cent and 3.5 per cent respectively.

Organizational Changes A major development in the field of private foreign enterprise participation in the post-independence era has been the advent of technical collaboration agreements. A technical collaboration agreement is defined broadly as an agreement between a foreigner and an entity created under local law and owned by local public or private interests, in which the foreigner provides management services, technical information, or both, and receives payment in money.[7]

A significant feature of this type of arrangement is that it precludes foreign ownership of capital, and the payment received by the foreigner is in return for technical services rendered and not for equity contributions. Insofar as the foreign firm has no equity interests in the venture, it follows that technical collaboration agreements also preclude the exercise of formal control over operations by foreign firms.

A joint business venture is defined as one in which there is the commitment, for more than a short duration, of funds, facilities, and services by two or *more* legally separate interests to an enterprise, for their mutual benefit.[8] The emphasis in this form of organization is on the commitment of resources by both entities. The resources committed by the partners need not be entirely financial. They may be managerial and technical resources. The share of the partners in the equity structure is not strictly defined. It may be 50–50 or it may be skewed to some extent in favour of one of the partners. The most important attribute of joint ventures is that neither of the partners exercises exclusive control over operations. Decisions are taken jointly. The

appeal of joint ventures for developing countries lies in this attribute.

The number of technical collaboration agreements between Indian and foreign firms has risen substantially since 1956. A total number of 3,557 collaboration agreements was approved by the Government of India over the period 1948–70. Of those, only 366 agreements were approved between the years 1948–56 (Table 20.3). Over the period 1957–63 more than 1,700 collaboration agreements were approved, but only 246 of these involved foreign financial participation.[9] Thus, though joint ventures involving foreign capital participation have occurred, pure technical collaboration agreements have been the most important form of participation. Further, even in cases where foreign financial participation is involved, not all the agreements involve inflows of capital from abroad. The equity held by foreigners may merely represent an allotment by Indian firms, of a part of their equity to foreign firms, in lieu of royalty and technical-fee payments to be made for imports of technology, or in addition to such payments.

Collaboration agreements have also been heavily concentrated in technologically intensive fields of manufacturing activity. Table 20.5 shows the distribution of collaboration agreements by industry. Electrical machinery, nonelectrical machinery and machine tools, transport equipment, and chemicals accounted for more than 50 per cent of the agreements approved during 1957–70.

The foregoing has summarised the salient features of foreign enterprise participation in the Indian economy. The analytical issues of importance are the factors which influence the patterns of foreign-enterprise participation in India, and their impact on the economy.

Determinants of Foreign Enterprise Participation in India
As shown in the previous section, much of the foreign private investment in India in recent years is in the manufacturing sector. Export-oriented investment, mainly in plantations and mining, has declined appreciably. Such investment tends to be highly mobile, responding to

Table 20.5. Technical Collaboration Agreements Classified by Industry, 1957–70

	1957	1958	1959	1960	1961	1962	1963	1964	1965	1966	1967	1968	1969	Jan. to Dec. 1970	Total 1957 to Dec. 1970
1. Electrical Equipment, Apparatus, Components, etc.	4	6	9	46	69	63	52	35	22	21	24	16	16	21	404
2. Industrial Machinery (other than textile machinery)	6	3	8	34	47	29	40	68	40	44	19	25	32	43	433
3. Machine Tools & Accessories	—	4	6	26	35	17	26	33	14	19	21	15	3	12	231
4. Transport Equipment	5	7	13	38	23	26	24	26	7	12	11	4	6	14	261
5. Basic Chemicals	7	8	18	25	37	4	4	26	14	10	11	7	4	4	179
6. Chemical Products	3	2	9	8	13	38	24	25	20	5	12	5	7	10	181
7. Heavy Electrical Equipment (Generation and Distribution)	7	6	4	35	27	—	2	20	10	8	13	10	4	5	151
8. Iron & Steel Products	2	5	11	25	17	12	13	21	9	12	2	7	2	6	124
9. Instruments	—	1	1	19	9	12	21	20	17	7	8	—	7	1	124
10. Textile Machinery	1	1	4	15	15	4	5	15	18	10	1	7	3	6	105
11. Materials Handling & Construction Equipment	1	1	4	18	19	4	4	13	8	8	9	3	7	5	104
12. Castings & Forgings	1	8	1	9	10	5	12	27	5	6	1	1	1	—	79
13. Drugs & Pharmaceuticals	4	4	4	11	7	9	6	6	5	3	5	5	3	3	77
14. Ceramic & Glassware	2	3	2	10	11	10	5	8	3	4	—	2	3	2	65
15. Paper & Paper Products	2	—	—	9	10	5	5	4	5	2	1	2	1	1	49
16. Metal & Metal Products	2	1	1	3	6	6	8	5	1	1	5	2	2	4	47
17. Technical Consultancy	—	2	1	—	6	5	9	6	1	1	4	2	2	5	38
18. Agricultural Machinery & Implements	1	—	3	4	2	3	2	3	2	2	2	4	9	4	42
19. Fertilizers	—	—	—	—	2	1	1	—	3	3	3	1	—	1	12
20. Pesticides	1	2	2	1	1	—	—	—	—	—	—	2	—	—	12
21. Others	32	42	49	44	43	43	37	47	38	23	32	11	25	36	500
Total	81	103	150	380	403	298	298	403	242	202	182	135	135	183	3191

changes in competitive conditions and the host governments' policies and attitudes towards foreign private investment. The decline in the share of plantations in total investment in India is not only to be explained by the increasing attractiveness of the manufacturing sector, but also by the emergence of East African countries as a profitable outlet for investment in plantations. In fact much of the increase in the absolute value of investments in the Indian plantation sector has been due to a revaluation of the existing assets.

An obvious reason for the increasing importance of the manufacturing sector is the prevalence of profitable domestic markets for manufacturing goods. The policy of import-substituting industrialization much in vogue in the sixties afforded highly profitable markets behind the tariff walls. India's official policy towards foreign private capital emphasising investment in technologically-intensive industries may have also contributed significantly to the prevailing pattern of investment. Within the manufacturing sector, technologically-intensive industries like chemicals, metal products, machinery, and transport equipment have gained in importance at the expense of less technologically-intensive fields like beverages and tobacco, food products and textiles. The industries in which foreign investment has been expanding are in general oriented towards the home market rather than towards exports.

This pattern of investment is broadly in agreement with the exploitation of the monopoly-over-advantages theory of direct investment outlined earlier. Although more detailed data are needed to establish this proposition firmly, some stray evidence can be listed to support it. In a study sponsored by the OECD, Grant L. Reuber reports on a sample of 13 foreign private investment projects in India.[10] Of these 13 projects, 6 are classified as market-development type of investment, 2 as export-oriented and the remaining 5 as government-initiated. Market-development investments are characterized by their home-market bias, their responsiveness to the size and long-run potential of the home market, and they are mostly initiated by foreign firms. Moreover they are based on long-run considerations and

in many cases they may be unprofitable in the short run. In other words, they conform to the type of investment termed defensive investment. The fact that more than 50 per cent of the projects in Reuber's sample were of the market development type does not necessarily reflect anything about the whole population of foreign investment projects in India. It is, however, revealing that five of the six market-development projects were expansions of existing investment. In contrast, both the export-oriented investments were new or "greenfields" operations and of the five government-initiated investments three were greenfield operations. This suggests the long-run nature of the market-development type of investment and their responsiveness to the profitability of domestic markets. It may also be noted here that more than 50 per cent of the technical collaboration agreements were also concentrated in technologically intensive fields of manufacturing activity like electrical machinery, nonelectrical machinery, chemicals, and transport equipment. This significant trend towards domestic-market oriented investment has important policy implications. The host country may have a stronger bargaining power in its relationship with foreign investors seeking a foothold in its expanding markets.

It was noted in the previous section that although significant changes in the composition and organization of foreign direct investment have occurred, neither the total stock of direct investment nor fresh inflows of capital into India have been very high compared to some of the other Asian countries. This shows that the existence of profitable markets alone may not be enough to attract foreign capital. The "climate for foreign investment" that prevails in the country may be more important than profitable markets resulting from protectionist policies. By "climate for foreign investment" is meant the tax policies enunciated by the Government, its strictures regarding employment of local nations by foreign firms, its ability to provide social overheads, its policy on repatriation of profits, the assurances it gives regarding compensation in case of nationalization and its attitude towards private enterprise in general. The Indian policy statements, though not lacking in incentives for private foreign capital, display an ambivalent attitude towards it. Assurances regarding repatriation of profits and compensation in case of nationalization and tax incentives are offered. But the protracted negotiations which the policy of judging each case on its merits involves, the insistence that majority ownership of capital should rest in Indian hands, and the stipulations regarding employment of local nationals may have discouraged foreign investors. Further stipulations barring the entry of foreign firms into consumer goods industries may also have acted as a factor inhibiting capital inflows. The logic of barring entry of foreign capital into such industries is questionable. As Bhagwati and Desai argue, "if a foreign investor buys up a restaurant, this will bring into the economy foreign exchange which can be used to import 'essential' machinery. To argue, therefore, that foreign investment should be excluded from the restaurant industry is just a simple and widespread fallacy".[11]

It does not, however, follow that all regulation of foreign investment was ill-conceived. As shown in the earlier section, there is a need for policies to curb the adverse effects of foreign investment. Regulation of foreign investment in the interests of guarding the balance of payments position of the country and protecting small-scale domestic entrepreneurs against competition from large international firms may have been necessary. Demarcating the sectors of foreign-capital participation and the insistence on the need for foreign firms to contribute to the exchange earnings of the country may be justified. But it is the policy of judging each case on its merits, involving protracted negotiations and the expenditure of managerial time and resources by prospective investors, that is questionable.

Benefits and Costs of Foreign Enterprise Participation. There exist a number of a priori arguments for and against foreign-enterprise participation. But the nature of the subject precludes definite generalization and precise quantitative estimates. Apart from the fact that the issue is clouded by political considerations, it may be impossible to quantify all the direct and indirect effects of FPI. In what follows we will analyse some of the issues in the light of the available empirical evidence on foreign enterprise participation in India.

A major cause of concern with imports of private foreign capital and technology is its effect on the balance of payments of the country. The argument that it adversely affects the balance of payments of the host country is usually supported by data to show that outflows in the form of dividends, profits, royalty, and technical-fee payments exceed the inflows of private capital. Table 20.6 shows the data for India on net inflows of capital (including reinvested earnings) on account of direct investment and outflows of income for selected years. The outflows for each year have in fact been in excess of the inflows. Further, payments for imported knowhow in the form of royalties and technical fees also show a rapid increase, and indeed they have grown much faster than dividend payments on direct investment (Table 20.6).

It may, however, be erroneous to conclude, on the basis of the above data, that imports of foreign capital and technology have resulted in a net foreign-exchange loss to the country. The inflow-outflow comparison is too partial in its approach to the issue. It neglects all the direct and indirect export-generating and import-saving effects of foreign investment, and ignores the externalities resulting from foreign investment. More generally it ought to be recognized that the balance of payments is a general equilibrium phenomenon. In other words, the problem of balance of payments is an integral part of the total economy. Any positive contribution to the total productivity of the economy pari passu improves the balance of payments in the absence of diseconomies and other distortions. Insofar as each act of investment has been productive and contributes to total national income, the problem of servicing the foreign debt is taken care of.[12]

It is the net change in real income resulting from the introduction of a foreign private investment project that determines its balance of payments effects. It is conceivable that an FPI project may draw

Table 20.6. Net Inflows of Private Foreign Capital, Outflows of Income
on Account of Foreign Collaboration

(Million Rs.)

Year	Inflows on a/c of Direct Investment	Total Private Capital Inflows	Outflows of Investment Income	Dividend Payments	Royalty and Technical Fee Payments
1965	219.0	649.0	1343.0	194.0	101.6
1966	216.0	1719.0	2039.0	288.0	142.4
1967	248.0	1008.0	2306.0	267.0	133.3
1968	253.0	649.0	2397.0	269.0	162.2
1970	340.0	407.0	2742.0	NA	NA
1971	431.0	536.0	262.0	NA	NA

SOURCE: *Reserve Bank of India Bulletin*, June 1974, pp. 1056–57.

resources from other sectors in the economy, causing a reduction in output and employment in these sectors. If these sectors had been contributing to foreign exchange earnings it might result in a reduction in the exchange earnings of the country. The FPI project replacing the domestic project may contribute to exchange earnings. But as Paul Streeten points out, the economics of FPI are not the same as the economics of domestic investment. Money crosses the exchanges in the case of FPI, but not in the case of domestic investment.[13] Dividends and royalties have to be remitted in foreign exchange in the case of the FPI project.

It is thus important to assess the productivity of the FPI project relative to the alternatives to it. In other words, the opportunity cost of the resources employed in the FPI project needs to be taken into account in assessing its balance of payments position. This is the so-called "alternative position" assumption that figures in the literature on the balance of effects of FPI. The empirical estimates would be sensitive to the assumptions made regarding the alternative position; i.e., if the assumption is made that there is no alternative to the FPI project and it is an addition to the existing investment in the economy, it is likely that the balance of payments effects would be positive. But if an alternative exists in the form of a domestically financed project or an opportunity to import the product, the opportunity costs of having the FPI project in terms of its alternative need to be assessed.

One method of assessing the balance of payments effects of FPI, taking the above factors into account, is provided by the well-known Little-Mirrlees (LM) approach to social benefit-cost analysis of industrial projects.[14] The LM method of evaluating the benefits and costs of a project implicitly takes into account its balance of payments effects. In the LM approach, all material inputs and outputs of projects are evaluated in terms of foreign exchange. In other words, the price imputed to the inputs and outputs would be the c.i.f. price of imports, or f.o.b. price of exports, depending on whether the inputs and outputs are importables or exportables. The justification for such a procedure is that international prices are supposed to represent, through trade and balance of payments, the true social-opportunity costs of inputs and outputs in production. But what if some goods are nontradeables? The procedure in these cases is to iteratively break down the nontradeables into their traded and nontraded inputs until one is left only with the traded goods and labour. All trades components of the nontradeables are then valued on their foreign exchange terms as suggested.

How is labour to be valued? In the LM method it is to be valued at its shadow wage rate, meaning its opportunity cost, or marginal product in an alternative project. This marginal product is again to be valued in terms of foreign exchange. This will be the employment effect of the project on the balance of payments. In addition, employment of labour in the project may also have a consumption effect on the balance of payments. Increased employment may result in increased consumption and worsen the balance of payments. In this case, the increased value of consumption in foreign exchange terms has to be deducted from the value added of the project in arriving at its balance of payments effect.

The balance of payments effects of the project are thus the value-added of the project (already estimated in foreign exchange) minus the consumption effects of the labour employed in the project. In other words, it is the net savings resulting from the project expressed in foreign exchange that gives the balance of payments effects. The foregoing account of the estimation procedures, however, relates to any project, be it foreign or domestic. Also we need a criterion to choose between projects competing for limited investment funds. The index used to judge whether to accept a particular project is the one normally used in investment appraisal—the net present value criterion, or alternatively the internal rate of return criterion. In the former case the time streams of the net benefits accruing from the project over its life are discounted back to the present. The discount rate to be used in so doing is to be based on the social opportunity cost of capital to the economy. If the resulting present value of the benefits of the project is positive, the project is to be accepted. The internal rate of return is nothing but the "yield" of the project. By definition, it is the rate of return or the discount rate that makes the present value of the benefit streams zero. If the internal rate of return of the project is greater than the social opportunity cost of capital, the project is to be accepted. Now if we need to compare an FPI project with a domestic one, all that needs to be done is add or subtract all the foreign financing flows resulting from the FPI project in estimating the benefits and costs outlined above. These flows relate to foreign exchange inflows accompanying FPI, and outflows due to dividends and royalty payments. The criterion for accepting an FPI project is then the internal rate of return. If the internal rate of return is higher for the FPI project than that of a domestic project, it is to be accepted.

(Assuming that both internal rates of return are higher than the relevant social discount rate or the social opportunity cost of capital to the economy).

The LM method, though it has its limitations, is a major step in evaluating the efficiency and implicitly of the balance of payments effects of FPI projects. That this method is operational is evidenced by a number of case studies that have employed it. One such study is that of Deepak Lal for four chemical projects in India.[15] Lal has estimated the internal rate of return for four chemical projects involving both foreign financial, and technical collaboration. These projects are in effect in the nature of joint ventures. The internal rate of return was calculated both at market prices and shadow prices as suggested by the LM method. As all four projects were new the "alternative position assumption" was that the only alternative to the project was importing the product. The social opportunity cost of capital in India was estimated to be around 6 per cent.

In general Lal's results show that the internal rate of return was higher than the social opportunity cost of capital only on the assumption that the government would continue to maintain its high tariffs on competing imports. Only one of the projects, manufacturing polyethelene products, was found to be profitable, with an internal rate of return in excess of 20 per cent, whatever the basis of the calculation. It was also found that externalities in the form of labour training were unimportant as all four projects were highly capital-intensive. The financial flows abroad associated with the projects are reported to have little effect on the evaluation of the projects examined. Thus, in general the projects appear to be "socially efficient" only in the presence of high tariffs. The issue then is whether the country wouldn't have been better off importing the product on a strict criterion of efficiency. But it could be argued that the government's tariff policy has other aims besides its effect on the efficiency of the projects under consideration. As these are relatively new projects, it could be argued on infant industry grounds that they are likely to become efficient in the future, even at international prices. Further, as Lal argues, there may not be any alternative to FPI in high-technology industries like chemicals if the establishment of such industries is deemed essential.

Other case studies of the balance of payments effects of FPI made under the auspices of UNCTAD have not been able to arrive at any conclusive results. It was found that in the case of 159 firms operating in India, Iran, Jamaica, Kenya, Malaysia and Colombia, 55 per cent were found to have a positive impact on the balance of payments. However, 60 per cent of the firms fell around the demarcation line between positive and negative impact, and only 21 per cent showed clearly positive, and 11 per cent a clearly negative impact.[16] The results were sensitive to the alternative-position assumption made.

The foregoing review of the empirical evidence available indicates that generalizations regarding the effects of FPI could be highly misleading. Obviously there is a need for more case studies of the sort conducted by Lal and UNCTAD.

Capital-intensity of FPI and Effects on Employment

An often-voiced criticism of FPI relates to the capital-intensity of the operations of foreign firms and the wage policies they pursue. Foreign firms transplant techniques perfected abroad. These are techniques designed for capital-rich and labour-poor economies and are ill-suited to capital-poor and labour-rich developing countries. In addition, FPI is likely to endanger employment opportunities in other sectors of the economy which may tend to imitate such techniques. Such imitation may be due to a xenophilic preference for foreign technology, or the compulsion felt by local firms to adapt such techniques in order to survive in a competitive milieu. Foreign firms also generally tend to pay relatively high wage-rates. Such a wage policy may be dictated both by a need for skilled labour and by a desire to appease local, national and trade union sentiments against their operations. But such a wage policy may push up wage rates in the economy as a whole, forcing domestic firms to substitute capital for labour. All this

tends to militate against employment creation in the economy.

A recent study shows that foreign firms operating in Indian industry are in general more capital-intensive in their operations than their Indian counterparts. It is reported that in the case of 22 out of a sample of 34 industries, foreign firms were more capital-intensive than domestic firms. The ratios of average productive capital per employee in foreign firms to that of domestic firms in the 22 industries varied between 100.6 and 402.8 per cent. An alternative measure of capital-intensity is the average value added per employee. This measure takes into account the flow of the contribution of capital as a factor of production to the production process and not its depreciated book value. On this measure also, foreign firms were found to be more capital-intensive. The average value added per employee in foreign firms was seen to exceed that of domestic firms in the case of 31 industries out of a sample of 34 industries. The variation in the ratio of average value added per employee of the foreign to domestic firms was around 103 to 397 per cent.[17] The experience of Indian firms wiih technical collaboration agreements with foreign firms has been similar. It is found that in general, Indian firms with technical collaboration agreements are more capital-intensive in their operations than Indian firms with no such foreign technical connections.[18] Further, the proposition that foreign firms tend to pay higher wage rates and salaries than domestic firms is also borne out by the evidence in the studies cited here.

Empirical evidence thus strongly supports the criticism that foreign firms tend to be relatively capital-intensive. It is, however, necessary to distinguish between the capital-intensity stemming from the "foreignness" of FPI, and that stemming from the trade, resource allocation, and financial policies of the developing countries. To an extent the capital-intensity of foreign firms is due to their "foreignness". As the Development Assistance Committee of the OECD puts it, for most foreign investors the path of least resistance lies in duplicating developed-country systems of manufacture or construction, the result of decades of innovation so as to substitute more and more intricate, automatic and hard-to-maintain capital equipment for increasingly expensive labour.[19] The foreign firms' reluctance to experiment with technologies and products appropriate to the factor endowments, income levels and local conditions of the developing countries may be entirely rational on economic grounds. It is less expensive to transfer a tested technique than invest in a new one.

To the extent that the higher capital-intensity of FPI is due to the "foreignness" of FPI there may not be much that developing countries can do about it, except invest in R & D to restructure and adapt the imported technology to local conditions. But there is much that they can do in the area of trade and resource allocation to alleviate the problem of capital-intensity of foreign firms. Most developing countries, including India, with their enthusiasm for industrialization have encouraged foreign firms to invest in capital-intensive activities. Many of the incentives offered to foreign investors by developing countries encourage capital-intensive operations by artificially reducing the cost of capital. Generous depreciation allowances, lower tax rates for designated industries, tax holidays for new and "priority" industries and concessionary tariff rates on imports of machinery and equipment, are some of the incentives that encourage capital-intensive operations. In India all companies pay a corporate income tax at 65 per cent, except those with a substantial public interest (i.e., government and general-public share holdings) which pay at the rate of 55 per cent. In addition, dividends remitted are taxed at 24.5 per cent and a surtax on corporate profits in excess of 10 per cent of capital employed is also levied. But these basic tax rates are reduced by a number of concessions. For newly-established firms a tax holiday of five years is provided, during which time no tax is paid on profits up to 6 per cent of capital employed, and there is no tax on dividends paid out of these profits. There is also a development rebate of 20 per cent on new plant and equipment.[20]

Apart from these tax incentives the imperfections in the capital market contribute significantly to the relative capital-intensity of foreign firms. It is now a well-established fact that in most developing countries factor prices do not reflect their underlying factor endowments. The market rate of interest is often artificially low relative to the wage rate, despite the fact that most developing countries are labour-rich and capital-poor. This fact, however, should influence both domestic and foreign firms to substitute capital for labour. But in addition foreign firms find themselves better placed to borrow than domestic firms. They have access to both the host country and their parent country capital markets. Further, even in the host-country capital markets they have better credit-worthiness than domestic firms. This is found to be so in the Indian capital market.[21] These imperfections reduce the effective rate of interest for foreign firms. In addition, the overvalued exchange rates maintained by most developing countries also favour the importation of capital-equipment. All this in essence amounts to granting a subsidy on the use of capital to foreign firms. On the one hand such policies may have encouraged capital deepening in what are already capital-intensive industries, and on the other hand they may have directed FPI towards capital-intensive types of activity. Developing countries may be able to alleviate this problem by subsidising the employment of labour instead of capital, and encouraging FPI into labour-intensive sectors of activity.

Over-import of Technology The rapid increase in the number of Indo-foreign technical collaboration agreements has posed a number of highly debatable issues. Has India imported too much and the wrong kind of technology? Are technical collaboration agreements a viable alternative to FPI? On the basis of available information it is difficult to assess whether or not over-imports of technology have occurred. In the early years, a number of agreements were approved in "inessential" consumer goods industries like toys, footwear, ink, toothpaste. But the number of agreements is a poor guide to the extent and nature of the assistance offered. Further, as Bhagwati and Desai point out, the argument is better made against the very establishment of these industries than in arguing that imports of technology should not be allowed into these industries.[22]

It is difficult to arrive at any settled conclusions on the contribution of technical collaboration agreements to the productivity of Indian industry. The quality and extent of technology imported under the agreements is not amenable to quantification. Moreover, detailed information on the terms and conditions under which technology has been imported is also not available. The available evidence on the issue is confined to interfirm efficiency comparisons. The productive performance of firms operating with foreign technology is compared to that of firms operating without the benefit of such technology in various industry groups. The limitations of this sort of exercise are well known. The firms being compared, though belonging to the same industry group, may not be producing similar products. The number of technical collaboration agreements a firm has contracted may be a poor proxy for the amount of technology it has imported.[23] Despite such limitations, the only available empirical evidence on the impact of technical collaboration evidence relates to interfirm efficiency comparisons. Various indicators of productive efficiency of firms such as labour productivity, capital productivity and total factor productivity have been estimated for a sample of firms operating with and without imported technology in different industry groups. The results vary as between industries. In some industries like electrical goods, basic industrial, chemical, and pharmaceuticals, the performance of firms operating with borrowed technology was found to be better than that of Indian firms operating without such technology. In some industry groups it was the foreign subsidiaries (FPI firms) which had the best performance. But the total factor productivity index for purely Indian firms was not far below that of foreign firms or Indian firms operating with borrowed technology. Moreover, during the period 1964–65 to 1969–70 the purely Indian firms registered a consid-

erable improvement in the index of total factor productivity, and the increase was much higher than that of other firms.[24] Although no broad generalizations are possible on the basis of these results, it is indicative that foreign collaboration does not always result in better utilization of factors of production and increased productivity.

It is indeed open to question whether technical collaboration agreements are a viable mechanism for transfers of technology.

The success of these agreements as transfer mechanisms depends on the will to transfer on the part of foreign firms, and the local firms' ability to assimilate and utilize the borrowed technology. The extent of knowledge transferred may depend on the degree of lender involvement through asset ownership and managerial control. Technical collaboration agreements are by definition bereft of foreign participation and control. The knowledge transferred under these agreements may not be very extensive. In the Indian case, much of the knowledge transferred under the technical collaboration agreements has been limited to the loan of blueprints, drawings, designs, process charts, flow sheets, etc. The technical involvement of foreign firms was much higher in the case of joint ventures involving foreign financial participation. It included the training of Indian engineers and managers abroad, assistance in plant construction, and help in procuring raw materials and marketing the product.[25]

The success of a technical transplant also depends on the knowledge-importing firm's ability to absorb the knowledge. The effective utilization of imported knowledge depends on the ability of local firms to restructure and adapt the imported knowledge to suit local conditions, and the availability of local sources of supply for components which meet the specifications and standards required by the foreign technology. The often-cited success story of Japanese industry in the field of technology-imports illustrates the significance of these factors.[26] The distinguishing characteristic of Japanese industry has been its ability to restructure and adapt imported knowledge by means of indigenous research efforts. The presence of a well-integrated sector of small subcontractors that could produce components to prescribed engineering standards and under tight production schedules also explains the success story of Japan. These basic elements are yet to take shape in India. Paradoxically enough, the success of technical collaboration agreements seems to call for the very skills and abilities which many of the less-developed countries lack. The foreign firms entering into technical collaboration agreements may have been of very little assistance in restructuring their knowledge to suit local conditions. In the Indian case it was found that such assistance, if it had occurred at all, was mostly in the case of joint ventures.[27]

Further, there is the issue of the control exercised by foreign firms. Theoretically, foreign firms cannot be expected to exercise control over operations when their involvement is confined to technical assistance. However, in practice they may be able to stipulate various restrictive clauses in agreements which enable them to exercise a certain degree of effective control over operations. These restrictive clauses relate to exports, sources of supply of raw materials, production standards, and minimum royalty payments. Table 20.7 summarises the data on restrictive clauses stipulated by foreign firms in the case of Indo-foreign collaboration agreements. The data relate to a sample of 1951 agreements surveyed by the Reserve Bank of India. The agreements are classified according to (a) foreign technical collaboration agreements entered into by foreign subsidiaries in India with their parent firms; (b) agreements involving both foreign technical and financial participation; and (c) purely technical collaboration agreements contracted by Indian firms.

Restrictions relating to exports are the most important. Total prohibition of exports is in a minority, while area restrictions, stipulating the countries to which Indian firms may or may not export, obtained in more than 53 per cent of the agreements surveyed. Of the other types of restriction the most important one

Table 20.7.   Restrictive Clauses in Indo-foreign Technical Collaboration Agreements

Type of Restriction	Number of Agreements with Restrictive Clauses			
	Subsidiaries	Minority Foreign Equity Participation	Pure Technical Collaboration	Total
1. Export restrictions:	56	230	169	455
(a) Total prohibition of exports	3	15	18	36
(b) Area restrictions	19	118	202	239
(c) Permission of collaborators needed	32	80	37	149
2. Sources of supply of materials and equipment	14	46	94	154
3. Restrictions on production pattern	2	36	27	65
4. Payment of minimum royalty	1	14	40	55
5. Restrictions on sales procedure	6	7	5	18
6. Others	1	1	1	3
TOTAL NUMBER OF AGREEMENTS WITH RESTRICTIONS	63	251	213	327
TOTAL NUMBER OF AGREEMENTS	144	445	462	1051

SOURCE: Reserve Bank of India, *Foreign Collaboration in Indian Industry—A Survey Report*, Bombay, p. 106.

relates to sources of supply. Nearly 30 per cent of the agreements surveyed by the Bank were of this type. Further, pure technical collaboration agreements involving no foreign financial participation accounted for a majority of the agreements with such restrictions. Export restriction clauses are a device by which foreign firms attempt to guard the markets for their own products, or for the sales of firms in foreign countries to whom they may have sold licences. Such restrictions may, therefore, not only be necessary to shelter their own markets from Indian competition but also to preserve their market for technology. Foreign firms may permit exports to certain countries whose markets they find difficult to service. Thus, such export restrictions are in the nature of a market-sharing device. They are, however, a control device to the extent they can influence future market prospects for India. Restrictions on sources of supply of raw materials and components may not only tie Indian firms to a particular source of supply but also enable foreign firms to charge a mark-up on the plant and equipment they supply. Such mark-ups may provide the foreign firm with an additional avenue of returns, especially when the Government has imposed a ceiling on the rates of royalty to be paid.

It is difficult to assess whether or not the growth in technical collaboration agreements has resulted in widespread technological gains to the economy. A study on foreign investment and technology by the National Council of Applied Economic Research has concluded that "imported technology has been widely diffused in the economy... imports of technology and associated equipment have played an important role in industrial expansion as well as in the prevention of monopolistic conditions".[28] On the other hand, Michael Kidron, in his study on foreign investments in India, states that imported skills do not permeate the economy to any great extent.[29] The conclusion of the National Council Study is based on a comprehensive examination of the distribution of collaboration agreements and royalties paid on imported knowhow by different industrial

groups and different size classes of firms in Indian industry. Michael Kidron's conclusion is based on casual observation and case studies. As argued earlier, the number of agreements approved in different industrial groups does not provide a satisfactory guide to the nature and extent of the technology imported, the terms and conditions on which it is imported, and its effective utilization. Similarly, casual observation and stray case studies may not provide enough evidence to pass judgement on the role of technical collaboration agreements. However, an examination of the nature and characteristics of these agreements does raise a more general issue. Are such agreements which are of an arm's length nature, preferable to direct foreign investment? It can be argued that in view of the many limitations that beset these agreements, they may not be a very effective mechanism for transferring technical knowhow to countries at an intermediate stage of development, such as India. They may be more suited to relatively developed economies like Japan which have the requisite skills and resources to restructure and utilize the imported knowhow. Furthermore, these agreements also pose problems of regulation and control. It is, therefore, possible that direct investment with more lender involvement through asset ownership, and joint ventures involving foreign financial participation, may be a preferable mechanism for importing foreign skills and knowhow. This conclusion is, however, predicated on the assumption that the host countries undertake measures to enlarge effective competition in their own economies and judiciously regulate the sectoral distribution of foreign-capital participation. This is not to say that technical collaboration agreements should be discarded altogether. The need to accelerate development being paramount, none of the means available to do so can be dismissed. They can be effectively utilized if domestic research and development efforts are directed towards improving the absorptive capacity of the economy. Such agreements may be eminently suitable in the case of sectors and industries which are capable of restructuring and assimilating imported knowhow.

Conclusions

Foreign private investment is perhaps the most sensitive and challenging issue in the field of development economics. The foregoing review shows its complex ramifications. It is impossible to state whether or not India has benefited from the import of technology and capital. Individual cases of FPI may have ranged from the enormously beneficial to the disastrous. The case studies cited in this paper and the available evidence on FPI and technical collaboration agreements have important policy implications. FPI has been attracted to Indian manufacture industries with profitable domestic markets. This has been more often than not due to the governments' tariff policies, which strengthens the Government's bargaining power for better terms and conditions. This is not to say that the regulations regarding areas of participation, wage policies, and dividend remittances need to be stiffened. But the country may be in a better position to transfer incomes from foreign firms to the domestic economy by fiscal means. In fact there may be a case for improving the "climate for foreign investment" with a view to attracting such investment, and transferring the maximum possible income from foreign firms to the domestic economy.

India's experience with technical collaboration agreements appears not to have been very happy. But there is no reason for discarding them entirely. The need is for efforts directed at increasing the absorptive capacity of the economy. In general, attraction and effective utilization of foreign capital and technology calls for a more effective policy framework and institutional change. It cannot be denied that foreign enterprise participation with its wide political and economic ramifications calls for effective regulation by the recipient countries. But regulations should not amount to crippling restrictions and unnecessary bureaucratic interference. In fine, foreign private investment poses a challenge to economic analysis and economic management. As is so often argued, effective regulation of multinational enterprises, the recent manifestation of foreign private investment, may be beyond the ability of any one single developing country. Trite as it may sound, international action is needed to effectively regulate the activities of multinational firms. The most important areas in which such action is necessary relate to the practice of transfer pricing by foreign firms, provision of information to developing countries on sources of technology, and assistance in the area of taxation.

REFERENCES

1. J.H. Dunning, *Studies in International Investment* (London: George Allen and Unwin, 1970), p. 2.
2. See C. P. Kindleberger, *American Business Abroad* (Yale University Press, 1969).
3. R.E. Caves, "International Corporations: The Industrial Economics of Foreign Investment", *Economic*, vol. 38, February 1971.
4. Michael Kidron, *Foreign Investment In India* (London: Oxford University Press, 1965).
5. Grant L. Reuber, *Foreign Private Investment in Development* (London, Oxford: Clarendon Press, 1973) p. 293.
6. A.I. MacBean and V.N. Balasubramanyam, *Benefit-Cost Analysis of Foreign Direct Investment with Special Reference to Asia* (Unpublished study).
7. J.S. Fforde, *International Trade in Management Skills* (Oxford: Blackwell, 1957).
8. J.W. C. Tomlinson, *The Joint Venture Process in International Business: India and Pakistan* (Harvard: M.I.T. Press, 1970).
9. Kidron, *Foreign Investment in India*, p. 260.
10. G.L. Reuber, *Foreign Private Investment.*
11. J.N. Bhagwati and P. Desai, *India: Planning for Industrialisation* (London: Oxford University Press, 1970), p. 224.
12. For a lucid discussion of this point see C.P. Kindleberger, *American Business Abroad* (Yale University Press, 1969).
13. P. Streeten, "New Approaches to Private Overseas Investment" in P. Ady (ed.), *Private Foreign Investment and the Developing World* (New York: Praeger, 1971).
14. The essential features of the LM approach sketched here is from A. I. MacBean and V.N. Balasubramanyam, *Meeting the Third World Challenge* (London: Macmillan, 1976), Ch. 8. For detailed discussion see Deepak Lal, *Appraising Foreign Investment in Developing Countries* (London: Heinemann, 1975).
15. For a detailed discussion of the methodology and estimates see Lal, *Appraising Foreign Investment*, pp. 95–144.

16. P. Streeten and D. Lal, *Main Findings of a Study of Private Foreign Investment in Selected Developing Countries* (New York: UNCTAD, 1973).

17. J.P. Agarwal, "Factor Proportions in Foreign and Domestic Firms in Indian Manufacturing", *Economic Journal,* vol. 86, September 1976, pp. 589–94.

18. V.N. Balasubramanyam, *International Transfer of Technology to India* (New York: Praeger, 1973).

19. "Development Assistance", 1970 *Review* (Paris: OECD, 1970), p. 17.

20. This information on Indian tax policy is taken from Lal, *Appraising Foreign Investment*, pp. 104–105.

21. J.P. Agarwal: "Factor Proportions in Indian Manufacturing", p. 592.

22. Bhagwati and Desai, *India: Planning for Industrialization*, p. 226.

23. For a discussion of the methodology and limitations of inter-firm efficiency comparison see Balasubramanyam, *International Transfer of Technology to India.*

24. "Survey of Foreign Financial and Technical Collaboration in Indian Industry 1964–70: Main Findings", *Reserve Bank of India Bulletin,* June 1974.

25. Balasubramanyam, *International Transfer of Technical Knowledge to India.*

26. See T. Ozawa, "Imitation, Innovation and Japanese Exports", in P.B. Kenen Lawrence (ed.), *Open Economy* (New York: Columbia University Press, 1968.)

27. Balasubramanyam, *International Transfer of Technical Knowledge to India.*

28. National Council of Applied Economic Research, *Foreign Technology and Investment —A Study of their Role in India Industrialization* (New Delhi, 1971), p. 17.

29. Michael Kidron, *Foreign Investment in India.* p. 303.

21

Economic Integration in South Asia

PREM P. GANDHI

Events have moved so swiftly on the Indian subcontinent since 1970 that they may have marked the end of the old geopolitical life of that region. Though it is too early to discern the full impact of the chain of events that started at the close of 1970, yet one can with some certainty note some of these changes. The creation of Bangladesh has written a new political equation in the area. The Simla Accord signed by India and Pakistan in 1972 visualizes the peaceful settlement of all political problems between them and suggests the possibility of increasing trade and economic cooperation. The three countries involved in the conflict of 1971 have resolved the problems of exchanging POW's, the return of refugees from India to Bangladesh, repatriation of political detainees in all three countries, and the eventual recognition of Bangladesh by Pakistan. Moreover, there have been exceedingly encouraging signs of economic cooperation between India and Pakistan, involving the resumption of postal and telegraphic communications, the signing of shipping protocol dealing with the resump-

tion of those services, trade agreements incorporating banking facilities and, most important of all, the Indo-Pakistan Cotton Agreement that comes closest to a regional market between them. At the same time, India and Bangladesh have establishd a Joint River Commission to regulate water supplies and to control floods in rivers flowing between these countries, and the Jute Agreement regarding the production and exchange of jute. This list of accomplishments is not exhaustive, nor does it suggest the effective long-term success of these measures, yet the fact that these countries have resolved these problems on their own (without any visible outside pressure from the world powers), is itself a major accomplishment that holds much promise. These measures have laid the political foundations and structure of cooperation that, if properly utilized, can lead to economic regionalism, which can prove to be very beneficial to these countries as well as to the countries around them, e.g., Nepal, Burma, Sri Lanka and Malaysia, in their fight against poverty and economic backwardness.

The increased strength of India on the subcontinent may have made the possibility of integration more difficult by causing uneasiness among its neighbours. It may also have revived old political frictions. The predominance of the Indian economy causes nervousness and suspicion about its objectives in any regional integration plan. At the same time, though the type or extent of integration is by no means defined or clearly appreciated in India, its attitude towards regionalism has been ambivalent: it has enthusiastically supported economic cooperation in the South Asian regions and Asia as a whole, while rejecting any stronger regional grouping. There have been a number of regional and international schemes of economic cooperation in which India and the other regional countries have been active members, e.g., the Asian Coconut Community, the Asian Pepper Community, the Asian Tea Community, the Asian Clearing Union, the Tripartite Agreement, RCD. Yet the discussion on economic integration in India as elsewhere in the region has remained at a very rudimentary level. This paper proposes to push this discussion by surveying the economic justification of regionalism and its relevance to India and the South Asian region. The paper is accordingly divided into two major sections. The first section is concerned with the scope of economic integration and is mostly definitional, to lay out the broad outlines of regionalism. The second section concentrates on the exploration of various techniques of integration as they relate to the developing countries and the South Asian countries in particular, and the benefits that these countries can hope for.

I

Definition of Economic Integration

In surveying some of the interpretations given to economic integration, Balassa concludes that it is both a process as well as a state of affairs:

> Regarded as a process, it encompasses various measures abolishing discrimination between economic units belonging to different national states; viewed as a state of affairs, it can be represented by the absence of various forms

of discrimination between national economies.[1]

However, the mere abolition of discrimination may not be enough to achieve the optimum efficiency that underlies the justification for economic integration. In fact, Tinbergen distinguishes between negative and positive integration. Negative integration involves the abolition of a number of restrictive trade impediments and thus results in a better division of labour and specialization in the products most suited to the domestic conditions of the member countries. But it is positive integration that thrusts towards the kind of cooperation and coordination of national economic policies which make economic integration a more meaningful entity. Positive integration requires the creation of new institutions and their instruments, or the modification of existing instruments. In Tinbergen's definition, integration is the creation of the most desirable structure of international economy, removing artificial hindrances to optimal operation, and introducing deliberately all desirable elements of coordination or unification.[2] Economic integration par excellence of all countries would imply "one world" in political terms, going much beyond what the classical economists had either envisaged or advocated.

Economic integration should also be distinguished from economic cooperation. Though ECAFE (Economic Commission on Asia and Far East) and now ESCAP, have used the two interchangeably, the terms differ, both qualitatively and quantitatively. Economic cooperation is by far the looser version of the two. Economic integration, on the other hand, involves a substantial degree of formal commitment to removing economic barriers, and other quantitative restrictions in the way of economic interaction. The higher forms of economic integration may also involve some loss of national sovereignty through substantial governmental commitments in changing domestic economic policies. Such may not be the case in economic cooperation, though the distinction here becomes rather fine. In any event, as Ballassa notes, "distinguishing between cooperation and integration, we put the main characteristics of the latter—the abolition of discrimination within an area—in clearer focus, and it becomes possible to give the concept definite meaning without unnecessarily diluting it through the inclusion of diverse actions in the field of international cooperation".[3]

Types of Economic Integration

With this background, we can distinguish between a number of different types of economic integration involving various degrees of economic association and the resultant abrogation of national sovereignty. ECAFE lists the following types of economic integration schemes in descending order of political significance and degree of governmental commitment:

1. Economic union
2. Customs union
3. Free-trade union
4. Sectoral or partial integration
5. Preferential application of quantitative restrictions
6. Preferential applications of tariffs
7. Long-term trade contracts.[4]

These proposals for economic integration differ from each other not only in terms of the commitments, but also in the resultant benefits. Each succeeding scheme on the list is less formal than the previous one. Thus, the pros and cons of any given proposal would depend upon the participants' assessment of the relative economic, political, and social costs and benefits of regionalism.

At one extreme of the spectrum is economic union, which represents the complete economic integration of a group of countries. Under this scheme there is not only complete freedom of movement of goods and services, but also of the factors of production. Except for land labour, capital and entrepreneurship move unrestricted between the member countries in order to gain the maximum returns. Along with this unrestricted mobility, economic union necessitates the coordination and harmonization of national economic policies with the possibility of political integration. The best-known example is the European Economic Community, popularly called the Common Market,

comprising France, West Germany, Italy, The Netherlands, Belgium and Luxembourg, which the UK, Denmark. and Ireland have recently joined.

The customs union differs from the economic union in that integration is limited to the elimination of tariff barriers between the participating countries, with the establishment of common external tariffs against nonmembers. The Central American Common Market, when finally matured, may be one example of the customs union, another being the former Benelux.[5]

Free trade area differs from the first two in that it maintains national external tariffs against nonmembers while eliminating internal tariffs between member nations. In a way it implies the establishment of a common market in all the trade of the constituent territories while retaining the freedom of individual tariff preferences or arrangements with outsiders. The establishment of EFTA (European Free Trade Association) in 1959 and LAFTA (Latin American Free Trade Association) in 1960 are examples of such economic integration.[6]

Sectoral or partial integration implies the establishment of a common market only in one sector or industry like in the case of the European Coal and Steel Community in 1951 or the Free Trade Agreement between the USA and Canada in automobiles in 1965.

The fifth form of integration scheme is only concerned with the removal of quantitative restrictions such as quotas on the intermember trade, while retaining customs duties on such trade. Customs union, or free trade arrangement, implies the removal of all kinds of restrictions, both tariff and nontariff.

Preferential tariff arrangements as exemplified by the British Commonwealth countries, extend only to mutual tariff preferences. No reductions in tariff, nor any elimination of such tariffs on Commonwealth trade are implied. A margin of preference is given in favour of goods originating within Commonwealth countries as against those of outsiders.

The last scheme is only a form of bilateral trade contract arranged between two countries. Since it is the weakest of all such proposals, the results on economic integration are also the least. Such a proposal may be considered a scheme for economic cooperation rather than economic integration.

In other words, in the traditional western economic literature, as Balassa has noted from its lowest to its highest forms, integration has been said to progress through the freeing of barriers to trade (trade integration), the liberalization of factor movements (factor integration), the harmonization of national economic policy (policy integration) and the complete unification of these policies (total integration).[7]

However, this "stages" theory of integration has been criticised both for its dependence on the classical orthodoxy of international trade as well as for its irrelevance, particularly to present-day conditions in the developing and the centrally planned economies that are characterized by planning and state intervention in the markets. For example, according to Kitamura "the attempt to coordinate and harmonize national economic policies will be an important instrument even in the earlier stages of integration process..." as well as that "in certain circumstances... integration may be accomplished to a considerable extent without lifting the existing trade barriers".[8]

In the same vein Balassa mentions the distinction between "market integration" and "production-and-development integration" proposed by the Hungarian economist Imre Vajoda. Both these are techniques to trade integration. While "market integration" is "the guarantee of unhindered sale of each other's products within the framework of the social system of participating countries", the latter is said to involve "raising to an international level and programming the production of those branches of industry which... cannot be developed to an optimum size within national boundaries".[9]

In a way then, the two techniques to trade integration emphasise different approaches. While traditionally, regional integration has started from trade liberalization, leading to the restructuring of production in the developed countries of Western Europe; in the developing countries and in the centrally planned economies, it may be

necessary to start from the production end, and then go on to its resultant effect on the growth of intraregional trade. In the first case, emphasis is placed on the disadvantages of import substitution, and thus on the scope for trade liberalization and export promotion ipso facto. On the other hand, by emphasising the development of the production structure on a regional scale, attention is focused on the considerable savings in production and distribution costs that may emerge through large-scale production, fuller utilization of existing capacities, greater specialization in production, joint management, and the coordinated use of jointly-owned resources.[10] Our discussion on "plan harmonization" later in the paper should be viewed in this context.

Economic Justification of Regional Integration

The case for economic integration in any form, is made mostly on the grounds of potential gains revolving around resource allocation and efficiency. In the traditional analysis, increase in productive efficiency is tantamount to a rise in real income and thus, to economic welfare. The argument is based on the idea of comparative advantage, i.e., countries produce those products regarding which they have a relative advantage, and by exchanging them with other countries for products in which they have a relative disadvantage, each country is naturally benefited. Based on the principle of comparative advantage, Ricardo and his followers advocated universal free trade as an international economic policy, believing that it would result in an optimum allocation of a given stock of resources, and in the process lead to higher levels of real income. This argument, couched as it is in static terms, assumes constant technology or unchanged production methods. Thus, within the static framework, productive efficiency occurs from a redistribution of productive resources from higher to lower cost sources so that more is produced with a given amount of resources than is possible under restrictive trade.

The static version of global free trade requires the existence of ideal conditions such as perfect competition, or lack of monopoly and governmental interference, constant cost, absence of external economies, perfect elasticity of foreign demand, full employment, and wage and price flexibility. It is the lack of such ideal conditions that led to dissatisfaction with the static version, pushing the development of the dynamic theory of free trade.

The dynamic benefits of universal free trade refer to the improved methods of production obtained by the widening of national markets through trade. Dynamic efficiency means technological change that is helped by the large-scale economies resulting from the increased size of the market, increased competition, lessened uncertainty and increased investment.

In fact, the historical record of the nineteenth century attested to the virtues of free trade. With the reductions in tariffs and rapid improvements in transportation, international trade grew rapidly in the nineteenth century, leading to tremendous economic growth, a side effect which the classicists had not suspected. In the light of this record, trade was later labelled an "engine of growth" by Sir Dennis Robertson. The principle of comparative advantage in its dynamic aspect of affecting economic growth, thus assumed the pivotal role in the economists' belief in, and advocacy of, universal free trade, until the experience of the developing countries started to shake it in the late 1950's. To be sure, the nineteenth century experience meant economic growth with trade not only for the advanced countries of Europe, but also for the less developed countries through a process which Nurkse called "the transmission of growth", working through the increased demand by developed countries for the primary products of underdeveloped countries In a way it is this aspect of trade that changed after the Second World War.[11]

This part in the chain of thought has been popularized by economists like Nurkse, Myrdal, Prebisch, Singer, and others who have been concerned with the process of development in the developing countries and the role that international trade plays in it. Thus, arguments run on the lines that trade based on comparative advantage, both in its static and

dynamic aspects, is not conducive to economic development. In its static version, trade may reallocate resources in the developing countries in sectors, mostly in the primary-producing sectors. The reallocation runs counter to the very process of economic development, aiming as it does at diversification of the economic base. In the dynamic context, trade contributes to the growth process only where exports lead imports so as to provide greater resources to help expand the economic base. However, in reality, exports of developing countries suffer due to a lag in the growth of demand in developed countries for the products of developing countries. The imports of underdeveloped countries, on the other land, rise rapidly under the necessities of development which require greater amounts of capital goods and other manufactured items, leading to a net import balance. The result then is that if trade is left free, as the classical economists believed, this unfavourable balance of trade would imply an outflow of productive resources which actually retards economic development instead of helping it. ECAFE sums up the discussion thus:

> Thus the limitation imposed on the possible rate of economic growth by the slow growth of exports finds its expression in a growing gap between export prospects and import needs. The gap may be bridged to some extent by foreign capital imports and external assistance. But, from the point of view of selfsustained growth, external economic aid should not constitute a permanent basis for economic development, and insofar as foreign loans necessitate interest and repayment servicing in the future, the extent to which capital imports can be made use of depends ultimately upon export earnings prospects.[12]

Apart from the argument presented above, the structure of world trade itself has changed. While in the nineteenth century the pattern of the international division of labour had resulted in the exchange of manufactured goods, raw materials and foodstuffs in approximately the same proportion, in the twentieth century almost two-thirds of such trade takes place between industrialized countries and of manufactured products. Moreover, the bulk of trade among developed countries is set within the framework of a regional block of western European countries belonging to the Common Market. The success of the European Common Market is itself the most important reason for the increasing interest in economic integration, so much so that there are serious discussions on, and schemes for regional integration in every part of the world, e.g., Free Trade Area between the US and Canada, or its wider version of the Atlantic Free Trade Area between the US and Canada, the countries of the Common Market, and Japan, Latin American Free Trade Association (LAFTA); Central American Common Market (CACM); the Andean Common Market (ACM); the Caribbean Community (CARICOM); the East African Community (EAC); ComeCon (Eastern European Countries and USSR) In Asia itself there are at least half-a-dozen schemes of regional cooperation between various countries, e.g., Regional Cooperation for Development (RCD), the Association of Southeast Asian Nations (ASEAN), some of which overlap.

The theory of regional integration in the form of either a customs union or its looser version, a free trade area, explores the question of preferential tariff cuts. The central concept of the classical static theory of trade was that under "ideal conditions" free trade would maximize world income. This gain would be due to the resultant productive and allocative efficiency. But it did not necessarily follow from this that free trade would also be the best policy for each individual country. Since the gains from free trade were not evenly divided but dependent upon the terms of trade, i.e., the reciprocal demand conditions, the basic case for free trade was thus modified by a number of arguments for protection. Moreover, since universal free trade was not possible under the existing political conditions, especially in the post Second World War period, interest shifted from universal to regional free trade. (Exceptions from universal free trade to regional free trade are only "second-best" solutions where any country or set of countries finds it difficult to pursue "first-best" policies that would

optimize welfare under puritan conditions). Where "utopian solutions" are limited by constraints, suboptimal policies have to be followed, and formidable gains and losses are balanced between alternative trade policies. The whole idea of regional integration is the most important application of the idea of "second best".

Trade Creation and Trade Diversion

In a pioneering study on "The customs union issue", in 1950, Jacob Viner warned international economists "that a move towards free trade was not necessarily beneficial (unlike a move to free trade) from the viewpoint of world welfare". Based primarily upon his distinction between trade creating and trade diverting effects, he showed that the discriminatory system of a customs union cannot guarantee such a rise. Trade is created when two countries form a union and their production structure is affected by their comparative advantages. But by forming such a union the two countries are also according each other protection, and so discriminate against the rest of the world. Trade is diverted from the outside world in favour of the partner. In this manner, overall production in the world is adversely affected, especially if the non-member country's products were cheaper prior to the formation of the customs union. In simple terms, the gains in production for union members are offset by the losses for nonmembers. Whether or not there would be an increase in the world's welfare will depend upon the extent of the net gains achieved in this fashion.

Since then the idea has been greatly elaborated and improved by Meade, Lipsy and others. Later refinements in Viner's model have included the consumption effects, which he had ignored, and have also included increasing costs, as opposed to Viner's assumption of constant costs. Taking into account the various modifications in the basic Viner model, at least three conclusions are of particular interest. First, a customs union is more likely to lead to a net increase in economic welfare if the economy of the partner countries is actually very competitive (or similar) but potentially very complementary (or dissimilar), e.g., India and Pakistan. Secondly, there will be a net increase in economic welfare through the formation of such a union if the initial duty rates are higher on imports into the partner countries (a condition that exists on the Indian subcontinent). Third, a customs union is likely to raise welfare if each of the two countries is the principal supplier of the exported products to the other and if each is the principal market for the other of the products that it imports.

Record of Performance of Economic Integration Schemes

Of all the schemes of integration, the European Common Market is not only the lone "success story" but also is the dominant integration scheme in the world, of developed, developing, and for that matter market-type or centrally-planned economies. The inclusion of Britain, Denmark, and Ireland has not only increased its membership but it has also weakened the position of its only competitor, the European Free Trade Association. In evaluating the achievements of EEC, Balassa has noted that tariff elimination among the member countries led to an increase of intraregional trade between 1959–71 of nearly sixfold, as against a fourfold increase in their total exports and imports. As a result, the share of intra-EEC trade in the total rose from one-third in 1950 to one-half in 1971. Of this total increase in intraregional trade, trade creation outpaced the trade diversion effects, particularly in manufactured goods. On the other hand, trade diversion effects that have occurred in the case of foodstuffs, chemicals, and simple manufactured goods have been offset by increased imports of capital and equipment due to increased investment activity. The net result is that between 1959–70 the volume of total imports into EEC countries rose at an average annual rate of 11.3 per cent, compared with 9.6 per cent in the pre-Common Market period. The volume of extra-area imports during the same period increased at a rate of 8.7 per cent a year against the 8.3 per cent annual increase between 1953-59.[13]

In spite of the tremendous increase in the intra-EEC trade and the beneficial effects of integration on economic growth, little progress has been made in regard to "production-and-development" integration. In technologically sophisticated industries, such as aircraft, space, computer, and electronics, where efficient operations are limited by the size of national markets, there is as yet no common policy in the EEC. This fact has retarded the development of technologically advanced industries in the European Common Market. Similarly, though "the anticipated gradual spillover into such adjoining issue-areas as fiscal harmonization, concentrations and mergers, competition, investment and social policy, and the reform of the common agricultural policy did occur",[14] yet there has been a noticeable failure on the part of the EEC to progress towards the Economic and Monetary Union (EMU) that was supposed to have been completed by 1980.[15]

But the greatest disappointment has been the lack of any progress towards regional integration in the host of integration schemes that now exists among the many developing countries of the world. None of these schemes has lived up to expectations. Among the various factors that account for the lack of development towards either "market integration" or "production-and-development integration" in the manufacturing sector of this type of country, Balassa mentions "considerations of national sovereignty, the difficulties of estimating benefits and costs, uncertainty as regards future changes in prices and costs, and the problems encountered in intergovernmental negotiations".[16]

For example, among the economic factors that retard the progress of regionalization are those connected with the economic structure of the South Asian region, as elsewhere in Asia and the developing countries—underdeveloped and largely homogeneous. Though neither of the economic factors alone preempts the possibility of economic integration, together they raise serious problems. Economic underdevelopment can be cured by industrialization which necessitates the heavy importation of capital, machinery, and technology. These are the very areas where intraregional trade is of no help because of the economic homogeneity of Asian countries. All of them are underdeveloped and primary-producing countries with very little diversification. These economies have little to contribute to the solution of each other's problems. In fact, their solutions lie in their interrelationship with the developed countries. Thus, in surveying the scope for regional cooperation among the developing countries of the world one always points to the lack of international trade between them as one of the basic factors hindering such a step. Since each one of the developing countries can do little to help the other, they have little to gain from integrating with each other. To secure concessions by liberalizing trade with each other is not so important as arranging credit, aid, and investment from the developed countries. Therefore, one witnesses the various preferential trade arrangements which the developing countries of Asia have with the developed and industrialized countries of Europe and America. These trade relationships grew essentially out of their past colonial relationship. However, none of these arguments should be considered permanent because of the very fact of their changing economic structure.

But the key to the prospects of economic integration lies in terms of the political factors. Integration, particularly at the higher stages, involves not only the freeing of trade but also the harmonization of economic policies which may require instituting a regional decision-making apparatus and hence a certain diminution of national sovereignty. Therefore, it has been emphasised "that the conflict between national sovereignty and economic self-interest can be resolved only if there is a political interest and the political will to do so. Economic integration thus appears as a part of a political process whose final outcome is determined by essentially political factors".[17] (The failure of the EEC to form EMU is a case in point). In Asia, unlike in Europe and Latin America, there has been suspicion and distrust among the regional countries. Strangely, in political terms, Asia is much less homogeneous than any other region. The range varies from representative governments to communist type regimes, with monarchy and military dictatorships in

between. All of this accounts for differing political values and ideologies. Moreover, while in other continents there have been forces present for political integration and cooperation, particularly since the end of World War II, Asia has witnessed trends towards political fragmentation. The division of India and Pakistan in 1947, separation of Burma in 1937, the split of French Indochina into Laos, and North and South Vietnam, the division of Korea into North and South, and its separation from Japan, the separation of Malaysia and Singapore, and so on, have all contributed toward the political disintegration of Asia. At the same time, their involvement with the two superpowers has widened the political cleavage between the Asian countries. Since all of them have gained political independence after World War II, the internal political conditions and economic reality are forcing them not only towards economic independence through development programmes, but also towards political and economic nationalism. The manifestation of this last item is that Asian countries have developed the strategy of national self-sufficiency at any cost in every field, a situation which runs counter to the fundamentals of economic integration and cooperation.

Over and above the obstacles mentioned here, the scope, nature, and type of economic integration schemes are not very clear to most South Asian countries. Should the regional integration sheme be extended to other countries in Asia, all but Mainland China, North Korea, and North Vietnam, or to some subregional groupings? Should it take the form of a customs union, free trade area, or sectoral integration? In view of the diversity of socioeconomic political structures in Asia, what role should be assigned to nonregional members or the advanced countries of Asia itself?

In view of the various considerations and the problems involved in welding together an organization comprising such a diverse group, it may be more practical to initiate a scheme of regional integration involving only a few countries. The present study proposes to concentrate on the South Asian region composed of

Bangladesh, Burma, India, Malaysia, Nepal, Pakistan and Sri Lanka. This amounts to recognition of the fact that integration at the subregional level is rationalized as a "third best" choice since neither the "first best" (i.e., global integration) nor the "second best" (total regional integration), may be workable in the face of the diversity of socioeconomic political factors.

Table 21.1 presents the South Asian

1969. By the same token, over two-thirds of the region's population lives in the rural areas. Overall, it suffers from economic poverty as reflected in low capita income. The explanation of the low capita income again lies in terms of the predominance of agriculture, which for the most part is conducted at subsistence level due to low productivity. Foreign trade is very important for the region both in terms of attaining the

Table 21.1.   South Asia—1972-1973*

Country	Area (km)	Population ('000)	% Growth (63–72)	Density (Per km)	GDP (Millions)	Per Capita GDP	Share of Agriculture in GNP
	1	2	3	4	5	6	7
India	3,280,483	547,949	2.2	172	NA	NA	NA
Bangladesh	142,776	71,470	NA	NA	5,803	92	56.0
Burma	678,033	28,885	NA	NA	1,975	68	38.0
Malaysia	332,633	10,583	3.2	26	4,041	370	31.0
Nepal	140,797	11,555	1.8	81	1,027	90	68.0
Pakistan	803,940	64,892	2.4	70	7,447	116	34.0
Sri Lanka	65,610	12,711	2.3	199	2,308	177	32.0

SOURCE: For Columns 1, 2, 3, 4, United Nations, *Statistical Yearbook,* 1973 (New York, 1974).

For Columns 5, 6, 7, United Nations, *Yearbook of National Accounts Statistics,* 1974, vol. III, International Tables (New York, 1975).

region's economic profile. The region and the component economies contain the essential elements of economic underdevelopment—smaller output, predominance of the primary sector, lower per capita income. At the same time, the region, as a whole, has one of the heaviest concentrations of population outside Mainland China, with a rate of population-growth that is one of the highest in the world. The "dual" characterization of the region is given by the fact that the agricultural sector accounts for 31–56 per cent of the gross domestic product of the individual countries.

The significance of this can be placed in perspective when one understands that a small increase in agricultural production, the kind this region has witnessed since 1967, can have appreciable effects on the economic growth-rate which for the region's economies has been between 5.5 per cent and 8.5 per cent in 1968 and

necessary capital and industrial products as well as for increasing the domestic output. The significance of it varies in individual countries—40 per cent in Malaysia to less than 5 per cent in India. For most of the countries in the region, the bulk of export earnings is derived from a single commodity—rubber in Malaysia, tea in Sri Lanka, rice in Burma. The bulk of foreign trade is conducted with the industrialized countries, and there is a very small amount of intraregional trade.

In other respects, in spite of the national differences in their outlook, the group is relatively more homogeneous. For one thing, all these countries except Nepal are former colonies of Britain with the common bond of the English language, and a civil service, administrative system and legal framework derived from Britain. The countries involved are also contiguous. There has been a great deal of population movement between them in the past.

Mostly this has been the movement of surplus labour from India and Pakistan to the rest. Till the recent past, Nepal had a common market with India, with special and economic interests due to its landlocked position. It is in this light that we may analyse India's objectives, its position, and the results in promoting regional integration in South Asia.

II

Economic Integration in South Asia

The case for economic integration among the developing countries such as in South Asia is not watertight. Any case for economic integration among the developing countries must be based on its merits and its contribution to the process of economic development. How far does the creation of a regional group affect the fundamental problems of the developing countries, e.g., increasing the opportunities for profitable investment, both domestic and foreign, broadening the export base, achieving balance of payments equilibrium, mobilizing unemployed and underemployed resources, and avoiding economic dualism? International trade has been suggested as a vehicle for economic development and yet trade, if left free, leads to an import balance resulting in the loss of productive resources that retards economic development instead of helping it. To overcome the problem of lagging export proceeds, developing countries place increasing emphasis on import substitution which is practised without any consideration to the cost and prices. That is, if a country like India finds it difficult to increase its exports, due either to low foreign demand or short domestic supply, and has meanwhile to import manufactured goods, capital equipment, machinery, and industrial raw materials for development and industrialization, it has to ration its limited foreign exchange by controlling or licensing imports, curtailing foreign travel, etc. The result of such controls is that domestic production of the previously imported products is encouraged—a process that gives no consideration to the comparative advantage or cost of production. If such im-

port substitution continues, the real cost to the country could be quite high. On the other hand, if the domestic market for a product such as steel is not large enough to absorb the output of a minimum-sized plant, it would lead to excess capacity (underutilization of the plant) and wastage of capital which the country can ill afford in the initial stages of its developmental process. Thus, in order to have import substitution, industries would continue to need protection on the basis of "infant industry" considerations.

Both these arguments are considered as the basis for economic integration or regionalism. Economic integration requires a mutual relaxation of trade barriers and exchange controls, which would lead to the expansion of trade. Since the increase in trade causes the demand for the country's exports to rise, it would also help in overcoming the smallness of the market, so that plants would now produce the desired maximum output, and the surplus would be exported abroad. Thus, economic integration of the region is viewed as the strategic weapon to combat economic underdevelopment.

However, both these arguments, though considered necessary for regionalism, not necessarily a rationalization for free trade. For one thing, regional integration in South Asia may lead to general increase in trade, but the bulk of regional trade is not among the South Asian countries but between them and the industrialized countries of the West and Japan. As Table 21.2 suggests, this lack of intraregional trade is attributed to the competitiveness of their existing economic structure, i.e., the homogeneity of their economies which are mostly agricultural, with a small industrial base. At the same time, the needs of industrialization are such that these countries have to trade with the developed ones. Thus, regional integration among the South Asian countries would not only involve little expansion of intraregional trade, but if steps are undertaken to increase this mutual trade with, say India, which is a relatively more industrialized country than others in the region, it would imply diverting trade from the low-cost countries of the West to high-cost Indian products, i.e., trade

Table 21.2. Intraregional Trade in South Asia, 1973*

Country	Total Value of Imports CIF (Million Indian rupees)	Total value of Exports FOB	Value of Interregional Exports (Million Indian rupees) and % of Total						
			India	Bangladesh	Burma	Malaysia	Nepal	Pakistan	Sri Lanka
India (Rupee)	42946	47399	—	2311 (4.8)	25.3 (0.05)	292 (0.6)	4987 (1 05)	—	125.3 (.26)
Bangladesh (Taka) BT1=0.746 IR.	49101	1998	NA	—	NA	NA	NA	NA	NA
Burma (b) (Kyat) Kyl=1.52 IR.	2983	33.91	148.4 (4.4)	NA	—	99.0 (2.9)	NA	299.9 (8.0)	541.0 (15.9)
Malaysia (Dollar) M$1=3.11 IR.	325685	395576	3927.3	NA	0	—	NA	0	0
Nepal (Rupee)	—	—	—	—	—	—	—	—	—
Pakistan (Rupee) PR1=0.157 IR.	7562	7401	NA	NA	65.8 (.88)	55.8 (.75)	NA	—	103.3 (1.39)
Sri Lanka (Rupee) CR1=1.02 IR.	5165	4748	22.2 (0.46)	NA	NA	NA	NA	462.3 (9.7)	—

*All data on trade was given in local currencies and was accordingly converted into Indian rupee (IR).

bFigures on Burma pertain to 1972.

SOURCE: United Nations, *Yearbook of International Trade Statistics*, Vol. I (Trade by Commodity), (New York, 1975).

398   International Economic Relations

diversion. Moreover, the development process requires a total increase in the exports of a country rather than a diversion of the existing trade. On this account, whether or not regionalism means a total expansion of the export base of the countries in South Asia, is left open to question.

In recent years, the idea of regionalism among the developing countries has been pushed on other grounds, some of which are relevant to our purpose. ECAFE, for example, does not heavily stress the lack of complementarity as a hindrance to regionalism. In fact, as it puts it, "What is relevant to the possibility of further expanding this volume of intragroup trade is not the degree of complementarity as such, as the extent to which the full volume of intragroup trade, determined by that degree of complementarity is prevented from realizing itself by the interposition of artificial barriers or other means of economic policy".[18]

In other words, what regional cooperation has to achieve is increasing the flow of intraregional trade between the less, rather than the more, complementary economies of the region. With such considerations, countries like Malaysia and Japan, having a highly complementary economic system, would have already exploited the trade possibilities between them. But the competitive economies of Burma and India, or India and Pakistan, have more to gain by trading with each other, if they can mutually relax their economic or trade and other artificial barriers. Rather than worry about the lack of intraregional trade at present, because of the absence of complementarities, the emphasis here is to create new complementarities or what LAFTA has called "complementation agreements".[19]

Specialists on regional integration among the ECAFE countries also argue that mere relaxation of trade barriers is not enough in the context of the present economic conditions of the region. Free trade requires an efficient price and market system to provide the necessary incentives for the firms to produce. In the context of the South Asian economies, the market system is not only inefficient because of the economic structure, but

it is also fraught with inelastic supply curves, imperfect mobility of resources, and governmental interference. In such a case there is no guarantee that free trade would encourage production and economic growth. In other words, deficiency of demand may have been an important factor in limiting growth in the developed countries, which the widening of the market can cure. In South Asia, like other developing areas, growth has been inhibited by the supply inelasticity. Free trade in that vein can hardly solve the problem of supply deficiencies. Among the factors limiting supply are (1) inability to transform; (2) need for intermediate goods; (3) disequilibrium in factor markets; and (4) misallocation of resources through misguided protectionism. Furthermore, free trade itself leads to the concentration of gains in those countries that have the initial advantage of industrial infrastructure, such as India. This possibility alone would weaken any attempt on India's part to push for a scheme, especially when the mood of its neighbours is one of suspicion and hostility. Free trade also runs counter to economic planning as the main instrument of economic development. Therefore, regional economists stress the idea of "plan harmonization" as a method of regional integration.

Plan harmonization refers to the coordination of national developmental plans ECAFE and the other specialists have consistently stressed this aspect of cooperation which is defined as "partial or comprehensive extension of national economic planning to a regional or subregional plan for the allocation of productive resources".[20] Such a scheme would require intergovernmental consultation, exchange of information, and negotiations. Sooner or later this may lead to agreements on production and investment policies which may be undertaken at the regional, rather than the national level. Regional investment plans would involve intergovernmental agreements on national specialization which itself would push the idea of economic integration. Thus, "the goals of integration can be attained, at least in principle, by the alternative means of 'agreed specialization' through intergovernmental negotiations without subjecting the participating countries to brutal and blind market forces and to the disruptive side effects of free trade".[21]

In a way, this approach is a complement to the trade liberalization method of economic integration. The only difference between "plan harmonization" and the classical prescription of free trade is that "freedom of commodity movements will be a dictated rather than a dictating circumstance in the plan harmonization strategy".[22] This would help the participating governments to develop the habit of consulting and trusting each other. Moreover, by agreeing to a regional investment strategy, the members will avoid wasteful competition with each other, conserve and allocate scarce capital better, apply import substitution on a regional rather than national level, have better distribution of the gains from integration, achieve economies of scale, and hence receive the benefits from greater efficiency and economic growth.[23]

Within this broad system of plan harmonization, at least three forms of integration have been suggested:

1. Vertical integration, where each country specializes in the production of an item and gives it to the other members for further processing before the finished product is distributed in the entire regional market. Such an arrangement is possible in industries whose products undergo several stages of production, e.g., iron and steel, jute, and rubber;

2. agreed specialization in independent products in industries where the production process is not divisible but the entire regional production is geared for regional demand on the basis of production quotas and market sharing;

3. horizontal integration, where the members produce competing products, e.g., jute, tea, rubber, coconuts. The member countries produce these goods which enjoy world monopoly, but, with few exceptions, due to the lack of cooperation among them, they are deprived of their share in the international trade consistent with their output levels. All these forms of integration apply not only to existing production but particularly to future lines of production, thus adding to the possibility of regionalization.[24]

For India and its neighbours to receive such benefits, economic integration schemes must be carefully considered. With proper organizational machinery, and the establishment of regional institutions, most of the fears of unequal distribution of integration gains and the supremacy of a given member—India—can be dispelled. It is often argued in India that because of its vast market, there are not many benefits which the country can reap from regional integration. Though the argument is true to some extent, there are other considerations that are far more important. The crucial ones are that India, like any other country, cannot and does not have the advantage in producing everything. Import substitution, having gone to extremes, has resulted in serious misallocation of resources. The excess capacity in most of the sectors is one sign of the inefficiency of the Indian economy.[25] Though it is hoped that this excess capacity is only short run, the time lag between the creation and the full utilization of capacity can be much longer in the developing economies. It is worth noting that a large population is not the same thing as a large domestic market. Low per capita income does not generate sufficient demand to realize the economies of scale. Balassa, for example, has emphasised that "no developing country has a market for manufactured goods one-half of that of France, a medium-sized industrial nation, it is between one-fifth and one-half of the size of the French market in four countries (India, Brazil, Mexico and Argentina), and between one-tenth and one-twentieth in another two (the Philippines and Turkey). The comparison becomes even more unfavourable if the value of manufacturing consumption is expressed in world market prices since in most developing countries protection has raised domestic prices in the world market."[26]

But the most persuasive case for regionalization and its benefits to India can be made on the grounds that it may provide India a way out of the structural problems which it is facing. Such structural problems have developed as a result of India's efforts to industrialize through development planning, where the scope and importance of international trade has been underestimated. Though it is true that the foreign sector accounts for only 5 per cent of total production in India and that till recently even this ratio has been declining as exports have grown more slowly than total output, yet the foreign sector is extremely important as international trade provides the possibility of enlarging the domestic transformation through imports of foreign capital rather than restricting it to those permitted by the available domestic capital. Aside from this, the very objective of industrialization, particularly of the heavy capital goods sector, is to put India on a self-sufficiency basis, i.e., the declining role of imports of capital goods towards the eventual independence from such imports, was to be achieved through a plethora of economic policies that were designed to provide protection (through import restriction) to the domestic industrial sector. Thus, industrialization through import-substitution came to occupy a central place in the scheme of economic development in India. Among such policies, domestic policies included a powerful and comprehensive industrial licensing system, and occasional price and distributional controls, while the foreign policy instruments relied on the use of quantitative restrictions along with frequent reliance on import and export incentives for the nontarget industries. The two together amounted to an automatic and anticipatory protection of the domestic industries. In a way then, the objective of industrialization and the policies designed to achieve this have led not only to an increase in government bureaucracy, promoting corruption and administrative inefficiencies, but also to smuggling, black marketing and the resultant tensions and strains in Indian society.[27] Moreover, there has been an increasing gap between the export and import performance leading to a foreign exchange scarcity that has intensified each year. The greater the foreign exchange scarcity, the tighter has become the need for import controls and substitution in the heavy industrial sector. But the effect of the foreign exchange scarcity has been to create a bias towards foreign inputs, capital and technology, that is inconsistent with the domestic factor endowment. It has also led to the creation of additional capacity despite the underutilization of the existing one, resulting in high cost and prices. Consequently, the need to conserve foreign exchange actually has had an adverse impact on export performance and scarcity of foreign exchange.[28]

A final comment on the Indian position is based on the benefits that would accrue to the private sector. Since economic integration would involve the harmonization of national economies, this will act as a direct incentive to the private sector. India's private sector possesses the necessary management skills, investment ability and the inspiration to take a larger role in economic development, and can be stimulated to a greater extent by the country's willingness to open up both domestically and internationally. This may prove to be highly beneficial to India in the long run since Indian investors have a tradition of dealing with the countries of South Asia. No doubt in this venture the excesses of the Indian private sector can be checked by the overall regional economic policy and institutions.

For the rest of the members in this regional scheme, the gains can be equally great. With no exception, the six members are small, with limited production capabilities and market. Each one trying to stimulate economic development will face these limitations and thus be handicapped. These limitations are particularly true for capital goods, industrial raw materials, and pertrochemicals. Moreover, the necessary availability of skilled manpower and management cadres is extremely limited in these countries. Thus, in order to achieve a more rational allocation of their limited resources, it remains in their interest to cooperate in such a scheme. Any fears of economic dominance can be allayed with the proper regional institutions. More realistic regional, political, and diplomatic cooperation will go a long way in soothing and overcoming the initial hostility.

Conclusion

In making out a case for regional integration, we by no means overlook the complexities involved in such a scheme, most of which are political in nature. One of the problems has been the hostilities that have existed on the Indian subcontinent. The situation has changed since the Indo-Pakistan conflict of 1971, and the signing of the Simla Agreement in 1972. Moreover, as a further justification for cautious exploration of the issue of economic regionalism in the area, one can mention a number of successful regional cooperative schemes that have involved the member countries of the South Asian region. The kind and extent of regional cooperation that has existed in Asia so far has taken the form of trade promotion and/or the strengthening of the infrastructure which promotes intraregional trade directly or indirectly. This has been the state of affairs in South Asia. Where do we go from here? Much more discussion on the cost/benefit of regional integration vis-a-vis cooperation is needed. Within regional integration schemes, techniques to achieve it range from free trade to economic unions. Trade integration itself can be brought about either through "market integration" by reducing the barriers to intraregional trade or through "production-and-development integration" by agreeing on multinational industrial programmes and investment allocation. All of these have to be placed within the political constraints of national sovereignty. Yet one can visualize at least some range that would provide a sub-optimum—a "second best" or "third best" solution, a maximum-maximorum condition. Similarly, we can also propose detailed feasibility studies on individual sectors, industries, and projects where regional integration can be achieved, and hence can be made the basis of policy formulations among the respective governments in the region.

REFERENCES

1. B. Balassa, "Towards a Theory of Economic Integration", *Kyklos*, No. 1, 1961, p. 4.
2. J. Tinbergen, *International Economic Integration* (Amsterdam: North Holland, 1958), Chapter 1.
3. Balassa, *Economic Integration*, p. 5.
4. ECAFE, *Economic Bulletin for Asia and the Far East*, vol. XII, no. 1, June 1961, p. 3.
5. Countries in the Central American Common Market are Costa Rica, El Salvador, Guatemala, Honduras and Nicaragua. Benelux represented the Association of Belgium, The Netherlands and Luxembourg.
6. EFTA was organized in the face of establishing the Common Market to which England was opposed in the beginning. Initially, it included Austria, Denmark, Norway, Portugal, Sweden, Switzerland, and the UK, and was popularly called the "outer seven" as distinguished from the "inner six" which was applied to the members of the Common Market. Recently, several members of EFTA, e.g., England and Denmark, have joined the Common Market. LAFTA membership includes Argentina, Bolivia, Brazil, Chile, Colombia, Ecuador, Mexico, Paraguay, Peru, Uruguay and Venezuela.
7. Bela Balassa, "Types of Economic Integration", Paper presented at the Fourth World Congress of the International Economic Association in Budapest, Hungary, 19–24 August 1974, p. 1.
8. Ibid.
9. Ibid., pp. 1–2.
10. See International Bank for Reconstruction & Development, "Economic Integration Among Developing Countries", Bank staff working paper No. 186, September, 1974 (mimeographed).
11. To be sure, the advocacy of free trade did not mean the exclusion of tariff, particularly if it was designed to aid "infant-industry" or to generate revenues, in such countries as Canada, United States, Germany, etc. By the end of that last century protectionists' sentiments had grown to such an extent that there was a period of tariff warfare. Besides, there also existed a network of international investment that brought the necessary capital to the colonies for resource exploitation.
12. ECAFE, "Economic Development and Planning in Asia and the Far East", vol. XII, no. 3, December 1961, p. 56.
13. Balassa, "Types of Economic Integration", pp. 2–5.
14. Ernet B. Haas, "Turbulent Fields and the Theory of Regional Integration", *International Organization*, vol. 30,. no. 2, Spring 1976, p. 195.
15. Ernet B. Haas has suggested that the failure of progress towards EMU is puzzling since superficially it looks like a natural candidate

for successful spill-over. To him, "EMU failed because France and Germany disagreed fundamentally on the respective merits and priorities of monetary and economic policy as methods of management. Furthermore Britain wanted neither. The disagreement was in no small measure due to certain national practices (e.g., a tradition of firm monetary management in France) and popular fears (the German government's presumed need to reassure the country on price stability). Neither government, for purely domestic reasons, felt able to give way. The institutional consequence in monetary policy was the continuation of the pre-existing pattern of regular consultation among the governors of Central banks and the creation of a small currency guarantee fund, but no permanent consolidation of "the snake in the tunnel". "Turbulent Fields and Regional Integration", p. 195.

16. Balassa, "Types of Economic Integration", p. 12.
17. Ibid., p. 15.
18. ECAFE, *Economic Development*, p. 53.
19. As far as this author has been able to determine, the idea of plan-harmonization seems to have been enunciated by the United Nations Economic Commission for Latin America and was soon incorporated in the writings of ECAFE and UNCTAD. For a fuller treatment of plan-harmonization, see ECAFE, "Approaches to Regional Harmonization of National Development Plans in Asia and the Far East", *Economic Bulletin for Asia and the Far East*, 15, no. 3, 1964, pp. 33–81.
20. H. Kitamura and A.N. Bhagat, "Aspects of Regional Harmonization of National Development Plan", in Theodore Morgan and Nyle Spoelstra (eds.), *Economic Interdependence in South-East Asia* (University of Wisconsin Press, 1967), p. 44.
21. Ibid., p. 42.
22. Ibid., p. 44.
23. In a way, the plan-harmonization approach to integration applies the strategy of import substitution to the regional market. It should also be pointed out that plan-harmonization schemes have taken various forms in the current debate on regionalization including the discussion on "project approach" in regard to new investment for the production of regional goods and services, e.g., transportation and communication, public utilities, education and research, or international goods such as agriculture, mining, and manufacturing products; "package approach" that involves the simultaneous establishment of integration products in all member countries. Unfortunately, in all schemes of regionalization such as LAFTA, Andean Common Market, Central American Common Market, Caribbean Community, East African Community, Regional Cooperation for Development, efforts made to integrate industries have not been very successful. Among the factors responsible for lagging progress on this front are the divergent economic and political

interests cumbersome negotiating procedures, lack of feasibility studies and the characteristics of the industries where complementarity agreements are supposed to be undertaken.
24. Rameshwar Tandon has discussed these more fully in his article on "Regional Trade Co-operain South East Asia", in *Journal of World Trade Law*, vol. 8, no. 4, July/August 1974, pp. 388–400.
25. For example, prior to the declaration of Emergency in 1975, it had been estimated that rail-wagon building capacity was working at 39 per cent of installed capacity in 1970–71. Other manufacturing industries like cement machinery, printing paper, tea, leather and rubber products used only about 70 per cent or less. See *Far Eastern Review; 1972 Yearbook* (Hong Kong, 1971), pp. 180–192.
26. B. Balassa, "Regional Integration of Trade: Policies of Less Developed Countries", in Paul Streeten (ed.), *Trade Strategies for Development* (New York: Halsted Press, 1973), pp. 177–78.
27. Jagdish Bhagwati and Padma Desai have critically detailed the performance of the Indian economy till 1966 in their book *India: Planning for Industrialization* (London: Oxford University Press, 1970). Similarly, other empirical studies on the process of industrialization through import substitution have estimated the resulting effective rates of protection for different Indian industrial processes for 1961 and 1962 to be as high as 10,000 per cent, with others at almost as high negative values. See, for example, J. Bhagwati and Sukhmoy Chakravarty, "Contributions to Indian Economic Analysis: A Survey", American Economic Association, *Supplement to American Economic Review*, September 1969.
28. It should be pointed out that the experience of India is consistent with that of other developing countries that have tried import substitution as a development strategy. On the one hand, import-substitution aimed directly at industrialization occurs at the cost of agricultural development. Agricultural stagnation hampers the growth of primary products, their exports, and in many cases the countries may become the net importers of agricultural products. At the same time this neglect of the primary sector curbs the growth of the domestic market since the bulk of its labour force is employed in that and the sector itself contributes to a major portion of national income. On the other hand, the programme of import substitution in the industrial sector is itself retarded due to the limited growth of the exports of manufactured goods. This is partly attributed to the barriers put up by developed countries in the way of exports of manufactured goods of developing countries and mostly becuase of the economic policies in such countries that favour import substitution to export promotion. Moreover, since large and frequent devaluations are resisted in the developing countries, this policy instrument has not received the

full attention that it should have. Rather the developing countries resort to other commercial instruments, e.g., tariff barriers, import duties, etc., in dealing with their balance of payments problems. Nurul Islam, "National Import Substitution and Inward LookingStrategies: Policiesof Less Developed Countries", in Streeten (ed.), *Trade Strategies for Development*, pp. 76–92.

SUGGESTED READINGS

Berrill, Kenneth: *Economic Development: with Special Reference to East Asia*. New York. St. Martin's Press, 1964.

ECAFE: Various Publications starting as early as 1957.

Ganguli, B.N.: *India's Economic Relations with the Far Eastern and Pacific Countries In the Present Century*. Bombay. Orient Longmans, 1956.

Ghosh, Alak: *Indian Economy: Its Nature and Problems*. Calcutta. The World Press, 1971.

Gupta, Sisir: *India and Regional Integration in Asia*. New York. Asia Publishing House, 1964.

Kang, Shin Joe: *Economic Integration In Asia*. Hamburg. The Hamburg Institute For International Economics. Verlag Weltarchiv Gmbh, 1969.

Morgan, Theodore (ed.): *Economic Interdependence in Southeast Asia*. Madison, Wis. University of Wisconsin Press, 1969.

Onslow, Cronley: *Asian Economic Development*. New York. Praeger, 1965.

Singh, Lalita P.: *The Politics of Economic Cooperation in Asia*. Columbia, Mo. University of Missouri Press, 1966.

Singh, Manmohan: *India's Export Trends and its Prospects for Self-sustained Growth*. London. Clarendon Press, 1964.

Singh, Patwant: *India and the Future of Asia*. New York. Alfred A. Knopf, 1966.

Uppal, J.S.: *Economic Development in South Asia*. New York. St. Martin's Press, 1977.

Index